Praise for Stuart Piggin and Robert D. Linder's

The Fountain of Public Prosperity

Winner of

The Australian Christian Book of the Year Award 2019

'A monumental history of evangelical Christianity in Australia, eclipsing Patrick O'Farrell's *Catholic Church and Community* as the fullest account of any religious movement in the Australian experience. The sparkling prose and deep insight into the interplay between this form of Christianity and the national story will engage the general reader and challenge the professional student. After this landmark book, it will no longer be possible to dismiss or minimise the influence of religion on the rise and development of modern Australia.'

Dr Geoff Treloar
Australian College of Theology & University of New South Wales

'One of the great works of Australian history ... One of the great studies of evangelicalism globally.'

Dr Meredith Lake
University of Sydney, author of *The Bible in Australia* (2018)

'This magnificent work reveals the largely unknown but very significant extent to which these great currents shaped our nation: it is truly a must-read.'

Hon John Anderson AO
Deputy Prime Minister, 1999–2005

'A masterwork of Australian history.'

Dr Brian Dickey
Flinders University

'... this is an important book that rebalances Australian historiography and goes a long way to restoring the role Christianity played in our national story.'

Paul Collins
Australian Book Review

'Stuart Piggin and Robert Linder's *The Fountain of Public Prosperity* is a meticulous, magisterial work of scholarship.'

Roy Williams
The Australian

'Their book is a significant contribution to Australia's religious history. It is also an invaluable addition to the history of evangelicalism anywhere in the world and will be of interest beyond Australia. I recommend it be widely read and used for its breadth, thoroughness.'

Laura Rademaker
Australian Historical Studies, vol. 50, 2019

'… this is a very valuable work and should be read by every Catholic historian to balance any isolationism and reliance on the stereotypes that may remain in our approach. It is a veritable lode for mining. I loved the footnotes rather than endnotes, the index is comprehensive and the bibliography huge – valuable starting points.'

Michael Belcher
Journal of the Australian Catholic Historical Society

'I have no doubt that *The Fountain of Public Prosperity* makes a significant contribution, not just to Australian religious history, but to Australian history more generally.'

Ed Loane
Churchman

'… tapping into the undiscovered resources mined in this book is the safest route to reimagining Australia's future.'

Mark Powell
The Spectator Australia

'At a time when a post-secular, religiously pluralist future clearly awaits Australian society, such an attempt at a history of Australia that is both contestable in its conclusions and clearly reflective about its underlying intellectual and spiritual commitments is in my view an intellectual project to be welcomed.'

Douglas Hynd
Honest History

'This book is a magnificent achievement, and ought to be read as widely as possible.'

Rory Shiner
The Gospel Coalition

Attending to the National Soul

Stuart Piggin
is Conjoint Associate Professor of History at
Macquarie University, Sydney, Australia.

Robert D. Linder
is Distinguished Professor of History at
Kansas State University, Manhattan, Kansas, USA.

Attending to the National Soul

Evangelical Christians in Australian History 1914–2014

Volume II of

The Fountain of Public Prosperity

Stuart Piggin and Robert D. Linder

Attending to the National Soul: Evangelical Christians in Australian History 1914–2014

Monash University Publishing
Matheson Library Annexe
40 Exhibition Walk
Monash University
Clayton, Victoria 3800, Australia
www.publishing.monash.edu

Monash University Publishing brings to the world publications which advance the best traditions of humane and enlightened thought.

Monash University Publishing titles pass through a rigorous process of independent peer review.

ISBN: 9781925835366 (hardback)
ISBN: 9781925835519 (pdf)
ISBN: 9781925835526 (epub)

www.publishing.monash.edu/books/ans-9781925835366.html

Series: Australian History

Design: Les Thomas

Cover image: Sydney Harbour Bridge at night by David Iliff

A catalogue record for this book is available from the National Library of Australia

CONTENTS

For
Mark Hutchinson, Darrell Paproth

and

Geoff Treloar
in gratitude for decades of fellowship in scholarship

PREFACE AND ACKNOWLEDGEMENTS

Attending to the National Soul is the second of two volumes on the participation of evangelical Christians in Australian history. That their participation has been extensive and their influence salient is the major positive claim of these two volumes. In the first, *The Fountain of Public Prosperity*,[1] reasons why historians have ignored the evangelical movement in Australia were canvassed. In sum, secular historians could not see it; evangelicals, their focus on the Bible, would not see it; and difficulties of definition were so great as to justify surrendering to the view that it was all too hard. Yet it was the major manifestation of Protestant Christianity brought to Australia with the First Fleet. It continued to be the dominant presence in Australian Protestantism in the twentieth century, the period covered by the present volume.

The defining characteristics of evangelical Christianity were identified in the Introduction to the first volume. Its theology is grounded in the Bible and the Protestant Reformation while its vitality and experientialism flow from the Evangelical Revival of the 1740s. It is therefore well understood as biblical experientialism. Its 'evangel' or 'Gospel' is that Jesus is the only, but certain, way to eternal life through the forgiveness of sins and reconciliation with God. Through evangelism or mission, it seeks to introduce people to a personal relationship with Jesus, the experience of which is known as 'conversion'. It is therefore Gospel-focussed and mission-minded. Preaching the Gospel and world evangelisation continue as core commitments of the movement to the present day. Institutionally, the movement is a coalition of the like-minded across the spectrum of Protestant mainline denominations and sects. It fosters commitment among the laity as much as the clergy and it promises to be the means of making the best of both this world and the next.

Characterised as 'vital religion' by its eighteenth-century leaders,[2] it was 'vital' not only in its cultivation of an intense personal relationship with Jesus Christ and in its missionary passion. It was also vital in contrast with nominal Christianity which William Wilberforce had excoriated in his long-winded

1 Stuart Piggin and Robert D. Linder, *The Fountain of Public Prosperity: Evangelical Christians in Australian History, 1740–1914* (Clayton: Monash University Publishing, 2018).

2 Piggin and Linder, *The Fountain of Public Prosperity*, 24 and passim.

manifesto, the *Practical View*.[3] There he called not the church, but the nation, to practise a religion sufficiently faithful to its founder to foment a national conscience equal to its international responsibility. Evangelical Christianity sought to bring public standards into alignment with the values of the Kingdom of God. It is therefore thoroughly reformist and, never content with formalism or nominalism, it seeks to make everything and everyone 'more Christian'.

This second volume, while tracing the story through the next century, has concerns similar to the first. To what extent did evangelicals influence the development of Australian values and public opinion post-empire? Did they have the moral energy to generate public-spiritedness? How successful were they in communicating to their fellow Australians not so much the doctrines but the 'dynamic altruism' of faith?[4] And in the process, how effective were they in attending to the Australian soul, to the spirit of the nation, as well as to the cure of the souls of individual Australians?

The three major themes of the current volume – the transition of the evangelical movement from spiritual empire to an antipodean Christendom; the capacity of evangelicals to attend to the conscience and consciousness of the Australian soul; and the interaction of evangelical Christianity with secularism – all raise very difficult questions. The authors of this book, frequently intimidated by the enormity of the task and the need to attain some depth as well as breadth, have dug deeply in two mines: the history of war and the history of Sydney Anglicanism. Politician and Governor-General, Paul Hasluck, son of Salvation Army parents, observed that 'The influence of religion in the life of a nation, of a community or of an individual is a broad subject. Historians each peg out a claim and sink a shaft.'[5] Here two shafts have been sunk. Whether or not they have hit pay dirt, the ore of evangelical Christianity's influence on Australian history, will be up to the reader to decide. In particular, we must leave it to the reader to make an assessment of the quality of the ore we have uncovered. There is, however, nothing lacking in its quantity. Historians will not be surprised by the copious details on Sydney Anglicanism. The reader will find quite exceptional, however, the extensive treatment of evangelical involvement in World Wars I and II and in the wars

3 *Practical View of the Prevailing Religious Conceptions of Professed Christians in the Higher and Middle Classes in this Country contrasted with real Christianity* (1797).

4 Alan Atkinson, 'How do we live with ourselves? The Australian national conscience', *Australian Book Review*, 384, 2016.

5 Paul Hasluck, *Light that Time has Made* (Canberra: National Library of Australia, 1995), 59.

in Korea and Vietnam, constituting perhaps one of the most comprehensive treatments yet written of evangelicals and war.

Apart from those two principal subjects, this study seeks to follow the evangelical story of the major and some minor denominations within the evangelical family, across all states and territories, and through major vicissitudes in Australian history. Since we are mainly concerned with the engagement of evangelicals with public life and culture, the committed will find here too little about the inner history of their own denominations, apart from the Anglicans who might find too much! The commitments of the two authors (Australian Anglican and American Baptist) no doubt shaped the selection and interpretation of the evidence across this vast field. We are only too aware that those of a different or no faith would have painted a very different picture, darker in some parts and rosier in others. Roman Catholicism is here analysed only in its interactions with evangelical Protestants. Its inner history and its significant impact on the shaping of Australian life are already well covered in Australian historiography.

In *The Fountain of Public Prosperity* the authors acknowledged a very long list of those to whom we are indebted for assistance with this impossibly ambitious project. For this volume, we also wish to thank the more than two hundred professing evangelical Christians who were interviewed for their insights on the more recent past. Their recollections, now digitised and deposited in the archives of Moore College, are a mine barely tapped in the current volume and will repay attention from future scholars. We would like to give special thanks again to five historians who read early drafts of the current volume and gave much-needed advice, direction and correction: Brian Dickey, John Harris, David Hilliard, Meredith Lake, and Darrell Paproth. This volume is dedicated with the profoundest gratitude and affection to Mark Hutchinson, Darrell Paproth and Geoff Treloar, historians of Australian and global Christianity, who persevered with us through the three decades of research and writing on this project.

ABBREVIATIONS

ABC	Australian Broadcasting Commission
ABI	Adelaide Bible Institute
ABFM	Australian Baptist Foreign Mission
ABM	Australian Board of Missions
ABMS	Australian Baptist Missionary Society
ACC	Australian Council of Churches
ACC	Australian Christian Churches (Pentecostal)
ACL	Anglican Church League
ACL	Australian Christian Lobby
ACR	*Australian Church Record*
ACW	*Australian Christian World*
ACT	Australian College of Theology
ADB	*Australian Dictionary of Biography*
ADEB	*Australian Dictionary of Evangelical Biography*
AFES	Australian Fellowship of Evangelical Students
AFL	Australian Freedom League
AHRC	Australian Human Rights Commission
AIF	Australian Imperial Force
AIM	Australian Inland Mission
ALP	Australian Labor Party
AMC	Australian Missionary Council
AOG	Assemblies of God in Australia
APA	Australian Peace Alliance
APB	Aboriginal Protection Board
APCM	Asia Pacific Christian Mission
ARMA	Anglican Renewal Ministries of Australia
AWM	Australian War Memorial
AWU	The Australian Workers' Union
BCA	Bush Church Aid Society
BCSA	Bible College of South Australia
BCV	Bible College of Victoria
BEM	Borneo Evangelical Mission
BFBS	British and Foreign Bible Society
BGA	Billy Graham Archives
BGEA	Billy Graham Evangelistic Association

BHP	Broken Hill Proprietary Company Ltd.
BMS	Baptist Missionary Society
BRF	Baptist Revival Fellowship
BS	Bible Society
BSF	Bible Study Fellowship
BU	Baptist Union
BWA	Baptist World Alliance
C&MA	Christian and Missionary Alliance
CBS	Campus Bible Study
CCC	Christian City Church
CCCS	Colonial (later Commonwealth) and Continental Church Society
CDP	Christian Democratic Party
CE	Christian Endeavour
CENEF	Church of England National Emergency Fund
CESA	Church of England in South Africa
CICCU	Cambridge Inter-Collegiate Christian Union
CIM	China Inland Mission
CLTC	Christian Leaders' Training College, PNG
CMBC	City Men's Bible Class
CMS	Church Missionary Society
COC	Christian Outreach Centre
CPC	Chinese Presbyterian Church
CPSA	Church of the Province of South Africa
CRC	Christian Radicals Club
CRC	Christian Revival Centres
CSSM	Children's Special Service Mission
CO	conscientious objector
CWCI	Christian Women Communicating International
DCCM	Department of Cross Cultural Ministries (HMS)
EA	Evangelical Alliance
EFAC	Evangelical Fellowship of the Anglican Communion
EMU	Evangelical Members within the Uniting Church in Australia
ESL	English as a Second Language
EU	Evangelical Union
FCA	Fellowship of Confessing Anglicans
GAA	General Assembly of Australia (Presbyterian)
GAFCON	Global Anglican Future Conference

GNH	Good News Hall
HMS	Home Mission Society (Anglican Diocese of Sydney)
HNW	The House of the New World
HTA	Holy Trinity Adelaide
IBMR	*International Bulletin of Missionary Research*
ISCF	Inter-School Christian Fellowship
IVF	Inter-Varsity Fellowship
JCE	*Journal of Christian Education*
JRH	*Journal of Religious History*
KYB	Know Your Bible
KYC	Katoomba Youth Convention
LMS	London Missionary Society
MAF	Missionary Aviation Fellowship
MBI	Melbourne Bible Institute
MGC	Melbourne Gospel Crusade
ML	Mitchell Library, Sydney
MLA	Member of the Legislative Assembly
MLC	Member of the Legislative Council
MOW	Movement for the Ordination of Women
MST	Melbourne School of Theology
MTC	Moore (Theological) College
MTS	Ministry Training Strategy
MUP	Melbourne University Press
NAA	National Archives of Australia
NCTM	New Creation Teaching Ministry
NEAC	National Evangelical Anglican Congress
NESB	Non-English speaking background
NLA	National Library of Australia
NSW	New South Wales
NT	Northern Territory
OAC	Open Air Campaigners
OCF	Overseas Christian Fellowship
PCEA	Presbyterian Church of Eastern Australia
PCF	Parliamentary Christian Fellowship
PBI	Perth Bible Institute
PNG	Papua New Guinea
PSAs	Pleasant Sunday Afternoons
RA	Reforming Alliance (UCA)
RAHSJ	*Royal Australian Historical Society Journal*

REPA	Reformed Evangelical Protestant Association
RSL	Returned Servicemen's League, now Returned and Services League
RSSILA	Returned Soldiers and Sailors Imperial League of Australia (later the RSL)
RTR	*Reformed Theological Review*
SA	South Australia
SCD	Sydney College of Divinity
SCM	Sydney City Mission
SCM	Student Christian Movement
SDA	Seventh-day Adventists
SMBC	Sydney Missionary and Bible College
SMH	*Sydney Morning Herald*
SPCK	Society for Promoting Christian Knowledge
SPG	Society for the Propagation of the Gospel
SU	Scripture Union
TEC	The Episcopal Church of America
TLC	Truth and Liberation Concern
UAICC	Uniting Aboriginal and Islander Christian Congress
UAM	United Aborigines' Mission
UCA	Uniting Church of Australia
UFM	Unevangelised Fields Mission
WA	Western Australia
WBT	Wycliffe Bible Translators
WCC	World Council of Churches
WCSPL	Women's Compulsory Service Petition League
WCTU	Woman's Christian Temperance Union
WEC	The Worldwide Evangelisation Crusade
WMMS	Wesleyan Methodist Missionary Society
WPC	Westminster Presbyterian Church
WV	World Vision
YMCA	Young Men's Christian Association
YWAM	Youth with a Mission
YWCA	Young Women's Christian Association

PROLOGUE

A Redeemed Crusader's Life of Atonement

But we are on the Lord's side and I feel now I must put the burden on him and acknowledge to HIM my own ineptness. He will work and use us and we must trust HIM to perform his justice which is perfect.
(Mary Bennett[1])

Of all campaigners for Aboriginal rights in Australian history, Mary Bennett, teacher at the United Aborigines' Mission at Mount Margaret in WA, warrants nomination for the most determined. She would probably also take out the prize for the most outspoken. All six police protectors of Aborigines in WA in the 1930s, she alleged, drank too much and five were immoral. She knew so much about the police, she declared, because she taught their half-caste children. Well over half a century before the 'black armband' school of historians called time on the sanitised version of white/black relations, she condemned the white settlement of Australia as a disaster and a disgrace. She had no patience with the euphemisms employed by whites to describe their dispossession of Aboriginal people: 'dispersal', she insisted, meant 'killing', and, though unreported, there had been 'wholesale massacres'. Australia's record towards its Indigenous peoples deserved international censure. They had been deprived, she thundered, of their lands, their children forcibly removed, their families 'smashed', and their women enslaved, abused and the 'sanctity of their person' denied.[2]

It was all too much for Auber Octavius Neville, WA's Chief Protector, who agreed to a Royal Commission into the treatment of Aboriginal people, apparently to allow Mary Bennett to vent her spleen in an environment he controlled.[3]

---

1 Mary Bennet to Ada Bromham, quoted in Alison Holland, *Just Relations: The Story of Mary Bennett's Crusade for Aboriginal Rights* (UWA Publishing, 2015), 358.

2 Mary M. Bennett, *The Australian Aboriginal as a Human Being* (London: Alston Rivers, 1930), 115.

3 *Report of the Royal Commissioner appointed to investigate, report, and advise upon matters in relation to the treatment of Aborigines*, Perth, 1935.

He appointed as sole commissioner, Henry Mozeley, to get the right outcome. Mozeley, Bennett reported, bullied Aboriginal witnesses. He chronically dissented from her allegations, dismissing them as hearsay. He found it was not wrong to keep Aboriginal people in chains, because they did not complain and did not appear to be in discomfort. Neville, who himself testified at the Royal Commission, was incredulous that Bennett should be content with allowing 'half-caste' Aboriginal people to marry just anyone in plain contravention of the science of eugenics. She responded tartly that whites when marrying were not required to concern themselves with eugenics. She stoutly opposed Neville's assimilationist belief in 'biological absorption' which she argued amounted to genocide.[4] She was well ahead of her time, demanding land rights for Aboriginal people and the payment of reparation to them, and an end to the abominable practice of removing children from their mothers. Asked if she would prefer neglected children to remain with their mothers, she replied unhesitatingly that she would: far better to be neglected than removed.[5]

Mary Bennett (1861–1961) came from a pioneering, privileged and well-connected family. Her paternal grandfather, Alexander Christison, was a Church of Scotland minister. He was known in his parish as 'the Dominie', the term widely used in Scotland for a parson. Incidentally, it was the same title used by the Indigenous people of Port Jackson to address the first chaplain, Richard Johnson. On the wall of his kirk at Fouldon near Berwick-on-Tweed, his son Robert (Mary Bennett's father) had placed a plaque engraved with the words 'Seek Him that turneth the shadow of death into morning.'[6] That is precisely what Mary Bennett was to do with respect to the need of Australia's indigenous peoples. Robert, 'the Meenister's son', established a huge cattle station, Lammermoor, in northern Queensland and acquired a reputation as one who worked together with the Dalleburra Aboriginal people for the mutual benefit of all parties. Some 300 lived on the property with hunting rights and access to water and, for the most part, sparing the sheep and cattle so that Christison could make a fortune and they could live in a modicum of safety.

Christison was a founder of the Anglican Diocese of North Queensland where, in 1879, his friend George Stanton, an evangelical, was enthroned as bishop. On his behalf Christison did deputation work in Britain and then trained the bishop in bushcraft in the demanding Australian environment. In demonstration of his familiarity with the Psalms, he even suggested what

---

4 Alison Holland, 'A Scottish Inheritance? Mary Bennett, the Aboriginal Cause and the Legacies of the Past', *Journal of the Sydney Society for Scottish History*, 16, 2016, 105.

5 Holland, *Just Relations*, 348.

6 Amos 5:8.

should go in a bush service of worship.[7] In 1927, twelve years after his death, Mary wrote his biography.[8] By this time, Mary, whose own husband died also in 1927, had become committed to her calling[9] to work with and for the Aboriginal people. The biography of her father is a fierce indictment of the plight of the Aboriginal people combined with a romanticised account of her father's enlightened treatment of them.[10] She attached great weight to her father's name for his Indigenous labourers as 'faithfuls'. She came to the conclusion that Aboriginal labour and generosity had been essential to the successful development of the new nation.[11]

Bennett believed that her calling was propitious. The sensitivity of the British conscience on native peoples at that time assumed political significance. Her work entailed advocacy on behalf of Aboriginal people throughout the Empire, defence of them in the Australian courts, and educating them through missions. The last, which she characterised as 'lifting up civilisation's casualties', was the work she said she most loved.[12] She condemned living conditions in Gnowangerup, WA, where she arrived in 1930 and taught the Nyungar children there to spin and weave before moving on to the Forrest River Mission. Then, from 1932 to 1942, Bennett worked at the UAM Mount Margaret Mission, established by Robert Schenk in 1921.

It has been rightly observed that Bennett 'would not have been acceptable to Schenk, or the UAM, if she did not adhere to the conservative doctrinal beliefs'.[13] She was at one with her evangelical missionary colleagues in her view of the undesirability of such Aboriginal practices as infant betrothal, child marriage, polygamy and wife-lending. These she condemned on the twin grounds

---

7 Mary M. Bennett, *Christison of Lammermoor* (London: Alston Rivers, 1927), 11, 145–154.

8 Bennett, *Christison of Lammermoor.*

9 On the nature and strength of her call to work with and for Aboriginal people, see Holland, *Just Relations*, 53, 65–71. It was a call which preceded her galvanizing encounter in 1929 with Anthony Fernando, himself an unrelenting Christian activist. On Fernando, see Fiona Paisley, *The Lone Protestor: AM Fernando in Australia and Europe* (Canberra: Aboriginal Studies Press, 2012).

10 Mark Cryle, 'A "Fantastic Adventure": Reading *Christison of Lammermoor*' in F. McKenzie, Journeys through Queensland history: Landscape, place and society, Proceedings of the Professional Historians Association (Queensland) conference, Brisbane 3–4 September 2009 https://espace.library.uq.edu.au/view/UQ:202012/p9780646519197_3_223.pdf&bookreader=true#page/1/mode/1up accessed 27.4.17.

11 Holland, 'A Scottish Inheritance?, 96.

12 Holland, 'A Scottish Inheritance?, 103.

13 Alison Longworth, '"Was it worthwhile?" An historical analysis of five women missionaries and their encounters with the Nyungar people of south-west Australia', PhD, Murdoch University, 2005, 278.

that they originated in 'heathenism' and were detrimental to the wellbeing of women.[14] She had more confidence in the capacity of biblical teaching to protect women from abuse than she had in Aboriginal traditions. But she was far more disturbed by white male attitudes to Aboriginal women than she was by traditional Aboriginal attitudes. Her book *The Australian Aborigine as a Human Being* was published in 1930. It is a rich compound of biblical beliefs, social research, practical experience, compassion for the oppressed, empathy with Indigenous cultures, and feminist insights. It seeks to educate her readers and appeal to their consciences, especially those of Christian women. Its contents are arranged around a quotation from Dr Ramsay Smith, physician and anthropologist, in the *Official Year Book of the Commonwealth of Australia* for 1909:

> The problem of what to do with the race, the most interesting at present on earth, and the least deserving to be exterminated by us, and the most wronged at our hands, is not a difficult one to solve, were a solution really desired.[15]

Four of the seven chapters are under the heading 'The most wronged at our hands'. Her opening proposition is that 'There is a growing number of enlightened humane Australians who feel that the present position of the Aboriginals is unworthy of a great nation' (11). The first chapter begins (13) with a quotation from I Corinthians 15:45: 'The first man … a living soul.' Her evaluation of the Aboriginal person as a [hu]man and brother, of one blood with all humankind, and with an immortal soul is common to all evangelical missionaries. But to this she added an embryonic appreciation of the religious value of Aboriginal culture which was not yet common among missionaries: 'We could learn much from "our" Australian natives, who are … [a] Spirit force which we lose at our peril' (52). Rather than insisting on the benefits of 'civilisation', she deplored 'the influence of the white men, which was causing the boys to depart from the ancestral virtues and to become selfish and unwilling to share' (57). She had much greater respect for Aboriginal culture which aided their survival than she did for the culture of those settlers which hastened their destruction. As to any culpability by Aboriginal people for their own plight, the 'chief crime of black men' was that of 'defending their wives and daughters!' (60).[16] In a

14 Alison Holland, *Just Relations*, 111–117, 369f.

15 Bennett, *The Australian Aboriginal as a Human Being*, Contents page.

16 In *Christison of Lammermoor* (97), she complained of the injustice of punishing 'the crime of black men defending their wives, not the crime of white men molesting black women'.

rare gesture of diplomacy, she claimed to have 'no quarrel with the settlers: the objection is to the system'. But her denunciation of the 'system' left no room for diplomacy. It was 'analogous to slavery'. Natives are deprived of their hunting grounds, compelled to work for settlers, and prevented from selling their labour in a system controlled entirely by the employers and the police (101). Her severest indictment is found in chapter six on Aboriginal women:

> Some people assert, for convenience, that native girls are 'non-moral,' intending to imply that the white man who has a fresh native girl every week – as one boasted – does her no injury; they assert that people cannot be robbed of what they do not possess nor native girls of chastity (113).

She reported complaints of 'motor car loads of men from bush townships or construction camps bent on "ginsprees," in other words drink and prostitution orgies' (116).

Her solution? Aboriginal women 'need *their* homes, *their* families, and not to be interfered with' (120). If they are in need of protecting, men cannot be trusted to do that: women must be appointed to care for women (126). Her appeal is couched in terms which reveals the debt feminism owes to the Bible:

> Faced with the suffering of our fellow women, with the suffering of children – is it beyond a woman's wit to find a way of helping them? a way to back up the work of women for them? Or is feminism a failure? Are we passing by on the other side? (127).

In her role of sensitising consciences, she employed the words of Jesus[17] and Abraham Lincoln[18]: 'It is the business of each one of us to know what is happening on the fringes of settlement. It is the business of each one of us if through us offences come' (142).

At a conference of the British Commonwealth League, Bennett gave a paper entitled 'The Aboriginal Mother in Western Australia in 1933'.[19] She joined the Anti-Slavery and Aborigines' Protection Society and, to address the exploitation of Aboriginal labourers, she applied for help from the International Labour Organisation and the International Federation of Free Trade Unions. She demanded reparation for the dispossessed.[20] Her very public campaign

---

17 Luke 17:1.

18 Second Inaugural Address (1865).

19 Mary M. Bennett, *The Aboriginal Mother in Western Australia in 1933* (Sydney: K.A. Wood, Printer, 1933).

20 Anne O'Brien, *God's Willing Workers: Women and Religion in Australia* (Sydney: UNSW Press, 2005), 78.

worried those who wished to stay on good terms with the 'governing class'. Those who had lent their support at first, but who were not at one with her in their religious convictions, deserted her. Especially prominent was the well-connected Theosophist, Bessie Rischbieth, president of the Australian Federation of Women Voters. She became alarmed by Bennett's 'unpatriotic' condemnation of settler rapacity and was attracted to A.O. Neville's belief in 'absorption' of First Australians by the more powerful white culture. Rischbieth found Bennett too self-righteous; Bennett considered Rischbieth too worldly. They parted company permanently.[21] Apart from Robert and Mysie Schenk at the Mount Margaret Mission, those who continued their support for Bennett's campaign included an ex-missionary, Edith Jones, by now wife of an Anglican minister, Ada Bromham, a revered WCTU leader, and Helen Baillie, who was also descended from a wealthy squatter dynasty, albeit one not so altruistic as Bennett's father had been.

Helen Baillie's father was from a squatting family in Victoria's Western District. Her mother was the daughter of Walter Fellows, first vicar of St John's Toorak, Melbourne's most opulent suburb. She attended Aldworth Girls' Grammar School in East Malvern, a seriously academic Presbyterian school in the evangelical tradition. Many of its pupils became missionaries; others like Helen herself became nurses. Classes in Christian doctrine at the school were taught by John Gason, vicar of St John's Church of England, East Malvern. Helen characterised him as 'a Saint of the Evangelical School'.[22] Upon reflecting on the social application of the Gospel, Helen became a Christian Socialist.

Baillie was trained in midwifery in London. Returning to Australia, she read Bennett's *Christison of Lammermoor* on board ship and was challenged to join its author in her crusade on behalf of Indigenous Australians. She felt called to the special work of 'the education of Australians in a right understanding of these natives, so that Australia as a whole may have an enlightened policy for her Aboriginals', and she formed the 'Aboriginal Fellowship Group' for the purpose and served as its secretary. Baillie visited Aboriginal communities in the outback, using a chauffeur-driven car, and was shocked by the poverty and racism she witnessed. She was opposed to the removal of Aboriginal people

21 Lake, *Getting Equal*, 130.

22 Peter Sherlock and Patricia Grimshaw, 'One Woman's Concern for Social Justice: The Letters of Helen Baillie to Farnham Maynard, 1933–36', in Colin Holden, (Editor), *Anglo-Catholicism in Melbourne: Papers to Mark the 150th Anniversary of St Peter's Eastern Hill 1846–1996* (Parkville: University of Melbourne, Department of History, 1997), 85–98.

of mixed descent from missions to government 'homes'. She advocated the appointment of women as protectors, and that they should be trained for the position. She agreed with Mary Bennett that there was nothing to be proud of in the history of the treatment of the First Australians. On the centenary of the emancipation of slaves in the British Empire and the death in the same year (1833) of William Wilberforce, she enthused: 'Could we not celebrate it by a determined effort to promote justice and humanity towards our own aboriginals, the original inhabitants of our land?' Baillie was one of a number of disciples of Mary Bennett,[23] sharing with her not only a commitment to professional competence in an altruistic profession, but also a resolute prophetic stance on humane race relations based on clear biblical principles.

Mary Bennett was not compliant, nor male, nor minister, nor theologian. She laboured among the least influential and she did not enjoy great success. She was not well known in her own lifetime and she almost disappeared from Australian history before anyone found a place for her. Historian Geoffrey Bolton doubted if she were sufficiently important to justify inclusion in the *Australian Dictionary of Biography*.[24] But she was such a champion of Aboriginal women and such a critic of white men that she is now revered by feminist historians,[25] even though they are inclined to neglect the study of missionaries on the grounds that they are not feminist enough.[26] In the case of Mary Bennett, recruited by UAM missionary Rod Schenk, there is a reluctance among feminist historians to identify her as a missionary: she was a teacher at the mission, they argue, more interested in education than in evangelisation. Such historians do not overlook entirely her religious motivation. Marilyn Lake, for example, is unenthusiastic about Bennett's 'perspective' in that it was that of 'a missionary and imperialist'. Yet she makes the large concession that her 'confidence and authority' for insisting on the freedom of women to choose their own marriage partner is derived from the Christian teaching on 'the intrinsic value of every human being'.[27] Alison Holland recognises her 'strong Protestant, Calvinist faith'[28] and acknowledges that 'Like reformers all over the empire, hers was a Christian agenda for change which utilised

---

23 Alison Holland, *Just Relations*, 273.

24 Holland, *Just Relations*, x.

25 Marilyn Lake, *Getting Equal: The History of Australian Feminism* (St Leonards: Allen & Unwin, 1999); Holland, *Just Relations;* Holland, 'A Scottish Inheritance?', 85–110. See also, Sue Taffe, *A White Hot Flame: Mary Montgomerie Bennett – Author, Educator, Activist for Indigenous Justice* (Clayton: Monash University Publishing, 2018).

26 Longworth, "Was it worthwhile?", 47, 279.

27 Lake, *Getting Equal*, 128.

28 Holland, 'A Scottish Inheritance?', 109.

the humanitarian moment to demand salvation and justice for Aboriginal people.'[29] But they do not give Christian influence the attention it warrants, and historian Anne O'Brien has called for this deficiency to be addressed.

It is not enough, O'Brien argues, to refer only in passing to the Christian backgrounds of those of feminist convictions. The role of Christianity in their life and work calls for closer analysis. O'Brien affirms categorically that 'the most active feminist advocates of Aboriginal women's rights were deeply committed Christians'.[30] She adds that downplaying the religious dimension does not help the feminist cause: 'To recognise the Christian basis of Mary Bennett's feminism is not to dilute it, rather the reverse'. 'In particular,' insists O'Brien, 'Mary Bennett's ideas need to be seen in the context of her life as a faith missionary'.[31] It is a just call. History is the discipline of context, and for Alison Holland in her monumental study of Bennett, written subsequent to O'Brien's exhortation, the contexts of feminism and human rights discipline her argument. Bennett's Christianity is never denied, but the nature of its influence is not analysed. The Christian vocabulary of faith, hope and compassion, of sacrifice, mission and crusade, of repentance, conscience, ethical awakenings, reconciliation and atonement, is all present, but how it shaped her thought and action is rarely explored.

Yet Holland has apparently begun the hard work of heeding O'Brien's plea, acknowledging explicitly that:

> For their part, the missionaries at Mt Margaret were devoted servants of God – faith missionaries – for whom working among the Aborigines was accepting a call. Beyond government permission, they required faith in God, self-righteousness, stoicism, Aboriginal co-operation and the support of the wider Christian community. Mary Bennett was among them.[32]

Here is a significant historiographical development. It begins to replace a binary approach to the limitations of missions in contrast to the perspicacity of feminism with the acknowledgement that, at least at this point in history, there was a fruitful synergy between them. Admittedly, Holland continues to employ the secularist rhetoric on Christian missions as passé and culturally aggressive: Mt Margaret was 'clearly part of a global missionary assault …

29 Holland, *Just Relations,* 52.

30 O'Brien, *God's Willing Workers*, 79.

31 O' Brien, *God's Willing Workers*, 79, 82.

32 Holland, *Just Relations,* 166f.

part of a broader Anglo-imperial modernist project that emerged in the first decades of the twentieth century'.[33] Yet she is able to recognise that it was an 'assault' and a 'project' not without benefit to Aboriginal people:

> the aims of the Schenks and Bennett fitted demands for citizenship and progress being made by many Aboriginal leaders in the southeast and southwest at this time who were, in turn, part of a global indigenous movement seeking access, opportunity, education, paid work and equal civil rights.[34]

It is always important to get history as right as possible, but this area of history, as Holland frequently notices, has obvious implications for the future. If a negative or anachronistic assessment of Christian missions were to lead to the sidelining of Christian thinking and practice it could impoverish Australia's future, especially that of Indigenous Australians. That is the perspective foundational to this study. And, although Mary Bennett's tireless activism was exceptional in its focus and persistence, it well exemplifies the themes of this study of the influence of evangelical Christianity on Australian history: its internationalism both in empire and missions; its public-spiritedness and persevering civic engagement in the interests of sensitising the Australian conscience; and its capacity for desecularisation in a rapidly secularising world through the invocation of biblical principles as social norms.

Because she was connected to the humanitarian wing of international evangelicalism, Bennett felt supported in her opposition to the more selfish aspirations of Australian nationalism and she drew strength from the work of women missionaries especially to India and China. She prized the principles of imperial humanitarianism, especially that of benevolent trusteeship, and was aware of the debt they owed to the vital religious faith of the slave trade abolitionists. Yet she was aware that, in the hands of acquisitive politicians and pastoralists, 'protection' had become a cloak for exploitation and 'civilisation' an excuse for cultural aggression.[35] British Empire justice fell short of the justice demanded by the Kingdom of God, and Bennett exemplified those evangelicals who, by the middle of the twentieth century had begun to see that to promote God's Kingdom, it was not necessary to insist on loyalty to the United Kingdom. She put the matter with characteristic robustness a month before her death in 1961: 'I grew up a shocking imperialist but not so

33 Holland, *Just Relations,* 195.

34 Holland, *Just Relations,* 195.

35 Holland, *Just Relations,* 12f.

shocking as to accept their blasphemies'.[36] She, then, is part of a complex story, one peopled with humanitarians and evangelicals as well as pastoralists and police: 'For Aborigines, the Empire not only brought the threat of destruction but also furnished the tools of adaptation and survival.'[37]

Bennett's public crusade for justice for Aboriginal people was deeply rooted in Christian faith and strengthened by it. In the face of sustained opposition, she did not withdraw into a private faith. Because she understood her work as a calling of divine origin; she had abundant moral energy to withstand all opposition and to remain unapologetic in her identification with the plight of Indigenous Australians. Because she believed that all Australians were equal in the sight of God, she committed herself to a practical and public-spirited campaign to raise Indigenous people to equality with those who dispossessed them. Because she believed in co-operating with all people of good will in the best of causes, she worked with people of many different faiths, but, when any withdrew their support, while despondent, she was not diverted from pursuing her calling. She was happiest when serving the disadvantaged alongside those who shared her faith. By intellect and upbringing, they were not as well equipped as she for public advocacy, but they were not her inferior when it came to perseverance in their engagement with the most needy.

What she achieved fell far short of what she hoped to achieve, but her impact on the Aboriginal rights movement after the Second World War was tangible. Because she was able to face the horrific reality of devastation wrought on the original population, she was committed to sensitising the conscience and educating the consciousness in the interests of developing an Australian soul accepting of all and more in alignment with its Christian heritage. Her humanitarian crusade was threatened rather than aided by the forces of secularisation which reputedly swept all before them and which sought to remove church involvement from public policy. But Bennett chose to exercise her ministry, with a feminist's focus on the rights of women, through the most conservative of evangelical agencies under the direction of the most uncompromising of missionaries. To demonstrate that such was neither surprising nor extraordinary is the purpose of this book. Dissenting from the *a priori* secular dismissal of the value of Christian missions, it seeks to make a small contribution to 'the larger humanitarian story in Australian history not yet fully told'.[38]

36 Quoted in Holland, *Just Relations*, 7.

37 Deryck M Schreuder and Stuart Ward, (eds), *Australia's Empire, Oxford History of the British Empire* (Oxford: OUP, 2008), 14. This quotation is from the 'Introduction' written by the editors.

38 Holland, *Just Relations,* 361.

INTRODUCTION

On National Consciousness and the National Conscience

'It is not a civic theocracy that we need, nor privatised religion, but the public opening up of the word of Christ to the world – and of the truth about his influence on its cultural history.'
(Edwin Judge)

This study of evangelical Christianity in twentieth-century Australia, as highlighted in the Prologue above, is the story of three of its relationships: with the culture; with secularism; and with the state. The culture is here characterised as the consciousness and the conscience of the 'Australian soul'. Secularism is here understood as a rival ideology, instinctively hostile to all religion, but especially to the Christian tradition in which it was conceived and nurtured and to which it owes most. The state is shorthand for the public domain, including not only the political, legal, educational, health and welfare spheres, but also the commercial system and the world of work.

What is the national soul of Australia and how did Christians in the evangelical family attend to it in the twentieth century? To answer the second question first, in the First World War, they attended to it by committing themselves as unreservedly as any part of the population to the war effort. They gave extravagant demonstration of their belief that those who loved Christ must be fully engaged with Australians at the point of greatest need, which was to defeat the enemy. Protestant Christians were in the forefront of those who enlisted or encouraged young men to enlist. They were among the first to sacrifice themselves and to find meaning in the sacrifice of those slain on the battlefield. They cared much for the physical wellbeing of members of the armed forces and they were attentive to the anxiety of their families. Before war's end, however, the harshest reality drove them to the realisation that this understanding of the greatest need of the Australian soul was more profligate than wise. They needed then to attend to a soul which was sorrowing and despairing rather than excited and optimistic.

Towards the end of the twentieth century a vocal minority of evangelicals gave attention to nothing but the close study of the Bible and to the preaching of the Gospel.[1] They condemned as outside the Gospel's mandate the concern for social welfare and counselling for the psychologically needy, and for national, social, economic and political stability. They believed that the best way to engage most proficiently with all Australians was to be focused on the Gospel for that is what all Australians most needed. The majority in the evangelical family criticised this stance as altogether too narrow: it reflected a failure to respond either to the fullness of the Gospel or to the needs of the Australian soul. It also failed one of evangelicalism's acid tests: evangelistic effectiveness. But, whether broad or narrow, evangelicals, when true to their own profession, were determined to engage all Australians with the love of God in Christ. They were not at liberty to abandon attending (or, as they would have said, ministering) to the Australian soul.

The Public Spirit of Christianity

To identify the content and benefit of that ministry to the Australian soul is one of the challenges of the current study. It will be argued, in sum, that it is a ministry which has sensitised the national conscience and helped shape the national consciousness. The most obvious benefit of faith in Christ to the individual soul is eternal life, but what benefit does the nation receive from those who have that faith? It is a benefit too little acknowledged in history considering how extensive it is. It includes public spirit, civic duty, patriotism, national pride, an orientation to reform, altruism, moral energy, and to informing the national conscience with self-sacrificing compassion and a freedom which is functional rather than libertine. Evangelical Christians have not had a monopoly on these national assets, but typically they contribute them to the community's 'social capital'. Together with a way of understanding the world and constructing national consciousness, they are the substance of what Christianity brings to the history of nations.

As we shall see, it is possible from existing sources at either end of the twentieth century to identify how church-going is positively correlated with civic-mindedness or public-spiritedness. At the beginning of the century churches assumed they had a civic role largely because their communities

---

1 A survey of Australian Protestant denominations in the early 1990s showed that more than twice as many preferred the combination of social action with evangelism to an exclusive focus on evangelism. Peter Kaldor, *Winds of Change: The Experience of Church in a Changing Australia* (Homebush West: Lancer, 1994), 61.

expected them to exercise that function. At the unveiling of a monument in commemoration of a mine disaster in the Illawarra coalfields, south of Sydney, in 1902 twelve speeches were scheduled, the last five by ministers of religion in the accepted order: Church of England, Catholic, Presbyterian, Methodist, Congregational. Only the last had mercy on the long-suffering crowd and waived his right to speak.[2] Ministers of religion were civic functionaries and their flocks were strongly represented in the ranks of community organisations. By the end of the century ministers were no longer automatically given civic roles,[3] but the members of their congregations were still on average far more involved with community organisations than those who were not churchgoers.[4]

Patriotism and nationalism are commonly associated with civic-mindedness, and Protestant churchgoers were also at both ends of the period under review more patriotic than Catholics and non-churchgoers, expressed greater pride in being Australian and were more willing to fight for their country.[5] But the love which evangelical Christians had for their country was not uncritical. They always wanted to improve it: one way to attend to the national soul was to reform it. Another manifestation of the evangelical care for the national soul has recently been characterised as the 'dynamic altruism'[6] of faith, best exemplified by William Wilberforce who associated it with 'true patriotism' and 'public spirit'. It is the source not so much of doctrinal correctness but of moral energy and it is a principal ingredient in the national conscience. To attend to the national soul, then, is to nurture the national conscience through the dynamic altruism which is an essential response to the hearing of the Gospel: 'by their fruits ye shall know them' (Matthew 7:20).

The Secular Spirit

Religious faith, however, attends to the consciousness of the national soul as well as to its conscience. Any study of religion in Australian society in the twentieth century has to respond to the issue of secularisation which, it is commonly assumed, has delivered Australia, along with many Western nations, to

2 Stuart Piggin and Henry Lee, *The Mt Kembla Disaster* (Melbourne: OUP, 1994), 244.

3 Yet, in current post-secular, multi-faith Australia, when religion is perceived as a potential threat to national security, training for 'civic leadership' is offered to heads of faith communities.

4 See Conclusion, below.

5 Gary D. Bouma and Beverly R. Dixon, *The Religious Factor in Australian Life* (Melbourne: MARC Australia, 1986), 34–37.

6 Alan Atkinson, 'How do we live with ourselves? The Australian national conscience', *Australian Book Review*, 384, 2016.

a post-Christian destination. To begin to reframe this 'settled sociological and historical truth'[7] is one of the purposes of this study. It is a challenge which, given the influence of secularism, must be faced if we are to have any hope of recognising Christianity's contribution to the national soul. For example, one respondent to the concept of dynamic altruism in the national conscience, complains that this is a 'moral matter' which has a 'religious connotation'. He prefers to meet Australia's need with science:

> There is no right or wrong in nature. There is only what is most efficient for survival and development. The faculty nature has endowed us with is not conscience, the moral or religious sense, but consciousness, the awareness of reality and of what is most efficient for our survival and development.[8]

This is a very secularised view of religion, denying to it any role in consciousness or in defining reality. It just assumes that religion is somehow subconscious and unreal, and it does not expect this assumption to be contradicted. It also assumes that religion and science are incompatible. There is no recognition of the possibility that religion might be as significant in the formation of consciousness as it is of the conscience, or that reality is ultimately to be understood as the world as it is perceived by God, or that science was conceived in the womb of biblical precepts. As indeed was secularism itself, which has been characterised as religion's 'Siamese twin', that is, joined at the hip at birth. This suggests the important possibility that our modern understanding of religion may be no older than our understanding of secularism.[9] Secularism claims to do what Christianity has claimed as part of its role, namely to structure knowledge and expectation to give its adherents meaning and purpose. So understood, Australia, along with much of the Western world, might be as 'christianised' at the end of the period under review as it was at the beginning. Edwin Judge, Emeritus Professor of History at Macquarie University, in 1996 declared:

---

7 Stephen Chavura and Ian Tregenza, 'Introduction: Rethinking Secularism in Australia (and Beyond)', *JRH*, 38.3, 2014, 299; Graeme Davison, 'Religion', in Alison Bashford and Stuart Macintyre, (eds.), *The Cambridge History of Australia* 2 vols (Port Melbourne; New York: CUP, 2013), vol.2, 221.

8 Rodney Crisp, https://www.australianbookreview.com.au/abr-online/archive/2016/185-september-2016-no-384/3531.

9 Brent Nongbri, *Before Religion: A History of a Modern Concept* (New Haven: Yale University Press, 213), 4.

> People in the churches should not accept that our age is post-Christian. It is profoundly christianised in its basic attitudes. The place of the churches is not to disabuse people of this, but to reintroduce them to the Master whom they ignorantly worship.[10]

Among the plethora of definitions of 'secularisation' and 'secularism', secularisation is here understood as the retreat of religious concerns in the public square, the reduction of religion's power to shape the national culture or consciousness, and the decline in religious belief and practice. Secularism is an ideology, the belief that religious influence on society is usually weak and unimportant and always detrimental. Historians typically assumed rather than proved that Australia's heritage in the twentieth century was secular. This study questions this assumption. But more importantly, it is also necessary to remove the debate from the religion vs secularity binary model. Secular Australia, it will be argued, has been significantly shaped by Christian values. In turn, it will be acknowledged that Christian Australia manifests secular values, but often those values required a Christian culture in the first place for their conception and maturation. The irony of the historical development of ideological secularism is that smuggled into it are numerous biblical values, which must be traced to the influence of Jerusalem rather than to the astringent Aristotelian logic of Athens. At the same time, the churches, even those eager to be seen to be untouched by secularism, have allowed their values to be shaped by Athens as well as Jerusalem. All Australians are more Christian than they know, and all Australian Christians are more secular than they know. All Australians wear a Gospel-sourced imprint.

To argue that Australia is still one of the most 'christianised' of nations raises the question of how dependent the secular nation is or should be on the Christian sources of its inspiration. It is a fact, for example, that the 'secular' education Acts of the nineteenth century in the Australian colonies were largely the work of that common Christianity advanced by civic Protestantism. But does that mean that Christianity should continue to have a significant role in state education in the early twenty-first century? Similarly, should Christians be so determined to create a Christian schooling system apart from the state secular system? Are not both, and therefore the nation, the poorer for giving an exclusive binary institutionalisation of the religion/secular divide? The answer to that is not an obvious 'yes': competition between the systems could be good for both. But aligning schooling systems with ideological secularism

10 Edwin Judge, *Engaging Rome and Jerusalem*, (North Melbourne: Australian Scholarly Publishing, 2014), 178, cf. xxviii.

on the one hand and fundamentalist religions on the other would surely be culturally impoverishing for the nation.

Ancient History Made Modern

Ironically, Australia has a history which, while apparently in retreat from Christian thinking, makes manifest the critical importance of understanding the earliest history of the Christian church. Members of the early church first sought to live at peace within the wider community of those who were not Christians. That is probably the aim of most Christians today – only a minority accept that to be a Christian in Australia it is necessary to be a culture warrior and oppose all that is not Christian in our political, legal and educational systems. Then, when Christians were persecuted for their faith, their leaders developed the position that it was not unreasonable to belong to an association that stood for the truth even if it involved breaking the law. As Australian laws become more incompatible with Christian ethical standards, there will be increasing tension between church and state.

The Roman state, following its era of persecution of Christians, inaugurated toleration of Christianity along with other religions in return for their prayers for the safety of the state. This pragmatic pluralism is paralleled in the modern world by the extensive use by governments of churches in welfare, hospitals and education, which is a recognition of the social capital generated by the Christian impulse to altruism. Finally, under Constantine Christianity became the official religion of the state, which is a position of privilege in the state which gave to Christianity a power which it found difficult to exercise without corruption. There are Christians in modern Australia on the right wing of politics who would be happy for their churches to have such power, but presumably the majority of Christians prefer freedom of religion as a statutory right.

In the fourth century AD (to continue with the ancient history which is so modern) Eusebius, Bishop of Caesarea, wrote a history of the church from the day of the apostles to the time of Constantine. He there argued that the Kingdom of God was evident in the progressive improvement of the present world and that the triumph of the church in history would result in the perfection of human society this side of eternity. At the beginning of the fifth century, the sack of Rome destroyed the belief that the coming of the Kingdom of God would result from the nexus of church and empire. At that time, Augustine, Bishop of Hippo, argued that the city of God would not triumph at the expense of the human state, but that both co-existed and that Christians are citizens of both and are called to commitment to both. In Australia, evangelical Christians followed Augustine in their belief that they are called to the twin commitments as citizens of heaven and citizens of the earthly city or nation state as it became. They did not identify the kingdom of God with the church and they did not believe that the nation state was perfectible within human history. But they did cling to the Eusebian belief that the preaching of the Gospel inaugurated the Kingdom of God in this life and that its coming was the principal agent in the progressive improvement and reformation of both church and society and they remained vigilantly attentive to both.

The Australian Soul Defined

Attending to the Australian soul is to attend to a complex reality. That soul might not itself be immortal in its corporate nature, but it does view reality in the light of eternity. It understands that it is the work of the Australian spirit, but a work, most Australians have hoped and still hope, is aided by divinity. Like the land it reflects, it is created, and therefore calls for reverence for the Creator and creation. It is a spiritual as well as a natural soul. It has sympathy with the Christian doctrine that humanity is enriched by recognition of its divine potential through Christ who became human so that humans might become divine. It is a secular soul in the sense that it is anti-sectarian, acknowledging that plurality enriches the human family. It applauds spirituality, welcoming the intensification of the religious commitment of its individual members, while insisting that such commitment must not be expressed socially in the public sphere. It is a soul with a significant past and a significant future: its Christian members understand it as present in the time between the two comings of the Lord, the first of which demarcates time in history.[11] It is a soul which calls for reflection on a divine purpose for this particular people at this particular time and place. It requires a philosophy of history in which there is a divine role for Australia within the community of nations. It is a soul, then, essential to the consciousness of Australians as well as to the national conscience.

It is also a soul with compassion at its heart – the altruism of faith – and is therefore supportive of social service. It is a generous soul which accepts

11 The secularists' campaign to replace BC/AD with BCE/CE is 'a pathetic example of historical obscurantism' for it seeks 'to suppress the reasons why the Christ-centred ages were so named, while retaining its method of counting'. Edwin Judge, 'The Religion of the Secularists', *JRH*, 38.3, 2014, 313.

that heart or compassion is a critical cultural characteristic.[12] It is a soul which understands love in terms of what can be done for another; it is not self-regarding. It is a passionate soul, learning from the passion of Christ, in revolt against the apathy extolled by the Classical philosophers. It is a soul with a bent for dynamic initiative, supportive of change in history. In particular, in ancient times, it sought a home in a new society, the church, and therefore it has an aptitude for innovation. The Australian soul is a very 'Christianised' one.

But, for all its 'Christianisation', the Australian soul is not a Christian soul. It is a Western soul, which means that it is a soul not at peace with itself. The self-sacrificing, relational Christian values of faith, hope and care for others, wrestle with the individualistic, self-referential Classical virtues of fortitude, prudence, temperance and justice. All Australians, Christian and non-Christian alike, are shaped by that tension, exacerbated by the rationalism and utilitarianism of the Enlightenment. Thanks to an institutional crossover, the church at the beginning of the twenty-first century favours the Classical virtues of moderation and changelessness, and is rebuked by a society for any hypocrisy, the 'acid test' for integrity bequeathed to our society by Jesus himself.[13] It is the wider society, not the church, which now moralises, pontificates and waxes indignant.

The conservative Protestant churches for many decades in the latter half of the twentieth century were uncomfortable with their prophetic role. They were discomforted by the secular command to keep out of the public domain. It took a liberal evangelical, Alan Walker, the Methodist, to insist that 'the whole Gospel' is concerned with 'the whole world'. But that might be too harsh a judgment on the contribution which even conservative evangelicals made to the national debate in the post-war decades of rapid transformation. Recently, the creativity, more varied than tentative, of evangelical leaders in the 1960s and 1970s has received close scholarly attention.[14] Rather than succumb to secular pressure to keep off the turf, they obeyed the higher command which had shaped their tradition of manning the barricades when the cause is right and, for that purpose, of joining with others outside their movement. They could have done better, but they were not entirely inept at addressing Australia's need as identified by Edwin Judge, namely 'the public

12 Augustine learned the word for heart from the Latin Bible (*cor*) from which the word 'cordial' is derived). Judge, 'The Religion of the Secularists', 317.

13 The forgoing analysis is based on Judge, 'The Religion of the Secularists', 307–319.

14 Hugh Chilton, 'Evangelicals and the End of Christian Australia: Nation and Religion in the Public Square 1959–1979', PhD, University of Sydney, 2014.

opening up of the word of Christ to the world – and of the truth about his influence on its cultural history'.[15] If Judge is correct, it might be valid to suggest that, at the beginning of the twenty-first century, in spite of the progress of secularisation, evangelical Christianity continues to be 'as much a public ethic as a personal credo'.[16]

Towards a New Christendom

In the first volume of this study on Australian evangelical Christianity, it was argued that the evangelical family of churches in the nineteenth century created an evangelical spiritual empire which closely paralleled the British Empire. The two empires engaged with each other often, sometimes critiquing, more often endorsing each other. Either way the mutuality was so substantial that it made little sense to let the story of one not illuminate the other. Just as the Australian colonies were among the most dynamic and prosperous of settler societies, so the evangelical denominations created omnipresent Christian communities, close to all Australians, powerfully shaping sedimentary attitudes and values. The two empires together constituted the British, or better English-speaking (Anglophone), part of Western Christendom.

The present volume, apart from exploring how evangelical Christianity attended to the national soul and how it related to secular challenges, tells the story of how Protestant Christians retreated from identifying the British Empire with the fast-expanding empire of the Spirit which evangelical Christianity was in the nineteenth century. For some, it was not a willing retreat. So intertwined had the two empires become, so like the Kingdom of God had the kingdom of British culture come to appear to patriotic British settlers, that to surrender the latter felt like losing the main game. To concede that Australia was no longer 'a Christian country' seemed as much a betrayal of one's religion as of one's nationality. British heritage and the Christian faith seemed to be identical. Looking back on the Australian nationalism of the 1890s, secular historians have ignored the story of the two kingdoms, one imperial, the other, evangelical. Doctrinaire secular historians have left the religion out on the grounds that it is either insignificant or malign. They prefer Australian nationalists to British Australians, overlooking the fact that in the early twentieth century most Australians were comfortably both at the same time. Heritage historian, Graeme Davison, suggests that the 'scaffolding of

15 Judge, *Engaging Rome and Jerusalem*, 179.

16 Boyd Hilton, *The Age of Atonement: The Influence of Evangelicalism on Social and Economic Thought, 1795–1865* (Sydney: UNSW Press, 2005), 203.

biblical narrative traditions, the cultural system from which secular nationalism had emerged, may have been less visible in Australia, but it may have been just as formative as it was in countries where it lay closer to the surface of public life'.[17] Ironically, the story of secular nationalism emerged out of the submerged story of biblical Christianity. Its roots were overwhelmingly British, White and Christian.[18] From them the strongest plant which grew was 'civic Protestantism', Australia's 'forgotten nationalism'.[19]

In the second half of the twentieth century, the Christian story was submerged even deeper in secular history. Arguably, in the 1960s the walls of the two kingdoms came tumbling down, and the current volume is an account of why and how Christians failed to maintain the synergy of the two. It was not so much that any decline in the British Empire made Christians think they must defend it in the interests of the survival of their own movement. Historians of Empire might assume that it is axiomatic that the decline of Empire must be accompanied by the decline of Christianity since they appear to be contemporary phenomena. But it is not the assumption of the authors of this book. Very rapidly – it was the work of the 1960s and 1970s – most evangelicals lost their appetite for defending the British Commonwealth. It is a story devoid of Humpty Dumpty dramatics. Barely noticed, the British Empire 'quietly dropped through the trapdoor of history, without any heroic anti-imperial struggle'.[20]

Any decline in the parallel spiritual empire, by contrast, was felt keenly at least by evangelicals. Depleted by two world wars, they now faced the twin powers of secularisation and multiculturalism.

Evangelicals then sought to articulate other understandings of the relationship between church and society in the pursuit of what has been termed daringly 'the next Christendom of the global South'.[21] It is not an entirely satisfactory term: it is not sufficiently comprehensive to describe the range of experimentation in evangelical churches in recent decades and it is not a term which evangelicals themselves would employ. But it is a valuable term:

---

17 Graeme Davison, *Narrating the Nation in Australia* (London: Menzies Centre for Australian Studies, 2010), 10, cited in Chilton, 'Evangelicals and the End of Christian Australia', 62.

18 James Curran and Stuart Ward, *The Unknown Nation: Australia after Empire* (Melbourne: MUP, 2010).

19 Richard Ely, 'The Forgotten Nationalism: Australian Civic Protestantism in the Second World War', *Journal of Australian Studies,* 20, 1987, 59–67.

20 Deryck M Schreuder and Stuart Ward, (eds), *Australia's Empire, Oxford History of the British Empire* (Oxford: OUP, 2008), 2.

21 Chilton, 'Evangelicals and the End of Christian Australia', iv, 8.

it differentiates this Christendom from Western Christendom; it argues that Australia retains a high degree of 'christianisation' in spite of secularisation; it implies that Australian evangelicals have accepted the plurality of a globalised, multicultural world and the challenge of mission to and in that world; and it recognises the exponential growth of Christianity in the global South at a time when Christian adherence was declining dramatically in its traditional Western heartland. While Australian evangelicals lived in a terrain over which the cold winds of secularism blew as fiercely as anywhere, they were located in the hemisphere where Christianity was experiencing the most rapid growth in its history. They were tied to this explosive advance by a still vital missionary movement and they had the theology to see the significance of the changing nexus between empire, nation and global community. They could see by sight as well as wishful thinking that Europe's religious decline did not have to be the future for Christianity in Australia.

It is counter-intuitive so to argue, but probably evangelical theology was ahead of Australian culture in one important respect. Theologically most, not all, evangelicals had always understood that to be Protestant it was not essential to be 'White' and 'Anglo-Saxon'. Theirs was a theology which had already served them well in their successful labours to abolish the slave trade on the grounds that all members of the human race are brothers (and sisters – they tended not to say that then) under the Fatherhood of God. It was a theology which became the principal factor in humanitarian advocacy for Indigenous Australians against the extremes of settler rapacity. It exposed the error of social Darwinism which justified putting down 'weaker' races. It was a theology, particularly in its Calvinist manifestation, that justified missionary multiculturalism: the belief that God was calling out for himself a people from every nation and that the subjects of the Kingdom of Heaven would be the redeemed from every race and nation. It is true that for much of the history even of the twentieth century the White majority of Australia fair had 'a British soul', perhaps even more British than that of the inhabitants of the British Isles.[22] Australian Evangelicals, appreciative of Britain's Christian heritage, did little to question the spiritual probity of the 'British soul', and it was the British themselves, overseers of a multicultural commonwealth of nations, who expressed disquiet at Australia's 'whites only' immigration policy.[23] White supremacy and ethnocentric 'Britishness' were not ultimately

22 Neville Meaney, 'Britishness and Australian identity: The problem of nationalism in Australian history and historiography', *Australian Historical Studies*, 32.116, 2001, 80.

23 Meaney, 'Britishness and Australian identity', 85.

compatible with Christian theology: from the first Pentecost the Christian church was multicultural and that too would be its eternal state.

Unlike Islam, Christianity has proven remarkably adaptable to all cultures, but it ultimately refuses to be imprisoned by any of them. So, just as it has transcended or departed in critical ways from the culture of the British Empire, it will not concede sovereignty to all the cultures combined in multicultural Australia. Evangelical Christianity has itself always been a multicultural movement, both nationally and internationally. Through its missionary arm, it learned that all find and accept Christ in a way consistent with their own culture and that all in the Christian community will learn from each other's cultural insights. Therefore, all cultures are to be respected. They have also found over time that in the matter of evangelism, always a core concern, people are not easily won to faith if their culture is disrespected: multiculturalism is critical to evangelistic effectiveness. The effect of Christian commitment is not to raise one culture above another. It cannot demand that any Christian should leave any culture. Monocultural evangelicalism is not an option for Australian evangelicals.

Yet for evangelicals, no culture, nor multiculturalism, can have ultimate authority. Christian multiculturalism does allow converts the freedom to leave their own culture, or at least try to, if they feel so called. Evangelical Christianity throughout Australian history has consistently challenged English imperialists, Scottish patriots, Indigenous traditionalists, European or Asian immigrants, with the claim that their culture is not their highest loyalty. Missionary historian Andrew Walls's observation on the cultural context of Christianity is as true of Australia as elsewhere:

> Throughout Christian history two forces are distinguishable in constant tension. One is an indigenizing principle, a homing instinct, which creates in diverse communities a sense that the Church belongs there, that it is 'ours'. The other is a 'pilgrim' principle that creates within the Christian community the sense that it is not fully at home in this world, so that it comes into tension with society from its loyalty to Christ. The one tends to localize the vision of the Church, the other to universalize it. The two principles are recurrent because each springs directly out of the Gospel itself.[24]

24 Andrew F. Walls, *The Missionary Movement in Christian History: Studies in the Transmission of Faith* (Edinburgh: T&T Clark, 1996), 53f, cf. 7–9.

With the refinement forced on them by history, the evangelicals increasingly focussed on the contribution which vital Protestant Christianity could make to the developing nation, without compounding it with the contribution of race and imperialism. The new focus felt like a narrowing at times, a disengagement from many of the aspirations derived from the imperial spirit. It also felt as if they were being pushed under by an ideology which wanted them to go away so that the separation of church and state could become a reality in a way it never was in the nineteenth century. Australians from the 1960s defaulted to the secular, not to nominal Christianity as they had a century earlier. Evangelical Christianity, in reaction, became more 'religious', fostering in the twentieth century, first fundamentalism and then Pentecostalism, accentuating the need for biblical truth and spiritual experience.

While conservative evangelicals, therefore, have let slide the label, if not the concept, of a 'spiritual empire', many, as we argued above, have been less happy to surrender the designation of Australia as 'a Christian country'. The latter see Australia as a Christian nation in need of becoming more Christian. Other evangelicals want to argue that there can be no such thing as a Christian nation, and that Australians have chronically exhibited such anti-Christian behaviour that there is no justification for seeing Australia as an exception to the rule. Both groups, however, seem to have been equally committed to making Australia 'more Christian'.[25] In an age of apparent rampant secularisation, they have seized on opportunities to make it so. There was the spiritual opportunity in 1959 with the phenomenally successful Billy Graham crusades; there was the cultural opportunity in the 1970s, unleashed by Gough Whitlam's 'new nationalism' when the 'Jesus people' sought to forge a way for the faith outside the mainstream churches; there was the political opportunity of the first decade of the twenty-first century when prime ministers on both sides of the political divide supported the interdependence of church and state in the delivery of social welfare and the definition of national values. Evangelicals have proved to be tenacious desecularisers.[26] Nevertheless,

25 'Historic evangelicalism is a religion of protest against a Christian society that is not Christian enough … Evangelical Christianity, in a word, assumes Christendom.' Andrew Walls, 'The Evangelical Revival, the Missionary Movement, and Africa', in Mark A. Noll, et. al., *Evangelicalism: Comparative Studies of Popular Protestantism in North America, the British Isles, and Beyond 1700–1990* (New York; Oxford: Oxford University Press, 1994), 311.

26 Stuart Piggin, 'Power and Religion in a Modern State: Desecularisation in Australian History', *JRH*, 38.3, September 2014, 320–340.

in the last four decades of the twentieth century, Australia looked more like 'secular Australia' and less like 'Christian Australia'.

Ironically, as evangelical Christians became less confident that Christ would have his way in Australia, they became increasingly confident that Christ must have the world. Precisely because it is a missionary movement, evangelicalism has always been an international movement.[27] A 'Christian nation' was not a big enough ambition for evangelical leaders. So, having flirted for a moment in the 1970s with 'gumleaf' theology in the interests of developing a genuinely indigenous theology,[28] most theologians have looked for more satisfying bases for their systematic theologies. Having fallen for the 'British Empire' in the nineteenth century, evangelicals had a shorter fling with 'Australian nationalism', but it, too was foredoomed. There were always voices identifying both alliances with promiscuity, but evangelicals persisted in risking that outcome. Britain's and Australia's experience of empire, in which they were brought into contact with other peoples, races and cultures, was a major factor in forging the national conscience as they wrestled with the consequences of the conspicuous failures of that contact. In this development, churches experienced in cross-cultural mission, might have eradicated the paternalist and colonial mindset more quickly than other Australian institutions. Evangelical Christians arguably found it easier than most Australians to know which part of their cultural baggage to discard as being unhelpful, but they did not find it any easier to come up with one alternative. Instead, they came up with many, and the movement has become so divided that some want to discard certain members of the family and others want to suggest that the word 'evangelical' has passed its used-by date, and that we live in a post-evangelical, as well as a post-Christian, world.

The three major streams of 21st century evangelicals[29] – conservative, progressive, Pentecostal – do not co-operate with each other as much as members of the evangelical family did in the nineteenth century, but neither do they spend as much time today as they did in the 1980s criticising each other. Indeed, on 5 March 2016 the two most powerful movements within the Protestant churches in Australia, Hillsong, a Pentecostal church, and the Anglican Diocese of Sydney, both now with significant multicultural and international ministries, held a joint service to commemorate the bicentenary of the Bible

27 Glen O'Brien and Hilary M. Carey (eds.), *Methodism in Australia: A History* (Farnham: Ashgate Publishing Company, 2015), 208.

28 Chilton, 'Evangelicals and the End of Christian Australia', 289–294, 356.

29 Brian Stanley, *The Global Diffusion of Evangelicalism: The Age of Billy Graham and John Stott* (Downers Grove, Illinois: IVP Academic, 2013), 236f.

Society in NSW. It was a significant event which represented not only the openness to the Spirit championed by Pentecostals and faithfulness to the Bible championed by Sydney Anglicans. It also represented the progressive branch of the family by highlighting the need to address reconciliation with the original Australians.

In practice, each of the streams is focussed on working out its own engagement with the world, both at home and internationally, and that includes the involvement of each in civic culture, public affairs and in politics. There is evidence, especially in the current century, that evangelicals, long accustomed to living in a coalition of families, are coming to embrace plurality as integral to the Gospel, and they are becoming more accepting of diversity both within and outside the movement. Evangelicals continue to esteem mission as central to their movement, and their involvement with missions overseas has exerted a reflex influence on the home churches as it always had. In an increasingly multicultural world it has become easier to accept that the vitality of non-Western Christians well justifies the perception that Australia is more in need of receiving missionaries than sending them. Part of the appeal of missionaries from non-Western cultures is that they reinforce the hard-won convictions of Australian Christians, that secularism is not invincible, that the Gospel shapes both consciousness and conscience, and that a post-imperial Christendom need not be nationalistic, monocultural, individualistic or bigoted. It could be patriotic, committed, distinctive and passionate. It would not be a Christendom in the old sense of a reigning theocracy at war with secular democracies. The legacy of the evangelical impulse for revival and renewal in Australia as elsewhere is more likely to be pluralism and religious freedom as new light is found in Jesus and his Word by those who are loyal to both above all and dependent on his Spirit.[30]

---

30 Mark Shaw. *Global Awakening: How 20th-Century Revivals Triggered a Christian Revolution* (Downers Grove, Ill.: IVP Academic, 2010), 213.

PART A

Faith under Fire, 1914–1945

Chapter One

EVANGELICAL CHURCHES AND THE HOME FRONT DURING THE GREAT WAR, 1914–1918

'The War is a new and potent discipline of Christian faith and life.'
(Rupert Murdoch's grandfather)

Norman Makin, trade unionist, journeyed to the Yorke Peninsula of South Australia in September and October 1916 to speak against the proposed referendum to allow the government to conscript young men for military service. He had little idea what kind of reception awaited him, but he soon found out.[1] At the time, Makin worked at the railway shops at Islington in North Adelaide and served as secretary of the local branch of his trade union, the Amalgamated Society of Engineers. Born in Petersham, Sydney, in 1889, his family moved to Broken Hill in 1898. It was there, in 1903, that Makin accepted Christ as his Saviour at the substantial Sulphide Street Wesleyan Church, a decision which he later described as 'surely the greatest of all moments in my life'. In that same year, Makin joined the Shop Assistants' Union as a junior member. These two decisions would largely determine almost every aspect of what became a long life of public service.

Before long, he was a Sunday School teacher and an active Methodist local preacher. Moving to Adelaide in 1911, he successfully pursued both meaningful employment and his former girlfriend who had moved there from Broken Hill a year previously. He found a job with an agricultural machinery manufacturer and two years later married Ruby Florence Jennings. He also transferred his church and union memberships and continued his interest in

1 Norman Makin, *The Memoirs of Norman John Oswald Makin* (Adelaide: J. M. Main Bequest of Flinders University, 1982), 6–7, 18–29, 44–53.

both Christian work and the labour movement. Before long, he was heavily involved in union activities and Labor politics.

With the advent of World War I in 1914, Makin was faced with the decision of whether to volunteer for the first AIF and then whether to support the government's proposal to introduce national conscription for overseas service. Makin decided to do neither. Although not a pacifist, his biblical beliefs led him to reject forced participation in violence. He also wanted to maintain union solidarity in its growing opposition to the war.[2] At the bidding of his union, he stood unsuccessfully for a seat in the federal parliament in 1915.

In 1916, also at the request of his union, Makin agreed to speak on the Yorke Peninsula on behalf of the anti-conscription forces. There were friendly receptions in the Kadina-Wallaroo-Moonta triangle, where Cornish Methodist copper miners, staunch union men all, dominated the audiences. There was a great swell of support at Moonta, and the meeting took on what Makin described as a 'revival atmosphere'. The Town Hall at Kadina was packed with the 'Cousin Jacks' and even some 'Cousin Jennys' as Makin and his companion spoke for two hours. There were many shouts of 'hear, hear', 'amen' and 'preach it, brother'. However, they met with stony silence at Yorketown, organised hostility at Maitland, and well-planned mockery at Wirrabara.[3]

But it was at the farming town of Bute that Makin felt the full force of rejection. It was there that he incurred the wrath of a contingent of women conscription supporters. After hiring a hall for a meeting, Makin encountered these women in the front rows, all knitting socks for the soldiers and engaged in highly audible discussion. Makin was unable to be heard above what he described as a 'babble of voices' and a 'regiment of obstruction'. When Makin shouted that he 'had paid for the hall', it only added to the amusement of those who had come to the meeting. After an hour of frustration, the anti-conscription trade unionists gave up and left the building. As they departed, they were pelted with rotten eggs from the surrounding darkness. It was impossible to see their assailants or to dodge the stinking chook grenades. The following morning an anonymous perpetrator laced their breakfast with some kind of laxative. They spent the remainder of the day on the run. It was a memorable moment in the political career of a man who would go on to serve as a Member of the Federal House of Representatives

---

2 Makin, *Memoirs*, 46–8; Donald J. Hopgood to Arnold Hunt, 9 September 1994; Arnold Hunt to Robert D. Linder, 13 September 1994; Harold Makin, son of Norman Makin, interviewed by Linder, 19 July 1995.

3 Makin, *Memoirs*, 48–51.

from 1919 to 1946 and again from 1954 to 1963; as Speaker of the House 1929–1931; as a member of Prime Ministers John Curtin's and Ben Chifley's War-time Cabinet, 1941–1946; as the first Australian Ambassador to the United States, 1946–1951; and as the first President of the United Nations Security Council, 1946–1947.[4]

The 'cult of empire patriotism'[5]

In Australia, on the eve of the War, there was strong sentimental attachment to Britain, and pride in being part of 'the greatest Empire in the history of the world'. In 1909, as part of that Empire's growing concern with military developments in Europe and Asia, the Commonwealth Parliament had passed the Defence Act by which Australia formally adopted compulsory home military service. This Act was amended in 1911 following a visit by the British Secretary of State for War, Lord Kitchener, who recommended that the country provide for a fully trained citizen army of 80,000 men. The government then introduced compulsory military instruction for cadets beginning at age twelve and continuing to age eighteen, at which time they became a part of the Commonwealth Army and received periodic training for a further seven years. Even so, on the eve of the war, the Australian standing army was small and the Royal Australian Navy, formed in 1911, in its infancy.[6] The country's ultimate protection against any potential aggressor lay with the British Royal Navy. Such was the state of Australia's national defence on the eve of the Great War.[7]

---

4 Makin, *Memoirs*, 50; and *SMH*, 22 July 1982, 10.

5 *Church Record*, 26 October 1917, 1. These are the words of the Rev. Stephen Taylor, Anglican rector of St Paul's, Wahroonga, in criticism of those who acted as if 'serving the Empire was their religion'.

6 Rowan Strong, *Chaplains in the Royal Australian Navy* (Sydney: UNSW Press, 2012), 35–37.

7 For the social and political background of Australia on the eve of the war, see Gavin Souter, *Lion and Kangaroo: The Initiation of Australia, 1901–1919* (Sydney: Collins, 1976), 155–94; Stuart Macintyre, *The Oxford History of Australia vol.4: The Succeeding Age, 1901–1942* (Melbourne: OUP, 1993), 122–41. For the diplomatic and military background of the war, see John Barrett, *Falling In: Australians and 'Boy Conscription', 1911–1915* (Sydney: Hale and Iremonger, 1979). The standard history of Australian participation in the war is still C.E.W. Bean's monumental *Official History of Australia in the War, 1914–1918*, 12 vols. (Sydney: Angus & Robertson, 1921–1934). The leading historian of Australian religion and World War I is Michael McKernan. See his *Australian Churches at War: Attitudes and Activities of the Major Churches, 1914–1918*, (Sydney and Canberra: Catholic Theological Faculty and Australian War

The churches were no better prepared for war in 1914 than the government. The 1911 census disclosed that 99.76 percent of Australians adhered to some form of religious belief, with 98 percent claiming affiliation with the main Christian bodies: 39.4 percent claimed to be Anglican, 22.96 percent Catholic, 12.86 percent Presbyterian, 12.61 percent Methodist, and 2.4 percent Baptist. Lutherans were strong in South Australia and Queensland where they had about 25,000 adherents in each State. In 1914, nearly all Presbyterians, Methodists, Baptists, Congregationalists, Lutherans and the smaller Protestant bodies could be counted as evangelical, with perhaps one-fourth of all Anglicans falling into that category. In total, evangelical groups claimed perhaps 40–45 percent of the population on the eve of the war.[8]

Although the struggle first to survive and later to build a prosperous settler society in an unfamiliar land left little time for theological reflection, a few Australian religious leaders had expressed what were the then prevailing sentiments concerning war and empire. Paramount among them was the venerable Rev. Dr. W.H. Fitchett, the founding and long-serving President of the Methodist Ladies' College in Kew, Victoria. Famous in Australia, famous throughout the Empire, he is unknown to secular historians today. His enormously popular book *Deeds That Won the Empire*, first serialised in the Melbourne *Argus* in the mid-1890s, is essential reading for understanding Australian thinking about war – at least before the war. It glorified the courage, intelligence and compassion which he believed characterised the spread of British Christian civilisation in the preceding centuries and sold more than 250,000 copies in the period leading up to the war.[9]

Memorial, 1980); *The Australian People and the Great War* (Sydney: Collins, 1980); and *Padre: Australian Chaplains in Gallipoli and France* (Sydney: Allen & Unwin, 1986). See also Robert D. Linder, *The Long Tragedy: Australian Evangelical Christians and the Great War, 1914–1918* (Adelaide: Openbook Publishers, 2000); Colin Bale, 'A Crowd of Witnesses: Australian War Graves Inscriptions on the Western Front of the Great War', PhD, University of Sydney, 2006.

8 Ian Breward, *A History of the Australian Churches* (St. Leonards: Allen & Unwin, 1993), 120–1, 196–7; McKernan, *Australian Churches at War*, 5–23; W. W. Phillips, 'Religion' in Wray Vamplew, ed., *Australians: Historical Statistics* (Broadway: Fairfax, Syme & Weldon Associates, 1987), 418–35.

9 William Henry Fitchett, *Deeds That Won the Empire* (London: Bell's Indian and Colonial Library, 1897), preface. Fitchett's work was a favourite of Winston Churchill, and John Monash, Australia's greatest military commander, carried a copy with him during the entire course of the war. C. Irving Benson, 'The Life and Times of Dr William Henry Fitchett', *Heritage: A Journal of the Methodist Historical Society of Victoria*, 11, 1960, 9–10. It was claimed that by 1921 its sales exceeded 900,000 copies. J.E. Carruthers, *Memories of an Australian Ministry, 1868–1921* (London: The Epworth Press, 1922), 275.

The real significance of Fitchett's work was the manner in which it helped to promote what has become known as 'civil religion' in Australia.[10] Most of the pro-war sentiment among the churches, especially in the Protestant denominations, was fuelled by a civil religion then integral to the ethos of the British Empire. Civil religion is a scholar's term used to describe the general faith of a state, nation or empire which focuses on common beliefs about the history and destiny of the state, nation or empire in question. It is a religious way of thinking about politics which provides a society with ultimate meaning which, in turn, allows a people to look at their political community in a special sense and thus achieve purposeful social integration and a sense of destiny. It was a religion which sacralised blood, understood in terms of race and sacrifice. The celebrated 'crimson thread of kinship', the phrase coined in 1890 by NSW premier Sir Henry Parkes, signified that the bond between Anglo-Celtic peoples throughout the Empire was a sacred one.

Empire Day was the focal point of British civil religion in Australia at the time of the First World War. It was a day which compounded civil religion and Protestantism rather than distinguishing between them. In fact, Empire Day came into existence largely through the efforts of evangelical Anglican leader, Archdeacon Francis Bertie Boyce, rector of St. Paul's Church of England, Redfern. In 1901, Boyce had founded the British Empire League in Sydney. His suggestion that Empire Day be celebrated in state schools and by the public at large on Queen Victoria's birthday finally won acceptance, and so the first Empire Day was observed on 24 May 1905.[11]

With the outbreak of hostilities in 1914, civil religion came to serve the needs of the Empire, especially in terms of moral support for the war and the enlistment of young Christian men in the Australian Imperial Force (AIF). The line between piety and patriotism became increasingly blurred and the flag at times seemed to replace the cross in the thinking of many church leaders. The sacrifice of soldiers on the battlefield was readily linked to the sacrifice of Christ on the cross. When the War came, no responsible statesman or churchman welcomed it, and many deplored it. Nevertheless, love of Empire and British civil religion, along with the widespread belief that the Allied side occupied the high moral ground, dictated an enthusiastic reception of Britain's declaration of war on Germany and the other Central Powers. The

10 Richard V. Pierard and Robert D. Linder, *Civil Religion and the Presidency* (Grand Rapids: Zondervan, 1988), 11–29; Richard Ely, 'The Forgotten Nationalism: Australian Civic Protestantism in the Second World War', *Journal of Australian Studies*, 20, 1987, 59–67.

11 Souter, *Lion and Kangaroo*, 109–13.

prevailing emotions in the country during the early months of the war were sheer excitement and a surge of tribal loyalty. The churches were in step with everyone else in their response to the war. In 1914 there was barely a dissenting voice. Civil religion had triumphed over Christian theology which had the resources to proffer an alternative view, but very few were looking for such.

Mobilising the Churches behind the War Effort

In Australia leading evangelical ministers typically supported the war because they saw it as an opportunity for national and individual moral renewal. As the Rev. Patrick J. Murdoch, pastor of the Camberwell Presbyterian Church in Melbourne and grandfather of Rupert Murdoch, noted in the preface of his book of war sermons, published early in 1915:

> The War is a new and potent discipline of Christian faith and life. It raises questions for the thoughtful Christian man to which he must find an answer. It is deeply affecting the inmost life of the chastened nations, and will make, in them and in innumerable individuals, the opportunity of moral renewal.[12]

The expressed hope of some that the war would deepen the spiritual and induce revival surely betrayed an anxiety that the 'Christian nation' was not as 'Christian' as they would have liked.[13] But probably the majority of evangelical clerical leaders supported the war effort because of their belief in the God-ordained and essentially righteous nature of the British Empire.[14] On 'Empire Intercession Day', Sunday 3 January 1915, the Rev. Peter Fleming, minister of Flinders Street Baptist Church in Adelaide, preached a sermon entitled 'Praying for Victory. Why It is Just to Fight the Enemy'. He maintained that in the process of building a world-wide empire, Britain had annexed territory only to 'give truer freedom under her liberty loving flag'. By contrast, he accused Germany of being consumed by an unholy imperialist lust which would result in the enslavement of nations and international anarchy. He characterised the German invasion of Belgium, an 'innocent and martyred nation', as 'the vilest thing in history'. Accordingly, he urged that although

---

12 Patrick J. Murdoch, *The Laughter and Tears of God and Other War Sermons* (Melbourne: Arbuckle, Waddell and Fawckner, 1915), 3.

13 Murdoch, *Laughter and Tears of God*, 11f.; Stuart Piggin, *Faith of Steel: A History of the Christian Churches in Illawarra, Australia* (Wollongong: The University of Wollongong Press, 1984), 177–80.

14 Joan Beaumont, *Broken Nation: Australians in the Great War* (Sydney: Allen & Unwin, 2013), 18f.

not everyone could shoulder a rifle, 'let every godly man and woman make it a daily petition to God that right may win'.[15]

Sydney's Church of England Archbishop John Charles Wright echoed Fleming's sentiments. In July 1915, he issued a pastoral letter to the clergy of his diocese urging the young men of the parishes to do their godly duty and enlist in order to replenish the ranks after the heavy casualties of the first months of the war. Later in the month, at an immense recruiting rally in the Sydney Exhibition building, Wright asserted: 'Talking is no good. We've got to draw the sword. We've got to draw it in the Name of God. Talking will not do it ... We must give up killing Kruger with our mouths'.[16]

As well as backing the war in principle, the evangelical leadership was active in helping to recruit men to serve in the AIF. Among notable evangelical clerical and lay leaders who filled these various roles were Archbishop Wright; Sir Joseph Carruthers, former Premier of NSW and brother of the Rev. Dr. J.E. Carruthers, editor of *The Methodist*, the official paper for that denomination in NSW; the Rev. Octavius Lake, possibly then the most influential Methodist leader in South Australia; the Rev. Dr. Ronald G. Macintyre, Professor of Systematic Theology at St. Andrew's College, Sydney; the Rev. Dr. E.H. Sugden, Master of the Methodist Queen's College, Melbourne; Donald Mackinnon, Victorian Attorney-General and Presbyterian stalwart; Edward Lucas, South Australian MLC and widely-known Methodist lay leader; and Louise Steadman and Annie Hunt, leading Methodist laywomen in South Australia, the latter of whom had four sons serving in France.[17] Among those most effective in recruitment through the 'Coo-ee March' October 1915 and the 'Wallabies March' November 1915 – January 1916 was John R. Lee who had come to Australia in 1911 from Cliff College, Derbyshire, to work in Methodist Home Missions. He enlisted in 1915, showing his occupation as 'water diviner'. He soon rose to the rank of Recruiting Sergeant/Major and was a highly persuasive platform speaker and recruiter.[18]

The evangelical churches also took part in the war effort by extensive fund-raising on behalf of the victims of the fighting and for various programs and facilities for the troops. Belgium occupied a special place of concern in

15 *The Australian Baptist*, 5 September 1915, 11.

16 *The Church Standard*, 2 July 1915, 10; *Sydney Diocesan Magazine*, 1 September 1915, 10.

17 Ernest Scott, *Australia During the War: The Official History of Australia in the War of 1914–1918*, vol.9 (Sydney: Angus and Robertson, 1938), 333–4, 400–1; Owen Parnaby, *Queen's College, University of Melbourne: A Centenary History* (Carlton: MUP, 1990), 36.

18 Daryl Lightfoot, 'A Cliff College Contingent and Rev. John Wilkinson of Narrabri: A WW1 Tragedy', *Archiv-Vista*, 1, 2015, 22.

the minds of many Christians during the early days of the war because of the stories of German cruelty to the Belgians, later revealed as fabrications, flowing from the British press. At the Armadale Presbyterian Church in Melbourne, young Brian Lewis remembered saving his pennies for the starving Belgians: 'Belgium was "Gallant Little Belgium" and the people were the "gallant starving Belgians" and from now on, if we did not finish our porridge we were told how much the Belgians needed it'.[19] Churches also raised large amounts for the Red Cross Fund and for the Repatriation Fund to help returning soldiers. Few of these churches reported any decrease in their regular giving or in monetary support for overseas missions as they raised substantial sums for the war effort.[20]

In addition, evangelicals gave funds for the construction and maintenance of facilities for army and navy personnel.[21] Church tents and huts for the recreational use of soldiers, as well as for spiritual ministrations, sprang up at every army post. Typical was the way in which the Methodists and Presbyterians cooperated to care for the troops in Queensland camps in Soldiers' Rest Tents. They were open to all troops and provided with furniture, literature, newspapers, writing paper, envelopes, pens and ink. There were also opportunities for games and for conversation with friends and with the chaplain. Services were held in the tents each evening, ranging from Bible studies to evangelistic meetings.[22] In NSW, each denomination provided facilities for its own soldiers and any others who cared to use them. Dorothy Wright, the Archbishop's wife, took a special interest in these projects and spearheaded

---

19 Brian Lewis, *Our War: Australia During World War I* (Carlton: MUP, 1980), 34. This is a childhood memoir of the conflict, especially as it affected Lewis's family and the Armadale Presbyterian Church (now the Armadale Uniting Church), Melbourne. Brian Lewis himself went to war in 1940, serving as a sergeant with the Second AIF, and with the British Ministry of War Transport, ending with the rank of brigadier. He was Professor of Architecture at the University of Melbourne, 1947–1971 (Information furnished by his son, Francis B. Lewis, Judge of the County Court of Victoria, to Linder, 19 October 1994).

20 Apart from the various funds associated with the war effort, churches supported funds of long standing, such as the Hospital Fund of Victoria. The churches of Victoria designated a Hospital Sunday each mid-October when the collections of every congregation were donated to the hospitals. Brian Lewis, *Sunday at Kooyong Road* (Richmond: Hutchinson of Victoria, 1976), 72–86.

21 Don Wright and Eric G. Clancy, *The Methodists: A History of Methodism in NSW* (St. Leonards: Allen & Unwin, 1993), 135.

22 *Australian Christian World*, 11 August 1916, 10–11; Richard Bardon, *The Centenary History of the Presbyterian Church of Queensland* (Brisbane: W. R. Smith and Paterson, 1949), 172–3.

a drive to raise money for billiard tables for 'the boys' to use.[23] St Stephen's Presbyterian Church in Sydney developed a special ministry to navy personnel on board the Training Vessel HMAS *Tingira*, through which passed some 3,400 naval cadets preparing for service on the high seas. The Rev. F.L.A. Schoeffel, a member of the St Stephen's ministerial staff and Presbyterian Chaplain to His Majesty's Fleet, regularly visited the cadets. Many were enrolled in the Minister's Bible Class, a number of whom eventually were received into full church membership.[24] George MacDonnell, Methodist chaplain, served on the *Tingira* throughout the war. An advocate for the White Cross Society and the Naval Temperance Society, his special concern was for the moral purity of the cadets. The Naval Board valued his services and considered him underpaid.[25]

Christian Endeavour groups also found creative ways to support the troops. In 1917, Dr. Francis E. Clark, President of the Australian Christian Endeavour Society, encouraged young people to start planting vegetable gardens to help with the war effort, and reported that thousands responded. Hundreds of evangelical churches sponsored first-aid classes for their members as a part of national defence. In many ways, the evangelical churches of the nation were more fully mobilised during the Great War than the country as a whole.[26]

Turning on the Brethren

Enthusiasm for the war developed another ugly side when some evangelicals turned on fellow travellers who declined to volunteer for the armed forces or who were from a different ethnic background. The Rev. John Flynn, later 'Flynn of the Inland', received a white feather in 1915. By this time, Flynn was superintendent of the fledgling Australian Inland Mission (AIM) of the Presbyterian Church, the base from which he later would establish his celebrated Flying Doctor Service. Flynn detested war but worried that he might lose influence for Christ if people thought him to be a coward, and he sought counsel from his close friend, the Rev. Frank Rolland. In Rolland's view, Flynn's situation was different in that the AIM was his child and it

---

23 *Sydney Diocesan Magazine*, 1 January 1915, 4; 1 September 1915, 5; 1 September 1916, 9; 1 December 1916, 5; *The Church Standard*, 8 December 1916, 8.

24 Graham W. Hardy, *Living Stones: The Story of St. Stephen's, Sydney* (Homebush West: ANZEA Publishers, 1985), 67.

25 Strong, *Chaplains in the Royal Australian Navy*, 109f.

26 *The Australian Baptist*, 30 November 1915, 12 and 1 January 1918, 3.

was at this time too young to survive on its own. Flynn opted to remain at his post and the next year received a second white feather.[27]

In the case of the German Lutherans, it was as if the entire denomination had been sent a gigantic white feather from Australian society, this in spite of the fact that many German-Australians had volunteered for service. Thousands of Lutheran German-Australians were arrested and detained by the authorities. The War Precautions Act of 29 October 1914 gave the federal government wide discretionary powers to make regulations 'for securing the public safety and defence of the Commonwealth'.[28] Many German place names were changed in the German-Lutheran parts of South Australia, NSW, Queensland, Victoria, Western Australia and also Tasmania, where Bismarck became Collins Vale. At least 81 names were altered by State parliaments. The mean-spiritedness even extended to dachshund-kicking and changing the name of German sausage to Belgium sausage.[29]

A number of evangelical leaders did urge caution lest innocent people, especially German-Australian Christians, be wronged. The Rev. William T. Shapley, pastor of the Jamestown Methodist Church in South Australia and a noted Methodist leader, preached reason and restraint: 'Let us beware lest the sword of justice should be forged in the fires of hate into a dagger of malice'.[30] The sentiment expressed in 1915 by the secretary of the Bethshan Holiness Mission must have been common among evangelicals. The Mission, on the NSW Central Coast, was headed by Elliot John Rien whose father had been a Lutheran:

> Bro Max Stuckrad was sent in by the Lord for a little time which ended by us inviting him to become a member which invitation he accepted. He has indeed been a great blessing. Although our countries are at enmity one with the other Praise Him there are no enemies to those who are in Christ Jesus. In receiving one of the Lord's little ones to

27 B.R. Keith, 'Rolland, Sir Francis William (Frank) (1878–1965)', *ADB*, online edition. He received the first knighthood conferred on an Australian minister of religion.

28 Frank K. Crowley, *Modern Australia in Documents*, 2 vols. (Melbourne: Wren, 1973), I:224.

29 Everard Leske, *For Faith and Freedom: The Story of Lutherans and Lutheranism in Australia, 1838–1996* (Adelaide: Openbook Publishers, 1996), 153. In South Australia alone, the Nomenclature Act of 1917 changed the names of 69 towns, districts, rivers and mountains 'of enemy origin'. Trevor Schaefer, 'The Treatment of Germans in South Australia, 1914–1924', BA Honours Thesis, Department of History, University of Adelaide, 1982, 36,44.

30 *Australian Christian Commonwealth*, 14 August 1914, 14.

> shield him as it were for a while we found we entertained Strangers [angels] unawares.[31]

Nevertheless, as the carnage mounted in Europe, a number of evangelicals began to voice their concern that the Germans in Australia were not being dealt with severely enough. One of the most persistent critics of German Lutherans was John Verran, former Labor Premier of South Australia and loyal son of the Methodist Church. In 1915, he made the wild claim that all of the Lutheran schools in his State had been established at the instigation of the Kaiser himself. Three times – in 1915, 1916 and 1917 – he sponsored legislation aimed at disfranchising German-Australians, and three times his bills were rejected. His rhetoric, however, helped create antagonism against German Lutherans at the local level. Also in South Australia, when Methodist minister Charles E. Schneider changed his name to Taylor in 1916, Octavius Lake enthusiastically endorsed the decision and expressed the hope that many more would follow Schneider's example.[32]

One evangelical minister who did not follow Schneider's example and Lake's advice was the Rev. Charles E. Schafer, an Adelaide Methodist evangelist and noted temperance advocate. When Schafer was in Tasmania in March 1916, campaigning for an early closing referendum there, his opponents called attention to his German surname in an attempt to discredit him. One of the leading defenders of late closing was R.J. Snowball, federal secretary of the Licensed Victuallers' Association. He remarked: 'If you go to hear the temperance advocate with the very German-approaching name of Schafer, you ought to learn a little more about his ancestors'. Schafer replied in detail to Snowball's innuendo, and he and his supporters carried the issue when a few days later Tasmanians voted by a two-to-one margin in favour of 6 o'clock and against 10 o'clock closing. The pro-liquor forces, it was said, did not then stand the chance of a 'Snowball in hell'.[33]

Despite repeated protestations of loyalty, popular violence against Lutherans escalated around the country as the war progressed. Broken windows and other

---

31 Bethshan Holiness Mission, *Annual Report*, 1915.

32 South Australia: Parliament. *Official Reports of the Parliamentary Debates* (Adelaide: I.L. Bonython & Company, 1915), 2630; Arnold D. Hunt, *This Side of Heaven: A History of Methodism in South Australia* (Adelaide: Lutheran Publishing House, 1985), 300; *Australian Christian Commonwealth*, 4 August, 1916, 12.

33 Hobart *Mercury*, 22 March 1916, 7 and 23 March 1916, 6; Hunt, *This Side of Heaven*, 280, 284; Marilyn Lake, *A Divided Society: Tasmania During World War I* (Clayton: MUP, 1975), 44–7.

exterior damage of church buildings was common, and, in a few cases, they were defiled with animal offal and human excrement. During the course of the war, vandals burned down five Lutheran church buildings.[34] The South Australian Parliament passed legislation declaring that all Lutheran day schools should cease operation no later than 30 June 1917. Forty-one schools closed, affecting 1600 scholars. This was a major blow to the Lutherans because of the intimate connection between faith and education in Lutheran life. Early in 1918, the authorities suspended the publication of all Lutheran church papers in German. The South Australian government also brought pressure to bear which resulted in the closure of the Lutheran mission at Bethesda while sporadic harassment made it difficult for the Hermannsburg mission in the Northern Territory to continue.[35]

The federal government interned 6,890 of whom the majority were Lutherans. Nearly all Lutheran pastors came under suspicion and most were considered 'devotedly pro-German' by the authorities.[36] In Queensland, ten German-Australian pastors – eight Lutheran and two other evangelicals – were interned for long periods. Among them, the Rev. Friedrich Gustav Fischer of Goombungee was born in South Australia in 1876 of parents who were also Australian born. He was arrested on the recommendation of the Defence Minister, Senator George Pearce, in order to relieve the anxiety of local citizens and 'to keep German residents in check' by example. He spent from 1915 to 1919 in the Holsworthy concentration camp near Sydney. Two other German-Australian ministers, Heinrich Niemeyer and his son William, were detained and interned at the same camp. The elder Niemeyer was the founding Apostle and Head of the Apostolic Church of Queensland, an Irvingite community which had transformed the scrub around Hatton Vale into a flourishing agricultural settlement in the period 1883–1914. Arrested in 1916 at age 63, the elder Niemeyer was held until April 1918, when he was released because of rapidly deteriorating health. The son, finally freed in September 1919, buried his father in February 1920.[37]

---

34 At Edithburgh and Forster in South Australia, at Netherby and Murtoa in Victoria, and at Toowoomba in Queensland.

35 Alfred Brauer, *Under the Southern Cross: History of the Evangelical Lutheran Church of Australia* (Adelaide: Lutheran Publishing House, 1985), 376; Jürgen Tampke and Colin Doxford, *Australia, Willkommen: A History of the Germans in Australia* (Kensington: UNSW Press, 1990), 185; John Harris, *One Blood: 200 Years of Aboriginal Encounter with Christianity* (Sutherland, NSW: Albatross, 1990), 382–3, 403.

36 *Argus*, 14 May 1915, 6; Gerhard Fischer, *Enemy Aliens: Internment and the Homefront Experience in Australia, 1914–1920* (St. Lucia: University of Queensland Press, 1989), 77.

37 Leon Trosky, *History of the New Apostolic Church in the Australian District* (Ipswich: Privately Printed, 1990), 12–19; and Fischer, *Enemy Aliens*, 102–8.

Dr. Eugen Hirschfeld was another high-profile Lutheran in Queensland affected by the war. Hirschfeld had migrated to Queensland in July 1890, at age 24, immediately following graduation from medical school in Germany. He became a naturalised British subject in 1893 and embarked on a highly successful career as a distinguished physician and medical researcher. He regularly attended St. Andrew's Lutheran Church, Wickham Terrace, Brisbane, the only Lutheran congregation in Australia on the eve of the war to be affiliated with the Lutheran Church of Prussia. In 1906, the German government named him its consul in Brisbane. In this capacity, he wrote to Lutheran pastors, promoting the German heritage in Australia and attempting to establish a German language society. When war came, he was forced to resign from the Queensland State Parliament, was interned on 11 February 1916, and, along with his pastor, C.E. Treuz, deported from the Commonwealth in 1920.[38]

The voices of those few non-Lutheran evangelical leaders who spoke against internment became muted as the church honour boards filled, sons perished in battle, and the wounded and maimed began to return to Australia.[39] In the meantime, the German Lutheran community of Australia quietly celebrated the 400th anniversary of the beginning of the Protestant Reformation on 31 October 1917.[40] As they did, the Lutheran settlements of the Barossa Valley in South Australia began to receive word that more and more of their own sons had fallen in battle in the service of their adopted country: names like Heuzenroeder, Juttner, Kindler, Lehmann, Riebe and Schroeder.[41]

From Imperial Righteousness to National Repentance

The growing carnage in 1915 and 1916 turned many against the war and caused a shift in the rhetoric of evangelical leaders from themes of duty and the righteous cause to those of sacrifice, repentance and renewal. The (Protestant) Council of Churches in South Australia sponsored a service of intercession and remembrance at the Adelaide Exhibition Hall on 3 October 1915. The address of the main speaker, Methodist stalwart Rev. Henry Howard, had

38 Fischer, *Enemy Aliens*, 110–20; and Tampke and Doxford, *Australia, Willkommen*, 184–5.

39 Philip Dowe, Anglican rector at Bulli, NSW, criticised the policy of internment in his parish newsletter in 1915. *Parish Gazette*, June 1915, 1.

40 Th. Hebart, *The United Evangelical Lutheran Church in Australia* (North Adelaide: Lutheran Book Depot, 1938), 133–4.

41 Schaefer, 'The Treatment of Germans in South Australia, 1914–1924', 21–2; Leske, *For Faith and Freedom*, 153.

twin emphases: that a son's or brother's life had not been wasted, and that 'a call to the colours'[42] was one of exemplary sacrifice. Howard intoned:

> Every drop of Australian blood that had stained 'the ringing plains of windy Troy' was calling to its kindred blood to render certain that its shedding should not be in vain. There was no call like that of sacrificial blood poured out in a great cause, and at its challenge there was only one thing for honourable men to do, unless they were to remain under the lash of perpetual self-rebuke, that was to drink of the same sacrificial cup … The most dull and common-place life by such supreme sacrifice became transfigured.[43]

Other evangelical leaders expressed their increasing apprehension over the growing slaughter. The Rev. James Heaton, pastor of the Mount Morgan Methodist Church in Queensland, wrote plaintively to Premier T.J. Ryan in August, 1916: 'Our town has given 800 or 900 men to the war. Our only return so far is the daily news of wounds and death'.[44]

This heightened sense of sacrifice led almost inexorably to a call for national repentance in order to make certain that God's favour was not lost, and the sacrifices were not in vain. It was during 1916 that evangelicals began to link sacrifice with repentance and renewal. The Rev. E.S. Tuckwell's presidential address to his fellow-believers at the annual meeting of the South Australian Baptist Union, September 1916, was typical of this attitude:

> After the war, when the cost of victory is realised, will not a great religious revival take place? … When we come to count up the enormous sacrifice the war has demanded, it will surely be only natural for the nation to turn to the Church for guidance. We are being taught great lessons, and if we could retain for a couple of decades the spirit of sacrifice and the sense of unity this war has engendered, and use them wisely and well, what a great moral uplifting there would be.[45]

Also in response to the growing slaughter and linked to the idea of sacrifice was the birth of Anzac Day. Spearheaded by the ANZAC Day Commemoration Committee of Brisbane and its honorary secretary, Anglican high churchman Canon David Garland, the idea of setting aside April 25 as Anzac Day spread

---

42 That is, the flag.

43 *Australian Christian Commonwealth*, 8 October 1915, 7.

44 Rev. J. H. Heaton to T. J. Ryan, 23 August 1916, Home Office, COL/A1207, 6849 of 1916, Queensland State Archives, Brisbane.

45 *The Australian Baptist*, 3 October 1916, 2.

quickly throughout Australia.[46] The first Anzac Day, 25 April 1916, was an occasion for pride, the commemoration of self-sacrifice, and self-assessment. At St. Andrew's Cathedral, Sydney, on the Sunday following Anzac Day (designated as 'Anzac Sunday'), Archbishop Wright declared to the assembled throng:

> Anzac – It is a new word in the world. But it is a word that ought to live ... We thank God for the bright roll of fame that is being compiled on blood-stained battlefields to enrich the annals of Australia. At the same time, we humbly pray that we may have endurance and perseverance worthy of this great self-sacrifice ... We pledge ourselves before God that the dead shall not have died in vain, but that we shall hold right on, until, as well in peace as in war, the right is throned in victory.[47]

A broad cross-section of the evangelical community took part in the first Anzac Day in Wollongong in 1916. A Methodist preacher spoke of the heroism at Gallipoli, Presbyterian and Salvation Army representatives offered prayers of intercession, and a Church of England minister read from the Bible and urged his audience 'to put on the whole armour of God'. The service closed with the singing of the national anthem. This routine would become standard fare for such celebrations in the decade which followed.[48]

Pacifists

Not all evangelicals supported the military prosecution of the war or participated in its celebratory rituals. At first, their voices were faint, but then grew more distinct as the human cost of war mounted. Before the conflict was over, non-violent evangelical Christians represented the main body of opposition to the war and to its corollary, conscription, on religious and moral grounds.

Even before the outbreak of hostilities, the Australian Freedom League (AFL) had represented evangelical pacifist interests by opposing militarism in

---

46 John A. Moses, 'ANZAC Day as Religious Revivalism: The Politics of Faith in Brisbane, 1916–1939', in Mark Hutchinson and Stuart Piggin (eds.), *Reviving Australia: Essays on the History and Experience of Revival and Revivalism in Australian Christianity* (Sydney: Centre for the Study of Australian Christianity, 1994), 170–84; John A. Moses and George F. Davis, *Anzac Day Origins: Canon D. J. Garland and Trans-Tasman Commemoration* (Barton: Barton Books, 2013).

47 *Sydney Diocesan Magazine,* 1 May 1916, 5–6.

48 Susan Westwood, 'A Study of the Attitudes and Activities of the Church of England in the Illawarra During the First World War', BA Honours Thesis, Department of History and Politics, University of Wollongong, 1980, 45, 57–8.

general and the new Defence Acts of 1909 and 1911 in particular. Although mostly Quaker in composition, the AFL also included in its ranks a number of Baptists, the most prominent of whom was the Rev. Martin Luther Murphy, minister of the Alberton Baptist Church in South Australia. Seventh-day Adventists (SDAs) officially rejected combatant status for members, but allowed individuals to serve as medical corps personnel as conscience permitted. The Christian Brethren also had a tradition of non-involvement in war and resisted the idea of killing other human beings. Like the Baptists and SDAs, the Brethren left ultimate decisions up to individual conscience. Few, if any Brethren, went to war in 1914.[49]

As a denomination, Baptists generally embraced the war effort. Yet a number of Baptist ministers and lay people opposed the concept of war. Early in the war, a spirited debate on the ethics of war appeared in the pages of *The Australian Baptist*.[50] In Melbourne, the Rev. Frank Clemens, pastor of the Murrumbeena Baptist Church, was a member of the Melbourne Peace Society and an outspoken Christian pacifist. In Sydney, W.R. Dovey, a well-known insurance actuary and Baptist lay leader, observed:

> Happy is the family which is under the sway of the rule of non-resistance for love's sake. Blessed would a community be in which this principle was dominant. But, alas, Christianity has not made enough progress for non-resistance to be acted on a large scale.[51]

The Church of England in Australia was the denomination most in support of the war, especially in terms of its clerical leadership. Yet even among Anglicans there were those who urged caution lest loyalty to the Empire

49 Barrett, *Falling In*, 81–127; William N. Oats, 'The Campaign Against Conscription in Australia – 1911–1914', *Journal of the Friends' Historical Society* (1989), 205–19; William N. Oats, *A Question of Survival: Quakers in Australia in the Nineteenth Century* (St. Lucia: University of Queensland Press, 1985), 43, 83–4, 319–20, 351, 382, 385; Arthur J. Ferch, ed., *Journey of Hope: Seventh-Day Adventist History in the South Pacific, 1919–1950*, (Wahroonga, NSW: South Pacific Division of Seventh-day Adventists, 1991), 82–92; Elisabeth K. Wilson, 'Brethren Attitudes to Authority and Government With Particular Reference to Pacifism', MHum Thesis, Department of History, University of Tasmania, 1994, 8–10, 89–91; Robert D. Linder, 'The Peaceful Evangelicals: Refusing to take up the Sword, 1914–1918', *CSAC Working Papers*, 1. 18, 1994.

50 F.J. Wilkins, *Baptists in Victoria: Our First Century, 1838–1938* (Melbourne: The Baptist Union of Victoria, 1939), 61, 79, 127–8; Robin Harvey, grandson of Francis Clemens, interviewed by Linder, Melbourne, 25 October 1994; *The Australian Baptist*, 18 August 1914, 1; 9 February 1915, 9; 20 April 1915, 10; 4 May 1915, 2, 10; 14 December 1915, 8; 18 September 1917, 2; 1 January 1918, 1.

51 *The Australian Baptist*, 18 August 1914, 1; 22 September 1914, 5.

become blood-lust and patriotism degenerate into hatred. Voices of restraint among evangelical Anglicans included those of Francis Bertie Boyce, rector of St. Paul's, Redfern, Stephen Taylor, rector of St. Paul's, Wahroonga and editor of *The Church Record,* 1916–1926, and Philip Dowe, rector of the Church of England, Bulli.[52]

Most Congregationalists joined their fellow evangelicals in backing Britain's war against 'the godless Huns'. This denomination, however, produced the most consistent and outspoken voice against the war on moral grounds, the Rev. Albert R. Rivett of Sydney. In August 1914, Rivett formed the Australian Peace Alliance (APA), an umbrella organisation aimed at establishing communications between the various peace groups in the country. The number of such groups affiliated with Rivett's organisation increased from thirteen in 1915 to fifty-four in 1918.[53] The main instrument for expressing Rivett's Christian pacifism was his own monthly magazine, *The Federal Independent.* He commiserated with several Congregational, Methodist and Presbyterian ministers who had been driven from their pulpits as a result of tensions created by their criticism of the war: 'Surely things are out of joint when earnest spiritually-minded men have to cut themselves adrift from the ministry of the churches because their loyalty to Jesus Christ makes continuance therein impossible'.[54] Rivett's criticism of the war cost him the pastorate of the Whitefield Congregational Church in Sydney in 1915.[55] Among those co-denominationalists who agreed with Rivett's views were the cultured, Socialist sympathiser, the Rev. Dr. L.D. Bevan, of Collins Street Independent church in Melbourne, afterwards the grand old man of South Australian Congregationalism, and Frank Tudor, a teetotal deacon from Richmond, Victoria, and leader of the federal parliamentary Labor Party from 1916 to 1922.

---

52 McKernan, *Australian Churches at War*, 5–6; Francis Bertie Boyce, *Four Score Years and Seven: The Memoirs of Archdeacon Boyce* (Sydney: Angus & Robertson, 1934), 81–2; Piggin, *Faith of Steel*, 174; *The Daily Telegraph*, 3 August 1914, 7; *The Church Record*, 26 October 1917, 1.

53 G. Lindsay Lockley, Biographical Card Index of Congregational Ministers in Australia, 1798–1977, Uniting Church Archives, North Parramatta, NSW; Janet Morice, *Six-Bob-A-Day Tourist* (Ringwood: Penguin Books, 1985), 47; Malcolm Saunders, 'The Origins & Early Years of the Melbourne Peace Society, 1899–1914', *RAHSJ*, 79, 1993, 111–2.

54 *The Federal Independent*, 15 November 1916, 13.

55 *The Federal Independent*, 15 August 1918, 10; Edward S. Kiek, *Our First Hundred Years: The Centenary Record of the South Australian Congregational Union* (Adelaide: The S.A. Congregational Union and Home Mission, 1950), 71; Janet McCalman, *Struggletown: Public and Private Life in Richmond, 1900–1965* (Carlton: MUP, 1984), 38–9, 98–9.

Presbyterians also supported the war with considerable enthusiasm, but here, too, a number of clergy and laity dissented from the majority view. Outstanding among them was the Rev. Dr. James Gibson of Queensland. He repeatedly warned the elect of God not to be misled by the siren song of the state. Gibson, thrice Moderator of the Presbyterian Church of Queensland and Moderator-General of the Presbyterian Church of Australia, 1920–1922, used his position as editor of the official Queensland Presbyterian magazine, *The Presbyterian Messenger*, to speak out against the war. Gibson's followers and the pro-war party engaged in a bitter debate over the war at the Annual Meeting of the Queensland General Assembly in May 1917. Even though Gibson himself was not present, his sympathisers managed to modify a proposed loyalty resolution which, even in its watered-down version, passed by only a 16 to 11 vote. In Melbourne, the Rev. Donald Cameron, Director of Home Missions for the Victorian Presbyterian Church, and in Sydney, the Rev. David Brandt, minister of the large and influential Chalmers Presbyterian Church, and several prominent Presbyterian laymen expressed similar views.[56]

The Methodists were the most giving of their sons to the god of battle while at the same time in many ways the most questioning of the war. They were particularly wary lest military life ruin or damage their young men's spiritual well-being. The Revs. W.H. Beale, Frank W. Walker and Albert Morris were among those Methodist clerical leaders who consistently opposed violence and war. The Rev. Dr. Samuel J. Hoban, Superintendent of the Methodist Central Mission, Sydney, openly expressed reservations about the Great War because of the negative effect military service would have on the morals of Methodist troops.[57]

The Rev. B. Linden Webb, Methodist parish minister in the small country town of Hay, became the most eloquent spokesperson for Christian non-violence in the war period. From January to March 1915, Webb preached three sermons on the current conflict. Later published as a small book entitled *The Religious Significance of the War*, they constitute the most tightly argued case for biblical pacifism produced during World War I in Australia.[58]

56 Richard Bardon, *James Gibson, M.A. D.D.* (Brisbane: W. R. Smith & Paterson, 1955), 9–16, 33–5, 85, 90–1, 101; McKernan, *Australian Churches at War*, 115, 117–8; *Argus*, 23 February 1915, 7; *The Daily Telegraph*, 3 October 1916, 8; *ACW*, 1 June 1917, 19; *The Messenger*, 13 December 1918, 794.

57 *The Australian Christian Commonwealth*, 12 November 1915, 10; Wright and Clancy, *The Methodists*, 129–36; Don Wright, *Mantle of Christ: A History of the Sydney Central Methodist Mission* (St. Lucia: University of Queensland Press, 1984), 108.

58 B. Linden Webb, *The Religious Significance of the War* (Sydney: Christian World, 1915).

Based on an exegesis of John 18:36, Matthew 24:12–13 and 2 Corinthians 10:3–4, Webb stressed 'the moral damage of war'. This conflict was a moral issue which Christians could not ignore: 'The war is not in keeping with our profession of Christianity; it is the outcome of materialism, worldliness, godlessness'.[59] He concluded his first sermon with a prophetic word, alluding to the competing ideals of Christ and Napoleon:

> ... when the Christian Church shall live for the ideals of Christ; when national leaders shall work towards them, then and then only shall we be on the way to rid humanity of the cruel curse of war. If we as a nation have a mission to be the world's peace-makers, His is the way to do it.
>
> Thus, not only in the lives of individual Christians, but in the 'Kingdoms of this world' Galilee shall vanquish Corsica. 'Not by might nor by power, but by my Spirit, saith the Lord of Hosts'.[60]

He concluded his final sermon with the question, Pascalian in its thrust: 'It is of very little moment to the Churches if I am wrong; but if I am right, what then?'[61]

Though himself a Christian pacifist, Webb nevertheless did not attempt to dissuade men from his church from enlisting in the armed forces, and many did so.[62] When his book began to circulate in NSW in June 1915, a brief but spirited debate over its merits broke out in *The Methodist*. Many individuals, lay and clergy alike, agreed with Webb, while others, mostly clergy, declared Webb a hopeless dreamer. The exchange revealed that the young minister had little support from the main leaders of his denomination and that his own parishioners listened to his case against war with grudging respect. However, as the community mourned its dead, and attempts to persuade the remaining young men to volunteer were stepped up, Webb's position became

---

59 Webb, *The Religious Significance*, 12.

60 Webb, *The Religious Significance*, 20. The biblical citation is from Zechariah 4:6. See also John Mathew, *Napoleon's Tomb* (Melbourne: Melville & Mullen, 1911); Malcolm Prentis, *Science, Race and Faith: A Life of John Mathew* (Sydney: Centre for the Study of Australian Christianity, 1998), 198–210.

61 Webb, *The Religious Significance*, 39; Robert D. Linder, 'Galilee Shall at last vanquish Corsica: The Rev. B. Linden Webb Challenges the War-Makers, 1915–1917', *Church Heritage*, 11, 2000, 171–83.

62 In July 1915, the membership of the Hay church stood at 50 full members and 20 junior members. Before the end of the war, 15 who were members or children of members had enlisted in the AIF. Minutes of the Hay Methodist Quarterly Meeting, 13 July 1915, Minute Book, Hay Methodist Quarterly Meeting, 1906–1933, Q.M. Rolls, Box 1, F, F2/3/M4, Uniting Church Archives, North Parramatta, NSW; *The Riverine Grazier*, 4 April 1916, 2.

more difficult.[63] On 18 October 1916, he submitted his resignation as both the minister of the Hay congregation and as a clergyman of the Methodist Church. He moved to Moss Vale where he taught elocution, farmed, peddled apples door-to-door, and sold clothes, all without success. After the war, he applied for reinstatement as a Methodist minister and was happily accepted back by the NSW Conference.[64]

Evangelicals and the Great Conscription Controversies

Mounting casualties in 1916, particularly following the Somme offensive initiated in July, and a dramatic drop in the number of recruits, created a political crisis in the Australian nation and a moral crisis in the Australian churches. In the first seven weeks of engagement on the Somme, the AIF sustained 28,000 casualties out of a total force of around 100,000 men. The sheer concentration of casualties was far greater than at Gallipoli.

The British, who had already introduced conscription, speculated aloud that without reinforcements to maintain them at full strength Australian divisions would have to be broken up. Prime Minister Billy Hughes returned from England in July 1916 determined to convince his Labor Government that conscription was the only solution to the military's demand for men. However, the majority of his party remained adamant in their opposition to compulsion. Therefore, Hughes suggested a plebiscite on conscription, and the ballot was scheduled for 28 October 1916.[65]

Evangelical Christians were split over conscription. On the one hand, Archbishop Wright was in many ways typical of evangelical clergy. He was convinced that conscription was as much a moral as a political question, and he campaigned in its support, urging a crowd in Sydney on the eve of the referendum: 'Do not show the white feather!' On the other hand, the Rev.

---

63 See the following pages of *The Methodist*: 26 June 1915, 2 and 6; 3 July 1915, 6; 10 July 1915, 6; 17 July 1915, 6; 31 July 1915, 7 and 11; 7 August 1915, 15; 14 August 1915, 9. Also see Linder, 'Galilee shall at last vanquish Corsica', 175–9.

64 Patricia Webb Ruffels, 'B. Linden Webb', unpublished manuscript furnished to the authors by the daughter of B. Linden Webb, 6 July 1995, 1–6; Linder, 'Galilee shall at last vanquish Corsica', 179.

65 Scott, *Australian During the War*, 337–9; Ken S. Inglis, 'Conscription in Peace and War, 1911–1945', in Roy Forward and Bob Reece (eds), *Conscription in Australia* (St. Lucia: University of Queensland Press, 1968), 22–65; Alan D. Gilbert, 'Protestants, Catholics and Loyalty: An Aspect of the Conscription Controversies, 1916–17', *Politics*, 6.1, 1971, 15–25; D.J. Murphy, 'Religion, Race and Conscription in World War I', *Australian Journal of Politics and History*, 20. 2, 1974, 155–63.

A.R. Rivett told his readers: 'A Church which takes up the position of conscripting life, involving as it does a violation of human liberty, the outrage of conscience, and in thousands of instances the disruption of the family, to say nothing of the spiritual ruination of men, whatever else it may be, is not a Church of Jesus Christ.'[66]

Methodists were divided on the issue, with most clergy in favour and most lay people opposed. In South Australia, the Revs Octavius Lake and Henry Howard gave their unswerving support, while the Rev. Dr George Brown, President-General of the Methodist Church of Australasia in 1916, took pains to point out that his denomination did not authorise any human being to speak as its representative on a purely political question. The Rev. Albert Morris took issue with Lake and Howard and preached popular anti-conscription sermons to his Brompton Methodist congregation in Adelaide and addressed numerous 'no' rallies for the Adelaide Anti-Conscription Council. He was aided by the energetic young Methodist lay preacher, Norman Makin.[67]

In Victoria, most Anglicans supported the initiative while Presbyterians and Baptists were not so certain. In Tasmania, Presbyterian home missionary Arthur Prowse pounded away at the conscription issue: 'Already 4,000,000 soldiers and as many civilians have perished. Their bodies, if laid side by side with sightless eyes to Heaven, would cover five square miles. A ghastly Carpet of Death affronting to God and humanity. How much larger will you vote for it to grow?'[68] Illawarra clergy were mostly silent on the issue, perhaps because the Labor Party, which dominated the region and to which so many of their church members belonged, was strongly opposed to conscription. In Western Australia, the State Labor Party Congress avoided a split after a raucous debate, mostly thanks to the effort of Jabez Dodd, a dedicated Methodist layman and prominent party leader, who cooled tempers with a conciliatory speech.[69]

---

66 *SMH*, 24 October 1916, 7; 26 October 1916, 8; *The Federal Independent*, 15 October 1916; Alan D. Gilbert, 'The Churches and the Conscription Referenda, 1916–17', MA Thesis, Department of History, Australian National University, 1967.

67 *Australian Christian Commonwealth*, 20 October 1916, 9; 27 October 1916, 6; *The Adelaide Advertiser*, 26 October 1916, 6; P.M. Gibson, 'The Conscription Issue in South Australia, 1916–1917', in J.I.W. Brach (ed.), *University Studies in History*, 4.2, *1963–1964*, (Nedlands: University of Western Australia Press, 1964), 69–70; Arnold D. Hunt, 'Methodism Militant', in Arnold D. Hunt and Robert P. Thomas (eds), *For God, King and Country* (Salisbury: Salisbury College of Advanced Education, 1979), 8–9; Makin, *Memoirs*, 47–51.

68 *The Zeehan and Dundas Herald*, 27 October 1916, 2; Lewis, *Our War*, 218.

69 Piggin, *Faith of Steel*, 182–3; *Illawarra Mercury*, 15 August 1916, 2; J.R. Robertson, 'The Conscription Issue and the National Movement in Western Australia', in Frank K. Crowley, ed., *University Studies in Western Australian History*, III, 3.3 (Fremantle, WA: S. H. Lamb, 1959), 6–8.

Available evidence suggests that evangelical clerical leaders were mainly pro-conscription, while the clergy-at-large and rank-and-file members were split over the question. The 1916 referendum failed by the narrow margin of 1,160,033 to 1,087,557.[70]

But this did not settle the issue. At the beginning of 1917, Hughes, expelled from the Labor Party for his support of conscription, became leader of a new coalition, the Nationalist or 'Win the War' Party. He then obtained a dissolution of Parliament and, in May 1917, won control of both the House and the Senate, while Labor's representation was reduced to a third or less in both houses. Frank Tudor, a devout evangelical Congregationalist, long-time champion of the trade unions and member of parliament for the federal seat of Yarra, Victoria, became the new leader of the federal opposition. Those who joined Tudor as Labor loyalists included Norman Makin, by this time MP for Hindmarsh. Makin and fellow Methodist from Queensland, James Page, acted as intra-party peacemakers and helped keep the Laborites from further cannibalisation. The Labor Party was thus held together during one of the most difficult periods in its turbulent history.[71]

Hughes announced on 17 November 1917 that another conscription vote would be held on 20 December.[72] The bad feeling of the first conscription campaign became raw hatred during the second. Once again, most of the clerical leadership of the churches, including those of an evangelical persuasion, supported the proposal. For example, the Rev. Dr Carruthers, now President of the General Conference of the Methodist Church of Australasia, sent 'yes' exhortations to all State presidents. The Sydney Anglican hierarchy, the main leaders of the Congregational and Presbyterian churches and ranking Salvation Army officers gave their support to an affirmative vote.[73]

Methodist minister C.E. James, writing in the influential interdenominational journal, the *Australian Christian World*, advocated conscription and attempted to respond to what he identified as three types of opposition to it: first, Christian pacifists like the Quakers, whose sincerity he conceded; second, the politically biased, like the Parliamentary Labor Party, who used the issue for partisan purposes; and, finally, Roman Catholic extremists, whom

---

70 Scott, *Australia During the War*, 352.

71 Leslie C. Jauncey, *The Story of Conscription in Australia* (South Melbourne: Macmillan, 1968), 245–7; John Faulkner and Stuart Macintyre, *True Believers: The Story of the Federal Parliamentary Labor Party* (Crows Nest: Allen & Unwin, 2001), 43–9.

72 Scott, *Australia During the War*, 397–414.

73 Hunt, 'Methodism Militant', 9–10; Gibson, 'The Conscription Issue in South Australia', 70.

he considered a subversive element in Australia. He pointed to Melbourne Archbishop Dr. Mannix as the leader of this last group and highlighted the divisiveness of his leadership. In his analysis, James identified Mannix as the focal point of sectarian strife during the second conscription controversy – strife which far exceeded anything yet seen among Australian Christians.[74] Mannix attacked Hughes for sponsoring a 'Lottery of Death' and a 'Blood Vote' and repeatedly made remarks which antagonised Orange Loyalist Protestants. Because of Mannix, the controversy in Victoria was more bitter than in any other State – and perhaps because of Mannix, Victoria shifted in the second referendum from a 'yes' to a 'no' majority.[75]

Observably, most evangelicals retreated into silence during the second conscription campaign. Thus, there were no official denominational endorsements of conscription on the part of South Australian Congregationalists and Presbyterians in 1917 as there had been the year before. In 1916, the editor of *The Australian Baptist* had supported conscription. In 1917, he fell mute. In the Illawarra, the silence was even more deafening than in 1916. Most evangelical clergy in this Labor-dominated area thought of enlistment as a matter of conscience and a test of character and faith, desirable features of a voluntary system, but eliminated by conscription.[76]

More evangelicals were openly critical of the conscription proposal in 1917 than previously. In Queensland, for example, the Rev. Dr John Graham Hughes, the energetic minister of the Rockhampton Baptist Tabernacle, received considerable press attention during the weeks before the December plebiscite by making numerous anti-conscription speeches in his area. At a pro-conscription rally in Rockhampton on 7 December 1917, Hughes created an uproar by remaining seated during the singing of the national anthem. The incident occurred when the main speaker, John Adamson, Federal Labor MP for Rockhampton and himself an evangelical clergyman, offered to allow anybody in the audience who disagreed with his pro-conscription views to have a turn at the podium following his own presentation. The Baptist minister took him at his word and moved to a place on the platform. However, following Adamson's speech, instead of turning next to Hughes, the chairman of the

---

74 *ACW*, 23 November 1917, 12.

75 Scott, *Australia During the War*, 241–3; Lewis, *Our War*, 272–5; McKernan, *Australian Churches at War*, 120–3; *Argus*, 29 January 1917, 9; Michael Gilchrist, *Daniel Mannix: Priest & Patriot* (Blackburn: Dove Publications, 1982), 38–52; B.A. Santamaria, *Daniel Mannix: The Quality of Leadership* (Melbourne: MUP, 1984), 74–94; Brenda Niall, *Mannix* (Melbourne: Text Publishing, 2015).

76 Gibson, 'The Conscription Issue in South Australia', 71–3; Piggin, *Faith of Steel*, 182–3.

assemblage called for the singing of the national anthem, normally the signal that such a gathering had come to an end. After the first verse, with Hughes still in his seat, the meeting disintegrated amidst pandemonium.

Hughes afterward defended his loyalty to king and country. He explained that he had not stood because, 'I had not received British fair play and justice'. This explanation did little to staunch the indignation, and Hughes was vilified in the press. In keeping with Baptist principles, Hughes made it clear that he was speaking for nobody but himself. However, a large number of men from his congregation were in the armed forces and its membership was split over his outspoken opposition to conscription. He was asked to resign from his pulpit in January 1918.[77]

In NSW, two evangelical leaders of the Labor movement were particularly outspoken critics of conscription, especially during the campaign of 1917. William Davies, a miner and Methodist local preacher from Wollongong, became an official for the Illawarra district of the Miners' Association shortly before the outbreak of the war. He opposed conscription in 1916, and, in March 1917, won a seat in the NSW Legislative Assembly. He was to hold it for the next 32 years. During 1917, Davies spoke with great eloquence at numerous anti-conscription rallies, and his criticisms, often based on biblical as well as economic grounds, were especially sharp. He was fond of citing the teachings of Jesus concerning peace and non-violence, claiming that Christ would have no individual conscripted to participate in war against his will. Mark Gosling, a devout Sydney Anglican from Petersham, was the second NSW Labor leader to speak out consistently against conscription. An officer of the Painters' Union and a branch president of the Australian Labor Party, Gosling was chairman of the Petersham and District Anti-Conscription Campaign in 1917. In 1920, he was elected as a Labor Party Member of the NSW Legislative Assembly, a position which he retained for more than a dozen years. The influence of these two Labor leaders among evangelicals was considerable, perhaps crucial, in deciding this question in the State.[78]

---

77 *Rockhampton Daily Record*, 8 December 1917, 6–7; *Rockhampton Morning Bulletin*, 11 December 1917, 3, 10; 12 December 1917, 4; 13 December 1917, 4; 19 December 1917, 5; 21 December 1917, 8; Minutes of Church Members Meeting Held in Baptist Tabernacle, 2 January 1918, Rockhampton Baptist Tabernacle, 18. Raymond A. Wilson, *A Reminiscent History of Rockhampton Baptist Tabernacle* (Rockhampton: The Baptist Tabernacle, 1992), 57.

78 Michael Hogan, *The Sectarian Strand: Religion in Australian History* (Ringwood: Penguin Books, 1987), 180–1; *SMH*, 22 February 1956, 6; Heather Radi, Peter Spearritt and Elizabeth Hinton, *Biographical Register of the NSW Parliament, 1901–1970* (Canberra: Australian National University, 1979), 114.

A number of evangelical lay women around Australia also exercised important leadership in opposition to the second conscription referendum. Celia John, a prominent member of Collins Street Independent Church in Melbourne, was exceptionally active in this cause. In Brisbane, Margaret Thorp, a Quaker peace activist, created a sensation when she became the spark which ignited a pitched battle between opposing women's groups at the Brisbane School of Arts in July 1917. She was the leader of a Brisbane organisation known as the Women's Peace Army (WPA). Her main theme was that 'Christ has shown them a better way' to conduct human affairs than war, and that military conscription represented nothing less than Christ recrucified. She pledged to give public testimony of this conviction at every opportunity. Therefore, when the Women's Compulsory Service Petition League (WCSPL) announced a rally for 9 July 1917 to bring pressure to bear on Prime Minister Hughes to impose compulsory service immediately, without recourse to a second plebiscite, she decided to act. At the appointed hour, Thorp and about 30 followers joined some 200 members of the WCSPL for their gathering at the School of Fine Arts. When the chairwoman read a statement of support for legislated conscription to be sent to the Prime Minister, Thorp arose from her seat and began to speak in opposition. She had uttered only a few sentences when she was shouted down. When she tried to continue, physical violence followed. One woman grabbed her and tried to force her out the door. Some of Thorp's followers came to the rescue, and, reported the press, the rally quickly degenerated into 'a seething mass of struggling women'. Thorp and her little band were driven from the hall, shouting 'three cheers for no conscription', whereupon the victorious WCSPL forces broke into a rendition of the national anthem. Thorp won a growing following over the course of the next few months preceding the second plebiscite.[79]

Among the men in the trenches, as on the home front, the clergy tended to favour conscription while the rank-and-file resisted it. John Gilbert 'Gib' Jacob, a young Methodist from Adelaide, was typical of many godly Diggers. In a letter to his brother, dated 20 April 1917, he revealed that most of his Christian mates, including himself, opposed conscription: 'No-one here cares for victory, all they want is peace – the sooner the better'.[80] Gib Jacob

---

79 Gilbert, 'The Churches and the Conscription Referenda, 1916–17', 116–7; Raymond Evans, '"All the Passion of Our Womanhood": Margaret Thorp and the Battle of the Brisbane School of Arts', in Joy Damousi and Marilyn Lake (eds), *Gender and War in the Twentieth Century* (Melbourne: CUP, 1995), 239–53.

80 John G. Jacob, *Home Letters of a Soldier-Student,* 2 vols., (Adelaide: G. Hassell & Sons, 1919), vol. 1, 73–9.

voted against conscription in December 1917. On 7 July 1918, he was killed in action at Hamel, near Villers Bretonneux in France.

In December 1917, the Sydney-based Anti-Conscription League circulated throughout NSW a broadsheet entitled 'A Manifesto from Protestant Ministers' with the subheading 'Conscription and Christianity'. It was signed by nine Protestant leaders, seven of whom were known evangelicals, including Rivett. They affirmed:

> We believe that when our fellow Ministers preach Conscription in the name of religion, they are speaking not in the name of the Christian religion but of that other religion which we have described as the religion of the State, and that if we take care not to confuse these two things, but seek an answer to the question in the light of Christian principles, we shall recognise the incompatibility of Christianity and Conscription.[81]

The 'no' vote once again prevailed, but this time by a larger margin: 1,181,747 against and 1,015,159 in favour.[82]

An analysis of the results in South Australia suggests that large numbers of rank-and-file evangelicals voted against conscription. A study of the Angas electorate showed that this heavily evangelical area with large numbers of Lutherans voted substantially against conscription. As church historian Arnold Hunt has pointed out, despite the advice of many of their clergy, the predominantly Methodist areas of Norman Makin's South Australia voted heavily against conscription in both referenda. Thus, South Australia with its large evangelical constituency twice turned down the conscription proposal by substantial majorities, though religion may not have been as important a factor in the rural areas as the need for farmers to preserve their labour force.[83]

Even though it appears that the majority of those evangelical clergy who spoke on the issues were pro-conscription, there is a long history of independent thought among evangelical laity which explains why they could ignore their

81 'Manifesto from Protestant Ministers', *The Federal Independent*, 15 December 1917, 3.

82 'A Misleading Manifesto', *The Methodist*, 29 December 1917, 7; Scott, *Australia During the War*, 423–4, 427.

83 Hunt, *This Side of Heaven*, 291; Gibson, 'The Conscription Issue in South Australia', 70, 73–4; Jenny T. Stock, 'Farmers and the Rural Vote in South Australia in World War I: The 1916 Conscription Referendum', *Australian Historical Studies*, 87, 1985, 391–411. Alan Gilbert's statement that 'the major Protestant Churches officially and emphatically came out in favour of a YES vote' needs to be modified. It is doubtful that this statement applied to the evangelical Protestant rank-and-file. Gilbert, 'Protestants, Catholics and Loyalty', 15–25.

leaders' advice and still consider themselves loyal Christians.[84] It is a mistake to assume, as some historians have, that public evangelical pronouncements were identical with popular evangelical opinion.

Evangelicals and the Fellowship of Sorrow

Life on the home front was not all controversy and division. After the initial outbursts of enthusiasm and early gestures of sacrifice, it became largely business as usual, both in the churches and in Australian life in general. Arnold Hunt read through some 200 issues of the official South Australian Methodist paper for the years 1914 through 1918. He was struck by the way in which the normal life of the church continued:

> The Women's Guilds and the children's societies still carried on. New churches were built: Gartrell, Wasleys, Pinnaroo, Kingscote, to name a few. The weekly life of the congregations was maintained; often, one imagines, by many people whose hopes and fears were daily focused on some khaki-clad son or sons on the other side of the world. There was, in the words of a leading chaplain, 'a wonderful fellowship of sorrow'.[85]

Nor was the War incompatible with church growth. In Queensland, the Presbyterian Church grew from 33,755 members in 1914 to 39,679 in 1919. In NSW and South Australia, Methodists enjoyed remarkable growth, especially in view of the fact that so many of their sons were killed in the war. NSW Methodists increased in membership from 24,291 in 1914 to 27,821 in 1919, while the membership of the Methodist Church in South Australia grew by ten percent in the five years following 1914, from 20,764 to 22,926. These patterns were typical for the evangelical churches which published membership figures.[86]

Life on the home front also reflected long-term commitments related to the war on the part of the evangelical clergy. They took the lead in organising

84 McKernan, *Australian Churches at War*, 58–9.

85 Hunt, 'Methodism Militant', 13. For examples of business as usual in the evangelical churches, see Raymond Nobbs, *You Are God's Building* (Wahroonga: St Paul's Church, 1987), 95; Piggin, *Faith of Steel*, 171–2; *The Australian Baptist*, 11 August 1914, 4; Brian Dickey, *Holy Trinity Adelaide* (Adelaide: Trinity Church Trust, 1988), 98.

86 McKernan, *Australian Churches at War*, 99–100; *The Methodist*, 14 November 1914, 7; Hunt, 'Methodism Militant', 1; Piggin, *Faith of Steel*, 172; Stephen Judd and Kenneth Cable, *Sydney Anglicans* (Sydney: Anglican Information Office, 1987), 178–9; Joan Mansfield, *A Church on the Highway: Pymble Presbyterian Church, 1895–1977* (Pymble: Pymble Council of Elders, 1985), 24.

corporate public prayer services among the churches, which, as in Sydney, occasionally even included Jewish rabbis, and at which all people were welcome. As the casualties mounted, these corporate ventures also came to include communal memorial services where the grieving could find comfort and be assured that the death of a loved one in the war had some meaning. The crowds at such services could be enormous, often overflowing the churches and the halls where they were held.[87] A particularly emotional event was the 6 August 1916 anniversary of the Battle of Lone Pine and the Suvla Bay operation at Gallipoli held at St. Andrew's Cathedral, Sydney: 'In the morning the members of the Returned Solders Association paraded and filled up the greater part of the Cathedral. Many hundreds were unable to gain admission'.[88]

The clergy of all churches agreed to deliver the notification telegram informing relatives of a soldier's death. They soon came to rue accepting such an undertaking. The sight of the local minister coming through the front gate came to fill with dread those with sons and husbands in the armed forces. Brian Lewis's mother, with four sons in the army, nearly fainted one day early in 1917 when she saw her Presbyterian minister walking up the path to the front door to pay an unscheduled but normal parish visit. She asked him to be good enough to phone before he came the next time. Many clergy would never forget the pain involved in such ministry. Nor did the people forget. A whole generation would associate the sight of a pastor or priest with terror, pain and death, and a whole generation of churches, evangelicals included, would suffer from this mental connection.[89]

Another area of long-term commitment on the part of evangelicals was related to their hope for an increase in spiritual vitality as a result of the war. Evangelical churches organised 'Go-to-Church Sundays' and urged people to 'give your soul a chance', but large numbers of individuals still engaged in secular pursuits on Sundays. The churches were more successful at hitching temperance to the patriotic bandwagon. On 3 April 1915, King George V announced that he would be a total abstainer for the duration of the war, and many evangelical clergy across the country enthusiastically endorsed a 'Follow the King' movement. It translated into a nation-wide campaign to close pubs at 6 pm. In all of the areas where early closing won the day, evangelical

---

87 *The Methodist*, 15 August 1914, 1; *Sydney Diocesan Magazine*, 1 September 1914, 21; and *ACW*, 30 November 1917, 16.

88 *Sydney Diocesan Magazine*, 1 September 1916, 9.

89 Lewis, *Our War*, 250–1. McKernan was unable to find any archival evidence that the government ever formally requested clergy to deliver death notices. McKernan, *Australian Churches at War*, 73, 184.

women, through the well-led WCTU, were instrumental in obtaining the victory. By 1917 public houses and hotel bars Australia-wide generally were closed on Sundays and only open from 9 am to 6 pm on weekdays, and public drunkenness became rarer for the remainder of the war. The ten o'clock staggers disappeared and the stage was set for what was to become the alleged 'six o'clock swill' of inter-war legend and lore.[90]

The General Strike, 1917

Evangelical churches understood their role as caring for the national soul in war-time primarily in terms of maximising public support for the war effort. But the national soul was no more at peace with itself than was the nation with its military enemies. Industrial unrest threatened national unity. Throughout 1916, the government of Australia was conducted in an environment of almost perpetual crisis. Rank-and-file workers were becoming increasingly frustrated and discontented with their working conditions. Many were convinced that the employers were using the war as an excuse to turn the clock back on hard-won changes. Railway workers struck on 2 August 1917. Within a week the strike involved 30,000 rail, tram, mine and wharf workers, and within a month, 76,000 workers throughout NSW were idle.[91] This was a moment of truth for the evangelical movement which instinctively saw itself as a third way, a bridge, between conflicting parties. Parts of the evangelical family had a long and rich association with the labour movement. They readily understood that attending to the national soul in this situation called for a just assessment of the workers' claims instead of assuming that class warfare was the fault of the workers. The public prosperity which they believed the Gospel facilitated was not for the exclusive benefit of capitalists.

Among those who led the strikers was Welsh Church of God lay preacher, Albert D. Willis.[92] Arriving in Sydney in 1911, Willis, a coalminer, soon became president of the Illawarra Miners' Association. The war and the ensuing conscription controversy disrupted Willis's plans for a reorganisation of the miners' unions and ultimately led to his ill-fated involvement in the 1917 general strike. Willis and E.J. Kavanagh, a Congregationalist, and two

90 Walter Phillips, '"Six O'Clock Swill": The Introduction of Early Closing of Hotel Bars in Australia', *Historical Studies*, 19, 1980, 250–66.

91 John Iremonger, John Merritt and Graeme Osborne (eds), *Strikes: Studies in Twentieth Century Australian History* (Sydney: Angus & Robertson, 1973), 51–80.

92 I.E. Young, 'A.C. Willis, Welsh Nonconformist, and the Labour Party in NSW, 1911–33', *JRH*, 2, 1963, 303–13; Piggin, *Faith of Steel*, 161–8.

others were jailed and charged with conspiring to strike and neglecting their duty as public officials. After a spectacular trial, the charges were dropped. In reality, neither Willis nor Kavanagh was enthusiastic about the timing of the strike, but, as good union men they supported it once it began. In Kavanagh's case, the police had confiscated a notebook he was carrying at the time of his arrest. It contained, in shorthand, the main points of a speech he had made about the strike. The police paid £200 to have the notes translated, hoping they would assist in securing Kavanagh's conviction. Instead, they revealed his personal distaste for the action and ensured his acquittal![93]

Willis assumed that, as in Wales, there was a basic compatibility between miners' lodges and Protestant churches, and he proceeded to become acquainted with a number of Sydney clergy, including the recently returned soldier, Anglican Dean A.E. Talbot. This friendship led to Talbot's sensational defence of the labour movement and, by inference, the strike, in the Church of England Provincial Synod in Sydney in August 1917. As the editor of *The Church Record* put it, the Dean's speech became the 'most generally discussed topic in Sydney' that week. The Provincial Synod met from 15–17 August. On 16 August, the Rev. Dr. L.B. Radford, Bishop of Goulburn, moved an anti-strike motion. Archdeacon Boyce and Dean Talbot both questioned the wisdom of giving the appearance of a deliberate attack by the Church of England on the working class. Several of the synod's lay members accused Talbot of defending the strikers and, by implication, of disrupting the war effort and supporting social anarchy.[94] A compromise motion was finally passed which deplored but did not condemn the strike, and which blamed the decay of morals and religion for the industrial troubles then plaguing the community. A local newspaper reported that, when the procession of strikers was in progress on the last day of the synod debate, a man stood on the corner of Bathurst and George Streets holding aloft a large sign bearing the words: 'Give cheers for the Dean of Sydney when passing St. Andrew's'. Consequently, as the workers passed that point, a continuous thunderous noise could be heard in the Chapterhouse where the synod was in session.[95]

By October 1917, the striking workers, hungry and discouraged, drifted back, and the strike was broken. The government had totally defeated the workers, thus ensuring a decade of poisoned industrial relations. As for the evangelical churches, it was too evident that the workers appreciated Dean

---

93 Young, 'A. C. Willis', 306–7; *SMH*, 14 September 1917, 8; 18 October 1956, 7.

94 Young, 'A. C. Willis', 306–7; *Church Record*, 31 August 1917, 1; *SMH*, 17 August 1917, 5.

95 *SMH*, 18 August 1917, 12.

Talbot's support because it was so unexpected. There were significant evangelical congregations with working-class membership especially in some inner-city suburbs of Australian cities, but increasingly evangelical congregations were becoming middle class. The ministers of these congregations largely lost contact with working people. By the late 1920s they were not well placed to take a leading role in the re-emergence of the labour movement as an important force in national life. This impaired the dynamic altruism of evangelical Christianity in Australia in the inter-war period when it was sorely needed.

Overall, the War uncovered propensities within the evangelical movement which threatened to weaken its public role. The support it gave to the British Empire at the beginning of the War received less unanimous approval at the end of the War. The uncritical identification of the Kingdom of God with the British Empire began to erode within the churches. In retrospect, that was not all loss, and those courageous clergy and people who withstood the patriotic tsunami witnessed to a higher truth. But the evangelical movement, which had reached a pinnacle of influence before the War, lost momentum. There was unprecedented division within the movement over war-related issues as denominational leaders parted company, not only with many of their lay members, but also with local ministers who often sided with their own church members. The confidence with which denominational leaders began the War was quickly diminished by the overwhelming horror of loss of life on an unprecedented scale. As the agony dragged on, denominational spokesmen had less to say as their capacity to discern the divine purpose died with the men in the trenches, whose ghastly experience must now be chronicled.

Chapter Two

CHRISTIAN SOLDIERS AND THE FRONT LINE DURING THE GREAT WAR, 1914–1918

We only know, from good and great
Nothing save good can flow;
That where the cedar crashed so straight
No crooked tree shall grow;

That from their ruin a taller pride,
Not for these eyes to see,
May clothe one day the valleyside …
Non nobis, domine.

'Non Nobis, Domine' (Not unto us, O Lord, Psalm 115)

(Charles E.W. Bean, Australian official war correspondent, written in December 1915, when leaving the graves at Gallipoli)

One of the ironies of the Rev. B. Linden Webb's futile pacifist stand against the war was that many of the Christian men in the ranks of the Australian armed forces agreed with him. The views of these 'godly Diggers', however, have been overlooked. The stereotype is of the average Australian soldier who was 'not religious' given little reason to change his opinion of religion because its chief representative, the chaplain, was ineffective. Evidence to the contrary has been submerged, probably unconsciously, as the assumption that the typical Digger was essentially without religion was as obviously true as the fact that the earth is flat. Truth is no more obvious in history than it is in science. The alternative view that soldiers were commonly very interested in religious issues and valued the presence and ministry of chaplains has made a late appearance in the writing of Australian history, but is already well on the road to acceptance.[1] Colin Bale has concluded that 'significant numbers of [soldiers] appear to have been more interested in religion than has often been thought'.[2] Michael Gladwin has argued that 'The archival record is far richer than most historians have suggested in revealing a positive relationship between chaplains and the AIF'.[3]

Godly Diggers

A popular judgment concerning the religion of the Diggers of the Great War comes from the pen of historian Bill Gammage. His influential book *The Broken Years* is based on the letters and diaries of some one thousand Australian soldiers who served at the front. Gammage tried to determine with what assumptions and expectations they volunteered for service, in what ways their outlook was amended by their wartime experiences, and what new attitudes they evolved and brought back to Australia following the war. He believed that what happened to these soldiers would reveal something of the change which came over Australia itself as the days of Empire gave way to the tradition of Anzac. In a discussion of the sources of his study, Gammage reported:

> But, as though to mock the attachments of gentler times, there are three particular omissions: religion, politics, and sex, and of these perhaps the most surprising is religion. These pages instance men who enlisted to defend their God, who remained devout Christians through every

1 The pioneering revisionist work in this area is Robert D. Linder, *The Long Tragedy: Australian Evangelical Christians and the Great War, 1914–1918* (Adelaide: Openbook Publishers, 2000). As the centenary of World War I approached studies questioning the stereotype of the non-religious Digger have multiplied: Colin Bale, 'A Crowd of Witnesses: Australian War Graves Inscriptions on the Western Front of the Great War,' PhD, University of Sydney, 2006; Colin Bale, 'In God We Trust: The Impact of the Great War on Religious Belief', in Peter Bolt and Mark Thompson, *Donald Robinson selected works. Vol 3: Appreciation* (Sydney: Australian Church Record, 2008), 303–314; Gary Kent and Daniel Reynaud, *Faith of the Anzacs* (Warburton: Signs Publishing, 2010), ch. 6; Michael Gladwin, *Captains of the Soul: A History of Australian Army Chaplains* (Newport: Big Sky Publishing, 2013). Similarly, Rowan Strong reports 'a rather stronger religiousness among RAN sailors and officers than previous historians have indicated'. Rowan Strong, *Chaplains in the Royal Australian Navy* (Sydney: UNSW Press, 2012), 292.

2 Bale, 'In God We Trust', 307.

3 Gladwin, *Captains of the Soul*, 75, 83.

> travail, and who, if they became fatalists, became so by trusting God entirely. Yet the average Australian soldier was not religious. He was not a keen churchman: he avoided church parades … He distrusted chaplains, and sometimes detested them, because he was an Australian, and because they were officers, enjoying the privileges of leaders but not the concomitant risks and responsibilities of battle.
>
> Most Australians found little in war to prompt consideration of a higher divinity. Some turned to God in moments of stress, but the majority kept their minds squarely upon the world around them, displaying a practical concern for the exigencies of battle, and a preoccupation with questions of food and rest, dead mates, leave, and the next fight. Not often during that blind struggle did they consider the Almighty being who supposedly directed their existence.[4]

Yet Gammage's assessment is not consistent with the evidence in his own book which is replete with religious imagery and references to Christianity and brimming with morality and moral judgments. Most historians of the war seem incapable of seeing the religious sentiments of the people of the time though they were stated plainly enough. Consequently, the pages of most accounts of World War I highlight 'all the usual suspects': larrikins, no-hopers, sentimental blokes, radical individualists, cynics, socialists, communists, even feminists – but seldom devout Christians. A re-consideration of the evidence in the context of the nature of Australian religious faith in the period 1914–1918 rather than from a more recent perspective is required.

AIF Chaplain Kenneth Henderson cautioned readers of his memoirs that it is unwise to draw any confident generalisations concerning the impact of the war on the religion of the Diggers. This is especially true, he notes, because the Australian soldier tended to bluff in such matters. Most combat troops remained basically Christian even though often personally alienated from organised religion. Almost all retained a belief in Providence, or what they sometimes called 'Destiny', and in the power of prayer. Most never lost their belief in and/or respect for Jesus Christ and almost all retained a pragmatic faith. If there was a 'typical' Australian Army religion perhaps it was best expressed by a remark made by a Digger to his padre after a particularly heavy artillery bombardment one day in France: 'We've been praying like hell!'[5]

---

4 Bill Gammage, *The Broken Years: Australian Soldiers in the Great War* (Canberra: Australian National University Press, 1974), xiv-xv.

5 Kenneth Thorne Henderson, *Khaki and Cassock* (Melbourne: Melville & Mullen, 1919), 154.

The representation of the World War I Diggers as 'romantic larrikins' has been popularised through novels like George Johnston's *My Brother Jack*, as well as through more serious studies such as John Laffin's *Digger: The Legend of the Australian Soldier*. It is most powerfully perpetuated in film and television, especially in such TV docu-dramas as the 1985 classic 'ANZACS'.[6] In this five-part television series, the romantic larrikin theme is strongly emphasised, with Paul Hogan playing a central role as Private Pat Cleary, 'the Australian larrikin – irreverent, shameless, humorous and irrepressible'.[7] The official account of the making of the series begins with a description penned in 1916 by Phillip Gibbs, an English war correspondent and admirer of Australian valour:

> They were gipsy fellows with none but the gipsy law in their hearts, intolerant of restraint, with no respect for rank or caste unless it carried strength with it, difficult to handle behind the lines, quick-tempered, foul-mouthed and primitive men, but lovable, human, generous souls when their bayonets were not red with blood.[8]

This picture of the romantic larrikin in uniform is half true – but only half. While many of the Australian volunteers were, in fact, larrikins in the mould of Pat Cleary and Paul Hogan, many were not. Large numbers of devout Christians, Protestant and Roman Catholic, enlisted to serve 'God and country'. The majority of these were evangelicals not given to swearing, smoking or drinking and they never abandoned their fundamental values of honour, decency, dedication to a fair go, devotion to duty, abhorrence of violence, and respect for human life.[9]

> Foremost among those who do not fit the larrikin stereotype are the more than a thousand soldiers of Aboriginal descent who fought in World War I.[10] Almost all of them were from evangelical mission

---

6 George Johnston, *My Brother Jack: A Novel* (London: Collins, 1964); John Laffin, *Digger: The Legend of the Australian Soldier*, rev. ed. (South Melbourne: Sun Books, 1990); John Cribbin, *The Making of ANZACS* (Sydney: Collins/Fontana, 1985).

7 Cribbin, *The Making of ANZACS*, 118.

8 Cribbin, *The Making of ANZACS*, 1.

9 The religious composition of the First AIF was about 80 percent Protestant and 20 percent Roman Catholic. Since the Protestant churches were overwhelmingly evangelical at this time, it means that the majority of the troops came from an evangelical religious background. Jeffrey Grey, *A Military History of Australia*, 3rd ed. (Cambridge: CUP, 2008), 91–2.

10 Noah Riseman, 'Diversifying the Black Diggers' Histories', *Aboriginal History*, 39, 2015, 137.

> stations, such as the Point McLeay and Point Pearce Stations in South Australia. Among the large number of Aboriginal soldiers killed in action was Private Henry Thorpe, who gave his life, and in so doing won the Military Medal for 'conspicuous courage and leadership'.[11]

Of the thousands from evangelical churches who served, four illustrate well this theme of 'godly Diggers': Owen Lewis, a Presbyterian; Alf Stewart, a Congregationalist; John Ridley, a Baptist; and Fred McLaughlin, a Methodist. These four men, and others like them, are represented in the assessment of Brian Lewis, Owen's brother, who grew up in an evangelical church during the war but who in later life was himself no friend of organised religion. Drawing upon his broad knowledge of the Melbourne scene, he concluded that the AIF was made up mostly of wowsers and larrikins, in approximately equal numbers:

> No body of troops which have ever been assembled could have been as morally divided as those which left Australia early in the war. Many of those who rushed to join in the first hysteria had felt a deep moral compulsion and the proportion of such men increased as the war went on. Next year at Wesley College I would learn one of the new war songs:
>
> Young Galahad has gone to fight
> In countries o'er the sea,
> For King and Empire, God and right
> And Truth and Liberty,
> Nor ever went a nobler soul
> Nor e'er a truer heart.
>
> And this was not a ridiculous exaggeration. They had the same high calling as had Sir Galahad, and like him, were 'pure'. They had never known the love of a woman and many never would; they were puritanical in the best sense of the word. They did not drink and most did not smoke; they were at one extreme. At the other were those who went in because they were out of work and the pay was very good. A uniform would give them prestige and a lot of free beer. Their morals were non-existent; they were the larrikins of the Melbourne 'pushes', anti-police, anti-authority and anti-discipline. They followed a pattern of rebellion against the ridiculous excesses of the military system.

---

11 John Harris, *One Blood: 200 Years of Aboriginal Encounter with Christianity* (Sutherland, NSW: Albatross, 1990), 612–4.

> Some made superb soldiers in action, many made deplorable soldiers out of action.[12]

Brian Lewis's brother Owen was one of those 'Young Galahads'. There is a poignant window into the evangelical soldier's soul in a letter written on 27 April 1915, by nineteen-year-old Owen to his father, pleading for permission to enlist. Owen was the fourth son of the family, studying engineering at the University of Melbourne at the time and doing brilliantly. His letter to his father illustrates the evangelical conscience and mind in action:

> It is hard to explain exactly what is impelling me to go but there is something allied to conscience which bids me go. I believe in a hereafter and if following the will of my conscience I enter it sooner than under ordinary circumstances I do not think that anyone should regret it.
>
> What comes to me a great deal is, that I am abiding here in comfort while others perhaps having people dependent on them are fighting my battles and giving up their lives for me. Death must come to us all sooner or later and there is no way so noble of leaving than that in which you 'Lay down your life for your friends'.[13]

The father did not give his consent and insisted that Owen finish the academic year. The obedient son acquiesced, and again topped the examination list. However, he finally enlisted early in 1916, and was killed in action in France on 12 April 1918.

Alfred (Alf) Stewart was 25 years old and a letterpress machinist in Sydney before his enlistment. He hesitated to volunteer because he could not bear the thought of killing other human beings. When he finally joined the AIF on 26 August 1915, he wanted to be a stretcher-bearer. Instead, he was assigned to a rifle company in the 17th Battalion.[14] He was the only surviving son (five brothers died at birth or in infancy) in a family which included a widowed father and three sisters. His father had been a Congregational missionary in the Outback earlier in life and the family were all active members of the Kogarah Congregational Church. A non-smoking teetotaller, Alf accepted Christ as Saviour as a teenager and served his church in many different capacities, including as a Sunday School teacher. After the war, he planned

---

12 Brian Lewis, *Our War: Australia During World War I* (Carlton: MUP, 1980), 134.

13 Lewis, *Our War*, 127.

14 Alfred R.M. Stewart, *Diaries of an Unsung Hero*, researched and compiled by Margaret Willmington (Blaxland: Mark Webb of B-in-Print, 1995), 4–5, 63.

to study for the ministry. He was by common consent of his extended family and army mates an eminently decent young man.[15]

Stewart embarked for France on 20 December 1915 and participated in some of the fiercest fighting on the Western Front in 1916 and 1917. He kept a war diary in which he recorded his innermost thoughts and commented on his military commanders, chaplains, church parades and the Christian fellowship he found among his mates. He recorded on 29 July 1916 that 'for comfort's sake I read dear Ma's favourite chapter John 14. It took me out of myself for a while. During those terrible bombardments one can always find comfort in prayer, but the nerve strain is awful'.[16] On another occasion, he recorded his first Easter Sunday under fire, 23 April 1916:

> We had Holy Communion in the officer's shelter at 10 am during which some fragments of exploded shell and mud landed at the open door. The Chaplain shook hands as we went out and said, 'I hope you will all be able to remember this service next Easter Sunday'.

Following 'one of the hottest bombardments', he wrote:

> There was simply one continuous roar, hiss, crash, heat & concussion. I must admit I did feel a bit afraid, but suddenly it came to me, why should you be afraid, when you honestly believe that God is taking care of you; and I felt ashamed and offered up a little prayer and instantly I lost all fear and though I was shaking a bit, I never felt afraid.[17]

After being wounded in August, 1916, Stewart was sent to England for convalescence. He visited relatives and attended church at every opportunity, with a record-setting four services in one day on 1 October 1916.[18] Lance Corporal Stewart was offered sergeant's stripes in September 1917, shortly before the battle of Polygon Wood. He said that he would think about it. Then, during heavy fighting on 20 September, there was a call for volunteers to rescue Sgt Malcolm Watson lying wounded in No Man's Land. Alf responded, and was bringing him in when hit in the legs by machine gun fire. Another Digger managed to drag the two men to a shell hole where they were awaiting stretcher bearers when a direct hit by enemy artillery fire killed them both.[19]

---

15 Stewart, *Diaries,* 7–8, 108, 137; letter of Margaret Willmington to Linder, 10 July 2000.

16 Stewart, *Diaries*, 133.

17 Stewart, *Diaries*, 78.

18 Stewart, *Diaries*, 174–5.

19 Stewart, *Diaries*, 63, 255.

The childhood dream of John G. Ridley, son of a Sydney publisher, was some day to be a soldier. When hostilities began in 1914, the eighteen-year-old Ridley longed for the day when his parents would agree with his plans to volunteer. However, before he could enlist he was converted to Christ in the Burton Street Baptist Tabernacle, and, like Ignatius Loyola before him, vowed to become a soldier for the King of Kings.[20] Ridley joined the AIF in August 1915, and by the beginning of the new year found himself with the 53rd Battalion in France. 'Brave as the bravest, cool and manly in action', according to Roman Catholic Chaplain John J. Kennedy, Ridley was soon promoted to sergeant.[21] It was as a nineteen-year-old sergeant that he repeatedly took his section into combat, including the battle of Fromelles in July 1916. On the evening of 19 July, Ridley blew his whistle and led his men over the top and into a hail of German machine gun and rifle fire. After passing over rough ground covered with bodies of the dead and wounded, strewn with barbed wire and pocked by shellfire, the sergeant guided his men into a water-filled ditch which had at one time been a German trench. Then, as he raised his head too high, a bullet found its mark:

> It was a terrible smack. It makes me shiver when I think of it. Something like a terrific blow from a cricket ball, but ten times worse. It stunned me with the force of it, and for a moment I hardly knew how I had been hit. Then the blood rushed out of my mouth and down my face in a torrent.[22]

As he began to thrash about in the water, two of the sergeant's men grabbed him to keep him from drowning. They worked desperately to staunch the flow of blood from the wound in his throat and to keep him from choking on his own blood. They managed to apply a field dressing and pull their wounded leader back to their own lines.

Ridley did not die that day and lived another sixty years. After recovering from this severe wound, he was promoted to lieutenant and sent back to his unit. In cooperation with Len Greenberg, close friend, fellow-Baptist and YMCA Secretary for the Fifth Division, Ridley organised what he called

20 Harold E. Evans, *Soldier and Evangelist: The Story of Rev. John G. Ridley, M.C.* (Sydney: Baptist Historical Society of NSW, 1980), 9–14.

21 John J. Kennedy, *The Whale Oil Guards* (Dublin: James Duffy and Co. Ltd., 1919), 118–20. Roman Catholic Padre Kennedy wrote of Ridley: 'He is a Baptist and I am a Roman Catholic, but I say of him most sincerely that he is one of the most perfect Christians I have ever met.'

22 John G. Ridley, *Milestones of Mercy* (Sydney: Christian Press, 1957), 55.

'the Bible Circle of the 53rd Battalion'. Meeting mostly in YMCA facilities behind the lines or makeshift shelters near the front, the circle included all ranks and many different denominations as they gathered regularly for Bible study, song fests and an occasional 'fellowship tea'. Ridley reported that many found Christ and large numbers sustained their faith in these circumstances, so much so that he referred to one period when something like a 'miniature revival' occurred. The Bible Circle numbered 50 or more at times.[23]

Frederick A. McLaughlin was one of four Methodist brothers from Victoria, all with a firm personal faith in Jesus Christ and a good church background, who joined the AIF in 1916.[24] In 1917–1918, Fred, along with his brothers Bert and George, participated in some of the most intense fighting on the Western Front, especially in the Arras and Ypres sectors. During those months, all three men read their New Testaments regularly, shunned participation in the more profane aspects of military life, attended church and/or YMCA services whenever possible, and kept their faith. Fred sought out Christian fellowship at every opportunity. He had close ties with a number of Methodist families in England near his training base in Brightlingsea. On one occasion while on leave, he caught a train at 10:00 pm on a Saturday night in Edinburgh, arrived in London at 8:00 am on a Sunday morning, and attended the celebrated Wesleyan Central Hall in the afternoon and again in the evening. 'Splendid service', he commented in his diary, noting that the evening sermon was on 'The Blood of Christ Cleanseth Us from All Sin'.[25]

On 28 August 1918, shortly after his promotion to Corporal, McLaughlin was cited for creative initiative and bravery under fire near the town of Vaux, and two months later was awarded the Military Medal. He spent 424 of his 710 days in France in the trenches. The object of the daily prayers of their mother and against great odds, all four McLaughlin men returned from the war. Fred McLaughlin remained an active Christian layman the rest of his life and, to the benefit of the national soul, became Prime Minister John Curtin's private secretary during World War II.[26]

---

23 Evans, *Soldier and Evangelist*, 21–7; and John G. Ridley, 'The Romance of a Bible Class', n.d., 1–7, typescript provided to the authors by Ruth Ridley, daughter of John Ridley.

24 William and Barbara Ross (eds.), The War Diary of 2nd Corporal F.A. McLaughlin, M.M., 1918, MS in the possession of Barbara McLaughlin Ross, Blackburn, Victoria (hereafter The War Diary of F.A. McLaughlin).

25 The War Diary of F.A. McLaughlin, preface and 11; Barbara McLaughlin Ross, daughter of Fred McLauglin, interviewed by Linder, Blackburn, Victoria, 30 July 1998.

26 The War Diary of F.A. McLaughlin, 79. See chapter 6 below.

In retrospect, what is surprising is that so many maintained their spiritual integrity in the face of incredible pressures to conform to a profligate lifestyle. Recent studies have shown that the incidence of venereal disease was no higher in the Australian armed forces during the conflict than in pre-war civilian life.[27] Sapper Henry W. (Harry) Dadswell discovered after demobilisation in 1919 that many civilians harboured misguided notions about the character of their nation's fighting men during the war. Dadswell, a former Church of England Sunday School pupil from Victoria, reported that he was frequently accosted by non-veterans who offered to buy him a beer or give him cigarettes. When he informed them that he neither drank nor smoked, they were nonplussed: 'And you a soldier!' they would exclaim in surprise. Dadswell noted that this expression, 'and you a soldier!' began to irritate him greatly, especially when he recalled the men of his old outfit, the 5th Division Signal Company. He records: 'I thought of the boys, some of the finest, clean-living boys you could meet anywhere. There were no canteens in the 1st AIF and about half of our unit neither smoked nor drank. The standards of behaviour and honesty were very high'.[28]

Enlistment among Evangelicals

A reason why so many of the diggers were 'godly' was that the manse-parsonage-rectory yielded so many recruits for the AIF, and clergy often volunteered for military chaplaincy to be with their men. From scattered statistics compiled by historian Michael McKernan, it seems that a minimum of 326 Protestant ministers served as chaplains and an additional 137 enlisted in the ranks.[29] Of that number, it appears that at least 195 of the chaplains and 100 of those who enlisted in the ranks were evangelicals at the time they volunteered. These numbers, however, may be too conservative, as ministers of 'Other Protestant Denominations' who enlisted in the ranks were not included in McKernan's statistics.

27 Judith Smart, 'The Great War and the "Scarlet Scourge": Debates About Venereal Diseases in Melbourne During World War I' in Judith Smart and Tony Wood, eds., *An Anzac Muster: War and Society in Australia and New Zealand, 1914–1918 and 1939–1945* (Monash University Publications in History No. 14, Clayton: Monash University, 1992), 58–85.

28 Henry W. Dadswell, Diary of a Sapper, MS 828, 137, Australian War Memorial Archives, Canberra.

29 Gladwin, *Captains of the Soul*, 32, 66 accepts Linder's calculation of 414 clergy of all denominations who served as chaplains.

Irving Benson, historian of Victorian Methodism, notes that between 40 and 45 Methodist ministers from that State joined the AIF in various capacities from chaplains to infantrymen, one-third of the total of 134 mentioned by McKernan. Given the heavy enlistment of Methodist clergy throughout every other State in the federation, it seems likely that the total of Methodist clergy enlistees was much higher.[30] Twenty percent of South Australian Methodist ministers enlisted in various capacities in the AIF, both as infantrymen and as chaplains. In Western Australia, where most of their clergy were young single men working in pioneer situations, the Methodist churches were denuded of ministers and home missionaries. The WA Methodist Conference reported that many preaching stations remained vacant during the greater part of the conflict. Sisters Rose and Elsie Rudeforth became co-pastors of the Gingin Methodist Church in 1916 following the enlistment of their regular minister and served there to the end of the war.[31]

In mid-1915, Chaplain A.E. Talbot, on leave as Dean of St. Andrew's Cathedral, observed: 'I have been wondering whether the readers of the *Diocesan Magazine* realise the contribution which the Clergy are making to this Force apart from the Chaplains. This contribution is by no means inconsiderable'. He catalogued the young men from the diocese he had encountered at the front. There were two sons of the Rev. J. Howell Price of St. Mary's, Balmain, both of whom were lieutenants in the First Infantry Brigade; Sergeant Stretch, wounded son of the Rev. J.F. Stretch, Bishop of Newcastle, who was assigned to the Second Infantry Brigade; Minor Canon Statt of Newcastle; the Rev. L.M. Andrews, formerly vice-principal of the Bush Brotherhood in Dubbo; the Rev. J.H. Gregg-MacGregor, and the Rev. Spencer E. Maxted – all NSW clergy and all in the Army Medical Corps. The Dean also mentioned that he had met a number of former students of Moore Theological College at the front, some now dead, some wounded.[32]

In a homecoming celebration of his return from the war held at St. Andrew's Cathedral in 1916, the Dean continued his compelling account of Sydney Anglicans in the war, many of them clergy, sons of clergy or theological students. He recounted how Major Horace Price, another son of the Rev.

---

30 McKernan. *Australian Churches at War*, 41, 95–7; Irving Benson, *A Century of Victorian Methodism* (Melbourne: Spectator Publishing Company, 1935), 353–61.

31 Robert D. Linder, *The Long Tragedy*, 105.

32 *Sydney Diocesan Magazine*, 1 October 1915, 6–9. Church of England Padre F. W. Wray listed ten NSW Anglican clergy he had encountered serving in the ranks at Gallipoli. F. W. Wray, Papers of Chaplain F. W. Wray, diary covering 22 January 1915 to 30 December 1916, File 3, DRL 648, Australian War Memorial Archives, Canberra.

J. Howell Price at Balmain, had recovered and buried the body of the Rev. Dr. Everard Digges La Touche, former Diocesan Missioner and Lecturer in Theology at Moore College, a line officer killed leading an infantry charge at Gallipoli. He also mentioned two other sons of a Sydney Anglican clergyman who were wounded at Gallipoli. One was combat correspondent and later war historian C.E.W. Bean,[33] and the other was Major J.W.B. Bean, a medical doctor. The Rev. C.H.W. Clark, incumbent Clerk of the Cathedral and father of future historian Manning Clark, was present at the celebration and gave the official welcome home on behalf of the congregation. Clark was so impressed by Talbot's presentation that he himself enlisted the next year as a stretcher-bearer in the Army Medical Corps.[34]

The evangelical theological colleges of Australia all suffered from the effects of the war as large numbers of their students and potential students enlisted in the ranks. At Moore College, after a steady increase in the number of students at the beginning of the century, there were only seven new men in 1915. In 1917, the college produced only three men for ordination as deacons, an all-time twentieth-century low. At the Baptist Theological College of NSW, by 1919 eighteen students had enlisted since the beginning of the war and only seven full-time ministerial aspirants remained in college. At the Presbyterian Theological Hall in Sydney, the number of students declined from fifteen in 1915 to eight in 1917 because of enlistments in the AIF, despite the official view that, although free to enlist, theological students should be discouraged from doing so. In 1916, serious consideration was given to the possibility of closing the Hall for a year and employing the remaining students as home missionaries. A number of ministerial students from Melbourne College of the Bible (Churches of Christ) enlisted, including J.C. Clark, who was killed in action. In South Australia, the Rev. Samuel Roberts, four lay preachers and at least a half dozen Parkin Theological College (Congregational) students enlisted at the outbreak of war. The college kept its doors open during the conflict only with the greatest difficulty.[35]

The number of ministers' sons who enlisted in the AIF was so large that it appears, from reading the church papers of the evangelical denominations, that there was not one eligible or fit man left in Australia among the sons of evangelical ministers. The Rev. J. Howell Price, rector of St. Mary's Church

---

33 K.S. Inglis, *C.E.W. Bean, Australian Historian* (St. Lucia: University of Queensland Press, 1970).

34 *Sydney Diocesan Magazine*, 1 April 1916, 6–8; Manning Clark, *The Puzzles of Childhood* (Ringwood: Viking Books, 1989), 55–7.

35 Linder, *The Long Tragedy*, 106.

of England, Balmain, had five sons in the army, while Ballarat Presbyterian minister John Walker had four sons at the front. In South Australia, five sons of Methodist minister Charles Nield enlisted, while fellow ministers William A. Potts and John Blacket each had three sons in the armed forces. Brisbane Methodist minister A.C. Plane, who himself served more than a year in uniform as a chaplain, had two sons in the army. Multiple enlistments from one evangelical ministerial family were far from uncommon.[36]

As to those who were lay members of evangelical churches on enlisting, an impressionistic survey of the church papers of the era suggests that the numbers must have been in the tens of thousands. Queensland Presbyterian historian Richard Bardon claimed that men from his denomination constituted 18 percent of the total enlistments in the armed forces in World War I, or about 75,000 troops. This is well above the 12.86 percent of the total population which identified itself as Presbyterian in the 1911 census. Yet, scattered evidence supports Bardon's figures. For instance, on 13 October 1916, *The Messenger*, a Presbyterian weekly, listed those members of the NSW Presbyterian churches who had fallen in battle since the last issue. It gave the names of 82 killed in action, the overwhelming majority of whom were officers. Further, Anglican reports indicated that many of the battalion and company commanders killed and wounded at Gallipoli had been active churchmen in the predominantly evangelical Sydney diocese. Memorial stained glass windows and honour boards in evangelical Church of England parishes in this diocese also attest to the large number of officers these churches contributed to the AIF in general. Evangelicals furnished an unusually high number of officers for the armed forces because they were likely to be better educated and more deeply imbued with a sense of duty than those from other backgrounds.[37]

Baptists also contributed heavily to the number of fighting personnel. The Wellington Baptist Church in country NSW, with only 75 official members on its roll, had by June 1917 sent 42 men to the front. By the end of the war, another 15 men from the church fellowship had enlisted, including the Rev. F.J. Dunkley, the minister, who became an army chaplain. In South Australia, a Baptist widow named Swift was left with ten sons, six of whom were in the armed forces by the end of 1917. Five of the six were members of the Edwardstown Baptist Church and one of those was a lay preacher. It was reported that the sixth son had 'given himself to Christ since his enlistment'.

---

36 Judd and Cable, *Sydney Anglicans*, 175; *Riverine Grazier*, 3 November 1916, 2; Hunt, *This Side of Heaven*, 284.

37 Bardon, *The Centenary History of the Presbyterian Church in Queensland*, 172; *The Messenger*, 13 October 1916, 655; *Sydney Diocesan Magazine*, 1 April 1916, 7–8.

Annie Sexton, the talented daughter of the prominent South Australian Baptist minister and Aboriginal rights advocate, the Rev. John Henry Sexton, served as a nurse in Egypt.[38]

The Salvation Army also contributed heavily in terms of men and, indeed, women: nearly a hundred Salvation Army women served as nursing sisters during the war. The pages of *The War Cry*, the official Salvationist public-ation, were filled with obituaries. Many Salvos served as bandsmen who also served as medics, while most served in the ranks. Many bandsmen lost their lives at the front because they frequently worked as stretcher-bearers. Few were officers because most came from the working class. Private Francis Inglis, a Salvo from Ararat in Victoria, served with distinction in France in the early years of the conflict. In 1916, his commanding officer promoted him to corporal and made him battalion mess caterer. His new assignment meant that he spent most of his time in comparative safety away from the trenches. Unfortunately, his new duties included the purchase of liquor for the use of officers and men. When he refused to buy the alcohol because, he said, 'it would do violence to my conscience', he was reprimanded, demoted and returned to the line. He was killed in action in 1917.[39]

Of all the evangelicals, the Methodists seemed the most eager to enter the fray. Irving Benson reported that hundreds of Methodist Sunday School scholars in that State enlisted at war's beginning, including two – Lieutenant W.R. Dunstan and Captain W.J. Symons – who won the Victoria Cross at Gallipoli. Another former Victorian Sunday School scholar and teacher at Albert Park Methodist Church who enlisted in the first AIF in August 1914, John Linton Treloar, would later become Director of the Australian War Memorial in Canberra. The small Newlyn Methodist Church in rural Victoria provided 25 of its sons for the armed forces. Methodist women also gave of themselves unstintingly, as attests the honour roll of 18 young women from Methodist Ladies' College in Melbourne who served as nursing sisters during the war.[40]

In South Australia, the Parkside Methodist Church already had 105 men at the front in May 1916 when it dedicated its first honour board. By the end of the war, the Malvern Methodist Church had 165 names on its honour board; the Kent Town Church, 97; the Payneham Church, 79; the Prospect North Church, 74; the Unley Church, 57 – all fairly large churches at the

---

38 *ACW*, 15 June 1917, 15; *The Australian Baptist*, 18 December 1917, 3.

39 John Bond, *The Army That Went with the Boys: A Record of Salvation Army Work with the Australian Imperial Force* (Melbourne: The Salvation Army, 1919), 71–176.

40 Benson, *Century of Victorian Methodism*, 357–8, 361; John L. Treloar, *An ANZAC Diary* (Armidale: Alan Treloar, 1993), 40, 92.

time. However, even the smaller churches of the South Australian Methodist Conference contributed disproportionate numbers to the military: 35 from the Forest Range Church in Adelaide Hills; 60 from the Sydenham Road Church in Norwood; and 33 from the small Yatala Church near Alberton Railway Station. In 1917, the Ovingham Methodist Church reported with pride that there was only one young man left in its congregation, and he had been rejected by the army on medical grounds.[41]

Wesley Church, the largest Methodist congregation in Perth, which claimed about 500 members and adherents in the period, contributed 35 young men to the armed forces. Of this number, ten were killed in action, including four with the surname of Rowland, descendants of the original Methodist Rowland family who first came to Perth on board the *Tranby* in 1830. Lieutenant Colonel Robert E. Jackson, Major Samuel Jackson and Lieutenant David Jackson, all highly-decorated war heroes, were among active church members of the Wesley Church who distinguished themselves in the war. John Wallace Laurance, son of the Rev. T.C. Laurance, minister of the church in the 1870s and 1880s, was also an enlistee. Devout Methodist Rowland John Robert (Bob) Pennington of the South Perth Church volunteered and became the first from the area to be killed in action. He was only the first of a large number of young Methodists to perish who had been active in the South Perth YMCA before the war. So many young men from its constituency were killed, wounded or psychologically shattered by the conflict that the South Perth YMCA permanently closed its doors for lack of clientele in October 1920.[42]

It was the same in NSW and Queensland. In Linden Webb's Hay Methodist Church, in spite of his public anti-war sentiment, young men gave themselves in abundance, including the sons of many of his church officers. Both of his Senior Stewards' sons enlisted, one of whom, Rupert Butterworth, had been the church choirmaster. One of the sons of his Junior Steward, J.E. McMahon, lost an arm at the Battle of Lone Pine, Gallipoli. The Newcastle Methodist City Mission, long known for its ministry to men, had a picture taken of one of its wartime gatherings which revealed how depleted it was of males: it showed 95 women and children and five adult men in attendance. Indeed, 95 of its active male members had enlisted.[43] Because of their almost universal support for the war, the evangelical churches probably bore a disproportionate burden of the cost. The great personal price they paid in terms of the death

41 Hunt, *This Side of Heaven*, 286.

42 Linder, *The Long Tragedy*, 109.

43 Linder, *The Long Tragedy*, 109f.

of their members had long-term effects at least as significant as their loss of moral certainty and authority in public discourse.

Another special concern of evangelicals was to ensure that the resources of the various 'Patriotic Funds', such as the Red Cross, the Australian Comforts Fund, the YMCA and the Salvation Army, reached the front line. Presbyterian Thomas Henley, a Sydney building contractor, State parliamentarian and evangelical lay leader, served as Honorary Commissioner of the Australian Comforts Fund. Having lost his oldest son early in the war, Henley travelled to Egypt in 1915 at his own expense as Commissioner for the Citizens War Chest Fund. He organised the allocation of comforts to Diggers from distribution points in Alexandria, Marseilles, Le Havre and London, and personally accompanied the goods to see that they reached the men for whom they were intended. To overcome objections to civilians entering the battle zone, Henley had to be gazetted as a lieutenant colonel.[44]

The two evangelical organisations which ministered most directly to the social, physical and spiritual needs of the troops were the YMCA and the Salvation Army. The YMCA furnished a place to deliver the goods contributed by the Red Cross, the Comforts Fund, church groups and similar organisations. It supplied recreational space and a lounge area for conversation and letter-writing. It cooperated with the padres in distributing New Testaments to the troops and it provided a place for religious meetings of various sorts, from evangelistic services to Bible studies. Methodist Chaplain James Green rejoiced at being able to hold joint services with Salvation Army Chaplain William 'Fighting Mac' McKenzie and William Owens of the Sydney YMCA in the organisation's facilities at Gallipoli.[45]

YMCA work during the war was led by some exceptionally talented individuals, such as Alec and William 'Cairo' Bradley in Egypt and Len Greenberg in France. Cairo Bradley, co-founder of the Egypt General Mission, had been working in the Middle East since 1898. With the advent of the Great War, he was released to minister to the Allied troops in the area, mostly in conjunction with the YMCA. He was joined in the work by Archie Law, who was stationed in Egypt with the Australian Army Medical Service. Bradley ran evangelistic meetings and he and his wife opened their home to the soldiers,

44 Aeneas Macdonald, *One Hundred Years of Presbyterianism in Victoria* (Melbourne: Robertson & Mullens, 1937), 159; *SMH,* 15 May 1935, 15; *The Bulletin*, 22 May 1935, 14; Thomas Henley, *After the War: Christendom and the Coming Peace* (London: Hodder and Stoughton, 1917), urged the Christian churches to cooperate in establishing 'a league of nations' following the war.

45 *The Methodist*, 14 November 1914, 7; 17 April 1915, 14; 17 July 1915, 6.

and 'scores' of them found Christ in this 'home away from home'.[46] After the war, Cairo Bradley worked among demobilised soldiers and eventually became a well-known Anglican evangelist in Sydney. Law later became an important figure in Victorian evangelical life in the 1920s.[47]

The Salvation Army began its war work when, in mid-August 1914, Colonel Wiebe Palstra and Commissioner Jeannie Hay opened a tent at the Broadmeadows training camp near Melbourne. It was the embryo of what later became known as the Army's Red Shield war work. Soon Salvation Army huts and hostels appeared at all military installations, both in Australia and overseas. By 1918, the Salvos had in operation 182 huts, 87 soldiers' hostels, 220 rest rooms (coffee stops) and 57 ambulances (mobile first aid stations), with over 800 Salvationists doing full-time work in military camps. Over the course of the war, they dispatched more than 500,000 telegrams on behalf of soldiers to friends and relatives and sent an average of 600 parcels each month to Australian prisoners-of-war.[48]

Evangelical Padres

Evangelical ministers responded with enthusiasm to the call for chaplains (or padres as they were then better known) for the AIF. Of the 414 clergy who served as padres during the war, at least 196 or 47 percent were evangelicals. Only 86 (20.7 per cent) were Catholics, whereas 25 per cent of the population at the 1911 census were Catholics. Catholic bishops were reluctant to relieve priests of their parish duties[49] and filling quotas for Roman Catholic chaplains proved difficult. Protestants, by contrast, formed long queues for the privilege of service. Evangelical padres, imbued with the values of civic Protestantism, were accepting of the harsh reality that defending their godly nation required the sacrifice of their youth. At the same time, they were eager to follow their young men to the front to make certain that no Australian soldier was lost to the Christian cause.[50]

To rationalise the allocation of chaplains, the Defence Department allowed four per brigade, with each brigade consisting of four battalions of 1000 men each. An individual chaplain lived with a particular battalion but was expected

46 Alex Gilchrist, interviewed by Margaret Lamb, 31 July 1986.

47 Linder, *The Long Tragedy*, 113.

48 Barbara Bolton, *Booth's Drum: The Salvation Army in Australia, 1880–1980* (Sydney: Hodder and Stoughton, 1980), 210–5; Bond, *The Army That Went with the Boys*, i-ii.

49 Gladwin, *Captains of the Soul*, 34.

50 McKernan, *Australian Churches at War*, 41–4, 182–3.

to serve all the members of his denomination within the brigade. Chaplains were allocated proportionately to the four major denominations (Church of England, Roman Catholic, Presbyterian, Methodist) on the basis of the 1911 census and on the assumption that the men of each church would enlist in about the same percentages as the denomination's strength in the community. After strong representations, the so-called 'Other Protestant Denominations' (for example, Baptist, Congregationalist, Churches of Christ, Salvation Army), all historically evangelical in nature, were given a few chaplain slots as well. This meant that about one hundred regular chaplains served at any one time during the war. There were far more evangelical clergy who volunteered for the military chaplaincy than there were slots available.[51]

The switch of the bulk of the AIF from the Middle Eastern Theatre of Operations to France created new challenges for chaplains. Gallipoli, though highly dangerous, was intimate, and the padres moved freely through the trenches with the men. In France, the scale of the war was immensely larger. The shift from the cramped quarters of Gallipoli to the instability of frequent trench rotation and the mobility of troops on a wider front in France made the chaplain's job much harder. There were far fewer opportunities for large church parades in or near the front lines in France mainly because of the greater number of aircraft and, especially, because of the greater concentration of heavy artillery.[52]

Evangelical padres often overcame these obstacles by means of networking and holding interdenominational church parades for their troops. A poignant example of evangelical cooperation during the war involved a padre and a medical corpsman at Gallipoli, namely, Chaplain Andrew Gillison, a Presbyterian, and Corporal Robert R.H. Pittendrigh, an ordained Methodist minister in the ranks. Gillison was the first Presbyterian chaplain appointed by his denomination. He was minister of St. George's Presbyterian Church in East St. Kilda, Melbourne, before the war. He joined the AIF in October 1914, and, at age 46, sailed for Egypt the following December. He was attached to the 13th Battalion, 4th Infantry Brigade, and accompanied it to Gallipoli in April 1915.[53]

Pittendrigh, a 32-year-old stretcher-bearer in the Australian Medical Service, had been ordained at the Stanmore Methodist Church, Sydney, on 5 November 1914, shortly before enlisting in the AIF. He wanted to be a chaplain but there were no more openings for Methodists, so he enlisted in

51 McKernan, *Australian Churches at War*, 40–1; McKernan, *Padre*, 1–3.

52 McKernan, *Padre*, 134–6; Henderson, *Khaki and Cassock*, 24–5.

53 McKernan, *Padre*, 6–8; McKernan, *Australian Churches at War*, 51–2.

the ranks. Pittendrigh told friends that he had joined the Australian forces, 'not only to serve his King as a soldier, but to serve his Divine Master by such testimony and service in the ranks as comradeship with men in camp and on the battlefield would afford opportunity'. As an older, more mature man, he was a natural leader and quickly advanced to the rank of corporal. Like Gillison, he soon found himself at Gallipoli.[54]

On Sunday, 22 August 1915, Gillison had been ministering in the front lines when he bumped into Pittendrigh patrolling the area for wounded. Gillison immediately recognised the younger man because they had shared their common spiritual concerns on a number of previous occasions. They met on the crest of a knoll at a place called Aghi Dere, near the scene of a recent fiercely-fought engagement. There they heard the cries for help of a wounded Australian about 50 yards in front of their position. A medical officer advised: 'Don't go out there, the Turks have it covered with rifles and machine guns'. Gillison and Pittendrigh, in spite of this warning, crawled out from their trench. They had almost reached the man when the Turks opened up with machine gun fire, hitting them both. They managed to get back to their trench, but there the chaplain collapsed. He was shot between the shoulders, and the bullet came out near his heart. With last words for his wife and children in Melbourne, he died at 2 pm. It appeared that Pittendrigh, although suffering from multiple wounds, was not in mortal danger. However, after evacuation to a hospital ship, he later died of his injuries.[55] Theirs was an effort worthy of the ANZAC legend.

The most revered of the chaplains was William 'Fighting Mac' McKenzie of the Salvation Army – 'a soldier's soldier and a chaplain's chaplain'. Born in Scotland in 1869, McKenzie's reputation for rowdiness and frequent punch-ups as a boy earned him the nickname 'Fighting Mac', a sobriquet particularly appropriate in light of his subsequent career in both the Salvation and Australian Armies. In 1884, McKenzie's family migrated to Queensland, where his father became a sugar cane planter near Bundaberg. Three years later, at age 17, young Billy McKenzie, following a profound spiritual crisis, underwent a life-changing experience when he accepted Christ as his Saviour. He soon joined the SA and quickly rose through the ranks to become an officer and administrator.[56]

---

54 *The Methodist*, 26 June 1915, 8; 14 August 1915, 10; 18 September 1915, 8.

55 *The Methodist*, 25 September 1915, 2; War Diary of Chaplain Ernest N. Merrington, cited in McKernan, *Padre*, 120–3; Robert D. Linder, 'Comrades in Arms: Australian Evangelical Cooperation in World War I, 1914–1918', *Lucas*, 18, 1994, 51–71.

56 McKernan, *Padre*, 2–6, 81–3; Bolton, *Booth's Drum*, 79, 212–5; Adelaide Ah Kow, *William McKenzie: ANZAC Padre* (London: Salvationist Publishing and Supplies, 1949), 5–55.

At the outbreak of the war, McKenzie, aged 44, immediately volunteered and was accepted as a military chaplain. Attached to the 4th Battalion, 1st Brigade, he sailed on 19 October 1914 on the *Euripides*, one of the first troop ships to leave Australia. He quickly made his presence felt among the 2,500 men on board. He conducted church parades, prayer meetings, community singing and sports competitions. Big, strong and physically fit, he was fond of joining in the men's recreation, especially boxing.

McKenzie landed with his battalion at Gallipoli in 1915. He spent much of his time with the troops in the front-line trenches. They came to revere him because he served them without regard to creed, and did everything possible to meet their material, as well as their spiritual, needs. One Digger recalled that at Gallipoli there had been a particularly dangerous and slippery path over some hills which periodically came under Turkish shell fire. It made carrying the wounded to safety extremely hazardous. One day they found that during the night Mac had cut steps into the rocky slopes the whole way over the wretched journey. His life soon assumed legendary proportions, and rumours abounded that he even led charges, armed only with a shovel. When the troops begged him not to expose himself to danger, he responded: 'Boys, I've preached to you and I've prayed for you, and do you think I'm afraid to die with you?'[57]

The Diggers extolled him as 'big hearted', 'incorruptible', 'considerate of the feelings of the individual', 'one of the bravest of the brave', 'a friend of sinners', and 'a man of deep mysticism combined with unalterable common-sense'. Scores accepted Christ through his ministry, and hundreds were buried under his ministrations. The death, gore and misery affected McKenzie deeply, and he lost five stone during the Gallipoli campaign. Following the battle of Lone Pine on 6 August, he personally buried 450 men over a period of three weeks. In his own words: 'the smell of the bodies after the first four days was overpowering and frequently I had to leave the graves to retch from the effects of the smell'. He further observed: 'War is indeed "Hell" and no adequate description can picture its ghastliness.' For his efforts at Gallipoli, he was awarded the Military Cross by the Australian High Command and promoted to lieutenant-colonel in the SA. He was mentioned in dispatches and word circulated that several officers who were killed in action intended to recommend him for the Victoria Cross, had they lived.

In France and Belgium in 1916–1917, McKenzie continued to live in the trenches with his boys, often carrying soldiers' packs when physical exhaustion

57 Quoted in Ah Kow, *William McKenzie*, 41.

beset them. He was at Pozières, Bullecourt, Mouquet Farm, Polygon Wood and Passchendaele, and endured the brutal 1916–1917 winter on the Somme. He ran canteens, organised concerts, counselled sufferers, wrote hundreds of letters of consolation to loved ones at home, and preached to large, receptive crowds in the rest areas behind the lines. It was also in France that his Voice (the term he used for his 'guardian angel') renewed its watchcare over him. This Voice had first called him when a young man to seek out the SA in Bundaberg in order to find Christ as Saviour. It was the same Voice which on occasion during his career had directed him to places of particular need. Now, in France, it warned him of danger and guided him to men in distress. On one occasion, he was burying some dead British soldiers who had lain exposed for a fortnight on a ridge in view of the enemy trenches. He had interred seven of them when his Voice told him to drop everything and run. As he dived into a shell hole about 25 yards away, an artillery round fell on the spot he had abandoned moments before. He mentioned this phenomenon in a letter to his wife:

> At all times of great danger, when engaged in such work, I am quietly conscious of this guardian angel's presence. I cannot see him nor can I tell who or what he is like, but I hear his voice sometimes saying 'Do not go there!' 'Get out of here!' 'Lie down in that shell hole!' 'Be careful!' or 'You are quite safe'. 'Wait five minutes here!' and such messages. I could give six instances in the past week when a prompt attention to his instruction has saved me from those big shells. I now know that if I pay heed and obey God I shall continue unharmed until my work is finished, so if I fall on the field you will know the reason.[58]

Eventually the strain took its toll, and reports filtered home that Mac needed to be relieved. The military authorities finally reluctantly acceded to the SA's request to order McKenzie home, and he returned to Australia early in 1918. Tumultuous crowds greeted him at every State capital and many smaller cities. He was the most famous man in the AIF. People travelled hundreds of miles to grasp the hand last to touch the body of their darling boy or to thank him for some kindness he had shown to a loved one. One mother journeyed nearly 300 miles to kiss the hands of the man who literally had pieced together the remains of her beloved son, blown to bits by shell fire, in order to give him a Christian burial. After the war, along with Billy Hughes, McKenzie was

58 Ah Kow, *William McKenzie*, 51.

the one man every Digger wanted to greet, and so immense were the throngs accosting him that his hand was left raw and bleeding.

Other evangelical padres ministered long and well to the Diggers of the Great War. To name a few: Church of England William E. Dexter, dedicated, tough, six-times wounded, Australia's most decorated World War I padre; Church of England Joseph J. Booth, energetic, disdainful of church parades, always in or near the front lines with his men, recipient of the Military Cross, and future Archbishop of Melbourne (1942–1956); Presbyterian Ernest N. Merrington, popular preacher yet thoughtful and well-educated, sensitive, always concerned with the wounded; Methodist A.C. Plane, plain-spoken, down to earth, caring to the point of exhaustion and despair; and Methodist James A. Gault, whimsical, fun-loving, creative and much-beloved by the troops.[59]

Spencer E. Maxted, a Sydney Anglican clergyman, enlisted first in the ranks and served as a stretcher bearer. He was finally appointed chaplain in January 1916 and sent to France. As the slaughter mounted at the Battle of Fromelles on 20 July 1916, Maxted joined his old stretcher-bearer mates to help bring in the wounded. After helping at least 150 men to safety, utterly exhausted, he sat down to rest and was immediately blown to bits by a shell. He was awarded the Military Cross posthumously. In one of the few references he made to padres in the war, C.E.W. Bean averred that, 'Chaplain Maxted, working in his shirt-sleeves and without puttees, rendered, until he was killed, services of mercy never to be forgotten by those who benefited from them'.[60]

Bean never wrote an account of the chaplains as he intended. His considered assessment of their contribution to the war effort would have been invaluable. Michael Gladwin, after working through the 'substantial body of evidence for the AIF's appreciation of their chaplains' pastoral and social concern', concludes:

> Soldiers and their families were universally grateful for chaplains' care for the dead and wounded; for the chaplains' concern for the spiritual and physical welfare of the living; and for the chaplains' role as a mediator between them, their loved ones, and the Army.[61]

---

59 Linder, *The Long Tragedy*, 133–8.

60 *Sydney Diocesan Magazine*, 1 October 1915, 8; McKernan, *Padre*, 147–8; C.E.W. Bean, *The Australian Imperial Force in France, 1916*, vol. 3 of *The Official History of Australia in the War of 1914–18*, 12 vols (Sydney: Angus & Robertson, 1923–1938), 437.

61 Gladwin, *Captains of the Soul*, 75.

It is a nice summary of the chaplains' role in attending to the national soul. It was essentially a mediatorial role of multiple dimensions, connecting soldiers to their communities at home and channelling various supports to men in the trenches, and the spiritual dimension of connecting those in danger to God, and bridging the divide between life and death.

The Vacant Pew

Of the more than 400,000 men recruited for the Australian Imperial Force – and they constituted 40 percent of all men of military age in the nation – at least 60,000 did not return. Another 213,061 were wounded. Countless others came home scarred in mind and spirit. For a country with a population of only four million inhabitants, the price of victory was enormous.[62]

Chaplain A.E. Talbot buried hundreds at Gallipoli, including, as we have seen, Digges La Touche. After his return to Australia in 1916, the Dean of Sydney related: 'I had a choir of 12 men the day before Lone Pine. I have only been able to trace one of them since'. Lieutenant C.L. Luscombe, Sydney Anglican lay leader, was killed in action on 1 March 1918. The afore-mentioned John Howell Price, rector of St. Mary's, Balmain, saw his five sons go off to war. Only two returned. In the Illawarra region, Anglican losses were also heavy. By February 1916, 110 men from St. Michael's parish, Wollongong, had enlisted. By the armistice, St. Michael's had lost 55 of its young men in the war.[63]

At Ashfield Presbyterian Church, Sydney, where the Rev. Robert J.H. McGowan was minister, 106 men and two women of a congregation of about 500 served in the AIF. Of those who enlisted, 22 never returned. The evangelical citadel of Toorak Presbyterian Church, Melbourne, also a congregation of about 500, listed 127 names on its honour board: two women who were army nurses and 125 young men. Of that number 24 died in the war. The Rev. John Walker, Presbyterian minister at Ballarat, saw four sons go to war. Three were killed in action in France, including his eldest, the Rev. Arthur D. Walker, while serving as a line officer, late in 1917. Even rural Scrub Hill Presbyterian Church near Creswick in Victoria, with less than 100 communicants, contributed 22 young men, of whom six died in service.[64]

62 *SMH*, 12 November 1918, 6; Michael McKernan, 'War', in Wray Vamplew (ed.), *Australians: Historical Statistics* (Broadway: Fairfax, Syme & Weldon Associates, 1987), 410–4.

63 *Sydney Diocesan Magazine*, 1 April 1918, 7; Piggin, *Faith of Steel*, 171.

64 Linder, *The Long Tragedy*, 146f.

Baptists, too, paid a heavy price in loss of life. Of the 57 men from the modest Wellington Baptist Church in NSW, eight were killed in action and ten returned home wounded. Ten of the fifty members who enlisted out of the Kew Baptist Church in Victoria, died while on active service. Six of the dead had been church officers. Seven young men from the influential Hobart Baptist Church failed to return. Among them was Cecil Salisbury, only son of church lay leader John Salisbury. Cecil Salisbury, a graduate of the University of Tasmania, had been Secretary of the Sunday School. He was the first man from the university to be killed in action.[65] The Bible Circle of the 53rd Battalion, which John Ridley was instrumental in organising and leading, lost fifty percent of its membership in the last Allied offensives of the war.[66]

Methodist losses were also heavy, perhaps more so than among any of the other denominations. Of eighty Methodist ministers nationwide who enlisted in the ranks, 12 were killed, 22 survived but abandoned the ministry after the war, and 46 returned to church work. Of 29 known Methodist ministerial student enlistees, six were killed in action and 15 dropped plans to pursue ordination following the armistice. Especially prominent among the Methodist dead were 'sons of the parsonage' and local preachers: in other words, those most likely to be future leaders of the church. In Victoria, for instance, sixteen Methodist ministers and probationers who enlisted in the ranks fell in combat.[67]

In NSW, the deaths of local preachers in the ranks were reported with routine monotony in the pages of *The Methodist*. Sergeant Ray Colwell, the son of Methodist leader and AIF Chaplain Rev. Frederick Colwell, was killed in action in France in June 1917. Young Colwell, a well-educated apprentice journalist and prominent local preacher, was, in the words of *The Methodist*: 'one of many bright promising young men nobly sacrificed for the Empire, which the Church could ill spare'.[68] Many of the South Australian Methodists who had eagerly rushed to the colours in record numbers never returned to their churches. John Blacket and George Davies, who had been teachers at the Methodist Prince Alfred College in Adelaide, were killed in action in France in 1916. By 1917, the Rev. Octavius Lake, editor of the *Australian Christian Commonwealth,* sounding much like St. Bernard of Clairvaux, the medieval monastic leader who claimed to have emptied the villages of France

65 Linder, *The Long Tragedy*, 147f.

66 Evans, *Soldier and Evangelist*, 70–8.

67 McKernan, *Australian Churches at War*, 97–8; and Benson, *Century of Victorian Methodism*, 357 and 361.

68 *The Methodist*, 3 July, 1915, 3; 18 September 1915, 8; 23 June 1917, 5; 14 July 1917, 5.

to go forth on the Second Crusade, declared that there was not an eligible or fit young man left in the parsonages of South Australian Methodism.

Eventually every Methodist congregation in the State had an Honour Board which bore mute testimony to the high percentage of young men in the churches who had volunteered and to the many who perished. Large congregations had larger numbers who enlisted and died: Malvern, 165 joined, 32 killed; Kent Town, 97 joined, seven killed; Payneham, 79 joined, 14 killed; Prospect North, 74 joined, 17 killed; Unley Park, 57 joined, 14 killed. Even the smaller congregations paid a heavy price for imperial glory. When the small country church at Yongala dedicated its Honour Board, it contained the names of four sons of the Potter family, three of whom died in the war. Arnold D. Hunt estimated that at least four percent of the total membership of the Methodist Church of South Australia, or about 850 individuals, perished in the conflict.[69]

The Bitter Fruits of Victory

When the war ended, in all parts of the nation, United Churches Victory Thanksgiving Services were held. At such a gathering in Wollongong, the Rev. Charles A. Stubbin, rector of St. Michael's Church of England, concluded that the victory was evidence that 'God had set his seal on the side of righteousness and truth. It was for us as a people and as individuals to establish righteousness and justice in our land'.[70] According to South Australian Methodist leader Octavius Lake, Christianity would share in the fruits of victory: 'The Church … feels that she has come to the birth of a new age, that there is opening before her the doors of unparalleled opportunity, and the password among all evangelical sects and denominations is, "Let us go up at once and possess the land, for we are well able!"'[71]

There was some justification for optimism. Numerous evangelical chaplains had established good rapport with their troops. Many had risked, and some had given, their lives for their men. The war had produced a number of genuine evangelical heroes, such as Gillison, Pittendrigh and McKenzie. The evangelical churches had heavily supported the non-violent aspects of the war, such as the work of the Red Cross and the Comforts Fund as well as their interdenominational arm, the YMCA. The Salvation Army was universally praised by the troops in the camps and at the front for its humane work and

69 *Australian Christian Commonwealth*, 4 August 1916, 4; Hunt, 'Methodism Militant', 1; Hunt, *This Side of Heaven*, 285–7.

70 *Illawarra Mercury*, 15 November 1918, 4.

71 *Australian Christian Commonwealth*, 2 August 1918, 2.

civilising influence. The evangelical churches had retained their integrity, not succumbing to the intense pressure from bereaved relatives to say prayers for the dead nor, though some came close (see Henry Howard below), did they adjust their theology to allow death in the service of the Empire to substitute for genuine faith in Jesus Christ.[72]

There is much evidence of young evangelical men who endured the heartbreak of the war to return to serve their churches and the wider public with enthusiasm and distinction. Included in this number were Presbyterian Dr. Charles Duguid, a surgeon with the Light Horse in the Middle East and later a distinguished humanitarian and Aboriginal rights activist; Presbyterian Sir John McLeay, who as a Lance Corporal won the Military Medal for gallantry at Villers Bretonneux and who later served for many years first as Lord Mayor of Adelaide and later as Speaker of the Federal House of Representatives; Methodist Digger Wybert Symonds, after the war a distinguished South Australian educator; Medical Corpsman Archie Law, who served in Egypt and later became an evangelist with the Victorian Open Air Mission and a key figure in the operation of the Upwey Conventions.[73] Clearly the war did not block the development of all evangelicals into model citizens and may even have contributed to that outcome. Furthermore, many evangelical churches during the inter-war period sustained slow but steady growth. In most of the nation, evangelicals, along with Roman Catholics, constituted the most vigorous expression of Christianity.

On the other side of the ledger, however, evangelical faith in the efficacy of sacrifice did not stand up to the reality of the horrors of modern warfare. When more than 250,000 Australian soldiers were repatriated, two-thirds of them in 1919, it was found that nearly 40 percent of them were sick or wounded. It was in this context that the terrible cost of the war became increasingly evident: the wholesale slaughter of the cream of Australian manhood. This reality dampened any joy in victory. Early in the war, Methodist preacher at Pirie Street Church in Adelaide, Henry Howard, had spoken of 'sacrificial blood', the 'sacrificial cup' and the 'great act of self-sacrifice' which had characterised the fallen heroes of Gallipoli. He declared of those who died: 'Their

---

72 *Church Record*, 1 January 1915, 1; 16 July 1915, 8; *Church Standard*, 9 July 1915, 4; *The Methodist,* 23 June 1917, 10.

73 Charles Duguid, *Doctor and the Aborigines* (Adelaide: Rigby, 1972), xiii-xvi and 52–92; Stewart Cockburn, *The Patriarchs* (Adelaide: Ferguson Publications, 1983), 1–5 and 51–5; *The Keswick Quarterly and Upwey Convention News*, 1, no. 2 (May 1926), 7–8; Evans, *Soldier and Evangelist*, 64 and 66. For a recent populist and controversial interpretation of one result of the war, see Col Stringer, *800 Horsemen: God's History Makers* (Robina Town Centre, QLD: Col Stringer Ministries, 1998).

voluntary service and sacrifice in the cause of the world's freedom includes them all among the elect of God'.[74] But by the time all was quiet on the Western Front, the theme of sacrifice had lost most of its appeal. According to Chaplain Kenneth Henderson, by the last year of the war the young men who had answered the call to sacrifice – at least those who had survived to that point – had come to ask: 'How can God let it go on?'

The Rev. Peter Fleming of Adelaide's Flinders Street Baptist Church articulated the growing awareness of the cost of the war, when on Sunday, 6 July 1919, he addressed a large throng at what was billed as a 'Peace Thanksgiving Service' in the Adelaide Town Hall. Only four and a half years earlier, he had spoken to another large gathering of many of the same people at an Empire Intercession Day on the topic of 'Praying for Victory'. He had lost one beloved nephew and saw another shattered by his war experiences, and he himself had observed first-hand the horrors of the Western Front. After pondering 'what might have been', he declared:

> We are sure of the righteousness of our cause, and we were, and are, proud of the valour of our splendid men – their daring and their dying, but it took all that sense of the justness of our cause and the pride of our heroes to sustain us under the daily anxiety and the anguish of the long tragedy.[75]

The long-term negative imprint of the war was felt in the psyche of traumatised individuals, in the morale of Christian denominations, and in the soul of the nation as a whole. By the end of hostilities, John G. Ridley, the young sergeant who, as we have seen, was badly wounded at the battle of Fromelles in July 1916, had attained the rank of lieutenant and, for acts of conspicuous bravery under enemy fire, had been awarded the Military Cross. After recovering from his severe wounds in a hospital in England, he rejoined his unit in 1917 and fought with distinction to the end of the war. However, he was far from well and often had to hide his pain in order to avoid being sent home and discharged. He was left with a legacy of oppressive headaches and other ailments which were to cause him periodic distress for the remainder of his life. The first of two serious breakdowns in his health occurred in 1921, shortly after he had finished his studies for the Baptist ministry and delayed the launching of his productive evangelistic career for at least three years.[76]

74 *Australian Christian Commonwealth*, 8 October 1915, 7.

75 *The Register*, Adelaide, 7 July 1919, 5.

76 Ridley, *Milestones of Mercy*, 53–6 and 105–24.

Anglican Chaplain Kenneth Henderson suffered nervous exhaustion after two gruelling years of front-line ministry and had to be invalided out of service in mid-1918. Nor would he ever be the same again. He would spend the remainder of his life dealing with the ghosts of his two dead brothers, killed in action at Gallipoli, and the theological problems which the war raised in his mind. In the end, he left the formal ministry and entered religious broadcasting.[77]

Former Methodist Sunday School scholar John Linton Treloar eventually became the first Director of the Australian War Museum in Canberra. The war had challenged his Christian faith. He never ceased to be or act like a Methodist, but he wore his religion lightly for the remainder of his life.[78]

Young Tom Playford, descendant of a long line of evangelical ministers and lay leaders, volunteered early in 1915 and served with the 27th Battalion in Gallipoli, Messines, the Somme, the Ancre, the Ypres Salient, Passchendaele and Pozières. Corporal Playford was badly wounded at Flers on 5 November 1916, near the end of the costly Somme campaign. After a year of convalescence, he rejoined his battalion and fought with it until the end of the war, by which time he had risen to the rank of First Lieutenant. A devout Baptist before the war, Playford went on to become the longest-serving Premier in South Australian history, but never fully recovered from his war experiences – physically, psychologically or spiritually.[79]

The negative actual effect of war on the churches outweighed the positive effects which were more hoped for than attained. The widespread revival and national repentance that evangelical churchmen had prophesied at war's beginning did not transpire. The pro-war posture, with its attendant calls for sacrifice and more sacrifice, hastened the decline of popular acceptance of Anglicanism as the unofficial 'national church'. So bitter were the fruits of victory that those who gave most – such as the Methodists – appear to have lost most.

The negative imprint of war was felt in the soul of the nation. Those who returned from the great adventure retained memories of strange lands, devastating experiences, strong comradeships and bitter losses. These were the memories that shook the foundations of life, warped some and remade

77 Robert Trumble, *Kenneth Thorne Henderson: Broadcaster of the Word* (Richmond, VIC: Spectrum Publications, 1988), 13–23.

78 Michael McKernan, *Here Is Their Spirit: A History of the Australian War Memorial, 1917–1990* (St. Lucia: University of Queensland Press, 1991), 37–9 and 199–200.

79 Stewart Cockburn, *Playford: Benevolent Despot* (Kent Town, SA: Axiom Publishing, 1991), 7–55; and Interview with the Rev. Tom Playford, son of Tom Playford, by Linder, Loebenthal, SA, 19 March 2001.

others, and set them apart forever. Those who served on the home front or who avoided the war as much as possible were also changed forever. Things would never be the same. Ideas of genuine nationhood danced in the heads of many as they sacralised Gallipoli, built their war memorials and created the Anzac tradition. The sectarian strife which erupted during the great conscription controversies of 1916 and 1917 continued unabated during the 1920s and 1930s and poisoned Protestant-Catholic relations as never before in Australian history. The war had blunted the moral consciences of many who now accepted conflict as normal, and too many joined with considerable enthusiasm in the bitter sectarian and ideological struggles of the inter-war period.

Were survivors able to sustain the hope that their sacrifice and that of those who made the supreme sacrifice had created a better world? More than one politician and historian saw the conflict as the birthplace of Australian nationhood, with Gallipoli and the Anzac Legend as the core of the new national identity. The collective images of death on the battlefield for a worthy cause – as they emerged in the 1920s, especially in the 'war memorial movement' – contributed to the growth of an Australian national self-consciousness. The national soul, nurtured in blood, had been bought with too high a price to go unattended. It was a soul made sacred by so much sacrifice that it could not be allowed to be violated by selfishness. Moralising about what constituted worthy behaviour, so congenial to the evangelical, was legitimated. There was a shift from a British to some sort of Australian civil religion.[80] It was more Australian because so many Australians had died; it was slightly less British because of a feeling that Britain had asked too much of its dependencies; and it was civil because it was a religion as wide as the public itself. Normally historians dwell on the differences between civil religion and Christianity. But in one critical way, this Australian civil religion was more Christian than Christians, depleted by the enormity of loss, could easily articulate. Christianity always inculcates in those it influences, whether they are particularly conscious of it or not, the values of faith, love and that hope which is more

---

80 K. S. Inglis, 'The Anzac Tradition', *Meanjin Quarterly*, 24.1, 1965, 25–44; Richard Ely, *Unto God and Caesar: Religious Issues in the Emerging Commonwealth, 1890–1906* (Melbourne: MUP, 1976); Alistair Thomson, 'The Anzac Legend: Exploring National Myth and Memory in Australia', in Raphael Samuel and Paul Thompson, eds., *The Myths We Live By* (London: Routledge, 1990), 73–82; John Moses, 'ANZAC Day as Religious Revivalism: The Politics of Faith in Brisbane, 1916–1939', in Mark Hutchinson and Stuart Piggin, eds., *Reviving Australia* (Sydney: Centre for the Study of Australian Christianity, 1994), 170–84; and Donald Horne, 'Celebrating Our Differences', excerpts from the First Barton Lecture, *The Australian*, 9 February 2001, 13; Mervyn F. Bendle, *Anzac and Its Enemies: The History War on Australia's National Identity* (Sydney: Quadrant Books, 2015).

than optimism. It is a galvanising, unrelenting orientation to the future. It is a hope against all hope (Romans 4:18), a hope beyond all hope, a hope not contingent on things seen, a hope which makes history without being dependent on it. Australia would recover and have a bright future in spite of all. This understanding of hope is another of Christianity's unique gifts to civilisation and has been secularised so that all (Christian and secularist alike) believe in the inevitability of change, and with it the possibility of transformation of the bleakest of pasts into the brightest of futures. It was hard for any to see that at the end of World War I, but it would be a major factor in galvanising Christians not to give up on attending to the national soul.

Chapter Three

MENDING THE BROKEN

Evangelical Churches in the 1920s and the Great Depression

'It's not only the pig sty with which we have to deal,
but with the pig'
(R.B.S. Hammond)

Between the wars Australian evangelicalism suffered the most intense internal convulsion in its history, occasioned by the onslaught of modernism. It is tempting in these three chapters devoted to the inter-war years to start at the point of greatest intensity. But we will resist that temptation and persevere with the structure of this history which is to treat the external impact of the movement before addressing its internal history. Much as inner anxiety afflicted the movement in these decades, caring for the national soul called for the courage of compassion for all Australians recovering from war and struggling with economic depression. The future of the evangelical movement was at stake, but so too was the future of the nation. It was a new age, requiring a new economy to address the needs of post-war reconstruction and world-wide economic recession.[1] Evangelicals, the English-speaking world over, approached this task with the conviction that they had much to offer towards the social and political arrangements required for this purpose and for the resurrection of Christian civilisation out of the holocaust of war. Any suggestion that this was a period when evangelicals retreated from their

1 William Coleman, Selwyn Cornish and Alf Hagger, *Giblin's Platoon* (Canberra: ANU ePress, 2006).

commitment to social reform and national regeneration, either in Australia or elsewhere, is to be firmly rejected.[2]

The magnitude of the challenge galvanised evangelicals, but that was a factor of faith and not of sight. The Great War and the Great Depression threatened the fundamentals both of Western civilisation and of Christian faith. Almost 60,000 young Australians were killed in the War. The idealism of most Australians died with them, and its orphan-child, public-spiritedness, was imperilled in the ensuing materialistic age, making money in the 1920s and surviving in the 1930s. Neither in the nation nor in the Church was leadership strong. It was a challenge for the Repatriation Department, although an impressively large and generous welfare scheme, to restore the lucky country and make it 'a land fit for heroes'.[3] The 1920s was a time of building war memorials to dot the geographical and mental landscape, some 1,455 of them, at once testimony to indomitable courage and constant reminders of what might have been.[4]

Politics were volatile and at times wildly experimental. The Australian Country Party was formed in 1919 and the Communist Party of Australia in 1920, both with a measure of evangelical participation. In 1921, in part to counter the formation of the Communist Party, the Labor Party abandoned its original pragmatic socialism as the chief means of making Australia 'a workingman's paradise' and swung left, adopting a more doctrinaire socialist platform that advocated the nationalisation of the means of production, distribution and exchange. The Labor Party now attracted increasing numbers of Roman Catholics into its leadership ranks. Evangelicals began to gravitate toward more conservative parties or away from all political involvement.

A new method of preferential voting in federal elections took effect in 1919, and compulsory voting was introduced in 1924. The move of the Commonwealth parliament from its temporary Melbourne home to an unfinished capital in the hills of southern NSW occurred in May, 1927. The war had delayed the building of the city designed by Walter Burley Griffin of Chicago. On 9 May, Canberra, which had been selected as the national capital before the war, largely because of the persistence of the American

2 Geoffrey R. Treloar, *The Disruption of Evangelicalism* (London: IVP, 2016), 252, 270.

3 Brian Dickey, *No Charity There: A Short History of Social Welfare in Australia* (Sydney: Allen & Unwin, 1980, 1987), 110f., Stephen Garton, *Out of Luck: Poor Australians and Social Welfare 1788–1988* (Sydney: Allen & Unwin, 1990), 112f.

4 Ken Inglis, *Sacred Places: War Memorials in the Australian Landscape* (Carlton South, VIC: MUP, 1998), 1–11 and 484–5.

ex-patriot and sometime preacher-politician, King O'Malley, was christened to the prayers and hymns of the shivering assemblage.[5]

Like politics, society in general became more experimental and volatile and less homogenous following the war. A coterie of Australian intellectuals and artists, with bohemian proclivities, began to attack the old societal norms. Norman Lindsay used his considerable artistic and intellectual gifts to ridicule Christianity in general and evangelicals in particular, especially the wowsers of his Methodist forbears.[6] On 10 March 1929 Donald Friend, budding artist and diarist, at the age of 14 then living in East Sydney, went to church, and reported that 'Church has plenty of room for improvement. Why on earth are there not a few robes and jewels, and candles. I long for delicious chants and invocations in Latin and French.' A month later he was confirmed by John Charles Wright, Archbishop of Sydney, and observed of the experience 'Am horribly impressed and reformed to a monstrous degree.'[7] Precocious brats have always had trouble with Sydney evangelicalism.

Nevertheless, the Protestant churches still dominated the rhythm of life of the overwhelming number of Australians in the interwar period, especially on Sundays. This rhythm, now lost, centred around the family, work, church, sports and simple amusements. Monday through Friday and sometimes Saturday morning were for work. Saturday afternoon was free for sports and the evenings for dances or the new cinemas. Monday was for washing the family's clothes. Sunday was for church and general relaxation. No places of amusement and hardly any shops were open, and in the afternoon half the Protestant children of the country were in Sunday School. In South Australia in 1933, this meant approximately eight percent of the total population of the State or more than 43,000 children.[8]

---

5 See Bob Ellis, 'King O'Malley', in Russel Ward, (ed.), *The Greats: The 50 Men and Women Who Helped to Shape Modern Australia* (North Ryde: Angus & Robertson, 1986), 138–43; Arthur R. Hoyle, *King O'Malley: 'The American Bounder'* (South Melbourne: Macmillan of Australia, 1981).

6 Even in his children's book *The Magic Pudding* (Sydney: Angus & Robertson, 1918), Lindsay makes fun of Bunyip Bluegum's Uncle Wattleberry. The ridicule of the whiskered older koala reflects Lindsay's pathological hatred of his maternal grandfather, the Methodist minister and distinguished missionary-anthropologist, Thomas Williams. Norman Lindsay, *The Scribblings of an Idle Mind* (Melbourne: Lansdowne Press, 1966), 19–24, 48–58; U.E. Prunster, 'The Pagan in Norman Lindsay', MA thesis, University of Sydney, 1983.

7 Ian Britain (ed.), *The Donald Friend Diaries: Chronicles & Confessions of an Australian Artist*, (Melbourne: Text Publishing, 2010), 21.

8 Wray Vamplew, (ed.), *Australians: Historical Statistics* (Broadway: Fairfax, Syme & Weldon Associates, 1987), 26, 434.

Immigration was encouraged partly because the Australian birth rate was falling. Perhaps because of the memory of the agonising losses of too many sons in the war, Australian couples preferred smaller families. Or was this because of a growing recognition that, in an urbanised society, material prosperity increased in inverse proportion to the number of children in a household? Or perhaps one of the country's most successful new industries, unnerving many an evangelical heart, Eric Ansell's condom factory in Richmond, had something to do with it.

At the beginning of the 1920s, only a few people had cars and almost nobody had a wireless. By the end of the 1930s, many had cars and most had a wireless. By the early 1930s, Australia was one of the half dozen most motorised nations in the world. The wider availability of the automobile robbed the local church of its unique role as the community centre. The Australian Broadcasting Commission, formed in 1932, encouraged fine music, and the ballet won a following. A serious audience for the arts was growing and education was again on the national agenda. Among those who promoted the arts in Melbourne in the 1930s were newspaper magnate Keith Murdoch and his wife Elisabeth, son and daughter-in-law of prominent Presbyterian minister Patrick Murdoch.

Technology also served practical needs such as those required by public transportation and nation building. On 16 November 1920, Wilmot Hudson Fysh and a group of Scots-Australian Presbyterian friends established the Queensland and Northern Territory Aerial Services Ltd (QANTAS), the future national airline. Fysh, a decorated returned service man, was the son of Tasmanians Frederick Wilmot Fysh and Mary Reed Fysh. The Fysh and Reed families had been friends and co-workers with Hudson Taylor, the founder of the China Inland Mission. Hudson Fysh's mother had served twice as a missionary to China with the CIM before her son's birth in 1895. Therefore, Fysh's pious evangelical Christian parents named their son after the great missionary-statesman. In 1921, Hudson Fysh helped the Rev. John Flynn set up his flying doctor service, and from 1928 to 1947 QANTAS provided a plane and pilot for the Australian Inland Mission of the Presbyterian Church.[9]

One of the most spectacular technological achievements of the interwar period was the construction of the Sydney Harbour Bridge. The greatest single-arch bridge yet built, it was a structure for the future and the ages, wide enough to carry four tracks of railway and six lanes of cars. Begun in

9 Wilmot H. Fysh, *Qantas Rising: The Autobiography of the Flying Fysh* (Sydney: Angus & Robertson, 1965), 3–9, 201–12.

1926 and opened on 19 March 1932, it was designed and supervised by the brilliant railway engineer and city planner John Job Bradfield, who regularly attended St. John's Church of England, Gordon. At Lavender Bay, the Rev Frank Cash photographed the bridge at every stage of its construction, wondering at its capacity to reveal 'divine inspiration in the modern universe'.[10]

Most Australians were still deeply attached to Britain. Tempers flared, and relations were strained in 1932, however, when the English cricket team visited Australia and used dangerous 'bodyline' bowling in the hope of neutralising the genius of Donald Bradman.[11] Nevertheless, migration from Britain was still encouraged and British ships still dominated Australian ports throughout the interwar period. During the 1920s, four of every five ships, measured by tonnage, were British, and half of all exports went to Britain.

Influenza Pandemic and Post-War Malaise

Beginning in January, 1919, the Spanish Influenza pandemic reached Australia, killing 12,000 Australians and millions world-wide. Churches, schools and meetings were closed, and the Anzac Day marches planned for April 1919 were cancelled. Strict quarantine regulations delayed the landing of troopships and each State closed its borders in an attempt to isolate the little understood disease.[12] In North Hobart, a run-down section of the Tasmanian capital, victims died in large numbers. In September 1919, local churches formed an Emergency Clothing Committee that set out to discover the extent of hardship created by the epidemic. Hobart was divided into thirteen districts, each of which was supervised by a clergyman. The Rev. E. Herbert Hobday, pastor of the Baptist Tabernacle, was in charge of North Hobart. Through

10 *SMH*, 29 December 1936.

11 Don Bradman sang with Paul White in the choir at Bowral Church of England, and when Paul White wrote his autobiography, *Alias Jungle Doctor,* he sent a copy to Bradman, who acknowledged it. Paul White was of the opinion that 'Bradman did not have a faith'. But Bradman's values owed much to the influence of his devout mother, Emily. 'When considering the stature of an athlete, I place great stress on certain qualities which I believe to be essential in addition to skill. They are that a person conducts his or her life with dignity, with integrity, with courage and perhaps most of all modesty. These virtues are totally compatible with pride, ambition, determination and competitiveness'. (Sir Donald Bradman, Bradman Museum, Bowral).

12 Humphrey McQueen, 'The 'Spanish' Influenza Pandemic in Australia, 1918–1919', in Jill Roe (ed.), *Social Policy in Australia: Some Perspectives, 1901–75* (Stanmore: Cassell, 1976), 131–47; Lucy Taska, 'The Masked Disease: Oral History, Memory, and the Influenza Pandemic', in Kate Darian-Smith and Paula Hamilton, (eds.), *Memory and History in Twentieth Century Australia* (Melbourne: OUP, 1994), 77–91.

visitation he discovered that almost every family in North Hobart had lost at least one member to the flu and that housing conditions were deplorable. He organised his church for action, appointing Ruby Livingstone as a full-time 'Sister' to work with the needy. The women and young men of the church then helped to establish the Ware Street Mission as a permanent church outpost to help the poor of North Hobart. This included both personal evangelism and advocacy of public programs to correct the conditions that bred disease.[13]

Even more enduring than the impact of the flu pandemic was that of the returned men on the Australian community in the 1920s. Australian historian Patsy Adam-Smith recalled her own childhood memories of the sights and smells of the maimed:

> We lived in a world where men were called 'Hoppy', 'Wingy', 'Shifty', 'Gunner', 'Stumpy', 'Deafy', 'Hooky', according to whether they lost a leg, an arm (or part of one), an eye, their hearing, or had a disfigured face drawn by rough surgery into a leer … And we listened through the thin walls when our parents came home from visiting a 'returned' uncle in hospital: 'I can't stand it. I can't go again.' It is mother. Your father's voice comes, strangled, like hers. 'You'll be alright.' 'No, but the smell. When he coughs … and breathes out … it's … oh, I'm going to be sick.' But she goes back next Sunday and the next until the day you go to school with a black rosette on your lapel, and the flag is flying half-mast for your Uncle Dick who was gassed.[14]

This same psychological and emotional damage manifested itself in almost all returned men, including the most stable and devoutly Christian among them.[15] For some time after the war there was a shortage of ministerial candidates in the evangelical churches. This was especially true of the Methodists who gave so many of their sons to the war. Many had not returned, and a number of those who did return no longer desired to enter the ministry. Men who had been too young to serve felt the war's impact and they too were lost to the ministry. In the case of the NSW Methodists, only four candidates for the ministry presented themselves for training in 1921, and that number did

---

13 Laurence F. Rowston, *One Hundred Years of Witness: A History of the Hobart Baptist Church, 1884–1984* (Hobart: The Hobart Baptist Church, 1984), 32–3; Laurence F. Rowston, 'The Influenza Epidemic and the Ware Street Mission', *The Tabernacle*, 40.3, 1998, 1–2, 4–5, 7.

14 Patsy Adam-Smith, *The Anzacs* (Ringwood: Penguin Books, 1991), 3.

15 Roslyn Otzen, *Whitley: The Baptist College of Victoria, 1891–1991* (South Yarra: Hyland House, 1991), 71–2.

not increase substantially until twelve volunteered for theological training in 1928 and again in 1929. The shortage of ministers did not seem to affect attendance in the evangelical churches, although, by hovering around pre-war levels, there was clearly no room for complacency.[16]

Evangelicals and the Great Depression

The economic crisis that hit the New York Stock Exchange in October 1929 quickly spread around the globe. The Australian economy was more afflicted than most, with levels of debt and unemployment only worse in Germany in the Western world.[17] Governments were woefully slow to offer assistance to the victims: it was not until April 1930 that South Australia introduced the first government-funded food dole for the unemployed. Australia, considered at the beginning of the twentieth century a 'social laboratory' because of progressive provision for pensions and allowances paid for out of consolidated revenue, could no longer afford this level of welfare, leaving the poor and unemployed lethally unsupported.[18] After the first decade of the twentieth century there was no significant developments in Australia's social security system until World War II. The leaders of the trade unions were also tragically unequal to the challenge of addressing the plight of their jobless brothers. In 1929, Australia had 901,000 card-carrying members of 189 different unions. By 1932, membership had declined to 740,000, with twenty unions disappearing altogether.[19]

The Depression was a great a test for the churches and charities as it was for governments and unions, and they, too, failed the test. They were already fully stretched by the demands of the indigent in the 1920s which was far from a prosperous decade for the working classes.[20] The churches represented the 'old ways' of doing charity, and the combined efforts of all the denominations did not prove equal to the task, giving painful proof of the need for a welfare state. The evangelical churches stand not only accused of this inadequacy, but also of being more interested in saving souls than in feeding and housing

---

16 *Minutes of the Twentieth Annual Conference of the Methodist Church of Australasia, Victoria and Tasmania Conference*, 1921 (Melbourne: Methodist Conference Offices, 1921), 85, 232; Wright and Clancy, *The Methodists,* 169; Vamplew, (ed.), *Australian Historical Statistics*, 418–35; Treloar, *The Disruption of Evangelicalism,* 235.

17 C. B. Schedvin, *Australia and the Great Depression: A Study of Economic Development and Policy in the 1920s and 1930s* (Sydney: Sydney University Press, 1970).

18 Garton, *Out of Luck,* 101, 123f.

19 Gerald Stone, *1932* (Sydney: Pan Macmillan Australia, 2005), 212–223.

20 Garton, *Out of Luck,* 119f.

bodies. That might be true, but they nevertheless probably fed and housed more bodies than any other community organisations. They are also accused of attending to their own survival as churches or denominations, or of responding in a piecemeal way to the prodigious need, of adopting a band aid approach, of reacting to symptoms of poverty rather than addressing causes. Evidence for all those charges is readily found, but the evangelical movement was so integrated at every level of society and its leaders so committed to finding solutions that it did a lot better than that. Among its leaders were those who combined compassion with pragmatism which enabled them to give practical assistance to the needy and occasionally to experiment with prophetic departures from socio-economic norms.

At the onset of the Depression, most evangelicals responded in a manner similar to the various government and public agencies: piecemeal and without a full understanding of the immensity of the calamity that had befallen them. In Melbourne, on Christmas Day, 1929, Christian retailer and philanthropist Sidney Myer, owner of Melbourne's leading department store, the Myer Emporium, put on a lunch attended by 11,000 diners who consumed a ton of ham, a half ton of corned beef, 22,000 bread rolls, 33,000 pickled onions and countless servings of peaches, sweets and cake. Myer, who had been raised in Russia as an orthodox Jew, was led to faith in Christ by Edwin Lee Neil, whom Myer had appointed as the managing director of the Myer Emporium.[21] During that same Christmas season, a Salvation Army soup kitchen dispensed 8,000 free meals each week until its resources were exhausted. Melbourne churches likewise shared clothing and food with countless needy people during the period.[22] All were emergency measures. But it was as well that the churches took such measures all over Australia because the emergency was real, and the hungry and homeless could not wait for the effect of new financial and economic measures to reform the capitalist system.

Among the evangelical churches, the Methodists and the Salvation Army were the best prepared to assist the needy. Within Methodism the Central Missions in Australian cities were the major sources of aid to the needy. They all had assistance programs of some kind in operation before 1929. The Newtown Mission was helping 2,070 people a year by 1932. By the mid-1930s, the Sydney Central Mission was assisting 150 men a day in some way. The Newcastle Central Mission initially provided free daily breakfasts for between seventy and eighty men as well as other relief for

21 Ambrose Pratt, *Sidney Myer: A Biography* (Melbourne: Quartet, 1978), 112.

22 Michael Cannon, *The Human Face of the Great Depression* (Mornington: M. Cannon, 1996), 61–66.

families. In 1931, it opened a hostel for men that remained open through the World War II Era. As late as 1937, the Newcastle Mission was serving over 50,000 free meals a year.[23]

In Queensland, the Albert Street Methodist Church and the Central Methodist Mission in Brisbane, under the leadership of the Rev. Harold Wheller, opened hostels for men, with lunches and evening meals provided. The church's annual report for 1930–1931 stated that in eighteen months the Mission had provided 140,000 free meals. The 1931–1932 report revealed that the total food consumed that year amounted to eight tons of cooked meat supplied by Foggitt Jones & Company (owned by a Methodist layman), forty-eight tons of bread, one and a half tons of sugar, one ton of butter, one ton of tea, 115,200 buns, 18,000 gallons of milk plus fruit, cakes and scones in great quantity and lettuce that was supplied daily by another Methodist, A.L. Evans. Yes, evangelicals loved statistics. Clothing was provided for those in need and essential foods taken to women and children. The Methodist Sisters of the People did much of this work, and the Mission soon opened a separate hostel for women from which food and clothing were distributed.[24]

In Perth, the Wesley Church and the Central Mission, under the leadership of the Rev. C.A. Jenkins, provided food, clothing and counselling for tens of thousands of people during the 1930s.[25] The Sisters of the People, among whom were qualified nurses, became the main agents of its social ministries. The Dorcas Society, the Girls' Friendly Aid Society, the Labour Bureau, the Haven of Hope for unfortunate young women, special relief programs, and numerous people's concerts and lectures were the means by which the Mission ministered to Perth's needy.

Methodist relief work in Melbourne was conducted principally through seven central missions. At Wesley Church the Central Mission was headed from 1933 by Irving Benson who responded energetically, if conservatively, to the crisis brought on by the Depression. Born in England in 1897, Benson migrated to Victoria in 1916, and was ordained in Wesley Church, Melbourne, in 1922, and eventually became its senior minister. He soon became a noted public figure in Melbourne, the spiritual confidant of many community leaders. He was associated with a wide range of community organisations including Toc H, the Miller Homes, the Library Association of Victoria, the

---

23 Wright, *Mantle of Christ*, 178–181.

24 F.R. Smith, *The Church on the Square: A History of the Albert Street Church* (Brisbane: The Uniting Church Centre, 1990), 91–94.

25 Wesley Lutton, *The Wesley Story: Centenary of Wesley Church, Perth, Western Australia, 1870–1970* (Perth: Western Australian Newspapers, 1970), 13–17.

Victorian State Library as a trustee, the Free Library Service Board, and the Councils of Queen's College and the Methodist Ladies' College. Something of a celebrity himself, he was accused of being 'a celebrity hound' as he wooed many of the leading political and social figures of his day. Because of his outspoken opposition to liquor and gambling, he was also referred to as 'the head wowser' of Melbourne.[26]

Benson's twin concerns were evangelism and social issues. He always preached for decisions for Christ and never abandoned the historic Methodist message of salvation by faith in Christ alone. On the occasion of his retirement in 1967, he declared, 'I have constantly preached the five cardinal points of Methodism: every man needs to be saved; every man can be saved; every man can know that he is saved; every man must witness that he is saved; and every man can go on to the experience of perfect love'. It was the last point that drove his social concern, which was consistent with traditional Methodist opposition to the so-called personal sins of the day: alcohol, gambling and breach of the Sabbath. But he also on occasion spoke out for social reform that would protect women from male exploitation and on behalf of the aged and the poor. He pushed his agenda through his long-running newspaper column, his several books, his personal contacts with powerful people, but most of all through his Pleasant Sunday Afternoons (PSAs) held at the Wesley Church and for many years broadcast over national radio.[27]

The PSAs attracted prime ministers, ambitious politicians, other leading citizens and international celebrities. It canvassed important political, social and community issues. As he became increasingly identified with public life, he closely followed politics by radio and prayed for parliamentarians in Melbourne and Canberra. He once remarked that after listening to debates in Canberra he also made certain that he prayed for the Australian people![28]

---

26 Renate Howe and Shurlee Swain, *The Challenge of the City: The Centenary History of Wesley Central Mission, 1893–1993* (South Melbourne: Hyland House, 1993), 97–119; A. Harold Wood, *'Not Lost but Gone Before': Memories of 100 Christian Men and Women* (Mitcham: Meerut Publications, 1987), 16–19; and Shirley Horne, 'Benson, Clarence Irving' in Dickey, Brian, (ed.), *Australian Dictionary of Evangelical Biography* (Sydney: Evangelical History Association of Australia, 1994), 38–39. Hereafter *ADEB*. For a highly negative view of Benson, see Keith Dunstan, 'Gamble on our Future Success', *Herald Sun*, 11 September 1993, 33.

27 Harold Wood, Principal of the Methodist Ladies' College in Melbourne, notes that ABC national radio took Benson off the air in 1942 because of the strong objections of the United Licensed Victuallers' Association to Benson's continuous attacks on the liquor industry. Wood, *'Not Lost but Gone Before'*, 17. But, see also Howe and Swain, *The Challenge of the City*, 113–115.

28 Wood, *'Not Lost but Gone Before'*, 18.

Methodist circuits also launched programs and cooperated with government agencies to help the unemployed. The Unley Methodist Circuit in Adelaide was particularly active, supporting relief work carried out by the Unley Unemployment Association. Local churches established food and clothing outlets for the needy and ministers invited those who were suffering to make themselves known so aid could be given. On one Sunday morning during the depression, the Rev. Percy Chennell, minister at Goodwood Methodist Church, received seventy applications for help. Churches in the circuit also tried to hire unemployed men in their congregations to do any work that they might have available.[29]

Of all of the various evangelical agencies, the Salvation Army was the best prepared to cope with the early waves of broken, desperate people. The Salvos ran soup kitchens, remade clothes and taught women the art of living on a minimal income. However, the Army was soon overwhelmed. For one thing, their facilities, although extensive, were limited, a reality which attracted criticism. The unemployed put a black ban on the Bennett's Lane soup kitchen in Sydney on the grounds that the soup was always the same and the men had to wait outside in the cold because the premises was too small to accommodate them.

In the 1920s, when most people, including the government, paid little attention to the forgotten sections of society, the Salvation Army began to provide extensive, long-term help for homeless and/or unemployed men. On Foster Street in Surry Hills, Sydney, it opened in 1923 Foster House, a five-storey building with dormitory style accommodation for 220 men. It was filled to capacity and often overcrowded from 1930 to 1939. In the early 1930s, the Salvos established camps for undernourished and starving children from the Sydney slums in order to feed them adequately and allow them to escape their crowded, shabby homes for a week. During the period, it was common for Salvationist Arthur McIlveen, later famed as the 'Padre of the Rats of Tobruk' in World War II, to come home and say to his wife, 'I have given our salary away again today, Lizzie'. 'The Lord will provide', responded Lizzie.[30]

The Salvation Army established soup kitchens in many parts of Australia and labour bureaus to seek work for the unemployed. Accommodation was found for the homeless. SAOs knocked on the doors in the slums ostensibly to distribute *The War Cry*, but really to seek out the destitute too proud to ask

---

29 Donald V. Goldney, *Methodism in Unley, 1949–1977* (Eagle Farm: William Brooks and Company, 1980), 176–177.

30 Howe and Swain, *The Challenge of the City*, 121; and Bolton, *Booth's Drum*, 156, 232, 261.

for help. The Army was trusted then as now, and school teachers regularly reported evidence of needy families to the Salvation Army.[31]

By contrast with the Methodist Central Missions and the Salvation Army, the Church of England was not as well prepared as it might have been to give assistance to the needy. In Sydney, its Home Mission Society (HMS) was then still more committed to helping poor parishes than poor people. But at the beginning of the depression the poor already had a Church of England hero in the person of the Rev. R.B.S. Hammond, rector from 1918 of St Barnabas, Broadway. Dubbed by the media as the 'Mender of Broken Men', Hammond was an impatient individualist and a compassionate activist who devoted his life to showing Christ to the world through a blend of evangelical theology and Gospel-based practical Christianity. Born in rural NSW in 1870, the son of a stock and station agent, Hammond was converted to Christ in the famous Grubb mission in 1891.[32] He began his ministerial career in Melbourne in 1894 and moved to Sydney in 1899.[33] Between 1904 and 1911, as an inner-city missioner, Hammond transformed the Mission Zone Fund[34] of the Church of England Home Mission Society into the spearhead of the Church's ministry to the inner city. He evangelised in the streets and in the factories and urged those who would listen to give up alcohol. His ministry in the tough neighbourhoods of Surry Hills flourished as his church services saw a ten-fold increase in attendance. Further, his successful special 'men's meetings' demonstrated that working class males were interested in the gospel. It is said that over 4,400 men came to Christ through Hammond. When he did not receive the support he believed that he needed from HMS, Hammond resigned and established his own social service structures based in the parish of St Barnabas, Broadway. The parish had fallen on hard times and there had been discussion of selling the church building. Hammond turned things around, and the church soon became a centre for welfare activities that reached well beyond the parish and his denomination.

While a parish missioner, Hammond had established the first 'Hammond Hotel' for seven destitute men in Newtown. Two additional hotels followed in Surry Hills. At Broadway, he expanded this work with a fourth hotel in

31 Bolton, *Booth's Drum*, 132.

32 See *The Fountain of Public Prosperity*, ch. 18.

33 On R.B.S. Hammond see Bernard G. Judd, *He That Doeth: The Life Story of Archdeacon R.B.S. Hammond* (London: Marshall, Morgan & Scott, 1951); Stephen Judd, 'Hammond, Robert Brodribb Stewart', *ADEB*, 148–150; Meredith Lake, *Faith in Action: HammondCare* (Sydney: UNSW Press, 2013), 1–112.

34 The Mission Zone Fund was designated for work in the 'slums,' or what at the time was the industrial heart of Sydney. Judd, *He That Doeth*, 41.

an abandoned warehouse that housed 120 men. Even before the Depression dramatically increased the need for such facilities, this ministry provided over 3,500 beds and tens of thousands of meals annually as well as clothing and shoes. The St. Barnabas' Employment Bureau found scores of jobs for the needy. To resource this ministry of relief for the poor and unemployed he used political and commercial means, enlisting the support of Sir Philip Game, the State Governor, and some business houses. He spoke each Monday night at a Business Men's Bible Class at Toc H rooms in Griffiths Brothers Tea Rooms. The singing of the 100 men present was so powerful that crowds would gather outside in George Street just to listen to it.

St. Barnabas' Broadway became the headquarters for what Hammond deemed to be practical evangelism. The notice board fronting Broadway became famous for its pithy sayings on practical Christianity and its anti-grog messages. For many years, Hammond and the publican across the street, who also had a signboard, exchanged witticisms to the point that their word duels became a part of Sydney legend.[35] Hammond also attracted large crowds by his powerful and eloquent preaching. He was a big man (a former footballer in Melbourne) with a striking physique that conveyed the impression of great reserves of restless energy. He had a commanding stage presence, an uncanny ability to 'read' his audiences, a facility for brilliant repartee, and an infectious sense of humour, all of which gave him considerable power over his audiences.

Hammond believed that alcohol was one of the most significant causes of the poverty that he saw all around him. Therefore, he became first a temperance advocate and then a prohibition crusader. He was president of the Australasian Temperance Society from 1916 to 1941 and of the NSW Temperance Alliance from 1916 to 1925 and again from 1927 until his death in 1946. He even made two trips to the USA, one in 1917 and one in 1919, and published the results of his study of the movement there in 1920. He and other St. Barnabas staff visited drunks at the Regent Street Police Court each day. More than 8,000 came under Hammond's ministry in 1925 alone, and about twenty percent of them signed a total abstinence pledge and joined the St. Barnabas' Brotherhood. But Hammond had greater plans to help the poor, to which we will return below.

In Melbourne, maverick Ridley College graduate Reginald Gordon Nichols performed feats of service similar to Hammond's for the victims of the Depression. After a successful career in business, he offered himself for

---

35 Some of Hammond's messages read: 'Salvation, like air and water, is free'; 'Try loving people; you can hate them without trying'; and 'Alcohol promises you heaven and gives you hell'. Judd, *He That Doeth*, 201.

ordination in the Church of England in 1910. He later graduated from the University of Melbourne and Ridley College, settling in at the working class and run down parish of St. Mark's Fitzroy in 1922. Nichols soon reversed the parish's fortunes and made the church a hub of evangelistic outreach and social ministry for the disadvantaged in Melbourne. Nichols was a product of 'muscular Christianity' who revolutionised worship services at the church and built new facilities for the working people of the district.[36] Reputedly, he had a 'silver tongue' and conducted his ministry like 'a business directed with the maximum acumen and the minimum of cost'. He developed a community or 'settlement' that provided physical nourishment and educational and social opportunities for needy men and women. By 1934, he could claim with some justification that his church was 'the best equipped in Australia for social work'.[37]

When the Depression broke in late 1929, Nichols, his staff and supporters immediately began to dispense the usual necessary items to keep hungry, unemployed men and their families alive. He also introduced several innovative services in his parish and beyond. Perhaps the most unique and successful of these schemes were his 'penny dinners'. By 1930, the Health Officers for Melbourne City Council found that thirty-seven percent of children in state schools were malnourished – with the percentage much higher in the tenement districts. Nichols responded to this need by shifting the priority of social work in the parish from relief parcels dispensed at St. Mark's to a program that provided fifty children from local schools with a hot meal at lunch time each school day. To allow poor families to retain their dignity, the children were selected by their headmaster and then charged one penny for each meal. The system was immediately successful.[38] After one week the number of dinners had doubled, and within two weeks had risen to 240. The number of children and schools served by this program increased each year thereafter until by 1935 more than a thousand children were being fed each day.[39] Other schemes and experiments met with varying degrees of success, all made possible by Nichols's dynamic and workaholic personality, his devotion to Christ, his willingness to work outside the confines of organised religion,

---

36 David A. Pear, 'Two Anglican Responses to the Depression and Second World War in Melbourne: A Study in Churchmanship', MTh Thesis, Melbourne College of Divinity, 1985, 30.

37 Pear, 'Two Anglican Responses', 32–37.

38 Pear, 'Two Anglican Responses', 105–106.

39 The details of the 'penny dinners' program are contained in Pear, 'Two Anglican Responses', 106–108.

and his use of new technology such as radio and the movies. Unfortunately, he suffered a 'breakdown' during World War II: 'he was arrested for "having sent obscene words by post" and was subsequently convicted'.[40] He died at age 72 in obscurity at a rest home in Castlemaine, Victoria on 18 July 1960.

In Melbourne, too, all three parties within the Church of England – evangelical, Anglo-Catholic and Liberal – responded in their own ways to the needs of the community without criticising the social welfare enterprise of others. The unlikely harmony manifested itself in the pan-theological cooperation in promoting the social welfare work of the Mission of St. James and St. John during the depression years.[41]

In Adelaide, St. Luke's Church of England in Whitmore Square, another Adelaide evangelical congregation, was located in the poorest quarter of Adelaide and was the main centre of evangelical Anglican social work in the diocese. Under the leadership of the Rev. J.B. Montgomerie, rector from 1933 to 1939, St Luke's made a name as a dispenser of social welfare in the city. Montgomerie especially was concerned for disadvantaged children in his parish and used the press and the radio to publicise the need. He was thus able to run out of his church 'the cheapest restaurant in Adelaide'. A hot two-course meal was served daily during the winter, free to 200 needy children from the nearby Sturt Street School, and at the price of one penny to others. Along with the food, the church gave the children lessons in gentility and good behaviour and an introduction to the Gospel. Montgomerie's spouse, Brucinda, organised the meals assisted by a volunteer 'band of 80 ladies from the City and Suburbs' who responded to the rector's radio broadcasts.[42] In Perth, ten members of the Church Army arrived in 1932, led by Captain John Cowland.[43] Their purpose was chiefly evangelistic, but was so effective that the Church Army, with its focus on ministry to the poor, was established in Anglican dioceses throughout Australia.

---

40 David Pear, 'Nichols, Reginald Gordon Clement (1888–1960)', ADB, online edition.

41 Barbara B. Darling, 'The Church of England in Melbourne and the Great Depression, 1929 to 1935,' MA thesis, Department of History, University of Melbourne, 1982, v-vii and 136–140; Keith Cole, *Commissioned to Care: The Golden Jubilee History of the Mission of St. James and St. John, 1919–1969* (Melbourne: Ruskin Press, 1969), 1–47.

42 Judith Rafferty, '"Till Every Foe Is Vanquished": Churches and Social Issues in South Australia, 1919–1939,' PhD, School of Social Sciences, Flinders University, 1988, 264–265; David Hilliard, *Godliness and Good Order: A History of the Anglican Church in South Australia* (Adelaide: Wakefield Press, 1986), 109; *St. Luke's Church, Whitmore Square, Adelaide, 1855–1955, Centenary Booklet,* 1955.

43 Brian H. Fletcher, *An English Church in Australian Soil* (Canberra: Barton Books, 2015), 173.

In the early days of rampant unemployment, Baptists tried various schemes to help. Those in the Sydney orbit established 'the NSW Baptist Labour Exchange' with the goal to match Baptists to available work. The lists, however, grew so long that resources were insufficient to administer the scheme. In the end, NSW Baptists, like most of those elsewhere left it up to the local churches to reach out to those in need.[44] Petersham Baptist Church, under the leadership of Joshua Robertson, was one such church which responded vigorously to the challenge. In July 1930, Robertson led the membership to agree to donate the entire evening's offering to relief, and to continue this practice as long as there was demonstrable need. There followed the establishment of a Women's Relief Committee that raised money and ran a clothing pool. Petersham residents recall seeing the large figure of the Baptist pastor bearing armloads of groceries to the sick and watched him as he mowed the lawns of the elderly who did not have the ability or funds to do it themselves. He was also seen sitting on the kerb at daybreak comforting a troubled milkman. When he left his Petersham pastorate in 1946, the City Council of Petersham passed a minute of appreciation that said in part that he had 'rendered yeoman service to the community in civil and philanthropic works and, during the economic depression, earned the heartfelt thanks of many an unfortunate family by his deeds of charity, many of which were anonymous.'[45]

Since many of the members of the Baptist churches of Queensland were working men, the Great Depression heavily impacted the denomination in that State. A Social Service Committee (SSC) was formed and charged with helping 'members of the household of faith' to weather the crisis. This was done by providing financial and material assistance and by attempting to find work for those needing jobs. Though limited in terms of success, the SSC was an early, first step in the denomination's venture into the provision of social welfare.[46]

Baptists and Churches of Christ in South Australia mostly left it up to the local churches to try to come to grips with the economic crisis. The South Australian Baptist Union's Social Services Department tried to find

---

44 *The Australian Baptist*, 15 January 1929, 3; 30 September 1930, 1; Ken Manley, *From Woolloomooloo to Eternity: A History of Australian Baptists*, 2 vols. (Milton Keynes: Paternoster, 2006), 1:439–444.

45 Peter Young, 'Rev. Joshua Robertson,' unpublished paper read to the Baptist Historical Society of NSW, 16 October 1980, 7–8.

46 David Parker (ed.), *Pressing on with the Gospel: The Story of Baptists in Queensland, 1855–2005* (Brisbane: Baptist Historical Society of Queensland, 2005), 68–70.

Baptists work, preferably with Baptist employers. The Baptists also operated two inner city missions that continued to function during the period, now adding counselling and crisis care to their children's outreach programs and their soup kitchens. In the main, denominational leaders called for 'sacrifice', and urged local churches to establish unemployment committees, practise economies, balance their budgets, and be practical and merciful. Taking this cue, the North Adelaide Baptist Church established a workshop to assist the unemployed to help themselves, and other South Australian Baptist churches did likewise.[47]

The Churches of Christ in Queensland had a Social Service Department that, under the leadership of the Rev. Charles Young, took action to alleviate suffering on a trans-congregational level in 1931. The Department solicited foodstuffs and clothing from church members. Goods were sent to a central depot at the Ann Street Church in Brisbane, from which 400 parcels were distributed to needy families. A total of 4,000 free meals were provided on Sundays to hungry travellers transiting through Yeronga Park in Brisbane during the worst years of the depression.

Among the Presbyterians, Eva Holland, daughter the Rev. Edward Holland (a missionary to Jamaica who introduced sugar farming to Queensland), was the key to the denomination's urban social strategy in Sydney in the 1930s. Holland guided the work of the denominational Social Service Committee and personally established Women's Clubs in places like Woolloomooloo where they provided fellowship, instruction on practical issues, and garments for the needy. One of her disciples, Marion Rennie, duplicated her efforts in Ultimo, as did others elsewhere in the inner city. On the eve of the Great Depression in 1929, it was reported that the Burnside Presbyterian Homes for Orphans had more than 400 occupants and the number was still increasing. It had been founded in 1911 by the wealthy Presbyterian laymen James Burns who, in a manifestation of sanctified competition, generously endowed the homes so that the Presbyterians would not be seen to be behind other denominations, especially Catholics, in providing for needy children. Reputedly, it became the largest orphanage in Australia, but was considered progressive and enlightened in its provision for the children to be housed in discrete communities of about thirty. As with many charities, it resisted government control on the grounds that this threatened its distinctively Christian mission.[48] It received

47 *The Australian Baptist*, 13 October 1931, 5, 12; 10 July 1934, 6; Manley, *From Woolloomooloo to Eternity*, 2:439–444; Rafferty, 'Till Every Foe Is Vanquished', 244–245, 280–281.

48 Garton, *Out of Luck*, 92.

minimal state supervision until the 1970s, but children raised in the homes report mainly positively on their experiences.[49]

The Presbyterians and Congregationalists usually left it up to local churches to respond to the crisis of the Depression, and some churches did well. St. Andrew's Presbyterian Church in the heart of Perth, under the leadership of the Rev. George Tulloch, was active in relief work, again especially directed to helping children. Church agencies ministered to the poor and needy of the city, but Tulloch himself took a special interest in children's shelters. He was instrumental in establishing Burnbrae, a Presbyterian Home for Children at Byford near Perth, and shortly before his death in 1946 was active in the purchase and preparation of Benmore, a home for adolescent boys at Caversham.[50]

New Departures in Social Welfare

With its incarnational theology, Catholic Christianity in the Anglican tradition might be supposed to have been more creative in social welfare provision than evangelical churches. Evidence that this was the case was the creation in 1933 of the Brotherhood of St Laurence by the Rev. G.K. Tucker. It sought to address not only the symptoms, but also the causes of poverty.[51] It appointed a research officer to strengthen its advocacy for justice for the poor. Liberal Catholics within the Church of England, such as Bishop Ernest Burgmann and Archbishop Geoffrey Sambell, influenced by the Christian socialism of Archbishop William Temple and academic, R.H. Tawney, were to contribute significantly to the creation of the welfare state.[52]

The instinctive first reaction of evangelicals to the crisis of the Depression was to see it primarily as a moral rather than an economic problem. But there were evangelicals who broke new ground in the quest for solutions to the Great Depression. In NSW, a few leaders who lived close to the working poor understood that the economic and social order needed immediate and primary

49 Mark Hutchinson, *Iron in Our Blood: A History of the Presbyterian Church in NSW, 1788–2001* (Sydney: Ferguson Publications and the Centre for the Study of Australian Christianity, 2001), 253; Kate Shayler, *Burnished: Burnside Life Stories* (Hazelbrook: MoshPit Publishing, 2011).

50 No author, *Fight the Good Fight: In Memoriam, Revd. George Tulloch, E. D.* (Perth: St. Andrew's Church, 1946), pamphlet held in the Battye Library, Perth, See esp. 19–20.

51 Stephen Judd, Anne Robinson, and Felicity Errington, *Driven by Purpose: Charities that Make the Difference* (Greenwich: HammondPress, 2012), 53.

52 Bruce Norman Kaye, Colin Holden, Geoffrey R. Treloar, and T. R. Frame, *Anglicanism in Australia: A History* (Carlton: MUP, 2002), 152.

attention. Among them was the Methodist Dr. E.E.V. Collocott, who insisted that while current relief efforts were urgently needed, any solution that did not also seek the radical reform of human institutions was inadequate. He was joined in this sentiment by the Rev. Rupert Williams, Superintendent of the Sydney Central Mission, who knew that it was too simple to blame the current labour unrest on the Communists or those who were suffering. It was, he said, the responsibility of the Christian Church to stir men to action in order to reform the social system.[53]

In Adelaide, the Rev. Samuel Forsyth, Superintendent of the Adelaide Central Mission (1929–1952), established the Kuitpo Labour Colony for the unemployed in rough forest country south of Adelaide. The SA State government provided subsidies that gave continuity to the project, but it was only a temporary charitable facility. In the 1940s, it was transformed into a residential institution for the rehabilitation of alcoholics. Nevertheless, it provided shelter and food and a fresh start for hundreds of hapless people during the most desperate years of the Depression.[54]

The Rev. Tom Willason, Superintendent of the Port Adelaide Mission (1924–1935), devised an innovative relief scheme in the hardest hit spot in Australia. Port Adelaide was a working-class community that had suffered periodic and severe unemployment in the 1920s. With the coming of the Depression, Willason and his wife Ethel (a full partner in his enterprise) ministered amidst increasing misery and squalor. In March 1931, there were 3,119 unemployed single men in Port Adelaide, representing fifty-five percent of all those unemployed in the Adelaide area. The 1933 federal census reported that the Port district contained 3,632 unemployed men, well over forty-two percent of the Port work force. It was the worst unemployment rate in Australia.[55]

More than half of Willason's congregation were themselves out of work by mid-1930. Willason's response was to establish a cooperative 'fishing fleet' to create employment, based on the principle of self-help rather than on handouts. With the aid of Captain J.A. Olsen, one of his church members, Willason devised a program with a dual purpose: unemployed men with fishing and shipping experience would engage in both an employment venture and an

53 Wright and Clancy, *The Methodists*, 178.

54 Brian J. Chambers, 'Need, Not Creed: A History of the Adelaide Central Methodist Mission, 1900–1952', MA Thesis, Flinders University, 1986, 147–210; Hunt, *This Side of Heaven*, 323.

55 Brian Dickey and Elaine Martin, *Building Community: A History of the Port Adelaide Central Mission* (Adelaide: Port Adelaide Wesley Centre, 1999), 70–73.

attempt to revamp the depressed fishing industry. The 'fishing fleet' concept received credibility when Willason himself produced a master mariner's certificate from his pre-conversion days at sea. The venture was a modest success. But it ended in 1934, largely because of the hostility of the existing fishing businesses, which did not welcome a competitor with charitable backing in a highly competitive industry. Nevertheless, for a few years at the height of the Depression the sale of fish after each trip enabled a number of families to come off the dole. Moreover, as historians Brian Dickey and Elaine Martin have pointed out: 'It showed care and concern, it broke the bounds of convention, it suggested that a central mission could undertake new and creative projects for its constituency'.[56]

A.B. Lalchere, minister of the Five Dock Church in Sydney, established in November 1929 the Methodist Unemployment and Relief Fund. It sought to offer men a period of casual work and pay them for it and continued to operate beyond World War II. In Melbourne, Os Barnett, a Methodist lay preacher, campaigned for a Babies Home to care for those whose parents were indigent. He knew how to win the support of people of all religions and none. He made an impact on the Victorian premier, Albert Dunstan, and became a member of the Victorian Housing Commission.[57]

In Sydney, R.B.S. Hammond launched a scheme designed to be a long-term solution to the problem of destitute families who had suffered or who lived at the mercy of slum landlords. Established as a settlement near Liverpool on the outskirts of Sydney, the scheme was simple: destitute families who already received public assistance in the form of unemployment benefits and child endowment would be able to participate in a home ownership plan whereby families with three or more children could purchase modest wooden homes on one acre plots of land for an initial payment of five shillings per week, with no deposit and no interest. This procedure allowed families to own their own homes in about seven years. The initial purchase of thirteen acres two miles from Liverpool was completed only when Hammond surrendered his life assurance policy to consummate the deal. Christian volunteers who camped on the site of what was now called 'Hammondville' cleared the bush and built the first roads on the property.

The first home was officially opened on 20 November 1932. Within two years there were more than fifty homes, a shopping centre and post office, a school and a community hall. By 1939, Hammondville was a community

56 Dickey and Martin, *Building Community*, 81.

57 Breward, *A History of the Australian Churches*, 126.

of 110 cottages sitting on 225 acres of land, and Hammondville itself was a new Sydney suburb. It proved to be one of the few successful land settlement schemes in Australian history and an enduring testimony to Hammond's vision and foresight.

In November of 1935, the Social Service Department of the Churches of Christ in South Australia endorsed the view that 'to save herself and the world the church must reconstruct the social system'.[58] In the same month, *The Australian Christian Commonwealth* published a letter in which the writer declared that Christians should blame 'none but ourselves if we do not insist on some of the principles of Christ's perfect social order being the foundation of the future.'[59] Unfortunately, the letter did not specify what these principles were. But the importance of the proposal did not lie in its practicality or specificity, for it was general and vague, but in the fact that it indicated an understanding that solutions to social and economic problems needed to be structural as well as personal.

The suggestion sprouted wings, however, with the formation of the Inter-Church Social Research Council in April 1936 as a result of a public meeting in the Adelaide Town Hall in December 1935. The new Council's purpose was 'to ascertain causes of poverty and to recommend such action as will result in its abolition'. The Council included representatives from the Baptist Union, the Churches of Christ, the Church of England, the Congregational Union, the Methodist Church, the Society of Friends and the Salvation Army. The Australian Student Christian Movement, the Woman's Christian Temperance Union and the Young Men's and Young Women's Christian Associations were invited to send 'associates' who had no voting rights. The plan was for the Council to examine the issue of poverty, its causes and possible means of abolition, and to issue three reports. The first two reports analysing the problem and causes of poverty were published in September 1936 and January 1938, respectively. The economic analysis in these reports clearly indicated that the Council seriously considered structural change as a necessary part of the solution. The third report was to have suggested ways of abolishing poverty and periodic economic crises leading to poverty. Unfortunately, World War II intervened and the third report was never published.[60]

---

58 *The Australian Christian*, 1 November 1934, 693.

59 *Australian Christian Commonwealth*, 30 November 1934, 16.

60 Rafferty, 'Till Every Foe is Vanquished,' 297–298.

Evangelicals in Politics, Business and Public Life

Because evangelicals possess a passion for maintaining the right and/or reforming the wrong, they commonly are found on all sides of politics. They are typically activist, but are extremely diverse in their social sentiments, a symptom of their individualism. In the 1920s and 30s, they occupied the full spectrum of political commitment, from the extreme right wing in their support of the New Guard, to the extreme left wing, in their sympathy for Communism. Most, of course, were found between the extremes, towards the conservative end of the spectrum, but with a significant number, especially in the Methodist tradition, identifying with the aspirations of the Labor Party. Then, among those actively engaged in politics, were those who maintained their zealous commitment to evangelical faith, and others who owed their values to evangelical influence in their youth, but who, in the heat of the political struggle, withdrew from regular religious practice.

Among the most interesting politicians of the period with strong evangelical associations were Robert Gordon Menzies and John Smith (Jock) Garden. They could not have been more different. Menzies, prime minister, 1939–41 and 1949–66, began his political career with the National Party, then switched to Joe Lyons's United Australia Party in 1934, and finally after Lyons's death, led a new UAP government as prime minister in 1939. Menzies identified himself as a Presbyterian, and there is no reason to doubt that he was an orthodox believer. His father, James Menzies, was a Presbyterian elder at Ballarat and later a Methodist local preacher and Sunday School teacher at Jeparit, where Robert was born. Grandmother Elizabeth Menzies, whom young Robert visited often, was a devout Presbyterian who only allowed four books in her house: the Bible, the Presbyterian hymnal, *Ingoldsby Legends*[61] and *Pilgrim's Progress*. Menzies was also influenced as were many Australian University students by the oratory and writings of the evangelical mystic, Henry Drummond.[62] During his time as a law student at Melbourne University, Menzies heard C.H. Nash deliver a lecture on the authority of the Bible. At one point Nash held high his copy of the New Testament and proclaimed: 'In this book is all I know of Jesus Christ and all I need to know of what God has in store for me'. Menzies later testified that as a consequence of this dramatic

61 A collection of myths and legends written by English clergyman, Richard Harris Barham.

62 R.G. Menzies, *Afternoon Light: Some Memories of Men and Events* (Melbourne: Cassell, 1967), 9. Drummond (see vol. 1, chapter 13) had attempted to reconcile science and religion in the very influential *Natural Law in the Spiritual World* (London: Hodder & Stoughton, 1883).

scene, he never gave up reading the Bible.[63] It shaped the way he thought of the civil as well as the spiritual sphere. Four years before his death in 1978 he had conferred on him the Freedom of the City of Kew in Melbourne. In his speech in response, he observed:

> You know I think it was the Apostle Paul who said that 'we are all members one of another.'[64] It is a lovely phrase, you know. It is a lovely expression. It means that no man lives to himself, that every man who lives in a community is a member of that community. He shares his membership with other people in it and, political friend or political foe, he owes them every good thing that he can contribute to the life of the country.[65]

In 1920 Menzies married Pattie Leckie at the Kew Presbyterian Church. In Canberra, he fraternised with the Rev. Hector Harrison, pastor of the Presbyterian Church of St. Andrew, where his daughter, Heather, was married in 1955. Harrison and Presbyterian minister, Dr. Fred McKay, 'Menzies' old friend', of the Australian Inland Mission, conducted the wedding ceremony. McKay later presided over Menzies' funeral at the Scots Church in Melbourne in 1978.[66] Perhaps Menzies' greatest contribution to Australian religion and politics was his role as 'the godfather of modern Liberal Party morality'. In other words, Menzies was able to project his own original evangelical values into the political process in such a way as to attract those who held similar views.[67]

Jock Garden, by contrast, was a maverick, a Communist, trade union leader, and an evangelical Christian minister. Like Menzies, Garden was of Scottish descent, coming to Australia in 1904. In 1906, Garden was a Churches of Christ preacher in Harcourt, Victoria. By 1909, he was a member of the Labor Party and a Baptist minister at Maclean, NSW. By 1913, he was in Sydney where he plied his sailmaker trade and became president of the Sailmakers' Union and its delegate on the Labor Council of NSW. He soon dominated the Labor Council as its secretary, and it became his power base

---

63 Darrell N. Paproth, *Failure Is Not Final: A Life of C.H. Nash* (Sydney: CSAC, 1997), 127–128, 236.

64 Ephesians 4:25

65 Heather Henderson, *Letters to My Daughter: Robert Menzies, Letters, 1955–1975* (Millers Point: Pier 9, 2011), 272.

66 A. W. Martin, *Robert Menzies, a Life*, 2 vols. (Carlton: MUP, 1993–1999), 1:1–18, 2:305, 565; Malcolm Prentis interviewed by Linder, 20 November 2008.

67 Suggested by Australian sociologist Bruce Wearne interviewed by Linder, 25 July 2004.

until 1934. He remained, throughout, an active member of the Churches of Christ. Whether in the pulpit, the Trades Hall or on the Sydney Domain, he proved himself a powerful and inspirational speaker. His personal life was blameless, and he was a teetotaller and a temperance advocate. His less than admiring biographer, Arthur Hoyle, judged him to be courageous, generous and good-natured, and observed that if Garden 'could not make people pious, he would make them better off'.[68]

After years of radical politicking within Labor ranks, Garden and W.P. Earsman launched the Communist Party of Australia in 1921. Garden would remain a Communist until 1926. During this period, he once declared: 'If Jesus were alive today, he would be a Communist.'[69] In 1922 he was elected to the Executive Committee of the Communist Party International (Comintern) and selected to represent Australia at the Fourth Comintern Congress in Moscow. This meant that he would be shadowed for much of his life by the Australian Special Intelligence Branch.

The Congress ended on 5 December 1922, and Garden headed for Lossiemouth, Scotland, where he still had relatives and friends. Instead of promoting Communism there, he spoke of the great opportunities in Australia and resumed his evangelistic activities. He was asked to speak at a revival meeting at the United Free Presbyterian Church in Lossiemouth at which more than 1200 people were present. Speaking on the theme of 'young men the rapids are below!' some fifty people responded to his appeal to accept Christ as Lord and Saviour. As one of them remembered sixty years later, 'We stayed saved.'[70]

The next few years brought with them strenuous political activity, exciting confrontations at open-air meetings, and threats on his life. After contending with NSW Labor leader J.T. Lang, Garden resigned from the Communist Party in 1926 and reached a rapprochement with 'the Big Fella'. More than anyone else Garden was responsible for the foundation of the Australasian Council of Trades Unions in Melbourne in 1927, and in 1929, he rejoined the Labor Party. He won the federal seat of Cook in 1934 as a Lang Labor candidate. During his time in Canberra he and Lang had a final falling out, and Lang saw to it that Garden lost pre-selection for Cook in 1937. In 1940, he was defeated in his final bid for the federal parliament. His career

68 Arthur Hoyle, *Jock Garden: The Red Parson* (Canberra: Privately Printed, 1993), 39, 154.

69 See one-page typescript, J.S. Garden/Percy Grainger file, Box 136, Manning Clark Papers, MS 7550, National Archives, Canberra.

70 Quoted in Hoyle, *Jock Garden*, 37.

in public politics ended, he drifted from business to business, preaching on the side. He was charged at various times with financial scams, but always acquitted. He died on 31 December 1968, given a Churches of Christ funeral, and farewelled this world as the only evangelical minister who was ever invited to a meeting of the Comintern of the International Communist Party in Soviet history.[71]

In the world of business, evangelicals were strongly represented, in demonstration of the Protestant work ethic. They were typically entrepreneurial, caring for their employees, paternalistic, and civic-minded. Prominent examples include carmaker Henry Holden in South Australia and Fletcher Jones in Victoria. Holden, a convinced Baptist, began what would become the highly successful Holden automobile empire in Adelaide in 1917. By 1923, he was employing over a thousand men and producing 240 car bodies per week. He enjoyed a close, if paternalistic, relation with this workforce. He fostered generous social welfare arrangements and good labour relations, using a factory consultative council. He had a passion for quality and demanded much from his workers, each of whom he knew personally. He was remembered as a generous and humane employer. His civic contributions were legion. He was mayor of Kensington and Norwood for eight years, a member of the Norwood School Board, and a founding member of the Municipal Tramways Trust where he initiated moves for the electrification of the system. He acted as chief magistrate in the eastern suburbs and was chairman of a committee formed to draft a bill for town planning. In 1904, he established the Norwood Cottage Homes for the aged poor. He was president of the YMCA and supported the government's Parkside Mental Asylum. He was a deacon and Sunday School superintendent in his local church for many years and was president of the Baptist Union of South Australia in 1899.[72]

(David) Fletcher Jones was likewise a legend among businessmen in Australia in the interwar period. He was a dedicated Methodist lay leader. A returned serviceman from the Great War, Jones began with a hawker's wagon in western Victoria and eventually built a vast business empire. He ran his business on consultative and co-operative principles, involving his employees in the management of his business because he believed that spiritual growth was achieved through productive and satisfying work and that the object of business should be social advance rather than individual profit. He was a staunch Labor Party supporter until the advent of Gough Whitlam in

71 Hoyle, *Jock Garden*, 140–156.

72 Sydney A. Cheney, *From Horse to Horsepower* (Adelaide: Rigby, 1965).

1972.[73] When he died in 1977, his company employed almost 3,000 workers in four factories and in thirty-three stores all over Australia. Gregarious and affable, a non-smoker and a teetotaller, he was exceptionally active in both his local community and in the Warrnambool Methodist Church.[74] He was revered as one of the most forward-looking, worker sensitive, and humane of Australian businessmen.[75]

Holden and Fletcher Jones were masters of all they surveyed, combining robust, outward faith, with conspicuous success in the realms of business and public life. But, perhaps increasingly, evangelicals were finding it harder to keep it all together. It was a reflection on the growing specialisation and secularisation that some seemed to feel it necessary to depart from the evangelicalism of their youth in order to make their way in the world. This might have been truer of the reflective types than of business men who typically found faith and commerce mutually galvanising. Two evangelicals who returned sadder but wiser from the war would make names for themselves in journalism and radio broadcasting. Church of England chaplain Kenneth Henderson left the ministry after the war in the conviction that churches must depart from colonial and traditional views and foster a national outlook that was more 'personal and experimental'.[76] His real contribution to the world of religion came with his selection to oversee religious broadcasting for ABC Radio in 1941, a position he held until 1956. He died in 1965, a man of faith, but it was not clear what kind of faith. In a similar manner, after experiencing the horrors of the Western Front, a young Methodist minister named Dick Boyer, who served as a line officer in the Great War, returned to civilian life shaken and cynical. He abandoned his earlier faith sometime in the 1920s and became a stockman and a major figure among Australian graziers. After performing many civic good deeds in the interwar period, he was appointed to the board of the ABC in 1940, becoming chairman in 1945. He held this position until his death in 1961, guiding the ABC through many periods of political controversy. Geoffrey Bolton, his biographer, judged him to be a 'humanist'

---

73 Jones believed that Whitlam was an agnostic and, therefore, he publicly renounced his formidable support of the Labor Party.

74 A Trades Union Secretary once introduced Jones: 'Meet Fletcher Jones, the only clothing manufacturer in Australia who doesn't own a race-horse.' Fletcher Jones, *Not By Myself: The Fletcher Jones Story*, 2nd ed. (Cheltenham: Kingfisher, 1984), xvi.

75 John Lack, 'Jones, Sir David Fletcher', *ADB*; Jones, *Not By Myself*, xviii-xix, 95–97, 194–198 and 214–232.

76 Graeme Davison, 'Religion', in Alison Bashford and Stuart Macintyre, (eds.), *The Cambridge History of Australia* 2 vols (Port Melbourne; New York: CUP, 2013), vol.2, 224.

when he died. But he was no 'secular humanist': he thought often and deeply about faith and retained a connection with the Presbyterian Church till his death.[77] The Boyer Lectures are sponsored annually by the ABC in his honour.

The commitment of the churches to engagement in public life is well illustrated by the extensive use they came to make of broadcasting. Cautious at first, evangelicals began to use the new radio technology in the mid-1920s. In 1924, the Congregational Church in Pitt Street, Sydney, then still a strong evangelical institution, broadcast one of its services. The Salvation Army soon followed with a broadcast of Christmas music in Adelaide on Radio 5DN that same year. In 1925, 5DN began regular broadcasts of services from a variety of churches. In 1931, the Roman Catholic Church formed the Catholic Broadcasting Company Ltd and founded Radio 2SM, and the evangelicals obtained a licence to establish radio station 2CH in Sydney, sponsored by the evangelical-oriented NSW Council of Churches. Frederick Stewart, a prominent businessman and Member of Parliament, provided the financial backing. When the station began broadcasting in 1932, Stewart announced at its opening that 2CH's mission was 'to educate, to evangelise, and to edify'. Sunday was dedicated to the churches, and free time was allocated for daily devotions from Monday through Saturday amidst the regular non-religious programs. This arrangement continued for many years.

In the meantime, during the 1930s, many religious broadcasts began to fill the airwaves from a variety of stations all over Australia. In this period, the Seventh-day Adventists made effective use of radio to evangelise the public, most notably with the 'Advent Choir' heard from Radio 2UE and the ministry of Pastor Charles Boulting over the radio in Mildura. In 1938, Adventist leader Laurie C. Naden established the Advent Radio Church as a popular, regular feature on at least seven stations throughout Australia. It was also during the 1930s that several evangelical ministers became household names in certain areas, such as Baptist minister Leslie J. Gomm in Newcastle, and Anglican priest Reginald G. Nichols in Melbourne who became a noted radio personality as 'Brother Bill'. Also in Melbourne, Methodist ministers J.H. Cain and Irving Benson became celebrated radio preachers through their effective use of the new medium. From the late 1930s Anglican college principal T.C. Hammond in Sydney also gained considerable notoriety as a radio personality as he engaged in his sometimes fierce controversies over the airwaves with the

77 Robert Trumble, *Kenneth Thorne Henderson: Broadcaster of the Word* (Richmond: Spectrum Publications, 1988); Geoffrey C. Bolton, *Dick Boyer: An Australian Humanist* (Canberra: Australian National University Press, 1967), 1–17; Marion Consandine, 'Boyer, Richard', *ADB*.

star of Roman Catholic radio, the Rev. Dr. Leslie Rumble. By the end of the decade, evangelicals throughout Australia were regularly and fully engaged in the use of radio as a means of religious outreach.[78]

In terms of social improvement in particular, evangelicals in the 1920s and 1930s continued to expend a great deal of energy trying to persuade Australians to give up grog and gambling. Fresh from victories during the war when hotel drinking hours were restricted and intrigued by the great American experiment with prohibition beginning in 1920, many Australian evangelicals believed that prohibition was the way of the future in the Western World. Methodists, Baptists and Churches of Christ generally backed the movement in Australia while large sections of the Church of England, the Presbyterian Church and the Lutherans were not so sure. Yet Sydney Anglican ministers Francis Bertie Boyce and R.B.S. Hammond were among those most dedicated to the movement to eradicate alcohol from society in the belief that it was one of the most significant causes of the poverty that they saw all around them. Hammond especially pushed for prohibition and exalted in the title 'the Wowser'. In one big push, the NSW Temperance Alliance managed to place the matter of prohibition on the ballot in 1928. There was great enthusiasm for this cause, but few funds. His opponents, on the other hand, spent lavishly. On 2 September, the voters rejected prohibition by an overwhelming majority of 826,762 to 331,085. Even though Hammond and many other evangelicals still harboured the dream of a drink-free nation, it was never to be.[79] It is doubtful, however, that this is evidence of a growing divorce between evangelical culture and common culture. Prohibition was a step too far, but most Australians did not support unrestricted access to alcohol. A NSW referendum to open hotels on Sundays as late as 1969 was lost overwhelmingly. The opening of hotels on Sundays a decade later was not the will of the people, but resulted from a deal between the powerful liquor industry and the NSW Labor Government.

Catholics and most Anglicans were tolerant of minor forms of gambling, such as raffles and bingo, especially when these were organised in order to raise funds for churches or charity. Among evangelicals, however, gambling had no

---

78 Bolton, *Booth's Drum*, 90–91; Clancy and Wright, *The Methodists*, 115; Breward, *A History of the Australian Churches*, 100–101; G.R. Treloar, 'T. C. Hammond the Controversialist', *The Anglican Historical Society Diocese of Sydney Journal*, 51.1, 2006, 20–35; Bridget Griffen-Foley, 'Radio Ministries: Religion on Australian Commercial Radio from the 1920s to the 1960s', *JRH*, 32.1, 2008, 31–54.

79 Robert B.S. Hammond, *With One Voice: A Study of Prohibition in the U.S.A.* (Sydney: NSW Alliance, McDonnel House, 1920); Judd, *He That Doeth*,122–151; *SMH*, 22 May 1928, 12; Rafferty, 'Till Every Foe is Vanquished,' 82–131.

appeal whatsoever and for them it was a sin. It was an offence against the eighth and tenth commandments, which forbade stealing and coveting the possessions of another. It encouraged greed and an inappropriate concern for materialism. Further, it was unjust in that the benefits it provided for a few were at the expense of many. Following this line of reasoning, most evangelicals opposed gambling in all its forms, while the Calvinists among them opposed it on the theological grounds that, since all was predestined, there was no such thing as luck.

In the 1930s, the South Australian government planned to expand opportunities for legalised gambling through the establishment of betting shops and a state lottery. The evangelical churches mobilised their resources and fought against these proposals, with some success and with increasing skill and assurance. They learned how to lobby against gambling as well as to preach about it and how to extract some concessions from the government. In the struggle, the most effective voice raised against gambling came from a new and extraordinarily effective campaigner, the Rev. Percy H. Chennell, the Methodist minister at Kapunda. In 1934, he published a powerful little book entitled *The Sport Without a Smile* that added to the theological and moral arguments against gambling and to the anecdotal evidence about the effects of the practice in South Australia. He introduced historical evidence from Britain and Australia, an analysis of available statistics, and made a study of the role and effect of gambling on the Australian economy. This greatly fortified the anti-gambling forces and reached out to others who shunned moral and theological arguments. It helped greatly to turn back the pro-gambling element in the SA parliament and helped assure the Christians at least a partial victory until the next concerted libertarian campaign in the 1960s and 1970s. The state lottery was defeated, but the betting shops were authorised under what was supposed to be strict government control with the promise that they would drive illegal bookmakers out of business. It was a losing battle, but the evangelicals were determined not to give the gambling and liquor industries free rein.[80]

* * *

Despite the psychological trauma inflicted on survivors by the war and the depletion of its leadership, the evangelical movement between the wars, as we

80 Percy H Chennell, *The Sport Without a Smile* (Adelaide: Gillingham & Company, 1934); Judith Rafferty, *Percy Chennell: The Man Who Killed the Lottery* (Malvern: Uniting Church Historical Society, 1990).

have seen, was able to generate a wide range of innovative ministries for the relief of want. Its membership across the denominations included significant working class representation, especially in the Methodist and Baptist churches as well as the Salvation Army and in some inner-city Anglican congregations. This enabled the movement to be responsive to victims of the Depression. Caring for the national soul in the inter-war decades called for practical activism in support for the economically most vulnerable. A national conscience of care for the unemployed and deprived was nurtured by evangelicals just as they had fostered the national conscience of sacrifice in the Great War. There was no hint among the churches of any inclination to withdraw from the public domain. They continued to accept responsibility for promoting public-spiritedness, dynamic altruism and moral energy. Some, a minority, even sought to contribute to the development of a new social system, to restructure the economy away from the vicissitudes and inequalities of Capitalism.

Focussing on individual initiatives is required by the history of evangelicalism as it is a movement which prizes individual effort. Clearly, all this effort was evidence of general self-sacrifice and occasional creativity. But this was not enough. Neither the early emergency measures taken by the churches in response to the Depression, nor the later more mature schemes for social reconstruction, nor the political commitments of numbers of socially-engaged evangelicals, had been sufficient to save all Australians from the worst effects of homelessness and unemployment. Their failure bore testimony to the enormity of the challenge, demonstrating that governments would have to be responsible for the massive social engineering required for the erection of the welfare state. That was not to come until during and after the Second World War. But then, as will be shown, churches retained a major role in welfare delivery, earned by their demonstrated effectiveness in that role. This policy of church and state interdependence in welfare delivery, in marked contrast to that of other Western countries, was the outcome of unpredictable political realities, reflecting the uneven power which churches were able to exercise in the different States and legislatures.

Just how effective in social welfare and caring for the national soul the churches were between the wars will be debated by historians. The churches would probably have done better had they not been distracted by a major challenge to their very essence: theological liberalism, or as it was more commonly known at the time, modernism. It brought to some of the older denominations, where evangelicalism had reigned undisturbed, confidence-sapping uncertainty.

Chapter Four

THEOLOGICAL WARFARE BETWEEN THE WARS

'If what Dr Angus tells us is true, there is no hope for any of us. There is no message of the Cross. There may be a philosophy; but there is no gospel of salvation to preach, only ethics'
(Wilfrid L. Jarvis).

Theological liberalism or modernism, clearly on the rise before World War I, now laid siege to the citadel of Australian evangelicalism. It was not a battle purely internal to the movement. Many Australians were interested in the issue of the Bible's authority and were attracted to liberal Protestantism and were often intrigued by what it had to offer.[1] In this respect, attending to the national soul called for an intellectual response in defence of a consciousness grounded in Christian truth. The fiercest battle against modernism was waged in the 1930s, mainly within the NSW Presbyterian Church. There theologian Samuel Angus came to personify opposition to the belief, fundamental to evangelical Christianity, that the Bible is the unique Word of God. Fear of contamination from Angus was felt in all denominations (even Roman Catholic) and all States of the Commonwealth. An earlier battle over modernism was fought in the 1920s by the Methodists in a controversy over theologically-liberal content in *Peake's Commentary on the Bible*. Western Australia had its own modernist *cause célèbre* when in 1929 Nicholas Richards, pastor of Trinity Congregational Church in Perth, gave a series of lectures denying the historical value of the New Testament. These battles within Methodist, Congregational, and Presbyterian denominations were part of the war against theological liberalism then endemic to Western Protestantism. That they were fought in the 1920s and 1930s rather than earlier suggests that

1 For a history of (mainly) liberal Protestant thought in Australia, see Wayne Hudson, *Australian Religious Thought* (Clayton: Monash University Publishing, 2016).

they were not responses to the Great War. Any decline of faith in the Bible cannot be traced to a hypothesised decline in faith in the goodness of God resulting from the horrors of war. Extreme trauma is as likely to strengthen faith as weaken it: the need for grace to survive is usually greater than the need for intellectual answers to the problem of evil. If anything, the Great War discredited rather than reinforced liberalism's questioning of the Bible. The War did not precipitate, but rather forced the postponement, of the battle between modernism and biblical authority.

By the beginning of World War II the evangelicals had found able leaders to defend the faith, assisted by a renaissance in evangelical scholarship. But that was a late development: for most of the 1920s and early 1930s, the situation was parlous. In England, to which most Australian evangelicals continued to look for guidance, evangelical Christianity was at a low ebb, 'in vigour of leadership, intellectual capacity, or largeness of heart',[2] and, for the next two decades, it was 'bumping along the bottom'.[3] In Australia by 1939, clerical Presbyterianism, Methodism, and Congregationalism had largely surrendered to the forces of modernism.

Secularism was also on the march. At the University of Sydney, John Anderson, Professor of Philosophy, gave no quarter in his frontal attack on Christianity in his endeavour to make universities off limits to those who entertained religious views. His strident atheism provoked resistance from all branches of the Lord's army, including modernists. Samuel Angus engaged Anderson with the weapons of the new, liberal 'essential Christianity'; Father Patrick Ryan with the forces of Roman Catholic tradition; and T.C. Hammond, with conservative evangelical apologetics.

Fighting modernism and secularism were only two of the battles Sydney Anglicans engaged in between the wars. There was the ongoing sectarian warfare with Roman Catholics, and there were also struggles within. Archbishop Mowll engaged in an open, painful dispute with his own non-evangelical clergy. There was in addition a rear-guard, hushed-up action against a clandestine cult of sinless perfectionists, who had infiltrated the major evangelical parachurch movements, the Intervarsity Fellowship and the Scripture Union. Evangelicals were now fighting on so many fronts that they had far less time and energy to engage with the wider community in constructing a Christian

---

2 Adrian Hastings, *A History of English Christianity, 1920–1985* (London: Collins, 1986), 200.

3 David L. Edwards, 'Evangelicals All', *Church Times,* 29 November 1985, quoting Dr Jim Packer.

nation. It was a movement in danger of turning in on itself in spite of the voluminous, though uncoordinated, reactive care work done by the churches.

Samuel Angus

When Dr Samuel Angus and Katherine Walker Angus, his wealthy American-born, chronically-ill spouse, disembarked from the RMS *Orsova* at Circular Quay in Sydney on 26 February 1915, they did not plan to die on Australian soil, though both did. Like most of the academic neophytes who came to Sydney and Melbourne in that era, Angus expected to spend a time of apprenticeship in 'the colonies' and then return to the Mother Country to take up his real life's work. In the meantime, he would attempt to bring as much enlightenment as possible to antipodean Presbyterians.[4]

Angus's outward appearance and demeanour were those of a cultivated British gentleman. He was no mate or digger, and he knew precious little about the land where he would spend the remainder of his life. He had earned the BA and MA degrees in Classics at University College, the Royal University of Ireland at Galway, studied in the United States at Princeton Theological Seminary, and then obtained an MA in 1905 and a PhD in 1906, both in Classics, from Princeton University. He had studied and taught at the Hartford Theological Seminary in Connecticut in America from 1906 to 1910; and, in the years 1910 to 1913, had undertaken further postgraduate work at the Universities of Marburg and Berlin in Germany and Edinburgh in Scotland. His academic credentials were impressive and dazzled many Australians, especially those in the churches, who assumed that education would always support orthodoxy.[5] There was no reason to doubt what his galaxy of evangelical referees said of him and what he himself affirmed when he took his ordination vows and pledged his allegiance to the Westminster Confession of Faith on 2 March 1915: that he was an orthodox Presbyterian and a loyal evangelical son of his church.[6] He would surely help guide believers through

---

4 Susan Emilsen, *A Whiff of Heresy: Samuel Angus and the Presbyterian Church in New South Wales* (Kensington: UNSW Press, 1991), 78–95.

5 Angus outlined his own career in his 'Biographical Catalogue', January 1932, Samuel Angus File, Alumni Records Sequence Number 5272, Princeton Theological Seminary Archives, Princeton, New Jersey, USA.

6 'Commission of the New South Wales General Assembly', October 1913, in *Blue Book* (Minutes of the General Assembly of the Presbyterian Church of NSW), 1914, 4; 109–12; *Minutes of the Presbytery of Sydney*, 2 March 1915, 41–4; Presbyterian Church of Australia, *The Procedure and Practice of the Presbyterian Church of Australia* (Sydney: Presbyterian Church of NSW, 1926), I:123, 186–8.

the treacherous shoals of the new biblical scholarship and stabilise 'the good ship orthodoxy' in Australia.

All was well for the first dozen or so years of Angus's teaching ministry in Sydney. His first book, *The Environment of Early Christianity* (1915), was well received and deemed a useful monograph by both evangelical and non-evangelical reviewers. Behind the scenes during this period, however, Angus, along with seven other Sydney clergymen, formed a private theological discussion group, which came to be known as 'The Heretics Club'. It was born on 8 June 1916, and, according to future member Anglican Canon Arthur Garnsey, 'was largely the product of Angus's fertile and lively mind'. Membership was limited to ten, and soon included six Presbyterians, two Anglicans, one Congregationalist and one Methodist. Angus was elected its first secretary. The club's objective was to make possible the adventurous discussion of theological matters in a comprehensive, experimental and free-ranging spirit, which challenged what its members perceived to be the prevailing opinions in the Australian churches of the day. Significantly, at its second meeting, Angus presented the first paper to be read before the group: 'The Christology of the Epistle to the Hebrews'. Clearly Angus was in the process of rethinking his evangelical convictions early in his Australian sojourn – but not yet openly.[7] It was in the Methodist church, rather than the Presbyterian, that theological controversy first threatened to tear down the walls of the orthodoxy shared by all members of the evangelical family.

The Methodists and Dr A.S. Peake

In the 1920s the controversy over *Peake's Commentary on the Bible,* greatly troubled Methodists Australia-wide, perhaps because Peake was 'one of their own'. Heavily indebted to British Methodism from their beginnings in Australia, most Methodist ministerial theological institutions in the interwar period used *Peake's Commentary*, or at least included it in their training syllabus. First published in 1919, it almost immediately brought the questions of biblical authority, experience and doctrine to the fore.

Arthur S. Peake, son of an English Primitive Methodist minister and himself a local preacher in that denomination, was Britain's foremost Methodist scholar

7 David Garnsey, *Arthur Garnsey: A Man for Truth and Freedom* (Sydney: Kingsdale Press, 1985), 180–9; Ken J. Cable, 'The First and Second Book of Chronicles: A History of the Heretics Club', in William W. Emilsen and Geoffrey R. Treloar (eds), *The Heretics Club 1916–2006* (University of Sydney: Origen Press, 2009), 1–28; Geoffrey R. Treloar, 'The Heretics, 1916–2016', *St Mark's Review,* 242, December 2017, 6–19.

at the turn of the century. Born in 1865, he became a distinguished authority on the Bible and well versed in the methodology of the new higher criticism from study at Oxford and in Germany. He spent 37 years at the Primitive Methodist Theological Training College in Manchester, during which most of that time he also served as Professor of Biblical Criticism and Exegesis at the University of Manchester. More than any other in world Methodism, he was responsible for introducing Protestants to the literary-historical analysis of the Scriptures.[8]

Six years in the making, Peake's influential general Bible *Commentary* finally appeared in 1919. Peake was the editor and a major contributor to the work. In the Preface, he explained the purpose of the volume:

> The present work is designed to put before the reader in a simple form, without technicalities, the generally accepted results of Biblical Criticism, Interpretation, History and Theology. It is not intended to be homiletic or devotional, but to convey with precision, and yet in a popular and interesting way, the meaning of the original writers, and reconstruct the conditions in which they worked … It has been the desire of the promoters that it should be abreast of the present position of scholarship, and yet succeed in making the Scriptures live for its readers with something of the same significance and power that they possessed for those to whom they were originally addressed.[9]

Peake had no intention of altering the basic teachings of Christianity, only clarifying their source. He argued that the critical study of the Bible was not destructive of devotion to its climactic figure, Jesus Christ. He was one of that first generation of 'liberal evangelicals' trying to come to terms with the new scholarship.

He was 'too liberal' for many Methodists in Britain, America and Australia. In 1921, prominent Methodist layman and philanthropist G.E. Ardill,[10] Secretary of the newly formed and short-lived Christian Fundamentals League in Sydney, criticised Peake's *Commentary* for its 'destructive tendency'. He objected to Peake's claims that the Genesis story of beginnings was

---

8 John T. Wilkinson, *Arthur Samuel Peake, 1865–1929: Essays in Commemoration* (London: Epworth Press, 1958), 9–12, 57; John T. Wilkinson, *Arthur Samuel Peake: A Biography* (London: Epworth Press, 1971), 1–17.

9 Arthur S. Peake (ed.), *Peake's Commentary on the Bible* (Edinburgh: T. C. and E. C. Jack, 1919), Preface, ix.

10 Brian Dickey, *No Charity There: A Short History of Social Welfare in Australia* (Sydney: Allen & Unwin, 1980, 1987), 82f.

incompatible with present knowledge about the earth's creation, that much of the Old Testament was allegory, and that Jesus was fallible when he spoke on matters of history and science. He was joined in his opposition to Peake by the Rev. Isaac Rooney of South Australia who asserted that it would be a miracle if students retained their faith after studying the *Commentary*. The Rev. Dr J.E. Carruthers, long-time Methodist leader and power broker, also opposed Peake mainly because he believed that Peake substituted natural for supernatural Christianity.[11]

In Victoria in the early 1920s, W.H. Fitchett, evangelical elder statesman and now octogenarian, locked horns over the Peake *Commentary* with younger 'liberal evangelical' theologian, Arthur E. Albiston, and others of a similar theological persuasion. Fitchett had become increasingly concerned following World War I over trends in ministerial education at Queen's College, the Methodist theological training school at the University of Melbourne. Fitchett, whom we met in chapter 1 as a fierce advocate of the imperial idea, was well read, an impressive preacher, and a fierce apologist for the Christian faith. He wielded considerable influence among Victorian evangelicals in general through *The Southern Cross*, the interdenominational weekly that he had founded in 1882. But by the 1920s, he was frail and by all accounts past his prime.[12]

Albiston, the son of a Methodist minister, was twenty-five years Fitchett's junior and only recently embarked on his career as Professor of Theology at Queen's College, a position he held from 1920 to 1939. Unlike Fitchett, he published nothing and left few literary remains. His influence came largely through his preaching style, especially his mellifluous voice, and, like Angus, through his devoted former students.[13] When Fitchett attempted to take his case to drop Peake's *Commentary* as a required text for theological students at Queen's College before the Victorian and Tasmanian Methodist Conference of 1921, Albiston worked behind the scenes to block him. The Rev. A. Percy Bladen, the Conference President, ruled that Fitchett's resolution was out of order. He was denied permission to speak and his resolution

---

11 *The Methodist*, 8 January 1921, 12; 6 August 1921, 9, 12.

12 Benson, 'The Life and Times of Dr William Henry Fitchett', 3–16; Wood, '*Not Lost but Gone Before*', 48–51; Robert D. Linder, 'William Henry Fitchett (1841–1928): Forgotten Methodist 'Tall Poppy', in Geoffrey R. Treloar and Robert D. Linder (eds.), *Making History for God: Essays on Evangelicalism, Revival and Mission* (Sydney: Robert Menzies College, 2004), 197–238.

13 Wood, '*Not Lost but Gone Before*', 1–4; A. Harold Wood, *A.E. Albiston: Preacher and Teacher* (Mont Albert: Privately Printed, 1989), 1–46.

dismissed on a technicality without debate. He later learned that a committee dominated by Albiston had counselled dismissal.[14]

When debate on his resolution was denied, Fitchett published it in *The Southern Cross*. He then wrote and printed a small booklet from his notes for the presentation he had not been allowed to make at Conference in 1921. It was forty-seven pages in length and appeared early in 1922 with the title *A Tattered Bible and a Mutilated Christ: Ought a Christian Church to Accept This?* The little booklet became the outline of *Where the Higher Criticism Fails*, a much more substantial work published later in 1922. Fitchett's thesis was that many of the higher critics appeared to 'rob the Bible both of its message and its authority'. He asserted that after they have questioned the reliability of the Bible and the deity of Jesus, Christians are left without a God-Man able to save sinners. Christianity without Christ, he concluded, 'would leave Jewish history without an explanation, and the Bible without meaning'. On the one hand, he argued, it is reasonable for 'the common man' to look to Christian scholars for guidance in these matters. On the other, it seemed that, in recent years, that guidance often made 'theories' appear as facts. The higher critics robbed Christians of the Christ they knew, and gave them 'a Christ whittled down into insignificance; a Christ convicted of ignorance and mistakes'. Therefore, Fitchett concluded: 'The Christ of his hymns and prayers beneath the acid of the Higher Criticism turns out to be a mournfully unmiraculous figure'.[15]

Fitchett continued to argue until his death in 1928 for the maintenance of the supernatural element in historic Christianity over and against naturalistic materialism. Undoubtedly the majority of the Methodist ministers in the pulpits and the overwhelming majority of the people in Methodist pews in the period agreed with him. However, the spirit of the times was against him. For one thing, the Australian Methodists were still reeling from their losses in World War I, and most had little appetite for theological concerns that seemed to be calling for more conflict. Further, the intellectual tide was running in favour of the higher critics who too quickly took control of the Methodist theological colleges. An entire generation of Methodist ministers were being inculcated with what seemed at the time 'the certainties' of the

14 Dallas Clarnette, 'An Historical Introduction', in W.H. Fitchett, *A Tattered Bible and a Mutilated Christ: Ought a Christian Church to Accept This?* reprt. ed. (Ballarat: Harry Brown & Co., 1972), 3–4. Clarnette concluded (p.4) that '1921 was the year that Victorian Methodism officially apostasised from Biblical and Historical Christianity'.

15 W.H. Fitchett, *Where the Higher Criticism Fails* (London: The Epworth Press, 1922), 18,19, cf. 149.

new scholarship. By the end of the 1930s, the liberal evangelicals had given way to genuine theological liberals. The former were open to biblical criticism on the grounds that it clarified the meaning of Scripture. The latter, in the belief that it undermined Scripture, took reason as their authority instead. The eventual results for the Methodist denomination proved to be devastating as Methodists drifted from their historical theological moorings. The tide was receding for evangelical Methodism.

Samuel Angus's True Colours

In January 1923 Samuel Angus, hitherto restrained in his expressions of heterodoxy, let down his guard in a widely-reported address on 'The Bible' to a Student Christian Movement Conference at Parramatta. Angus urged his young hearers not to deify the Bible because it was a human-made book, containing mistakes and, on occasion, images of God that were repugnant to modern Christians. In response, the Victorian Presbyterian leader J. Lawrence Rentoul privately counselled Angus to refrain from 'modernist pronouncements', eschew subjective interpretations of Jesus and the Bible, stop undercutting orthodoxy, and return to his evangelical heritage.[16]

Appropriately considering the long-term influence Angus would exercise among Methodists, the earliest evangelical attack came from their ranks and not from NSW Presbyterians. Angus had begun teaching Methodist students in 1918 as a member of the new Joint Theological Faculty (Presbyterians, Methodists, Congregationalists) formed to strengthen common theological education among evangelical Protestants. Agitated by reports from Methodist students of Angus's 'modernist' teachings, the denominational leader, Dr J.E. Carruthers and J. Ward Harrison, minister of the Botany Methodist Church and editor of the holiness magazine *Glad Tidings*, moved during the 1923 Conference that Methodist students be withdrawn from Angus's classes. Their motion was defeated, but the Conference agreed to set up a committee to inquire into the matter.

There ensued three major confrontations over Angus within the Presbyterian Church in the periods 1929–1933, 1934–1936 and 1939. The first broke out in 1929 when he published *Religious Quests of the Graeco-Roman World.* His colleague at St. Andrew's Theological Hall, the denominational politician R.G. Macintyre, reviewed it critically in *SMH*.[17] Macintyre alleged that Angus's

16 J.L. Rentoul to Samuel Angus, 21 August 1923, MSS in File Folder: Angus, Rev. S., 1922–29, Box 6/3, Ferguson Memorial Library, Sydney.

17 *SMH*, 9 November 1929, 11.

book was deliberately provocative, privileged pagan philosophy over Christian theology, and dismissed both the virgin birth and traditional Presbyterian teaching about the sacraments as derivative from pagan religion.

A number of Presbyterian leaders also expressed concern over reports of Angus's increasingly open opposition to established church doctrine and creeds. Chief among them was Robert J.H. McGowan, pastor of Ashfield Presbyterian Church. He defeated Angus for the Moderatorship of the NSW Presbyterian Assembly in 1931 by a vote of 116 to 14, a stark measure of increasing discomfort with Angus. Then, in April 1932, the Methodist Conference voted to withdraw their theological students from further instruction by Angus, a decision that prevailed until 1937.

The first official charges against Angus were laid by Joseph Fulton, a retired Ulster-born Presbyterian minister. In May 1932, Fulton petitioned the NSW General Assembly to examine allegedly heretical teachings in the theological college that were white-anting the Church and driving it towards Unitarianism. Sydney newspapers became fascinated with the case, with *SMH* adopting an anti-Angus stance while *The Daily Telegraph* and *The Sun* were in Angus's corner.

Throughout 1933 McGowan appealed to the various courts of the Presbyterian Church to consider the Angus case: the Presbytery of Sydney, the NSW General Assembly, and the General Assembly of the Presbyterian Church of Australia. To the second Angus gave his assurance of adherence 'without mental reservation' to the Presbyterian doctrine of the church. It, therefore, expressed its confidence that Angus did not hold beliefs concerning Christ that were contrary to the faith of the Church as expressed in its historic creeds.[18]

The second period of confrontation, dragging on painfully from 1934 to 1936, began with the publication of his most theologically radical book, *Truth and Tradition*. It was first and foremost a polemic, a work of controversy designed to shock rather than persuade his opponents. He argued that the church must rethink its historic beliefs. Its Calvinist God must be rejected in favour of the Father of the Prodigal Son, the Trinity must be discarded because it was incomprehensible and irrelevant, the virgin birth must be abandoned because it was historically impossible, the atonement must be dismissed as untenable, Jesus as Emmanuel, God with us, was to be replaced by Jesus the Divine Son, and the physical resurrection of Jesus must be strongly challenged as ancient myth.

---

18 Rowland Ward, *The Bush Still Burns, the Presbyterian and Reformed Faith in Australia 1788–1988* (St. Kilda: Presbyterian Church of Eastern Australia, 1989), 338.

Ultimately, he maintained, his Church must choose between creed and conduct, fiction and faith, tradition and truth, Presbyterianism and true Christianity.

The response was swift. Macintyre, in his *The Theology of Dr Angus,* which appeared on 9 May 1934, expressed his 'deep shock' at the new revelation of Angus's views. To Macintyre, it was now clear that Angus rejected the basic doctrines of Christianity. Another major attack followed from the pen of Roman Catholic apologist Dr Leslie Rumble, who on 15 May released his new book *Dr Angus – or Christ.* He denounced Angus's departure from Christian orthodoxy and assured his audience that this kind of thing would never be tolerated in the Roman Catholic Church.[19]

The NSW General Assembly met in an atmosphere of crisis in May 1934. There was now great fear that the Angus issue would split the Church. After more accusations, hand wringing, solemn promises and compromises, the body again voted to do virtually nothing. Angus again repented and promised to behave himself, and the Assembly by a 174 to 83 vote declared its belief that the Presbyterian Church was sufficiently broad to allow for people of different views to exist within its ecclesiastical family.[20]

Angus's wife died in November 1934, and Angus himself was ailing badly and entered hospital for treatment, most likely for some form of cancer. After convalescence, Angus resumed his duties at the theological college in March 1936. McGowan and A.J. Carter, minister of the Church at Ebenezer/Portland Head, appealed the case to the forthcoming General Assembly of Australia to be held in Sydney in September, and over one-third of the decisions made at the 1936 Assembly were related to Angus, mainly because of a massive petition from concerned Presbyterian ministers and elders of the Church outside of NSW. The petition asked that the General Assembly address the denials made by Angus in *Truth and Tradition* of the Supreme and Subordinate Standards of the Church to which every officeholder was pledged. It asked for decisive action and was signed by 111 ministers and 250 elders, none of whom was from NSW. It signified the widespread unrest now present in the churches that could no longer be ignored.[21] The General Assembly adopted a resolution intended to be a compromise that everybody could live with while at the same time making the displeasure of the churches

19 R.G. Macintyre, *The Theology of Dr Angus: A Critical Review* (Sydney: Angus & Robertson, 1934), 11; Leslie Rumble, *Dr Angus – Or Christ* (Sydney: E. J. Dwyer, 1934).

20 *Blue Book*, 1934, 59, 69–72, 150.

21 *SMH*, 11 September 1936, 12; Presbyterian Church of Australia, *Blue Book:* Minutes of Proceedings of the Federal Assembly of the Presbyterian Churches of Australia and Tasmania (Sydney: The Church, 1936), 191–7.

known to Angus. The resolution ended by declaring the case closed.[22] The matter was not closed, of course, but it did signal the awful realisation among Australian Presbyterians that if somebody won, everybody lost.

The third and final battle of the Angus Wars within the Presbyterian Church ensued in 1939, with the publication of Angus's *Essential Christianity*.[23] The patience of the champions of orthodoxy in other denominations was past exhausted. In a widely publicised sermon, Wilfrid L. Jarvis, pastor of the Sydney Central Baptist Church, declared 'If what Dr. Angus tells us is true, there is no hope for any of us. There is no message of the Cross. There may be a philosophy; but there is no gospel of salvation to preach, only ethics'.[24] Most Presbyterians who read *Essential Christianity* saw it as yet another defiance by Angus of the deliberations of the official standards of the Church. It contained many of the same 'modernist themes' found in more brazen form in *Truth and Tradition*. It seemed clear that Angus had breached the trust of the 1936 resolution and that something needed to be done.[25]

The Angus case therefore again dominated the proceedings of the National General Assembly in Melbourne in September 1939. German forces had invaded Poland on 1 September, and Australia was again at war. Therefore, the meeting was held in an atmosphere of deep gloom. After a day-long debate on the Angus problem, it was resolved because of the uncertain times to postpone consideration of the matter to the next Assembly in 1942. The resolution to defer the matter passed by a vote of 155 to 100, indicating continuing strong concern that further steps were needed to deal with Angus.[26] With that action, even though those present had no way of knowing this, the Angus case was over. The crisis of Australian survival in World War II and Angus's continuing decline in health precluded any further pursuance of the matter in 1942. Moreover, Angus's scholarship and his liberal theology were now badly out-of-date, and the war destroyed what was left of the optimism of theological liberalism and its vision of a new world order. Events had simply overtaken the issues involved in the Angus case and made it irrelevant. Theology in general had moved on to neo-orthodoxy and its repudiation of liberalism, and the Australian evangelicals were beginning to renew themselves from within.

---

22 Presbyterian Church of Australia, *Blue Book*, 1936, 40–2.

23 Samuel Angus, *Essential Christianity* (Sydney: Angus and Robertson, 1939).

24 *SMH*, 8 May 1939, 16; Wilfred L. Jarvis, *New Testament Christianity and the Philosophy of Dr S. Angus* (Sydney: W. L. Jarvis, 1939).

25 For relevant correspondence, see Box 6/3, Ferguson Memorial Library.

26 Presbyterian Church of Australia, *Blue Book*, 1939, 72–8.

At the 1942 National General Assembly nothing further was done with Angus. Australian fortunes were at a low ebb as the nation braced itself for a possible Japanese invasion, and Angus himself was obviously near to death. Even though there were still several petitions concerning the case from his old opponents, by common consent they were ignored. Instead, it was moved: 'That all communications dealing in any way whatsoever with the case of Dr Angus be discharged from the Business Paper of this Assembly …' This motion was unanimously approved. And with that, the most famous heresy case in Australian history came to an end.[27]

The end was also near for Angus himself. With a heightened sense of his own mortality, he attempted to complete a number of academic and personal projects. He concentrated on what might be called social criticism, political ethics and personal memoirs. His *Man and the New Order*, published in 1942, presented little hope for Australia's present and future prospects and promoted social Darwinism. He argued the case of the social conservative, anticipating the future right-wing political career of his university friend and associate Enoch Powell, Professor of Greek at the University of Sydney (1937–39). Angus denounced the wartime socialist government of John Curtin and prophesied a bleak, collectivised future for Australia.[28]

Angus also published in September 1943 a bittersweet autobiographical work entitled *Alms for Oblivion: Chapters from a Heretic's Life*.[29] It is an account of shattered dreams and a lament on Australian society. His final years were dogged by reactions to his right-wing political views, his stated pro-German sympathies, and his alleged anti-Semitism. He remained a fascist sympathiser and harboured pro-German sympathies until the outbreak of World War II in 1939, when his career as a political commentator came to an abrupt end. Angus died of cancer on 17 November 1943. His estate was probated at £31,694, most of which was left to his relatives in Ireland. Perhaps that was his final farewell to the land in which he had invested so much of his life as an intellectual missionary and in which he had experienced so much anguish.

The Theological Struggle in the West

In WA, the argument over the Bible and the new scholarship seemed to engulf the entire Perth Christian community rather than being focused on

27 Presbyterian Church of Australia, *Blue Book*, 1942, 43.

28 Samuel Angus, *Man and the New Order* (Sydney: Angus & Robertson, 1942), 27–33, 61–75, 102, 120.

29 Samuel Angus, *Alms for Oblivion: Chapters from a Heretic's Life* (Sydney: Angus & Robertson, 1943).

any one major evangelical denomination. The central figures in the Perth controversy in 1929 were Carment Urquhart, pastor of the Maylands and Victoria Park Baptist churches, and Nicholas Richards, pastor of the Trinity Congregational Church in Perth. Urquhart founded the Perth Bible Institute (PBI, now Perth Bible College) in 1928 and served as its principal from 1928 until his death in 1945. Its four-point platform was a reflection of Urquhart's view of himself: 'interdenominational, evangelical, biblical, and missionary'. Though basically a shy man, on the speaker's platform Urquhart could be fierce and uncompromising. He saw evolution and higher criticism as threats to the Christian faith and wrote a number of books against them.[30]

Urquhart's concern to defend the evangelical faith became a *cause célèbre* in Perth in 1929 when Nicholas Richards began a series of Wednesday evening lectures on 'What Is the Bible?' in which he introduced the new ideas of biblical criticism to his audience. A Welshman, Richards held an MA from Oxford University and a BD, a prestigious theological degree in the early twentieth century. His substantial education, his keen sense of humour and strong personality, and his cultivated accent immediately gave him a prominent place in the Perth community. He arranged for a radio broadcast of Trinity's morning services to the public each Sunday.[31] He was up to date and apparently upset by what he considered the narrow-mindedness of many of his colleagues. He was prepared to enlighten them, which he did in his sermons, evening lectures and denominational addresses. By 1929, he had a reputation as a stirrer in the community and had come to the attention of the evangelical leadership of Perth, including Urquhart, George Tulloch of St. Andrew's Presbyterian Church in central Perth, Edward Hogg, a prominent Baptist minister, and Herbert King, rector of St. Matthew's Church of England, Guildford. Tulloch, in particular, became Urquhart's close friend and firm supporter, both in this conflict and in the life of PBI. Known as 'Roaring George', Tulloch was an eloquent and passionate preacher who had little use for theological liberals.[32]

---

30 Irene M. Spice, *Carment Urquhart and His Vision, the Perth Bible Institute* (Perth: Privately Printed by Irene Spice, 1993), 21–85, 195–202; Richard K. Moore, *A Centenary History of the Baptist Denomination in Western Australia, 1895–1995* (Perth: The Baptist Historical Society of Western Australia, 1996), 112, 298–299; Rev. Max Wells interviewed by Linder, 28 July 1995; Hensley White to Linder, 15 December 1996.

31 Muriel Brockis, *A History of Trinity Congregational Church, Perth, Western Australia, 1914–84* (Leeds: W.S. Maney and Son, 1988), 20–22; *The West Australian*, 15 June 1929, 6.

32 Brockis, *History of Trinity Congregational Church*, 24; Spice, *Carment Urquhart*, 26–29; Laurie and Ruth Galloway interviewed by Linder, Perth, 27 July 1995.

On Sunday morning 21 July 1929, Richards spoke on 'The Man Who Worked No Miracles,' in which he explained away Jesus' reported wonder-working powers. This broadcast brought a storm of protests. It resulted in a sermonic rebuttal from King at St. Matthew's Church that was quoted at length in *The West Australian*. Urquhart and Tulloch organised a series of lectures to refute Richards' views on three successive Wednesday evenings: 'The Bible and Higher Criticism', 'The Bible and Darwinism', and 'The Bible and Science'. These talks drew large crowds and were later published in book form as *Is The Bible True?*[33] At best the response of the evangelicals was a holding action until the next generation of evangelical scholars could test the validity of the new learning.

The Bible Colleges

The anti-modernist rather than anti-intellectual response to liberalism was chiefly the work of Bible colleges which proliferated across Australia in this period. They were formed, however, not only in response to the modernist takeover of most of the already existing theological colleges, but first and primarily to train future missionaries and lay leaders. Presbyterian minister W. Lockhart Morton, at the suggestion of Hudson Taylor, founder of CIM, established what was to become Angas College in Adelaide in 1893 for the training of male missionaries.[34] In the wake of the 1912 Chapman-Alexander Mission to Australia, Adelaide evangelical leaders in 1914 founded the Chapman-Alexander Bible Institute on the Moody Bible Institute pattern. Angas College collapsed when Morton returned to Melbourne in 1920 and CABI ceased to exist in 1926. The Bible college with the longest continuous existence in Australian history is the Sydney Missionary and Bible College, established in 1916 by the Rev. C. Benson Barnett, a returned CIM missionary. SMBC described itself as Bible-centred and interdenominational in character and was originally intended to be primarily a missionary training school.[35]

Melbourne Bible Institute (MBI), Adelaide Bible Institute (ABI) and Perth Bible Institute (PBI) followed in the 1920s. MBI (from 1978 the Bible College of Victoria, and from 2010 the Melbourne School of Theology)

33 Carment Urquhart, *Is the Bible True?* (Perth: Perth Bible Institute, 1929).

34 Darrell Paproth, 'Faith Missions, Personality, and Leadership: William Lockhart Morton and Angas College', *Lucas*, 27 & 28, 2000, 64–89.

35 David Parker, 'Fundamentalism and Conservative Protestantism in Australia, 1920–1980,' PhD, University of Queensland, 2 volumes, 1982, 2:541–543; Susan Emilsen, 'Barnett, Charles Benson', *ADEB*.

was established to train missionaries and lay workers in biblical knowledge and evangelism.[36] The original impetus for the founding of MBI came at the end of 1919 when the CIM Council invited C.H. Nash, noted Melbourne Anglican evangelical leader, to become the founding principal of a Bible institute for the training of missionaries.[37] From the college's inception in September 1920, however, Nash made it clear that he also intended MBI to be an evangelical institution of higher learning. Nash believed that the most dangerous enemies of the church were those within who embraced and taught higher criticism and the new science that, in his judgment, undermined the authority of the Bible.[38] The ethos and mission of the new school were made explicit in a public statement Nash issued in August 1920:

> The Melbourne Bible Institute stands four-square for the whole-hearted acceptance of the entire sacred volume of the Old and New Testaments as from God. This is God's Book for the plain man, and to such He will interpret its full meaning progressively by His Holy Spirit ... If the Book is from God, it will bear without loss the sincerest and most searching examination. There is nothing to hide, and nothing to explain away. Its genuineness will defy the acid as well as the sledge-hammer of criticism.[39]

Evangelical Christians in Adelaide, under the leadership of local businessmen James Butler, Samuel Barnett and A. S. (Alec) Jackman and the Rev. Reg Burrow, established the Adelaide Bible Institute (ABI) in 1924. Known initially as the Worldwide Evangelisation Training Centre, the name was quickly changed to ABI (From 1973, the Bible College of South Australia). The initial name, however, indicated the main emphasis of the new institution on evangelism and missions. Local Baptist, Methodist, Presbyterian, Churches of Christ, Brethren Assemblies and independent evangelical churches and leaders enthusiastically supported ABI in its early years. Its initial curriculum

---

36 Darrell Paproth, 'The Melbourne Bible Institute: Its Genesis, Ethos and Purpose', in G.R. Treloar (ed.), *The Furtherance of Religious Beliefs: Essays on the History of Theological Education in Australia* (Sydney: Centre for the Study of Australian Christianity, 1997), 124–155.

37 Paproth, *Failure Is Not Final,* 90–97; John H. McCracken, with Paul and Helen Shelley, *Summing Up: John Harold McCracken1906–1999* (Aranda, ACT: Privately Printed by Heather and Paul Shelley, 2003), 112–113.

38 Paproth, *Failure Is Not Final*, 90–108; W.S. Clack, ed., *We Will Go: The History of 70 Years Training Men and Women for World Missionary Activity* (Melbourne: Bible College of Victoria, 1990), 14–16.

39 Clack, *We Will Go*, 14.

focused on biblical studies and practical theology. It soon added apologetics to fortify its students against the increasing attacks on traditional evangelical beliefs.[40] The Perth Bible Institute was founded in 1928 by the Baptist, Carment Urquhart, who, as we have seen above, was a doughty warrior in defence of evangelical orthodoxy against any modernist inroads.

The Australian Bible colleges have been remarkable for the continuity they have achieved in evangelical doctrine, Keswick piety, and interdenominational comity. They enjoyed until recently a distinctive constituency: faith missions, conventions for the deepening of the spiritual life, evangelistic organisations, independent churches, and lay men and women who felt the need for systematic Bible knowledge. Of the 8,000 students enrolled in Australian Bible Colleges to 1980, it has been estimated that 40% became full-time Christian workers.[41] The stature and long tenure of the early Bible College principals – Morton, Nash, Barnett, Urquhart, and C.J. Rolls – gave the colleges a critical influence in shaping Australian evangelicalism in the second quarter of the twentieth century and protecting it from modernist inroads. The Bible colleges were normally opposed to biblical criticism, theological liberalism, the theory of evolution, and the social gospel. They commonly affirmed premillennialism and biblical inerrancy, and inculcated an appetite for fighting for right doctrine, understood as the virgin birth, atoning death, bodily resurrection, second coming and deity of Christ. These characteristics ensured that the evangelical movement would continue to produce evangelists and missionaries in significant numbers which was the main reason for the foundation of Bible colleges in the first place.

New Reformed Evangelical Leadership

The chief value of the typical Bible college reaction to modernism was that it held the fort until the more extreme and unverified claims of rationalism, science and biblical criticism were tried and found wanting, an outcome still some decades away in the future. The pressing challenge of the moment for the evangelical movement was to find new leaders who could defend the faith intellectually whilst maintaining missionary and spiritual vitality. Liberalism

40 John D. Calvert, 'A History of the Adelaide Bible Institute (ABI), 1924–1962, with Special Reference to the Development of Its Theological Education,' MA Thesis, University of South Australia, November, 2000, 59–70; Bruce S. Bryson, *My Father's House: The Bryson Story of Life on Four Continents* (Adelaide: Gillingham Printers, 1993), 58–59, 105–106.

41 David Parker, 'The Bible College Movement in Australia', unpublished paper, 9th Conference South Pacific Association of Bible Colleges, August 1980, 4–7.

was perceived as killing that vitality, and even liberal evangelicalism seemed to sap it, so the solution was to find leaders who were conservative in faith and powerful in intellect.

Sydney Anglicans resolved the problem with a typically drastic response to a providential opportunity. Within a short space of time in the mid-1930s the liberal evangelical troika of archbishop, Moore College principal, and dean of the cathedral, was removed by death. Conservative evangelicals, determined to appoint a 'definite' evangelical and 'an initiating father in God', elected Howard West Kilvinton Mowll as archbishop.[42] Mowll was a big man with a big voice and, many said, a big heart. 'He's gigantic; he's magnetic; he's courageous; and he's humble' exclaimed one Sydney admirer.[43] He was the most effective of evangelical ecclesiastical leaders to emerge on the Australian scene between the wars, and his episcopate (1933–1958) turned out to be the most momentous in the history of the Sydney diocese. His goal and that of his followers was to make the diocese impregnably evangelical in practice and in spirit. Its reputation as the Protestant Vatican began to spread throughout the world-wide Anglican Communion. Its touchstone of biblical truth as central to Christianity came to be the clearest understanding of evangelical faith in Australia and beyond.

Mowll kept the deanship of the cathedral to himself until 1947 when Stuart Barton Babbage was appointed. Most significantly, Mowll orchestrated the appointment of Thomas Chatterton Hammond as principal of Moore College. Hammond had been the head of the Irish Church Missions based in Dublin for seventeen years before coming to Sydney aged fifty-nine. His Irish Protestant background had moulded his approach to the proclamation of the Gospel, and many in the diocese approved of his uncompromising opposition to theological liberalism and Roman Catholicism.[44] What really attracted Mowll to Hammond, however, was not his pugnacity, but his scholarship. Hammond had been a gold medallist at Trinity College Dublin and was a prolific writer.[45] He was not an original thinker, but he was a deep thinker who became an able theologian.[46] He has been characterised as 'a genuinely Anglican theologian in the evangelical tradition, with a deep respect for

42 Judd and Cable, *Sydney Anglicans,* 226.

43 *Anglican Church Record*, 13 April 1933, 1.

44 Warren Nelson, *T.C. Hammond: His Life and Legacy in Ireland and Australia* (Edinburgh: Banner of Truth Trust, 1994), 71–81.

45 There are almost 100 entries under 'T.C. Hammond' in the Moore College Library catalogue.

46 Nelson, *Hammond*, 92–94.

both Calvin and Butler and arguing for what he on more than one occasion termed a "moderate Calvinism".'[47] His strongly objective theology did not express itself in the Keswick style of spirituality then in vogue, and he set a new fashion of verbal muscularity since accepted by many as the acceptable face of Sydney evangelicalism.

But not by all. Too soon, Mowll, with Hammond's help, found himself in conflict with those in the diocese whose views were theologically different from his own.[48] In the Memorialist Controversy of 1938, a group of so-called 'middle churchmen' within the diocese resisted Mowll's drive to promote a permanent evangelical hegemony in Sydney. Their disenchantment culminated in a Memorial presented to the Archbishop asking for a conference on the basis that:

> in a living church, there must always be a considerable diversity of thought and feeling ... we feel bound to say that Diocesan life in Sydney has for some time been marred by the unhealthy dominance of one school, namely, that of a rather rigid, conservative evangelicalism ... we feel bound to say that time after time we have been baffled by a certain intolerance in members of the dominant party.[49]

There were fifty clerical signatories, with Canon Garnsey, Warden of St Paul's College in the University of Sydney, as their leader.[50] On Hammond's robust advice, Mowll handled the matter legalistically rather than pastorally. He asked each Memorialist to complete a questionnaire as a precondition for a meeting. The Memorialists ignored the requirement and the conference never took place. Correspondence between Garnsey and Mowll was made public. The coming of World War II rescued the Archbishop from further discomfiture, and when Garnsey died in 1943, the controversy died with him, but not the after-effect.[51] 'There comes a time in the life of a diocese when its character is set in concrete. It takes a jack-hammer to change it.' So observed historian Ken Cable, with reference to the history of the Diocese of Sydney.

---

47 Robert Banks, 'Fifty Years of Theology in Australia, 1915–1965, Part One', *Colloquium*, 9.1, 1976, 40.

48 Marcus Loane, *Makers of Our Heritage: A Study of Four Evangelical Leaders* (London: Hodder and Stoughton, 1967), 180–181.

49 Extract 'The Memorial – 1938', quoted in *Anglicans Together*, 50, 2013, 3.

50 This represented approximately one-fifth of the total number of clergy in the diocese. Marcus Loane, *Archbishop Mowll: The Biography of Howard West Kilvinton Mowll* (London: Hodder and Stoughton, 1960), 144.

51 Loane, *Archbishop Mowll*, 144–149; Judd and Cable, *Sydney Anglicans*, 238–240; Garnsey, *Arthur Garnsey*, 162–163.

Historians will debate when the concrete hardened, that is, when the diocese became conservatively evangelical in its inimitable Sydney way. Was it 1938 when the fifty 'memorialists' met with uncompromising rejection from their Archbishop?[52] The majority of Sydney Anglicans apparently preferred the stability of concrete. Judd and Cable note concerning Mowll's first years: 'He wore out chaplains and assistants, but won the hearts of many church people, old and young alike. This high profile, high energy leader gave them a sense of belonging to an active, living Christian community larger than their parish: the Diocese of Sydney'.[53]

It was a more anti-Catholic diocese than ever. Hammond's role as a 'defender of the faith' was especially apparent in his legendary debates with Dr Leslie Rumble of the Roman Catholic Church which were broadcast in Sydney. 'Dr Rumble's Question Box' on Radio 2SM was the best known religious program in Australia until Rumble's retirement in 1968.[54] As a former Anglican himself, Rumble had a solid knowledge of the Bible and tried to use biblical citations to woo Anglicans back to Mother Rome while claiming the Scriptures as the book of the Church. Hammond relished the thought of going on air to refute Rumble and took to the airwaves on Radio 2CH soon after his arrival in Sydney in 1936. He established a pattern whereby he responded to Rumble's 'Question Box' answers by selecting from them for comment certain Roman Catholic doctrines that he considered to be unbiblical. Often these responses were printed in pamphlet form and eventually many of them published as a book, *The Case for Protestantism*.[55] The repartee became so popular that the two radio stations arranged their schedules so that listeners could hear both Hammond and Rumble on any given Sunday evening.[56]

Among Hammond's prolific writings, one book made him famous around the evangelical world: *In Understanding Be Men*.[57] It was not intended to be a systematic theology and, though produced in the 1930s at the apogee of modernism, it did not try to answer the new scholarship. Instead, it buttressed the

52 Stuart Piggin, 'The Properties of Concrete: Sydney Anglicanism and its recent critics,' *Meanjin*, 65.4, 2006, 184–193.

53 Judd and Cable, *Sydney Anglicans*, 230.

54 Leslie Rumble, *Radio Replies in Defence of Religion* (Sydney: Pellegrini, 1934; Griffen-Foley, 'Radio ministries', *JRH*, 32.1, March 2008, 32–36.

55 T.C. Hammond, *The Case for Protestantism* (Sydney: Author, 1960).

56 T.C. Hammond, *Reply to Dr Rumble: Marriage and Education* (Sydney: Criterion Press, n.d.); Donald W.B. Robinson, 'The Reverend Bernard George Judd (1918–1999)', *Lucas: An Evangelical History Review*, 25 & 26 (1999), 180.

57 T.C. Hammond, *In Understanding Be Men: A Synopsis of Christian Doctrine for Non-Theological Students* (London: IVP, 1936).

old evangelical truths with a masterful knowledge of the Church Fathers and Reformation theology, while clearly articulating standard evangelical belief, albeit with a Calvinistic bent. It served its purpose of shoring up evangelical belief in pews and pulpits at a time when such literature was not plentiful. It put backbone into the faith of evangelicals, providing them with a theology rather than just a vague notion of what it was to be a Christian.[58]

Liberalism and Catholicism were easy enemies to identify. But an increasing suspicion of all formulations of the faith which departed in any way from the shibboleths of orthodoxy made conservative Sydney Anglicans condemn those who might have been their friends. One both conservative in theology and powerful in intellect was Swiss Reformed theologian, Karl Barth. The English version of Karl Barth's famous commentary on the Epistle to the Romans appeared in 1933. Barthianism was a powerful refutation of liberal Protestantism. Many Australian Protestants, who had been led into dangerous waters by the liberalism of Samuel Angus, scrambled on board Barth's lifeboat and paddled their way tentatively back towards the safety of the evangelical shore. Evangelicals liked much of what they heard from Barth. Not only did he affirm the rebelliousness of humankind beginning with Adam, 'the man who sinned at once', and the righteousness and omnipotence of the transcendent God, who revealed himself through Christ alone and saved by grace alone, but he insisted that the Bible was the sole source of knowledge about God. Many evangelicals, especially those with a taste for theology, were captivated. Stuart Barton Babbage recorded that his personal addiction to theology dated from his reading of Karl Barth and he even gave his wife Barth's writings to read on their honeymoon. The leading New Testament scholar, Sir Edwyn Hoskyns, according to Babbage, observed that the 'the evangelicals had the ball at their feet, if only they knew it'.[59]

But they either did not know it, or they knew better. His brand of neo-Calvinism was too extreme even for them. Barth wanted to rescue the Christian faith from any dependence on human culture, on history, reason, experience, the visible church, or political power. He argued that the resurrection of Christ should be thought of as a 'non-historical event' because it was too central to the revelation of God to be subjected to the lawlessness of historical relativism. He denied that human society had any affinity with the Kingdom of God, and encouraged the Church to ignore the world. He exalted God by obliterating man. Evangelicals were happy to use this ammunition in

---

58 Nelson, *T.C. Hammond*, 131–134, 159–165.

59 Stuart Barton Babbage, *Memoirs of a Loose Canon* (Melbourne: Acorn Press, 2004), 19, 36.

their bombardment of the liberals, but they could not accept that the Word should be so divorced from the world.

Fundamentalists, too, wanted to separate from the world. But Barth's position was distinguished from that of the fundamentalists in that he insisted that the Bible only became the Word of God when it was interpreted by the Holy Spirit in the life of the believer. Fundamentalists were not the only evangelicals who felt uneasy at Barth's apparent downplaying of the authority of the Bible in its own right. T.C. Hammond, more disposed than most evangelicals to detecting the heresy in the fairest-sounding words, perceived immediately that Barth was no ally of evangelical truth and warned that 'it would be dangerous to allow so stout an opponent to remain unassailed in our rear'.[60] Another who went to great lengths to find Barth wanting was Presbyterian evangelist, Harold Whitney.[61] But, in developing a considered biblical response to Barthianism, mainstream evangelicals brought about a resurgence in Calvinism which excited them. The advent of the *Reformed Theological Review* in 1942 was symptomatic of the revived Calvinism. It was conceived by Robert Swanton, a Melbourne Presbyterian, who was to serve as its editor for over forty years. It fostered evangelical scholarship and Reformed convictions. Swanton had studied history at Melbourne University, writing a thesis on John Dunmore Lang, and in the late 1930s had studied theology at Basel, Switzerland, with Karl Barth himself.

Mowll did more for the cause of the theological defence of Calvinist orthodoxy than appoint Hammond. He also reached out to prominent non-Anglicans. He counted as a personal friend G.H. Morling, who served as the principal of the NSW Baptist Theological College (now named after him) for a remarkable 40 years. Morling had gifts unusual in evangelical circles and seemed an unlikely warrior of the church in its struggle with liberalism. He had a mystical emphasis that drew from a rich variety of spiritual traditions. He did his master's thesis on Francis of Assisi and was a devotee of the Quakers.[62] By nature eirenic and moderate, Morling was probably forced to commit himself and the college more peremptorily to a conservative view of biblical inspiration than he might otherwise have done. With reference to the Angus controversy, he affirmed that the college's policy was 'one of sound

60 T.C. Hammond, *Reasoning Faith: An Introduction to Christian Apologetics* (London: IVF, 1943), 80.

61 H.J. Whitney, *The new heresy* [Katoomba: H.J. Whitney, 198–?].

62 Morling told H. Watkin-Smith he would be quite happy to be a Quaker (comment made at the 1990 Baptist Historical Society AGM, 17 April 1990).

evangelical teaching as opposed to modern theological conceptions',[63] but he left up to C.J. Tinsley, the influential pastor of Stanmore Baptist Church and who could be a harsh critic of modernism, to boast that the college 'had one of the strongest evangelical platforms of any college in the world, being based wholly and solely upon the Word of God'.[64]

Morling was not primarily an apologist or controversialist. He was an exegete and homilist who thought that the best defence of the Bible was to teach it exegetically and experimentally in conventions, in his Thursday night Bible School in which up to 200 people of all denominations enrolled, and in the pages of the *Australian Baptist* where he conducted the Australian Baptist Bible School for a decade. Probably the most important thing he did for the defence of the Bible was to train his students to share his passion for it. But does Morling's rather devotional approach explain why few of his students became what Old Testament scholar John Thompson, from 1966 Reader in Semitic Studies in the University of Melbourne, called 'really solid'?[65] They preached the Word, but neither their doctrine nor their theology was particularly robust, and they rarely made hearty controversialists.

Secularism Rampant: Professor John Anderson

It was at the University of Sydney between the wars that, for the first time in its history, the advocacy of atheism flourished. This was the mission of John Anderson, Challis Professor of Philosophy, a post he held from 1927 to 1958. Anderson broke the idealist philosophical tradition which had prevailed there hitherto, and set Australian philosophy 'on its characteristic course': 'realist (in the sense of being concerned with the ways of working of real things in the world, rather than having our ideas as the central focus of philosophy), materialist, atheist and more interested in criticism than in synthesis or moral uplift'.[66] Anderson rejected all absolutes, except for free thought. He excluded religious people from the Freethought Society, which he founded and of which he was president. He delivered an address for the Freethought

63 Cited in E. Ron Rogers, *George Henry Morling: 'Our Beloved Principal': Baptist Theological College of New South Wales Australia 1923–1960: a definitive biography* (Macquarie Park: Greenwood Press in association with the Baptist Historical Society of NSW, 2014), 109.

64 Rogers, *'Our Beloved Principal'*, 131.

65 John Thompson interviewed by Linder, 28 August 1987.

66 James Franklin, *Corrupting the Youth: A History of Philosophy in Australia* (Sydney: Macleay Press, 2003), 2,3.

Society in which he declared that war memorials were political idols and that religious ceremonies associated with them only served to impede rational evaluation. He gave a series of lectures to the New Education Fellowship entitled 'Religion and Education' in which he argued that religion was always incompatible with education and should be excluded from all involvement in University education. He was particularly cross with students who joined religious societies, which they did, he believed, to 'safeguard themselves in advance against learning anything'.[67]

Anderson assiduously cultivated his students, having lunch with them in the Union, taking afternoon tea with an élite coterie off campus, and often inviting them to his Turramurra home on the weekends for tea and tennis. He delighted them in the classroom with his anti-establishment remarks and his frequent resort to witty sarcasm, including many wisecracks about religion. Under his tutelage, a number of students who entered the university with a religious commitment left with none. He subverted the faith of such future literary luminaries as Donald Horne and James McAuley.[68] Having maintained, in the name of freedom of speech and academic freedom, his right to say what he wanted, Anderson spent most of his time criticising. Franklin concludes that 'there was something emotionally difficult, perhaps arid and cruel, in the relentless "criticism" of the Andersonian school'.[69] In consequence, the University of Sydney during the interwar period changed from a rather benign institution of higher learning into a bastion of militant secularism. It is little wonder that religious liberals like Angus as well as Roman Catholics and evangelicals all opposed his views.

Samuel Angus, as we saw above, was among the first to withstand the Andersonian onslaught, giving public lectures in defence of Christianity in various university venues. He coached members of the Student Christian Movement on how to respond to atheistic arguments. In their eyes, Angus 'effectively silenced' Anderson's claims that cast doubt on the historicity of Jesus.[70] Angus's campaign against Anderson's atheism and public opposition to religion turned many of those who heard him into 'devotees' who came to feel that the Church could not survive without him.[71] Father Paddy Ryan, the

---

67 Franklin, *Corrupting the Youth*, 17f.

68 Donald Horne, *An Interrupted Life* (Sydney: HarperCollinsPublishers, 1998), 187–195, 576–577.

69 Franklin, *Corrupting the Youth*, 37

70 Emilsen, *A Whiff of Heresy*, 180–4.

71 Mark Hutchinson, *Iron in Our Blood: A History of the Presbyterian Church in NSW, 1788–2001* (Sydney: Ferguson Publications and the Centre for the Study of Australian Christianity, 2001), 249.

voice of Catholic apologetics in Sydney in the 1930s and 1940s and opposed to evolution and communism, also stood up to Anderson, debating him in 1936 and again in 1939.[72]

Anderson especially delighted in attacking the Sydney University Evangelical Union, whose members he considered dangerously anti-intellectual. The EU of the 1930s was a spirited group led by such able students as Paul White (the future 'jungle doctor'), Donald Robinson (a future archbishop), and Bill Andersen, a future lecturer in Education in the University of Sydney, none of whom was either anti-intellectual or dangerous. In withstanding Professor Anderson's atheism, they had a champion in the new principal of Moore College, T.C. Hammond. He possessed a sharp intellect, a photographic memory, a robust sense of humour, plenty of courage, a heart for evangelism, and eloquence consistent with the Irish stereotype. His powers of disputation were formidable. He was well equipped to engage John Anderson, which he did in memorable combat, greatly heartening the evangelical student troops.

Donald Robinson and other evangelical students arranged a debate between Anderson and Hammond on 7 August 1941. Bill Andersen recalls walking over to the debate with Hammond who told him that he had not made any special preparations for it. It was not so much a debate as two lecturers diametrically opposed to each other. Anderson was a logical positivist while Hammond was an idealist and quoted great slabs of Plato off by heart during the debate. Anderson identified Marxism and the EU as examples of credulity.[73] He asserted that the Apostle John had invented Jesus and that he could 'disprove the Resurrection from the New Testament … but I haven't got one on me'. An EU student sitting near the front proffered him one, but reportedly this did not help because Anderson had little knowledge of the New Testament text. Hammond pounced, exposing Anderson's ignorance of the resurrection accounts, so central to the evangelical proclamation of the Gospel. Anderson reiterated his belief that there was no place for religion in the university because religious people could not think objectively and with open minds. To him, in any case, truth was relative. Hammond maintained that truth was not relative, and nobody, not even philosophers, have truly open minds. He argued that it was unreasonable to expect Christians to be completely open-minded about what they believed to be established truth, because that would mean that they did not really believe that it was either established or true.

---

72 Franklin, *Corrupting the Youth*, 74–76.

73 Anderson was himself a former Marxist, but apparently not a former Christian.

Honi Soit, the student newspaper, reported: 'In spite of dramatic gesture and smokescreen eloquence, Canon T.C. Hammond was kept strictly on the defensive in the "Christianity, Faith and Credulity" debate last Thursday.' Anderson, the paper concluded, had exposed the evangelical Christians to be the obscurantists that they were. Others felt that the two disputants had merely passed each other like ships in the night. The evangelicals were delighted with their representative and believed that the shallowness of the rationalist cause had been exposed. Commented Donald Robinson: 'It was an amusing evening. We thought we had put ourselves on the map'.[74]

Sinless Perfection

Conservative evangelicals made no attempt to hide their hostility to Anderson's atheism or Angus's modernism. Defending the Christ of faith and the historicity of the Bible was a fitting activity in the public domain. But not all their fights were fit for the public gaze. They were embarrassed and tried to keep under wraps an aberration of holiness teaching which they labelled 'sinless perfection'. This is the belief that it is possible in this life to 'eradicate sin', to achieve 'entire sanctification', or 'perfect love'. These were terms familiar to those raised in the holiness movement which owed its pedigree chiefly to John Wesley. To the cognoscenti, they were terms which denoted different aspects of the quest for holiness. Their opponents had difficulty understanding precisely what each term meant, and they bundled them together under the label of 'sinless perfection' and condemned them as heretical. Sinless perfection is the doctrine that, by an instantaneous experience of the Holy Spirit, sin is eradicated in believers. This meant either that they were not able to sin or that they were able not to sin any more. Its opponents considered it an easy doctrine to refute on the simple pragmatic grounds that they were all too aware of their own sinfulness and, if pressed, had no difficulty in detecting it in everyone else!

The problem was that it seemed to have a lot going for it. First, it was conceived and luxuriated in the environment of missionary and holiness conventions to which the evangelical movement then owed so much of its spiritual power. Second, scriptures could be cited in its support: (Romans 6:11 'reckon ye yourselves to be dead indeed unto sin'; 1 John 3:9 'Whosoever is born of

74 Donald Robinson interviewed by Linder, 9 January 1995; *Honi Soit*, 14 August 1941, 5. T.C. Hammond, *Abolishing God: A Reply to Professor John Anderson* (Melbourne: S. John Bacon, 1943), 12–13, 18–24; A.J. Baker, *Anderson's Social Philosophy* (Sydney: Angus & Robertson, 1979), 118, 142.

God doth not commit sin … he cannot sin, because he is born of God'). Third, it was embraced by some family members of well-known evangelical Anglican and Brethren dynasties: the Grants, Decks, Youngs, Griffiths, Neils, and Agnews, and they were not only well-connected and wealthy, but they were well educated too. Why, some were university graduates, even doctors! Fourth, it flowered quickly in all the major non-denominational evangelical institutions: the Inter-Varsity Fellowship and the Scripture Union, the Crusaders Union and the Inter-School Christian Fellowship. Like all civil wars, it was hard to fight, dividing not only the evangelical movement, but families within the movement for decades to come.

Decisive action against those who entertained perfectionist views was taken on 9 March 1938 when the Council of the South Sea Evangelical Mission interviewed two of its young missionaries to the Solomon Islands, Ronald Grant, son of Will Grant, a Sydney dentist, and Alan Neil, son of Edwin Lee Neil, managing director of the Myer Emporium in Melbourne. Both Ronald Grant and Alan Neil had witnessed remarkable scenes of revival in the Solomons. It transformed Islanders at one 'place of heartbreak' where pagan practices had thrived even among baptised Christians, and at another it lasted for three months of blessing.[75] It was therefore not surprising that Grant and Neil longed for an even deeper experience of the Holy Spirit. They confessed to the SSEM Council that they had not yet received the blessing of 'entire sanctification', but they were seeking it. After praying for the 'fullest enduement for service', Alan Neil believed that God gave him 'more victory and more power in service'. He reported that he had initially 'mentally rejected' Wesley's teaching on entire sanctification. But that was 'without prayer' and, after much prayer and reading he had come to embrace it as 'the truth of God'. Asked what entire sanctification is, Neil replied that it is 'the fullest indwelling of Christ' following upon God's dealing 'with the root of sin', adding 'This is a miracle'. Ronald Grant concurred, informing the Council: 'I read Wesley and Paget Wilkes. In the matter of sanctification Paget Wilkes holds what I hold.[76] I believe that by a sudden act sin within me is rendered inoperative, and from then on a continuous resurrection life can be lived.'

75 George Strachan, *Revival – Its Blessings and Battles: An Account of Experiences in the Solomon Islands* (Laurieton: SSEM, 1989); Alison Griffiths, *Fire in the Islands: The acts of the Holy Spirit in the Solomons* (Wheaton: H. Shaw Publisher, 1977).

76 A. Paget Wilkes was an Anglican evangelical who founded the Japan Evangelistic Band in 1903 and wrote a number of influential devotional works promoting the Wesleyan doctrine of entire sanctification, including *The Dynamic of Service* (1924) and *Sanctification* (1931).

The Council was chaired by Northcote Deck, for 19 years a medical missionary with SSEM. Deck was a cousin of Florence Young, founder of SSEM.[77] She was also present at this epochal meeting of the Council, though the verbatim minutes of the meeting do not record that she said anything.[78] Another member of the Council, the Rev James Douglas Mill, however, said plenty. He declared entire sanctification an 'untenable' position. He had been the minister of Chatswood Baptist Church for fifteen years from 1921. When he started at Chatswood he found it had many supporters of 'sinless perfectionism'. He preached against it, emptied the church and had to start again. Since then 'serious lapses' had occurred in those who held this view and a number were 'now away from God'. In his strong stand at Chatswood, he had been supported by Florence Young herself and other members of the Deck and Young families. He and his supporters were therefore in no mood to tolerate what they perceived to be an outbreak of sinless perfectionism in the Solomons.

Neil and Grant agreed that what they believed was radically different from what 'the Mission and Keswick believe'. Keswick taught the 'second blessing' which does not eradicate one's sin, but is essentially a matter of being filled with the Spirit for the ongoing battle with inward corruption. Neil and Grant never identified entire sanctification with sinless perfection, but Mill obviously did, and the rest of the Council concluded that their view was incompatible with continuing in the employ of the Mission. The minutes record that Neil and Grant agreed that they had reached the parting of the ways and they invited the Council to ask them to resign. But the chairman insisted that it was not for the Council to ask them to resign: the resignation should come from them. All agreed, and the minutes of the meeting conclude with the following:

> A.N and R.G. then offered to resign & retired to write out their resignations. It was suggested that for the public the announcement of their withdrawal upon the Mission should be worded something like this 'It has seemed the guidance of God that Mr. R. Grant and Mr. A. Neil should withdraw from the work'.
>
> A.N and R.G. handed in resignations. Accepted by Council with deep regret (motion carried unanimously).

77 *Fountain of Public Prosperity*, ch. 19.

78 A transcript of the minutes of the SSEM Council for 9 March 1938 was shared with the authors by historian David Hilliard.

> Lovingly commended to God in prayer by Dr Deck. Mrs [Frances] Neil[79] would be asked to send in resignation. Meeting closed with prayer.

Seventy-five years later, Ronald Grant's daughter, Elizabeth, reported thus on the meeting: 'Ronald was initially shocked. A belief was attributed to him which he had never held and which he regarded as unbiblical. In effect, he was prevented from saying anything in his defence and then required to promise not to discuss it. He kept that promise.'[80] The belief he never held was 'sinless perfection', but he did hold the doctrine of 'entire sanctification', which the unsympathetic identified with sinless perfection. The unsympathetic included the committee of the Katoomba Christian Convention which also took drastic steps, rejecting all further association with Grant and Neil.[81]

But that did not stop them. On 10 June 1938, a new evangelical paper, *The Edifier*, published an article entitled 'The Reality of Entire Sanctification' by Alan Neil. In promoting the full-blown Wesleyan view of sanctification, Neil wrote of 'uttermost salvation' and the need for to be 'fully sanctified':

> the searching of the Spirit goes on till there comes a time when the searching ceases, and the Holy Spirit gives the witness that the whole of the self life is experimentally crucified, put to death, with Christ, and it is no longer I but Christ living within … [and] you know you are cleansed from all sin.[82]

The article caused a furore which stunned *The Edifier's* editor, Eric Daley. Neil's former principal at MBI, C.H. Nash, responded with a series of articles on the Holy Spirit, insisting that no-one reaches perfection in this life, but that did not lessen the onus on the Christian to lead a holy life. Nash could see the spiritual potential in Neil, and consoled him in a constructive and healing manner.[83]

Nash's role in the containment of perfectionism was probably critical. Influenced deeply himself by Keswick teaching, Nash came to reject firmly all optimistic views about our power over sin. 'As long as I remain in a mortal

79 Ronald Grant's sister.

80 Libby Wilson, 'Ronald Rutherford Grant' in Stuart Braga, *All His Benefits: The Young and Deck Families in Australia* (Wahroonga: Stuart Braga), 244f.

81 David Hilliard, 'The South Sea Evangelical Mission in The Solomon Islands: The Foundation Years', *Journal of Pacific History*, 4, 1969, 41–64.

82 *The Edifier*, 10 June 1938. Ronald Grant always insisted that his teaching subscribed to the 13th chapter of the Westminster Confession, 'Of Sanctification' (Letter from Mary Grant to Stuart Piggin, 27 August 1993).

83 Leonard Buck interviewed by Margaret Lamb, 15 November 1986.

body,' he wrote, 'I expect to have to endure the conflict between flesh and spirit and how … to be delivered from that conflict except by a moment by moment hiding in God's grace I have not yet discovered (to my shame).'[84] Nash's commitment to the older Augustinian view that sanctification involves lifelong conflict explains in part why in Melbourne sinless perfectionist teaching was contained within a small group, known as 'The Group' or 'the Royal Family', of whom Alan Neil and Ronald Grant were leading members. They sought to live in close communion with God, though it was cultish in its exclusivity.[85]

Sinless perfectionism was thus excluded from the SSEM, the Katoomba Christian Convention, the Upwey Convention, and *The Edifier*. That left the IVF, EU, CSSM, SU, Crusaders, and the CMS League of Youth. In September 1939, the SUEU resolved its problem with a spill and an election for all committee positions. As it was the custom for the outgoing committee to nominate the incoming committee, five of the seven nominated by the committee of 1938–39 were committed to the sinless perfectionist position, including Humphrey Deck as president, Philip Deck as secretary, and Lloyd Sommerlad. But Harvey Carey, medical student, later Professor of Obstetrics and Gynaecology at the University of NSW, had other ideas. He believed that there was a danger that the preoccupation with perfection would displace the more traditional commitment of the EU, namely evangelism, and that the EU would become a perfectionist coterie powerless to witness for the Gospel. He decided to stand for the presidency and successfully lobbied support from those opposed to sinless perfectionism. Engineering student Alwyn Prescott was elected secretary: he had looked at those who professed to be sinless, and concluded that it was quite obvious that they were not.

At the 1940 annual general meeting of the SUEU 86 members were present. The attendance was ominous for the perfectionists, for they were not popular and could not win elections. They attempted to limit the number of voters by refusing to allow postal voting and disenfranchising evening students.[86] It was a vain move: their ticket was defeated resoundingly. John Hercus, a Baptist and later a surgeon and revered lecturer and writer in an apologetic vein, was elected president over Alan Lane by 66 votes to 20, and Donald

---

84 David Chambers, *Tempest-Tossed: The Life and Teaching of the Rev. C.H. Nash, M.A.* (Melbourne: Church Press Publications, 1959), 139f.

85 Morag Zwartz, *Fractured families: the story of a Melbourne church cult* (Boronia: Parenesis Publishing, 2004).

86 SUEU Minute Book, 18 September 1940, Sydney University Evangelical Union papers, acc.549 series 27, University of Sydney Archives, Fisher Library, Sydney.

Robinson secretary over Philip Deck, by 65 votes to 21.[87] Hercus informed the Grant-dominated IVF executive that it had lost the confidence of the SUEU.

In other organisations, the axe fell more swiftly. The SU and the CSSM had the structures and constitution necessary to contain the problem: CSSM staff worker, Heather Drummond, was asked to resign by a more experienced and mature council than was available to the EUers. In the Crusader Union, some teachers threatened to have the union excluded from schools if the problem were not dealt with. Jack Dahl, a member of the Crusader Union's Council, sought to organise gatherings at which T.C. Hammond would refute the tendency. In Sydney, the Crusader Union leaders imposed a rigorous discipline on those who espoused perfectionism, not permitting them to teach it in the meetings of the union. Any who did not agree to accept this discipline had to move out. Friends and relatives parted rarely to see one another again, and the divisions kept happening for decades as the movement managed to get its hooks into new members.

Not until 1943 was control of the IVF wrested back from the perfectionists. Lindsay Grant, Ronald's youngest brother, had held the position of IVF General Secretary from 1936. A contemporary claimed that, as well as he knew his Bible, Grant was not well grounded in Christian doctrine.[88] His spirituality was far more a matter of practice than of theology.[89] The practice had echoes of the Oxford Group with which the Evangelical Union had earlier wrestled, including group confession of weaknesses and failings.[90] Lindsay Grant was replaced by Paul White as IVF General Secretary and the perfectionists withdrew from their old friends. It was a peremptory, hurtful separation. In 1947 Lindsay married Del Agnew and settled in Sydney. Del severed all links with the Melbourne group, led by Alan Neil and Ronald Grant, who had married her own sister Nancye in 1938. The Sydney group, with Del as high priestess, began exercising an autocratic rule over the members of the movement which, in the time-honoured manner of cults, became a commune. The claimed basis of Del's power was that she had a prophetic capacity to discern evil in the lives of others and the spiritual power to eradicate it. She

87 SUEU Minute Book, 25 September 1940.

88 Bruce Bryson, interviewed by Brian Dickey, 15 December 1988. Myrrh digital repository, Moore College Library, https://myrrh.library.moore.edu.au:443/handle/10248/8768.

89 Win Dunkley to Margaret Lamb, 12 August 1990.

90 On the Oxford Group, see David Bebbington, *Evangelicalism in Modern Britain* (London: Unwin Hyman, 1989), 235–240.

controlled every detail of the lives of commune members, including marital relationships and the care of children. Family break-ups were engineered. Couples were ordered to break up, with no appeal. In 1952 Del's marriage with Lindsay ended in an arranged divorce which scandalised his former friends. Lindsay married another from the inner circle, Margaret Debenham, in 1963, and they all continued to live in the commune. The scandal split the group. Heather Drummond never accepted the divorce. She detached herself from the group and returned to the church.

As befits a cult, Lindsay and Del Grant's commune remained hidden from the public gaze. But an evangelical spiritual élite had been traumatised. Members of divided families who had stayed out of the cult became hypersensitive to holiness aspirations and nervous of related revivalist and Pentecostal teachings. They learned more about how to fight to keep the movement orthodox than they did about how to keep themselves holy. In the evangelical movement as a whole, spirituality had been demoted and orthodoxy promoted. For if this manifestation of perfectionism was at first suffered within élitist families, the reaction to it was applied to all branches of the wider family, already traumatised by the legacy of war, the deprivations of economic depression, and the inroads of theological liberalism.

* * *

By the beginning of World War II significant changes had come over the movement in Australia. Evangelicals were better educated, had more intellectual resources to defend the faith, and their leaders had weathered the storms of liberalism without (for the most part) descending into fundamentalism or withdrawing into sectarianism. But it was now more defensive in its theology, narrower in its social commitments, and less confident about its significance in the shaping of the Australian nation. Even the overseas missionary movement which served to open the horizons of many conservative evangelicals may be understood partly as an opportunity to express orthodox faith in an environment uncontaminated by liberalism. Evangelicalism had become more self-absorbed, more concerned to meet the needs of its own supporters, and more anxious to keep their approval. It was a more hard-edged, less devotional movement than it had been at the beginning of the twentieth century. Its members now knew better how to fight to preserve their movement than how to preserve either their own sanctity or the national health.

Chapter Five

WINNING SOULS AND SHAPING THE AUSTRALIAN SOUL

Inter-War Missions

'I believe that the Man who flogged the money-changers from the temple still calls all men to the heights of moral courage and spiritual peace. I should like to feel that there lies my allegiance'
(R.M. Williams)

Reginald Murray Williams (1908–2003), bush clothing entrepreneur, was given a state funeral in Queensland. Premier Peter Beattie said of the nation's greatest leather worker: 'When you pull on a pair of R.M. Williams's boots everyone knows you walk taller. It's not just the size of the heel, it's the spirit of the man who made them in the first place.'[1] The spirit of the man is instantly recognisable as an Australian spirit. It might be argued that they don't come more Australian than RM (as he was popularly known) and what it means to be an Australian obsessed his imagination. What did it mean to be an Australian between the wars? Was Christianity any part of it? Jesus certainly was. For RM, as for historian Manning Clark who shared in the obsessive search for the Australian character, Jesus was a lifelong part of the obsession. In the imagination, what one makes of oneself and what one makes of Jesus are two sides of the one coin. So, if RM does epitomise the Australian identity, analysing the impact of evangelical Christianity on his understanding of

1 *The Age*, 12 November 2003.

Jesus and on his life experience would be one measure of its role in shaping Australian history.

RM's autobiography reveals a man deeply concerned over religious issues which is hardly part of the stereotypical Australian. But his many reflections on religion read like a creed of stereotypical Australian faith, offering insights into the troubled national soul. Its title, *Beneath Whose Hand*,[2] is taken from Kipling's Recessional. Its opening words (p.1):

> More than a personal history, this book is a story of adventure; the adventure that might be encountered in any life that keeps as guidelines the rules governing the human spirit. It represents also a search for those rules, a seeking after knowledge.

That, like the title, sounds humble enough. The Christian thinks, 'this seems promising. This is the story of a seeker who believes that the human spirit is governed by rules'. But, before the first page is out, RM distances himself from the orthodox believer with the claim 'this account is not just the boring story of a just man'. Here already is the Australian stereotype. For 'just man', read 'justified man', read 'Christian', read 'boring'. That Williams's reserve about the church is more Australian than personal is suggested by the fact that he did not work out these views for himself. His father helped (192). He just would not go to church, although his wife never missed it. Like most Australian males, RM's father was scared of his wife, and respectful of social convention, and so no work was ever done on the Sabbath. In Adelaide in 1926, RM attended the evangelistic meetings of Gipsy Smith and, at the end of his life, could still hear 'the thunder of the spellbinder's voice' (12). He knew his Bible, which his mother had packed in his swag, and which he read in filial obedience to her. He knew the words of Jesus and he knew hymns and their 'nostalgic' tunes. But he was never christened, and, although his balanced assessment was that 'the Church in Australia has a stabilising influence' (192), he does not appear to have attended church much. He was not willing to be married in a church nor 'to accept the dictatorship of a church in such important matters as my private life' (91). Religion in Australia, or, at least, its stereotype, is like that. It is supported – with reservations, particularly about institutions and their claims to authority. It is tentative, nervous, adolescent in its desperation to assert personal autonomy. It always apologises for itself.

---

2 R.M. Williams, *Beneath Whose Hand: The Autobiography* (South Melbourne, Macmillan, 1984).

RM remembers those hymns; they are part of his imagination; but they are just 'nostalgia', surely the lowest form of imagination.

As one of the few white men who could not only survive, but actually thrive, in the Outback, Williams was invited to help a number of missionaries in their work among the most isolated of Aboriginal tribes. Rod Schenk asked him to build a large concrete tank for the Mount Margaret Mission of the United Aborigines Mission at Laverton in WA. Sixty years later he received a cassette message from Schenk's widow, Mysie, thanking him for constructing the water tank which was still in service, and ending with the exhortation: 'Dear Reg, we did miss your fellowship when you left and we long to see you back in that fellowship with the Lord Jesus … Trust Him and learn to lean on Him. He is the water of life and the water of life means more to our native people than anything else.' Williams wept. He saw Jesus in Mysie, the one who stretched wide his arms and said, 'How often would I have gathered you in but you would not hear' (15; Matthew 23:37).

In 1927 Williams joined a team headed up by missionary Bill Wade to make a census count of the Aboriginal population in the area of about a million square miles between Laverton to the west and Oodnadatta in SA to the east. RM admitted frankly to hating this uncompromising zealot, but there were few he respected more, and none who influenced him more. Wade, an ex-sailor, had been converted from a thoroughly reprobate life and joined the Salvation Army. He testified constantly to all people about being 'saved by grace'. Williams was embarrassed and sceptical. But he had to concede that Wade could be totally trusted with women – in this RM thought him unique. Admirably too, Wade did leave a trail of men behind him seriously 'wondering if they might perhaps need religion' (25).

What most impressed RM about Wade was his courage. Wade, 'strengthened by belief' (33), was indomitable. Because he was totally convinced that he was called by a sovereign God to this ministry, Wade would take his camel train beyond the point of no return, trusting that water would be found. He threw his arms around warring Aboriginal people who threatened to spear his party, protesting that he was their friend, an act which worked and which left Williams 'almost convinced' (31). Neither would RM ever doubt Wade's achievement: this vast area was made over to the custody of the Aboriginal people, and no white can enter it without a permit. Wade went on to establish a mission in the Warburton Ranges and gave his life to the work. 'He was impossible,' concluded RM, 'but truly great' (36). Fifty years later, RM saw a television program which featured an Aboriginal evangelist who was having a 'marked impact on his people' and who had been raised in Wade's mission.

There could be no doubting the efficacy of Wade's work, RM reflected, when he saw 'this black John the Baptist, born in wilderness and carrying the banner that Bill must have put in his hands' (66).

Then, in 1935, Charles Duguid, the first lay Moderator of the Presbyterian Church and President of the Aborigines Protection League, invited RM to accompany him on a trip into the Musgrave Ranges in north-west SA. They stayed at Ernabella station while they explored the area, and Duguid planned the establishment of a mission where Aboriginal people would be left free to follow their own way of life. He asked RM to convene a committee to establish the mission, and RM took considerable satisfaction in Ernabella's success as 'a bastion against white intrusion'. Again, RM saw the power of religious motivation, and acknowledged the fruitfulness resulting from 'the march of religion' (66).

Religion is a problem as well as a strength. 'We are cursed because we believe we have sinned against God' (92). The sinner is troubled, not only by what he has done, but by what he has left undone. Chief of these for RM, since he refers to it more than once – thrice in fact – is that he has not taught his children – his many children by two marriages – religion (147,176,198). Maybe it was to correct that omission that the motivation for the writing of his autobiography is chiefly to be found because it is full of religion.

Jesus was for Williams what expatriate Australian poet, Peter Porter, called the 'Master Haunter'. 'Jesus', says Williams, 'has cast a long shadow on history, and I suspect that He is badly represented.' At the end of his autobiography, Williams asks (193):

> … if the Man Jesus were to step inside my door or come knocking, would I know Him? A man of the road, with straw, perhaps, from some lonely haystack still clinging to His uncut hair, garments creased and road-stained. Would I welcome Him? I might. What would He say to me, looking through my façade of respectability into my soul? … I am torn by the tragedy of it all. How do I follow Him? How would I know God if I saw Him? I shall look for Him among the uncouth, the sorrowful, the have-nots. Maybe He will be there. And will He know me?

His final advice? '"Seek and ye shall find", is probably the best.[3] I cannot guarantee that you will find it but at least the seeking will be good for you' (194). Very Australian: 'Seek and you might find'. It is true in the spiritual

---

3 The reference is to Matthew 7:7.

realm as on the goldfields or in the outback in need of water. His final wisdom on the subject of religion is also very Australian: 'It is possible, quite possible, that religion cannot be transmitted by words' (198). To be haunted but helped, to practise Christian charity if not believe its creedal confessions, and to be humbled by the transcendent mystery, was the experience of those influenced by evangelical faith without accepting it – perhaps the majority of Australians between the wars.

Evangelical Women

Another difference between the stereotypical Australian in the early twentieth century and the typical evangelical Australian is that the former was male, whereas the latter was as likely to be female. There is no difference between the sexes in grades of heroism. Mysie Schenk, the typist who joined her husband in the hardest of mission fields in the Warburton Ranges and continued on there after his death, was a case in point. In 1925, approximately 59 percent of Australia's cross-cultural missionaries were women. Between 1914 and 1932 the CMS sent out 153 missionaries of whom 104 were women. Between 1915 and 1938 the Methodists sent out 223 missionaries of whom 141 were women, while in the period 1914 to 1938 the Baptists sent an extra 58 missionaries of whom 43 were women to their celebrated mission in Bengal.[4]

Apart from missionary work, evangelicalism increased the ways for women to express themselves in their home churches and communities. The Woman's Christian Temperance Union reached its peak in this period as a training ground for social activists. Among the leaders to emerge from the WCTU was Hilda Burnard. A member of Goodwood Methodist Church, Adelaide, she became WCTU state president. She lobbied for prison reform, temperance legislation, women's ordination, and Aboriginal rights. She spearheaded WCTU and YWCA support for the establishment of the Aboriginal Advancement League of SA. She became its vice-president and president, serving alongside Charles Duguid's wife, Phyllis.[5]

In the Australian stereotype the Outback is a male preserve, but evangelical women, especially unmarried women, found new and exciting opportunities for service there. In May 1926, the Sydney press widely reported that Sister Grace Syms and her assistant Mary de Labilliere had been sent by BCA in a new Church of England Motor Van Mission vehicle to provide spiritual

---

4 Janet West, *Daughters of Freedom* (Sutherland: Albatross, 1997), 256.

5 Ian Burnard, 'Burnard, Hilda Agnes', *ADEB*; Alison Holland, 'To Eliminate Colour Prejudice: The WCTU and Decolonisation in Australia', *JRH*, 32. 2, 2008, 256–276.

ministry to people in the far west districts of NSW. The two braved bush fires, crossed flooded creeks, and made their way through untracked areas in order to bring the Gospel of Jesus Christ to people in the Outback.[6]

Expanded women's ministries were given a boost by Maude Royden's visit to Sydney in 1928. Royden was just orthodox enough to intrigue Sydney Anglicans. Oxford educated, she was the daughter and sister of baronets. In 1917, she was appointed Assistant Preacher at the Congregational City Temple in London. During her Australian visit, she preached at St. Mark's Church of England, Darling Point. Suffragette Jessie Street's influence in this parish may have had something to do with the invitation, since she was a leading parishioner there.[7] Sydney Archbishop J.C. Wright asked Royden to speak to clergy on the topic of 'The Divine Mystery of Sex'. It was deemed a superb talk, and Canon (and future bishop) W.G. Hilliard was one who was impressed and began to rethink his views on the subject of the ordination of women.[8]

Monica Farrell, a former Roman Catholic and well-known Protestant evangelist in Ireland, represented yet another type of evangelical woman leader. T.C. Hammond knew of her reputation and persuaded her to migrate to Australia in 1937 and she quickly made her mark. At the Mt. Kembla Church of England near Wollongong, for example, from 13 to 20 February 1938 she spoke eighteen times in eight days to perhaps a thousand people, and the number of communicants at Mt. Kembla doubled. In the 1940s she felt called to a wider area of service beyond NSW and became a freelance worker. Later, she established the interdenominational Light and Truth Gospel Crusade, and continued her evangelistic campaigns in Europe, North America and Australia, using Sydney as her home base. Eloquent, humorous, pugnacious and fiercely anti-Catholic, no male told Monica Farrell what to do. She said that she answered only to God.[9]

The Pentecostal tradition, with its openness to prophetic ministries, made room for outstanding women to express their abilities and gifts. Janet Murrell

---

6 Sydney J. Kirkby, *These Ten Years: A Record of the Work of the Bush Church Aid Society for the Church of England in Australia, 1920–1930* (Sydney: Bush Church Aid Society, 1930), 27–28; Margaret Rodgers, 'Sydney Women should be Trail Blazers', *The Southern Cross*, August 2003, 9.

7 West, *Daughters of Freedom*, 321–324.

8 *SMH*, 29 May 1928, 12; Maude Royden, *A Threefold Cord* (London: Macmillan, 1948).

9 C.K. Hammond, 'Farrell, Monica', *ADEB*, 110; Stuart Piggin, *The Fruitful Figtree: A History of All Saints Anglican Church, Figtree, 1888–1983* (Wollongong: All Saints Anglican Church, 1983), 33; Monica Farrell, *Laughing with God* (Glebe: Protestant Publications, 1957).

Lancaster and Mina Ross Brawner were but two who assumed critical leadership roles in the 1920s and 1930s.

Janet Lancaster in 1909 established the first permanent Pentecostal church on Australian soil. Her Good News Hall in North Melbourne became a focal point of Pentecostal preaching and activity until it closed its doors in 1935. GNH sponsored a visit from two foreign Pentecostal super-stars of the 1920s, namely, Smith Wigglesworth from England and Aimee Semple McPherson from the United States. Lancaster's most enduring legacy was her promotion of the role of women in ministry. Many found opportunities for service at GNH, including Winnie Andrews, Florrie Mortomore, Pauline Heath, Annie Dennis and Mina Brawner, all leaders in early Australian Pentecostalism.[10]

Mina Ross Brawner gave 28 years of ministry to Australia. She worked first as a Seventh-day Adventist missionary from 1900 until 1912. Then, after training as a medical doctor and experiencing a filling of the Holy Spirit at Aimee Semple McPherson's Angelus Temple in Los Angeles, she worked again in Australia from 1927 to 1943, holding evangelistic meetings that emphasised divine healing in Sydney, Ballarat, Melbourne and Brisbane. She visited prisons, set up food distribution centres and soup kitchens for the poor, and established fourteen churches and two Bible colleges.[11] She defended her right to lead services and preach in a series of articles in 1929 and 1930, later published as a book:

> Imagine my surprise on being informed by older labourers in the Lord's vineyard, that … a woman might preach, or sing, or pray in public (provided she wore a hat), but she must not anoint with oil when praying for the sick; must not hold office as pastor, elder or deacon; must not teach men (only women and children); must not officiate at the Lord's table nor pass the elements; must not solemnise marriages or administer water baptism …
>
> Charging God with the folly of anointing and equipping his handmaidens for service, and then disqualifying them because they are what he made them (his handmaidens) … My sense of justice was outraged, but only momentarily, remembering that I am my Lord's love-slave, pledged to serve him in any capacity he chooses … and with this resolve I opened my Bible to study the status of 'Woman in the Word'.

---

10 Barry Chant, *Heart of Fire* (Adelaide: The House of Tabor, 1984), 111–121.

11 'God Has Broken the Curse', Healing and Revival Press website, 2006, www.healingandrevival.com (accessed 22 June 2009).

> ... at the earnest request of many of God's children, I have decided to publish these papers on 'Woman in the Word,' and to send them forth with the prayer that God will so use them and that ... my sisters in Christ will rise in their God-given liberty and do with their might what their hands find to do.[12]

Theologian Shane Clifton has analysed Brawner's writings and pronounced them, unlike those of Janet Lancaster, orthodox, compelling and 'representative of some of the best elements of Pentecostal spirituality'. He adjudges her to have been a 'first wave feminist' and a strong voice for all women everywhere.[13]

C.H. Nash and the Melbourne 'Clapham Sect'

Evangelicalism was not primarily a clerical movement, and just as women tested the waters of opportunity afforded by the movement, so lay men, too, played an increasing role in this period. The evangelical business men of Melbourne in particular strengthened the home base for a rash of evangelistic and missionary enterprises. They developed over two generations probably the strongest, the best-organised, and the most determined network of lay evangelicals in Australian history.

At the head of this powerful network of laymen was a clergyman, C.H. Nash, but he became arguably the most influential Melbourne clergyman of his generation precisely because he devoted his attention to the nurture of lay people through the Melbourne Bible Institute (MBI), the Upwey Convention, and the City Men's Bible Class (CMBC). His close friend and founding President of the MBI from 1920 until his death was Edwin Lee Neil, managing director of the Myer Emporium. Another who warmly supported the MBI was Hervey Perceval Smith, managing director of the Palace Hotel, the founder of the Melbourne Gospel Crusade, formalised in 1920, and dedicated to the proclamation of the three Rs: Ruin by the fall, Redemption by the Blood of Christ, and Regeneration by the Holy Ghost. In 1924, he opened the Keswick Book Depot, and in 1926 appeared the first number of *The Keswick Quarterly and Upwey Convention News*, which Smith edited and published. Smith is in many ways an evangelical archetype: lay rather than clerical; significant because of his fellowship with other like-minded

12 Mina Ross Brawner, *Woman in the Word* (Melbourne: Victory Press, 1931), 7–8.

13 Shane Clifton, 'Pentecostal Hermeneutics and First-Wave Feminism: Mina Ross Brawner, MD', *The Pentecostal Charismatic Bible College Journal* (October 2006), http://pcbc.webjournals.org/ (accessed 25 June 2009).

warriors rather than as an individual; more interested in God's multifarious contemporary activities in the world than in biblical or theological scholarship; committed to working out the implications of his conversion in terms of evangelising others and progressively dealing with not necessarily sinful but unhelpful personal habits such as smoking and drinking; and turning away from some political interests and amusements, not to withdrawal and separation from the world, but to engagement with such social problems as care for the poor and slum clearance.[14]

Among other worthies of their generation were William Buck (a Melbourne firm of Chartered Accountants still bears his name), Alex Eggleston (founded a firm of architects and designed the 1000 seat auditorium for the Upwey Christian Convention), James and John Griffiths (tea importers), Horace John Hannah (a remarkable bibliophile), T. Graham, A. Kenny, Dr John James Kitchen, Dr D. Stewart MacColl, David Ernest Renshaw, Charles Alfred Sandland, and Frank Varley (son of Henry Varley, the evangelist). Two evangelists, Walter Betts[15] and George Hall, were associated with the group. It was Kitchen's vision to establish MBI to train missionaries, and it was Hall's vision to establish the CMBC in 1927 to bring to the commercial young men of Melbourne the challenge of life-long service to Christ. The CMBC met in the Griffiths Brothers Tea Rooms in 64 Elizabeth Street Melbourne and was attended by between 140 and 200 men. Out of the MBI grew in 1928 the Borneo Evangelical Mission (BEM)[16] and in 1931 the Australian Council of the Unevangelised Fields Mission (UFM).[17]

The convergence of these activist evangelical societies in Melbourne birthed the CMS League of Youth in 1928. Max Warren, English missionary statesman, said: 'From the League of Youth in Australia and New Zealand has come a stream of recruits for missionary service which has no parallel in the church life of those countries'.[18] In Melbourne, too, the Methodist Local Preachers Branch was very vigorous and had an impact on evangelical life in Australia, as teams of these local preachers went all over Australia and New Zealand. For many years, it held a Holiness Convention each King's Birthday

14 Will Renshaw, *Marvellous Melbourne and Spiritual Power: A Christian Revival and its Lasting Legacy* (Moreland: Acorn Press, 2014), xii, 71–92, 188–196.

15 Dallas Clarnette, *50 Years on Fire for God: The Story of Walter Betts* (Kew: The People's Church, 1967).

16 Shirley Lees, *Drunk before Dawn* (Sevenoaks: OMF, 1979).

17 John and Moyra Prince, *No Fading Vision: The First 50 Years of APCM* (n.p.: Asia Pacific Christian Mission, 1981).

18 Genevieve Cutler, *The Torch: The Story of the CMS league of Youth* (Lilydale: Church Missionary Society, 1976), 7.

weekend in Melbourne. It was conducted entirely by laymen. George Hall, who had been trained in America under Dr R.A. Torrey and Dr Campbell Morgan, and who knew evangelical life in the USA intimately, said that the Methodist Local Preachers Melbourne Branch Holiness Convention was the greatest spiritual force he had ever experienced.[19]

The Convention Movement

C.H. Nash's lay army plotted for eternity which is not the same as plotting to win control of a denomination. The former requires holiness and prayer, the latter too often guile and politics. Ecclesiastical politics prevailed in synods and assemblies, but the evangelicals developed another institution for the higher work of discerning the divine purpose, namely the convention. In the interwar period conventions for the deepening of the spiritual life and for the fomenting of missionary zeal became a major source of strength and morale-building. Among the most successful and enduring were the Katoomba Christian Convention in NSW and the Upwey (from 1950, the Belgrave Heights) Convention in Victoria.

By the 1920s, the Katoomba Convention had become a week-long gathering of evangelical clergy and lay leaders during January of each year. The number of people at Katoomba grew from 52 in 1904 to nearly a thousand in the late 1920s. Although each speaker was free to choose his own subject as the Holy Spirit moved him, almost invariably the addresses followed the Keswick pattern of emphasising the deepening of the spiritual life, holy living and missions.[20]

The Upwey Convention of Victoria was first held in December 1918. John Griffiths was elected the first president of the convention[21] and was succeeded by the Open Brethren medical doctor J.J. Kitchen who served on the executive council for almost 20 years. Generously supported by Melbourne business and professional men, Upwey was without money worries, and could concentrate on its primary mission to promote holy living and missionary concern among its constituency.[22] Upwey's teaching concentrated on biblical aspects of the practical Christian life and on missions and studiously avoided

19 Leonard Buck to Margaret Lamb, 14 December 1990.

20 Stuart Braga, *A Century Preaching Christ: Katoomba Christian Convention 1903–2003* (Sydney: Katoomba Christian Convention, 2003), 40.

21 Darrell Paproth, 'Griffiths, John Moore', *ADEB*; 'Past Upwey Conventions', *The Keswick Quarterly*, May 1926, 9–12.

22 Darrell Paproth, *Failure Is Not Final* (Sydney, Centre for the Study of Australian Christianity, 1997), 83, 92–93, and 134–135.

controversial matters. In 1933, the auditorium at Upwey was expanded to seat 1,200 as the numbers attending increased during the Great Depression; in 1934, 2,000 attended.

During the 1920s, conventions also arose in other states. The Kingston Convention in Tasmania followed the Upwey pattern. It began at Easter in 1925 and was so successful that the following summer the committee of the Open-air Mission ran a nine-day convention at Kingston Beach. Their motto, 'The perfecting of the saints for the work of ministry', differed from the motto ('All One in Christ Jesus') of other Australian conventions.[23] The Queensland Evangelisation Society sponsored the Mt. Tamborine Convention, which clearly reflected the same emphases as Katoomba and Upwey. In South Australia, the convention meeting at Victor Harbour became simply the Keswick Convention. The Kalamunda Convention in Western Australia began in a large tent under the leadership of the Perth Bible Institute in 1929. In each State the conventions fostered evangelical unity and boosted morale.

Missions to the Outback

The Presbyterians, Anglicans and Methodists all established significant ministries in the Outback. In 1912 John Flynn had been appointed foundation superintendent of the Australian Inland Mission (AIM) of the Presbyterian Church of Australia. Through its medical work, later supplemented by patrol padres, nursing hostels, aircraft and the pedal radio, it sought to maintain a 'mantle of safety' over the people of the outback. Flynn was not an evangelical, and the AIM, consistent with the inclination of its founder for ecumenicity, was careful to insist that creed was not its primary concern.

In 1919, a group of Anglican evangelicals, who were very concerned with creed, formed the Bush Church Aid Society (BCA), largely in response to the various bush brotherhoods that Anglican High Churchmen had established. The BCA was an instrument of wider evangelical influence in the Australian Church at a time when Sydney was becoming more isolated. The new society was empowered 'to call, train and support clergy, Bush brothers, catechists, lay-evangelists, teachers, Bush nurses and Bush deaconesses'. It could provide hostels and missions if invited by the bishop. Sidney James Kirkby, rector of Ryde, was appointed foundation secretary.[24]

23 R.S. Miller, *Fifty Years of Keswick in Tasmania* (Launceston: Tasmanian Keswick Convention, 1975), 7.

24 Donald Anderson, 'Defending an Evangelical Society and an Evangelical Diocese, Sydney James Kirkby, 1879–1935', MA, University of Wollongong, 1985; T.E. Jones,

BCA grew out of the work of the Colonial and Continental Church Society (CCCS) which had been operating in Australia for a century. In 1922 Kirkby proposed to the CCCS in London that the range of churchmanship acceptable to the Society be broadened. To this the CCCS Committee responded that since the BCA was an Australian Society it was at liberty to make such a change. The Australians were reminded, however, that the BCA was founded 'to further Evangelical work in the Bush areas' and that, should the change be made the CCCS would have to stop its grant 'in fairness to the views of the Society's supporters'.[25] Duly reprimanded, the antipodeans re-endorsed the purity demanded of evangelicals and withdrew the proposal. The surprising reality, here, has only recently been uncovered in the unpublished research of Brian Roberts, long-serving National Director of BCA. Roberts has discovered that BCA, when founded in 1919, was not prepared to cut the apron strings with London. It did not become a legal entity until 1936 when it was registered in NSW and set up with Memorandum and Articles of Association. The period between 1919 and 1936 represents a process of indigenisation in which BCA passed from interdependence to independence.

By the end of 1921 the BCA was working in the Dioceses of Bathurst and Riverina in NSW, Gippsland, Bendigo and Wangaratta in Victoria, Willochra in South Australia, and Bunbury and Perth in Western Australia. As early as 1922 the BCA 'Mail-bag Sunday School' was established and, at its peak in 1939, 4,500 children were being serviced by 60 volunteers. BCA missioners experimented with novel means of transport. Motor vans travelled vast distances on appalling roads for evangelistic, pastoral, and colportage purposes. This mobile ministry was continued into the 21st century.[26] The Rev. Len Daniels in 1928 became the first 'Flying Parson' in history when he took delivery of a 'Moth' aeroplane, 'The Far West'. From this developed the 'Anglican Flying Medical Services'.[27]

In the Methodist Inland Mission Harry and Dorothy Griffiths were among those who gave a lifetime's service to the Outback.[28] They commenced min-

---

'These Twenty Years': A Record of the Work of the Bush Church Aid Society for Australia and Tasmania (Sydney: BCA, 1939); Helen Caterer, *Australians Outback: 60 Years of Bush Church Aid* (Sydney: AIO, 1981); Brian Underwood, 'The History of the Commonwealth and Continental Church Society', MA, Durham University, 1972.

25 General Minutes, CCCS, 1 August 1922, 16 January 1923.

26 On the use of vans in evangelism and mission work, see the four booklets by R.M. (Bob) Armstrong in the 'Wheel Tracks' Pictorial Albums series.

27 Helen Caterer, 'Australia's First Flying Padre', *Decision,* September, 1982, 5; Len Daniels, *Far West* (Sydney: Church of England Information Trust, 1959).

28 Harry Griffiths, *An Australian Adventure* (Adelaide: Rigby, 1975), 1–6; E.R. Sexton, *'Griff'* (Adelaide: SA Methodist Historical Society Publication, 1969), 4–6.

istry in the Outback early in 1931. Harry became Director of the MIM in 1946 and retired in 1970, his name by then written all over the Australian Inland.[29] Not only had he faithfully preached the Gospel, but he also stitched up wounds and pulled teeth, debated theology with station hands, cut hair, transported stockmen and Aboriginal people hundreds of miles to hospitals, performed baptisms and marriages, shoed horses, patched tyres and repaired motor vehicles. He supervised the construction of the Alice Springs Bath Street Methodist Church in 1934 and the Griffiths House, a children's hostel, in 1941. 'Griff', as he came to be known, was active in the Alice Springs RSL Club (even though a teetotaller), and he and his fellow members were instrumental in having Anzac Hill granted to them as Anzac Reserve. Griffiths suggested a memorial to the Anzacs be erected on the crown of the hill and he was responsible for its design.[30] Today, Harry and Dorothy Griffiths' remains are interred on Anzac Hill.

Indigenous Concerns

Beginning in World War I and extending through the interwar period, a number of important missions to Aboriginal people were established.

In Table 1 it is noteworthy that the focus of Christian missions had moved on from the States of NSW, Victoria and Tasmania, to the north and west of the continent, that the Methodists in this period made up for lost time, that the UAM was also strongly involved in the multiplication of mission stations, and that the smaller evangelical denominations, the Baptists, Open Brethren, the Churches of Christ, the Salvation Army and the Assemblies of God were now all contributing to missions to Indigenous peoples.[31] It is a fine example of 'holy emulation' among evangelicals as their missionary societies responded to consciences newly awakened in the twentieth century to the plight of the original inhabitants of the land.[32] Missionaries sided with Aboriginal people in their ongoing violent confrontations with police and white station owners and labourers. But they also commonly sided with governments in their new policy of assimilation especially of children of mixed descent whilst maintaining the segregation of 'full-blood' Aborigines on mission stations. Thus the

29 Griffiths, *An Australian Adventure*, vii.

30 Griffiths, *An Australian Adventure*, 103, 149, 166.

31 Harris, *One Blood*, 389–760.

32 Among those who initiated the burst of church-based missions were non-evangelical Anglican bishops such as George Frodsham, Bishop of North Queensland, and Gilbert White, Bishop of Carpentaria. In 1907 White invited evangelical missionaries to work in his diocese. Harris, *One Blood,* 696.

Table 1. Aboriginal Mission Stations 1914–1939

Name of Mission	Church	State / Territory	Commencement Date
Mornington Island	Presbyterian	Qld	1914
Cowal Creek	C of E	Qld	1915
Purga	Salvation Army	Qld	1915
Croker Island	Methodist	NT	1915
Goulburn Island	Methodist	NT	1915
Goulburn Inland Mission	Methodist	NSW	1916
Angurugu, Groote Eylandt	CMS	NT	1921
Emerald River, Groote Eylandt	CMS	NT	1921
Mt. Margaret	UAM	WA	1921
Milingimbi	Methodist	NT	1921
Elcho Island	Methodist	NT	1922
East Arm Settlement (Leper Station)	RC	NT	1923
Lockhart River	ABM	Qld	1924
La Grange (West Kimberley)	RC	WA	1924
Oodnadatta	UAM	SA	1924
Oenpelli	CMS	NT	1924
Gerard	UAM	SA	1925
Gnowangerup	UAM	WA	1926
Palm Island	Baptist	Qld	1927
Colebrook Home	UAM	SA	1927
Badjalang	UAM	WA	1930
Derby (Leper Station)	UAM	WA	1930
Nepabunna	UAM	SA	1930
Channel Island (Leper Station)	RC	NT	1930
Palm Island	RC	Qld	1931
Balgo Hills	RC	WA	1931
Doomadgee	Brethren	Qld	1932
Warburton Ranges	UAM	WA	1933
Sister Kate's Home (Perth)	C of E	WA	1933
Ooldea	UAM	SA	1933
Rockhole (Balgo)	RC	WA	1934
Yirrkala	Methodist	NT	1935
Port Keats	RC	NT	1935

(*continued*)

Name of Mission	Church	State / Territory	Commencement Date
Edward River	ABM	Qld	1935
Tennant Creek	RC	NT	1936
Phillip Creek	AIM	NT	1936
Davenport	Brethren	SA	1937
Derby (Leper Station)	RC	WA	1937
Ernabella	Presbyterian	SA	1937
Umeewarra	Brethren	SA	1937
Alice Springs/Arltunga	RC	NT	1937
Roelands Native Mission Farm	Church of Christ	WA	1938
Finniss Springs	SA	UAM	1939
Kellerberrin	Baptist	WA	1939
Daintree River	AOG	Qld	1939

'rescue humanitarianism' of the missionaries entered into an 'odd alliance' with 'settler racism',[33] a situation which contributed to dramatic scenes in the ongoing conflict between the original and incursive populations. Christian missions were not then as heavily subsidised by governments as they were to become after World War II. But co-dependence between church and state rather than independence was the rule in Aboriginal uplift, just as it was in other areas of welfare.

Massacres of First Australians continued: at Forrest River (WA) in 1926 and at Coniston Station (NT) in 1928. Arguments over the cause and number of victims in both calamities have figured in the 'History Wars' between the 'Black armband' and the 'White whitewash' schools of historians. Chief campaigner for the latter, Keith Windschuttle, does not deny that there was a massacre at Coniston Station, but he does deny the Forrest River massacre, maligning in the process the most vocal witness for the prosecution, missionary Ernest Gribble.[34] In the Coniston massacre at least 31 Indigenous people were killed, and it might have been as many as 170. The only positive observation that might be made about these massacres is that they may have been the last in which there was any element of official involvement by the forces of the law and they may have brought to an end a frontier war which had agonised

33 Peggy Brock, et al., *Indigenous Evangelists and Questions of Authority in the British Empire 1750–1940* (Leiden, Boston: Brill, 2005), 15.

34 John Harris, 'Counting the Bodies: Aboriginal Deaths in Colonial Australia', *Zadok Paper*, S115, 2001, 6f.

on for well over a century. But it did not bring to an end police brutality nor the struggle of Indigenous people for justice.

Indeed, one of the most amazing episodes in the history of Aboriginal missions was still to come. The event was referred to in the media Australia-wide and beyond as 'the Peace Expedition'. In 1932 five Japanese fishermen were killed at Caledon Bay on the eastern coast of Arnhem Land, NT. A police party was sent from Darwin to investigate, and one of their number, Constable A.S. McColl, was speared to death. The police planned a punitive expedition. Missionaries in Arnhem Land were appalled at the prospect and prevailed on the Commonwealth government to allow a party of CMS missionaries to embark on a peace expedition instead, unarmed and unprotected. The Prime Minister, Joseph Lyons, aware of the findings of the 1927 Wood Royal Commission into the Forrest River massacre, gave them six months to complete the exercise.

In the party were Hubert Warren who had been one of the early missionaries at the Roper River Mission and Alf Dyer who was then at the Oenpelli Mission. Dyer, given to visions and rash of judgement, had already resolved to go on the expedition alone having taken the matter to the Lord in prayer. He was given a verse from Scripture to affirm this leading: 'For if thou altogether holdest thy peace at this time, then shall … deliverance arise … from another place; … who knoweth whether thou art come … for such a time as this?' (Esther 4:14).[35] When Dyer joined the other members of the mission party in Darwin, one of them wrote:

> Having heard that CMS had had to restrain him from going overland, on horseback, entirely unaccompanied, to quieten the Caledon Bay blacks, and that he ranked with Warren in experience of the wild tribes, I had pictured Dyer a man of gigantic physique. Instead, he proved to be a thin little, malaria-ridden scrap of humanity who, especially in the shorts, shirt, and skull-cap which he wore aboard the lugger, looked like a wizened-up pirate.[36]

When the missionaries eventually arrived at Caledon Bay they were greeted with cheers rather than spears. They found that the Japanese had been killed for interfering with the women, but that Constable McColl had been killed

35 A.J. Dyer, *Unarmed Combat: An Australian Missionary Adventure* (Sydney: Edgar Bragg, [c.1954?]), 56; Keith Cole, *Oenpelli Pioneer: A Biography of the Founder of the Oenpelli Mission, the Rev. A.J. Dyer* (Melbourne: CMS Historical Publications, Melbourne, 1972).

36 Dyer, *Unarmed Combat*, 14.

by one Dagiar from a different tribe from Blue Mud Bay south of Caledon Bay. Dagiar, too, claimed that he speared the policeman when he witnessed him molesting his youngest wife. The missionaries persuaded those who confessed to killing the Japanese together with Dagiar to go to Darwin to face the trial which they were confident would acquit them. Warren returned south to a hero's welcome, while Dyer accompanied the accused to Darwin on an eleven-day voyage during which the Aboriginal people frequently abandoned ship and had to be retrieved. When they landed in Darwin, the Aborigines were immediately seized by the police and clapped in irons. They were demented with terror, expecting instant execution. Dyer received hostile letters from all over Australia, denouncing him for having deceived and betrayed the First Australians. 'These letters I took and laid on the Litany desk in Christ Church like King Hezekiah "to cast them upon the Lord".'[37] After disgraceful trials in which the accused were not even permitted to speak in their own defence, the killers of the Japanese were each sentenced to twenty years and Dagiar was sentenced to death. An appeal to the High Court, initiated by Warren, led to the quashing of all the sentences. Dagiar was released into Dyer's care, but disappeared and was never heard of again.

So vociferous were complaints at the treatment of the First Australians following the Peace Expedition, that a beginning was made in changing the procedures in court cases involving Aboriginal people. At about the same time, a more significant change in governmental policy was implemented: assimilation was to replace segregation.[38] Today it looks like a patronising and racist policy, but at the time it was a humanitarian breakthrough.[39] It signified a shift in understanding about the destiny of the Aboriginal people: they were no longer seen as a dying race. But assimilation was not about a future for Aboriginal people AS Aboriginal people.

Amidst the disaster and suffering of the Aboriginal people, missionaries continued to do the work to which they felt called: evangelising, encouraging Aboriginal people to live at peace with one another and with whites, acquiring sensitivity to Aboriginal cultures, and (the work of too few too late) translating the Scriptures into indigenous languages, the work of decades. At the new Methodist mission at Milingimbi in Arnhem Land, NT, the Rev. Thomas Theodor Webb and his wife, Eva, began in 1926 an exceptionally fruitful

37 Dyer, *Unarmed Combat*, 67.

38 Harris, *One Blood*, 763.

39 Brian H. Fletcher, *An English Church in Australian Soil* (Canberra: Barton Books, 2015), 184, 224.

ministry.[40] Aboriginal theologian, Djiniyini Gondarra, born at the mission in 1945, reports that it had been a very difficult place with frequent tribal wars. The Webbs brought reconciliation and restoration and were much loved for their 'pioneering, faithful witness'.[41] Webb never doubted that Christ could liberate from the fear of evil spirits and sorcery, but insisted that every ministry should be consistent with the culture. He closed the mission's children's home so that children could be with their parents during their schooling rather than with missionaries. He spoke up boldly for justice for the Aboriginal people and was among the fiercest objectors to police punitive expeditions.[42]

Australia lost one of its great missionary-scholars on 20 October 1922, when Carl Strehlow, in search of medical help, died at Horseshoe Bend, NT.[43] Strehlow had earned the title of 'ingkata', meaning a trusted leader and teacher, from the Aranda (Arrernte) people whom he served on the Lutheran Hermannsburg Mission. Among his converts was the future artist Albert Namatjira. Strehlow's most lasting contribution to the Aranda people, however, was his Bible translations. Word of Strehlow's passing spread quickly and Hermannsburg, already enjoying revival,[44] experienced a fresh spiritual vibrancy as believers held evangelistic meetings all over the mission area. Building on Strehlow's legacy, cresting the wave of revival, and led ably from 1926 by a new mission director, Friedrich W. Albrecht, it was a 'golden age for Hermannsburg'.[45]

German-speaking missionaries had always shown a deeper sensitivity to Aboriginal cultures than English speakers.[46] That now was beginning to

---

40 Arthur F. Ellermore, 'Methodism among the Aborigines', in James S. Udy and Eric G. Clancy, *Dig or Die* (Sydney: World Methodist Historical Society, 1981), 245f.

41 Djiniyini Gondarra, *Let My People Go* (Darwin: Bethel Presbytery, 1986), 2.

42 John Blacket, *Fire in the Outback* (Sutherland: Albatross Books, 1997), 49f.; David Andrew Roberts and Margaret Reeson, 'Wesleyan Methodist Missions to Australia and the Pacific', in Glen O'Brien and Hilary M. Carey (eds.) *Methodism in Australia: A History* (Farnham: Ashgate Publishing Company, 2015), 205.

43 Theodor G. H. Strehlow, *Journey to Horseshoe Bend* (Adelaide: Rigby, 1969).

44 Brock, *Indigenous Evangelists*, ch. 6.

45 Harris, *One Blood*, 381–410; Maurice Schild, 'Carl Strehlow's Work on the Aranda and Loritja Tribes – A Plea to Publish', *Lutheran Theological Journal*, 34.3 (November 2000): 147–153; Barbara Henson, *A Straight-out Man: F.W. Albrecht and Central Australian Aborigines* (Carlton: MUP, 1992).

46 'There were some significant differences between English and German speakers in their approach to indigenous societies. Germans showed great interest in learning and recording local languages, and were themselves outsiders in the British empire. German missionaries often arrived with poor English so that they were even more ready to preach and teach in an indigenous language.' Regina Ganter, 'German Missionaries in Australia', http://missionaries.griffith.edu.au/introduction#whygermans, accessed 25 April 2017.

change. A significant step was taken when Keith Langford-Smith, son of Sydney Canon S.E. Langford-Smith, worked on the CMS Roper River Mission Station in the NT. In 1932, he used a CMS publication to call attention to three things that were essential to any Aboriginal mission: (1) a knowledge of the native language; (2) a knowledge of Aboriginal laws and customs; and (3) a knowledge of the Aboriginal beliefs and myths integral to their world view.[47] Such axiomatic thinking had been a long time coming and, though it helped pave the way for all subsequent missionary work in northern Australia, it was not easily realised. For a start, Aboriginal people themselves were often very reluctant to share such knowledge.[48]

A mission where the new cultural sensitivity attained practical implementation with transformative results was established in 1937 at Ernabella in South Australia by Presbyterian medical practitioner and social activist, Dr Charles Duguid with, as we have seen, the help of R.M. Williams and of Bob Love, an experienced Presbyterian missionary to the Aboriginal people who was to become Superintendent of Ernabella in 1941. There the Pitjantjatjara were free to practise their culture and were taught in their own language. Together with Albrecht and Williams, Duguid campaigned successfully to have large areas of the south-west of the Northern Territory reserved for Aboriginal occupation rather than allowing the development of privately-owned pastoral properties.

Significantly contributing to the increased sensitivity to the needs of Aboriginal people was the experience of women missionaries nurtured in the feminism they had themselves helped to create. Those who had worked in India and China gave encouragement and advice to women working in the less glamorous missions in Australia. Recent research on women missionaries has revealed instances of startlingly progressive thinking within the context of conservative moral and theological thought. Such radical conservatism is the hallmark of evangelical women in their attention to blots on the national soul.

Easily the most important change, however, in the fraught history of the Aboriginal encounter with Christianity was the emergence of able Aboriginal Christian leaders. One Indigenous preacher who began to make his mark in the 1930s was Doug Nicholls. Converted in the Northcote Church of Christ in Melbourne, he became a Church of Christ minister. His fame as an Australian rules footballer, his sincerity and wit made him a popular speaker to white groups. He looked after a growing community of Aboriginal people in Fitzroy, Melbourne, at the end of the 1930s. It became the first

47 *Church Missionary Gleaner*, July 1932, 12–13.

48 This is a major contention of Laura Rademaker, *Found in Translation: Many Meanings on a North Australian Mission* (Honolulu: University of Hawai'i Press, 2018).

Aboriginal Church of Christ in Australia with himself as pastor. With the establishment of the Aborigines' Advancement League in 1957, the organisation selected Nicholls as its full-time field officer and he became a political activist. Appointed Governor of South Australia in 1976, he had to retire the following year because of ill health, still the only Indigenous Australian to serve as governor of any colony, state or territory.[49]

Among evangelical Aboriginal leaders who came to prominence during the interwar period, David Unaipon was exceptional.[50] He had first earned a measure of fame as an inventor, but during this period he became a much sought-after evangelist and public speaker. Unaipon's two causes were the welfare of the Aboriginal people and the propagation of the Christian Gospel, and he believed that these two causes were mutually reinforcing.[51] Today, his face adorns the Australian $50 bill, which gives due recognition of his brilliance, and is evidence perhaps that his interpretation of Indigenous history was acceptable to many in white society. He criticised organisers of the 1938 National Day of Mourning for harping on the narrative of failure in Aboriginal history. He wanted instead a narrative of gratitude and success. He thought traditional Aboriginal beliefs, on which he wrote extensively, were of anthropological interest only – he no longer believed them himself.

But Unaipon's was not the only route to emergence as an Aboriginal survivor and leader. There were Indigenous Christians who were beginning to construct a narrative alternative to both failure and success, namely one which called for the necessity of struggle with hopefulness. Chief among those in the evangelical Aboriginal community who led the fight for the rights of Indigenous people during the 1930s were William Cooper[52] and William Ferguson. Born near Echuca in 1861, Cooper founded the Australian Aborigines League in 1933. He petitioned King George V to intervene to prevent the extinction of the Aboriginal race and to grant Aboriginal people representation in the federal parliament. Though his efforts came to naught, he continued to press for Aboriginal rights in Victoria throughout the 1930s.

Cooper's counterpart in NSW was William Ferguson, an Aboriginal elder in the Dubbo Presbyterian Church. In 1937, he launched the Aborigines'

---

49 Mavis Thorpe Clark, *Pastor Doug: The Story of Sir Douglas Nicholls, Aboriginal Leader* (Melbourne: Lansdowne Press, 1972); 'Doug Nicholls', Collaborating for Indigenous Rights web exhibition profile, National Museum of Australia, accessed 16 November 2016 at http://indigenousrights.net.au/people/pagination/doug_nicholls.

50 On Unaipon, see Brock, *Indigenous Evangelists,* ch. 11.

51 Hilary, M. Carey, ' The Land of Byamee: K. Langloh Parker, David Unaipon, and Popular Aboriginality in the Assimilation Era,' *JRH*, 22.2, 1998, 200–218, see 213.

52 On Cooper, see *The Fountain of Public Prosperity*, chapter 14.

Progressive Association at Dubbo and travelled widely, inaugurating branches of his movement all over NSW. He pressed for a governmental inquiry into the corrupt Aboriginal Protection Board which then had supervision over Aboriginal affairs and was supported in his efforts by several key evangelical leaders. The Parliamentary Committee of Inquiry heard much evidence of shocking living conditions and mismanagement on Aboriginal reserves. Still, the government refused to budge.

Meanwhile, Cooper conceived of the idea of a 'Day of Mourning' on the sesquicentenary of white settlement on 26 January 1938. On the appointed day, Cooper, Ferguson, Nicholls and their supporters rallied in Sydney from all over the eastern States. A manifesto was circulated entitled 'Aborigines Claim Citizenship Rights', calling for an end to the Aborigines Protection Board, for proper education, for laws to prevent the exploitation of Aboriginal labour in the Outback, for an end to domestic service by Aboriginal girls, and a termination of all discrimination and injustice towards Aboriginal Australians. Their efforts culminated in a sympathetic meeting with Prime Minister Joseph Lyons, his wife Dame Enid Lyons, and John McEwen, Minister for the Interior, at Parliament House. Nothing but sympathy came of it. With the Great Depression on their minds and another war looming on the horizon, few of those with political power were willing to risk a white electoral backlash by espousing the Aboriginal cause. The problem was that Cooper and Ferguson had believed that they were speaking to an essentially Christian white community that would recognise that their claims were just and right. Though they died disillusioned, future events would prove them true prophets if without honour in their own country.[53]

Overseas Missions

In 1935 Archbishop Henry Frewen Le Fanu of Perth was elected Primate of the Church of England in Australia and Tasmania (as it was known until 1981). Le Fanu's appointment broke a 63-years-old tradition that the Primacy should be in Sydney, 'the mother see in Australia'. Howard Mowll, the vanquished and disappointed Archbishop of Sydney, congratulated Le Fanu at a missionary rally in the St Andrew's Cathedral Chapter House. Le Fanu responded:

> We love the Church of England and all that it stands for. It floats along and does its job fairly well; everybody growls at it. It does not fire the imagination, and some people are not in love with it. We do not talk as

53 Harris, *One Blood*, 608–633.

> much as we ought to about it. But our missionaries show that they are people who are prepared to take their lives in their hands. It is a good thing to meet people whose lives have been changed, and who are ready to go through anything for their Master. I love them, for they are still ready to show the marks of the nails in their hands.[54]

A church with missionaries was a church with a pulse. The immediate post-war decade was actually one of considerable expansion in missionary activity by Australian evangelicals. It is often observed that Australians were not good at initiating new denominations like the Americans, but typically what Australians were good at in the spiritual realm has not been noticed. In fact, they were very good at initiating new non-denominational missionary societies, and moving into new fields of missionary endeavour. Evangelicals themselves thought of commitment to overseas missions as a good barometer of spiritual health. In 1926, Australia was the third largest financial contributor to overseas missions behind the United States and Great Britain. In that year, a meeting of the missionary societies of the various denominations was held in Melbourne under the chairmanship of John R. Mott and in 1927 the National Missionary Council of Australia was formed.[55] *The Keswick Quarterly and Upwey Convention News* in the 1930s and 1940s carried reports on thirty-nine overseas missionary societies and forty-eight home mission societies. It was said that donations could be left with the editor to be distributed to about 50 mission organisations and they would always find their way to the right place.[56] In 1938 there were at least 613 Australians serving on the foreign mission field.[57]

The Bishop of Mombasa, R.S. Heywood, visited Australia in 1926 and promoted the cause of a new diocese, Central Tanganyika, in what is now Tanzania, and appealed to the Australian church for help. CMS of Australia and Tasmania accepted the responsibility for the area. George Chambers

---

54 *SMH,* 15 March 1935, 11.

55 On Mott's visits to Australia in 1896 and 1903, see *The Fountain of Public Prosperity,* chapter 17.

56 Renshaw, *Marvellous Melbourne and Spiritual Power*, 81–89.

57 David Turnbull, 'Australia and Carey's Legacy', unpublished paper presented at the Conference of the New Zealand Association for the Study of Religion, Wellington College of Education, Wellington, 1992. Turnbull points out that the figure of 613 foreign missionaries in 1938 is a conservative estimate since Australians serving in 'international societies' like the CIM and the SUM were not counted as Australian missionaries.

from Sydney was consecrated its first bishop in 1927, and the first party of Australian missionaries sailed for Africa in March 1928. Chambers was reputedly a dynamic leader of men and especially women, including Katie Miller (the real founder of the Church at Berega), Deaconess Narelle Bullard (who established Kongwa Hospital and who was also pastor, evangelist and preacher, believing that she had received a definite call to preaching as well as nursing), and Ruth Minton Taylor (a teacher at Mvumi School). By 1938 Chambers had a team of 24 Australian missionaries of whom 17 were women.

In 1931, MBI-trained Albert Drysdale went to the Fly River in New Guinea to establish a base for the Unevangelised Fields Mission (UFM), a newly-formed faith mission. Not only did its council not ask for financial support, but it expected its missionaries not to ask for any either. Drysdale wanted to work with and for the unreached Gogodala people to the north east of the Fly. Among the Gogodala, the old men realised that their tradition was seriously under threat, and they resolved to revert to their old ways and remove the missionaries' heads. Warned of their intention, the only missionary then at Balimo, Frank Briggs, went to meet his potential murderers. His grasp of their language was so poor that he doubted that he could make himself understood let alone persuade them to continue to welcome the new ways. He found that he was able to talk freely to them in their own tongue for two hours and won them over in what he naturally believed was a double miracle.[58]

UFM also worked in the Heart of Amazonia Mission (Brazil). Its Australian missionaries included two of *The Three Freds*[59] who in 1935 disappeared without trace on the Xingu River, where they had been attempting to reach the Kayapó Indians.[60] Yet, within two years friendly contact was made with the Kayapó, some of whom confessed to killing the missionaries, and, in 1942, just seven years after their martyrdom, a convention of Xingu Christians was held.

A conspicuous example of the reflex spiritual benefit for home churches of their engagement in overseas missions was the influence of the East Africa Revival that began in 1933 in the Rwanda CMS mission. The revival influenced Australian Christianity chiefly through three instruments: CMS missionaries in East Africa and visiting Australian church leaders, such as Marcus Loane, who took news of the revival back to Australia with them; African pastors,

58 Prince, *No Fading Vision*, 42.

59 Fred Roberts and Fred Dawson.

60 Horace Banner, *The Three Freds* (London: UFM, 1938); Horace Banner, *The Three Freds and After* (UK: UFM, 1961).

such as Festo Kivengere, who visited Australia and spoke at conventions; and Roy Hession's book *Calvary Road*, a classic of evangelical spirituality arising from the revival, which was widely read and faithfully followed. The revival resonated with the Keswick emphasis on holiness and strengthened the convention movement in Australia, raising the spiritual temperature of the movement at the very time when it was threatened by the chilly winds of liberalism, and it kept alive in the evangelical movement the expectation of revival.[61]

Evangelistic Missions and Revivals

Evangelistic campaigns of the inter-war years in Australia were taken by the best-known English-speaking evangelists on the international evangelical stage. They included Rodney 'Gipsy' Smith, William Booth-Clibborn, grandson of William Booth, Catherine Booth-Clibborn (William Booth's daughter who left the Salvation Army and became a Pentecostal), Gavin Hamilton, Hyman Appelman, Lionel Fletcher, Oswald Smith, Garry Love, W.P. Nicholson, William 'Cairo' Bradley, J. Edwin Orr, John Robinson, the Rev Bill Watts (known as 'Hallelujah' Bill), Bishop John Taylor Smith, Aimee Semple McPherson and Smith Wigglesworth.[62] They were all strongly individualistic evangelists in their style and methods. Australian-born Lionel Fletcher, the 'Empire Evangelist' was hailed as 'the outstanding evangelist of the interwar period'.[63]

Liberalism within the churches discouraged support for evangelistic campaigns and revivalism, but the passion for evangelism and the conversion of the unsaved continued to be fundamental to evangelicals. So too was pragmatism, and evangelistic rallies worked. Support for them both by organisers and attenders was still sufficiently strong to generate well-attended campaign meetings and a variety of types of evangelistic campaign. Gipsy Smith's 1926 campaign, for example, attracted large crowds in all mainland capital cities, and 80,000 signed 'decision' cards, made up, it has been suggested, 60 per cent of re-dedications and 40 per cent new converts.[64] Not surprisingly, given the

---

61 Colin Reed, *Walking in the Light: Reflections on the East African Revival and its Link to Australia* (Brunswick East: Acorn Press, 2007).

62 J. Edwin Orr, *Evangelical Awakenings in the South Seas* (Minneapolis: Bethany Fellowship, 1976), 151–160.

63 Geoffrey R. Treloar, *The Disruption of Evangelicalism* (London: IVP, 2016), 243.

64 Walter Phillips, 'Gipsy Smith in Australia, 1926: The Commonwealth Evangelistic Campaign', in Mark Hutchinson and Stuart Piggin (eds.), *Reviving Australia: Essays on the History and Experience of Revival and Revivalism in Australian Christianity* (Sydney: CSAC, 1994), 185–201.

horrors of World War I, there were evangelistic campaigns which stressed the end times and the second coming of Christ. Among second advent evangelists were the Baptist William Lamb, who followed world events closely, particularly in Russia and Israel,[65] and Harry Howe, Anglican rector of Christ Church, Gladesville in Sydney, whose 'Prophetic Chart' mapped out the future, the ruling theme in his preaching.[66]

Evangelism in local parish or church missions was still seen as the only legitimate way of growing a church, especially in the smaller evangelical denominations. The Gospel of the new birth, not cultural Christianity, was what all Australians needed. Dr G.R. Cairns of Seattle, for example, conducted a mission tour of 13 months under the direction of the Baptist Evangelistic and Propaganda committee and a record number of baptisms for a year, 561, was attributed to it.[67] In evangelistic missions especially for children, Alex Brown, CSSM missioner from 1924, and Vincent Craven, General Secretary of SU Australia, led the way. There were healing missions, such as that associated with Australian-born High Anglican, James Moore Hickson, who attracted huge crowds across the English-speaking world, including to the centre of Sydney Anglicanism, St Andrew's Cathedral. Healing also featured in the missions conducted by the Pentecostal revivalists, Smith Wigglesworth and Aimee Semple McPherson, whose claims to miracle-working lent fascination and notoriety to their meetings.[68]

The appeal of the exotic was also found in the ministry of Catherine Booth-Clibborn, who had acquired the nickname 'La Maréchale' (the Field-Marshall). On visiting Australia in 1926 she was so struck by the great potential of the nation as a force for the spread of the Gospel beyond its shores that she wrote the hymn 'Let Australia set the Pace'.

> Hear the cry from every nation,
> Bound and struggling for release;
> See, above earth's desolation,
> Comes the wondrous Prince of Peace.

---

65 Michael Petras, 'The Life and Times of the Reverend William Lamb (1868 -1944)', *The Baptist Recorder*, 101, 2008, 1–11.

66 H.G.J. Howe, *The Dawning of that Day* (Sydney: [H.G.J. Howe], 1922). This book went through five editions before Howe's death in 1932.

67 BUNSW, *Annual Report 1921–2*, bound with the Minute Book, Baptist Association, Epping, NSW.

68 Damon S. Adams, 'Divine Healing in Australian Protestantism', *JRH*, 41.3, 2017, 346–363.

Chorus:

"Go and tell" of His redemption,
Let Australia set the pace;
Christ alone brings full salvation,
Reaching every tribe and race.

The Booth-Clibborns fell out with the Salvation Army when they followed for a time the extravagances of the Australian prophet, Alexander Dowie.[69] But the essential unity of those evangelicals who had a passion for souls and who put evangelism above orthodoxy is evidenced by two historical fragments. John Ridley, the finest of Baptist evangelists, wrote a poem testifying to his personal admiration for Catherine's evangelistic zeal:

I trace thy fervent feet
To many a haunt of Hell;
And hear thy voice so sweet
The gospel message tell;

And sinners in their shame
And women of ill fame
Will ever bless thy name,
La Maréchale.[70]

Then on 19 June 2012, an earth tremor in Melbourne caused the top shelf of books belonging to Will Renshaw, historian of the evangelical heritage, to collapse. On top of a pile of books now jumbled on the floor he found a book personally inscribed by 'The Maréchale' to Miss Renshaw, an unmarried aunt, for a 'real service rendered' in 1936.[71] The sanctified unity of those hungry for souls was not easily fractured by a little heterodoxy.

The preaching of the Gospel followed by an appeal to accept Christ was by now the standard fare especially in evening services in many evangelical churches, especially in Methodist and Baptist churches. The converted had heard it all before, but, it was reasoned, they loved it, and the unconverted, who it was hoped would also be in attendance, needed to hear it. In Sydney, C.J. Tinsley, pastor of the Stanmore Baptist church, built up what became the premier Baptist congregation in Australia with a vigorous evangelistic outreach.

---

69 On Dowie, see *The Fountain of Public Prosperity*, chapter 18.

70 John Ridley, *The Passion for Christ* (Stanwell Tops: Ambassadors for Christ, 1963), 72.

71 Will Renshaw to Darrell Paproth, email 22 June 2012.

Tinsley's slogan 'We must preach or perish; teach or tarnish; evangelise or fossilise' became a familiar refrain in Baptist life in the 1930s.[72]

Open air preaching reached its zenith as a form of evangelism in the inter-war years. Open Air Campaigners, which developed into an international ministry, originated in Australia. The name was suggested by Roy Gordon, the greatest of open air preachers. Jim Duffecy, converted in an OAC beach Sunday School at Coogee, a Sydney suburb, in 1923 and who was to become Director of OAC International, wrote of Gordon:

> As an open air evangelist to adults I have never seen his equal. I believe he ranked with Whitefield, Booth, and the other greats. Working mainly in Sydney and NSW, his ministry at city parks, factories and Sunday evening city meetings will long be remembered. Crowds of fifteen hundred miners would gather around the wagon for hours as he preached to them during depression days on the Newcastle coalfields. Thousands were converted under his unique open air ministry.[73]

Woe betide the heckler who tried to belittle the Gospel when Gordon was on the platform. Duffecy was not so naturally gifted, but with disarming candour he revealed something of the psychological state of those who believed themselves called by God to do the work of an evangelist:

> If I waited until I had a burden for souls, I would never get the burden. I never go to an open air meeting without thinking that I would rather be a *student* of the Word than a *preacher* of it, especially if the open air meeting looks as though it may be a difficult one!
>
> I don't love souls until I look into their faces in the open air, so I trick myself into going to them. I use two books to do it and each supplements the other. The first book is my Bible … the other one is my diary. The first one tells me *what* to preach and the other one *when* to preach it. I try to keep the last one sensibly full so that I have to go to preach the first one. I often go in fear and trembling (I find that knocking knees get better if you kneel on them), but I always come back rejoicing. I find that I get less ulcers from relaxed working than guilty sitting.[74]

---

72 Stanmore Baptist Church 40th Year Memorial Book Presented to Pastor C. J. Tinsley, 27 May 1941; John G. Ridley, *C.J. Tinsley of Stanmore: A Love of the Evangel* (Sydney: Greenwood Press, n. d.).

73 Jim Duffecy, 'Roy Gordon goes Home', *Intercom,* December 1971.

74 *Intercom,* December 1971.

In Melbourne, open air preaching was well supported between the wars. A score of open air preachers, attached mainly to the Melbourne Gospel Crusade and the Evangelization Society of Australasia, braved the hecklers at Yarra Bank in Melbourne, which has been compared with the Domain in Sydney and Mars Hill in Athens, as well as other sites in the city and suburbs. The preachers included such respectable evangelical veterans as Frank Varley, H.P. Smith, Charles A. Sandland, Leonard Buck and George Hall. Disruptive youth were removed by those police 'in full sympathy with the work'. The magic lantern was used to project images and gospel texts onto sheets attached to walls so that the message might be received through eye-gate as well ear-gate. The message? 'Let the stern facts of sin and judgment be fearlessly proclaimed, in the power of the Spirit, and we shall see more broken hearts.'[75]

Local revivals continued to accompany evangelistic campaigns, and, as with all genuine revivals, spread the influence of the Gospel beyond the churches into the wider community. A revival in Cessnock on the NSW coalfields reduced the hold of Communism on the miners. In 1929, the coalfields had been the subject of first a coal miners' strike and then a lockout by the management. The Communist leaders of the Miners' Union were stirring up the miners to use direct action. In the midst of the anxiety, the Protestant churches of Cessnock (Baptist, Methodist, Presbyterian, Salvation Army) promoted an evangelistic campaign with Frederick B. Van Eyk, a Pentecostal from South Africa, and Albert Banton as evangelists. The meetings had phenomenal success with hundreds converted. In Pentecostal folklore, many of the 'red' activists were converted and revealed their caches of explosives stored in readiness for the insurrection. The plentiful conversions defused the situation and deprived the unions of so many Communists that they never recovered their dominance.[76]

Revivals too were instrumental in addressing the needs of Aboriginal people. Aboriginal pastor Peter Morgan testifies that revivals were surprisingly common among his people. Morgan's experience provided evidence that the

75 Renshaw, *Marvellous Melbourne and Spiritual Power,* 124–137; Robert Evans, *The Evangelisation Society of Australasia: The Second Period, 1919–1945* (Hazelbrook: the author, 2011).

76 Bob James, '"Lots of Religion and Freemasonry": The Politics of Revivalism during the 1930s Depression on the Northern Coalfields,' in Hutchinson and Piggin (eds), *Reviving Australia,* 233–248.

evangelical movement in Australia had long witnessed phenomena consistent with full-blown Pentecostalism. He testified in a 1993 sermon:

> I come from the Atherton tablelands. Where I come from, revival broke out in 1934 so it's a long time. 1934. Now the Holy Ghost fell upon our people and they were drunk for weeks. They couldn't go to the shops to the supermarket otherwise they speak in tongues. They were drunk, they were drunk, you would think they were under the influence, but they were drunk in the Spirit, and they couldn't speak a word for weeks in English. They spoke in tongues … My cousin who came through this revival in 1934, I said to him, 'Your face is shining'. He says, 'Yeah'. He says, 'I know that'.[77]

The visiting evangelist most interested in chronicling revival was J. Edwin Orr, who was born and raised in Belfast in Ireland, engaging in city-wide evangelism with Christian Endeavour. He first visited Australia in 1936, covering the continent and holding twenty meetings a week over six weeks. At the conclusion of this campaign, Orr left a written account of his 'impressions of Australia'. He noted that the twin sins of Australians were 'gambling and pleasure-craze', and observed that, 'The average Australian is not religious: he is not anti-religious either: he is just indifferent'. He reported that the major denominations supported his evangelistic efforts and that evangelical unity was apparent everywhere he went. He said that although there were some liberal theologians among the Presbyterians, Methodists and Congregationalists, all three of these groups welcomed his meetings, especially the lay people. Orr recorded that 10,000 people indicated that they were in need of personal spiritual 'revival' and there were 1,200 first-time decisions for Christ.[78] Orr ministered again in Australia in 1938–1939, touring the main country towns and many outback posts, and reported good results everywhere.

In retrospect, reformed alcoholic Arthur Stace, who chalked in copperplate the word 'Eternity' on the footpaths of Sydney streets, has become the most celebrated convert of interwar evangelism. His conversion came through the preaching of R.B.S. Hammond, while the inspiration to write the word 'Eternity" (half a million times over 35 years) came from a sermon preached

77 Peter Morgan, recorded address given to the National Praise and Worship Conference, Lighthouse Christian Centre, Wollongong, NSW, 28 September 1993.

78 J. Edwin Orr, *All Your Need: 10,000 Miles of Miracle Through Australia and New Zealand* (London: Marshall, Morgan & Scott, 1937), 114–121.

by John Ridley on Isaiah 57:15, 'For thus saith the high and lofty One that inhabiteth Eternity, whose name is Holy; I dwell in the high and holy place, with him also that is of a contrite and humble spirit, to revive the spirit of the humble, and to revive the heart of the contrite ones.' The word 'Eternity' was lit up on the Sydney Harbour Bridge at the New Year's fireworks display to welcome in the third millennium. It was witnessed by more than a million around the harbour and over a billion world-wide. Following the cessation of the pyrotechnics, as the word 'Eternity' remained the sole illumination in the darkness, the vast assemblage around the harbour foreshore broke the silence with spontaneous applause, testifying to the profound shaping of the Australian soul in the most distinctive of Christian values: humility in the light of eternity. It was a moment of poetic wonder:

> I saw 'Eternity' the other night
> illuminated left to right
> across the harbour – Word of light:
>
> a sign in darkness proving sight
> and comprehension of the night,
>
> a script in time, a trace in air
> of what is. Always. Everywhere.[79]

Other well-known inter-war converts include Marcus Loane, future Archbishop of Sydney, Paul White, the 'jungle doctor', and Stuart Barton Babbage, later Dean of Sydney and of Melbourne. Loane was converted at a mission held at St. Paul's Chatswood by Edmund Clarke, a visiting CSSM missioner. Clarke had visited Australia in 1913 and returned in 1922, in receipt of the support of Brethren business man, J.B. Nicholson. On the last night of the Chatswood meetings, Loane sat at the back of the church with his mother and a sister. Clarke ended his sermon with an appeal for personal commitment to the Lord Jesus. Loane recalls glancing at his mother and sister and wondering what they would think: 'But I knew that God had spoken, and He gave me grace to respond.'[80] His contemporaries, White and Babbage, were converted at missions conducted by W.P. Nicholson[81] whom Babbage remembered as 'a fiery, tub-thumping, hell-raising Irish evangelist'. White was

---

79 Kate O'Neil, 'Eternity: For Arthur Stace', unpublished poem.

80 John R. Reid, *Marcus L. Loane: a biography* (Brunswick East: Acorn Press, 2004), 4.

81 Stanley Barnes, *All for Jesus: The Life of W.P. Nicholson* (Minneapolis: Ambassador Publications, 1996).

converted in Sydney on 3 December 1926 at the Nicholson United Mission and that evening signed a 'My Decision' card. Babbage was converted with 'far reaching consequences' at a Nicholson mission in Auckland in 1932.[82]

Student Work

The evangelical taste for texts, doctrines, and apologetics made it a cerebral faith as well as an emotional one. It is therefore not surprising that between the wars, it was successfully defended and propagated at universities and that evangelical student societies flourished there. Many very able students entered Sydney University with the exhibitions awarded under the University Amendment (Exhibitioners' Fees) Act of 1918. Before the First World War the Australian Student Christian Movement (SCM), formed in 1896, had a near monopoly in the field. As the debate over modernism hotted up after the War, the SCM's choice of leadership imported an increasingly liberal theology which divided its broad membership. The reaction of Paul White to his undergraduate experience of SCM at the University of Sydney, was indicative:

> When I got up there the one Christian organisation that I heard about was the Student Christian Movement. I went along to a study circle, and the leader (a prominent Methodist minister) started to tear leaves out of the Bible, and tell me that I really needed to rethink the whole of my faith; that I had swallowed too much without thinking. I didn't like it, and I told him so. I was at the advanced age of nineteen, and perhaps I was a little bit *gauche*, because after three or four of those particular bible studies, it was suggested that perhaps they would go more smoothly if I didn't attend.[83]

At Sydney University in 1919, an Arts undergraduate, John Deane, called a meeting of protest against the widened basis of membership of the SCM. Those who came withdrew from the Sydney University Christian Union and began a meeting for prayer in a room in the clock tower. This became known as the Sydney University Bible League.

In response to liberalism both within SCM in universities in England, evangelicals formed the Inter-Varsity Fellowship (IVF) in 1928. It was a move precipitated not only by the questioning of Christian fundamentals, but also by the abandonment of the priority of evangelism. In the years immediately

82 Stuart Barton Babbage, *Memoirs of a loose Canon* (Brunswick East, Vic.: Acorn Press, 2004), 11.

83 Paul White interviewed by Margaret Lamb, 3 March 1986.

prior to 1928 the World Student Christian Federation sought to replace the strident nationalism thought responsible for the Great War with an internationalism designed to funnel relief funds to dispossessed students. In the process it came to focus on relief exclusive of evangelism.[84] Evangelicalism was already an international movement, and the evangelicals who formed IVF were eager to establish Evangelical Christian Unions, not only in every British university, but in every university in the British Empire and beyond. The IVF sent its vice-chairman, a young medical student called Howard Guinness, to Canada to begin that work. It was an ideal appointment: Guinness was a pioneering, individualistic, maverick. In the middle of his tour of Canada, Guinness received from Brethren philanthropist, J.B. Nicholson, a telegram inviting him 'to extend to Australia [his] … work as a representative of the Christian Union of Great Britain'.[85]

Guinness arrived in January 1930, and in Melbourne on 14 March 1930 the Evangelical Union (EU) was launched 'in utter dependence upon God', as the Minutes record.[86] Fifty-five students became members on that day. On 3 April 1930, the Sydney University EU emerged out of the pre-existing Sydney University Bible Union. There is some evidence that the EU at the University of Queensland may have pre-dated those at Melbourne and Sydney Universities. Dr J.E.C. Aberdeen, a botanist with the University of Queensland, recalls that the Queensland EU may have started as early as 1929, on the heels of the organisation of Evangelical Unions in Britain.[87] In Guinness's second visit to Australia in 1933, similar student associations were established in every Australian university.

The work of the IVF in Sydney began with a commitment to evangelising students when they were still at school. Guinness said: 'our first target was the schools for we believed that a Christian witness in any University was largely dependent on the Christians who joined it from school. School then was the place to confront students with the living Christ before their attitudes hardened and spiritual truths were rejected in the name of reason or expediency.'[88] In 1930 J.B. Nicholson called together 25 young men and women,

---

84 Benjamin L. Hartley, 'Saving Students: European Student Relief in the Aftermath of World War I', *IBMR*, 42:4, October 2018, 295–315.

85 Joy Parker, *A Vision of Eagles: Fifty Years of Crusaders in NSW* (Sydney: The Crusader Union of NSW, 1980), 7.

86 The primary minutes seem to be lost. Harold McCracken, *Summing Up* (Canberra: Heather and Paul Shelley, 2003), 119; David E. Angus. *Decisive Years: Experiences of Christian University Students* (Melbourne: David E. Angus, 2005), 3.

87 Dr John E.C. Aberdeen interviewed by Margaret Lamb, 8 December 1989.

88 Parker, *Vision of Eagles*, 7.

mainly from the newly-formed EU and the Katoomba Convention, who were committed to Guinness's vision, and the Crusader Union was launched. Its founding Secretary was Dr Paul White who asked people to pray for him while they cleaned their teeth.[89] The Crusader Union confined its mission to independent schools. Within government schools a separate evangelical student group, the Inter-School Christian Fellowship (ISCF) was formed.

In June 1935 members of the SUEU debated the motion to change the name of their society to the Sydney University Christian Fellowship. In supporting the motion, it was argued that the word 'Evangelical' created confusion for students who thought SCM was what they were looking for, whereas the EU was what they really wanted. Furthermore, it was acknowledged that there was a 'natural dislike' to the name, 'especially in the colleges'. Those opposed to the motion argued that the name formed a reproach which was 'so necessary in keeping members up to the mark'. Thirty-five attended the meeting which debated the motion. The motion was lost very narrowly, by 17 to 15 with three abstentions.[90]

In 1935 W.P. Nicholson spoke at a mission at Sydney University. When he began to speak, several students in the back of the room 'yelled cat-calls, stamped their feet, sang songs, and threw "an irritant powder" around the room'. Afterward, the Rev. David Hughes, a Methodist minister who chaired the gathering, said that he had spoken to wharf labourers at Woolloomooloo, at the Sydney Domain, and at Hyde Park in London, and had never heard such foul language or the name of Jesus so scorned as he had at this meeting.[91] Were such unpleasant experiences indicative of a widening gap between evangelical culture and common culture? Evangelicals were certainly committed to maintaining the engagement of the two cultures while never giving up on the ambition to reform the popular culture. But they were probably more successful at engaging the more educated than the workers. By the beginning of World War II many old hands had come to the rescue of the evangelical student movement. These included Nash, Hammond, Paul White, Principal Morling, Marcus Loane, Howard Guinness (who took up a parish in Sydney), Stuart Barton Babbage, Leon Morris, Frank Andersen, John Thompson, and John Laird. Basil Williams, from New Zealand, was appointed as the first IVF travelling staff worker, and his four years of service strengthened the

89 Parker, *Vision of Eagles*, 65.

90 Minutes of the SUEU, 10 and 27 June 1935, acc.549 series 27, University of Sydney Archives, Fisher Library, Sydney.

91 *SMH*, 1 August 1935, 9.

movement all over Australia. It resulted in a more cerebral faith, adept at informing the consciousness as well as sensitising the conscience.

* * *

Evangelical Christians between the wars continued to try hard. They tried hard to defend the authority of the Bible and the truth of the Gospel. They tried hard to win souls and to shape the soul of the nation. They were unnerved and divided by liberalism, but by the beginning of World War II had recruited able apologists. Capable laity took responsibility for running the institutions essential to its expansion: conventions, Bible colleges, evangelistic and missionary societies. Liberalism within denominations increased the supply of evangelicals to non-denominational societies not contaminated by liberalism. The movement held its own and won back some of the kudos it had lost through World War I. In the process, it won many to vital faith and influenced the majority of Australians, including R.M. Williams, with its values and concerns. But it was a more inward-looking and defensive movement than it had been before World War I, and no sooner was it on the road to recovery than it was battered again by the brutality of war.

Chapter Six

RELUCTANT COMBATANTS

Evangelical Responses to World War II

'War is, without question, the negation of all that Christ taught and meant, and yet, as in bitter irony, there are professedly Christian men who defend it, as their forefathers defended slavery.'
(The Rev J.W. Burton, *The Methodist*, 27 February 1932, 4.)

The churches were taught a number of hard lessons in World War I, and World War II gave them all too much opportunity to prove that they had learned those lessons. Especially at the beginning of the first war, they had glorified military service and the honour of making the supreme sacrifice in the defence of the nation. They had been too quick to identify what God's purpose might be in that crisis of civilisation. They had not counted the cost of total war and they were accused of doing too little to give practical support to the troops themselves. In World War II the churches, aware that their zealous support for the war effort at the beginning of World War I had hastened the advent of secularisation,[1] were less strident in their proclamation of the divine purpose, less eager to encourage their youth to go to war, and they were more determined to give practical help to those who did enlist.[2]

When German forces invaded Poland on 3 September 1939, Prime Minister Robert Menzies announced that Australia was again at war. The reaction to his appeal for volunteers was not as enthusiastic as that of the call to arms in 1914. From 1939 to 1945, with the help of conscription, Australia mobilised

1 Hilary Carey, 'Religion and Society', in Deryck M Schreuder and Stuart Ward, (eds), *Australia's Empire, Oxford History of the British Empire* (Oxford: OUP, 2008), 207.

2 Michael Gladwin, *Captains of the Soul: A History of Australian Army Chaplains* (Newport: Big Sky Publishing, 2013), 104.

993,000 men and women out of a population of some 6.9 million. Of that number 27,073 were killed in action or died, 23,477 were wounded in action, and 30,560 were taken prisoner, of whom 8,296 perished while in captivity.[3] The losses were about half those of World War I,[4] and enthusiasm for the war was less than half.

Attending to the Australian soul and sensitising the national conscience, therefore, elicited a more nuanced response from evangelicals than they had made at the beginning of World War I. There were possibly few more reluctant fighters in the Empire once the war began in 1939 than the young evangelical Christian men and women of Australia. They disproportionately volunteered for the Medical Service or other non-combatant roles once World War II was declared. Horace Hamer and Tom Wilkinson, two Christian servicemen from Victoria, recalled that up to twenty-five percent of their medical units were composed of evangelical Christians. Hamer became a stretcher-bearer with the 10 Field Ambulance in New Guinea, and Wilkinson was with the 2/9 General Hospital, also in New Guinea.[5] Many other evangelicals were assigned to intelligence units, especially the élite Central Bureau. Most, however, of those even of a similar religious persuasion, volunteered out of a sense of patriotism and a desire to defend their loved ones and their country against the enemy, and, therefore, ended up in various combat and support units in spite of the reluctance acquired through the nation's recent experience of total war.

The Medicos

If reluctant, the evangelical men and women who served in World War II were still among the most idealistic, and their commitment to find a way to serve their country was undiminished. William E.C. (Bill) Andersen was a conscientious objector (CO), but he saw combat in New Guinea anyway. Andersen was only sixteen years old when war broke out and a pupil at Fort Street Boys' High School in Sydney. Thanks to the Inter-School Christian Fellowship (ISCF) and the school Classics Master, Wilfred Porter, he had become a Christian in 1936. Porter was a member of the Christian Brethren

---

3 'World War II: 1939–45', National Archives of Australia website, http://www.naa.gov.au/collection/explore/defence/conflicts.aspx accessed 25 July 2016.

4 Jeffrey Grey, *A Military History of Australia*, 3rd ed. (Cambridge: Cambridge University Press, 2008), 152–3.

5 Horace Hamer and Thomas L. Wilkinson, interviewed by Linder, 27 June 2000.

and influential in guiding Andersen's thinking about the New Testament and Christian ethics. Andersen considered Jesus' words about 'loving your enemies' and decided to apply for CO status in the early years of the war. His EU friends at Sydney University whom Andersen described as 'just war people' made this decision difficult. Andersen had no sooner thought his own way through this dilemma when he was conscripted. However, his wish for non-combatant status was honoured and he was assigned to the Medical Service in 1943 as a male nurse in the 2/7 Field Ambulance.[6] He agreed with Hamer and Wilkinson (above) that about twenty-five percent of the medical personnel he encountered during the war were evangelical believers.

Andersen was encouraged by older Christians to let the other soldiers know from the first day that he was a Christian believer: 'nail your colours to the mast', they said. Andersen experienced little hostility when he used his Scripture Union notes to guide his Bible reading in his tent at night in full view of his mates. Soon other likeminded men in the unit identified themselves, and Bible study groups were formed. Andersen found that, wherever he was posted, there were always Christian believers around for close friendship and fellowship.

Troops scheduled for deployment to New Guinea were sent to the Atherton Tablelands in Queensland for final training in jungle warfare, and there were approximately 70,000 of them there at the time. All of the usual evangelical troop welfare agencies were also there: the Salvation Army, the YMCA and Everyman's, and all were exceptionally active. The Herberton Methodist Church became a focal point of evangelical worship on Sunday evenings when the Diggers took over and held an egalitarian service with no distinction of rank and no salutes. These services were packed Sunday after Sunday and many lives were changed as a result. Andersen enjoyed meeting four times a week with a small circle of believers that included Alan Begbie, the senior chaplain in the 6th Division; Vincent Craven, a YMCA officer and dynamic Christian leader in Sydney before the war; and Alan Dube, another energetic YMCA officer. Begbie had already served in New Guinea at the bloody battles at Buna and Gona, and after the war, became Chaplain General of the Australian Army from 1957 to 1974 and a major figure in Sydney Anglicanism.

Posted to New Guinea in mid-1944, Andersen's unit set up a field hospital under the command of Colonel Clive Selby. The action on the Kokoda Track had been concluded, but heavy fighting continued in northern New Guinea

6 Bill Andersen interviewed by Linder, 8 June 2001.

and the islands of the area. At one point, Andersen suffered from hypomania[7] and was repatriated to Australia for a few weeks for treatment. He graduated from Sydney University by means of correspondence courses, and Colonel Selby made him a teacher of his fellow troops in the war zone so that they could gain their Intermediate Certificates after the war. Andersen's Bible studies during the war also led him to join a Baptist church. Demobilised in 1946, he taught for many years at Sydney University and at Morling and Moore theological colleges in Sydney in the field of psychology. He also worked untiringly with such Christian organisations as Scripture Union, IVF and the Crusader Union, reaching an astonishing 75 years of service to SU in 2013.[8]

Among evangelical medical doctors who enlisted in the service during the war was Ronald Richmond Winton. Born in Campbelltown, some 60 kilometres south of Sydney, Winton grew up in a modest middle class home that valued education and good literature. With his head full of Rupert Brooke's poems and Dickens and Shakespeare, Winton won an Exhibition to study medicine at Sydney University in 1930. On graduation, he accepted a position as a junior resident at the Brisbane General Hospital in 1935. As an empire loyalist and idealist, he enlisted in the second AIF on 23 May 1940 and dedicated his life-saving skills to the war effort.[9] He gave more than six years of military service as a Medical Officer in various combat and administrative units. Like Andersen, he found evangelical soul mates everywhere he served. He initially was assigned as an MO of a Regimental Aid Post attached to the 2/2 Australian Anti-Tank Regiment and shipped to the Middle East. His unit was posted to the British base near present-day Gaza.

Winton's anti-tank unit was involved in serious fighting during 1941 in Syria and Lebanon. During that time, he often worked in an Advanced Dressing Station. In June-July, 1941, during heavy fighting at Merdjayoun in the Syrian campaign, Winton served as the anaesthetist for a surgeon who operated on the badly damaged leg of a young artillery officer who had performed heroically during an eighteen-day period of fighting that blunted a Vichy French tank attack on the city. His wounds had become septic necessitating the amputation of his leg. That young officer was Arthur Roden Cutler, Winton's fellow Sydney Anglican, who subsequently was awarded the Victoria Cross and became Governor of NSW.

---

7 Hypomania is a minor form of mania, marked by periods of great excitement and violence, in this case, growing out of the experiences of combat in wartime.

8 Bill Andersen, 'This Is My Story', *The Baptist Recorder*, July, 1998, 4–8.

9 Ronald Winton, *Johnny Head-In-Air: Memoirs of a Doctor Journalist* (Glebe: Book House, 2002), 24–37.

Winton's unit was recalled home in 1942 to defend Australia from a possible Japanese invasion. He was posted to the newly formed Second Division and made a staff officer, then sent to New Guinea. Near the end of the New Guinea campaign, he moved to the headquarters of the Australian Army in Lae and was promoted to Lieutenant Colonel. He was demobilised on 28 November 1946 and returned to civilian medical practice. In 1947, he became assistant editor of *The Medical Journal of Australia*. In 1957, he was appointed editor and served in that capacity for twenty years. He lectured in the history of medicine at Sydney University from 1962 to 1977 and supported the EU there while also serving on a number of international medical bodies. His obituary in *The Medical Journal of Australia* notes that 'The great guiding principle in his life was his deep Christian faith'.[10]

Secret Intelligence Work

Other evangelical men were attracted to or were selected for the intelligence branch, especially the highly secret intelligence unit known as the Central Bureau.[11] Their number included Will Renshaw from Melbourne and Donald Robinson from Sydney.

William Fletcher Renshaw was born on 26 January 1926 in Kew, Victoria, into a devout Methodist family. His father, David, was a Methodist local preacher. Renshaw matriculated at university at age fifteen and became a chartered accountant at age eighteen. Will admired his older brothers David and Allan, and could hardly wait to follow them into the armed forces as soon as he was old enough to do so. After registering for conscription on his eighteenth birthday, 26 January 1944, Renshaw enlisted in the RAAF,[12] training first as a wireless operator in Victoria. The RAAF soon discovered his brilliant mind and recruited him for the Central Bureau. He joined No. 5 Wireless Unit and was assigned to the Central Bureau's secret headquarters at 'Nyrambla', a large house in the Brisbane suburb of Ascot.[13] Although in the RAAF, he ended active service seconded to the US 6th Army as part of

10 Laurel Thomas, 'Ronald Richmond Winton: Obituary', *The Medical Journal of Australia*, 181.1, 2004, 26.

11 On the Central Bureau, see Alan Powell, *War by Stealth: Australians and the Allied Intelligence Bureau, 1942–1945* (Carlton South: MUP, 1996); Jack Bleakley, *The Eavesdroppers* (Canberra: AGPS Press, 1992).

12 William F. Renshaw, interviewed by Linder, 31 July 1998.

13 William F. Renshaw, Curriculum Vitae; and William F. Renshaw, War Service Diary, 16 Feb. 1944 to 31 Dec. 1945, 1–4.

General MacArthur's ultra-secret intelligence unit in St. Miguel near Manila in the Philippines.

Renshaw experienced military life in the raw, a shock for someone who had grown up in a loving Christian home where he never heard a swear word. He discovered that finding Christian fellowship in the armed forces was mostly a matter of self-identification by behaviour and going to Christian places that other believers in the service frequently visited, like local churches or Everyman's huts. He also discovered rich veins of Christian fellowship in churches of various denominations (Methodist, Baptist, Salvation Army), in Everyman's huts, and in Bible studies and Christian fellowship meetings. While posted to Point Cook near Melbourne, he placed on a bulletin board a notice convening Christian fellowship meetings and from twelve to fifteen men responded. Among them was Noel Vose, later the noted leader of Western Australian and then of world Baptists, but at the time simply another young Christian in the ranks of the RAAF. Renshaw and Vose became good friends and Renshaw occasionally took Vose home with him for a meal and family worship.[14]

The Central Bureau was a mixed unit of Australian and American troops attached to the US Sixth Army under General Douglas MacArthur. Their job was to monitor Japanese radio transmissions and to crack their codes. Those who agreed to serve in the Central Bureau took a vow of secrecy and silence that was only lifted fifty years after the conclusion of the war. They were told: 'Not only do you not exist, you never will have existed. You will remain for always unknown and unacknowledged. There will be no awards, no glory. There will be no medals for this unit.'[15] Renshaw had entered the clandestine world of 'Signit', a code name for Signal Intelligence, responsible for intercepting and decoding Japanese military messages.

Renshaw discovered other Christians attached to various Central Bureau units in Brisbane. Among them were Donald Robinson, a future Archbishop of Sydney; Alan Langdon, a future distinguished clergyman of the Sydney Anglican diocese; Robert Brown, a future Melbourne Baptist minister and columnist for *The Age*; Ted Brown, future Treasurer of the Fellowship for Revival of the Methodist Church of Victoria; and Geoff Charlesworth, a future leader of note in the Victorian Methodist Church. These men often saw each other at various Brisbane church services, especially at the dynamic Albert Street Methodist Church and the lively Baptist Tabernacle.

---

14 Renshaw, War Service Diary, 2; Renshaw interview, 31 July 1998.

15 'Allied Signal Intelligence Units and Other Secret Units in Australia During WW2', http://home.st.net.au/~dunn/sigint/sigint.htm, accessed 7 June 2006.

No. 5 Wireless Unit moved from Brisbane to San Miguel north of Manila in July 1945. There Renshaw began to employ his skills as a Japanese Kana Code intercept operator. He and his mates picked up messages indicating that the Japanese government had mobilised a force to resist the invasion of their homeland considerably larger than the Allies had originally anticipated, and that it was prepared to fight to the last man, woman and child. This intelligence was fed to the American government in Washington, contributing to the decision to drop the first atomic bombs on Japan in August 1945.

As the war wound down and then ended, Renshaw used the opportunity to experience his first cross-cultural missionary work in conjunction with several Australian and American padres. In his war diary, he especially praised the preaching and pastoral work of Edward (Ted) Roberts-Thompson, the RAAF chaplain attached to his unit. Roberts-Thompson was the former pastor of the Hobart Baptist Tabernacle and a future principal of Morling College in Sydney.

Renshaw returned to Australian soil on 27 October 1945, was finally discharged at Melbourne on 29 April 1946, and resumed his professional life as a chartered accountant. In the years that followed, he became a successful Melbourne accountant and one of the most energetic of the lay leaders of evangelical Christianity in that city. In particular, during those post-war years, he devoted time and money to the Melbourne Bible Institute, Christian higher education and the support of overseas missions.

In Sydney, Donald Robinson also was invited to join the Central Bureau. He was born in 1922 in Lithgow, the son of Richard Bradley Robinson, a Church of England minister and later a well-known Canon of St. Andrew's Cathedral and confidant of Archbishop Howard Mowll. Donald Robinson entered the University of Sydney to study Classics and English in 1940 and joined the University Regiment. He became one of the celebrated 'chocos' at age 19 when he was called up for active service with the outbreak of war in the Pacific in December 1941.[16]

Early in 1942, Dale Trendall, Robinson's former Classics lecturer at Sydney University, contacted him and asked him if he might be interested in what he called 'other work'. Trendall was one of those designated to identify bright young men and recruit them for the Central Bureau. After first swearing a vow of silence, he was interviewed by Trendall in Sydney University's Nicholson

16 Donald W.B. Robinson, interviewed by Linder, 28 May 2001. 'Chocos,' short for 'Chocolate Soldiers,' was the disparaging word used for the militia that in the early years of the war could not be sent outside of territorial Australia. AIF volunteers believed that the militiamen would melt away if they ever experienced the heat of combat.

Museum. Robinson remembers being asked a series of mysterious personal questions without ever being told what this 'other work' involved. He heard nothing for several months until he received an order out of the blue to report to the Central Bureau's Brisbane headquarters. He later recalled: 'I was in traffic analysis, which involves discovering everything you can from enemy messages without being able to read them. We could tell from the number of messages whether anything was afoot, and identify whether the messages were about weather or aircraft movement. You could often tell who was sending the message from the call sign used by the operator.' Typical of the culture of the Central Bureau was the fact that when Sydney University Professor of Mathematics, T.G. Room, later joined the Central Bureau in Brisbane, he and Robinson shared an office, but never talked to one another about their work. Nodding and a few civilised grunts was all there was to their relationship.[17]

Don Robinson was well settled into his Central Bureau work by early 1943. He described his Brisbane days as 'very stimulating', both in terms of Christian fellowship and his personal intellectual development. A typical Sunday found him at the local Church of England service at 8:00 a.m., at the City Presbyterian Church at 11:00 a.m., and at the Baptist Tabernacle in the evening. He participated in the Crusader Movement and the Evangelical Union at the University of Queensland. He met John Thompson, later a noted Old Testament scholar in Sydney, and Frank Andersen, later a respected Old Testament scholar in Melbourne. He sometimes lodged with Fred Schwarz, a Christian medical doctor and future famous anti-Communist crusader in the USA during the Cold War, and Heighway Bates, a future Christian leader in Western Australia. He saw Will Renshaw and Alan Langdon, and fellowshipped with numerous other future Christian leaders. He also developed his profile as a future Christian intellectual during his Brisbane days. He was able to read widely in theology and church history as a number of relatives and friends supplied him with books, and he also had time to study Greek.

His next assignment with the Central Bureau took him to the combat zone in New Guinea. He served in Port Moresby and then in the New Guinea highlands, surviving two air raids. It was while in the highlands that he felt most isolated during his time in the army, separated from other believers and from his beloved books. Following his New Guinea tour, the army sent Robinson to officers' training school, and then assigned him to Darwin

17 Robinson interview; and Richard North, 'Master Codebreakers,' *The University of Sydney Gazette*, 30.2, 2002, 11.

where he continued his intelligence work until the end of the war. He was able to secure early release from the military in August 1945 and immediately returned to his university studies.

Robinson's strong Christian background helped him sustain his faith while in the military. Both his mother and father wrote him frequent letters of encouragement, and various Christian friends helped make certain that he always had something at mail call. Further, he found the pastoral care of various Church of England, Salvation Army, and Presbyterian chaplains to be of great help. In the end, he judged that life in the army was an environment no more difficult in which to live a Christian life than it was at the university or in the community at large. His post-war world was devoted to higher education (having passed in 1950 the Third Part of his Theological Tripos at Cambridge University), teaching duties at Moore Theological College in Sydney, and church administration. He served as Archbishop of Sydney from 1982 to 1993.

Alan Langdon was conscripted for army service in 1941, but turned down on medical grounds. Therefore, he enrolled as a student at Sydney University and spent two years there studying education and foreign languages. In 1943, he was conscripted again in view of the urgent need for men with Japan threatening invasion. This time he was accepted and told to report to the Sydney Show Grounds at 6:00 am where his first military assignment was to peel potatoes. He was sent to Bathurst for infantry training and there entered into what he described as 'a completely new environment'. The conversations were laced with profanity and the talk was all of womanising and grog. However, as usual, there were other self-identified evangelicals in the group and a small fellowship of believers was established. Langdon himself read his Bible openly in a hut occupied by 38 Diggers and found the best place for prayer was the latrine. He also spoke up concerning the physical needs of the men, and this earned him the respect from the other soldiers and allowed him to 'live as a man among men' rather than to have to retreat into a spiritual cocoon.[18]

In the latter part of 1943, he was assigned to the Central Bureau. The general atmosphere was more genteel and the unit full of other evangelical Christian women and men. It was there that he met the young Methodist Geoff Charlesworth and struck up what was to become a life-long friendship. Renshaw and Robinson were also there and became good friends.[19]

18 Alan Langdon, interviewed by Linder, 24 April 2001.

19 Ray Ctercteko, interviewed by Linder, 13 July 2006.

Langdon and Charlesworth spent three months training with the Central Bureau in Brisbane. While there they fraternised mostly with Methodists and attended the very popular and serviceman-friendly Albert Street Methodist Church. They also attended the Baptist Tabernacle that was equally popular with the troops. Langdon also reported that, wherever he went in his Army career, he always found Bible studies that were troop-led and maintained.

Langdon and Charlesworth then proceeded to New Guinea in 1944 and participated in the landing at Hollandia, two of the few Australians among tens of thousands of Americans. They were then ordered to join a small Central Bureau unit in the Philippines, where once again they were surrounded by tens of thousands of American troops. There they participated in the famous 'GI Gospel Hour' that later metamorphosed into the Far Eastern Gospel Crusade. The two Australians found themselves in Manila when the war against Japan ended on 15 August 1945. Headquarters authorised leave for those who wished to travel in north Luzon Island, which Langdon and Charlesworth interpreted as meaning 'north of Luzon'. Therefore, they hitched rides on US and Australian aircraft bound for Okinawa and then Japan. They landed in Tokyo just one month after the first atomic bomb was dropped and two weeks after the surrender. Their goal was to find and visit Japan's most famous Christian, Dr. Toyohika Kagawa.

Kagawa was well known in the West because of his challenging books and his several lecture tours of North America. He had become a Christian as a young man and lived among the small minority Christian community in pre-war Japan. He suffered extreme prejudice because of his chosen faith and had been interned during the war, all of which gained him many admirers among Australian Christians. Langdon and Charlesworth badly wanted to find out if he was all right and to meet him. They travelled to the Tokyo suburb where Kagawa lived, and he heartily welcomed them into his modest home. They also attended the first church service following the Japanese surrender where young Langdon delivered greetings from the Christians of Australia to the assembled congregation of Japanese believers. Before Langdon left Tokyo on his way back to his unit, Dr. Kagawa gave him a letter and asked that he personally deliver it to his friend, Sydney Archbishop Howard Mowll, as soon as possible. Langdon kept his promise, thus assuring the success of his own future plans to study for the Anglican ministry as a result of his newfound visibility among Sydney Anglican leaders.

Following the War, though its members were sworn to secrecy for another fifty years, the Australian Central Bureau was given recognition as an

Outstation of Bletchley Park in Britain, the home of codebreaking during the War. Renshaw reports:

> We were each given individual citation certificates signed by the UK Prime Minister and special badges from the Queen's badge maker. Last year I was invited to have a brick with my name on it built into what is known as 'The Codebreaker's Wall' at Bletchley Park. However incomparably far greater with eternal consequence is to have one's name written in the Lamb's Book of Life. Hallelujah![20]

Another who found himself a part of the Australian intelligence service, ultimately responsible to the Central Bureau, was Lutheran missionary from Adelaide, the Rev. A.P. Harold Freund. He had been a missionary in New Guinea for more than six years when war with Japan broke out in December 1941. The Australian government almost immediately made him a coast watcher to observe and report movements of enemy shipping and other military activities.[21] He served in this capacity from February 1942 until July 1943, often in extreme danger. In May 1942, he was officially conscripted into the Australian Army with the rank of Sergeant in the hope that, if caught by the Japanese, he would be treated as a POW and not a spy.

Numerous Lutheran missionaries participated in coast watching from 1942 through 1943 and several lost their lives in the process. One such was Gustav Adolph (Dolph) Obst. Freund and Obst had gone to New Britain together to evacuate Australian troops who had been ordered to flee the Japanese invasion of Rabaul on 23 January 1942. In December 1942, Obst was caught reporting on Japanese sea and air traffic near Cape Gloucester in western New Britain and immediately executed. Other Lutheran missionary coast watchers from South Australia included Victor Neumann, Arthur Frederick (Pat) Zacher, David Rohrlach and Theodor (Ted) Radke, most of whom were lay workers on the various Lutheran mission stations. Many them had been conscripted into the New Guinea Volunteer Rifles or some similar military unit. Radke lost his life after capture by the Japanese. Freund and the other Australian Lutheran missionaries of German extraction in New Guinea, provided information vital to the successful Allied campaign against the Japanese.[22]

---

20 Will Renshaw to Stuart Piggin 27 February 2018.

21 A.P. Harold Freund, *Missionary Turns Spy* (Glynde, SA: Lutheran Homes Incorporated, 1989), 52–3, 172 and 176.

22 Freund, *Missionary Turns Spy*, 190–1; Grey, *A Military History of Australia*, 166.

Reluctant Combatants

Among combatants who were evangelicals, in apparently marked contrast to prevailing attitudes in World War I, most had no enthusiasm for armed conflict or were opposed in principle to war. Yet the belief that their faith required them to help protect their loved ones and their country prevailed. Ronald S. Bevington was one such. Born in England in 1911, he grew up in a devout Church of England home, studied for the ministry at Ridley Hall, Cambridge, and was priested in 1936, and the following year felt called to exercise his ministry in Australia. He was licensed in the Diocese of Sydney in early 1939, and at the same time enlisted in the Royal Australian Navy.[23] In June 1940 he was posted to the HMAS *Perth* as ship's chaplain.[24] In late 1940 he was engaged to Sheila Nicholson, granddaughter of the wealthy Christian businessman who was one of the leaders of the Christian (Open) Brethren Assemblies in Sydney.[25]

Perth spent most of 1941 protecting convoys from Britain to the Middle East and in transporting Australian troops to and from Greece and Crete, coming under heavy attack by German aircraft on several occasions. Sometime early in 1941, the ship's captain, Phillip Bowyer-Smyth, decided that all church parades should be voluntary, and thereafter the average attendance was seventy out of a ship's company of 640 men. Bevington also attracted an average attendance of around forty for the weekly Eucharist, daily Morning Prayer services and daily evening Bible studies.[26] Ship's records reveal that some of the crew viewed Bevington as 'a bit of a Bible basher' and that he was somewhat aloof. There is probably some truth to both observations. Bevington was an evangelical who took his faith seriously. He did not drink with his fellow officers when in port. *Perth*'s commanding officer judged him 'a very earnest Christian – heart and soul in his work'. Again, he noted: 'Has not had much experience of working with men and has found it difficult to catch the confidence of officers or ship's company – but has made progress'.[27]

23 Ray Ctercteko, interviewed by Linder, 13 July 2006.

24 R.S. Bevington, Personal Record, RAN, Series A3978, National Archives of Australia, Canberra (hereafter NAA); H. Ian Pfennigwerth, *The Australian Cruiser Perth, 1939–1942* (Dural: Rosenberg, 2007), 73.

25 See Margaret Lamb, 'John Beath Nicholson', *ADEB*.

26 Chaplain's Report, HMAS Perth, 15 January 1942, MP150/1, Item431/204/100–HMAS Ships, NAA; and Pfennigwerth, *Perth*, 73, 79 and 95.

27 R. S. Bevington, Personal Record, RAN, Series 3978, NAA. The evaluation period covered 7 June 1940 to 1 September 1941. In the same report, Bevington was rated 'Satisfactory' and judged to be a man 'of temperate habits'.

Following the Japanese attack on Pearl Harbor and invasion of Malaya on 8 December 1941, *Perth* was ordered to sail for the Java (Dutch East Indies/ Indonesian) Theatre. On 24 February *Perth* joined a multinational task force of eleven American, Australian, British and Dutch ships and engaged Japanese forces in the disastrous Battle of the Java Sea. *Perth* and the heavy cruiser USS *Houston* survived, only to run into Japanese warships which were protecting an invasion convoy of approximately 50 ships that had landed at Banten Bay, Java. Struck by four torpedos, *Perth* was sunk early on 1 March.[28]

What happened to the ship's chaplain? Bevington gave his own life jacket to a sailor who had none. He was last seen in the water, clinging to a piece of debris. The shore was within sight and, because he was a good swimmer, he decided to strike out for the tree line in the distance. He was never seen again. Nor were 680 other members of the ship's crew.[29] Sheila Nicholson heard on the radio that the *Perth* had been sunk and that 'her Ronald was missing'. She waited four long years to receive final word of his fate, hoping against hope that he had somehow survived and was a POW. She finally married in 1949 and had three children. Her son said that the family remembered that it was 'a great emotional tear' for Sheila to lose her fiancé and a sad memory with which she lived for the remainder of her life.[30]

Another reluctant idealist was Geoff Slinn, an active member of a Christian (Open) Brethren Assembly in Sydney. Slinn was born in Burwood, NSW, in 1912. He was well-educated, steadily rising in the management ranks of the Corinth Bank, and had a wife named Peggy. He worked extensively with primary school children both as a Scripture teacher in the Masonic School and as a teacher/social director for the CSSM. He loved to work with this age group even though he and his wife apparently could not have children of their own. He was opposed to taking up arms, as were most Christian Brethren of his day. But, like the Seventh-day Adventists, the Christian Brethren assemblies usually left it up to the individual conscience when it came to the decision whether or not to serve in the military.[31] He volunteered for the RAAF on 20 June 1942 having come to the realisation that the war was going badly

28 Pfennigwerth, *Perth*, 210–226.

29 Donald Robinson, interviewed by Linder, 9 July 2009; Kathryn Spurling, *Cruel Conflict: The Triumph and Tragedy of HMAS Perth* (Sydney: New Holland Publishers, 2008), 180; Rowan Strong, *Chaplains in the Royal Australian Navy* (Sydney: UNSW Press, 2012), 174–182; 292.

30 Sheila Nicholson Knox, interviewed by Robert D. Linder, 14 July 2009; Peter Knox, interviewed by Linder, 13 July 2009.

31 Elisabeth Wilson, 'Brethren Attitudes to Authority and Government, With Particular Reference to Pacifism', MA thesis, University of Tasmania, 1994.

at the time, that Australia was in danger, and that many of his mates had already signed up for some branch of the military. Among those mates was Ron Bevington whom Slinn had befriended through Christian Endeavour.

In his World War II diary, Slinn related his experiences in the RAAF for *every* single day that he was on active service.[32] He trained as a bombardier in Canada and in Britain in Lancaster bombers. But he was unnerved by the moral implications of bombing military and civilian targets. When visiting some of his English relatives in London, he first saw the immense damage and human suffering that the blitz had caused.[33] On 5 December 1943, he recorded his revulsion at modern warfare when as part of his training he attended a lecture on 'dirty methods of unarmed attack', which he described as 'really very horrible'. He attended a provocative play when on leave in London entitled 'There Shall Be No Night'. He recorded in his diary that night: 'The story was of a pacifist Greek doctor and how the war engulfed him, his family and his ideals. It set my mind thinking a bit'. On 27 March 1944, he wrote: 'Oh how I dislike this life!!' He requested that he be transferred to some unit other than Bomber Command. He was assigned to Squadron 138 at Tempsford Air Base in Bedfordshire, perhaps the most secret RAF airfield in World War II, reporting there on 18 May 1944. In the meantime, he spent his weekend passes and leave time attending church and sometimes playing the organ for services, leading children's events at church and at English CSSM meetings, and visiting relatives and English friends, including Ron Bevington's father. He found that the elder Bevington had turned his home into a place where retired clergy could live, an act carried out in honour of his lost clergyman son.[34]

As the war dragged on and he accumulated 'ops' over France, Belgium, Denmark and Norway, Slinn began to complain about being increasingly weary. On 19 September 1944, he reported: 'Slept fairly well – a bit nervy'. On 30 September 1944: 'Tired but slept in too late for breakfast! Got things ready for our trip to Denmark tonight. Still tired after lunch and slept in the Mess!' On 8 October 1944: 'feeling tired'. On 9 October 1944: 'Sleeping restlessly lately.' On 22 October 1944: 'Am feeling tired – seem to feel it most when I relax like this'. Slinn was showing obvious signs of combat fatigue.

---

32 Slinn, War Diary; typescript 'Excerpts from Geoff Slinn's World War II Diary' in the possession of the authors.

33 Based on various diary entries from 22 October 1942 to 1 August 1943. For examples of his observations of the London bombings, see diary entries 19 June 1943, and 4–5 August 1943.

34 Diary entries 28 November 1943, 26 April 1944, and 18–20 September 1944.

On 26 November 1944, on the eve of his thirty-sixth op, he wrote: 'We are going into Denmark – I prefer these jobs. Dull and misty outside'. On that night while on the way back from Denmark, Slinn's plane was shot down over the North Sea. He was reported 'missing in action' and no trace of his body or his plane was ever found. Back at Tempsford, his diary lay on the desk in his room. According to his habit, his last words were penned following his last diary entry: 'Monday 27/11/44', underlined, awaiting his return to report on that day's activities.[35]

Yet another idealistic yet reluctant warrior, twenty-year-old Jack Quinn, volunteered for the AIF in mid-1940, he said, in order to defend freedom and family. Forty years later, he reflected on his enlistment in responding to a questionnaire sent out by historian John Barrett of La Trobe University. In response to Barrett's query 'Did you have a personal desire to join?', Quinn wrote 'Not at all. I joined against my will'. At heart, he assured Barrett, he was a peaceful man, but he confessed that: 'I had little real knowledge … I had highly idealistic beliefs in the Empire standing for freedom and right'.[36]

Quinn was an active member of the North Sydney Baptist Church before he joined the AIF. Highly articulate and a bit brash, he was a quintessential young Baptist layman of the period. His opinions are particularly interesting in light of his strong religious commitment. When asked his view of COs, he replied that he 'respected views of those who were "Fair Dinkum," but found it hard to understand why they refused service, as my own views were sympathetic to their basic beliefs'. Of army chaplains, he commented, 'Well meaning but mostly useless and harmless. Some exceptionally helpful'. When asked in what ways the army life was a worthwhile experience to him personally, Quinn wrote, 'I learned much about human nature, and developed a more realistic philosophy, became more self-reliant and had a better appreciation of my own worth'.[37]

Quinn served with the 2/17th Battalion in Libya and India. He was one of the fabled 'Rats of Tobruk', and was twice wounded in that battle, once

---

35 Slinn was one of 264 airmen posted to Tempsford Airfield who were killed in action in 1944.

36 John Barrett, Australian Army Questionnaire, Australian War Memorial Archives, PR89/135, Box 47. Barrett's summary and interpretation of the results of his questionnaire were published in John Barrett, *We Were There: Australian Soldiers of World War II tell their Stories* (St. Leonards: Allen & Unwin, 1995), 325–8. See also Mark Johnson, *At the Front: Experiences of Australian Soldiers in World War II* (Melbourne: CUP, 1996).

37 Barrett, Australian Army Questionnaire. See the index of Barrett's book for references to Quinn.

only slightly but a second time severely. The second wound came when his commanding officer surrendered his platoon to the Germans. Quinn did not agree with his lieutenant's decision, tried to flee and was shot. He never fully recovered and was repatriated to Australia where he was discharged on 21 December 1943. He indicated on Barrett's questionnaire that he found returning to civilian life 'a bit hard'. However, his local church and his wife Doreen aided his adjustment to civilian life. He and Doreen became loyal members of the Epping Baptist Church in Sydney.[38]

The Home Front during World War II

On the home front, the churches immediately mobilised to support the nation and the men and women in uniform.[39] But they had learned from bitter experience in the First World War not to blow the ecclesiastical trumpet in celebration of military triumphalism. They were less enthusiastic about their young members going off to war and more practical in their support of those who did. Few doubted that the war against the Axis Powers was a righteous one, but the inordinate zeal of World War I was absent. South Australian Methodists, for example, rejected a request from the Department of the Army to make an appeal for recruits from its pulpits and in denominational publications. The predominant view was that the war had to be fought and won, but hatred of the enemy should have no place in the propaganda arsenal either of the church or the nation. Among the responses of individual evangelical churches to the war, St. Swithun's Anglican Church, Pymble, a Sydney suburb, was typical in illustrating the entire absence of a war-mongering spirit and the presence of the spirit of sacrifice.[40] Parish rector Arthur L. Wade penned this revealing commentary in the parish newsletter in June 1941:

> The list of names of men from our parish, or closely connected with our people, and for whom our prayers are asked, is a growing one. Many of our keenest and most earnest younger churchmen have already enlisted. They are not the type to glorify war, nor who love to fight for fighting's sake. Rather they are men who have earnestly faced the call

---

38 Michael Petras, historian and family friend of the Quinns, to Linder, 26 July 2010.

39 Michael McKernan, *All In!: Fighting the War at Home* (St. Leonards: Allen & Unwin, 1995); Katharine Massam and John H. Smith, 'There Was Another Weapon: The Churches on the Homefront', in Jenny Gregory (ed.), *On the Homefront: Western Australia and World War II* (Perth: University of Western Australia Press, 1996), 149–161.

40 Marcia Cameron, *Living Stones: St. Swithun's Pymble, 1901–2001* (Wahroonga: The Helicon Press, 2001), 80.

> not only of a country that needs men to fight its battle, but also the deeper struggle that lies behind that of the Nation – the struggle to retain for the future of the world all that Christian civilization holds dear … So, sadly, yet proudly, we enter week by week fresh names in our prayer list, while we often record at the same time another gap in the valued workers of the Church.[41]

Six young men from the church did not return, while five who had joined the RAAF won the Distinguished Flying Cross.[42]

Most in evangelical churches continued to assume that Australians were still a Christian people and that God would respond to their petitions. This was evident in the calling of national days of prayer. In the first two years of the war there were five such days, all endorsed by the federal and state authorities. The largest of these in SA, an ecumenical gathering held in Adelaide Oval on 8 September 1940, drew 33,000 people. In WA, 'Prayer for a just and peaceful end to the war engaged many Western Australians on the homefront. There were probably more people involved in the spiritual war effort than there were serving in active combat'.[43] In Sydney, regular services of intercession were held, with St. Andrew's Cathedral as the focal point. The Cathedral bells rang daily at noon to bring the city to prayer. Memorial and intercessory services were held, sometimes on an impromptu basis, when, for example, news of the sinking of the *Sydney* and *Perth* or the fall of Singapore were announced. There were also regular services for the relatives of POWs.

It was during the war years that Archbishop Mowll's greatness as a leader became evident. He went to extraordinary lengths to meet the needs of soldiers, both spiritual and recreational. In 1939 he established the Church of England National Emergency Fund (CENEF). Its auxiliary, the Sydney Diocesan Churchwomen's Association, mobilised 2,000 women under Mrs. Mowll's leadership. The grounds of the Cathedral were covered with makeshift huts for servicemen. There they found food, a bed, and friendship. It was a service described by the Governor-General's wife as 'pure Christianity'. At Dorothy Mowll's funeral in 1957 a man, standing outside the Cathedral on the site of the huts, stopped a passer-by and said, 'There are not many in the world like her. Many a time she put her hand on my shoulder and gave encouragement during the war.'[44]

---

41 *The Messenger*, June, 1941, 1.

42 Cameron, *Living Stones*, 92.

43 Massam and Smith, 'There Was Another Weapon', 149.

44 Stuart Piggin, *Spirit, Word and World: Evangelical Christianity in Australia* rev. ed., (Brunswick East: Acorn Press, 2012), 131f.

Among Baptists, too, women were prominent in the work that needed to be done on the home front. Mrs. J. Arthur Lewis, a Victorian Baptist leader, noted that the various Comfort Funds, the Red Cross, church hostels, canteen services and the YWCA were all 'largely built on the sacrificial services of women folk'. She also fretted about broken marriage vows and the damage that liquor was doing to wartime relationships.[45] Baptist women believed more in action than words. For example, the Baptist Women's Patriotic League in Newcastle, NSW, early in the war visited recruits encamped at the Newcastle Showground and helped with the alterations and repairs of the Diggers' allocated clothing.[46]

Keeping up morale required some explanation of why this disaster had befallen the whole world. One who attempted such an explanation was Howard Mowll's imported theologian, T.C. Hammond, principal of Moore College. At St Phillip's Church in Sydney, of which he was also the rector, Hammond gave a series of weekly talks during the lunch hour, published apparently in 1942 under the title *Fading Light: The Tragedy of Spiritual Decline in Germany*.[47] Hammond attributes the rise of Nazism to Germany's turning away, not from religious belief, but from God's word as the only true antidote to infidelity:

> The Germans set themselves to restore the great foundations of God, freedom and immortality, without having direct recourse to the Holy Scriptures. They did not banish God, but their devotion to proud learning checked them in presenting to the people of their land the unadulterated message of the Gospel. It is from that movement, the compromise between unbelief and real unadulterated Christianity as it is presented in the Scripture, that we can trace all our present evils (27–28).

His final warning:

> [this unbelief] is in our midst, for dozens of earnest clergymen and laymen still draw their inspiration from this German compromise, unmindful of the fact that those who started on this inclined plane one hundred years ago, have ended by deifying Adolf Hitler, and further than that human folly cannot go (28).

---

45 *The Australian Baptist*, 4 January 1944, 5.

46 *The Australian Baptist*, 11 March 1941, 2.

47 London: Marshall, Morgan & Scott, [1942].

Conscientious Objectors

In spite of the reservations which Australian Christians had about involvement in another war, conscientious objectors were not very popular with rank and file church members. Among the evangelical denominations, the Methodists were more inclined to take a definite stand against war as a way to resolve international disputes. In NSW, the Rev. F.W. Hynes, the editor of *The Methodist*, urged his co-religionists to seek peace and shun war. NSW Methodists led in the formation of a United Christian Peace Movement in 1937, the president of which was Methodist clergy stalwart E.E.V. Collocott.[48]

Christian pacifism was strongest in SA where many resolutions and individuals strongly backed the League of Nations as a way to prevent war. The most vocal of SA Methodist advocates of non-participation in any war was a group of ministers, especially Harold White and Edward Jew, along with a number of laymen, the most prominent of whom was the Adelaide solicitor, J.L. Treloar. For Jew, writing in 1935, the church's attitude toward war was clear: 'Christ was a pacifist'. He argued that Jesus' followers had to take his words and spirit seriously and, no matter how much it cost, refuse to support war in any form.[49] But when the war came, most of the peaceful evangelicals fell silent and the call for Christian non-violence melted in the harsh light of the threat to the Australian mainland.

Baptists had debated the principle of non-violence during the interwar period without result. Apart from a handful of ministers, such as W.H. Holloway of Melbourne and J.C. Chamberlain of Adelaide, there was not much support for the renunciation of force as the way to resolve international quarrels.[50] The best-known of Baptist COs was lay preacher, Phil Hancox, converted to Christ in 1928 at age 14 in the City Tabernacle Baptist Church in Brisbane. As war clouds gathered over Europe in the late 1930s, Hancox heard such comments as 'anyone who plays tennis on Anzac Day should be taken out and shot' and 'if a man won't fight for his country, he doesn't deserve to live in it'.[51] Such sentiments led him to consider what he should

48 Wright and Clancy, *The Methodists*, 180–1.

49 Minutes of Methodist General Conference, 1935, 156, cited in Hunt, *This Side of Heaven*, 347.

50 Holloway, in particular, argued that nationalism was the curse of the modern world and that war should be 'stripped of its false glory'. *The Australian Baptist*, 17 August 1937, 3. Also see Manley, *From Woolloomooloo to 'Eternity'*, 2, 501.

51 Phil Hancox, *Cavalry or Calvary? The Christian Dilemma* (West End: Christians for Peace, 1984), 1 and 14.

do if conscripted for military service. The outbreak of war in 1939 compelled him to come to a conclusion:

> I did not consult any Bible commentaries nor read any books on the subject, apart from the Bible itself. Within a few weeks I became convinced that war had no place in the life of a professing Christian. This for me was now a strong conviction.[52]

This set the stage for Hancox's confrontation with the authorities over his determination not to participate in the war in any manner whatsoever. He was hauled before a magistrate on 15 February 1942 to answer charges that he refused 'to take the oath or make an affirmation for service in the defence forces'. He said that his religious beliefs would not permit him to undertake either combatant or noncombatant military duties. Whereupon the magistrate lectured him, 'Mr. Hancox, you are a misguided young man', and sentenced him to six months at the Palen Creek Prison Farm outside of Brisbane.[53] Hancox spent four months on the farm before he secured early release on grounds of good behaviour. While there he discovered other evangelical COs among the thirty to forty members of the shifting prison population. The most outspoken of these, Harry Attwell, a Pentecostal preacher, became Hancox's closest friend while in confinement. Other evangelicals included Methodist Les Hoey and an unnamed member of the Salvation Army.[54]

In the years immediately following his release from prison, Hancox had difficulty finding a job and endured much criticism and rejection by fellow Baptists. However, he maintained a generous spirit and served his local church and the Baptists of Queensland well, finally winning the esteem and affection of his fellow believers. Before his death in 2000, he had been a long-time Sunday School teacher, choirmaster, deacon, and Men's Society president and was twice president of the Baptist Union of Queensland in 1964–1965 and 1972–1973. He spent his years following retirement in 1979 conducting evangelistic campaigns through Queensland, the United States, the Philippines and Indonesia.[55]

---

52 Hancox, *Cavalry or Calvary?*, 24.

53 Hancox, *Cavalry or Calvary?*, 45–54.

54 Philip Hancox, interviewed by Linder, 16 June 1998.

55 Phil Hancox, *My Adventures in Evangelism* (Brisbane: Privately Printed, 1995); and *The Queensland Baptist*, May, 2000, 10. In 2007, Phil Hancox was one of sixty-nine representative individuals worldwide and the only Australian whose name was chiselled in the Conscientious Objection Commemorative Stone in Tavistock Square, Bloomsbury, London, England.

Although not classified as COs because of their ministerial exemptions from military service, a number of evangelical ministers espoused pacifist sentiments during the war. Chief among them were Baptist Gilbert Wright and Methodist Alan Walker. Wright, pastor of the burgeoning Epping Baptist Church during the war and later principal of Morling Theological College, declared:

> Every true Christian hates war. It is hellish, devilish, horrible, and God Himself has given assurance that some day it shall be no more … When the blast and bitterness of war scar our very souls nothing but the spirit of Christ can subdue the fierce resentment and hunger for revenge that sweep over us … Love is still the greatest thing in the world and though almost obliterated today in the enveloping rain of tears and blood, individually we are to dedicate ourselves to demonstrate its eternal beauty and power.[56]

Early in the war, Walker, pastor of Cessnock Methodist Church, published 'A Peace Manifesto' in *The Coalfield's Chronicle*.[57] The manifesto declared war to be 'contrary to the will of God and the mind of Jesus'. It argued that 'the ethic of Jesus to love rather than hate' applied 'to national action no less than individual conduct'. It opposed conscription as 'an unwarrantable interference with the rights and liberties of the subject' and called for tolerance toward conscientious objectors should the government introduce a plan for universal military service.[58]

Lance Shilton, later Dean of Sydney, was another who did not want to kill another human being, but who also believed that he should serve his country in some capacity in time of war. When he was conscripted, he applied for the Army Medical Service and his request was granted. Because of a heart murmur, he was classified as unfit for overseas service and spent his four years in the military at various camps in Australia, mainly at Kapooka in Victoria.[59] Shilton, typical of evangelicals, was given to making stands, no matter the cost. On one occasion the men were paraded for instruction about the use of contraceptive devices by the unit Medical Officer (MO). It was assumed

---

56 Harold Gow and Ken Manley, *People with a Purpose: Epping Baptist Church, 1933–1983* (Epping: Epping Baptist Church, 1983), 29–30.

57 November 1939 issue.

58 Harold R. Henderson, *Reach for the World: The Alan Walker Story* (Nashville: Discipleship Resources, 1981), 41.

59 Lance Shilton, *Speaking Out: A Life in Urban Ministry* (Sydney: CSAC, 1997), 16, 28.

that they would engage in promiscuous sex while on leave and, therefore, it was necessary to take precautions against becoming infected with sexually transmitted diseases. When the MO called for questions, Shilton sprang to his feet and said: 'Sir, why didn't you mention anything about the commandment which says, "Thou shalt not commit adultery?"' The MO responded with a torrent of abuse, but many of the men came to him afterwards and said, 'I'm glad you spoke up the way you did'.[60]

John Curtin and the Evangelicals

Any study of the public role of religion must attempt to analyse its influence on the motivation of those with responsibility for the national destiny, especially political leaders. Though fraught with difficulty, it is a surprisingly rewarding subject,[61] as may be illustrated by an analysis of the impact of evangelical Christianity on Prime Minister John Curtin, who led his nation during most of World War II from 7 October 1941 until his death in office on 5 July 1945.[62] Curtin's religious development reflected many evangelical influences, especially personified in those closest to him: his wife, Elsie Needham; his private secretary, Frederick A. McLaughlin; ministers of religion, especially the Presbyterian Hector Harrison; and his politician colleagues, Norman Makin and Jim Hunter.

Born in Creswick, Victoria, in 1885, Curtin was the son of a police officer of Irish descent and reared a Roman Catholic. He left his church of origin and, after a brief stint in the Salvation Army, joined the Australian Labor Party and the Victorian Socialist Party. He became a heavy drinker, a problem that plagued him intermittently for much of his life. In 1917 he married Elsie Needham, a Labor Party activist, Methodist, and teetotaller. She helped to keep her husband from drinking himself to death. In Perth, he became editor for *The Western Worker*, the official trade union newspaper. He was elected to the Federal House of Representatives for the first time in 1928 and again in 1929, losing his seat in December 1931 as he simultaneously lost his battle

60 Shilton, *Speaking Out*, 31–2.

61 See, for example, Roy Williams, *In God They Trust? The Religious Beliefs of Australia's Prime Ministers 1901–2013* (Sydney: Bible Society, 2013); Greg Sheridan, *God is Good for You: A Defence of Christianity in Troubled Times* (Sydney: Allen & Unwin, 2018), 171–242.

62 Robert D. Linder, 'Presidents, Prime Ministers and Evangelicals: Christianity and Leadership in Two Countries', *Lucas*, 32, 2002, 7–54.

with alcohol.[63] Following this loss, Curtin settled down in Perth with Elsie, determined to beat his drinking problem.[64]

In September, 1934, Curtin recaptured his old Fremantle seat and after a pledge to Labor MPs that he would never touch alcohol again, he was elected the new party leader on 1 October 1935 and continued in that capacity until his death in 1945. In that role, he became, in the words of professor of politics, David Black, 'a puritan revolutionary' who emphasised self-discipline and practical morality.[65] With the fall of the Menzies government in late 1941, Curtin became Prime Minister, just in time to guide his nation during the most difficult days of World War II. He was sworn in as Prime Minister on 7 October 1941. Exactly two months later, Japan entered the war, an immediate threat to Australia. It was in this context that Curtin made rapid progress in his Christian pilgrimage. Too little has been written about this aspect of Curtin's life and career.[66] Curtin biographer, David Day,[67] gave some attention to the wartime prime minister's religion, but did not seem to comprehend the texture of Curtin's growing spirituality during the war, nor understand the nature of the faith of those who surrounded the prime minister during his period.[68]

Curtin's spiritual awakening seems to have begun in the 1920s in WA when he occasionally attended the Ross Memorial Presbyterian Church in West Perth to hear the Rev. Dr Julian Ralph Blanchard, its evangelical preacher. His wife now attended Presbyterian and Congregational churches in the Perth area.[69] She had grown up in a devout Methodist home in Tasmania. As a girl, she was active in Sunday School and played the organ in various Hobart

63 Elsie Curtin to the Rev. Hector Harrison, 12 December 1958, Hector Harrison Papers, NLA, Canberra, MS6277, Box 1, Folder 4.

64 J.A.J. Hunter to Lloyd Ross, 6 June 1958, Lloyd Ross Papers, NLA, Canberra, MS3939, Box 29, Folder 9.

65 Professor David Black, interviewed by Linder, 14 July 1997.

66 Roy Williams, *In God they trust?*

67 David Day, *John Curtin: A Life* (Sydney: Harper Perennial, 1999), 146–7.

68 Day misunderstands the nature of the evangelical Methodist faith of Fred McLaughlin, Curtin's private secretary during the war, and the appeal of the Moral Rearmament Movement to mainstream churches in the period before MRA began to change significantly following World War II. Day portrays McLaughlin as some kind of 'religious zealot', undermining McLaughlin's credibility, thus making it doubtful that he could possibly influence the Prime Minister. See Day, *John Curtin*, 481–3.

69 Hector Harrison, interviewed by Mel Pratt, 2 October 1973, 1:1/43–1:1/44, John Curtin Prime Ministerial Library, The John Curtin Centre, Curtin University, Perth, WA; Elsie Curtin to Hector Harrison, 18 December 1947, Harrison Papers, MS 6277, Box 1, Folder 4; *The Western Impact,* 4, 1980, 2.

churches. There is no evidence that she ever departed from her evangelical Christian faith,[70] and she continued with one Methodist practice to the end of her days: no alcohol was ever served in the Curtin home.[71] Contrary to the view of her biographer, Diane Langmore, she did not solve the problem of the prospect of a mixed marriage with the Catholic John Curtin by opting for 'a secular marriage and life'.[72] The Curtins, it is true, were married in a civil ceremony, but it does not follow that they then went on with a secular 'life'. Elsie rather continued to practise her Christian faith while remaining an active member of the Australian Labor Party. She sensed no conflict here and seems to have influenced her husband by her example.[73]

Elsie Curtin frequently visited the St. Andrew's Presbyterian Church when in Canberra and various Presbyterian churches while at home in Cottesloe, among them the St. Andrew's Presbyterian Church of Perth where the Rev. George Tulloch, an evangelical stalwart, presided. She developed a warm friendship with Hector Harrison and considered him a spiritual mentor in whom she could confide. Her evangelical connections were many. Her brother Leslie Needham was organist at the Rose Bay Presbyterian Church in Sydney, and her grandchildren were baptised in the Cottesloe Presbyterian Church in Western Australia. Most of her friends in Canberra were Presbyterian members of Harrison's congregation.[74]

After becoming Prime Minister, Curtin himself entered into a close friendship with Hector Harrison, who apparently became Curtin's main clerical mentor during the last years of his life. Harrison, a native of WA, had moved from St. Aidan's Presbyterian Church in the Perth suburb of Claremont to St. Andrew's, Canberra in May 1940, only a few months before Curtin became Prime Minister. Harrison always claimed that they got along so well because they were both from WA,[75] but they had one other important thing in common: both previously had been members of the Salvation Army. Harrison's father had been converted to Christ and delivered from alcoholism

---

70 Elsie Curtin to Hector Harrison, 10 March 1946, Harrison Papers, MS6277, Box 1, Folder 4; and Diane Langmore, *Prime Minister's Wives: The Public and Private Lives of Ten Australian Women* (Ringwood: McPhee Gribble, 1992), 116–7.

71 Langmore, *Prime Minister's Wives*, 126; Elsie Curtin to Hector Harrison, 10 March 1946, Harrison Papers, MS6277, Box 1, Folder 4.

72 Langmore, *Prime Minister's Wives*, 122, 153.

73 Elsie Curtin to the Rev. Hector Harrison, 8 May 1946, Harrison Papers, MS6277, Box 1, Folder 4.

74 Elsie Curtin to the Rev. Hector Harrison, 18 December 1947, and 19 December 1948, Harrison Papers, MS6277, Box 1, Folder 4.

75 Hector Harrison, interviewed by Mel Pratt, 2 October 1973, 1:1/43.

through Salvation Army preaching in Northam, WA. Harrison had grown up in an active Salvation Army home and joined the Salvos himself in 1916, at age fourteen. He eventually became an officer and worked for a time in the Melbourne slums before deciding to study for the Presbyterian ministry. He later claimed that he left the Salvation Army because it did not include the sacraments of baptism and communion in its ministrations. He also seems to have been attracted by the dignity and decorum of Presbyterian worship.[76]

A practical factor in their friendship was that the Prime Minister's Lodge and the Presbyterian manse were in close proximity in Canberra. They were neighbours who literally could see each other at will without the press or anybody else knowing about it.[77] Shortly before he died Curtin left specific instructions for his friend Hector Harrison to conduct his funeral in Canberra. Curtin stipulated that it be a religious celebration and that there be no intervening service between the one in Canberra and the graveside ceremony in WA.[78]

Another evangelical Christian important in Curtin's life during his prime ministerial days was Frederick A. McLaughlin, his private secretary, and 'a committed Christian and a keen Methodist'.[79] McLaughlin revealed that Curtin became dependent upon God and concerned about spiritual matters increasingly during the war years. McLaughlin reported that he had prayed with Curtin, both of them sometimes getting down on their knees. In addition, McLaughlin, a teetotaller, provided Curtin with moral support in his struggle with liquor. It was McLaughlin who was the trusted liaison between Curtin, Elsie Curtin and Hector Harrison concerning the funeral arrangements.[80]

Norman Makin, Labor Member of the House of Representatives from South Australia (serving from 1919–1946 and 1954–1963) and Methodist local preacher, was another evangelical on intimate terms with Curtin. Along with Curtin, Makin was one of the nine original members of the Advisory

---

76 Cuttings from various Western Australian newspapers, dated 1921–1924, Harrison Papers, MS6277, Box 1, Folder 1; Freda Whitlam, interviewed by Linder, 30 May 1997; Roger C Thompson, 'Pastor Extraordinaire: A Portrait of Hector Harrison', in Susan Emilsen and William W. Emilsen, eds., *Mapping the Landscape: Essays in Australian and New Zealand History in Honour of Professor Ian Breward* (New York: Peter Lang, 2000), 168–84.

77 *The Melbourne Herald*, 6 July 1945, 3.

78 Frederick A. McLaughlin to Hector Harrison, 23 June 1945, Harrison Papers, MS6277, Box 1, Folder 4.

79 Barbara Ross (daughter of F. A. McLaughlin), interviewed by Linder, 31 July 1997.

80 Hector Harrison, interviewed by Mel Pratt, 2 October 1973, 1:1/40–1/41; James Coulter, interviewed by Isla Macphail, 6 December 1995, 3–4, John Curtin Prime Ministerial Library, The John Curtin Centre, Curtin University, Perth, WA.

War Council created in 1940. When he became Prime Minister, Curtin made Makin Minister for the Navy (1941–1943) and later Minister of Aircraft Production (1943–1946). Makin had constant access to Curtin and often counselled him concerning spiritual matters.[81] On one such occasion, Curtin acknowledged: 'I am aware that there is a hereafter and that men are required to account for their misdeeds in this life'.[82] Makin also provided Curtin with the moral and spiritual support he needed to resist the bottle. He was always there to join Curtin in drinking water, juice or a soda at official gatherings.[83] As he lay dying, Curtin asked for Makin to come visit him. After he had told Makin of the arrangements he had made for his funeral, Makin prayed at his bedside. After trying to rally him with thoughts of the thousands who were earnestly praying for his recovery, Makin departed with a 'God bless you John'. Curtin died at 4:00 am the next day, 5 July 1945. Makin was the last person to see him alive.[84]

As the war ground on, Curtin had more and more frequently invoked God in his speeches as he called Australians to gird their loins and sacrifice for the war effort. He was distressed that so many Australians did not seem to understand or care that the country was fighting for its life. On one occasion, he declared in the hearing of the press corps: 'What this country wants is an Evangel'. One reporter who heard the remark muttered irreverently: 'The initials are right anyway'.[85]

When he was Prime Minister, Curtin frequently took long walks through the Botanic Gardens and the streets of Sydney with J.A.J. (Jim) Hunter, an old friend who for nearly twenty years represented Queensland in the Federal House of Representatives as a member of the Country Party. While they walked, they conversed about a wide range of subjects, including religion. Curtin at the time was becoming more and more interested in the basic teachings of Christianity. Hunter was himself an active Presbyterian, and he had two brothers who were Presbyterian ministers, one of whom was a theologian of note. Curtin revealed to Hunter the ache in his soul caused by the fact that as a young man he had abandoned his Christian faith and embraced rationalism. Curtin believed that his faithless years had brought with it alcoholism

81 *The Methodist*, 22 March 1930, 6; and Norman Makin, *The Memoirs of Norman John Oswald Makin* (Adelaide: The J. M. Main Bequest, 1982), 25–8.

82 Frederick A. McLaughlin to Hector Harrison, 26 June 1945, Harrison Papers, MS6277, Box 1, Folder 4.

83 Harold Makin, interviewed by Linder, 19 July 1995.

84 Norman Makin, *Federal Labor Leaders* (Sydney: Union Printing Party, 1961), 108.

85 Lloyd Ross, 'The Story of John Curtin', *The Sun Herald*, 10 August 1958, 43.

and a great spiritual void, and that only Elsie had saved him from total ruin. Now, as Prime Minister, he realised that he needed a power beyond himself to help him cope with the extraordinary burden of leading his nation during a war of national survival. The terrible burden of sending thousands of men into the jaws of death hung like a great weight on his mind and spirit, and eventually killed him.[86] It was on their last meeting shortly before Curtin's untimely death that the Prime Minister affirmed that, ultimately, it was not any particular church that was critical, but Jesus Christ. Among Curtin's last words to his old friend were: 'You are right, Jim. It doesn't matter what Church a man belongs to. The main thing is for him to live a decent straight clean life as near to Christ as humanly possible'.[87] Curtin, unlike R.M. Williams, appears to have been more helped than haunted by Christ. Out of the well-springs of his own growing spirituality, he came to find in Christ 'a present help in trouble', not only to address the strife in his own personal life, but also as a means to help rally all Australians in their hour of national peril.[88]

Curtin's funeral was a cathartic experience for the nation. The Sydney *Daily Telegraph* described Curtin's formal farewell at Canberra in July 1945, with the headline: 'Men Break Down at Ceremony in King's Hall'. The paper reported uncharacteristic behaviour at the nation's capital:

> Ministers and other members of Parliament wept openly at the memorial service for the late John Curtin in King's Hall, Parliament House today. For a quarter of an hour the lid of the casket was raised while members silently filed past to see their old colleague for the last time.[89]

Later Labor Party Leader and Governor-General Bill Hayden recalls as a boy walking through the deserted streets of South Brisbane on the day of Curtin's funeral. Every home seemed to have a radio on, as hushed and weeping, a shocked people listened to the service as it was being broadcast from Canberra.[90] When Curtin's funeral entourage reached Perth, the skies providentially cleared after twenty-eight consecutive days of rain. On Sunday 8 July, a crowd estimated at around 30,000 people listened as the military bands played 'Rock of Ages' and 'Abide with Me'. They then watched as Hector Harrison and Lincoln Sullivan, minister of the Johnstone Memorial Congregational Church of Fremantle, presided over Curtin's burial in the

---

86 Geoffrey Serle, 'Curtin, John (1885–1945)', *ADB*, online edition.

87 Hunter to Ross, 6 June 1958, Lloyd Ross Papers, Box 29, Folder 9, NLA.

88 Tony Stephens, 'The Man We Never Knew', *SMH*, 1 July 1995, 'Spectrum', 6A-7A.

89 *Daily Telegraph*, 7 July 1945, 1.

90 Bill Hayden, *Hayden: An Autobiography* (Sydney: Angus & Robertson, 1996), 39.

Presbyterian section of the Karrakatta Cemetery. Later that evening, Harrison conducted a memorial service in George Tulloch's St. Andrew's Presbyterian Church in Perth. This service, broadcast over radio station 6KY, was evangelical Christendom's final tribute to the fallen leader. In the end, Curtin died a believer. And he chose to lie among the Presbyterian faithful when it came to his final resting place.[91]

* * *

The churches in World War II made greater provision for the care of service men and women than they did in World War I, brought less pressure on them to enlist, and shared and at times led resistance to jingoistic manifestations of war-mongering. Maybe this meant the churches had learned the harsh lessons taught by the First World War. Maybe it signified that the three strands of imperialism, civil religion and Christian values had begun to unravel with the discovery that the three were not natural partners. Maybe Christians were beginning to wake up to the reality that it is never easy to stoke the fires of patriotism and sensitise the conscience at the same time. For the most part, the subjects of this research appear to have had tender consciences. Often evangelicals who enlisted appeared to be more disconcerted by the behaviour and values of their fellow soldiers than by the enemy. They typically sought and readily found opportunities for Christian fellowship. Prophetic voices of restraint also were raised during the war by a number of evangelical ministers and laypeople. Though not numerous, these conscientious objectors to violence and war made themselves heard and served as a reminder of the teachings of Christ concerning love for friends and enemies and reminding those caught up in the war that there was another way. Though not fully appreciated at the time, their voices of restraint served to remind evangelicals and other Christians of their faith commitments. But very few even of those most disposed to pacifism denied that this war against Germany and Japan was about as just as any war could be.[92]

The evidence that is available also supports the rather surprising conclusion that many emerged from the war with strengthened rather than weakened faith, and built on their experiences of war to achieve conspicuous success in

91 *The West Australian*, 9 July 1945, 5; *The Presbyterian* (WA), August 1945, 92.

92 Michael Gladwin, *Captains of the Soul: A History of Australian Army Chaplains* (Newport: Big Sky Publishing, 2013), 101.

their professions and vocations. At least this seems to have been true of those who were to become leaders within the evangelical movement.[93] This is not to argue that suffering is good for humanity, nor does it prove that this was true for the majority of Christian service men and women. Yet, the plentiful Christian fellowship enjoyed by evangelicals appears to have worked for many, strengthening them for the horrors which too readily threatened them. The dangers of war had proved a propitious context in which to evangelise, for recruitment of converts seems to have been unusually successful. War raised the sights to international horizons, and some, in consequence, developed a taste for cross-cultural missions which led to life-long engagement with the missionary movement.

93 The same was observed for British returnees. See Ernest Gordon, *Miracle on the River Kwai* (London: Fount, 1965), 228.

Chapter Seven

IN EXTREMIS

War-Time Ministries and Prisoners of War

'Tex, you are a damned fool. You don't have to be here.
But we're glad you are!'
(An Australian captain in New Guinea to
Chaplain Tex Morton)

World War II triggered a response from evangelical Christians which was central to its character, namely its capacity to initiate new ministries to meet the challenge of the hour or to adapt old ones for that purpose. These special ministries to the officers and ranks of the armed forces included the work of the military chaplains, the Salvation Army, the YMCA and their associated welfare officers and the newly formed Everyman's Welfare Service. These organisations reflected the heart of the evangelical movement in their commitment to evangelism and practical welfare. A sharper focus on ends was accompanied by the usual evangelical pragmatism in strategy. War-time ministries were often led by men used to making a difference, who were well connected with community and military leaders and were not bashful in using their connections. This chapter reviews these ministries to men and women at the front and also the experience of evangelical Christians who were prisoners of war. The simple evangelical spiritual disciplines of fellowship, Bible reading, prayer and hymn singing played a significant part in maintaining the morale of those imperilled by war.

The Chaplains

A total of 754 men served as padres in the Australian army during the war.[1] Of that number, consistent with the focus of this book, it is estimated that

1 Michael Gladwin, *Captains of the Soul: A History of Australian Army Chaplains* (Newport: Big Sky Publishing, 2013), 101.

nearly half were evangelicals. Leaving aside the Roman Catholic chaplains, evangelicals among the Protestant padres was at least sixty percent, or about 340 chaplains.[2] The chaplains themselves, aware that most service men and women attached little importance to such distinctions, commonly overlooked denominational distinctions and there was a pronounced reduction in sectarian tensions.[3]

According to historian John Barrett, the more than 3,700 returned men who responded to his 180 question survey in the early 1980s gave padres their hard-won approval,[4] with sixty-three percent expressing uncritical appreciation for their services. Appreciation of the value of chaplains seems to have increased as the war progressed.[5] 'Combat padres', those who accompanied their units into battle, earned the deepest respect of the men. Infantryman Peter Garrett, for example, recalled that when he was crippled by machine gun fire and behind Japanese lines, a group led by a chaplain had rescued him. In interviews with returned men, many of them voiced appreciation for the ministry of evangelical chaplains, such as Church of England padres Alan Begbie, Cecil Dillon, Rudolph Dillon, Francis Oag Hulme-Moir, Ralph Ogden and Roy Wotton; Methodist chaplains Frank Hartley, Arthur Jackson, Ivor Maggs and Lewis Trelawney Ugalde; Presbyterian padres A.R. Dean, R.H. Dean, Harold Wardale-Greenwood and Alexander McLiver; Baptist chaplains John Drakeford, Merlyn Holley, Malcolm McCullough, Harry Orr and F.H. Starr; and Churches of Christ padre Harold Norris.[6]

Testimony to the influence of chaplains is found in a letter Norris received in January 1943 from Sergeant Jeff Davis of 2/12 Battalion. Davis had become a Christian under Norris's ministry when he had been stationed at the Springbank Camp in South Australia the year before. In his letter, Davis explained that he attributed his loss of fear to his acceptance of Christ. He went on to observe: 'It seems to me that too many folk think of the Christian faith as a prize in heaven for being a good boy on earth. My faith is to me the incentive to make the best use of my life here on earth, knowing that it isn't the end of my life'. Eleven days later, Padre Norris learned of Davis's death at the further end of the Kokoda Track. Survivors discovered that Davis's

---

2 Rodney W. Tippett, 'Greater Than We Thought: Australian Army Chaplains in the South West Pacific Area, 1942–1945', MA (Hons), UNSW, 1989, 156–79.

3 Gladwin, *Captains of the Soul,* 125, 145–147.

4 Barrett, Australian Army Questionnaire, AWM Archives, PR89/135, Box 47; Gladwin, *Captains of the Soul,* 149.

5 Gladwin, *Captains of the Soul,* 119f.

6 Based on interviews with 75 World War II returned men, by Linder, 2001–2009, Morling Baptist College Archives.

last letter was one to his brother in the navy, urging him also to become a Christian. Chaplain Norris recalled that while his unit was resting near Port Moresby after it had taken part in the heavy fighting at Buna and Gona on the northern coast of Papua, a corporal from the 2/12 Battalion whom the padre had known in South Australia as a militant atheist came to him and revealed that he had been deeply impressed by Davis's Christian witness. The soldier told the chaplain:

> Jeff Davis was my friend. Jeff's life was changed when he accepted Christ as his Saviour. He got more 'kick' out of life than the rest of us. He never put himself first. It was always his men first. If I thought that the end of a life like Jeff's was death, I'd go mad. His life must go on; I want to be a Christian, and if I live after this war, I want to make something of my life and do the things Jeff would have done.[7]

Many of the evangelical chaplains distinguished themselves during the war. Three may be taken as examples: Baptist Harry Orr, Church of England Roy Wotton, and Methodist Frank Hartley.

Arthur Henry (Harry) Orr had served four years as pastor of the Bexley Baptist Church (1934–1938) and from 1938 to 1943 as assistant minister under C.J. Tinsley at Stanmore Baptist Church in Sydney. He enlisted at age thirty-two as an army chaplain on 30 March 1943. After graduating from the No. 2 Course for Chaplains in Sydney in September 1943, Orr was assigned first to the Bathurst training camp and then to the Darwin defence forces. He then spent most of 1945 in New Guinea where he was responsible for men in small outposts scattered along the coastal areas for several hundred kilometres around Lae during the final months of the war. He gave himself unstintingly to his work and did it so well that he was Mentioned in Dispatches.[8] On one occasion, Orr made a two-week trip of 250 kilometres on foot in Morabe Province to visit isolated clusters of from three to ten men at fifteen signals stations in dangerous and rough country with swamps and flooded rivers in western New Guinea.[9] Of the nearly one hundred letters to his wife that survive, all are cheerful and upbeat, except one, dated 1 May 1945, in which Orr complained:

---

7 Harold G. Norris, interviewed by R. W. Tippett, 25 July 1986; Tippett, 'Greater Than We Thought', 77–78.

8 Harry Orr to Lois Orr, 19 June 1944, 10 October 1944, 17 April 1945, Baptist Archives, Morling College, NSW.

9 Chaplain A. H. Orr, Report on Visitation of Signal Lines of Communication, Morobe-Amboga Area, Headquarters, Lae Base Sub Area, 29 June 1945, Morling Baptist College Archives.

> I feel very depressed and fed up this morning. The Army is getting on my nerves at the moment. I get sick of the filthy, profane language, a bit weary of the same old technique of battling for services and trying to do the real job. Just feel right down in the dumps. I'm suffering from a bit too much to do, I think. Just fed up with censoring letters.[10]

The times of achievement, however, far outweighed his disappointments. In mid-June 1945 at Bulolo in New Guinea, Orr exalted:

> I had splendid little services all the way up and on Wednesday night, at Bulolo, one I shall always remember. We had the usual sing song. It was in a house! Owned by one of the civvies before the war. The boys towed the jeep up to the house, connected a few wires, and lo, we had light from the car battery … The boys lifted the phone and fellows all down the road were listening in at their phones – and asking for request numbers! Then a service – in which all were very reverent and interested – and after a sing song, until quarter past eleven. They simply would NOT let me stop. I could hardly pull the groan box back and forwards. During the last sing song – we sang practically every hymn in the book – the fellows started talking about Sunday School days. Then they wanted to sing their old Sunday School hymns. And we did – Jesus Loves Me, Mothers of Salem, Jesus Bids Us Shine, When He Cometh, Hear the Pennies Dropping, and our Sunday School is over! All amidst the most surprising enthusiasm and accounts of Sunday School experiences. It was a revelation to me how deeply Sunday School teaching had gone – and also an indication of what can be done when the atmosphere is right.[11]

Orr's sense of humour helped. It seems that in one area where he held services, an officer had taught a parrot to swear. One Sunday morning Orr was preaching in a hospital chapel while next door others had gathered to hear the parrot. Orr told his spouse that 100 attended the church service, while 150 gathered around the parrot. The contrast struck Orr as funny rather than as a threat to his ministry.[12] He told his wife of counselling young soldiers deep into the night, then rising early the next day to move on to another

10 Harry Orr to Lois Orr, 1 May 1945, Baptist Archives. Chaplains were divided over whether censorship was an appropriate role for them. Gladwin, *Captains of the Soul*,108.

11 'GRIST FOR THE MILL: Glances at N. G. & Papua', from Harry Orr to Lois Orr, mid-June 1945, Baptist Archives.

12 Harry Orr to Lois Orr, 15 July 1944, Baptist Archives.

venue. It was a tough but rewarding life. Orr was apparently an inspirational speaker and, as his reputation spread, often had hundreds in attendance at his services.[13] He was able to lead many men to Christ. In one letter to his wife, Orr reflected on the value of his army experiences:

> I'm just back from my sojourn out on one of our sites, and did some very good work. Long conversations with ever so many blokes, prayer with some and preparatory conversion talks with some … Never while life shall last, will I have such an avenue of service … The experience I am gaining, the knowledge of human nature, the viewpoint of the fellows is invaluable, and will enrich my ministry for all time.[14]

After the war, Harry Orr became a leader of his denomination and established a Baptist mission on the Baiyer River in New Guinea. It was, as Orr observed, 'born through the travail of war service'.[15]

Whereas Harry Orr saw no fighting while on active service, Church of England Chaplain Roy Wotton did. Wotton was one of the 'combat padres' who served in the front lines with their men. He served briefly in North Africa before being rushed home as part of the 9th Division in order to prepare for a possible invasion of Australia by the Japanese. Once there, he became one of three chaplains attached to the 18th Brigade and sent north to Queensland to await orders.[16] His unit would soon be involved in heavy fighting on the Kokoda Track in New Guinea. Wotton believed that he had to earn the trust of his men by staying in touch with them and accompanying them into battle. As he and his men fought their way across the spine of the Owen Stanley Range, Wotton had many close encounters with the Japanese forces. On one occasion while in thick jungle, Wotton suddenly found himself face to face with a Japanese officer. The startled officer turned and ran, only to be tackled and captured by the Australian padre.[17]

---

13 Harry Orr to Lois Orr, 15 July 1944, 10 October 1944, 13 March 1945, 12 June 1945, 9 July 1945, Baptist Archives.

14 Harry Orr to Lois Orr, 30 August 1944, Baptist Archives.

15 Service of Thanksgiving for the Life and Ministry of the Rev. Arthur Henry Orr, 3 January 1993, Chatswood Baptist Church, Chatswood, NSW; Ron Robb, *Bethel: A Tradition of Faith at Work* (Ashfield: Ashfield Baptist Homes, 2002), 21–8; John Garrett, *Where Nets Were Cast: Christianity in Oceania Since World War II* (Geneva: WCC, 1997), 180.

16 Each brigade was assigned three chaplains: one Church of England, one Roman Catholic and one Protestant from one of 'the other denominations'. In effect, each chaplain served one of the brigade's three battalions. In Wotton's case, he spent most of his time with the 2/12th Battalion.

17 Roy Wotton, interviewed by Linder, 23 May 2001.

During one lull in the fighting in 1942, General Douglas MacArthur, the Supreme Allied Commander in the Pacific, summoned Wotton's commanding officer to Port Moresby for consultations. His CO took Wotton with him for the meeting. After MacArthur criticised the Australians for not making significant progress quickly enough, Wotton spoke up and suggested the American general come take a first-hand look at the Owen Stanley Range for himself. Wotton estimated that he 'added a number to the ranks of Christ during the war' as he comforted hundreds of wounded and grieving Diggers and stood by them in thick and thin. He buried more than 400 Diggers during his army career, almost all of them with the help of Sergeant Stuart Murray, who became his trusted assistant in both North Africa and New Guinea. Murray, an Aboriginal member of the Churches of Christ, married a daughter of Aboriginal evangelical leader Douglas Nicholls after the war and himself became an influential Christian figure in Victoria. He founded the Victorian Aboriginal Advancement League.

One of his fellow combat chaplains in New Guinea whom Wotton admired was Francis John Hartley. Frank Hartley had been the Methodist minister at Orbost, Victoria when he enlisted in the AIF on 31 January 1941. He left behind a new spouse to join the army in order to look after the spiritual needs of the 'boys' in the military. He served for nearly five years and saw intensive combat before returning to civilian life in late 1945. Hartley served as the Protestant chaplain of the 7th Australian Division Cavalry for most of the war. This unit was heavily engaged in Papua during the final fighting to drive the Japanese army back down the Kokoda Track and into the sea at Sanananda in late 1942 and early 1943.[18] Like other padres in New Guinea during the heavy fighting, Hartley had little chance to conduct formal services in the combat zone. He spent most of his time in personal conversations with his troops as he looked after their spiritual welfare. He supplied them with comforts and 'luxuries' like soap, biscuits, chocolates and cake. He also personally delivered the mail to frontline positions and helped construct and carry stretchers for the wounded and was especially punctilious in giving the dead 'an appropriate Christian burial'. As it was, he buried the majority of men of his unit. Of the 420 men who had gone into action, only sixty-two were left standing by the end of the campaign. All of the others had been killed, wounded or fell victim of malaria or scrub typhus.[19]

18 On the Sananada campaign, see Gavin Long, *The Six Years War: Australia in the 1939–45 War* (Canberra: AWM, 1973), 236–247.

19 F.J. Hartley, *Sananda Interlude* (Melbourne: The Book Depot, 1949), 62–63, 80, 85.

Hartley had many harrowing experiences as a combat padre. One of the most stressful occurred early in the Sananandaa campaign. On 20 December 1942, C Squadron had established a hotly contested forward post at the cost of heavy casualties, with thirteen wounded, of whom eight were serious stretcher cases. Under intense enemy fire they could not withdraw with their wounded and they refused to do so otherwise. In order to inform headquarters of their predicament, the commanding officer asked for three volunteers to make their way through Japanese lines. Two of the volunteers did not make it and the third, Corporal Ham Morton, did so only after he was badly wounded. The commotion associated with Morton's break through brought Padre Hartley and the unit's medical doctor to the Regimental Aid Post to see if they could help. It was the middle of the night and the problem was how to keep the bleeding stopped until morning when an operation could be performed. The only thing they could do was to take relays in holding their fingers on the pressure point. According to Hartley:

> I'll never forget my second shift. All were sound asleep and my relief was a good few yards away. My thumb went numb and I became cramped, so I lay down full length beside the patient. He was breathing heavily and peacefully, thanks to the morphia. I did not want to call out in case Ham was awakened. There was nothing to be done but be there and wait. My chief worry was whether I was unwittingly releasing the pressure. By this time all feeling had gone completely from my thumb. It was a strange experience, to be lying there, with the moonlight making ghostly shadows through the trees, knowing that a man's life depended on my keeping awake and keeping the pressure on. With such a responsibility on one's mind, it was impossible to go to sleep, however tired.[20]

Soon after dawn, the doctor, with his four helpers holding the patient down, operated and Morton's life was saved.

Christmas Day 1942 was a special occasion in that Hartley celebrated it under fire. To hold a church service was impossible, but he played Santa Claus by making his way through the jungle to his regiment's most forward outpost to deliver two large bags of mail and Comfort Funds parcels to the troops. The men were ecstatic when they saw the mail and, according to Hartley, 'their joy knew no bounds'. Hartley declared:

---

20 Hartley, *Sananda Interlude*, 24–25.

> I don't think I've ever felt more in the spirit of Christmas ... We had cared for the wounded and had brought hope to their lives. We had brought news from home to the lonely. We had contributed to physical comfort of the needy. The feeling of unselfishness was abroad ... One fellow expressed the feelings of us all, "The best Christmas present I've ever had in my life was to see those wounded go down the track, and then to know that they had got through".[21]

When the campaign to capture Sananada was over and the men who survived the ordeal were assembled at Dobadura aerodrome for the flight back to Port Moresby, Hartley held an evening church service for the survivors. Almost all of the remaining men attended. Hartley spoke briefly from 2 Corinthians 7:10: 'For godly sorry worketh repentance to salvation not to be repented of: but the sorrow of the world worketh death'. Hartley observed: 'It is godly sorrow that assists man to salvation. I have every reason to believe that the message went home. Many chaps spoke to me afterwards and there was a general resolve to do something better with our lives'.[22] Hartley was Mentioned In Despatches for his courage under fire and his devotion to the spiritual and physical welfare of his fellow Diggers.[23] On returning home he became the pastor of a Methodist church in Melbourne. He became a campaigner for nuclear disarmament and opposed Australia's participation in the Vietnam War. Menzies labelled him 'the pink parson'.[24]

Salvation Army Welfare Officers

Although the Salvation Army had only twelve official chaplains in the army during the war, it had nearly 400 welfare officers serving everywhere the Australian armed forces were deployed.[25] Barrett in his study of World War II Diggers reports that they were overwhelmingly positive in their response to the work of Salvation Army padres and welfare officers. Chaplain and welfare officer could make effective teams as one Digger testified:

> Our chaplain so often said 'Call me Digger' that we did call him 'The Digger'. And we had a Red Shield (Salvation Army) representative as

21 Hartley, *Sananada Interlude*, 38.

22 Hartley, *Sananada Interlude*, 83.

23 The Rev. Wesley Hartley, son of Frank Hartley, to Linder, 1 October 2010.

24 Gladwin, *Captains of the Soul*, 242.

25 Stanley (Tex) Morton, interviewed by Linder, 30 May 2001.

> a welfare officer whom we called 'The Professor'. The battalion was getting a bit on the nose because we were without soap of any kind, so Digger and Professor somehow acquired a gross of Palmolive shaving sticks and worked into the early hours cutting them up to give each man from colonel to cook's offsider an equal ration. I always thought Digger was the best soldier in the battalion, though he was not of my belief, and I can't speak too highly of the old Professor, with his pencils and paper and 'Write to your Mum, soldier'. When the main force of the battalion landed at Rabaul, I was in the first barge and one of the first ashore. Out of the bush came a voice, 'Coffee, mate – with or without?' It was the Professor. He'd landed the night before.[26]

Salvo welfare officers often served as unofficial padres for the forces. The most famous of these unofficial padres was Arthur William McIlveen, 'the Padre to the Rats of Tobruk'.[27] Born near Inverell, NSW, on 29 June 1886, McIlveen was the son of a poor farmer. The McIlveens were Presbyterians and Arthur was converted to Christ at an evangelistic mission in Inverell when he was in his early teens. To help support his family, he left school at age fourteen and became a tin miner for the next decade. The Salvation Army came to Inverell in strength early in the twentieth century and impressed young Arthur with their happy Christian faith and their dedication to Christ. In 1910, he threw in his lot with the Salvos and volunteered to train for the Army. Even though he was fifty-three years of age when the war began, he was appointed welfare officer to the 18th Brigade of the AIF and sailed for Britain in May of 1940. After training in the UK, the brigade was moved to Egypt and eventually to Libya. From the beginning of his wartime adventure, McIlveen served as an unofficial padre to the troops, and eventually was attached to the 2/9 Battalion that fought in the Battle of Tobruk from April to August 1941.[28]

Working under fire, McIlveen attended to the needs of Australian troops as well as German and Italian POWs. Diggers were especially impressed by his willingness to provide them with comforts, coffee, tea, biscuits, a cheery

---

26 John Barrett, *We Were There: Australian Soldiers of World War II tell their Stories* (St. Leonards: Allen & Unwin, 1995), 328.

27 Nelson Dunster, *Padre to the 'Rats'* (London: Salvationist Publishing and Supplies, Ltd., 1971); J. C. Salter, *A Padre with the Rats of Tobruk* (Hobart: J. Walch & Sons, 1946); Gladwin, *Captains of the Soul*, 110–113. FitzSimons does not mention McIlveen by name, alluding to him only as 'an old Salvation Army fellow who used to wander around with a wind-up gramophone'. This hardly explains McIlveen's enormous popularity with the Rats. Peter FitzSimons, *Tobruk* (HarperCollins Publishers, 2006), 410.

28 Darryl McIntyre, 'McIlven, Sir Arthur Wulliam', *ADB*, online edition.

word and a word of prayer in the front lines under intense enemy bombardment. Sprinting from trench to trench and to the various perimeter posts in the outlying areas burdened down like a pack mule by his supplies and a wind-up phonograph, he gained the special affection of the Diggers by playing his records on his battered old machine wherever he went. Major W.R.E. Isaacs, one of the Rats, later summed up the way the soldiers thought of him:

> The best-liked member of the garrison was Brigadier Arthur McIlveen of the Salvation Army. In rest areas, there was never any need for a compulsory church parade when it became known that Padre Mac would be doing the honours. At least one battalion used to get 100 percent attendances, and the surge of their singing 'Shall we gather at the river?' could be heard for miles.[29]

McIlveen maintained his close ties with the Rats following the war. In the 1950s, the Rats of Tobruk Association, in appreciation for his contributions to their spiritual and material wellbeing during the siege, bought a house for him and his family at Bexley in Sydney.[30]

Among Salvation Army welfare officers who served first in North Africa and later in New Guinea were Albert Moore and Stanley (Tex) Morton. Both were, like McIlveen, unofficial padres as well as welfare officers and both cooperated closely with the various military chaplains. Although they preached at every opportunity, they mostly counselled Diggers one to one. Morton served as a stretcher-bearer on occasion in New Guinea and worked with the medical doctors in the Regimental Aid Post. A captain in New Guinea once said to Morton: "Tex, you are a damned fool. You don't have to be here. But we're glad you are!"[31]

YMCA Welfare Officers

As in World War I, so in World War II the YMCA quickly mobilised and went with the troops. The Y, as it was often called, was still a basically evangelical organisation, staffed and supported by evangelicals in World War II. The majority of its welfare officers were either Methodists or Baptists, a great many of them ministers who could not obtain a chaplain's slot. Identified by its Red Triangle, the Y, like the Salvation Army, provided Australian armed

---

29 Dunster, *Padre to the 'Rats'*, 70.

30 Roy Wotton, interviewed by Linder, 23 May 2001.

31 Peter Brune, *A Bastard of a Place: The Australians in Papua* (Crows Nest: Allen & Unwin, 2004), 181; Morton, interviewed by Linder.

forces personnel with food, drink, toiletries and writing materials. Salvation Army and YMCA welfare officers always served different units and did not directly compete with one another. Many YMCA welfare officers often preached when a chaplain was not available and most witnessed to their faith and offered spiritual counselling.[32]

YMCA Forward Area Representative Sam Watson and his offsider Evan Shirrefs, both Baptists from Victoria, served in the Syrian Campaign in June-July 1941. Watson, an ordained Baptist minister, and Shirrefs, a Baptist layman, both from Melbourne, were travelling close on the heels of the troops in the battle zone one day near Merdj Ayoun in their large Austin Mobile Canteen when they ran into heavy shelling on the main road. Their mobile canteen, with its name 'Dinkum' painted on its front end, pulled over to allow a staff car to pass and crashed helplessly on its side in a deep ditch. Stranded and unable to extricate their mobile canteen from the ditch, the two Y representatives set up shop and for three days and two nights distributed lemon cordial and cakes to passing troops heading toward the front.[33]

Other YMCA officers gained a measure of notoriety for their service during the war. One of these was Henry Preston Black, nephew of World War I padre and NSW Baptist leader W. Cleugh Black. Harry Black, a fine physical specimen, had left school in 1934 at age 15 to support his family during the Great Depression. He enlisted in the militia in 1939, then joined the RAAF in 1940, and was called up in 1941. He learned to fly in Victoria, after which he was posted to Canada to complete his training as a fighter pilot. As he was about to complete his training, he developed chronic airsickness. Therefore, he was discharged and sent home. He returned to Australia just as the fighting on the Kokoda Track was at its height. Black pleaded to be allowed to join the YMCA and be sent to New Guinea. He was attached to the 2/7th Australian Division Cavalry Regiment that was involved in the final fierce fighting at the northern end of the Kokoda Track. There he served with Padre Frank Hartley on the Sananada Road, and he built a makeshift hut of bamboo timber just behind the front line and next to Hartley's padre's tent. Black called his little patch 'Guinea Glen' and Hartley his tent 'Padre's Paradise'. Black worked closely with Hartley, gathered in the comforts that planes regularly dropped close behind the lines, and then passed them on to the padre for delivery. Black also always had hot tea, pen and paper ready for Diggers who had been relieved from the front lines for a visit to his hut,

32 Angus S. Mitchell, 'Those "Y" Blokes', *The Rotarian*, 64.6, 1944, 32–3.

33 Jack Manning, 'Baptists of the Red Triangle with the AIF', *The Australian Baptist*, 23 November 1943, 4.

out of sniper range of the enemy. Black had set up his rest area beside a clear, rushing river where Diggers could bathe and wash their clothes. The two men also often went forward to collect the wounded and the dead, and bring them back behind the lines for treatment or an appropriate Christian burial.[34]

After Sananda fell in January 1943, Black traversed the primitive Bulldog Track to Wau three times before being attached to a parachute battalion. It was in this period that he, along with YMCA welfare officers Jack Manning, Bob Langdon and Bert Green, cooperated with Padre Harry Orr in ministry. Then in late 1944, he was assigned to the 2/11th Battalion, which captured Wewak in May 1945 in one of the final campaigns in the Pacific Theatre of Operations. Black returned to Australia in August 1945 and joined the staff of the YMCA. In 1948, he was appointed general secretary of the Y in Canberra. He was awarded the 1953 Coronation Medal for his YMCA work.[35]

Among other dedicated and distinguished 'Y blokes' were Stanley T. Earl, and William Clack. Stan Earl was a prominent Baptist minister in South Australia who had spent four years in the army in World War I. After beginning his YMCA service in SA, he was assigned as Senior Representative for the 7th Division, newly returned from the Middle East and posted to Queensland. He then accompanied the Division to New Guinea to support his welfare officers through the battles of Buna, Lae and Salamaua. After being told the YMCA could go to New Guinea with the army but could take no gear, Earl somehow managed to ensure that the Y units there were well equipped anyway. He returned to Sydney to assume the pastorate of the Granville Baptist Church in June 1944.[36]

Bill Clack of the Ballarat Baptist Church had studied at the MBI, hoping one day to become a missionary to China. His dream, however, was interrupted by the war. After graduation from MBI in 1941, Clack volunteered for wartime duty with the YMCA. He eventually ran the YMCA hut at the RAAF base at Nadzab in New Guinea. There he dispensed an average of 100 gallons of tea a day to service personnel. He ran welfare activities during the day and held church services and Bible studies at night in cooperation with Baptist Padre Alan Burrow of SA. He flew to outlying airstrips in small planes to care for the needs of airmen there, and on one such occasion barely survived a plane crash. He merely shifted the focal point of his ministry to the hospital where he recovered before going back to his Nadzab hut. After New Guinea, Clack

34 Hartley, *Sananda Interlude*, 58–63.

35 Harry Orr to Lois Orr, 25 May 1945, Baptist Archives.

36 *The Australian Baptist*, 11 January 1944, 3; 4 July 1944, 4.

spent time in Borneo and the Philippines and a year in Japan as a part of the occupation force. He became general secretary of the Launceston YMCA from 1947 to 1954, after which he was appointed secretary and men's superintendent of MBI where he served for the next twenty-one years.[37]

Len Buck and Everyman's Welfare Service

In September 1939 when World War II broke out Len Buck was thirty-three years old and, with a wife and four children, he was not a good prospect for military service. He ran an essential business (clothing manufacturer) which was also a basis for exemption from the military in Australia in the early years of the war. He was determined, however, to do something for God and to help his country resist fascist aggression. Therefore, he used his influence as the leader of a new evangelical movement in Melbourne known as the Campaigners for Christ to accomplish his goal of serving God and country.

Campaigners for Christ grew out of the City Men's Bible Class (CMBC) begun in the Griffiths Brothers' Tea Rooms in Melbourne in 1929 with the Rev. C.H. Nash as teacher. The CMBC drew several hundred young Christian businessmen to the Tea Rooms every Monday evening for fellowship and instruction in godly living, discipleship and evangelism. On 23 January 1936, at the conclusion of that evening's Bible Class, twenty-seven of the men present went to Len Buck's showroom in Flinders Lane to talk about starting a movement that would implement what they had been learning in the class. Included in this number were Buck and Harold Swanton, a loss assessor in the insurance industry, and many of the other well-known leaders of interdenominational evangelical Christianity in Melbourne. Swanton expressed his desire to 'campaign for Christ', and thus was born the lay evangelistic movement Campaigners for Christ.[38]

In late 1939 Buck convinced the Council of Campaigners for Christ to establish an organisation to address the spiritual and welfare needs of Australia's military personnel – 'welfare with a purpose' as he called it. Buck's concern was to proclaim Christ, 'warning every man, and teaching every man in all wisdom: that we may present every man perfect in Christ Jesus'.[39] After drawn out negotiations, the Australian Defence Force recognised Everyman's, authorised its welfare work and approved the first Everyman's Hut. The success of

37 *New Life*, 22 July 1999, 1 and 5.

38 Darrell Paproth, *Failure Is Not Final* (Sydney: Centre for the Study of Australian Christianity, 1997), 125.

39 Colossians 1:28 (KJV)

these early negotiations with the Defence Department owed everything to Buck's charisma. In the words of Charles Sandland, 'by his dignified bearing and distinctive uniform, he could well have been mistaken for the Colonel of the regiment. By his persuasive approach, he seemed able to demand from Generals, and whoever, almost any concession or support he felt to be needful'.[40]

Following Japan's attack on Pearl Harbour in late 1941, Buck requested permission to embark on an Everyman's mission to Malaya in response to the build-up of British troops there.[41] He secured permission to take to the war zone a three-ton Ford truck that he had converted into a Mobile Canteen in Darwin. His attempt to establish an Everyman's Hut near a RAAF aerodrome at Khota Baru in Malaya was thwarted by the Japanese invasion in early December 1941. As he withdrew with the Allied troops, he dispensed New Testaments and evangelistic booklets on tables alongside his canteen. According to Buck, he placed 200 Gospels and other Christian literature on a table: 'All went in a few minutes. The supply was replenished, and again the literature was rapidly taken'. He talked with Australian troops well into the night, discussing spiritual matters and the situation in which they found themselves.[42]

When the Allied columns reached Singapore, the concentrated bombing of the city began. On the evening of 11 February 1942, the Allied High Command gave permission for sixteen vessels to leave Singapore. As the sixteen ships left the harbour at dawn on 12 February, all but two were sunk. Buck was on board the *Empire Star* which, though bombed and strafed for six hours, escaped to the open sea. He arrived in Fremantle, Western Australia, by way of Batavia late in February 1942.[43]

Buck later recounted his harrowing experiences at meetings in Australian capital cities including one held on 18 March 1942 in the Collins Street Baptist Church in Melbourne with a thousand people in attendance. His account of his work emphasised the matters which concerned evangelicals. He told of how on one of his last days in Singapore amidst appalling slaughter, he noticed only two Asians drunk but thousands of British troops and civilians inebriated. He reported witnessing feats of unselfish heroism under fire and saw a number of people turn to God. After the ferocious bombing of the *Empire Star*, somebody said, 'Let's have a service'. Over 700 individuals

40 *New Life*, 16 May 1996, 1.

41 Alan Kerr, *Guided Journey: Some Experiences of a Lifetime* (Gundaroo: Brolga Press, 1998), 25.

42 *New Life*, 26 March 1970, 1; 20 March 1942, 5.

43 Keith Morgan to Linder, 10 October 2003.

gathered round and sang 'Abide with Me' and other old hymns. Commented Buck: 'God spoke to many that night'.[44]

Of all the ministries to the armed forces conducted by the churches in World War II, Everyman's was the most typical of the evangelical impulse. Arising itself from an evangelistic body (Campaigners), formed by a layman, it was non-denominational, practical and evangelistic. But why did Buck press on with this work when two other evangelical welfare agencies with ties to the military, the Salvation Army and the YMCA, already existed? Most evangelical institutions lose their evangelistic edge over time, and Buck might have thought that a new evangelical organisation was required to effectively evangelise the troops. During discussion of the formation of Everyman's in 1939, at a meeting of the executive council of Campaigners for Christ, Buck 'expressed a wish that we should do a work of a definite evangelistic character among the soldiers'.[45] An early Everyman's slogan was 'Welfare Work with a Purpose'. The purpose was evangelism.

According to Buck, Alfred E. Coombe more than anybody else in the Campaigners' organisation bankrolled Everyman's during World War II. Senior partner in the wool firm of John Sanderson and Company, President of the Australian Wool Board during World War II and a Presbyterian elder, Coombe was the most influential of Everyman's angels.[46] He had connections among the military high command. He knew Lieutenant-General Sir Brudenell White, the Army Chief of the General Staff in 1940, and gained an entrée with him for Buck to plead his case for the Campaigners' new religious welfare organisation. Buck was fearless in his approach to high-ranking military brass when it came to securing a place for Everyman's on or around military posts. Following his return from Singapore in early 1942, Buck secured from Brigadier D.V.J. Blake permission to establish an Everyman's recreation centre and hut at the soon to be opened Bonegilla Camp, fifteen kilometres east of Wodonga in Victoria. It was the first of its kind to be set up on Australian soil.[47]

Following Bonegilla, Everyman's spread rapidly to many locations around Australia, including an Everywoman's Hut, staffed by evangelical women, at Bandiana, five kilometres from Wodonga. Everyman's tearooms were

---

44 *New Life*, 20 March 1942, 5; *The Age*, 12 March 1942, 2; David Price, 'A Life of Service: Leonard E. Buck (1906–1996)', *Lucas* 21 & 22, 1996, 129–35.

45 Minutes of the Executive Meeting of Campaigners for Christ held in the home of Mr. L.E. Buck, Melbourne, 5 October 1939.

46 Leonard Buck, interviewed by Margaret Lamb, 18 May 1988.

47 Keith Morgan, interviewed by Linder, 24 July 2004.

established in all of the capital cities. The personnel who ran these huts and tearooms included Protestant ministers, missionaries who had returned to Australia because of the war and countless male and female civilian volunteers. All of this was organised and directed by a 'War Council' formed from the ranks of the Melbourne-based Campaigners for Christ on 3 July 1940, with Len Buck as its chief driving force, aided and abetted by many of Melbourne's leading businessmen, several ministers of religion and a politician, namely, the old Methodist stalwart W.A. Edgar.[48]

Everyman's personnel eventually appropriated officer status with the honorary rank of lieutenant. As the Commissioner of the organisation, Buck took for himself the honorary rank of colonel. None of this was official until Everyman's was finally accredited by the military years later during the Korean War (1950–1953).[49] Until then, all of Everyman's World War II activities were ad hoc, and rested upon Len Buck's negotiating skills and his strong faith and determination. Hundreds of soldiers, undergoing training in Townsville, found Christ as Saviour in the Everyman's hut and many believers found a home away from home where they could spend their free time in a Christian environment.[50] Buck also established at least two Everyman's huts in the Atherton Tablelands above Cairns, ministering to where hundreds of others, women as well as men. Bruce Bryson, who served with Everyman's during the war, recalls that the welfare service had established fifteen 'elaborate welfare huts and centres' by the end of the war.[51]

Everyman's welfare officers Stan Drew and Stan Nichols had an especially fruitful ministry among the troops in the Tablelands.[52] Drew, who focused on a 1,200-man unit, preached to a large, hushed audience on the eve of their departure for New Guinea. When he concluded his sermon, 'massive numbers' stood for prayer and to indicate that they had accepted Christ as Saviour. Drew, a moving preacher and a fine violinist, seldom had less than 300 men and women in his services during his period on the Tablelands. After the war, he remained with Everyman's and ministered effectively in Adelaide and Perth.[53]

---

48 Minutes of Executive Meeting, Campaigners for Christ, 3 July 1940, Melbourne.

49 'Our History', http://www.everyman.org.au/index.php/about_us/or_history/ (Accessed 20 July 2010).

50 Donald Horne, *An Interrupted Life* (Sydney: HarperCollins Publishers, 1998), 401.

51 Bruce Bryson, *My Father's House: The Bryson Story of Life on Four Continents* (Torrens Park: Gillingham Printers, 1993), 73.

52 Raymond Taylor, interviewed by Linder, 22 July 2004.

53 Morgan interviewed by Linder, 24 July 2004; and Irene Hart Playford, *Man with a Violin and A Vision: The Story of Stan Drew* (Perth: Pilpel Print, 2004), 7–10.

Stan Nichols, who had trained for the ministry at MBI, was another eloquent speaker and a compassionate and effective personal counsellor. His ministry on the Tablelands was legendary among the Diggers posted there. On one occasion, a soldier committed suicide in public while on parade, sending shock waves throughout the camp. Nichols took immediate action to head off an epidemic of suicides and console the men in the young soldier's company. He discovered that no effort had yet been made to notify the family of the soldier who had killed himself. Nichols, therefore, wrote a compassionate letter to his mother explaining the situation, but before he sent it he showed it to the approximately 150 men in the company and asked if it met their approval. It did, and this act made an enormous impact on the men.[54]

Everyman's efforts in the war shaped numerous future evangelical leaders, including Lt. Frank Gallagher who, influenced at the Everyman's Hut in Townsville, later became a Baptist minister in Sydney, and Ed Bentley who in Northern Queensland, found Everyman's Welfare Huts to be a 'home away from home', and after the war embarked on a seventeen-year career with Everyman's, working on its behalf all across eastern Australia.[55] Everyman's Welfare Service has served Australian military personnel in every conflict since the Second World War and continues to do so today.

Evangelical Prisoners of War

In his study of Allied POWs of the Japanese in World War II, Gavan Daws divides them into three basic tribes: The aristocratic British tribe, the individualistic American tribe, and the communalistic Australian tribe. The Australian tribe was built on the traditional practice of mateship. Daws argues that these three national tribes 'simply were what they were, for good and ill'.[56] But was there possibly another 'tribe' in the camps, one that transcended ethnic, cultural and national difference – one based on Christianity and Christian values rather than nationality and national values? At the very least, it is possible that vital Christian faith, where held by POWs, was a factor in their survival, a very practical manifestation of caring for the Australian soul. Furthermore, where mateship existed among Australian POWs, it might have done so in its most intense and pure form among enclaves of practising Christians in the camps. Case studies suggest the feasibility of

54 Ray Taylor, interviewed by Linder, 22 July 2004.

55 Maurice Edwin Bentley, interviewed by Linder, 24 July 2004.

56 Gavan Daws, *Prisoners of the Japanese: POWs of World War II in the Pacific*, rev. ed. (Carlton North: Scribe, 2008), 134–40; Gladwin, *Captains of the Soul,* 121,133.

this proposition. Arnold Jordan, Geoff Bingham, Florence Trotter, and Brian Morcombe all evidence the survival value of faith. On the other hand, believers were never tempted to imagine that their faith shielded them from the sufferings of their fellow Australians. Some such as Ted Skinner put self-sacrifice above personal survival; Chaplain Wardale-Greenwood at Sandakan constantly boosted the morale of his fellow-prisoners, only to perish with most of them;[57] others such as the missionaries on the ill-fated *Montevideo Maru* were drowned along with all the other passengers in the worst maritime disaster in Australian history.[58]

Arnold Oakley Jordan experienced a special kind of spiritual mateship in the POW camps in which he found himself while working on the Burma-Thailand Railroad in 1942–1945. Jordan, born in Burnie, Tasmania in 1911, accepted Christ as his Saviour in 1931 in the Yolla Baptist church. Convinced that he was called to the ministry, he attended MBI in 1933–1934. He enlisted in the Australian Army on 21 June 1940. Another reluctant warrior, Jordan applied for assignment as a medical orderly. Eventually attached to the 2/13 Australian General Hospital in Singapore, he was captured on 15 February 1942.

Jordan was first interned in the POW camp at Changi in Singapore. On 15 May 1942, along with 3,000 other men, he was assigned to A Force to labour on the infamous Burma-Thailand Railroad, ending up with the men who constructed the bridge over the River Kwai.[59] On the eve of his first workday on the railway, Colonel Y. Nagatomo, the camp commander, outlined to the assembled prisoners what Jordan called 'his blue-print for the suffering and crime that awaited us'. He made clear two concepts that constituted the ideological foundations of the camps. First, those who do not work do not deserve to eat. Second, soldiers should die rather than surrender, therefore, no prisoners of war deserve to live: the Samurai Code of Bushido applied to the POW camps under Japanese control.

As the horrors of the camps unfolded, Jordan and his fellow prisoners struggled to maintain their self-respect and their self-identity. Gradually a cluster of men gathered around Jordan and other Christian leaders in order to sustain their humanity and enable them to survive. When asked how he and his friends survived, Jordan said it was music, personal faith in Christ

57 Gladwin, *Captains of the Soul*, 138.

58 Margaret Reeson, *Whereabouts Unknown* (Sutherland: Albatross Books, 1993); Margaret Reeson, *A Very Long War: The Families Who Waited* (Carlton South: MUP, 2000).

59 Arnold Jordan, *Tenko on the River Kwai* (Launceston: Regal Publications, 1987). 'Tenko' is the Japanese term for a roll call.

and the support of his Christian mates. Not only did the men stage concerts and entertain themselves with self-generated music, but they also repeatedly recalled the words of well-known Christian hymns. Jordan often sang a familiar gospel song to revive his spirits:

> There is never a day so dreary,
> There is never a night so long,
> But the soul that is trusting in Jesus
> Will somewhere find a song.

Jordan carried his Bible with him and read it daily during his captivity. The Japanese never tried to take it away from him. He noted several times in his memoir that he was deeply sustained in his spiritual life: he may have been physically exhausted and mentally fatigued, but at the same time spiritually invigorated. He recalled that he preached on one occasion at the River Kwai camp. His text was Psalm 137:4: 'How can we sing the songs of the Lord while in a foreign country?' His answer: 'In a strange land of loneliness, we can sing the Lord's songs by making Christ, crucified for our sins and risen again for our justification, the centre of our circle.'

This circle of his Christian mates with Christ at the centre helped him to survive the brutality of the camps. The main problems were illnesses and a lack of food. Jordan survived attacks of beriberi and dysentery thanks to Ted Goulston, his best mate and, like Jordan, an evangelical. Jordan and Goulston enlisted within days of each other in 1940 in Tasmania, served in the same unit and spent their entire confinement together during the war. It was Ted Goulston who cared for Jordan during his most serious illnesses and nursed him back to health.

Other close Christian friends in the camps contributed to mutual survival. One was a British Tommy named George. He received a letter one day that revealed that his wife, mother and sister had been killed in a German air raid over Manchester. Nevertheless, his faith was unfailing. He often spoke of his desire to become a minister when his term of service expired. Another special mate was Moorbin, concerning whom Jordan remarked: 'Morb was a Pommie-Aussie with a voice from Lancashire that unfailingly proclaimed every passing rumour, both possible and impossible, as gospel truth. His steadfast faith in God, as well as in Dame Rumour, was a cheer to us all.'

There were still others, like Australian Alec Bell, who inspired even in death. Late in 1943, trying to escape, Bell was recaptured, placed in the guardhouse and nursed back to health, after which the Japanese shot him. Bell made his death count. During the week prior to his execution, he was allowed two visits from Australian Church of England Padre Frederick Bashford who later revealed that Bell was a man of faith who did not fear the ordeal of death that awaited him. He was taken to the place of execution early in the morning. According to both a Japanese Christian guard and the commander of the firing squad, Bell appears to have dominated his final minutes to such an extent that the Japanese officer was clearly shaken, remarking to Allied senior officers: 'Why should he thank ME, and shake hands with ME before he died'. He added: 'What strange words … I have done my duty, now you do yours! How sad it is that so brave a man should die for such a foolish attempt to escape'. At the camp church service the following Sunday evening, Padre Bashford announced the opening hymn, adding:

> The words of this hymn are Alec Bell's last message to us all. I want to tell you that he had no fear of his impending ordeal. He regarded death as a transition, as an entrance into a higher, fuller life … Alec Bell's last request to me was that, here tonight, we sing this, his favourite hymn … his final testimony to all men.

The hymn was 'Rock of Ages' with its closing verse:

> While I draw this fleeting breath,
> When mine eyes shall close in death,
> When I soar to worlds unknown,
> See Thee on Thy judgement-throne;
> Rock of Ages, cleft for me,
> Let me hide myself in Thee.

The Christian guard present at Bell's execution was Corporal Horowishi. Jordan noted that all knew that Horowishi was a Christian and were thankful. On being ordered to administer corporal punishment to an erring prisoner, Horowishi would pull his punches, saving many a POW from a senseless beating. Jordan commented: 'To a man, our camp honoured and respected Horowishi as a fellow-soldier of integrity and compassion.' Horowishi was, in a real sense, a Christian mate who transcended all ethnic, cultural and national lines, perhaps even obliterated them. After the war, Jordan returned to civilian life to continue his training for the Christian ministry. He spent many years thereafter first as a Baptist and then as a Presbyterian pastor.

Ted Skinner's story was tragically different. A young evangelical Christian from Tenterfield, NSW, Skinner volunteered for the AIF on 1 August 1941 and requested to be assigned to the Medical Service.[60] He was posted to the 2/10 Field Ambulance and dispatched to Malaya in February 1941. In February 1942, he was captured by the Japanese in Singapore.

In July 1942, the Japanese recruited B Force from among the Australian POWs. They were told that they were going to an area where food was plentiful and the medical personnel were told not to worry about medical supplies because they would be waiting at their destination.[61] Skinner was among the approximately 2,400 Australian and British prisoners who were sent to Sandakan. Of that number, only six Australians would survive. The Japanese gradually reduced rations and increased the beatings until most of the Australians had contracted malaria, dysentery, beriberi and various other tropical diseases. When it became apparent that an Allied invasion was imminent, the Japanese commander decided to move the remaining prisoners westward to the mountain town of Ranau, some 260 kilometres distant from Sandakan. The plan seemed to be to kill them all in order to eliminate any eyewitness accounts of the atrocities that had occurred in the prison camp over the previous three years. Most of the prisoners died en route to Ranau. Those who managed to survive the marches were later killed.[62]

One who lived to tell the tale was Gunner Owen Campbell who along with Corporal Ted Emmett and Privates Keith Costin, Sidney (Sid) Webber and Ted Skinner felt that they would never last until Ranau and, therefore, decided to make a break for it along the march route. On 7 June, Allied planes swept over the struggling column causing the guards and prisoners to seek cover. While the Japanese guards were busy saving themselves, the five men ran into the jungle, grabbing as many of the guards' food rations as possible. On 9 June, they made camp so that Campbell, who had malaria, could rest. The next day, Skinner came down with a severe case of dysentery, so the five fugitives decided to camp for a few days while he recovered. On 11 June, Emmett, Webber and Costin pressed on, leaving Campbell and Skinner behind. The two men stayed put from 12 to 15 June, during which time Campbell's condition improved while Skinner's worsened. All the while, Skinner tried to persuade Campbell to go on without him in order not to jeopardise his chance to survive. Campbell refused. On 16 June, Campbell

---

60 Edward Kenneth Skinner, War Record, B883, NX41647, National Archives of Australia, on line at http://recordsearch.naa.gov.au/ accessed 12 October 2010.

61 Don Wall, *Sandakan Under Nippon: The Last March* 5th ed. (Mona Vale: D. Wall Publications, 2003), 1–22.

62 George Duncan, 'Massacres and Atrocities of World War II', http://members.iinet.net.au/~gduncan/massacres_pacific.html (accessed 4 July 2010).

scouted the area to see if he could find water and catch some fish. When he returned, he found Skinner had taken his life by slashing his own throat.[63] Thus, Ted Skinner, described by his mates as a 'brave and gentle man', literally laid down his life for his friend. Campbell died on 3 July 2003, aged eighty-seven. Ted Skinner died in the jungles of northern Borneo on 16 June 1945, aged 27, in order that his mate might live.[64] More than 8,000 Australians died in POW camps during the war.

An evangelical soldier who lived to reflect deeply on the spiritual implications of his experience as a prisoner of the Japanese was Geoff Bingham. He was born in country NSW in 1919, the son of a prominent dentist. He came to faith in an unconventional manner, as he became aware of what he called 'a Presence' that seemed to be always with him. He began to attend an Anglican church and in his late teens decided to enrol in theological college, much against his father's wishes. He left Sydney's Moore College after only one year to enlist in the Second AIF in 1940.[65] With the outbreak of the war with Japan in December 1941, he and his fellow Diggers found themselves confronting an overwhelming force of Japanese invaders on the Malay Peninsula. By then he was Sergeant Bingham and a section leader. He was subsequently awarded the Military Medal for acts of outstanding bravery before his unit withdrew to Singapore Island for what was presumably to be their last stand in its defence.

It was while defending the northern part of the island that Bingham was badly wounded. After lying in pain for a day and part of a night, he was evacuated to a hospital and treated. After the surrender of all British forces to the Japanese on 15 February 1942, he was taken into Singapore city where his wound was cleansed of maggots, dressed, and his fractured bones reset.[66] Within a few days he was a resident of the War Camp at Changi. It was this place and, later, the equally infamous Kranji POW Camp, that were to be his home for the next three and a half years.[67] It was not only a deplorable situation to be in physically, a hell-hole of starvation and disease; it also ravaged

63 Wall, *Sandakan Under Nippon*, 91–6; 'What Happened on the Sandakan Death March?: Statement by Escaped Prisoner Owen Campbell', 12 January 1947, online at http://www.anzacday.org.au/education/activities/sandakan/evid_escapee.html. accessed 6 July 2010.

64 'Roll of Honour – Edward Kenneth Skinner', AWM records, online at http://www.awm.gov.au/research/people/roll_of_honour/person.asp?p=537795, accessed 10 October 2010.

65 Geoffrey C. Bingham, *Love Is the Spur* (Parramatta: Eyrie Books, 2004), 5–8.

66 Peter Elphick, *Singapore, The Pregnable Fortress: A Study in Deception, Discord and Desertion* (London: Hodder & Stoughton, 1995), 345–356.

67 Bingham, *Love Is the Spur*, 10–18.

the psyche: 'the humiliation of defeat, the early degrading of fighting men, the loss of Singapore, … the deeper humiliation of the Thailand experience, and the anger at separation from loved ones'.[68]

Bingham recorded his disappointment not only with several of the chaplains, but also with himself. Was it or was it not all right to scrounge, perhaps sometimes steal, food in order to stay alive? He wrote: 'I discovered that I very much wanted to live, and I was quite hungry. If being in rackets didn't matter, then why hold back from being in them?' Indeed, where was God amidst all the misery and suffering that now surrounded him – 'starved daily for two years without a break', as he put it?[69] Where was God? Bingham discovered that he was present to the suffering through the sufferings of his own Son. It was a presence which brought salvation, healing and hope, and enabled hitherto defeated and demoralised men to transcend their selfishness in the service of others. In Changi in 1943 he wrote the poem 'Angel Wings' which was to become a hymn sung in churches over six decades later:

> Angel wings, beating my face,
> Forcing me into grace.
> Dear eyes, loving my soul,
> Drawing me to the goal.
> Strong Word, piercing my brain,
> Bringing me holy shame.
> Pain's cry, welling within,
> Lifting me out of sin.
> Red hands, clotted with blood,
> Thrusting me up to God.

Typical of the evangelical, perhaps, Bingham's spirituality was intensely personal, but it resonated with some who formed with him a community of hope. Bingham and a handful of other prisoners became exceptionally close as they shared almost everything, including their food and their innermost thoughts and spiritual concerns. It was a community which transfused faith and hope into the wider prison community. It was a major factor in their survival, and it left Bingham with a settled conviction that spiritual renewal and revival were possible in every situation.

As the members of this close-knit spiritual community prepared to part and go their separate ways at the end of the war, a torrent of emotion swept over

68 Bingham, *Love Is the Spur*, 68.
69 Bingham, *Love Is the Spur*, 36–37.

them. According to Bingham, 'The British men grieved over the fact that they would not see us again'. Toby Critoph, his close mate and one of their spiritual inner circle, spoke for them all when he said to Bingham: 'What worries me is that you will go home, marry some girl and all your love will go to her and your children. Then you won't love us as you do now. That's fair enough. But we have never known the experience of love that we have had here'. Bingham explained that most men would not have used the word 'love' to describe their relationship but that a great affection based on their common experiences and their close spiritual connection certainly had grown up among them.[70] Bingham always struggled to describe this Christian community within the prison community – it was not, he insisted, a 'clique' because in addition to being an opportunity to deepen the spiritual life, it existed to serve those in most need who were not its members. It was best described, he concluded, as a 'community of love', which he subsequently realised was what every local church should be.[71]

At Chungkai and Nakawm Paeton, near the River Kwai in Thailand, POW communities were also transformed apparently by a similar discovery of healing power that 'comes from the Most High'.[72] The story of spiritual renewal as told by Ernest Gordon in his best-selling account,[73] begins when an Australian sergeant asks Gordon to lead an honest discussion group to explore 'the real dingo' of faith in such extremity. The group studied the Bible together and got to know Jesus as the one who went through experiences similar to those they were suffering. He was the 'Comrade-God who on the cross was slain, to rise again'.[74] Out of it grew a 'fellowship of freedom and love', a 'church without walls' which displaced the selfishness, discord, and anxiety with 'a wonderful sense of unity, of harmony, of peace'.[75] Gordon traces a score of public benefits which stemmed from the new spirit and renewed will to live unleashed by this fellowship in the prison community, including a jungle university to satisfy the hunger for education, a library, a range of artistic and artisan initiatives, an orchestra, dramatic society, community singing, and a production line to make artificial limbs for amputees. Just as Bingham had discovered what every local church should be, Gordon discovered what every community, every democracy, should be, and sought to build this Kingdom

70 Bingham, *Love Is the Spur*, 89.

71 Bingham, *Love Is the Spur*, 96.

72 Ernest Gordon, *Miracle on the River Kwai* (London: Fount, 1965), 112.

73 Gordon, *Miracle on the River Kwai.*

74 Gordon, *Miracle on the River Kwai*, 190.

75 Gordon, *Miracle on the River Kwai*, 118.

of God in peace time, but such dynamic altruism he found much harder to achieve in Britain than in a POW camp.[76]

Florence Trotter Syer was a sister in the Australian Army Nursing Service (AANS), a POW of the Japanese for more than three years, and one of the nurses whose story was told in the 1997 movie 'Paradise Road'.[77] Born in Sydney on 4 October 1915, Florence (Flo) Trotter grew up in a devout Presbyterian family in Eastwood, NSW. She trained for the nursing profession at Brisbane General Hospital, enlisted in the AANS in 1940, and was called to active service in January 1941. She was assigned to the 2/10 Army General Hospital, which was attached to the 8th Division destined for Singapore in 1941.[78]

The British High Command ordered the Australian Army nursing sisters in Malaya to evacuate the battle zone just days before the fall of Singapore. A group of sixty-five nursing sisters, including Flo Trotter and her unit, left Singapore on 12 February 1942 on board the *Vyner Brooke*. Their ship was bombed and sunk by the Japanese two days later. Of the fifty-three survivors of the air attacks, the Japanese killed twenty-one and took the remainder prisoner.[79] Thus began Flo Trotter's more than three years of captivity. Of the sixty-five nurses who left Singapore on 12 February, Flo Trotter and twenty-three others survived and returned to Australia.[80]

Shuffled from place to place on Sumatra, the nurses lived on decreasing amounts of food amid degrading physical conditions. The guards despised their prisoners, and Red Cross parcels were either lost or stolen by their guards. The camp commandant also withheld medicine from the prisoners, especially quinine for the malaria that plagued them all.[81] In mid-1942 the Japanese tried to force the sisters to become 'comfort women', sex slaves of the Japanese officers. By using their wits and, in the end, by the selfless sacrifice of four of the older sisters, most escaped this fate. At first, the sisters put off their tormentors by making themselves as unattractive as possible by rubbing dirt on their faces, wearing men's boots, keeping their hair closely

---

76 Gordon, *Miracle on the River Kwai*, 216–231.

77 Florence Trotter Syer, interviewed by Linder, Kenmore, Qld, 16 August 1998.

78 Betty Jeffrey, *White Coolies* (Sydney: Angus & Robertson, 1954), 1.

79 Jeffrey, *White Coolies*, iv, 2–25; Syer, interviewed by Linder.

80 Susanna De Vries, *Heroic Australian Women in War* (London: HarperCollins Publishers, 2004), 252.

81 Syer, interviewed by Linder; De Vries, *Heroic Australian Women in War*, 200–53; Pat Gunther Darling, *Portrait of a Nurse* (Mona Vale: Don Wall, 2001); Norman G. Manners, *Bullwinkel: The True Story of Vivian Bullwinkel, a Young Army Nursing Sister, Who was the Sole Survivor of a World War Two Massacre by the Japanese* (Carlisle: Hesperian Press, 1999).

cropped or sprinkling their hair with urine. The final showdown came when the Japanese demanded that they hand over four nurses to be comfort women in their club or face the loss of their already small rice ration. Four younger nurses were selected, but four older women agreed to replace them. The other nurses swore on a Bible that the names of the 'four volunteers' would never be revealed in order to spare pain to them and to their relatives, and no one ever broke that vow.[82]

Flo Trotter survived this horror, she indicated, through music, enduring friendships and faith in Christ. The music was organised by Margaret Dryburgh, a Presbyterian missionary to Malaya from Britain, and Norah Chambers, an English Christian woman imprisoned by the Japanese. Dryburgh was an accomplished pianist and choir director, and Chambers was a professional violinist. Dryburgh was a driving force in the prison camp, not only through her spiritual strength but also by constantly organising activities, writing poems, plays and songs and, together with Chambers, writing music for the camp glee club and voice orchestra. Dryburgh wrote both the words and music of 'The Captive's Hymn' which became an anthem for POWs on Sumatra. It was first heard in the camp in July 1942 when a trio sang it during a Sunday church service. It quickly spread through the camp and was sung at church services, concerts, and special occasions for the remainder of the nurses' captivity. The fourth of its five verses reads:

For our loved ones we would pray
Be their guardians, night and day,
From all dangers, keep them free,
Banish all anxiety.
May they trust us to Thy care,
Know that Thou our pains dost share.[83]

Flo Trotter's closest friends in the camps were other Christian women, especially the devout Sylvia Muir, Pearl Mittelheuser (known as 'Mitz'), Joyce Tweddell (known as 'Tweedie') and Ada 'Mickey' Syer, who was to become her sister-in-law after the war when Flo married her brother Frank. Margaret Dryburgh and the other missionary women in the camps led a

82 Syer, interviewed by Linder; and De Vries, *Heroic Australian Women at War*, 228–31; Barbara Angell, *A Woman's War: The Exceptional Life of Wilma Oram Young, AM* (Frenchs Forest: New Holland Publishers, 2003), 88–92.

83 https://singingtosurvive.com/2013/05/03/the-captives-hymn/ accessed 23 August 2016.

church service every Sunday throughout their ordeal and almost everybody in the camps attended.

Although the war ended on 15 August 1945, the camp commander did not inform the prisoners of this until two weeks later. When he finally assembled the prisoners to tell them that the war was over, he stood before them and said: 'The war is over sisters'. He did not say who had won, although it was easily inferred. Then, with an expressionless face and as if the events of the past three years had not happened, he announced: 'Now we can all be friends'.

Margaret Dryburgh was one of nearly a hundred missionary POWs held by the Japanese. Brian Morcombe was another who spent most of the war in a prison camp. In 1939, Brian volunteered for the AIF and requested the medical corps. He shortly thereafter asked for a ministerial exemption to go to the mission field and it was granted. Then he applied to the Borneo Evangelical Mission (now the Overseas Missionary Fellowship) and was accepted.[84] Morcombe arrived in Borneo in October 1941. Twelve months later, the Japanese invaders rounded up all of the foreign missionaries and teachers in the country and interned them in the POW camp at Kuching (also known as the Batu Lintang Camp) in Sarawak. Morcombe was incarcerated along with 3,000 other Allied military prisoners and civilians. By the time the camp was liberated in 1945, at least a thousand prisoners had perished there.[85]

Morcombe managed to survive more than three years of captivity by relying on his personal physical stamina, his medical skills, his personal religious faith and the support of his fellow Christians in the camp. Reassured that 'God had not forsaken us', he conducted Bible studies for his fellow inmates. He reported that the Japanese did not interfere with Sunday church services which were well attended, usually led by one of the imprisoned padres. Morcombe and American Christian and Missionary Alliance minister Herman Dixon were the main Bible study leaders.

Among official Japanese papers found at the camp following liberation were two 'death orders'. Both set forth the method of execution of every POW in the camp. The first order was scheduled for fulfilment on 17 or 18 August 1945, but was not carried out. The second order was scheduled for

---

84 Brian Morcombe, interviewed by Linder, 17 July 1997; for the story of the Borneo Evangelical Mission, see C. Hudson Southwell, *Unchartered Waters* (Hong Kong: Astana Publishing, 1999).

85 Morcombe interviewed by Linder; Agnes Newton Keith, *Three Came Home* (Boston: Little Brown and Company, 1947); and Keat Gin Ooi, *Japanese Empire in the Tropics: Selected Documents and Reports of the Japanese Period in Sarawak, Northwest Borneo, 1941–1945*, 2 vols. (Miami, OH: Ohio University Center for International Studies, 1998).

execution on 15 September. The dropping of the two atomic bombs on Japan that demoralised the Japanese military and the timely liberation of the camp most likely prevented the murder of over 2,000 inmates. Morcombe survived and lived to serve again as a missionary to the people of Borneo.[86]

* * *

What was the impact of the war effort on the evangelical movement? The impact of World War I appears to have been almost wholly detrimental owing to the shocking loss of life which wiped out a substantial part of the leadership of the movement and discouraged survivors. The impact of World War II was not so comprehensively negative. The response of the churches had been altogether more mature: less jingoistic and more practical. Instead of destroying the movement's leadership, the experience of war often refined it. Many of the returned men of World War II became clergy, missionaries, religious educators and professionals including medical doctors or lawyers following the war, and it is hard to deny that they were in many ways the better for the suffering they had witnessed and endured. An impressive number became denominational leaders: Noel Vose, Donald Robinson, Lance Shilton, Kenneth Short, Ron Rogers, Elvin Janetski, Marcus Loane, Francis Hulme-Moir and Clive Kerle, to name but a few.

The explanation of Frank Gallagher, who became a Baptist minister after the war, concerning why so many returned evangelical men opted for full-time Christian service following the war, is probably typical and to the point. It was based on what they saw as servicemen: 'There were so many who needed to hear'.[87] The evidence points to comparatively successful evangelistic efforts on the front line. The War also opened up evangelicals even more to the need for cross-cultural missions because many of them had served in Pacific and Asian countries, and many ex-servicemen and women became missionaries to those countries.

The War also opened the evangelical movement more to American influence and less to British as the Americans came to the aid of Australia in its most dangerous hour. The American influence was not all gain, but the reduction in allegiance to the United Kingdom as the repository of all that is best in the world was the essential requirement to refocussing evangelical enterprise on

86 Ooi, *Japanese Empire in the Tropics*, vol. 2, 636; Morcombe interviewed by Linder.

87 Frank Gallagher, interviewed by Linder, 16 July 2002.

building the Kingdom of God rather than the British Empire. But neither Australians in general nor evangelicals in particular were yet ready to depart from the British connection. Australians were not as demoralised after World War II as they had been after the First World War. They were not as troubled by the price they had to pay for victory. Appalling as it was,[88] it was a lower price than they had paid in the first war, and there was less doubt that their cause was just and that this particular war was a necessary evil. Christian and Australian values were still in close alignment. There was no call for serious self-reflection, let alone criticism.

The combined forces of evangelical Christians had made a genuinely useful contribution to the war effort and they had done it through the means they found most congenial, caring for the national soul and providing for the psychological and social needs of soldiers, including those who were wounded and imprisoned, and their loved ones. The confidence which Christian leaders had after the war was neither complacent nor untested, but it was not the best preparation for the challenges of future decades: wars in Korea, Vietnam and Afghanistan were not so obviously justified as the war against Hitler and the Japanese who bombed Australian cities. In later generations, those who fought in World War II readily supported sending young soldiers into battle with the steely resolve of those who had fought so well in a clearly-justified war and who had little doubt that taking up arms, if regrettable, was necessary at regular intervals in this fallen world.

88 Gladwin, *Captains of the Soul*, 136f.

PART B

Faith and the Secular Challenge, 1946–2014

evangelical, more interested in evangelism than churchmanship. He had been a member of the SCM at Sydney University two decades before the formation of the Evangelical Union. He was a tutor at Moore College in 1916 and CMS travelling secretary after that. He studied at Ridley Hall in Cambridge and then served as a missionary in India with CMS. In 1943 he was appointed Bishop of Tasmania. In 1952 when Orr was appointed to Tasmania he received counselling from Cranswick who was a family friend of the young woman who bore his child in Melbourne. The Bishop, a member of the University Council, referred Orr to a psychiatrist and believed until 1955 that Orr was dangerously compulsive in sexual matters and should be dismissed. It was also in 1955 that 18-year old student, Suzanne Kemp, kept a diary, written in German, allegedly of her sexual relations with Orr. Early in 1956 she wrote to Orr a letter full of religious imagery. Referring to her own state of mind she wrote:

> I am usually chasing a piece of music 'down the nights and down the days, down the labyrinthine ways of my own mind'.

This is a quotation from Francis Thompson's poem 'The Hound of Heaven' about Christ's pursuit of the soul. She wrote about her own confusion in religious terms, 'Forgive me for I know not what I do.' She explained that she had a 'desperate need' to be with him when she thought of Christ: 'Perhaps you and He have unconsciously swapped places in my mind.'[86] Shortly afterwards she confessed to her parents that she was in love with Orr, that he believed in free love and that they were lovers. Her outraged father complained that Orr had seduced his daughter, and the University Council dismissed him. In the ensuing trial Suzanne Kemp informed the judge that Orr did draw a comparison between himself and Christ in that both were illegitimate and that, just as Christ overcame this burden through love, so he would do the same.[87] Orr denied that he had made such a 'preposterous' suggestion. In court, he did not adopt the position that it was acceptable for him to indulge in free love with his students and that it was a private matter. That was not to become a common belief for another decade! He rather argued that she was seriously disturbed, that she was lying and had framed him, and that he had been dismissed without due process. This position he argued until his death a decade later during which time he remained unemployed. His full-time career was now that of the martyr.

86 Quoted in Cassandra Pybus, *Seduction and Consent: A Case of Gross Moral Turpitude* (Port Melbourne: Mandarin, 1994), 6,8.

87 Pybus, *Seduction and Consent*, 91

Orr embroiled colleagues and friends and his long-suffering wife in an increasingly hysterical defence, including the claim that it was a CIA conspiracy, which some left-wing academics were all too willing to credit. Strangely, from 1959 to 1964, when he withdrew from all involvement with the matter, Cranswick contended that Orr had been unfairly treated. By then the Presbyterian Church which accepted him back into membership in 1958 and Guilford Young, Catholic Archbishop of Hobart, were of the same opinion. The church in the 1950s still had 'moral weight' and was prepared to use it to redress perceived injustice, but that can be destructive when unaccompanied by common sense. That might be an argument for the separation of church from academy except that, when it came to Orr, few academics showed any more sense. Australia was on the slippery slope.

* * *

Equipoise was on the way out and with it the unity and confidence of the evangelical movement. But in the 1950s evangelical Christianity did a lot for Australia, and the 1950s did a lot for evangelical Christianity. It won the allegiance of a record number of Australians and it engaged the attention of a lot more. It shaped values and contributed to social harmony and economic prosperity. It exported all three along with the Gospel through an energetic and large missionary movement. It is to be found everywhere in the history of the period, justifying, especially in this period, the claim of the afore-mentioned David Stove who was not a believer – not in anything much except perhaps cricket: 'not to understand religion is … not to understand nine-tenths of human history.'[88]

---

88 Roger Kimball, 'Who was David Stove?', *The New Criterion*, 15.7, 1997, online at http://www.newcriterion.com/articles.cfm/Who-was-David-Stove--3368, accessed 30 January 2012.

Chapter Eight

CRUSADING FOR PEACE AND PROSPERITY, 1946–1965

'not to understand religion is ... not to understand nine-tenths of human history.'
(David Stove, philosopher)

The two decades following World War II were marked by laborious reconstruction, dramatic sociopolitical change, troublingly-high inflation and anxiety about world peace. Yet, the 1950s, in particular was a decade of equipoise, a stable decade of balanced rights and responsibilities, accompanied by a consensus on national values. That achievement, it will be argued, had a lot to do with the churches. It was an argument the post-war churches made at the time. They made their plans for growth and expansion in a period of social stability and economic prosperity which they contended are the fruits of religious observance. It could even be argued that the 1950s was the most religious decade in Australian history in terms of churchgoing and Christian obervance. Recently, a similar claim has been made for twentieth-century Britain and for the same reason: religious observance was running at record levels and the contagian of revival was caught all over Britain.[1] That is a harder claim to defend for Britain than Australia where the churches were at the height of their powers: they had never been so well supported or better attended. Contrary to the prevailing impression, the churches were remarkably alert to the need to be responsive to the by now quickly-evolving culture. They consciously sought to be more 'Australian'. The Anglican Church, for example, adopted a new constitution in 1962 which allowed it greater freedom to experiment, and in later decades developed new liturgies, prayer books,

1 Callum Brown, *The Death of Christian Britain: Understanding Secularisation, 1800–2000* (London: Routledge, 2001), 172f.; S.J.D. Green, *The Passing of Protestant England: Secularisation and Social Change, c.1920–1960* (Cambridge: CUP, 2011), 29–33.

and joined with other denominations in the production of new hymn books. Hilary Carey has argued that the process of becoming 'more Australian' was late, slow and painful,[2] but Brian Fletcher has rather emphasised how felicitously and competently the Anglican Church anyway conducted the process.[3]

The Role of Evangelical Christianity in Post-War Reconstruction

Post-war reconstruction was hampered by scarce material resources, inadequate capital, and arguments between the Commonwealth and States over powers to address the needs of the long-suffering population. It was also a dramatically growing population, thanks to a post-war baby boom and immigration, largely from war-ravaged Europe. Housing this population resulted in the rapid suburbanisation of cities and was followed by educational reforms especially in the tertiary sector. The skills employed in producing warplanes was redirected to the production of motor cars, beginning with the first Holden, 'Australia's own car', in 1948, and family weekends were never the same again. In 1956 television was introduced in time for the Melbourne Olympics, and entertainment was never the same again.

With the defeat of Ben Chifley's Labor Government in the 1949 federal election, the Liberal/Country Party coalition, headed by Robert Gordon Menzies came to power and held it until 1972, Menzies himself retiring undefeated in 1966.[4] His strong leadership was an undoubted factor in the nation's stability, relying heavily on the support of middle-class Protestants. Menzies not only appealed to their aspirations for home ownership and education, he also played on their fears. He became the determined opponent of Communism and sought to outlaw the Communist Party of Australia. He did not succeed, but he had plenty of ammunition to use for the purpose: the Soviet Union was now a nuclear power, had repressed the democracies of Eastern Europe, and was involved in spying on Australia, spectacularly exposed by 'the Petrov affair'; China went Communist in 1949; the fight against Communism in the Korean War (1950–1953) took 340 Australian lives; and Communists were controlling Australian trades unions and fermenting strikes which affected power

2 Hilary Carey, 'Religion and Society', in Deryck M. Schreuder and Stuart Ward, (eds), *Australia's Empire, Oxford History of the British Empire* (Oxford: OUP, 2008), 208.

3 Brian H. Fletcher, *An English Church in Australian Soil* (Canberra: Barton Books, 2015), 176, 191ff.

4 Judith Brett, 'The Menzies Era, 1950–66', in Alison Bashford and Stuart Macintyre, (eds.), *The Cambridge History of Australia* 2 vols (Port Melbourne; New York: CUP, 2013), 2. 112–134.

supplies and essential building materials. Other threats on the world stage included the withdrawal of Britain from India and its disastrous partition in 1947 and the withdrawal of other European powers in the decolonisation of South-East Asia and their replacement by unstable regimes.

Understandably, there was a widespread feeling which extended beyond the churches, that only a religious revival would save the nation from Communist control and moral decay. On Remembrance Day, 1951, Sir Edmund Herring, Rhodes scholar, decorated veteran of two world wars, barrister and Chancellor of the Church of England Diocese of Melbourne, issued a 'Call to the People of Australia', signed by four of his fellow chief justices and Protestant, Catholic and Jewish leaders. Australians must arise to repel the enemy from without, mainly Communism, and from within, namely moral decay and apathy. The call continued to be issued until 1957, but was not met with much enthusiasm. Sir Waldron Smithers, the Conservative MP for Orpington in Kent in England, wrote to the Archbishop of Canterbury suggesting that it would be a good idea to issue such a call in the UK. Archbishop Fisher replied that it should not come from clergymen and that its effect in Australia was not great.[5]

Herring was to become Chairman of the General Committee of the 1959 Billy Graham Crusade, and that did have a great effect in Australia. In fact, this period was the high noon of Australian Christianity – Catholic as well as Protestant. Evangelistic enterprise at both the local and national levels enjoyed unprecedented success. The 1950s began with Alan Walker's 'Mission to the Nation' and ended with the 1959 Billy Graham Southern Cross Crusades when the whole nation experienced a spiritual awakening. National values and Christian values, in theory identical before the 1960s, were brought into closer alignment in practice. The state lion lay down with the church lamb. Protestant and Catholic churches co-operated with Federal and State governments in pursuit of peace, prosperity and anti-Communism. There was little to question the proposition that Australia was a 'Christian nation'. Not more than half of one percent of the population claimed to have no religion, and the percentage identifying with a Christian denomination, hitherto about 90 per cent, actually rose between the census of 1947 and that of 1954. Marriages conducted by clergy were about 90 per cent, and three out of every ten Australians claimed to attend church weekly.[6] It was in the 1950s

---

5 Ruth Frappell, et. al., *Anglicans in the Antipodes* (Westport: Greenwood Press, 1999), 309.

6 Hugh Chilton, 'Evangelicals and the End of Christian Australia: Nation and Religion in the Public Square 1959–1979,' PhD, University of Sydney, 2014, 3; David Hilliard, 'God in the Suburbs: The Religious Culture of Australian Cities in the 1950s', *Australian Historical Studies*, 24.97, 1991, 399–419.

that Australian Christianity – Protestant as well as Catholic – managed for the last time for sixty years to increase the numbers of churchgoers at a rate higher than the rate of population growth.[7]

It was the strength of the Christian presence in Australia and its congruence with the prevailing values of Australians which helps to explain why this tumultuous time was one of peace and stability.[8] Journalist John Pilger, in his TV series on Australia, claimed that the 1950s was the only decade where a balance of individual freedom and community responsibility was attained: it was a decade of equipoise.[9] The historian Prime Minister Paul Keating was to hire as his speech writer in the 1990s agreed:

> In the 1950s, issues of heritage and identity, spiritual health, national cohesion and progress were central to all our lives, and happily coexisted with economic questions.[10]

It was an age when Australia's Christian heritage was expressed in the development of one of the most stable and safe of the world's democracies. Australia in the 1950s is a good illustration of the proposition (known as 'the Halévy thesis') that vital Christianity ferments national stability by restraining acquisitiveness and fostering mutuality. It was an age when there was little ambiguity about morals – at least among the middle class.

This was the period in which the evangelical movement reached the zenith of its influence on Australian society, and the time when it experienced its most exponential growth. Admittedly, not all evangelicals agreed that the late 50s and early 60s was the golden age for their movement. Stuart Barton Babbage, then Principal of Ridley College in Melbourne, wrote in 1963: 'At the present time, in most parts of Australia, the tide is running strongly

---

7 J.L.J. Wilson, (ed.), 'Churchgoing in Australia', *Current Affairs Bulletin*, 22.4, June16, 1958.

8 For the foundation of the argument, see Edwin Judge, '"On this Rock I will build my *ecclesia*": Counter-cultic Springs of Multiculturalism,' in E. A. Judge, *The First Christians in the Roman World: Augustan and New Testament Essays*, ed. by and James R. Harrison, (Tübingen: Mohr Siebeck, 2008), 619–668.

9 The 1950s was the decade most reviled by left-wing intelligentsia. For a more nuanced assessment, see John Murphy and Judith Smart (eds), *The Forgotten Fifties: Aspects of Australian Society and Culture in the 1950s* (Carlton: MUP, 1997); John Murphy, *Imagining the Fifties: Private Sentiment and Political Culture in Menzies' Australia* (Sydney: UNSW Press, 2000).

10 Don Watson, *Recollections of a Bleeding Heart: A Portrait of Paul Keating PM* (Sydney: Knopf, 2002), 113.

against evangelicals, and the situation is one of agonizing difficulty.'[11] But this agony was ecstasy compared with what preceded and followed it. For this was the period in which the movement enjoyed greater unity as its success meant that it did not obsess so much over liberalism or splinter over strategy. It rejuvenated the old denominations and created new ones; it strengthened its intellectual foundations and provided a better education for ministers and youth; it replaced concern for piety, understood as personal religious experience and practice, with a more engaged spirituality; and it focussed on what it did best, the making of disciples through the preaching of the Gospel and the study of the Bible. The biblicism of evangelicalism became more pronounced than ever, now buttressed by the scholarship of conservative academics in universities as well as theological colleges. In the process, evangelicalism reinvented itself, making this one of the most formative epochs in the history of Australian evangelicalism. Those fashioned by this new paradigm of evangelicalism continued to lead and define the movement at the end of the first decade of the twenty-first century.

But the Christian churches had long been a major presence in Australia. Why would they have been critical to national stability, and able to engineer equipoise, at this juncture in Australian history? It may be that the nature of the challenge it faced at this time was one it was peculiarly fashioned to address. The world was a different place and it called for a different understanding of Christian faith, just as the experience of death in a POW camp in Thailand had led one Australian sergeant to the conclusion that Christianity had to be the 'real dingo' or it was all over for him and his mates. Now in this post-war, but still very dangerous world, realism and neo-orthodoxy replaced idealism and liberalism. The conviction dawned that evangelicalism had to become a lot tougher to survive and thrive in an increasingly secular world. It was fertile soil for the nourishing of earnest, Reformed evangelicalism, which was destined to become the most powerful manifestation of evangelicalism in the second half of the twentieth century. Pietism and emotionalism were displaced by a defensive, rationalistic belief system, bastioned by new Bible scholarship and defended by apologetics now packaged in the readable, affordable literature published by the Inter-Varsity Press in London. The old evangelicalism of missions and revival and Keswick piety and millennialism still appeared to be strong, but new Reformed forces were emerging. The resulting displacement

11 Stuart Barton Babbage, 'Evangelicals in the Church in Australia,' *Churchman,* 77, 1963, 118.

of evangelicalism as heartfelt religion by an evangelicalism of the mind was comprehensive. Those who felt that an emotional vacuum had been created in their souls proved easy prey to the Charismatic movement of succeeding decades. That was another adaptation of a very adaptable movement for another age. But, to reiterate the themes of this study, by caring for the Australian soul in the immediate post-war decades, when the British Empire was in retreat, and the fires of secularism had at least been ignited, the evangelical movement made a substantial contribution to the equipoise of the Australian nation.

Involved in the reinvigoration and reinvention of the evangelical movement were leaders of diverse gifts and passions. There was not only the prophetic evangelism of Alan Walker, the unflinching anti-Communism of Fred Schwarz, and the moral conservatism of astute politicians such as Tom Playford, Premier of South Australia, and R.G. Menzies, Prime Minister, but also Stuart Barton Babbage's appreciation of cultural diversity, John Stott's theological precision in identifying Gospel priorities, and a cadre of academics determined to replace the speculative fancies of the theological liberals with the best scholarship. The symphony played by these evangelical leaders was still largely one of harmony: discords were the more pronounced for their rarity. The movement became both more robust and more flexible, with its innate potential to cause friction in the wider society offset by its capacity to be more strategic in the issues it chose to confront.

Alan Walker: Dreaming the Master's Dreams

The Mission to the Nation was launched by the Methodist Church in April, 1953. At its head was a relatively young man, an Australian, doubly unusual for a national crusade in Australia. Great faith had been put in him and that was a burden. Not everybody was happy and that, too, weighed on his spirit. He was not only sensitive to criticism; he could be devastated by it. Communion with a different spirit was required, and he experienced it:

> I walked into the stillness and gathering darkness of the Australian bush. Presently, in the stillness, an evening breeze stirred. I could hear it rustling in the leaves of the gum trees above me. Suddenly, there came to my mind the picture of Jesus talking to Nicodemus in Jerusalem: 'The wind blows where it will, and you hear the sound of it, but you do not know where it comes from or where it goes to. So it is with everyone who is born of the spirit.' There came to my mind, there in the Australian bush, a simple sentence: 'The wind is in the gum trees!

> The wind is in the gum trees!' It was to me a promise. We would hear the wind of the spirit blowing across Australia.[12]

Walker valued spiritual experiences, and forty years later he reported it as 'the second most important *experience* of my life.'[13]

Alan Walker (1911–2003) was an endangered species – a Christian 'tall poppy', arguably the most influential Christian in Australia in the second half of the twentieth century. He is one of a handful of Australian Christians who contributed to the progress of the Kingdom of God on the world stage. He was appointed to the fashionable Methodist parish of Waverley in Sydney at the tender age of 33. When he arrived, it was a relatively poorly attended 'wedding cake' church; when he left it was the vibrant 'church at the crossroads'.[14] The spire of the church cast a shadow right across Bondi Junction, symbolising to young church member Frank Kirby-Brown the church's protective mantel over the community. The Junction was a bus terminal, and bus drivers would stand at the back of the crowded congregations to listen to the singing of Wesley's hymns which continued long past the end of the service.

While at Waverley, Walker developed a good working relationship with Archbishop Howard Mowll.[15] He attended the first meeting of the World Council of Churches in Amsterdam in 1948, and, in the following year, was seconded as an Australian adviser to Dr Evatt in his work on Human Rights for the United Nations. Warwick Fairfax appointed him first religion editor of *The Sydney Morning Herald*, and for more than a quarter of a century he wrote the paper's Christmas and Easter editorials.[16] He received the OBE in 1955, and then duplicated his 1953–55 Mission to the Nation evangelistic campaign in Australia by leading a similar effort in USA in 1956–7. He became head of the Wesley Central Mission in the heart of Sydney in 1958 and led it for 20 years. He then served for a decade as Director of Evangelism for the World Methodist Council, preaching the Gospel in 78 countries. He was knighted in 1981. Then, until 1995, he served as principal of the Pacific College of Evangelism in Sydney later renamed the Alan Walker College of Evangelism.

Clearly, Sir Alan Walker was not your average Aussie. Yet he had a distinctively Australian pedigree: Convict and Christian. His great-great grandparents

12 D.I. Wright, *Alan Walker: Conscience of the Nation* (Adelaide: Openbook, 1997), 97.

13 Wright, *Alan Walker,* 97.

14 Wright, *Alan Walker,* 90.

15 Alan Walker, *A Vision for the World: Alan Walker Tells His Story* (Wantirna: New Melbourne Press, 1999), 30.

16 Forty-four of these were published as a book, *Herald of Hope* (Sutherland, Albatross, 1994).

were convicts. They produced three children out of wedlock before they married when their eldest son, John Joseph, was 20. With a reputation as an anti-religious, hard drinker, John Joseph on 3 February 1838 was brought to faith in Christ through the ministry of a Methodist circuit rider, the Rev William Schofield. Thus began a Christian dynasty which has produced to date sixteen ministers, of whom Alan was the 13th, and his two sons, Bruce and Chris are the 14th and 15th, and Chris's son, Ben, is the 16th. John Walker worshipped and preached in a little chapel, now the oldest Methodist chapel in Australia, erected first in 1828 and re-erected at Vision Valley, Arcadia, the conference centre created by Alan Walker.

If Alan Walker's Australian pedigree cannot be challenged, his evangelical pedigree has been.[17] He was sometimes accused – as he was on the closing night of the Mission to the Nation – of not preaching the Gospel.[18] Morally, he was a wowser, common among evangelicals, but socially, he was a radical, and this irritated many evangelicals, probably most of whom were social conservatives. But, in spite of any gainsayers, Walker must not only be included in evangelical ranks; he should be placed in the very forefront of those ranks. He never wavered from the conviction that the 'supreme task of the church [was] to evangelise, to win Australia for Christ'.[19] He believed that his primary calling was preaching the Gospel in evangelistic services in which he called for conversions and appealed to those convicted by the Holy Spirit to come forward and give their lives to Christ. His 1999 autobiography concludes with his ruling aspiration: 'I hope nothing will impair me proclaiming to the very end the story of Jesus. Always, always, I want to be able to say: "Oh that my Saviour were your Saviour too"'.[20] And, like all the best Methodists in the evangelical tradition, he believed in revival and longed and worked to promote 'national revival through a revived church'.[21]

Walker believed that the preacher of the Gospel had a prophetic mandate, his task to preach 'the whole Gospel for the whole world'. Foremost among the social questions that involved him in controversy and recrimination was his stand on the issue of war and violence. Walker was a pacifist. On his way home from England in 1939, with war clouds on the horizon, influenced

17 For an analysis and refutation of this charge, see Robert D. Linder, 'Alan Walker among the Sharks: Why the Most Important Christian in Australia in the Latter Half of the Twentieth Century was not also a Beloved National Figure,' *Church Heritage* 17, 2011, 2–23.

18 Wright, *Alan Walker,* 103.

19 Wright, *Alan Walker,* 79.

20 Walker, *A Vision for the World,* 154.

21 Chilton, 'Evangelicals and the End of Christian Australia', 2.

by the English Methodist statesman, Donald Soper, Walker vowed that he 'would never again support war or the preparation for war under any circumstances'.[22]

Walker was strongly opposed to the 'White Australia' policy, welcomed the enrichment of Australian culture from Asian sources, and supported the enfranchisement of Australian Aboriginal people. When Arthur Calwell, Immigration Minister in the Labor government of Ben Chifley (1945 to 1949), sought to deport Malaysian seamen who had been unable to leave Australia during the War and some of whom had married Australian wives, Walker campaigned against the government on the issue. Later he wrote:

> It became one of the incidents which led in a few years to the abandonment of White Australia. Never should it be forgotten, it was the Christian Church which ended the outrageous racism of Australia.[23]

New Left historian Humphrey McQueen recognises the contribution of the churches to the elimination of White Australia and a reduction in racism, but he rightly claims that this was the work of lone prophets with the majority of Christians timid and intermittent in their stand against racism.[24] He considers Walker's 1945 publication on immigration as 'virtually unprecedented' and 'far and way better' than any other secular or religious assessment of the policy.[25] Admittedly, it was not hard for him to shine in the long, gloomy struggle to dismantle the policy.[26]

Walker also maintained his criticism of unbridled capitalism throughout his life. His concern was always for economic justice. During his first pastorate at Cessnock in the 1940s, he had championed the cause of the miners. Later, in 1957, when being considered for the position of superintendent of the strategic Sydney Central Methodist Mission, at least two board members objected to his appointment on the grounds that his reputation as a socialist, internationalist and pacifist would dry up financial support for the mission. Nevertheless, Walker won the job and proved these concerns to be unfounded as he raised tens of millions of dollars in support of his many projects over the following years, especially from wealthy business people.[27]

---

22 Chilton, 'Evangelicals and the End of Christian Australia', 2.

23 Walker, *A Vision for the World*, 14.

24 Alan Walker, *White Australia* (Glebe: Christian Distributors' Association, 1946).

25 Humphrey McQueen, *Gallipoli to Petrov: Arguing with Australian History* (Sydney: Allen & Unwin, 1984), 146.

26 Gwenda Tavan, *The Long, Slow Death of White Australia* (Melbourne: Scribe, 2005).

27 Walker, *A Vision for the World,* 16–22, 59 and 60ff.

Walker was a wowser among epicureans. He never passed up the opportunity to speak out against corruption, gambling, prostitution and alcohol abuse. In 1965, he was heavily involved in campaigning against poker machines, a floating casino off the NSW coast, and television bingo. In his 1965 anti-gambling campaign, he criticised the newly-appointed governor-general for gambling at the races. In retribution, multi-millionaire Frank Packer, who controlled TV Channel 9 and who was fond of gambling, instructed his TV executives not to show Walker's Easter Mission Sunrise Service in 1966, as they had in the past. But Walker knew how to use the media without dying by it. He was a successful radio broadcaster, and for seven years 'I Challenge the Minister' appeared on television. So, when Packer's Channel 9 stopped televising Walker's Easter Sunday Sunrise Service, Channel 7 snapped it up.

Walker did not mellow. Like John Wesley his heart was strangely warmed, and more strangely, it stayed warm. Alan Walker was electrifying even in old age. He flogged many a dying horse into life: he was adept at 'arousements'. In spite of his still valuable sociological study of Cessnock[28] published by Oxford University Press when he was still a young man, he was no academic. He did not deal in abstractions; nor would he put two sides of an argument. It was essential, he insisted, to take a strong stance and to proclaim it fearlessly. Some took this for arrogance, but they did not know him. He sounded confident because he had taken the trouble to do enough reading and research to feel confident. Those who had grown accustomed to his public strength and media dogmatism were surprised on meeting him to find him so humble, so gentle, so prayerful, so – saintly!

His passion arose from dreaming, which he understood as dreaming the Master's dreams after him. Alan Walker's great optimism that the world could be changed into the likeness of the Kingdom of God galvanised him into organising concerted assaults on racism and war and other evils. His dreams became reality with the unprecedented regularity which marks the exceptional leader: National Christian Youth Convention, Life Line which was to spread to more than 300 cities across Australia and overseas,[29] Fellowship House and later Wesley Centre, Teenage Cabaret, School for Seniors, the Church of the Homeless, College for Christians, Singles Society, Vision Valley (the 'country club for everyone'), National Goals and Directions.

The sincere in all walks of life were attracted to him. Bill Hayden, Governor-General, rose a great while before dawn one day in 1997 to catch

28 *Coal Town* (Melbourne: OUP, 1944).

29 Lifeline was perhaps Walker's most important and innovative social service creation during his long ministry. Wright, *Alan Walker*, 160–2.

a plane to Sydney from Brisbane so that he could launch Don Wright's biography of Walker. It was not only Walker's practical Christianity which Bill Hayden professed to admire, but also his 'faithfulness to the Spirit'. This observation, remarkable on the lips of a self-professed atheist,[30] was perceptive, and identifies another characteristic of Alan Walker, all too rare even among Australian evangelical Christians. Walker's holistic evangelicalism not only included the whole Gospel and the prophetic mandate, but it was also open to experiences of the Spirit. Walker enjoyed the guidance of the Spirit at many cross-roads in his life, and he reports the falling of the Spirit on a number of the gatherings he addressed. Suddenly, sovereignly, the celestial fire would kindle, the atmosphere would change, eternal stakes were raised, and the outcome a guaranteed extension of the Kingdom of Christ in the hearts and lives of men and women.[31]

Walker was a practitioner of what he called 'responsible evangelism' made up of a clear call to experience conversion, a social conscience, and Holy Spirit power. These were actually the components of the evangelicalism of Walker's chief mentor, John Wesley. But the second and third elements were not integral to the mainstream evangelical paradigm constructed in this period which was built rather on new conservative scholarship on the Bible.

Evangelicalism and Politics

Capitalism, having overcome the challenges posed by depression, war and the Labor Party, regained dominance both economically and politically in Australian society, with the middle class as the chief beneficiaries. Evangelicalism found its greatest depth of support among the middle classes. Thanks to the growing prosperity, Catholics too, who traditionally identified with the working class, woke up to find they had become middle class. The political master of Australian politics, Robert Gordon Menzies (Prime Minister from 1949 to 1966), was happy not only to identify with the Protestants in their love for the Bible, but also with Catholics in their need to find the resources to run their independent school system. He also thought that he was appealing to both in his desire to outlaw the Communist Party, or, at

30 It was reported of Bill Hayden in October 2018 that, though a 'lifelong atheist', he had 'found God' and been baptised in St Mary's Catholic Church, Ipswich, at age 85. Hayden said, 'it was witnessing so many selfless acts of compassion by Christians over his lifetime, and deep contemplation while recovering from a stroke, that prompted his decision'. 'Atheist Politician finds God at 85', *Australian Prayer Network Newsletter*, 9 October 2018.

31 Walker, *A Vision for the World*, 25.

least if he could not get Catholics to vote for his party, he was happy to see them vote for the newly-created anti-Communist Democratic Labor Party rather than the Australian Labor Party.

Intentionally and unapologetically, Menzies governed to promote the values of the middle class in the belief that this would best benefit the country as a whole. On 22 May 1942 in a speech which has gone down in history as expounding the philosophy of the Liberal Party of which he was the founder, Menzies declared: 'the time has come to say something of the forgotten class – the middle class … who, properly regarded represent the backbone of this country.' What, he asked, 'is the value of this middle class?' His answer was that 'it has a "stake in the country". It has responsibility for homes – homes material, homes human, and homes spiritual.' Of 'homes spiritual' he declared:

> Human nature is at its greatest when it combines dependence upon God with independence of man … the greatest element in a strong people is a fierce independence of spirit … The home spiritual so understood is not produced by lassitude or by dependence; it is produced by self-sacrifice, by frugality and saving.[32]

Freedom with responsibility – the stuff of equipoise – and the fruit of the Christian Gospel. Menzies understood the political value of the Christian heritage to which all Australians, consciously or unconsciously, were heirs. Menzies, as we saw in chapter 2, had been President of the Melbourne University Students' Christian Union in 1916,[33] and, under the influence of evangelical leader C.H. Nash, adopted the habit of daily Bible reading, the chief spiritual discipline of evangelicals.[34] Menzies believed that the Christian religion was an essential part of education and therefore provided state aid to church schools and university colleges before many evangelical Protestants were happy to receive it. He was not a *laissez-faire* libertarian: he did not believe that all individuals should care for themselves. He was a Christian paternalist who cared about the Australian soul as much as he did

---

32 The text of 'The Forgotten People' is reproduced in the Menzies Virtual Museum, maintained by the Menzies Foundation, East Melbourne, 2002–2016, http://menziesvirtualmuseum.org.au/transcripts/the-forgotten-people accessed 19 November 2016.

33 A.W. Martin, *Robert Menzies: A Life*, vol. 1, 1894–1943 (Carlton South: MUP, 1993), 22.

34 Darrell Paproth, *Failure is not Final: A Life of C.H. Nash* (Sydney: Centre for the Study of Australian Christianity, 1997), 127f.

the Australian economy and attached greater importance to the former. He believed in partnerships between government and businesses and between governments and churches.[35]

On 13 February 1960 Menzies opened Bible House in Canberra, the national headquarters of the British and Foreign Bible Society, with a speech that would have left his evangelical hearers reluctant to vote for anyone else! Like a good sermon, it has three major points. He began by giving two reasons for entertaining the belief that the Bible is not only the world's best seller, but also the most widely read:

> Firstly, for all of us or almost all of us, the Bible is the most remarkable repository of religious history. Frankly, I don't think that any man could regard himself as educated unless he had become familiar with the great historic stories in the Bible.
>
> In the second place, and of course in the greatest place, the Bible is the repository of our faith and of our inspiration. Never out of date, always up to date, always difficult of application and therefore stimulating to thoughtful people. It is the great source of faith, and of course that is why we ought to read it. That is why so many of us … like myself, constantly do read it!

Then he argued that it was of critical importance to read the Bible itself rather than books about the Bible. He cited the Latin *melius est petere fonts quam sectare rivulos* – 'it is better to seek the fountain-heads than to divide up the little streams' and added:

> That is a perfect description, isn't it, for what our approach ought to be to this great and immortal book? Let's seek the fountain heads – it's all there! The story is there, the great history is there, the great Gospel is there, the whole spirit of Christianity is there.

Thirdly, in proof of the 'unbelievably great' English literature of the Authorised Version, he recounted a little experiment he conducted for a speech he gave at a school speech night. He took 100 words at random from a competent speech given in the House of Representatives and 100 words from the Bible. Of the 100 words given in the Parliamentary speech 15 were words of one syllable 'and all the rest had two or three or four and of course,

35 Brett, 'The Menzies Era, 1950–66', 114.

under the influence of the economists, five or six. And the 100 words from the Bible had 80 words with one syllable – 80!'

Then the great orator gave a resounding peroration:

> If I were, as I am not, an atheist or an agnostic or some other such unhappy person I would still take the Bible with me to a desert island for two reasons. One, that I would have a noble piece of literature to accompany me and two, because given ample opportunity to study it I might cease to be an atheist or agnostic.[36]

This may not have been the most logical of arguments, but it helps to explain why evangelicals so readily voted for his government and readily entered into partnerships with it in the provision of social welfare, hospitals and education. Menzies, like Lt. Governor La Trobe in Victoria a century earlier, put the spiritual before the material, or better went 'behind the material to the spiritual', thus projecting an apparently incontrovertible social vision with which middle-class evangelicals readily congenialised: 'He produced a coherent Australia. He developed its harmonics. He gave new unity, new stature, new dignity.'[37]

Evangelicals, Welfare and Social Justice

The complementarity, rather than the separation, of church and state has been the Australian experience for much of its history. It became a hall-mark of the later years of the Menzies' government. Financial support from governments for social services provided by any religious group which met government guidelines resulted in the dramatic expansion of social welfare. The relationship between church and state became one of pragmatic pluralism, and was far more developed in Australia than in other comparable Western countries. Welfarism was the policy of the Menzies government and the Labor governments of Curtin and Chifley which preceded it, with more provision for housing, education, even free milk for schoolchildren. Labor based its welfare policy on a new philosophy now widely accepted that those who had suffered the deprivations of war should be guaranteed a more secure life and that

36 Robert G. Menzies, Speech at the opening and dedication of Bible House, Canberra, 13 February 1960, Robert Menzies papers, MS 4936, Series 6 Box 258, folder 52, NLA, Canberra, recording available online at http://nla.gov.au/nla.obj-222158841, accessed 19 November 2016.

37 Sir John Bunting, quoted in Janet McCalman, *Journeyings: The Biography of a Middle-Class Generation, 1920–1990,* (Carlton: MUP, 1993), 233.

would be provided by the welfare state: 'Charity, once needs-based, became universal entitlement; in western countries compassion became nationalised.'[38] The succeeding Liberal/National Party government established in 1956 the Australian Council of Social Services (ACOSS), the welfare sector's peak lobby group. But it also funded church initiatives in child care and aged care. From about 1960, in contrast to the welfare provision in Britain, Europe and the United States which was a state provision, the Federal Government offered partnerships, including partnerships with churches, in the areas of welfare, education and immigration. Churches were expected to assist with the assimilation of immigrants. They were invited by governments to attend Australian Citizenship Conventions and be involved with the Good Neighbour Movement.[39] In response, evangelicals generally rethought both their attitudes towards the state and to social issues, many incorporating social concern as part of the Gospel, and skirmishing with those who thought the Gospel required only evangelism, not action on social issues.

The common perception about evangelical commitment to social welfare is that it was impressive and innovative in the nineteenth century, but that evangelicals became wary of it at the beginning of the twentieth century when the social gospel was identified with liberalism and as a poor substitute for the real Gospel. Then, particularly after World War II, as evangelicals became more preoccupied with theological purity, those who worked for social welfare organisations struggled to convince some church leaders that their ministry was to be as valued as that of the proclamation of the Gospel. The influential leader of the theological purity movement, Moore College Principal Broughton Knox, declared that Jesus never showed any concern for social justice, and that was because 'the call for social justice springs from envy rather than compassion'.[40]

In the early 1960s, Stuart Barton Babbage, then principal of Ridley College in Melbourne, was one church leader who thought the evangelicals were insufficiently involved in social welfare, especially human rights, and he deplored it:

> There are few [Australian evangelicals] who are alive to the sociological and cultural challenges of the present day and who have any profound understanding of international issues. There are few, if any, prophetic

---

38 Stephen Judd, Anne Robinson, and Felicity Errington, *Driven by Purpose: Charities that Make the Difference* (Greenwich, NSW: HammondPress, 2012), 54.

39 Chilton, 'Evangelicals and the End of Christian Australia', 97.

40 Quoted in James Franklin, 'The Sydney intellectual/religious scene, 1916–2016', *St Mark's Review*, 242, December 2017 (4), 34.

> voices: on such pressing and vital matters as the White Australia policy the evangelical voice is strangely muted. When evangelicals do speak on political and social issues, their thinking is generally shoddy and ill-informed, superficial and reactionary.[41]

In the next month, Babbage rampaged against censorship in the University of Sydney and he also condemned the church as 'smug', 'middle-class', 'stuffy, timid and unimaginative'.[42] He was no hypocrite. Having hurled mimic thunder at all aspects of church life, he took himself off to the United States for a decade-long ministry in which he berated Americans for their racism and stoutly argued that 'there is no impression without expression and that acceptance of the gospel has social as well as personal implications.'[43] He rejoiced when his second son, Christopher, married 'a strikingly-beautiful Afro-American'.[44] When the right-wing American philanthropist, J. Howard Pew, opposed Christian social action on the grounds that Jesus never took part in a demonstration, Babbage suggested to him that Jesus' cleansing of the temple might point to 'a different conclusion'.[45]

Babbage's fulminations were not hyperbole. Evangelicals had become as likely to resist social change as to promote it and were hesitant to take advantage of all the opportunities the Menzies' government offered. A conspicuous example was in the field of education. The 1961 NSW Education Act, based on the Wyndham Report of 1957, provided for the extension of schooling from eleven to twelve years and for greater provision for science education. Both measures made education more expensive, a great impost on Catholic schools which had always struggled financially. From 1963 Menzies' government gave state aid to science education in Catholic schools.[46] He was able to make this decisive break with past policy by capitalising on the panic, especially in America, following the launch in 1957 by the Russians of the first earth-orbiting satellite, Sputnik. Menzies made it a matter of national security that every Australian secondary school would have a science laboratory.

41 Stuart Babbage, 'Evangelicals in the Church in Australia,' *Churchman*, 77, June, 1963, 119.

42 Stuart Barton Babbage, *Memoirs of a Loose Canon* (Brunswick East: Acorn Press, 2004), 134.

43 Babbage, *Memoirs*, 138.

44 Babbage, *Memoirs*, 140.

45 Babbage, *Memoirs*, 150.

46 Benjamin Edwards, *Wasps, Tykes and Ecumaniacs: Aspects of Australian Sectarianism 1945–1981* (Brunswick East: Acorn Press, 2008), 161ff.

The Anglican Church in the Diocese of Sydney, apparently not sharing the same political imperative and more fearful of Catholics than of the Russians, appointed a committee of inquiry into state aid. It was chaired by future Archbishop, Marcus Loane. Edwin Judge, historian and synod member, was a member of it. The group was made up of academics and clergy: school heads and parents were absent. They argued that the first duty of Christian parents was to support the state system and that the religious needs of students in state schools could be met through the continuation of existing arrangements. This was at variance with the view of the head of the church's Department of Education, Alan Langdon. Hugh Gough, then Archbishop of Sydney, also thought it folly not to accept state aid, but Edwin Judge and Moore College Principal, Broughton Knox, were particularly determined in their support for state schools. The Anglican Diocese of Sydney never formally recanted its opposition to state aid, but the matter was removed from consideration by synod and left in the care of church school councils who judged it best to avoid the folly identified by Gough. Pragmatic pluralism, the reciprocity of church and state in welfare provision, continued to expand, if unevenly, as the century progressed, and conservative evangelicals continued to debate the wisdom of such engagement.

Communism and Fred Schwarz

Alan Walker was in the minority of evangelicals in support of socialism. Most evangelicals favoured capitalism and, during the Cold War, were fearfully anti-Communist. The best-known and the most intelligent of the evangelical anti-Communist crusaders was Fred Schwarz. Between 1931 and 1934 he was a science student at the University of Queensland. While there he was converted at a crusade in Brisbane taken by W.E. Booth-Clibborn, grandson of General Booth, founder of the Salvation Army. Schwarz joined, and soon led, the University's Evangelical Union, carried a large Bible and was known as a fanatic – Howard Guinness thought of him as 'a Pentecostalist'. Sydney evangelicals heard that Brisbane EU was influenced by Pentecostalism, and appealed for prayer about this undesirable development. But Queensland EU was not troubled. They had Fred, and he was a massive intellect and a great debater.

At his graduation ceremony, as he walked out to receive his degree, his long-suffering fellow students gave a robust rendition of 'Onward Christian Soldiers', which Schwarz correctly assessed as 'good natured yet not meant as a compliment'.[47] He graduated as a medical doctor in 1944. During his medical course, he had come into contact with Communist students, including Max Julius, a law student who came from a family of Communists and was president of the Student Union. It was in debating with him that he forged his conviction that Communism was not to be opposed on economic or political grounds, but on the basis of its 'false doctrines about God and man,'[48] a perspective widely shared among Australians.

Schwarz further honed his debating skills in the Sydney Domain, frequently taking on Communists, including the popular Stan Moran, an official of the Waterside Workers' Federation. In a famous exchange, he was asked by the Communist chairman of one of these meetings, 'what is dialectical materialism?' Without faltering Schwarz replied that 'dialectical materialism is the philosophy of Karl Marx, which he formulated by marrying the idealistic dialectic of Hegel to the materialism of Feuerbach, abstracting from it the concept of the inevitability of progress due to the conflict of opposites called the thesis and the antithesis, applying this concept to the history of economic and social progress, and deriving therefrom a doctrine of inevitable social change.' When the chairman responded with stunned silence which Schwarz took to be incomprehension, he added, 'Don't blame me; it's your philosophy, not mine; you are the one who believes it, not I.'[49]

Early in 1950 Australia was visited by two prominent American fundamentalists, Carl McIntyre and T.T. Shields. They invited Schwarz to America to speak on anti-Communism. He relished the opportunity and gave long, strongly-reasoned addresses without notes. From 1952, he wrote a series of anti-Communist booklets, beginning with *The Heart, Mind and Soul of Communism*. His most famous book in this genre was *You can Trust the Communists (to be Communists)* first published in 1960.

On the advice of Billy Graham and others, Schwarz formed the Christian Anti-Communist Crusade. Its mission was to preach Christ and 'educate people about the Communist menace'.[50] 'Anti-Communism *aided* evangelism', he insisted.[51] Senator Fulbright, the Chairman of the Committee on Foreign Relations of the US Senate and the most vocal opponent of American involvement in Vietnam, claimed that Schwarz was in it for the money. One who

47 Fred Schwarz, *Beating the Unbeatable Foe: One Man's Victory over Communism, Leviathan, and the Last Enemy* (Washington: Regnery, 1996), 17.

48 Schwarz, *Beating the Unbeatable Foe*, 22.

49 Schwarz, *Beating the Unbeatable Foe*, 39.

50 Schwarz, *Beating the Unbeatable Foe*, 104.

51 Schwarz, *Beating the Unbeatable Foe*, 105

defended Schwarz against this charge was Donald Robinson, then Deputy Principal of Moore College and later Archbishop of Sydney. He wrote to the *Sydney Morning Herald* on 28 February 1970:

> Dr Schwarz is an Australian of unusual ability and was formerly a medical practitioner in this city. He gave his first public address on the nature of Communism in 1946 to a meeting in Sydney at my invitation, and I have a reasonable knowledge of his attempt to awaken the general public to an awareness of the professed policies of Communism … to insinuate, as Senator Fulbright does, that he has mercenary motives in conducting his Christian Anti-Communist Crusade is ludicrous.[52]

Large claims have been made for the impact of Schwarz. Many prominent world leaders have confessed that they learned their anti-Communism from Schwarz, including President Fidel Ramos of the Philippines and Ronald Reagan. On the fall of Communism in the late 1980s Ronald Reagan wrote to Schwarz commending him for his 'tireless dedication in trying to ensure the protection of freedom and human rights'.[53] With Alan Walker's support for socialism and Schwarz's opposition to Communism, the evangelical movement was keeping up its capacity to produce those committed to the passionate trial of all options. This did not mean that all evangelicals were passionate ideologues: some, most successfully those in politics, were passionate pragmatists.

Tom Playford, Liberal Conservative Premier

One such was Sir Thomas Playford, SA's longest-serving Premier. He was the sixth generation of Playfords, Baptists and orchardists in SA. His father, also Thomas, was born in 1861 and died in 1945, not sharing his own father's political ambitions or any other form of ambition apparently. But he married one of sterner stuff, Bessie Pellew, who was a close critic of sermons, something of a 'divisive Baptist' and a Sabbatarian to the point of impracticality.[54] Their son (the premier) was a conservative in values yet with a marked strain of welfare socialism in his political practice. He served in the South Australian parliament for 35 years and was Premier continuously for nearly twenty-seven

52 Schwarz, *Beating the Unbeatable Foe*, 266.

53 Ronald Reagan to Fred Schwarz, 4 January 1990, in Schwarz, *Beating the Unbeatable Foe*, xx.

54 Walter Crocker, *Sir Thomas Playford: A Portrait* (Carlton: MUP, 1983), 14f.

years from 1938 to 1965. He was a natural leader, a benevolent despot, and the government took on his own character:

> His government was quiet-spoken in tone, but its will, like its honesty, was never in doubt. Some of its moral values were old-fashioned but nothing else about it was old fashioned except its dependence on rural-based political power long traditional in South Australia.[55]

He was as incorruptible as any politician in Australian history and has withstood the closest scrutiny from historians who have not merely parroted the accusations of his political enemies. After 35 years he left parliament with no more money than he entered it. He was never known to lie, and in commercial matters and political negotiations his word was his bond. He was 'deeply and innately fair-minded'.[56] He established the City of Elizabeth, although he knew, with its working-class population, that it would return a Labor parliamentarian. He refused all urgings to name it 'Playford', but instead used the opportunity to name the town after the young sovereign, a shrewd move calculated to attract desirable English migrants to the State, thus increasing the labour force.

Playford was never boastful of his own achievements, never keeping any record of them, was always eager to give the credit to others, and surprised everybody when he eventually succumbed, unlike his senator grandfather, to the much-offered knighthood. The Archbishop of Canterbury, Geoffrey Fisher, one who was given to expressing his judgments on men, in his visit to Australia in 1950, met Playford, and found him to be an 'excellent and upright man'.[57]

Apart from these qualities of character, Playford was very skilled politically and administratively: he had brains as well as backbone. He was just so competent. He was lucid, always on top of the facts, he never wasted a penny of the tax-payer's money and he ran a very lean public service. He refused to accept any gifts in office, was allergic to its frills, and exasperated his family by spending his own money attending public functions. He was physically strong and powerful; a prodigious sportsman; always vital and clear-headed. He had an excellent memory, a quick mind, a good, if formally uncultivated, intellect. He was never paralysed by fear, regret or resentments. 'The bandwagon was not his vehicle.'[58]

55 Crocker, *Playford*, 1.

56 Crocker, *Playford*, 2.

57 Edward Carpenter, *Archbishop Fisher – His Life and Times* (Norwich: The Canterbury Press, 1991), 482.

58 Crocker, *Playford,* 171.

Being a doer of the Word rather than a speaker of it, there are questions about Playford's religious position, an issue of perennial interest to evangelicals. Walter Crocker, one of his biographers, observes: 'I gained the impression that his views would not be orthodox; that while his cast of mind and his values were Christian, his outlook was that of the Stoic.'[59] Another biographer, Stewart Cockburn, wrote that the 'support of the principal Churches was still important to political leaders and Playford had it, not least because he was widely perceived as being a convinced Christian. Whether this was true or not is hard to say.'[60] His contemporary, William Slade, a cousin, surmised: 'Like all of us, he went to Church and Sunday School, in our case the Baptist Church. But he was never devout. I think he had his reservations about it all.'[61] When convalescing from terrible war wounds in Britain in 1917, between the 70 operations he suffered, he read widely, it is said in every area except 'sacred literature',[62] although he came to admire Milton's *Paradise Lost* greatly after the War. When his son, Tom, announced that he wanted to be a missionary, the absentee father – for that is what the premier was to his children, in spite of being named 'Father of the Year' – snapped 'Don't be ridiculous'.[63] He did not go to Church as often as his wife: he would sing loudly and out of tune and did not like being told to restrain himself! After the birth of Margaret, their first child, he said to his wife, 'You go to Church, Lorn[a], and I'll stay home and mind the baby.' After the 1959 Billy Graham crusades, which impacted Adelaide greatly as they did the rest of Australia, a Liberal backbencher asked if the government intended to do anything to remember the event. Playford responded with his usual clarity which brooked no argument, 'The government deals with the economic affairs of the State. It leaves spiritual affairs to the Church.'[64] His wife testified that he was not under the thumb of anyone, industry or church, and could not be counted on to do their bidding. Historian David Hilliard concludes: 'In fact, the influence of religious institutions diminished rather than grew over the 26 years and 226 days of Playford's rule; nor was Playford as firm in his commitment to Protestant Christianity as many supposed.'[65]

---

59 Crocker, *Playford,* 178.

60 Stewart Cockburn, *Playford: Benevolent Despot* (Kent Town: Axiom, 1991), 210.

61 Cockburn, *Playford,* 33, 210.

62 Cockburn, *Playford,* 54.

63 Cockburn, *Playford,* 62.

64 Cockburn, *Playford,* 210.

65 David Hilliard in Bernard O'Neil, Judith Raftery and Kerrie Round (eds.), *Playford's South Australia,* Adelaide, APH, 1996), 253.

How do we explain this apparent lack of ideology or dogmatism in his religion? Like all the Playfords, he was a dissenter, a non-conformist, and independency of mind was itself a religious conviction. Anglican evangelicals are not so prone to heterodoxy precisely because they are not habitual dissenters – they have not needed to be for their social survival. Playford was not particularly interested in theology as he was a man of action and practicalities and was never keen on abstractions and theories. All this meant that he was able to avoid the problem which bedevils most evangelicals when it comes to politics, namely their penchant for dogmatism which renders them habitually incapable of the pragmatism essential to political survival and success. Playford's pragmatism made him unusual even in political circles. He may best be described as an Independent Christian Utilitarian Social Democrat!

But there is no doubting the depths and influence of his religious faith. The prayers sent to him by his grandmother during the First World War were found in his wallet on his death. He chose as his wife, from among many who desired him, Lorna Clark, who came from an even stricter Baptist family than his own. Ironically, his Christian convictions not only protected his government against the charges of corruption, but they also cost him office. When asked by Donald Coggan, Archbishop of Canterbury, why he thought he lost office in 1965, Playford replied, 'I think, your Grace, I was not sufficiently liberal in matters relating to alcohol and gambling.'[66]

His son, Tom, believes him to have been a good Christian and a 'lovely man', recalling how he would sing the 23rd psalm with great vigour in the orchard, albeit out of tune, and how he claimed to his son on one occasion, also in the orchard, 'Tom, do you know what was the greatest tragedy the world has ever known? It was the crucifixion of Christ!'[67] Stewart Cockburn's assessment may not be far from the truth:

> The Christian faith which had dominated the lives of his paternal great-grandfather, his mother and his wife was never so obvious and unequivocal in him but it unquestionably influenced the formation of his character, his indifference to material possessions, and hence his integrity and probity in public life. He could sometimes fairly have been accused of cunning, deviousness, ruthlessness and arrogance as

66 Cockburn, *Playford,* 346.
67 Cockburn, *Playford,* 210.

> he pursued his ends. Sometimes he made mistakes. Yet, because of the qualities just mentioned, these less attractive propensities did not lead to the corrupting consequences of power observed in so many other political leaders.[68]

Playford was above party, and was described as 'a socialist at heart' and the 'best Labor Premier South Australia ever had'.[69] In his years in office, he reduced the Labor Party to uncritical compliance with his policies since they appeared to be in the best interests of the workers, and to a habit of 'brooding hopelessness and brooding self-pity'[70] over the gerrymander. There were twice as many country seats as Adelaide seats, irrespective of population, so that, as the city population grew with Playford's industrialisation policies, the value of country votes increased to almost four times that of city votes.[71] Those who lived in the bush, Australia over, found such a disparity easy to rationalise: it was a small compensation for the many disadvantages they suffered. They construed it as their entitlement and a manifestation of their premier's care for them. He would leave it to others to disappoint them by seeking to remove it, and that was a long time in coming.

It required a humanist civil libertarian, namely future Labor premier, Don Dunstan, to oppose him successfully, as Playford's values were so similar to those of the Methodists and Catholics in the Labor Party that they found it hard to fault him. Playford did not lose office until 1965, but the 1959 SA elections were the beginning of the end for him. Dunstan attacked the gerrymander, which he dubbed the 'Playmander', and he also attacked Playford's support for capital punishment. In 1959 this was a highly emotive issue thanks to the sentencing to death of Rupert Max Stuart for the rape and murder of a young girl. This was the most difficult issue Playford faced in his long premiership and to it his eventual demise has been attributed.[72] In any event, he was not determined to have Stuart hanged at all costs, and he approved the commutation of his sentence in October 1959. Ken Inglis, historian, who followed the case closely from the beginning and was one of the first to raise concerns about the trial, concluded that Stuart was 'probably

---

68 Cockburn, *Playford,* 349.

69 Crocker, *Playford,* 2.

70 Cockburn, *Playford*, 244.

71 Cockburn, *Playford,* 242.

72 K.S. Inglis, *The Stuart Case*, New ed. (Melbourne: Black Inc., 2002), 91, 336,

guilty'.[73] Playford had this in common with Inglis: he played with a straight bat, which is possibly rarer among politicians than historians.

The Stuart Case

At exactly the time Billy Graham was holding his crusades in Australia in 1959, Australians became engrossed by the protracted legal battle over the conviction of Rupert Max Stuart, an Arrernte (Aranda) man, for the rape and murder of eight-year old Mary Hattam in Ceduna, South Australia. So extensive and expensive was the process of being seen to give Stuart justice, including a Royal Commission, that it betrayed a deep national anxiety and guilt over the treatment of Indigenous people.[74]

It was a Catholic priest, Thomas Dixon, who first raised the possibility of Stuart's innocence, but the business of sensitising the Australian conscience on Indigenous disadvantage was by now becoming the business of all the churches. The linguistic expertise in the Arrernte language and 'Northern Territory English' of Theodor (Ted) Strehlow, the veteran Lutheran missionary born at the Hermannsburg Mission – the only white man ever raised in Arrernte society[75] – brought the police case into disrepute. On linguistic grounds Strehlow showed that the confession which brought about his conviction could not have emanated from Stuart. The police insisted that it was word for word as he dictated it, but Strehlow maintained that the police had beaten him and that, for fear of his life, he signed the confession which they had concocted. In prison, Dixon read to Stuart the only book ever printed in Arrernte, the Bible translated by Strehlow's father.[76]

Strehlow never doubted Stuart's innocence, but he was a passionate and increasingly paranoid soul, and he despaired that the 'slave-minded' SA churchgoers – with the Lutherans the most enslaved – would arise in protest.[77] Charles Duguid, a consistent critic of the protectionist policy of governments, put the Aborigines' Advancement League, of which he was founder, at the disposal of Stuart's supporters. The chairman of the Australian Board of Missions, Frank Coaldrake, encouraged concerned citizens to contribute to a fund to finance Stuart's legal defence.[78] Rohan Deakin Rivett, editor-in-chief of the

73 Inglis, *The Stuart Case*, 308

74 Inglis, *The Stuart Case*, 201, 277.

75 Inglis, *The Stuart Case*, 43.

76 Inglis, *The Stuart Case*, 94.

77 Inglis, *The Stuart Case*, 329.

78 Inglis, *The Stuart Case*, 64.

News Ltd which critiqued the Adelaide Establishment and the Stuart trial, was grandson of Alfred Deakin and of the Rev Albert Rivett, who opposed military conscription as we saw in chapter one. The Congregational Union of SA invited Don Dunstan, who had moved a private member's bill to abolish capital punishment, to address it and then sent a resolution to the government calling for its abolition.[79] A society which campaigned in 1959 to have Stuart's conviction reviewed was the John Howard Society, named after the eighteenth-century Congregationalist prison reformer whom we met in chapter one of volume one. When Stuart was due to be paroled in 1973 the Evangelical Fellowship of Aboriginal Christians collected offers of 15 jobs and 7 places for Stuart to stay in Adelaide.[80] In the event he was paroled to the Catholic mission at Santa Teresa established in 1952 for the Eastern Arrernte people near Alice Springs. Following more spells in gaol, he became an Arrente elder, was married and became a respected character. He died in 2014.

The Stuart case is a good bridge from the age of equipoise to that new, less stable age, and the support which Stuart received was a sign that the evangelical radicals would be well represented in that new age. Historian Ken Inglis put the transition well:

> Rupert Max Stuart had been locked away in 1959 from the Australia of Sir Thomas Playford and Sir Robert Menzies, when the watchwords for Aboriginal policy were protection and assimilation. He was released in 1973 into the Australia of Don Dunstan and Gough Whitlam, where people spoke a new language of self-determination and land rights.[81]

The new age was not all gain, and Stuart went into a world where the Christian missions had been replaced by government-controlled communities where alcohol abuse and the neglect of children were far more common than they had been in the days of the missions.[82] Stuart was returned to prison in Adelaide five times, mainly for drunkenness, until one-time Catholic priest, Pat Dodson, employed him as a field officer with the Central Land Council, thus putting Stuart on the road to respectability as a 'Law man' and later chairman of the Central Land Council.

Court cases can be wonderful barometers of social and spiritual pathology. Another court case engrossed Australians even more in the 1950s than the

79 Inglis, *The Stuart Case*, 211.
80 Inglis, *The Stuart Case*, 351.
81 Inglis, *The Stuart Case*, 357.
82 Inglis, *The Stuart Case*, 376.

Stuart case. In it, too, Christians were among the most vocal defenders of the accused, and in that, too, they probably got it wrong.

The Orr Case

The Orr Case was the product of all the negative forces of this era: uncritical anti-Communism, soft-headed radicalism, academic pretension, insecure parochialism, anarchic amorality, self-serving spirituality and gullible religion. It is more a part of the history of the Student Christian Movement than of the evangelical movement, and there would be evangelicals who would take this as an object lesson in what can happen when the Bible is not obeyed, when fear of sin is lost. But at least one evangelical was involved, and the Orr case was a dramatic anticipation of the swinging, sinning sixties. For both reasons to end this chapter with this cautionary tale seems justified.

Sydney Sparkes Orr was appointed to the University of Tasmania in 1952. He had arrived in Melbourne in 1946 from Belfast. He became a popular lecturer for the SCM with its appetite for radical theology. Orr's message was that the world might be redeemed through love and that no distinction was to be made between brotherly, free and Christian love. When his wife joined him from Belfast, she found him living with a young social worker whom he had met at a conference of the SCM.[83] The three lived together until the social worker, on falling pregnant by him, withdrew from the arrangement. He was appointed to Tasmania when the Chancellor, who was accustomed to having his own way, decreed that he did not want an atheist or moral relativist in the chair. Orr, demonstrably the least able of the four applicants short-listed for the position, was chosen because of his links with the SCM. It was argued that he was 'a real Christian and a scholar', who would speak out against Communism and would take a strong position on the moral issues of the day.[84] Regrettably, the selection committee was not privy to Sydney University philosopher, David Stove's assessment of Orr:

> He was an *absolute pariah*, before he became a martyr. Stupid, devious, boring, and, to add to his charms, a Christian of the purest 'creeping Jesus' kind.[85]

Among those who did not quite share Stove's clarity of conviction about Orr was the Anglican Bishop of Hobart. Geoffrey Cranswick was a liberal

83 Franklin, *Corrupting the Youth*, 53.

84 Franklin, *Corrupting the Youth*, 55, 204, 206.

85 Franklin, *Corrupting the Youth*, 60.

Chapter Nine

CRUSADING FOR SOULS, 1946–1965

'Oh that my Saviour were your Saviour too.'
(Alan Walker)

The Australian census of 1947 revealed that large numbers of Australians were aware of the church or denomination they stayed away from. Nominal Christianity was Australia's largest religion, a situation which the churches could not accept happily. Their solution? More church building in the new suburbs of the expanding cities[1] and (for evangelicals especially) more evangelism. The Australian Council of Churches called the churches to combine in a united Commonwealth Crusade. This was to happen in 1959 with Billy Graham's Southern Cross Crusade, but in the late 1940s the churches were focussed on denominational concerns. So, the ACC encouraged each of the denominations to organise their own campaigns, which for the most part they did. The Presbyterians, alarmed to learn from the census that they had slipped behind the Methodists to become the fourth largest denomination, organised the New Life Movement. The Baptists and the Churches of Christ needed no such bidding. John Ridley's evangelistic meetings attracted far more than Baptists. The denominational evangelist for the Churches of Christ, Ernest Christian Hinrichsen, was one of the nation's most effective evangelists for more than thirty years. He preached all over Australia in tent missions from the South Coast of NSW to the goldfields of Western Australia. He reputedly established more than 50 churches and led 30,000 to faith in Christ.[2] He also ensured that the training colleges of the Churches of Christ, at Glen Iris in Melbourne and especially Woolwich in Sydney, had evangelism as a core subject in the curriculum. Their graduates typically emerged with an

1 David Hilliard, 'God in the Suburbs: The Religious Culture of Australian Cities in the 1950s', *Australian Historical Studies*, 24.97, 1991, 408f.

2 E.C. Hinrichsen, *The Gospel under Canvas* (Melbourne: Austral Printing & Publishing Ltd, 1958).

appetite for evangelism, in emulation of the revered Hinrichsen, and with considerable benefit to the growth of that denomination.[3]

Overseas evangelists who reaped big harvests in Australia after the war included Hyman Appelman, Bryan Green, and Leslie Weatherhead. Howard Guinness, founder of the IVF in Australia, spoke at a series of successful University missions in the early 50s. Geoffrey Bingham, following his near-death, spiritually-deepening experiences in World War II, became a conduit of revival, first in Australia, and then on the mission fields of Pakistan and India. Alan Walker's Mission to the Nation, 1953–55, not only further consolidated Methodism in third place in the denominational pecking order, but raised questions about Australia's Christian identity not before articulated. Billy Graham's 1959 crusades across Australia were able to ride on a tide of religious interest higher than any previously experienced in Australian history.

Outreach to Youth

Of great significance for the future prosperity of the evangelical movement, new energy and increased resources were put into winning young people to Christ. Outreach to children was the special focus of the CSSM which employed children's missioners who, not only conducted beach missions and camps, but also held meetings for children outside of schools. Foremost among missioners in 1950s and beyond was Owen Shelley (1927–2014). On staff at SU, Owen organised camps, including Ag Camp, Camp Conqueror, Pioneer Camp on the Shoalhaven River, the junior boys' camp at The Grange in Mount Victoria, and sailing at Camp Bevington on Lake Munmorah. Shelley counselled 'never underestimate the under eight'.[4]

Ministry to teenagers was revamped by the wide acceptance of the pre-war change in methodology from ministry *for* youth to ministry *by* youth in recognition of the growing appreciation of peer influence.[5] The new stress on youth work was clearly true of Sydney Anglicans:

> Evangelism was the key to progress, with the under-25s as the main target group. A mission by youth to youth, organised for 1951, aimed at contacting all those confirmed in the diocese in the previous ten

3 Dennis Nutt, *A Crucible of Faith and Learning: A History of the Australian College of Ministries* (Rhodes: Acom Press, 2017), 33–42.

4 Phillip Jensen at the memorial service for Owen Shelley, *SU News*, Summer 2014, 15.

5 Ruth Lukabyo, 'From a ministry for youth to a ministry of youth: A history of Protestant youth ministry in Sydney, NSW 1930–1959', PhD Macquarie University, 2018.

> years. This focus on youth was to produce the enormous young people's fellowships that filled the churches in the fifties. The Youth Department maintained its aggressive outreach among diocesan young people through houseparties, rallies, and fellowship groups. It was part of a total program that began with plans for the diocese-wide Youth Mission of 1951 and concluded with the Billy Graham Crusade of 1959.[6]

Non-denominational evangelistic events especially designed for youth were also well patronised in this period. In Sydney, perhaps the best-known youth evangelist was Alex Gilchrist. He had served in Everyman's Welfare Service during World War II. After the war, he succeeded Cairo Bradley as NSW director of Campaigners for Christ. He was agreeable and personable, avoided strident moralising, and his pleasant speaking voice made him a popular Christian broadcaster and preacher. He gained considerable public notice when in 1950 he began live broadcasts with radio station 2CH each weekday morning and Saturday evenings. Once a month the Saturday evening broadcasts doubled as 'This is Life' rallies which members of youth fellowships in Sydney regularly attended, singing hymns in the trains going in and coming home, to the consternation of other passengers.

Geoff Bingham

Geoffrey Bingham, poet and mystic, was another exceptionally fruitful evangelist. In the hell-hole of suffering as a POW he had witnessed the depths to which the depravity of humanity could sink, but he came to believe that the love of God in the cross of Christ could outreach it. When subsequently counselling any who shared with him their deepest hurt he would impulsively gather them in his arms and assure them vehemently that God had already dealt with it on the cross and that it need not imprison their spirits any longer.

Following the war, he returned to Moore College, was Senior Student in 1952 and received first class honours in the Licentiate of Theology (ThL). He discussed the East Africa Revival with Marcus Loane and others, and reflected on the foundation premise of Keswick theology, that the believer is 'crucified with Christ' (Galatians 2.20). He read the works of Andrew Murray who infused the Reformed faith with the pietism of the Evangelical Revival. He studied Walter Marshall's *The Gospel Mystery of Sanctification* (1692) and discussed it with T.C. Hammond who declared that it was 'spot on', and *Born*

6 William J. Lawton, 'The Winter of our Days: The Anglican Diocese of Sydney 1950–1960', *Lucas*, 9, 1990, 13f.

Crucified (1945) written by L.E. Maxwell, an American fundamentalist. He also studied the works of the church's greatest theologian of revival, Jonathan Edwards. To synthesise such influences required a powerful intellect as well as a passionate heart, and Bingham seemed to be endowed with both as is evidenced not only by his preaching, but also by his literary and poetic output.[7]

The Gospel, he taught, promised more than the forgiveness of sins. Through the cross, guilt is destroyed, and through the destruction of guilt, the power of sin is destroyed. Living in the freedom which results from the destruction of the penalty and power of sin is the holy life. From 1953 to 1956 each Sunday he packed out the Garrison Church, Miller's Point, in Sydney.[8] The fires of revival fell: all-night prayer meetings just 'went like a flash'. Remarkable scenes of revival accompanied his ministry in Pakistan where he served from 1957 to 1966 as a missionary with CMS.[9] He analysed the success of his labours in terms of his preaching the Gospel of grace:

> The ministry we had in Pakistan was that of preaching the Scriptures, and especially the great themes. That seemed to raise the spiritual 'water-table' – so to speak – until eventually there was a great outflowing of grace and the Spirit in the truth of Christ. That is how I see what happened with Edwards and his ministry, and no less the Wesleys, Whitefield and the somewhat later English Evangelicals … My thinking is not in terms of revival, but in the power of the Gospel proclaimed in the power of the Spirit.[10]

Bingham's spirituality preceded that of the main influence of the Charismatic movement, and was a genuinely indigenous revitalisation movement of a type rarely experienced in Australian history. Perhaps his greatest work in Australia was in local church missions where revival was often experienced. The addresses he gave at these missions were on bondage to sin and Satan, the powers of darkness and of flesh and the world, and the true freedom which Christ gives from such powers. From August 1962, when he held a mission in the Parish of Thornleigh in Sydney, the tapes of his addresses with these themes were played over and over by those who heard him gladly, and his

---

7 Bingham wrote 197 books. In *The New Creation Hymn Book* (1993) there are 73 of his hymns, and 34 of his short stories were published in *The Bulletin*.

8 Martin Bleby, *A Quiet Revival: Geoffrey Bingham in Life and Ministry* (Blackwood: New Creation Publications, 2012), 139–154.

9 On the Pakistan revivals see Geoffrey Bingham *Twice-Conquering Love* (Blackwood: New Creation Publications, 1992).

10 Geoffrey Bingham to Stuart Piggin, undated letter c. September 1997.

teaching on the holiness and love of the Father in the efficacy of the cross became their regular diet. Scores were converted and many went into the mission field or the ministry.

During the Thornleigh mission, a prayer meeting of about thirty people was held in a private home. Bingham read from Psalm 24, 'Who shall ascend to the hill of the Lord? He who has clean hands and a pure heart.' Then he suggested that those present should come to the Lord and ask him to reveal himself to them. They all knelt down in a circle, someone began to weep, and a great conviction came over all of them. Some tried to pray, but dissolved in sobs. And then there came over one present an incredible sense of his own depravity in the sight of God. He was crushed and broke down and sobbed convulsively, and the others around him were prostrate on the floor, broken hearted. Then a gentle quietness came over the whole group, followed by a wonderful sense of God's total forgiveness. Then they sang and sang until they were hoarse, on and on, until someone said, 'It's half past four in the morning'.[11] Bingham was poet and lover as well as preacher and teacher, and his ministry was to the heart. Through it thousands of Australians were confronted with the holiness of God and comforted with the experience that Jesus cared for their souls.

Mission to the Nation

Bingham's ministry was mainly to local church communities. Alan Walker's was to the nation – literally. Starting in the Melbourne Town Hall on 8 April 1953, Walker's Mission to the Nation began with a bang, with 3,000 in the Town Hall and an equal number in nearby venues. The next morning he received congratulatory telegrams from Prime Minister Menzies and the leader of the Opposition, Dr H.V. Evatt. The goal of the Mission was Christian Australians and a Christian Australia.[12] Walker's vision of a Christian Australia was not the materialist nation of the capitalists, but a caring community of public housing for the poor, marriage guidance for the benefit of families, and social justice for Aboriginal people. Walker always made an appeal after his addresses for people to come forward and make a public confession of faith in Christ. Thirty years after the Mission, he continued to come across people who reported that they had made that act of faith and how important it continued to be for them.[13]

11 John Dunn interviewed by Stuart Piggin, 26 September 1986.

12 See Walker, *Heritage without end: A Story to tell the Nation* (Melbourne: General Conference Literature and Publications Committee of the Methodist Church of Australasia) which went through five editions in 1953.

13 D.I. Wright, *Alan Walker: Conscience of the Nation* (Adelaide: Openbook, 1997), 111.

In the first six months of the Mission, Walker preached in 52 centres throughout Australia, not only in capital cities. This gave him an Australia-wide profile, unprecedented for a Methodist minister. The Mission was well attended throughout 1953 and was favourably reported in the Press which was not averse to a religious revival, nor to the realisation that the country had an evangelist of 'world stature' in its midst.[14] The climactic Sydney meetings in 1953 were accompanied by a procession of witness of 25,000 and a youth rally which attracted 10,000 to the open-air stadium in Rushcutter's Bay.

Walker was in hot water in 1955 when the National Christian Youth Convention, which was part of the Mission to the Nation, criticised government expenditure on armaments. The Convention was considered by Walker to be the most important act of witness produced by the Mission, but paranoid conservatives believed the Methodist Church was an agent of Communism, and ASIO began to amass on file Walker's statements on Communism. The file on Walker up to 1959 alone was 180 pages long, and he later suspected it would be much bigger once the Vietnam War period was reached.[15]

The Mission to the Nation ran into the sand of petty jealousies, conservative reaction to its methods and message, and disappointment over not seeing revival. Yet, addressing as it did issues of common concern such as war, sex, racism, poverty and unemployment, it may have had a deeper impact on the nation as a whole than on the church in particular.[16] It was one of those rare occasions when an evangelical Christian had conceived and propagated national goals and political ideals consistent with Christian values. Walker was becoming 'the conscience of the nation' as a later governor-general was to call him.[17]

Billy Graham, 1959

Never before and never since the 1959 Billy Graham crusades in Australia's capital cities have Australians been so concerned with the Christian religion. The crusades were the most effective engagement with the Australian community ever achieved by evangelicals in Australia. Did Australia experience

---

14 *Sydney Sun*,11 April 1953.

15 *SMH*, 21 July 1990.

16 Even so, in the years 1953 to 1957, 8,044 people were added to the Methodist Church in Australia. Samantha Frappell, 'Post-War Revivalism in Australia,' in Mark Hutchinson and Stuart Piggin (eds.), *Reviving Australia: Essays on the History and Experience of Revival and Revivalism in Australian Christianity* (Sydney: CSAC, 1994), 255.

17 Wright, *Conscience of the Nation*, 113.

genuine revival in 1959 as Graham himself prayed that it would? He himself never doubted that his time in Australia was a 'God thing'. He had at that time received invitations to speak at crusades in more than a hundred different parts of the world. 'One invitation in particular captured my interest. For some reason I could not fully understand, although I believed it was the leading of the Holy Spirit, I had developed an overwhelming burden to visit the distant continent of Australia'.[18] Christians understand revival as a sovereign work of God, and throughout history it appears to have been generally associated with six forms of human behaviour which the historian can identify from evidence: they are longed for; they draw Christians together in unprecedented unity; they are born of ardent prayerfulness; they renew the Church; they convert many; they restrain sinful antisocial behaviour. They were all experienced in the Billy Graham Crusades in Australia in 1959.

i. The Expectation of Revival

A deep longing for, and expectation of, revival developed strongly in Australia in the 1950s. True, there was room for doubt about city-wide campaigns in the tradition of American revivalism. When in 1956 evangelist Oral Roberts had come to Melbourne 'with the largest tent in the world, it was disconcertingly pulled down around his ears'.[19] The Graham Team's preliminary research suggested that the Australia campaign would be small because the population was scattered and Australians had a reputation for being sports-loving, prosperous, and hitherto resistant to evangelists.[20] The modest campaign the team had in mind for Australia suggested that they were not expecting revival.

But Oral Roberts's experience did not prove that Australians were generally hostile to mass American-style evangelism. A member of the Young Communist League later confessed to being in a training exercise to burn down the tent. In mitigation, he explained, this was not for any ideological reason: it was just an opportunity to train in a commando-style operation![21] Evidence pointed to Australia's openness to evangelism rather than the reverse. At the end of the Mission to the Nation, the question of whether Australia needed a religious revival was put to a nation-wide Gallup Poll. The general

---

18 Billy Graham, *Just as I am: The Autobiography* (Sydney: HarperCollins, 1997), 325.

19 Stuart Barton Babbage, *Memoirs of a Loose Canon* (Brunswick East: Acorn Press, 2004), 119.

20 John Pollock, *Crusades: 20 Years with Billy Graham* (Minneapolis: World Wide Publications, 1969), 186; William Martin, *The Billy Graham story: a prophet with honour* (London: Hutchinson, 1992), 252.

21 Note of a discussion with Alan Gill, 26 May 1989.

feeling seemed to be that young people would lead a better life with the help of religion and that religious belief raised moral standards. Billy Graham himself was to come to the conclusion that Australians were suffering from more than social and psychological anxiety at the time. They were starving spiritually and seemed to sense it.

Table 2. Responses by denomination to the question: 'In your opinion does Australia need a religious revival?'

Denomination	Yes	No	No Opinion
Baptists	74	17	9
Methodists	64	22	14
Presbyterians	57	27	16
C of E	47	33	20
RC	44	35	21

Source: The *Advertiser* (Adelaide), 24 October 1953, 4.[22]

The Melbourne *Age* reported:

> The most significant and arresting feature of the evangelistic crusade … is the obvious fact that … it has demonstrated a passionate desire on the part of widely differing sections of the community for a revival of true religion comparable with the great revivals of history.[23]

The BGEA did much to create expectation. 'The Hour of Decision' was broadcast on more than 30 radio stations throughout the land. Billy Graham films were screened in cinemas. They reached the most unlikely places. We read, for example, of the initiative of the Rev Stuart Harper, then the pastor at Goombargana Hill, out of Albury. His little Baptist church was the only building on the hill. He invited Jerry Beavan, Director of Crusade Arrangements in Australia, to screen in the nearby small town of Walla Walla, a Lutheran stronghold, the film 'Miracle in Manhattan'. Beavan's visit (August 1958) was preceded by weeks of prayer, with members of other churches uniting with the Baptists for the occasion, and resulted in conversions and considerable impact on the district.[24] Such events, multiplied all over Australia, raised expectation.

---

22 The authors' thanks to Michael Petras for drawing our attention to this table.

23 *Age*, 14 February 1959.

24 *The Australian Baptist*, 20 August 1958.

ii. Unprecedented Unity

By 1959 Graham had already turned his back on the sectarianism of fundamentalism. He was concerned not to dwell on what divides Christians, convinced that 'the great divisions have always resulted from somewhat minor differences.'[25] The most unequivocal supporters of Graham in 1959 were Baptists and the Open Brethren.[26] The latter had always stressed the importance of unity among Christians as a biblical principle, but the Graham Crusades, to which they contributed a disproportionately high number of counsellors and advisors, afforded them the opportunity to experience the unity in practice. 'In that crusade,' observed their historian Kenneth Newton, 'Brethren men and women mixed freely with Christians from all denominations in a way they had not done previously.'[27] It was, he adds, 'one of the catalysts for a partial liberation of Brethren women'.[28]

Graham's remarkable appreciation of the importance of the Anglican Church was critical to his success. He did not win all Anglicans. E.H. Burgmann, Bishop of Canberra & Goulburn, said that Graham's view of the Bible was 'idolatrous',[29] while T.B. McCall, Bishop of Rockhampton, wrote in his diocesan magazine that aspects of the Graham crusades were 'objectionable, dishonest, distressing, and disgusting'.[30] But Graham's growing friendship with a number of senior Anglican clergy – R.C. Kerle, Marcus Loane, Archie Morton, Leon Morris, S.B. Babbage, H.M. Arrowsmith – goes a long way towards explaining the success of the Australian crusades. At the last meeting of the Sydney Crusade Graham waxed lyrical on the Sydney clergy. Seldom had he seen 'a city before where one man was so loved by so many from all walks of life as the late Archbishop Mowll, nor a city where the calibre of the clergy has been so high, so devout, so spiritual, so evangelical as in the City

---

25 Quoted in 'Billy Graham in Australia', *Current Affairs Bulletin*, 24.4, 1959, 55.

26 Stuart Piggin, 'Billy Graham's '59 Southern Cross Crusade: Evangelistic Efficacy and Baptist Bonanza,' *The Baptist Recorder*, 107, 2009, 1–13.

27 Kenneth J. Newton, *A History of the Brethren in Australia with Special Reference to the Open Brethren* (Indooroopilly, Qld.: Aberdeen Desktop, 1990), 90.

28 Lamb, Margaret, "'Out of all Proportion': Christian Brethren Influence in Australian Evangelicalism', in Geoffrey R. Treloar and Robert D. Linder (eds.), *Making History for God: Essays on Evangelicalism, Revival and Mission* (Sydney: Robert Menzies College, 2004), 105.

29 Quoted in 'Billy Graham in Australia', 57. Meredith Burgmann, the bishop's granddaughter, was not allowed by her mother to hear Billy Graham on the grounds that he was vulgar. 'ABC, Radio National, 'God Forbid', http://mpegmedia.abc.net.au/rn/podcast/2017/07/gfd_20170730_0605.mp3.

30 *SMH*, 2 May 1959.

of Sydney'.[31] The Southern Cross Crusade was preceded and accompanied by extraordinary inter-church unity. Ministers' fraternals, made up of ministers from all denominations in a region, had rarely enjoyed such unity of purpose. Their members were clearly gripped with excitement at the prospect of having 'God's chosen prophet', the man who had 'preached to more people than any man in the history of the world'.[32]

But this was not the limit of Graham's ecumenism. He sought and succeeded in obtaining the assistance of the secular arm. Graham brought with him to Australia a letter from Richard Nixon, requesting William Sebald, the American ambassador, to give any assistance that the members of his staff might be able to provide: 'Certainly,' Nixon concluded, 'it would be most difficult to find people who were more friendly in their attitude toward the United States than the Australians.'[33] The press, too, were united in their praise of the handsome young evangelist, giving 'unprecedented recognition with not one unfriendly voice'.[34] Ken Inglis observed that the newspapers were among the first converts.[35] Graham thought it 'a wonderful thing when the newspapers make religion front page copy almost every day'.[36]

iii. Extraordinary Prayerfulness

In the *Crusade Bulletin* for October 1958, Graham wrote, 'If spiritual awakening comes to Australia, it will not be as a result of organisation, publicity, preaching or singing. It will come as a result of prayer on the part of Christians all over the world.' With the crusades in full swing, he believed 'that more prayer has been made for the Melbourne and Sydney crusades than for any single event in the whole history of the Christian Church'.[37] The first 'vital National Prayer Offensive' was launched at an all-night of prayer in five centres in Melbourne on 21 September 1958. At least sixteen churches in Sydney and twenty in the country joined in praying for the southern capital. One attendee commented, 'never have I seen such spontaneity in prayer. I noticed through the night that there was never any lagging in the praying. There was

31 Film F, 10 May 1959, Collection 113, Billy Graham Archives, Wheaton College, Illinois, (hereafter BGA).

32 *Illawarra Mercury*, 7 April 1959.

33 Richard M. Nixon Pre-Presidential Papers, Federal Records Center, Laguna Niguel, California.

34 Film F 124, BGA.

35 K.S. Inglis, 'Sydney, Meet Mr. Graham,' *Nation*, 11 April 1959, 14.

36 Film F 130, BGA.

37 Crusade Bulletin, March 1959.

a very evident leading of the Spirit of God throughout.' The intensity of prayer continued to increase. The opening of the Sydney Crusade was something 'in the nature of a spiritual explosion'.[38] The 10 April 1959 evening of prayer had to be held in 51 centres.

iv. The Church is Revitalised

Four measurable indicators of the Church's revitalisation may be analysed: increased numbers of churchgoers, theological students, and missionaries, and increased Bible reading as measured by membership of the Scripture Union.

Evidence abounds of increased membership of individual churches after the crusades. Lance Shilton, for example, rector of Holy Trinity Adelaide,[39] wrote to Graham in 1962, indicating that 'where there is sympathetic and sincere follow-up by the Church to whom they are referred, the majority [75%] go on to spiritual maturity'.[40] A world record 646 inquirers were referred to Gordon Powell's church, St Stephen's Macquarie Street in Sydney, and 404 were added to Church membership. Two years later a survey revealed that 52% had not missed a communion, 24% had missed a few, and 24% appear to have dropped out.[41] The percentage of survivors (76%) is remarkably similar to Shilton's experience. Did church membership overall rise in Australia after the crusades? Readily available Church membership statistics only give figures for 1956 and 1961. They do show a higher than expected increase between those years. Both Anglican and Presbyterian figures reveal a healthy increase between 1961 and 1966, suggesting that the Crusades had fostered a capacity for evangelism in those denominations. The Methodists, however, peaked in 1961.[42]

The Baptists benefitted most. Graham himself is a Baptist, and Baptists traditionally are enthusiastic about evangelistic campaigns to increase membership. The Baptist percentage of decisions was five time higher than the population average.[43] With about 2% of the population, the Baptists scored 11.6% of the decisions, exactly the same percentage as the Presbyterians who had 10.7% of the population.[44] The Baptists also supplied nearly 30% of counsellors for the

38 Crusade Procedure Book, Sydney, Executive Minutes, 25 March 1959.

39 Collection 245, 2,2, BGA.

40 30 July 1962; Robert O. Ferm Papers, Collection 19 Box 5, folder 47, BGA.

41 'Never before in Human History', *Decision*, May 1984, 20.

42 Based on W. Vamplew, *Australians: Historical Statistics* (Broadway: Fairfax, Syme, and Weldon, 1987), 428–31.

43 F. Alleyne and H. Fallding, 'Decisions at the Graham Crusade in Sydney: A Statistical Analysis', *Journal of Christian Education*, 3.1, 1960, 39.

44 Alleyne and Fallding, 'Decisions at the Graham Crusade', 37, 39 n.5.

Sydney Crusade.[45] The unpublished research of Edward Gibson, one-time President-General of the Baptist Union, shows that up to 1953 a decrease in membership was as likely for Baptist churches as an increase, and that the percentage increase picked up in 1956, peaked in 1959 and 1962, then went into decline until the mid-1970s. Clearly the Billy Graham Crusades did not initiate the improvement in the denomination's membership, but it enabled it to grow even more rapidly in 1959 and to reach its highest rate of growth in 1962. The 1959 Crusades, then, were a very effective form of harvesting and an effective, but short-term, means of Church growth.

Numbers of theological students and missionaries increased dramatically in response to the crusades. In 1969 the Adelaide Bible Institute had a student body of 118, 25% of whom were there because of the 1959 crusades.[46] More than half of the Melbourne Bible Institute's 160 students in 1969 were products of 1959. The first year intake of 44 at Moore College in Sydney in 1960 was the largest in the college's history to that date, and the 1961 total enrolment of 104 students was the peak enrolment before recent years.[47] In 1961 Mary Andrews at Deaconess House surveyed her students about the impact of the Crusade. All said they had either been involved in it or converted at it, except an Indian student from Kerala, and she had participated in Graham's 1956 campaign in India![48] Missionary training received a similar boost. A great number of people who came forward for CMS service were converted at the 1959 Billy Graham Crusade.[49] Jack Dain, Federal Secretary of CMS, 1959–1965, reported that 'Over my years in CMS there was never a single course of candidates among whom there were not Graham converts.'[50]

The crusades' impact on Bible reading was probably enormous. Scripture Union membership in Australia leaped from 58,000 in March 1958 to 104,400 in November 1959.[51] In the weeks which followed the Sydney Crusade, it is reported that 183 Bible Study groups were established in the Central Business District of the city. One of them – led by the Rev Arthur Deane, then vice-principal of SMBC – lasted for a decade.[52] The Bible was again

45 'Billy Graham in Australia,' 56.

46 G. Bingham to Berryman, 12 October 1972, Collection 245, 14, 23, BGA.

47 Bill Lawton, '"That Woman Jezebel" – Moore College after 25 Years', Moore College Library Lecture, 1981, 22,32.

48 Mary Andrews to Stuart Piggin, 5 May 1989.

49 Irene Jeffreys interviewed by Linder, 22 September 1987.

50 A.J. Dain to Berryman, 28 September 1972, CN 245, 14, 23, BGA.

51 John Prince and Moyra Prince, *Tuned in to Change: A History of the Australian Scripture Union 1880–1980* (Sydney: SU Australia, 1979), 166.

52 Letter from Arthur Deane to Stuart Piggin, 16 April 1993.

widely accepted as the Word of God within Protestant churches. Theologians, thanks to Karl Barth's neo-orthodoxy, had begun the move back to the Bible, but Graham's uncompromising proclamation of the Bible as the Word of God strengthened that development.

The Crusade also made the laity more interested in evangelism. 'The rise of small group ministry had its roots in the 1959 Graham Crusade. The counsellor training and follow-up program for the Crusade validated the role of laypeople in the evangelistic and nurturing role of the local church.'[53] When Graham returned in 1968, 69 and again in 1979, the ranks of counsellors were awash with '59ers'. Graham had successfully mobilised evangelicalism's major task force, the laity.

v. Large Numbers are Converted

The 1959 Southern Cross Crusade took in Australia and New Zealand. During the fifteen weeks of the Crusade nearly three and one-quarter million people, or one quarter of the entire population of Australia and New Zealand, attended meetings. Because many people attended the crusade meetings more than once, the total number of individuals who attended would have been less than a quarter of the population. But of those who did attend, 150,000 responded to Graham's invitation to accept Christ. This response rate of 4.6% was more than double the average response rate at Billy Graham crusades world-wide.[54] This included 130,000 Australians, or 1.24% of the entire population. To that point it was the largest, most successful evangelistic campaign in human history. 'Never again will I doubt that the Gospel is the power of God,' wrote Bishop Kerle overawed, 'nor that men's lives can be changed through the foolishness of preaching.'[55] The unprecedented and incomparable national success of the '59 crusades is probably evidence that Australia in reality if not by reputation was one of the most evangelical of the world's nations. In Australia evangelicalism was 'comparatively mainstream'.[56]

Melbourne attendances totalled 719,000 with 26,440 enquirers. That is a response rate of 3.7%. Attendances at the Sydney Crusade totalled 980,000 with 56,780 enquirers, a 5.8% response rate. The crusades in other cities were

53 Judd and Cable, *Sydney Anglicans*, 298.

54 By 1989 Billy Graham Crusades were attended by 100 million and 2 million made public commitments to Christ. By 2005 when Graham retired 215 million had attended his crusades in 185 countries.

55 Crusade Procedure Book, Melbourne, BGA.

56 Hugh Chilton, 'Evangelicals and the End of Christian Australia: Nation and Religion in the Public Square 1959–1979, PhD, University of Sydney', 2014, 190.

taken by associate evangelists with Graham speaking at the final meetings, with results as follows: Perth, 5,396 inquirers and 106,800 in attendance (or 5.1%); in Adelaide, 11,965 and 253,000 (or 4.7%); and in Brisbane 10,661 and 291,000 (or 3.7%).[57] Graham had never known such a response. 'Spiritual hunger is the greatest I have ever known in my ministry,' he said, 'This is the work of the Holy Spirit.'[58]

vi. The Reduction of Sinful Practices in the Wider Community

The great revivals of the past have raised community standards, sometimes eliminating temporarily whole areas of criminal practice and immorality. At first sight it looks unlikely that the 1959 Crusades would have done that. Only 25% of decisions made at the Sydney Crusade, for example, were made by the unchurched. Only 5.5% were from so-called depressed residential areas and only 7.5% of those who were employed were in labouring or manual jobs.[59] At first glance the statistics show that all the crime indices except drunkenness[60] rose dramatically in the 1950s, suggesting that the frequently-voiced expressions of fear about juvenile delinquency and moral declension had some basis in fact. Then, in the 1960s, the indices rose even more steeply, suggesting at first sight that the Crusades had no quantitative impact on the community's standards.

Yet anecdotal evidence of such impact is plentiful and colourful. The *Sunday Mirror* which appeared the Sunday after the final meeting of the Sydney Crusade includes an article headed, 'THUG GIVES UP REVOLVER Burglar hands over tool-kit', in which magistrate A.E. Debenham claimed that 'The Billy Graham Crusade has cut crime in Sydney by an estimated 50 per cent'. This claim was accompanied by stories of a safebreaker handing the instruments of his trade to one flabbergasted counsellor, a gunman surrendering his revolver to another, businesses were reporting an epidemic of repayments of bad debts, while Church attendance in King's Cross, Sydney's red-light district, had risen to record heights. A keen Anglican all his long life, Debenham went to every Crusade meeting. The nature of his work involved protracted interviews with people brought before the courts. He did not

57 Report of the Billy Graham Crusades in Australia and New Zealand, 1959 (unpaginated), BGA.

58 Stuart Piggin, *Faith of Steel* (Wollongong: University of Wollongong, 1984), 242.

59 Alleyne and Fallding, 'Decisions at the Graham Crusade', 34–39.

60 S. K. Mukherjee, *Crime Trends in Twentieth-Century Australia* (Sydney: Australian Institute of Criminology & George Allen and Unwin, 1981), 82–84. Drunkenness offences in Australia peaked in 1951 and then declined throughout the 1950s and 1960s.

hesitate to probe their spiritual condition, and on the basis of such intimate discussions, he concluded that Billy Graham was having a deep impact on the human psyche in Sydney.[61] Many a dormant conscience was awakened. A young woman confessed to her university that she had obtained her degree through cheating. A bank employee informed a bank official that he had embezzled a small sum of money. Expecting to be dismissed, he was the means instead of the official's going to the crusade where he, too, was converted.[62] Billy's searching preaching even uncovered a spy! Frances Bernie, a member of the Communist Party during World War II and who worked in Dr Evatt's office in Canberra in the early 1950s, had been under investigation for passing on secrets to Russian Communists. In 1953 she professed to make a full confession to ASIO, but following the 1959 Graham Crusade, she contacted ASIO to make a yet fuller confession and 'clean' her 'troubled conscience'.[63]

Such copious anecdotes were an encouragement to look harder at the crime statistics. The number of convictions for all crimes committed in Australia doubled between 1920 and 1950 and then doubled again between 1950 and 1959 when the population increased by only one-quarter.[64] Then, in 1960, 1961, and 1962, the number of convictions remained fairly constant, resuming its dramatic upward trend in the middle and late 1960s.[65] Something which occurred at the same time as the Billy Graham Crusades slowed, even stopped, the further decline into criminality of community behaviour. The illegitimate birth-rate and the per capita consumption of alcohol give other rough indexes to non-criminal community standards. Again one is at first struck by the gigantic changes in behaviour which overtook Australian society in the later 1950s and 1960s. Ex-nuptial births as a proportion of total births fell in the 1940s and early 1950s to an historic low of about 3.9 per hundred. They then began to climb fiercely in the middle and late 1950s, heralding the permissive 1960s. In the period 1955 to 1965 this index rose every year to almost double the 1954 figure, but the year it rose slowest (.06%) was in 1960.[66] The illegitimate children not conceived in 1959 were not born in

---

61 Telephone conversation with Mr. and Mrs. A.E. Debenham, 18 May 1989.

62 *Decision Magazine*, June 1962, 13.

63 Desmond Hall and David Horner, *Breaking the Codes* (St Leonards: Allen & Unwin, 1998), 319.

64 The population increased by a steady rate of about 200,000 per year throughout the 1950s. See *Demography*, 1965, *Bulletin* No.83 (Commonwealth Bureau of Census and Statistics, Canberra, 1966), 4.

65 See S.K. Mukherjee et. al., *Source Book of Australian Criminal and Social Statistics, 1900–1980* (Canberra: Australian Institute of Criminology, 1981).

66 *Demography*, 1965, 80.

1960! Turning to alcohol consumption, Bureau of Statistics biannual figures show that, contrary to trends, the alcohol consumption for 1960–61 was 10% lower than the 1958–59 figure.

The unique global celebrity status of Billy Graham has been attributed to many factors, including the coinciding of his ministry with the advent of television.[67] Televangelism has not proved a guaranteed route to respectability, however. Graham's own character and the professionalism of his team were major factors. The most obvious factor is that he was superb at doing what evangelicals prize most highly: preaching. Can the identifiable changes in social behaviour in Australia in 1959 be attributed to the content of Graham's preaching? It was undoubtedly remarkably powerful, effective preaching. His oratorical powers have been compared with the hypnotic mesmerising of Hitler. But an analysis of the homiletics of his Australian crusades reveals no such pyrotechnics. His sermons were far from emotional rants. To today's observer they are surprisingly rational and systematic. He sought five outcomes in every sermon: comprehension, conviction, confession, cleansing, and calling. Graham first addressed the mind, in the interests of comprehension or understanding. He argued that humans are sinners in need of God and that God's response to the need was the cross of Christ. He then preached the law of God to bring the sinner under conviction. Here the appeal to the mind led to an effect on the emotions, since the mind and heart together must respond to God. Then, having worked through the comprehension and conviction phases, he made his appeal to come forward in response to the invitation to receive Christ. This invitation to make a public confession was really an appeal to the will – his hearers had to *do* something: they had to decide. To any who made a public confession, Graham affirmed that God responds with cleansing (forgiveness) and calling (to a life of self-sacrifice, purpose and destiny). A typical Graham sermon was a reproach to conservative evangelical preachers who never went beyond the first step of addressing the mind, and to more emotional preachers who ignored it.

Graham's preaching became the accepted model for the evangelistic sermon. Apart from addressing the mind, heart and will, other factors may explain Graham's effectiveness as a preacher. He preached from the Bible, accepting it as the Word of God, giving him confidence and authority. This meant his perspective was biblical, and he preached on such unpopular things as hell, the work of the Holy Spirit in convicting and converting, the absolute necessity of

---

67 Brian Stanley, *The Global Diffusion of Evangelicalism: The Age of Billy Graham and John Stott* (Downers Grove, Illinois: IVP Academic, 2013), 65–72.

prayer in any successful enterprise for God. He preached the Gospel, accepting the fact that it is foolishness to those who are perishing. He called for decision, explaining why it must be now and why it must be made publicly. He spoke in short, simple, energetic sentences: neither the sentence construction nor the argument is convoluted. He preached for revival. He preached for engagement. He spoke of the world's problems, then the individual's problems, and then of the cross as the solution to those problems. He paid careful attention to what he considered concerned Australians: the delinquency of youth; the keys to happy marriage and family life; the fear of atomic war. He thus made every sermon situational, occasional, relevant. The content of his preaching in 1959 was at least in alignment with behavioural changes in Australia. At the last meeting of the Melbourne Crusade, when a record 143,000 piled into the Melbourne Cricket Ground, Graham preached on the Second Coming of Christ. His words exemplified all of the above:

> 'Occupy until I come.' Don't just say, 'I'm going to sit down and wait for his coming.' No. That's sin against God. That's displeasing to God. Go back to your school. Go back to your home. Go back to your church. Go back to your social obligations. Work, as you have never worked. 'Occupy until I come.' Go down among the people. Help the poor. Love your neighbour, no matter what race he may be. Give food for the hungry. Get involved in the world in which we are living as a light and shining testimony for Christ.'[68]

By all the indicators accessible to the historian, then, revival did come to Australia in 1959. What has become clear in retrospect, however, was that the 1959 Billy Graham crusade was a peak achievement of the evangelical movement in Australia, rather than the harbinger of a brilliant new period of achievement for it.

Initiatives of the Mainline Denominations

There were signs of weakness among Protestant denominations in the immediate post-war decades, although over-all they appeared to be making small gains. Archbishop Mowll's vision was not only for his diocese, nor even for Australia. His strategy was missions to the East and to the young: he had been a missionary bishop in China and had been involved in student youth ministry in Canada. The key was Moore College to send out the missionaries

---

68 Film 130, 15 March 1959, BGA.

and the Youth Department to reach the youth. Evangelicalism is not above hero-worship, and Mowll's after-glow reaches into the present. This 'initiating Father-in-God' still represents the evangelical ideal of the consecrated life, made up of activism, orthodoxy, and holiness of life.

In Melbourne the evangelical cause did not prosper among Anglicans. Frank Woods was appointed Archbishop in 1957 by Geoffrey Fisher, Archbishop of Canterbury. Woods was reputedly of evangelical lineage, but Fisher hoped he would teach the church in Australia how to be Church of England, not rock bottom Protestant like Sydney or Anglo-Catholic like Adelaide and Brisbane.[69] Woods endeavoured to break down the isolation of parties by the doubtful means of placing evangelical curates with Anglo-Catholic incumbents. He also succeeded in achieving the right to appoint the clergyman every third time a Melbourne parish became vacant. At St John's Camberwell, which had been an evangelical parish, there were vestments and incense within a year of the adoption of the new policy. As a result, in Peter Adam's estimate, over sixty of Melbourne's parishes changed their churchmanship from evangelical to liberal Catholic, in the forty years following 1950.[70]

If the tide of evangelicalism in Melbourne and the Australia-wide Anglican church had been receding, it came in a little in 1965 with the election of Clive Kerle, co-adjutor bishop of Sydney, as Bishop of Armidale. Kerle was irenic and revered, but, to bring the diocese back into the evangelical fold, he joined forces with the outspoken and uncompromising preacher and evangelist, John Chapman ('Chappo'), who had been Youth Director of the diocese since 1960. Kerle was patient and, while he was careful never to appoint a clergyman to a parish with whom the people did not believe they could work, he did appoint evangelical clergy wherever he could. In the process, he reduced the average age of the clergy by 25 years and ensured that the diocese was changed from one Anglo-Catholic at its core to an evangelical 'satellite' of the Diocese of Sydney.

Post World War II Methodism manifested much vigour. It had become the third largest religious denomination in Australia ahead of Presbyterianism. Its congregations grew, some of them exponentially, such as Pirie Street Methodist Church in Adelaide, where women outnumbered men by almost three to one. Methodist youth work also grew, both Crusaders and Christian Endeavour. In Sydney the Methodists were ably led by Frank Rayward, superintendent

69 Ruth Frappell, et. al., *Anglicans in the Antipodes* (Westport, Connecticut: Greenwood Press, 1999), 327.

70 Peter Adam to the authors, 2 May 1990. In recent decades, however, the tide has flowed back in the evangelical direction.

of the Wesley Central Methodist Mission. Rayward, along with Walker, had stood out against the liberalising leaven of Samuel Angus. At the Methodist Ladies' College in Melbourne, the saintly A. Harold Wood, passionate for social justice as for souls, was principal for twenty-seven years from 1939, producing generations of citizens eager to serve.[71] But, while institutional Methodism prospered, the spirit of Wesley himself, so evident in Wood, no longer suffused the denomination as a whole: the spark of revival lit fewer fires among the working classes. It felt like its greatest moment in history had passed.[72]

The Congregationalists who had outshone the Baptists in nineteenth-century Australia had now slipped a long way behind them – white-anted by theological liberalism is the usual explanation. But the Congregationalists were Independents, and the independent-minded were quite capable of establishing pockets of evangelical vitality. In the Sydney suburb of Padstow, for example, Joseph Watt from northern Ireland was the secretary of the Independent Church, the first church to be established in the suburb. Watt's wife was suspicious of hymn-singing, and their son George, intense, serious and very encouraging of conservative evangelical missionary work, became the dominant force in the church after his father. George Watt's sister, Gertie, married a Hathaway, a poultry farmer, and their daughter, Margaret, is the mother of Ian Thorpe, the Olympic swimmer. By 1950 missionaries from the Padstow church had served in Africa, among the Aboriginal people of the Warburton Ranges in Western Australia and in the Solomon Islands. The church joined the Congregational Union in 1954. It chief ministry was its Sunday School with 120 members in the mid-50s and the Christian Endeavour work among the children of the district which, with the adjacent suburb of Revesby, became a working-class Bible belt. But such evangelical enclaves were becoming rarer in Congregationalism.[73]

Initiatives of New Denominations

In the environment of the post-war resurgence in Calvinistic Reformed theology, the Dutch Reformed Church in Australia was warmly welcomed by

---

71 Jane McCalman, *Journeyings: The Biography of a Middle-Class Generation, 1920–1990*, (Carlton: MUP, 1993), 105, 283; Ian Breward, *Dr Harold Wood: A Notable Methodist* (Melbourne: Uniting Academic Press, 2013).

72 McCalman, *Journeyings*, 37.

73 For a personal account of disenchantment with Protestant orthodoxy by a Congregationalist, see Maynard Davies, *Beyond My Grasp* (Sydney: Alpha Books, 1978).

conservative evangelicals as a worthy denomination and part of the evangelical family. Created by immigrants to Australia from war-ravaged Holland, it was well placed to strengthen the family ties, and was soon to become known as the Christian Reformed Churches.[74] In 1962 the Reformed Church of Australia at Kingston, Tasmania, opened the first parent-controlled Christian school in the tradition of Abraham Kuyper, the Dutch Calvinist scholar.

A number of American holiness churches were established in Australia in the early years after the war. Precisely because they were American and Arminian and perfectionist they were made to feel as if they were unworthy sects and so were not at first welcome in the family. These churches include the Wesleyan Methodist Church,[75] which struggled to establish its reputation as a respectable member of the evangelical family. It helped that George Beverley Shea, the much-loved soloist at Billy Graham crusades, was a member of the Wesleyan Methodist Church. But opposition from Reformed evangelicals left Holiness leaders sometimes feeling that they would do better to make common cause with Pentecostals:

> These evangelical leaders are good men, and do work hard for the Kingdom, but are absolutely opposed to entire sanctification, and they find it hard to recognize us as an evangelical group. Because of this being 'set off' by other evangelicals, it is easier for some among us to find 'fellow feeling' with the Pentecostals.[76]

Migrants enriched the mix. From Southern Italy and Sicily came many impoverished migrants, and they were not all Roman Catholics. Some were Pentecostals who in Italy had come to outnumber the evangelicals. In Australia their separate identity from other evangelicals was reinforced by the fact that they did not speak English with any facility. It was essential for them to have their own churches where Italian was spoken. In Sydney, they established the Punchbowl Italian Assemblies (sic) of God Church. Their

---

74 J.W. Deenick (ed.), *A Church en Route* (Geelong: Reformed Churches Publishing House, 1991).

75 Don Hardgrave, *For Such a Time: A History of the Wesleyan Methodist Church in Australia* (MacGregor: A Pleasant Surprise Ltd, 1988); Glen O'Brien, 'North American Wesleyan-Holiness Churches in Australia', PhD, La Trobe University, 2005; Glen O'Brien, 'Anti-Americanism and the Wesleyan-Holiness Churches in Australia', *The Journal of Ecclesiastical History*, 61.2, 2010, 314–343.

76 Leo G. Cox, letter to the *Wesleyan Witness*, 29 December 1951 (Indianapolis, Indiana, Wesleyan Archives). Quoted in O'Brien, 'North American Wesleyan-Holiness Churches in Australia', 169.

historian, Mark Hutchinson, argues that as a living faith, Pentecostalism made the hard lives of migrants bearable and meaningful.[77]

Wondrous developments were also found in occasional Aboriginal congregations. John Blacket of Khesed ministries in 2013 released a DVD entitled 'A Pocket of Fire' where all the talking heads are indigenous people. They tell the remarkable story of a little Assembly of God church established in the 1930s at Pinnacle Pocket near Atherton in Queensland. It was started by a Mr Coulter, who had come to farm there, having experienced the Welsh Revival. In 1959, this church at Pinnacle Pocket was handed over to an Aboriginal Pastor, Sterling Minniecon, and, according to Blacket's research, the church has produced more than forty Aboriginal evangelists. Among the most effective of them have been Sterling's own sons – Ray and Rodney. Ray was to become so disenchanted with the racism that he suffered within the church, seemingly still wearing colonial blinkers, that he gave it all away for a time. But for many Indigenous people the church was the only hope, and Ray says that what brought him back into faith and ministry was his heritage from Pinnacle Pocket which was 'like heaven'. He was taught there to worship and love God, a heritage from a revived church which made an indelible impression on him and, through him, on many thousands of Indigenous people.

Overseas and Aboriginal Missions

The period immediately after World War II covered the sesquicentenary of the modern missionary movement from Britain. It now reached a watershed in its history. The post-colonial era required foreign missionaries to hand over to nationals responsibility particularly for church growth and education. There were three major developments. First, the home base for cross-cultural ministries was strengthened and missionary policies were adjusted to the contexts of a new world. Second, Australian evangelical leaders responded to the closing by the Communists of China to missionary activity in 1949 by redirecting their resources and personnel to new areas, especially in Asia. Third, because the end of World War II coincided with the end of European empires, Christian missions, especially in Africa and India, had to operate in a post-colonial world calling for indigenous leadership.

The Anglican CMS illustrates all three developments. In 1945 the General Synod of the Church of England appointed the Anglican Missionary Council (AMC) to co-ordinate missionary work apart from home missions. The

77 Mark Hutchinson, *Pellegrini: An Italian Protestant Community in Sydney, 1958–1990* (Sydney: APS, 1999), 67.

Council was composed of equal numbers of representatives from CMS and ABM. The response of the South Australian branch of CMS was typical. It maintained a vigilant eye on AMC policies to ensure that the CMS lost none of its distinctive character in the process. In 1960 Irene Jeffreys, the SA branch's long-serving lay General Secretary was appointed by the CMS Federal Council to serve on the AMC. She was an outstanding missionary strategist, progressive in her thinking, and she channelled the best of CMS thinking into the AMC.

Much of the spiritual vitality of CMS in this period continued to come from the League of Youth, which had been formed in 1927. From 1948 the League held annual interstate conferences which attracted Leaguers from all States. It was a major opportunity for CMS to recruit missionaries, and many who attended testified to having their lives transformed by the Holy Spirit.[78] This was a sign that Keswick spirituality was still in this period considered essential to missionary vigour. Andrew Murray's reflection on CMS and spiritual motivation[79] was important to the Rev Geoffrey Fletcher, General Secretary of the NSW CMS from 1954 to 1964. He said that the 1954 Summer School was disappointing, so he decided to tie the Summer School to Keswick for purposes of inspiration, and later reported that the application of Keswick to CMS Summer School was 'the turning of the tide'. He recalled that the Summer School at which Geoffrey Bingham spoke was 'marvellous'.[80]

With the coming to power of the Communists in 1949 Christian missionaries were soon expelled from China. It looked and felt like the end of an era. In that same year, Amy Oxley Wilkinson, of the Marsden, Hassall and Oxley dynasties, died. She had worked in China with CMS from 1896 until 1920 running a school for blind boys. So remarkable had her work been for innovation and service that she had been awarded the 'Order of the Golden Grain', China's highest honour for a foreigner and only the second ever awarded to a Westerner.[81] How would China and indeed, the Christian faith, fare now that missionaries were expelled? Their work in China finished, the Australian missionaries were redirected to work in India, Pakistan, Ceylon, Malaya and Singapore, while some were redeployed at home. Mary

78 R.V. Davis, *A History of the Church Missionary Society of Australia, SA Branch, including WA, 1910–1960* (Adelaide: CMS, 1960), 59, 60.

79 Andrew Murray, *The Church Missionary Society and the deepening of the spiritual life* (Sydney: CMS, n.d.).

80 Geoffrey Fletcher, interviewed by Margaret Lamb,16 November 1989.

81 Linda and Robert Banks, *They shall see his Face: The Story of Amy Oxley Wilkinson and her Visionary Blind School in China* (Sydney: Acorn Press, 2017), 118.

Andrews, for example, was made principal of Deaconess House in Sydney. Neither she nor Archbishop Mowll, who appointed her and who had himself been a bishop in China, lost their enthusiasm for the conversion of China. In 1953 Mowll realised a long-held ambition by launching an appeal through both CMS and the ABM to send missionaries to South East Asia. In 1956 he was able to visit China.

In Tanganyika, for which CMS Australia had accepted responsibility in 1927, Alfred Stanway became Bishop in 1950. He was an indefatigable organiser – he needed to be. The education system in post-colonial Tanganyika was then expanding dramatically through grants-in-aid to all church primary, middle and secondary schools which conformed to approved standards. Churches too multiplied at the rate of one a week in the 1950s. Stanway agreed that Africans themselves now had to be given more responsibility. Parishes were organised into rural deaneries which provided a training ground for African leadership. Bishop George Chambers (see chapter 5) had started in 1927 with two African clergy; by 1960 Stanway had eighty-two. On 15 May 1955 Yohanna Omari was consecrated as the first African Bishop of the Diocese of Central Tanganyika. In 1959, together with Assistant Bishop, Festo Kivengere, he visited Australia, and both were hailed as living evidence of the effectiveness of Christian missions. In July 1959 Lance Shilton, who was then chairman of the SA branch of CMS, accompanied Kivengere on a tour of Aboriginal missions in Northern Australia. He observed that Aboriginal people were far more at home with Kivengere than they were with whites, and his revival experience in East Africa breathed on the smoking flax of the Indigenous in Australia.[82]

By 1960 CMS Australia supported 216 missionaries in 13 countries, including 71 in Tanganyika. But the largest single contingent of CMS missionaries (78) was to Aboriginal missions in the Northern Territory. It was claimed in 1963 that 'the proportion of missionary personnel [working with all missionary societies] to the native population is one in fifteen, surely making the north of Australia the most intensive and concentrated missionary field in the world!'[83]

In 1959 the major Christian missions, meeting in the National Missionary Council of Australia, adopted an agreed policy on Aboriginal people, urging that all existing reserves be retained for Aboriginal use and ownership. In 1963 the National Missionary Council insisted that assimilation was to be a strictly voluntary process – it was not to be forced on Aboriginal people – and

82 Colin Reid, *Walking in the light: reflections on the East Africa revival and its link to Australia* (Melbourne: Acorn Press, 2007).

83 Stuart Babbage, 'Evangelicals in the Church in Australia,' *Churchman,* 77, June, 1963, 117.

the Council acknowledged that the greatest obstacle to progress in relations between Aborigines and whites was land: 'It must never be forgotten that, for the most part, Australia was taken from the Aboriginal people by force without payment or compensation, or recognition of their inherent title to the land.'[84]

Consistent with this conviction, CMS in 1963 took out a mining right on behalf of the Aboriginal people of Groote Eylandt. CMS established the Groote Eylandt Aboriginal Trust into which they paid all royalties which soon exceeded $1 million annually. Only Aboriginal people had voting rights on the Trust, and CMS took nothing for itself. 'It is difficult to see how CMS could have done better.'[85] On the other hand, the Methodist Mission at Yirrkala in Arnhem Land could have done a lot better when it sold out to the mining company and sacked its protesting superintendent, Edgar Wells.[86] But Wells succeeded in mounting a petition to have Indigenous people granted land rights.[87] It took too long (three decades) for the petition to be granted, and by then the missionary contribution to this basic right was easily forgotten and overlooked.

Another vexing issue was the lack of progress in the translation of Scriptures into Aboriginal languages, in embarrassing contrast with the plethora of Bible translations in other parts of the world. During World War II, CMS missionary at Oenpelli, Nell Harris, translated Mark's Gospel into Gunwinggu, and CMS chaplain in Groote Eylandt, Len Harris, translated Mark and the Letter of James into Wubuy. But, instead of portending a golden age of Scripture translation, these initiatives came to nothing as 'the CMS did not care enough'.[88] When it did care enough in the 1960s to give missionary Judith Stokes freedom to devote herself to the ambitious project of translating the Scriptures into Anindilyakwa, the main Aboriginal language of Groote Eylandt, the frustrations were both unanticipated and legion. It was not a project welcomed by many of the Indigenous people themselves: they did not necessarily want their language 'reduced' to writing; they preferred the missionaries to teach them English; they appeared to favour using their language as a shield against the incursion of missionaries rather than as a means

---

84 *Four Major Issues in Assimilation: a Memorandum* (Sydney: National Missionary Council of Australia, June 1963).

85 John Harris, 'Anglicanism and Indigenous Peoples,' in Bruce Norman Kaye, Colin Holden, Geoffrey R. Treloar, and T.R. Frame, *Anglicanism in Australia: A History* (Carlton: Melbourne University Press, 2002), 240.

86 Harris, *One Blood*, 803–817.

87 Kirstie Close-Barry, 'Transporting concepts of Indigenous land rights between Fiji and Australia's North,' paper read at Colonial Christian Missions and their Legacies conference, Copenhagen, 28 April 2015.

88 Harris, *We wish we'd done more*, 36.

of communication with them.[89] Stokes enjoyed more success in translating hymns into Anindilyakwa. It was the highlight of her career, Stokes said, when Danabana and other Aboriginal women wrote a significant collection of hymns in Anindilyakwa.[90] Through such hard-won experiences, missionaries came to the realisation that cross-cultural mission was not a one-way street. Cultural exchange required mutuality, including respectful reflection on the possibility of authentic spirituality in 'ceremony' and 'the dreaming'.[91]

Baptists in this period both allowed for the indigenisation of its oldest missions in India and created new cross-cultural missions. A new work in New Guinea proved to be very successful. In India, the only country where Australian Baptist missionaries worked before World War II, the most dramatic changes were experienced. Following the partition of India in 1947, Australian Baptists worked among the Boro and Garo tribespeople in Assam, insisting that there was to be no Baptist mission work independent of the native church, a far-sighted acceptance of what missions had to be in a post-colonial world. Within a few years both the Boro and Garo churches, answering not to the missionaries but to indigenous Baptist Unions, were reporting dramatic expansion both numerically and financially. Typically, the indigenous churches conducted their own evangelism and built their own churches and schools; the missionaries chiefly did medical work. By 1970 all the Australian missionaries had left Assam, but the ABMS continued to support the work financially and with scholarships to ensure ongoing leadership training and with partnerships and ongoing visits born of friendship. By 2000 there were over four million Christians in North East India. It had become the 'Bible-belt' of Asia,[92] one of the finest fruits of Australian evangelical Christianity.

* * *

Evangelicalism's commitment to mission in post-World War II Australia facilitated some surprisingly successful evangelistic enterprises. The marriage

89 Laura Rademaker, *Found in Translation: Many Meanings on a North Australian Mission* (Honolulu: University of Hawai'i Press, 2018), 109, 116–126.

90 Rademaker, *Found in Translation*, 159.

91 Rademaker, *Found in Translation*, 174–5.

92 Tony Cupit, Ros Gooden and Ken Manley (editors), *From Five Barley Loaves: Australian Baptists in Global Mission, 1864–2010* (Preston: Mosaic Press, 2013), chapter 6; Richard Pierard, 'The Missionary Origins of the Bengal-Orissa-Bihar Baptist Churches Association,' *American Baptist Quarterly* 29, 2010, 31–45.

of Keswick-inspired spirituality with Reformed theology under Bingham fermented revival; Alan Walker's addressing national as well as individual needs kept alive the hope for a Christian Australia; Billy Graham's faith in the authority of the Bible, taught in the prayerful expectation of revival, revitalised the Australian church. The evangelical movement in Australia was now clearer than ever about what the Gospel said and how it was to be communicated for the salvation of souls, but it now prized clarity above peace, and thinking above feeling.

Chapter Ten

THE 'REWORKED PARADIGM'

Reformed Evangelicalism, 1946–1965

'A confident intellectualism expressive of a robust faith in God, whose Word is truth, is part of the evangelical tradition.'
(J.I. Packer)

The most distinctive development in international and Australian evangelicalism in the decades following World War II was theological: the construction of a much stronger intellectual case for the historical, philosophical and psychological truth of the Gospel. It was a development which owed more to Britain than to America. Although American evangelicalism after World War II started to have an observable influence on the shape of Australian evangelicalism, that was not as comprehensive nor as rapid as might be supposed. By this time, in any case, American evangelicalism was not what it had been in the 1920s. Its fundamentalism was no longer either dominant or unchallenged. In 1942 the National Association of Evangelicals was formed in the USA under the leadership of Harold J. Ockenga. He coined the term 'the new evangelicalism' to identify the movement and insulate it from the negative connotations which had come to characterise fundamentalism. It was Billy Graham who, contrary to the stereotyping of his critics, effectively led the campaign against both fundamentalism and revivalism and forged a new evangelicalism which enjoyed unprecedented evangelistic success.[1]

In Australia (as in Britain), American 'new evangelicalism' was not needed because the old evangelicalism had not gone so fundamentalist as in America.

1 Robert D. Putnam and David E. Campbell, *American Grace: How Religion Divides and Unites Us* (New York: Simon & Schuster, 2010), 82–90.

Australian evangelicals had not been sidetracked into attacks on evolution or the defence of premillennialism, and unlike the fundamentalists, were open to seeking support from the greatest of the English-speaking defenders of the faith: Reinhold Niebuhr, William Temple, T.S. Eliot, C.S. Lewis, John Baillie, and G.K. Chesterton, none of whom was an evangelical.[2] In Australia, post-war evangelicalism then continued to champion the Bible, but not in the anti-intellectual, closed-minded way attributed (often unfairly) to earlier American fundamentalists.

The Resurgence and Reconstruction of Reformed Theology

While fundamentalism was on the way out in America, in Britain conservative, Reformed theology in the Puritan tradition was on the way back. Its critics saddled it with the label of 'fundamentalism', but it was a different beast from the American species, and it was the British reconstruction of evangelicalism which chiefly influenced Australia. After World War II it was surmised that liberal evangelicals, such as Max Warren and Stephen Neill, would assume control of the evangelical movement in Britain. But in fact a new group of conservative evangelicals outflanked them: E.J.H. Nash ('Bash'), who reached 'top boys from top schools'; Martin Lloyd-Jones, the preacher; J.I. Packer, the theologian; and John Stott, the preacher/teacher. In 1950 the Westminster Conference was founded by Packer, Raymond Johnston and Martin Lloyd-Jones. The last saw this as a sign of revival in Britain and laid down its parameters: seventeenth-century Puritan theology combined with that of the eighteenth-century founders of evangelicalism – Whitefield, Howell Harris and Jonathan Edwards. Thus it was Lloyd-Jones who reintroduced evangelicalism to the Reformed theology which had been 'almost snapped off in the late nineteenth century, when Spurgeon seemed to lose to the rising tide of liberalism in the "downgrade" controversy.'[3] American fundamentalism made no contribution to the reconstruction of evangelicalism in Australia in the 1950s, but the theology of the Westminster Fellowship did.

An even greater contributor to the reshaping of Australian evangelicalism was John Stott, who a Catholic historian contended 'must be accounted one

---

2 Cornelius Van Til, *The New Modernism* (Philadelphia: Presbyterian and Reformed Publishing Company, 1947).

3 Christopher Catherwood, *Martin Lloyd Jones: Chosen by God* (Crowborough: Highland Books, 1986), 128.

of the most influential figures in the Christian world'.[4] Stott's success at All Souls, Langham Place, in central London, was due to his presentation of a clear message along with a willingness to interact with the broader culture and some of its values. Stott was neither world-denying nor anti-modern. He was a warm supporter of Billy Graham, unlike his older contemporary, Martin Lloyd-Jones. If, with help from Lloyd-Jones, evangelicals were identifying their differences from liberalism, from Stott, they were clarifying their differences from fundamentalism and emotional pietism. It was a product which Australian evangelicals bought. Archbishop Mowll invited Stott to become a coadjutor bishop of Sydney in 1956. Stott declined, but he did visit Australia in 1958, preaching to packed congregations in cathedrals and the main city churches of other denominations and to large crowds at university missions. His 1958 Sydney University mission became legendary in the annals of the Evangelical Union. The response to the Gospel in the reputedly secular nation was remarkable, anticipating the tsunami of spiritual commitment which accompanied the Billy Graham crusades in the following year. It was in 1958, too, that *Basic Christianity*, Stott's best-known book, was published. The most popular title of the Inter-Varsity Press, it is rational yet appealing to the heart, an exposition of evangelical faith as attractive as it is authoritative. In Australia, Stott had become easily the most revered of evangelical preachers. Not surprisingly, on the death of Mowll, later in 1958, he was nominated for election as Archbishop of Sydney. But he was always a reluctant starter for episcopal rank and he let his nominators know that he would be unlikely to accept if offered the position.[5] He never did become a bishop, but he was well on the way to becoming the leading Anglican international evangelical of his day. He had no appetite for ecclesiastical politics, but more than any other evangelical leader his prestige and clarity of thought ensured that another generation of evangelicals would understand that the Gospel meant they must attend to bodies and minds as well as souls and the national soul as well as the individual soul.

In 1961 the Evangelical Fellowship of Anglican Communion (EFAC) was formed at the behest of John Stott and Marcus Loane, then an assistant Bishop to Hugh Gough, Archbishop of Sydney. Stott recalls that EFAC began in correspondence between himself and Gough. As Gough was then the most senior Anglican Bishop, Stott felt that he was the obvious person

4 Adrian Hastings, *A History of English Christianity, 1920–1985* (London: Collins, 1986), 455.

5 Timothy Dudley-Smith, *John Stott: The Making of a Leader* (Leicester: InterVarsity, 2001), 321–326; 398–408.

with whom to canvass the creation of an international evangelical fellowship. At the 1958 Lambeth Conference, Marcus Loane, representing Howard Mowll, had felt a great sense of isolation as he battled for the evangelical cause. The Church Union paraded its Anglo-Catholic bishops in triumphal procession around the Albert Hall. There was no comparable organisation to bring evangelical bishops together. That struck John Stott as a great tragedy.

The formation of EFAC provoked the criticism that this was to institutionalise pan-evangelicalism, a world-wide evangelical Anglicanism, which was no better than pan-Anglicanism. Stott's defence against this charge accurately revealed the thinking of those who put evangelicalism first and Anglicanism second, a perennial issue. Anglicanism, argued Stott, is 'largely an historical phenomenon', the death of which in any part of the world would not be a matter of regret, whereas evangelicalism is 'a theological heritage', witnessing to 'Biblical truth as unchanging divine revelation'.[6] Clearly, Stott saw nothing wrong with pan-evangelicalism and was in effect its mastermind and spiritual and theological leader. Ironically, as the British Empire dissolved after World War II, the Church of England evolved into the World-wide Anglican Communion with two parties: pan-Anglicanism and pan-evangelicalism.[7] The long-term fruit of this was the holding in 2008 of GAFCON, the Global Anglican Future Conference, which was a meeting of conservative evangelical Anglican churches ranged over against the diversity of Anglicans who met at Lambeth under the Archbishop of Canterbury.

Work among Students

The new academic rigour in the evangelical movement at the end of the Second World War strengthened theological and Bible colleges and increased the appeal of evangelical Christianity to university students. At the University of Melbourne, the Student Christian Movement, then engaged in much social activism and known as the Labor Party at prayer, was actually larger than the Evangelical Union, which had been weakened by the War. But by 1949 that was no longer true, and in 1951 Canon Bryan Green, an Anglican evangelist from Birmingham, reinforced the ascendency of EU when he twice conducted missions in Melbourne. *Time* magazine hailed him as Britain's 'Billy Graham',

6 Timothy Dudley-Smith, *John Stott: A Global Ministry* (Leicester: InterVarsity, 2001), 52.

7 Stuart Piggin, 'Australian Anglicanism in World-Wide Context,' in Bruce Norman Kaye, Colin Holden, Geoffrey R. Treloar, and T. R. Frame, *Anglicanism in Australia: A History* (Carlton: MUP, 2002), 200–222.

but his reputation as a highly effective evangelist dates back to the 1920s. He had been the chief instrument in the conversion of Howard Guinness whom, for good measure, he had won over to evangelical Anglicanism. Green's Moorhouse Lectures in Melbourne in 1951 were published as *The Practice of Evangelism* and widely read. In the competition between EU and SCM, for competition it was, Green well and truly tipped the balance in favour of the EU. Apparently it did not hurt, according to a young woman and an SCMer in 1951, that Green was strikingly handsome.

Much of the scholarship foundational to the reinvigorated evangelical movement was conducted through the Inter-Varsity Fellowship,[8] and it was through the IVF that Australian evangelicals made a significant contribution to this renaissance.[9] The IVF had been formed in the UK in 1928 and in 1938 appointed its own Biblical Research Committee, followed in 1944 by the opening of the Tyndale House for Biblical Research in Cambridge. Eminent Brethren New Testament scholar F.F. Bruce observed in 1980 that at that date about 25–30 scholars associated with the Tyndale Fellowship were working in British Universities.[10] An effect of this scholarship was that the locus of evangelical enterprise moved from the heart to the mind.[11]

From 1953 to 1961 the Australian IVF was imaginatively led by Pennsylvania-born Charles Troutman. Along with a million other Americans, he had been in Australia during the War. Dr. John A. Thompson, a Baptist Old Testament scholar and Director of the Australian Institute of Archaeology, which specialised in biblical archaeology (later Reader in the Department of Middle Eastern Studies at Melbourne University), was in touch with Troutman before his return to Australia, keeping him informed of the Institute's publications.[12] Thompson explained to Troutman:

---

8 Derek Tidball, 'Post-war evangelical theology: a generational perspective,' *Evangelical Quarterly*, 81.2, 2009, 145–160.

9 Between 1943 and 1964 the IVF through the Tyndale Press published at least 47 academic monographs. Four of them were by young Australian authors destined to make a big impact in Australia: Alan Cole, *The New Temple. A Study in the Origins of the Catechetical 'Form' of the Church in the New Testament* (London: Tyndale Press, 1950); Leon Morris, *The Biblical Doctrine of Judgement* (London: Tyndale Press, 1960); Leon Morris, *The Wages of Sin. An Examination of the New Testament Teaching on Death* (London: Tyndale Press, 1955); Donald W.B. Robinson, *Josiah's Reform and the Book of the Law* (London: Tyndale Press, 1951).

10 F.F. Bruce, *In Retrospect: remembrance of things past* (London: Marshall Pickering, Rev. Ed., 1993), 127.

11 Mark Noll, *The Scandal of the Evangelical Mind* (Leicester: IVP, 1994).

12 In 1948 the Institute published five pamphlets all written by Thompson: *Records in Clay; Cities Walled up to Heaven; Unearthing Solomon's Stables; These Extra-Ordinary Documents; Luke, the Historian.*

> Our way is not so easy in this branch of IVF because we are constantly assailed for our 'fundamentalism' and out of date viewpoint. Out of date indeed!! Brother Charles, we evangelicals can hold up our heads as never before as we discover how very historical is the record of our faith as found in the Bible.[13]

At the invitation of Paul White, Troutman returned to Australia in 1953, intending to work for only a brief period as an IVF staff worker. His wife and two of his three children, however, contracted polio in the epidemic of that year. Consequently, Troutman protracted his stay until 1961.

Two years after Troutman's appointment, the controversy over fundamentalism came to a head in Britain and Australia. When Billy Graham was invited to preach in Great St Mary's Church at a mission of the Cambridge Inter-Collegiate Christian Union in 1955, there was a chorus of opposition to the holding of a 'fundamentalist mission' at Cambridge. The flood of letters to the *Times* lasted for weeks. John Stott's contribution to the debate was published in Billy Graham's *Crusade* magazine.[14] He explained that there are three characteristics of fundamentalism from which conservative evangelicals insist on distancing themselves: 'a bigoted rejection of all Biblical criticism, a mechanical view of inspiration, and an exceptionally literalist interpretation of Scripture'.[15] The new Archbishop of York, Michael Ramsey, who had been Professor of Divinity at Cambridge, weighed in with an article entitled 'The Menace of Fundamentalism', which was really an attack on the evangelistic enthusiasm of keen evangelicals. Ramsey, later Archbishop of Canterbury, maintained his strong anti-evangelical stance, insisting that it closed minds instead of opening them.[16] Stott replied again in *Crusade* in May 1956. But it was clear that the issue had become so big that it demanded sustained analysis.

Two major studies ensued, one by a High church critic in Australia, the other by an evangelical apologist. In 1947 the Society of the Sacred Mission, an Anglican religious community dedicated to training men for ordination, had established St. Michael's House at Mount Lofty, near Adelaide. Its greatest scholar was Gabriel Hebert. In his *Fundamentalism and the Church of God*, Hebert was quite candid about his aim:

---

13 John A. Thompson to Charles Troutman, 26 March 1950 (Troutman Papers in possession of the Troutman family).

14 November 1955.

15 Quoted in Alan Cole, 'Gabriel Hebert on *Fundamentalism and the Church of God*', *Reformed Theological Review*, 17.1, 1958, 12.

16 This was the Archbishop's message to ordinands at King's College London in the early 1970s.

> It is with conservative evangelicals in the Church of England and other churches, and with the Inter-Varsity Fellowship of Evangelical Unions, that this book is to be especially concerned.[17]

Hebert's approach was eirenical, but his basic argument was that conservative evangelicals could not claim justly that they avoided, not so much anti-intellectualism, but narrow intellectualism. The evangelicals did not have a consistent world view, nor a well-rounded theology, nor a sufficiently deep understanding of the Church. Hebert's attack provoked many refutations.[18] The most extensive refutation came from the pen of J.I. Packer. His *Fundamentalism and the Word of God*[19] became an evangelical classic. Along with Stott, Packer wanted to distance himself from fundamentalism. The dispute revealed the concern which evangelicals now clearly had to be considered intellectually respectable. More important it demonstrated that biblical interpretation had become the key concern of evangelicals. It has remained so ever since. Packer argues that, by contrast with the fundamentalist:

> The Evangelical is not afraid of facts, for he knows that all facts are God's facts; nor is he afraid of thinking, because he knows that all truth is God's truth; and right reason cannot endanger sound faith. He is called to love God with all his mind; and part of what this means is that, when confronted by those who, on professedly rational grounds, take exception to historic Christianity, he must set himself not merely to deplore or denounce them, but to out-think them ... A confident intellectualism expressive of a robust faith in God, whose Word is truth, is part of the evangelical tradition.[20]

Evangelicalism became a more confident movement as a result of its strong apologetic defenders. It also became a movement more critical of others. Troutman was far more determined than Howard Guinness, the founder of IVF in Australia, had been to distance the IVF from the SCM.[21] Troutman often expressed astonishment at the mess Guinness caused by too willingly accepting invitations to preach extended to him by the SCM. One SCM staff worker (an 'unrepentant liberal' in Troutman's view) replied to Troutman's

---

17 Gabriel Hebert, *Fundamentalism and the Church of God* (London: SCM, 1957), 10.

18 For example, Cole, 'Gabriel Hebert on *Fundamentalism and the Church of God*'; Martin E. Marty reviewed the book in *Christian Century*, 74, 1957, 1411–1413.

19 (London: IVF, 1958).

20 Packer, *Fundamentalism and the Word of God*, 34.

21 Robyn Boyd, *The Witness of the Student Christian Movement: Church ahead of the Church* (Hindmarsh: ATF Press, 2007).

invitation to cooperate in the Billy Graham Crusade by saying pleasantly 'I cannot conscientiously co-operate with Dr Graham's message or his methods of evangelism'.[22] Troutman refused to even consider the SCM leadership to be Christians: he stated that he was praying for their conversion. This represented a change for the Australian IVF which had been more pietistic, that is concerned with inner religious experience and personal devotional practices, and therefore less combative. Now the IVF was far more focussed: the Bible and evangelism became the twin concerns of Australian evangelicalism at its apogee in the early 1960s.

The evangelical movement in Australia not only became more solidly grounded in biblical scholarship, it also became better organised, especially in its mission to the young. Paul White had put this in train before Troutman arrived. White spoke of the 'unbreakable circle between the Scripture Union and the IVF', the mutual supportiveness and organisational continuity between members of the evangelical family. Troutman received the wholehearted support of SU Secretary, Colin Becroft, and school pupils from the Inter-School Christian Fellowships (ISCFs) and Crusaders transitioned into the EUs and staffed beach missions and camps. Following graduation, many EUers became teachers who in turn supported ISCFs, Crusaders, Scripture Union, and CSSM. Graduates were supported by the Graduate Fellowships in each State and professionally-related fellowships including the Australian Teachers Christian Fellowship, the Christian Medical Fellowship, the Australian Nurses Christian Movement, the Lawyers' Christian Fellowship, and the Research Scientists Christian Fellowship. The last saw its role chiefly in terms of apologetics and held science weekends, especially in NSW and SA for high school pupils whose faith, it was feared, was threatened by scientific rationalism. So by the end of the 1950s the burgeoning scholarship in Biblical Studies was buttressed by scholarship in ancillary disciplines and in the professions. Evangelicalism has always been involved in the development of professionalisation,[23] one of the cultures in which it most thrives, and evangelical professional groups sprang up like mushrooms.

Australian evangelicalism was not only more cerebral, less pietistic; it was also more international, less parochial. Troutman shared Archbishop Mowll's

---

22 In 'Confidential Report', Charles Henry Troutman, Jr., Papers, Collection 111 box 11, folder 16, 3, BGA.

23 Stuart Piggin, *Making Evangelical Missionaries* (Appleford: Sutton Courtenay Press, 1984), 29–47.

vision for the Australian evangelisation of Asia[24] and pushed the vision hard through the creation of the Overseas Christian Fellowship (OCF). By the 1950s increasing numbers of well-connected Chinese businessmen were settling in Australia. Unlike earlier generations of Chinese, they tended to be married and to bring their wives with them. Their children required education, and so they turned to the evangelical churches to provide fellowship, nurture, and networks which could help them to thrive in business. In addition to the business men, many Chinese students now came to Australian universities. The Chinese population of Sydney grew from 3,300 in 1947 to 8,500 in 1961. The Chinese population of Australia as a whole was 12,100 in 1947 and 23,600 in 1961.

The OCF was formed independently of the IVF in Adelaide in 1956 and in Sydney the following year. In building a link between the OCF and the IVF, Troutman was assisted in having an Asian as president of the SUEU. Lawrence Chia was a brilliant young Singapore national who was to make his mark in the fields of science and education as well as in Presbyterian and evangelical circles, rising to the rank of Associate Professor at the National University of Singapore and Chairman of the Evangelical Fellowship of Singapore. Through the OCF, Troutman promoted a concern for Asia in evangelical circles that was well ahead of anything felt in the general community.

In succession to Charles Troutman, Ian Burnard was appointed IVF General Secretary. Burnard was a South Australian of Cornish Methodist stock. He was led to Christ by Lyall Lush, commercial artist and publisher of Christian comics, who owed his faith to Howard Guinness, making Burnard the spiritual grandson of the founder of IVF in Australia. Burnard completed his BSc in pure mathematics in 1956 and retained a life-long interest in science, but he also loved history and lexicography. He had been President of the Adelaide EU and was from 1957 an IVF staff-worker.

During Ian Burnard's time as Secretary, Evangelical Unions became enormous, headed by student leaders of ability and an impressive biblical understanding. The Sydney University EU in the mid-60s comprised some 900 members, or about 1 in 17 of the entire student body. These remarkable statistics, duplicated in other universities, such as the University of New England, suggest that the suburban, family-oriented evangelicalism of the stereotype does not encompass all evangelicals in the 1950s – there was

24 W.J. Lawton, 'The Winter of Our Days: The Anglican Diocese of Sydney, 1950–1960', *Lucas* 9, 1990, 12, 15ff.

a young, engaged, student face to the movement which proved critically important to its future direction and development. Universities, even more than middle-class suburbs, were becoming the heartbeat of the movement.[25]

Ian Burnard was clear about the IVF's priorities. First, current issues were to be approached biblically. Second, the EU's proactive evangelism was to be maintained, and, in many a union refectory and on many a university lawn, Burnard modelled a fearless evangelism. He reinforced Troutman, encouraging students to focus on the Bible and evangelism. A study of the religious experience of the student body at the University of New England reveals that in the 1950s it was a remarkably religious community, with all student Christian societies enjoying strong support.[26] Attendance at churches and religious activities was high, as was daily prayer, observance of Christian moral values, and concern to apply those values to address social problems. In 1961 10% of all incoming students to the university claimed that they intended to be ministers or missionaries or serve in some Christian organisation, nearly 50% said that they attended church weekly and 54% said that they prayed every day.

When Burnard began as General Secretary, the OCF was not a part of IVF, but he fostered the links, and ensured that the same speakers spoke at their conferences as at IVF: Alan Cole, John Hercus, David Adeney. Among the members of OCF was Andrew Lu who was to become a leading Presbyterian layman and elder and session clerk in his own church, the Chinese Presbyterian Church (CPC) in Crown Street Sydney. OCF stressed Bible study and the evangelisation of Asian students, and this reinforced the evangelical nature of the CPC which in 1949 appointed Pui Sam Mo as its pastor, and every area of church life was transformed. The CPC held an annual house party on Australia Day. The January 1961 house party lives on in the annals of the church as a time when the Spirit came in revival power. A number of OCF members and staff workers were present. The speaker was the Rev Bernie Gook, Anglican Chaplain to the University of Sydney, and his subject was 'Am I a Christian?' Those present were brought to the astonishing realisation that there is a living God who does concern himself with 'the affairs of men'.[27] It was a transformative experience, always recalled with gratitude

25 This is also partly true of evangelicals in other parts of the English-speaking world. See Brian Stanley, *The Global Diffusion of Evangelicalism: The Age of Billy Graham and John Stott* (Downers Grove, Illinois: IVP Academic, 2013), chapter four.

26 D.R. Beer, '"The Holiest Campus', Its Decline and Transformation: The University of New England, 1946–79,' *JRH*, 21.3, 1997, 318–336.

27 Wendy Lu Mar, *So Great a Cloud of Witnesses: A History of the Chinese Presbyterian Church, Sydney, 1893–1993* (Surry Hills: Chinese Presbyterian Church, 1993), 29.

by such future leaders of the church as John Ting, Kathleen Kuo, Andrew Lu, and Shirley Ng.

In their desire to strengthen the intellectual content of Evangelicalism, Troutman and Burnard were assisted by University staff. The evangelicals in this period had their share of brilliant intellects, including Edwin Judge, Anna Hogg and Frank Andersen. Edwin Judge trained generations of students in the scholarly appreciation of the Judeo-Christian tradition. Educated in Classics in New Zealand and at Cambridge, Judge was well aware of his evangelical heritage. Charles Simeon had presided over the evangelical party at King's College, Cambridge. Each week, at the bidding of the Professor of Ancient History, Sir Frank Adcock, who recruited spies for the British in World War II and who then occupied Simeon's rooms, Judge sat with other students of the Classics reading through much of the corpus of Greek plays, very conscious of the Christian and Classical traditions on which the University was based. Another link between Judge and the Clapham Sect was forged in the winter of 1955–56 when he sat next to E.M. Forster, the novelist, at dinner at King's. Forster was a Fellow of King's, a member of the Bloomsbury Group, and his great aunt was Marianne Thornton, daughter of Henry Thornton, the banker and member of the Clapham Sect. Forster asked Judge if he could 'think of any differences in the general pattern of human behaviour that might be positively attributed to Christianity'.[28] Judge was to spend the rest of his life thinking of such differences, but on this occasion he suggested that the habit of self-deprecation might be attributable to the value which Christians attached to humility. Forster was a champion of the King's 'doctrine' that only two things matter: friendship and beauty. While not unappreciative of either friendship or beauty, Judge was implacably resistant to such a doctrine and he honed his scholarship in opposition to it. In commenting on the journey from the Clapham Sect to the Bloomsbury Group, a journey made by a number of the descendants of the Clapham fathers, Judge explains that that there is a major distinction between a 'sect' and a 'group'. A sect is made up of those who follow a cause. In departing from his evangelical heritage, Forster had taken leave of all causes, becoming President of the Humanist Society later in life. He began his humanist essay 'What I believe' with the words 'I do not believe in belief'.

Judge was appointed as a lecturer in ancient history at the University of Sydney in September 1956. He retained the Classicist's appreciation for

28 James R. Harrison (ed.), *The First Christians in the Roman World* (Tübingen: Mohr Siebeck, 2010), 59.

language and text. It was an appreciation acquired, not only from his Classical training, but from its uneasy partner, Bible Study. Judge's practice of studying the Classical and biblical, side-by-side, using the same methods, and considering them in the light of modern culture, has proven surprisingly fruitful in its application to the study of Australia's public culture. Judge argues that Australian culture is more than anything the product of the unresolved tension between Classical and biblical values. He founded, edited or contributed to a range of academic journals which defended, or rather explained, the Christian faith: *Prudentia* in New Zealand and *The Journal of Religious History*, *The Journal of Christian Education*, and *Interchange* all in Sydney.

Anna Hogg was raised in the Brethren. At Sydney University she shone in philosophy and won the admiration of her professor, the notorious atheist, John Anderson. She was the first woman to receive first class honours in philosophy at Sydney University. When a position was created at the Sydney Teachers' College in the philosophy of education, Anderson persuaded her to apply and warmly supported her appointment. As a senior lecturer in education, Anna Hogg was the first editor of *The Journal of Christian Education* launched by the Australian Teachers Christian Fellowship in 1958. Hogg explained that professional teachers could not be content merely to practise their craft and achieve results. Professionals, she wrote, have to understand the principles on which their practice is based.[29] *JCE* was apparently unique, another contribution of Australian evangelicalism to the world: it was soon going to twenty countries with a large uptake in North American tertiary institutions.

Frank Andersen was Judge's academic colleague from 1975 to 1980 at Macquarie University before becoming Professor of Studies in Religion at the University of Queensland. Born in Warwick, Queensland, Andersen first took degrees in Science before turning to Russian language and literature and then to theology. He was a genuine polymath who put his considerable scientific expertise and literary sensitivity to the computer and poetic analysis of the texts of the Hebrew Bible. His doctorate on Hebrew syntax was awarded with Distinction at Johns Hopkins University, where he worked under the supervision of the leading Old Testament scholar, W.F. Albright. Though an evangelical of pronounced warmth and piety, Andersen's objectivity in his scholarly pursuits was relentless. He was one of a new generation of evangelical scholars whose biblicism led to strenuous feats of the intellect as well as to devotion. He was a generous colleague and teacher and infected

29 'Editorial', *JCE*, 1.1, 1958, 3.

all with whom he worked with indomitable enthusiasm for linguistic tasks of extraordinary complexity. He suffered a number of personal tragedies and non-self-inflicted professional disappointments both before and after his study of the Book of Job which was published by the Tyndale Press in 1976. He concludes his preface to that commentary with the words: 'Everything is a gift, suffering the holiest of all: and healing of all hurts is to be found in the Body of One who was broken, the only *pharmakon athanasias*.'[30] He wrote sonnets through which cascaded the joy of his spiritual experience, but it was a joy based on a profound awareness of what God had done for him in Christ:

> At the roots of mind,
> Where consciousness draws nourishment from foul
> Repressions, that sump of life's accumulations –
> The pain and shock of birth, the infant traumas,
> Wrongs done to others and indignities received –
> at that deepest, most unconscious spring
> of all my life you put your innocent Word.[31]

The academic rigour, resulting from the surge in scholarship and the determination to give evangelicalism more intellectual muscle, attracted some who had been unmoved by the older more emotive evangelicalism. A case in point was Brian Dickey, a Sydney University undergraduate in the years 1957–61, who graduated with first class honours in History and the University medal, and became an Associate Professor of History at Flinders University in South Australia.

> I was converted at the SUEU Houseparty in August 1957, where Edwin Judge and Geoff Fletcher[32] were the teachers, ying and yang if ever there were. Edwin cool, clear, detailed, historically knowledgeable, Fletcher passionate, Bible hitting and as I now realise very Keswick. But it was a powerful combine and it did for me!
>
> The next term ... I attended the EU weekly public lectures as I gradually got involved in all this new stuff. Troutman was expounding the Creed to a crowded lecture theatre ... It was full solid stuff. At the same time,

30 Quoted by Stuart Barton Babbage in Edgar W. Conrad, and Edward G. Newing (eds), *Perspectives on Language and Text: Essays and Poems in Honor of Francis I. Andersen's Sixtieth Birthday, July 28 1985* (Winona Lake: Eisenbrauns, 1987), xvi.

31 'I am Yahweh, your Healer [Exodus 15:26]', Conrad and Newing, *Perspectives*, xxv.

32 CMS NSW State Secretary.

many of us were benefiting from History I with Bruce Mansfield … Mansfield[33] was using a succession of great Reformation texts in lengthy extracts to elucidate his lectures … These expositions made Luther and Calvin accessible, so it made perfectly good sense for me to buy and read the *Institutes* (purchased 13 July 1958). I read them on the train to and from home to uni, a good half hour run.

Our Bible study group meetings in 1958 were provided with thoughtful and solid study materials. By 1959 surely the stuff being developed by the Beeck brothers[34] was coming through, even more solid stuff indeed. Meanwhile John Stott did his thing for EU, Basic Christianity week by week, and then Billy Graham …

I had personal pastoral dealings with Troutman in Jan 1961 (by which time I'd got to know him fairly well). He was gentle, relaxed, well informed and moderate in his advice: a really lovely man close up in a study absolutely overflowing with scholarship, books everywhere to the ceiling.

Ted Fackerell the mathematician was the principal proponent at Sydney of Warfield and then the Dutch reformed scholars (he probably still is!) I dutifully bought the relevant volumes as they became available through Banner of Truth. But the thunderbolt was Packer's *Fundamentalism*. We lapped it up: I still have my copy. It was indeed just what we all wanted and needed, and it was by a man of nearly our generation.

In comparison with later ways of thinking about vocation encouraged in Sydney by Phillip Jensen at St Matthias, we were encouraged by Ian Burnard and Troutman to make the best of our academic competence, take the scholarships, pursue academic careers and influence the Christian community that way (hence the importance of Edwin Judge as a model).

All of which is intended to suggest that I certainly was engaged with Christianity intellectually as part of my spiritual formation. There was nothing sloppy, and emotionalism was at a discount. If therefore I was a product in Sydney of the refashioning of the evangelical paradigm,

33 Lecturer in early modern European history. On Mansfield's years at Sydney University (1952–76), see Bruce Mansfield, *Summer is almost over – a Memoir* (Canberra: Barton Books, 2012), 36–67.

34 IVF staff workers from WA.

> so be it. I haven't changed much. What I didn't get as a child was that warm and fuzzy emotional romantic middle class upbringing which for two-three generations was the seedbed for the Keswick style of evangelicalism. My childhood was lowscale on emotion, working class, solitary, intellectual and achievement driven. So I was fair game for the reworked paradigm.

The 'reworked paradigm' was enough to forge generations of scholars who saw no conflict between academic values and evangelical beliefs and who, like Dickey himself, occupied influential teaching and research positions in Australia's 'secular' universities.[35] Did the focus on the spiritual and academic make it difficult for committed EUers to see the social, cultural and political dimensions to life? The recollections of Doug Buckley, an engineering student at Sydney University in the 1950s, suggest that it did. The understanding we have of Sydney University in the 1950s, he complains, comes from the memories of celebrities such as Peter Coleman, Bob Ellis, Germaine Greer, Donald Horne, Clive James, Paddy McGuinness, and Les Murray. Members of the 'Sydney Push', they were all Arts students, on 'a different planet from most of us'. Their 'particular brand of malarky' would have been news 'to virtually all of us, certainly to me'. His celebrities were Charles Troutman, Howard Guinness, Dudley Foord, 'a leading Baptist always called Principal Morling', and T.C. Hammond:

> If anyone has listened to TC and left thinking Christianity is a matter of mere feelings and taste, not facts and rationality, it won't have been TC's fault. No vague, comfortable spiritualities for TC.

But he wondered even then if TC's rationality 'might have led to too high a view of that talent'. Buckley confessed that his fellow evangelicals had no patience with 'churchmen hobbled by party spirit', but that did not translate into empathy with those outside all the denominations or for liberals within the denominations. They rather saw the wider community 'mainly in terms of its need of Jesus'. For 'serious reflection on society', members of all the other Christian groups on the one hand, and the Andersonian sceptics on the other,

35 Catholic New Testament scholar, Frank Moloney, in his review of *The Content and Setting of the Gospel Tradition* (Grand Rapids/Cambridge: Eerdmans, 2010), edited by Mark Harding, Dean of the Australian College of Theology, and Professor Alanna Nobbs, Head of the Ancient History Department at Macquarie University, wrote: 'It represents the peak expression of the evangelical academic tradition in Australia'. *The Catholic Biblical Quarterly*, 74, 2012, 631.

'would have left us for dead'.[36] Evangelical suspicion of ecumenism and secularism issued in two spectacular clashes on university campuses, both in 1961.

The SCM/EU Divide

Liberal Christians were often as concerned as conservatives by the threat of secularism. Ecumenism was their solution, while conservatives considered theological liberalism was part of the problem. Ecumenists believed that the unity of Christians had evangelistic power and that division was a gift to the secularists and a cause of confusion to young university students now faced with a growing number of student Christian societies. At the University of New England, Methodist chaplain, James Udy, professed to being 'appalled' at the growing chasm between the EU and SCM.[37] The Australian Council of Churches (ACC) responded to this concern by holding a consultation in May 1961 at Ormond College in the University of Melbourne on 'The Church's Responsibility to the Universities'.

Almost fifty delegates were invited including leading churchmen, and representatives of the SCM and IVF, university chaplains and heads of university colleges. The consultation was carefully planned by the ACC Executive. Its vision was to increase the opportunities for the study of religion in universities by addressing fears that denominational differences could revive sectarianism and that fundamentalism threatened the open inquiry critical to the nature of the university. Preliminary papers were circulated for the edification of delegates. The Rev. David Taylor, Assistant General Secretary of the ACC, observed that fragmented, non-co-operative Christian work on campus 'repelled superior minds'. That diplomacy was not essential to ecumenism was demonstrated by his denunciation of 'Christians who have a small-minded religion, which shuts them off not only from the rationalistic unbelievers but from all great minds, past and present.'[38] Evangelicals were not made any more comfortable by Professor Charles Birch of the University of Sydney, who in the only formal address given at the consultation, condemned the 'anti-intellectualism' now all too common in religious groups in the university: 'Its effects on some lives is nothing less than disastrous. This Consultation

36 Doug Buckley, *Fragments from a Forgettory* (Hartwell: Temple House, 2007), 187–191.

37 Ian Walker, 'Church, College and Campus: The Sacred and the Secular in the Foundation of Denominational Colleges in Australian Universities, with particular reference to certain colleges in universities established in the period 1945 to 1975', PhD, UNSW, 2001, 217.

38 Walker, 'Church, College and Campus', 223.

should be concerned at ways of salvaging the wrecked lives such religion leaves in its wake.'[39]

Evangelicals quickly decided that this was not a consultation, but an ambush. In fact, one of the delegates, Bishop Marcus Loane reached that conclusion in advance of the consultation. At the last moment, Archbishop Gough withdrew and asked Loane to replace him. David Taylor called on him with the preliminary papers. Loane later recalled:

> He came over to see me and he gave me something – I could hardly believe my eyes – he gave me something which purported to be the report of the Conference, which hadn't met! Hadn't even met! It was all written out, recommending all sorts of things. I could hardly believe it! I fell out with him then and there. It was a bad start![40]

Loane thus became aware of the ACC's goal which was to close both the SCM and IVF and replace them with an ecumenical organisation responsible to the ACC. Loane was provoked into doing what he did best: defending evangelical truth. He emphatically declared at the consultation that he could never support any proposal to establish a Christian witness on campus which did not have as its central message the substitutionary death of Christ.[41] Loane was later accused of wrecking the consultation. His view was that it just 'fizzled-out' and nothing came of it.[42] In fact, the consultation had far-reaching effects, but they were the opposite of those planned by the ACC. When he became Archbishop, Loane, unlike his predecessor, Howard Mowll, distanced himself from both the Australian and the World Council of Churches. The newly fortified conservative evangelicalism, embraced by the IVF, stood for a sterner response to secularism than that adopted by the theological liberals. It proved a far more effective response in the long term, causing the IVF to wax and the SCM to wane, but it could be embarrassing at times, and just such a time was only months away.

The Secularist Push

There were voices even in this conservative period which questioned the moral consensus and the values hegemony of the churches, the more striking for their rarity. One who did so was the editor of *Punch* in the UK, Malcolm

39 Walker, 'Church, College and Campus', 225.
40 Walker, 'Church, College and Campus', 226.
41 Reid, *Marcus L. Loane*, 56.
42 Walker, 'Church, College and Campus', 232.

Muggeridge, then in his rampaging pre-Christian days. In a visit to Australia in 1955 he explained that he was out to shock. He had no difficulty in achieving his aim: everybody in Australia in the 1950s was easily shocked precisely because Christian values were so widely accepted. In fact, they were so widely accepted that nobody thought to define what they were! The Archbishop of Canterbury, never reluctant to judge his fellow men, explained that Muggeridge was a deliberately vulgar, coarse-minded individual, who had to be stopped.[43] Another who had to be stopped was John Anderson, Professor of philosophy at Sydney University, then secularism's most doughty champion in Australia. Anderson retired as Professor in 1958 and died in 1962, but he contended stoutly for materialist atheism until the end. He was not a libertarian himself, but those of his followers known as Andersonians, and who were part of the Sydney 'Push', did practise what Anderson preached.[44]

Anderson was such a threat that the evangelicals and Catholics combined forces to resist him. It followed hard on the failure of the ecumenical consultation on Christian activity in universities. The year 1961 is pre-Vatican II when sectarian rivalry between Catholics and Protestants was still robust, so Anderson did well to unite them. Austin Woodbury taught scholastic theology at the Aquinas Academy in Sydney. One of his students, Victor Kinsella, a surgeon, used some of Woodbury's weapons to attack the amorality of Andersonian empiricism and went so far as to argue that the University of Sydney should lose its Royal Charter for harbouring such a libertine. His allegation that Anderson was corrupting the morals of youth was entertained seriously by the Youth Policy Advisory Committee established by the NSW State Government in 1961.[45] Its chairman, Judge Adrian Curlewis, sent a copy of Kinsella's attack on Anderson to the Anglican Archbishop of Sydney, Hugh Gough. In a sermon he preached at St Andrew's Cathedral on 6 July 1961, to which he had alerted the media, Gough alleged that there were teachers in Sydney universities who were urging students to throw off the restraints of conscience, dispense with marriage and practise free love. Since immorality, he contended, has always undermined civilisation, it was the responsibility of the government to act. In the hysteria which ensued, Anderson emerged from retirement to defend freedom of expression. To the charge that only one philosophical position was

43 Frappell, *Anglicans in the Antipodes*, 321.

44 James Franklin, *Corrupting the Youth: A History of Philosophy in Australia* (Sydney: Macleay Press, 2003), 108.

45 Geoff Sherrington, 'Youth, State and Community: The Report of the Curlewis Youth Policy Advisory Committee in New South Wales', *Australian and New Zealand History of Education Society Twenty-First Annual Conference Proceedings* (Adelaide: St Mark's College, 1992), II. 125–38.

taught at Sydney University, Anderson made the interesting defence that 'if you give students all sorts of views, you are not encouraging a real grasp of philosophy'.[46] It is an argument akin to that used by defenders of the Moore College policy of teaching only Reformed theology to its students. Anderson was as dogmatic and combative as any Moore College lecturer has ever been:

> The academic world has to attack any religion which tries to lay down requirements not in accordance with reality. In any university the fight between secularism and religion is intense ... church-going minds are childish. We are dealing with people who are not really adults.[47]

A.K. Stout, Professor of Moral and Political Philosophy at Sydney University until 1965, had been appointed ostensibly to moderate Anderson's atheism. But he usually supported Anderson and told his students that Gough was an intellectual lightweight having only attained third class honours at Cambridge.[48] If it is a wonder today that anyone should have taken Gough's intervention in the Department of Philosophy seriously, that was partly because he represented the establishment: he was a patrician, married to Madeline, daughter of Lord Kinnaird, and he was the more imposing because he was tall, handsome, and very English. And Gough's intervention was helped by the fact that the Australian public had since 1956 been in a state of frenzied astonishment over the alleged sexual misconduct of another Professor of Philosophy, Sidney Sparkes Orr, as discussed above (chapter 8).

The press invited the Rev Dr Stuart Barton Babbage, then well established as a commentator on religious matters with a fine turn of phrase, to comment on the issue of academic freedom which Anderson's views raised. The loose cannon let loose, asserting that not allowing academics to speak freely was akin to McCarthyism and that the next step would be the rubber truncheon and the concentration camp. He did not mention any names, but Gough naturally saw Babbage's contribution as a hostile act.[49] Furthermore Gough had alienated the support of journalist and stirrer of the Anglican Church, Francis James. He had wanted to speak in synod and Gough had insisted that he resume his seat. James had resolved that 'Gough must go' and five years later, he achieved his goal.[50]

---

46 Quoted in Franklin, *Corrupting the Youth*, 99.

47 Quoted in Franklin, *Corrupting the Youth*, 99.

48 Franklin, *Corrupting the Youth*, 104.

49 Stuart Barton Babbage, Flotsam and Jetsam – a sequel to *Memoirs of a Loose Canon*, 2011, 17 (unpublished typescript in the possession of the authors).

50 Babbage, Flotsam and Jetsam, 17.

Marcus Loane, who took over administration of the diocese on Gough's departure, gave health concerns as the reason for Gough's unexpected retirement, and on Gough's death over thirty years later maintained this explanation: 'the nervous strain of seven strenuous years took their toll in a serious breakdown in health'.[51] It seems that Gough had become romantically involved with a woman of high social standing. Francis James, though not reticent in later life to tell the story, at the time persuaded his many media contacts not to publish the rumour.[52] Only *Oz* did so, with the satirical gloss that it was 'wild and patently ludicrous nonsense'.[53] Marcus Loane has been criticised for not being more open about it, but he was not motivated solely by the desire to protect the reputation of the church. He respected the wishes of the woman involved and her husband that the matter should not be made public, and even the church's gladdest detractors have been reluctant to reveal her name.[54] But no remnant of comfort is salvageable here. This was an all-too-easy victory for the forces of secularism.

Theological Education

The education offered in theological and Bible colleges in this period improved dramatically, thanks to greater interest in the life of the mind, to curriculum changes and structural stability. For example, Moore and Ridley, the Anglican evangelical colleges, added to their offerings the London BD, perceived as a qualification superior to the Licentiate of Theology offered by the Australian College of Theology.

Broughton Knox became principal of Moore College in 1959 and held the position for 26 years. Marcia Cameron's biography of him[55] shows him to have been a strange one and he came from a strange lineage. It is not surprising that a diocese shaped by him is also strange. But, as she also shows, in spite of his flaws, many loved him deeply, and his influence was enormous. He was

51 M.L. Loane, 'Obituary: The Right Rev Hugh Gough', *Independent,* 29 November 1997.

52 Interview of Francis James by Stuart Piggin, Margaret Lamb and Robert D. Linder, 19 June 1990; Marcia Cameron, *Phenomenal Sydney: Anglicans in a time of change, 1945–2013* (Eugene: Wipf & Stock, 2016), 104–107.

53 *Oz*, 28, June 1966.

54 Humphrey McQueen, 'Primates are Human', accessed 3 January 2017, on http://www.surplusvalue.org.au/McQueen/p_war_aus/Soc-Cu/pwar_aus_sc_archgough.htm

55 Marcia Cameron, *An Enigmatic Life: David Broughton Knox, Father of Contemporary Sydney Anglicanism* (Brunswick East, Acorn Press, 2006).

the main propagator of the new anti-pietistic, cerebral plant which took over the evangelical garden in Sydney in the 1960s.

Born in Adelaide in 1912, Knox was educated at the University of Sydney where he studied Greek alongside Gough Whitlam and demonstrated his independent spirit by not joining the Evangelical Union. He was trained for the ministry and ordained in England in 1941. Before serving as a naval chaplain in 1944–45, he joined with Stuart Barton Babbage in the Biblical Research Committee of the IVF and with Douglas Johnson in the production of scholarly evangelical literature. Knox acquired a reputation as an uncompromising champion of Reformation doctrine; when he perceived something was contrary to Scripture he had the memorable habit of uttering a sevenfold 'no'. He galvanised a generation of evangelicals to say 'no' to the advances of liberalism and the incursions of ritualism.

Within months of his appointment as tutor to Moore College in 1947, Knox made an unforgettable appearance as an 'expert witness' in a famous trial known as 'the Red Book Case' in which the Bishop of Bathurst was accused of advocating liturgical innovations incompatible with the law of the Church of England. The defendant's barrister, Mr Frank Kitto, K.C., later Judge Kitto, could not shake Knox's evidence. He began by trying to establish that Knox was not an expert witness, but the judge disagreed.[56] It was said that this was the first time Kitto was rattled by a witness.

Knox received his doctorate from Oxford in 1953 for a dissertation later published under the title *The Doctrine of Faith in the Reign of Henry VIII*. There, in an insight which is the key to both his faith and his personality, Knox observed that human sufficiency (as opposed to faith in God) 'taught the haughty to presume while the humble despaired and it gave little place for Christian joy'.[57] Knox may have looked and sounded like an academic, but his instincts and his heart were those of a warrior for the truth rather than of a speculator on truth. The truth in the Word of God was to be obeyed – personally – and was to be defended and error refuted fearlessly. He was more interested in engaging with God than with other professional theologians. But he loved theology and he loved arguing and he taught his students to love both. It was said that Knox and T.C. Hammond were both argumentative and loved a good fight. But, whereas the latter wanted to win

56 Arnold L. Wylde, *The Bathurst Ritual Case, with a Preface by the Ven. Archdeacon T. C. Hammond, MA, ThD* (Sydney: George M. Dash, n.d.), 22.

57 D.B. Knox, *The Doctrine of Faith in the Reign of Henry VIII* (London: James Clarke & Co, 1961), 274.

his opponents, Knox was content to lose them if he won the argument: truth is more important than being nice.

His belief that the Bible was the sole authority in all matters of faith and doctrine led him to insist that only doctrines found in the Bible should be taught as essential to salvation,[58] that the Bible is self-authenticating, and that the only revelation of God is 'propositional'. In 1960, he developed the last claim in an article entitled 'Propositional Revelation the only Revelation'.[59] He disputed the view that 'the Word of God' is not a series of propositions, but a series of events, that God's revelation is not in words, but in acts. Knox argued that this view is contrary to the revelation of the Bible itself which affirms that the words, or propositions formed by those words, are the means by which revelation takes place. An event is not revelatory, only the Bible's account of that event reveals God's mind: 'For an event to be revelational, it must be interpreted by God himself.'[60] To affirm propositional revelation was to affirm inerrant revelation.[61] God can and has not only made one inerrant proposition, but a whole series of them in the Bible, and excluded from it any erroneous proposition. Not to believe that is 'the height of impiety'. It followed that the chief work of the ministry was to teach the Bible where alone God reveals himself, the chief work of the theologian was to defend the inerrancy of Scripture, and the chief glory of the believer was to hear and learn the Scriptures. This emphasis has fashioned Sydney Anglicanism more than any other single influence. The height of piety became the proclamation and defence of the Word.

Under Knox, the general theology textbooks studied at Moore were changed from the older, evangelical Anglican works of Griffith Thomas, to the more continental, neo-orthodox theology developed by Gustav Aulen in *Christus Victor*, Nygren's commentary on Romans, together with a Barthian, Reformed emphasis. It was believed by the staff themselves that Knox had opened the way to what they characterised as 'the Biblical theology movement'. Vice-Principal Donald Robinson's capacity as an exegete of Scripture promoted the disciplined study of what the text was actually saying. This was further strengthened by Peter O'Brien and Paul Barnett in the research which led to their writing

58 'The authority of Holy Scripture' in D.B. Knox, *Thirty-Nine Articles* (Sydney: AIO, 1976), 15–20.

59 *RTR*, 19.1, 1960, 1–9.

60 Knox, 'Propositional Revelation the only Revelation,' 6.

61 By inerrancy, Knox meant not so much in an historical or scientific sense, but in its capacity to inculcate infallibly and authoritatively the truth about and from God pertaining to faith and morals.

of large commentaries on some of Paul's letters. Bill Dumbrell studied the over-all meaning of Scripture and infused into current evangelicalism a biblical philosophy of history as students came to understand the revealed purpose of God. A world view displaced the older more individual concept of personal redemption. Evangelicalism became stronger theologically and tougher intellectually. It was not all gain. Theology was becoming more specialised, like other disciplines in secular universities. It was in danger of losing contact with the spirituality of ordinary Australians. Perhaps as preaching and defending the Word became the core concern, the laity, and especially women, then largely denied opportunities to teach this theology, were marginalised.

In Melbourne Ridley College was also transformed in this period, presided over by two outstanding principals, Stuart Barton Babbage and Leon Morris. Babbage was appointed Principal of Ridley in 1953 and is credited with breaking up 'the Concordat', an agreement with diocesan authorities which curtailed the access of its lecturers to teach diocesan ordinands beyond their first year. Babbage's influence on Melbourne was extensive as he was not only Ridley Principal, but also Dean of St Paul's Cathedral, and a popular speaker at the Melbourne EU. He chaired the 1959 Melbourne Billy Graham Crusade. He gathered around him lecturers who were to achieve international recognition. Frank Andersen, mentioned above, began his stellar academic career at Ridley, as did Ian Siggins, the Luther scholar. Among students at Ridley in Babbage's time was Peter Thomson, who was to become at Oxford the mentor of Tony Blair, Britain's Labor Prime Minister, and Michael Ball, who was to become chairman of the National Capital Authority and inventor of the '100 National Treasures' concept to recognise Australians who make a difference. Halcyon days, but it was not all easy going: the fight over the Concordat was hard-won, and in 1962 Archbishop Woods replaced Babbage as Dean with Tom Thomas who was both full-time and not an evangelical.[62]

When Leon Morris took over, Ridley was (as usual) in dire financial straits. The student numbers, low at the beginning of Babbage's time as principal (1953–63), tapered off again at the end of it. Morris had been vice-principal of Ridley College from 1945 to 1959. He took two years off at Cambridge in 1950–51 to study for his PhD (his thesis later published as *The Apostolic Preaching of the Cross*). As vice-principal he had found it irksome that because of unresolved tensions between the diocese and the college, he was not allowed to lecture students doing the ThL, and the Archbishop (Joseph Booth, 1942–1956) did not seem to approve of him – he did not know why. He did get on very

62 Stuart Barton Babbage interviewed by Stuart Piggin, 19 April 2012.

well with Booth's successor, Frank Woods, Archbishop from 1957 to 1977. But, as the son of working-class parents from the coal town of Lithgow, he was tough and did not let adversity trouble him or approval influence him. 'I'm not very interested in what others think about what I'm doing, but I am passionately interested in being where God wants me to be, doing the work he wants me to do.'[63] So guided, he agreed to go to Ridley in the first place, left it in 1959 for study in America and Cambridge, and then in 1964 agreed to return to Ridley as principal in spite of a more congenial offer to stay in England and a more lucrative offer of a position in America. Celebrated for his defence of the penal substitution doctrine of the atonement, he wrote more than fifty scholarly books and commentaries. The royalties on these books, which sold widely throughout the entire evangelical world, were left for the benefit of theological students in the Leon and Mildred Morris Foundation.[64]

In Morris's time as principal (1964–1979), Ridley became the first of the affiliated residential colleges of the University to admit women students, and then it accepted women theology students. Morris never doubted that women should have the same opportunity as men to serve in every ecclesiastical office. In addition to teaching New Testament and doctrine, he taught Liturgiology, only because he had no one else to do it: 'As principal in a way you are top of the heap, in another way you have to gather up the fragments.' He took a great interest in the building of the chapel – the first Ridley had in its half-century existence, conferring at length with the architects on the liturgical principles which it was to express. It is octagonal – easier to build than a circle – but it still achieved the desired community feeling. The pulpit was elevated above the communion table, to symbolise the evangelical stress on the priority of word over sacrament. But while Morris was firm on these evangelical fundamentals, he enjoyed working with theologians from the full spectrum of churchmanship. He served on the General Synod Liturgical Commission and he considered the production of the AAPB (*A Prayer Book for Australia*, 1978) a major triumph since it allowed all Australian Anglicans to enjoy common prayer, whereas in some provinces of the Anglican Communion rites are drawn up in such an exclusive way as to make it impossible for some to use them conscientiously. He also served on the Doctrine Commission out of the same conviction that evangelicals should be involved in the wider church.[65] While contending that he was far too busy to know what Moore

63 Leon Morris interviewed by Margaret Lamb, 8 August 1986.

64 Barbara Darling, 'Shy Scholar a catalyst for Women's Ministry,' *The Melbourne Anglican*, 481, 2010, 16f.

65 Morris interviewed by Lamb.

College was up to, he suspected that because evangelicals were a minority in the Melbourne Church, they thus developed a broader sympathy and a firmer root than their Sydney counterparts. To be a Melbourne evangelical, he argued, 'you have to be thoughtful'. The danger for Sydney students was that they would have a positional view rather than a biblical one. Far better 'to have a deep conviction of the truth and flexibility in applying it'.[66] Thus his contentment to see women ordained as priests in the Anglican Church.

Ridley was more committed to being biblical than Reformed. But this was the age when Reformed theology flourished, strengthened by Continental as well as British scholars. In 1954 the synod of the Reformed Churches of Australia resolved to establish a theological college and (it was hoped) a Christian university modelled on the Free University in Holland founded 70 years earlier by Abraham Kuyper.[67] The Rev. J.A. Schep was appointed as foundation Professor of New Testament. He retired in 1964 when he adopted a Pentecostal position. The college's most venerable scholar was Klaas Runia, Professor of Systematic Theology from 1957 until 1971. He had been a minister of the Reformed Churches of the Netherlands, and had written his doctoral thesis at the Free University under the supervision of G.C. Berkouwer on Karl Barth's doctrine of Scripture. He became a valued contributor to the *Reformed Theological Review*.[68] Reformed dogmatics, he declared in his inaugural address as theology professor, must be scriptural, church-confessional, and theocentric. With reference to the last he rejected Barth's theology as ultimately false because it was Christocentric rather than theocentric. For the Reformed scholar, the science of theology was clearly the treasure of the Church, and Runia enthused in his peroration to his 'dear Students':

> Theology is a queen, beautiful as the dawn, adorned with many mysteries. I tell you honestly: theology has the love of my heart. I can only see it as a privilege to infuse into others this same love.[69]

Theology, though, was not invariably a queen of peace. In 1963 the Reformed Evangelical Church linked up with the Presbyterian Church of Eastern Australia, another small Calvinist denomination, to establish the John Knox

66 Morris interviewed by Lamb.

67 J.W. Deenick (ed.), *A Church en Route: 40 Years Reformed Churches of Australia* (Geelong: Reformed Churches Publishing House, 1991), 178.

68 Rowland Ward, *The Bush Still Burns: The Presbyterian and Reformed Faith in Australia, 1788–1988* (Wantirna: R.S. Ward, 1989), 379.

69 Klaas Runia, *Reformed Dogmatics: Its Essence and Method* (Geelong: Reformed Theological College, 1957), 29.

Theological College in Melbourne. Both the college and the denominations which supported it continued to be tempted towards Hyper-Calvinism and were therefore rocked by disputation over such issues as whether or not the Gospel is to be offered to all since Christ died only for the elect.[70]

* * *

The 1950s was a formative decade in the history of evangelicalism. The movement had navigated a course between fundamentalism and liberalism. Institutionally, it developed structures for imparting a formulation of the faith that was at once more biblical and more reasonable to school pupils, university students and academics, and theological college students and staff. Its lay supporters were better educated and more numerous, especially in the professions. Reformed theology toughened its presence in the world of ideas and its capacity to help believers withstand the cold winds of secularism. A concentration on evangelism and the Bible brought clarity to the movement's identity. It resisted the temptation to withdraw into a holy huddle. It was determined to engage with unbelievers and with the challenges of historical developments. All these strengths were also its perceived weakness: its simplicity and focus could be taken for simpleness and narrowness. Ironically, its mainstream Calvinist and Reformed ideology made the development of Arminian and experientialist alternatives the more imperative. The Charismatic movement was still very much in its infancy in the older denominations and would receive little support from them. But it would become more vital to the health of the evangelical movement as a whole as the movement moved away from Keswick pietism, first retreating from a preoccupation with religious experience, and then, over time, losing the discipline of daily devotional practices such as the Quiet Time.

70 Ward, *The Bush Still Burns*, 391–401.

Chapter Eleven

SHOCKS TO THE SYSTEM

Secular Challenges, 1966–1979

'Well, you know, that is not certain, not certain, not certain at all. Not certain. It might easily, easily, it might easily, quite easily, just fall away after 20 years or so. Just fall away.'
(Michael Ramsey, Archbishop of Canterbury, when asked in the early 1970s if the Church would survive into the next century).

Coming off a decade of equipoise, when Christian and social values were largely aligned, evangelicals were unprepared for the shocks of the 1960s and 1970s.[1] Don Dunstan, Labor Premier of South Australia, characterised the period as 'a king tide of change'.[2] Probably the most radical decades in Australian history, they witnessed the dismantling of the 'White Australia' policy, the Vietnam War, the new morality, and the Whitlam government. The churches favoured the first and with their experience of foreign missions were less averse to multiculturalism than most Australians, but they were tested by the reality that multiculturalism with Asians meant multifaith. The most conservative of them endorsed Australia's engagement in the Vietnam War as they were anti-Communist, but a large number of evangelicals opposed it, especially as the war dragged on. The new morality appeared to them to be the old immorality, and the Whitlam government was seen to be undermining traditional morality by its passage of the Family Law Act (1975) which allowed

---

1 David Hilliard, 'The Religious Crisis of the 1960s: The Experience of the Australian Churches', *JRH* 21.2, 1997, 209–28; Callum G. Brown, 'What was the Religious Crisis of the 1960s?' *JRH,* 34.4, 2010, 468–479.

2 Quoted by Angela Woollacott, 'Gender and Sexuality', in Deryck M Schreuder and Stuart Ward, (eds), *Australia's Empire, Oxford History of the British Empire* (Oxford: OUP, 2008), 331.

for no-fault divorce subsequent to a year of marital separation. Altogether conservative Christians were on the back foot and could rightly be accused of opposing the very principles they espoused in the nineteenth century: civilisation, progress and freedom. These ideals, when no longer viewed through the lens of Christian faith and morality, lost their appeal. At the same time, Christian faith and morality lost traction in the Australian soul. They were in some danger of becoming worse than irrelevant, namely meaningless.

From the perspective of evangelical spirituality, the 1960s was a glacial decade. Secularity, the exclusion of religion from public concerns and cultural convictions, was rampant and the religious tide ebbed. Australia, said sociologist Hans Mol in 1971, was either 'a Christian nation in search of a religion, or a heathen nation in flight from one'.[3] Liberal Christianity, in particular, was in big trouble, and at the universities the Student Christian Movement subsided dramatically and never really recovered. It became a social justice movement without theology.[4] Denominational membership which had been rising steadily from 1931 (though usually below population growth) peaked in the early 1960s. From the mid-1960s, mainline denominational membership began to slide.[5] Church attendance fell among the Australian population from 41% attending at least monthly in 1960 to around 24% in 1985. Sunday School attendance, still huge at the beginning of the 1960s, declined dramatically with the introduction of Sunday sport. Numerical decline was a feature across Western churches apart from the United States. The Archbishop of Canterbury, when asked if the Church would survive into the next century, responded: 'Well, you know, that is not certain, not certain, not certain at all. Not certain. It might easily, easily, it might easily, quite easily, just fall away after 20 years or so. Just fall away.'[6]

The 1970s was a time of Australian re-awakening and re-evaluation of the national identity and experience. Post-war 'baby boomers', now in young adulthood, experimented with new lifestyles, rejected traditional moral values, but held more firmly than ever to the value of material security. John Gorton, Liberal Prime Minister, 1968–1971, established the Australian Council for the Arts and the Australian Film Development Corporation which fostered

3 Hans J.J. Mol, *Religion in Australia: A Sociological Investigation* (Melbourne: Nelson, 1971), 302.

4 Renate Howe, *A Century of Influence: The Australian Student Christian Movement* 1896–1996 (Sydney: UNSW Press, 2009), ch12.

5 W.W. Phillips, 'Religion', in W. Vamplew (ed.), *Australians: Historical Statistics* (Broadway: Fairfax, Syme and Weldon, 1987).

6 Quoted in Monica Furlong, *C of E; The State It's In* (Hodder and Stoughton, 2000), 117.

cultural innovation and new interpretations of the Australian identity.[7] Large-scale immigration of those of a non-English speaking background, made assimilationist aspirations a pipe-dream, and hopes of a common national identity faded.[8] The works of Miriam Dixson and Anne Summers called attention to the role of women in Australian history, and Geoffrey Blainey and Henry Reynolds rescued the Aboriginal people from historical oblivion.[9] There was a recovery of interest in things spiritual, but not in the engaged spirituality of traditional Christianity. This was the spirituality of private experience.[10]

From the evangelical perspective, things could have been worse. Australia was actually not nearly as secularised as Europe, as measured by the percentage who attended church, prayed, and professed to believe in God. Further, in so far as Australia was increasingly influenced by America, it was subject to strong evangelical currents. In 1972 Dean Kelley published his influential study *Why Conservative Churches are Growing*.[11] In 1974 the National Council of Churches' *Yearbook of American and Canadian Churches* showed that conservative, missionary-minded churches were the only ones enjoying significant membership growth. The strength and resilience of evangelicalism in the USA surprised the prophets of Christianity's demise, and a cover story in *Newsweek* labelled 1976 'the year of the evangelical'. American evangelicals responded energetically to the 'great shock' of the sexual revolution with a conservative backlash. In Australia, the evangelical movement was as strong as it had ever been numerically and intellectually, but because of secularisation it was weaker culturally. There was no year of the evangelical or conservative backlash in Australia in the 1970s.

How did evangelicals understand the changes which overwhelmed Australia in the 1960s and 70s? Was it primarily a negative understanding: – a crisis

---

7 Paul Strangio, 'Instability, 1966–82' in Alison Bashford and Stuart Macintyre, (eds.), *The Cambridge History of Australia* 2 vols (Port Melbourne; New York: CUP, 2013), vol.2, 143.

8 James Jupp, 'Identity', in Richard Nile (ed.), *Australian Civilisation* (Melbourne: OUP, 1994), 78.

9 Miriam Dixson, *The Real Matilda: Women and Identity in Australia, 1788*–1975 (Ringwood: Penguin 1976); Anne Summers, *Damned Whores and God's Police: The Colonization of Women in Australia* (Ringwood and Harmondsworth: Penguin, 1976); Geoffrey Blainey, *The Triumph of the Nomads: A History of Ancient Australia* (London, Macmillan, 1976); Henry Reynolds, *The Other Side of the Frontier: Aboriginal Resistance to the European Invasion of Australia* (Ringwood: Penguin, 1982).

10 David Tacey, *Re-enchantment: The New Australian Spirituality* (Sydney: Harper Collins, 1999), 239.

11 (New York: Harper & Row, 1972).

from which there could be no return? A disaster portending moral declension demanding resistance? An eclipse of any hope for the development of a national conscience? Or were the changes to be seen more optimistically as an emergency calling for the contribution of social capital to address need? Was there an opportunity to find a new way to bring the Gospel to bear on the Australian soul and to write new chapters consistent with the romantic trajectory of their own history?

The Vietnam War

By the mid-1960s the Menzies government, jittery about Communism's incursion into Indochina, committed troops to oppose it in Vietnam. At the beginning of the Vietnam War, the majority of the Australian public supported the government's decision to join American intervention in Vietnam, although the conscription which soon followed was never popular. There is no evidence that evangelicals in large numbers differed from the public in general in their support of the conflict during its first years, nor in their distaste for conscription. Many accepted the 'domino theory' promoted by American and Australian governments that expansionist Communist forces must be deterred from invading the nation's Asian neighbours, otherwise the Communists would eventually reach Australia itself.[12]

Among evangelical leaders, Anglican Archbishop Hugh Gough of Sydney took a position of resolute support for the war. He visited Vietnam in 1965. Wearing military denims to demonstrate his affinity with the troops, he proclaimed that the defeat of the Vietcong was just a matter of time. He told a reporter, 'There is no question of who's going to win – it's just a question of when. The trouble has been to find the Comms, but if they come out and fight it could be over very quickly'. The remarks set off a firestorm of criticism by intellectuals and academics. Students in particular were outraged and posters soon appeared on the Sydney University campus with the slogan 'Gough Must Go'.[13] In Melbourne, Archbishop Woods, though, or perhaps because, he had a distinguished war record – he had to be fished out of the sea at Dunkirk – was a consistent critic of the decision to go to war in Vietnam.[14]

12 Jeffrey Grey and Jeff Doyle, (eds.), *Vietnam: War, Myth and Memory* (Sydney: Allen & Unwin, 1992).

13 *SMH*, 27 October 1967, 17.

14 Brian Porter, *Frank Woods: Archbishop of Melbourne* (Parkville: Trinity College, 2009), 39.

The 1964 National Service Act provided for the re-introduction of conscription. In total, 15,381 conscripts served in Vietnam, just over a quarter of the Australian armed forces sent there between 1962 and 1975. As in previous twentieth-century wars, around twenty percent of those Diggers who served in the armed forces during the Vietnam conflict were evangelical Christians.[15] Eric Trezise, who served with Everyman's Welfare Service in Vietnam in 1970–71, usually found from fifty to seventy dedicated Christians in each battalion and about another hundred or more who could be classified as 'seriously interested' in spiritual matters.[16]

One conscript, Nick Cooper, grew up in Wangaratta in Victoria. He became a Christian at age nineteen shortly before his army service through the witness of his girlfriend and future wife, Lois Schmidt. He was conscripted on 8 July 1970 and served in Vietnam in 1971–1972. He sustained his faith in Vietnam through Bible reading and prayer, and through Lois's letters and prayers and a steady stream of spiritual literature from the local Brethren church back home. He sometimes attended an Everyman's hut in Vietnam and used his carpentry and building skills at a nearby Catholic orphanage. After the war, he was 'very restless' and had a hard time settling down. He finally yielded to a call to the ministry and trained at the Bible College of Victoria from 1996 to 1998. In retrospect, he regarded the Vietnam War as 'immoral' and said that if he knew then what he had come to believe, he would have been a conscientious objector.[17]

Bryan Nicholls, later a Uniting Church minister, served in Vietnam, not as a 'nasho', but as a member of the regular army. He enlisted in 1956 and was posted to Vietnam from October 1965 to October 1966. Nicholls was not a Christian during his deployment to Vietnam. He knew one man in his unit who was an outspoken, Bible-believing Christian, and that individual was regarded as a good solder and treated well by his mates.[18] Nicholls personally attended only one religious event while in Vietnam and that was a Christmas Day communion service in 1965. It made a profound impression on him as an unnamed chaplain preached a sermon on Psalm 23 which made Nicholls aware of his own mortality. In 1968, after twelve years in the army, Nicholls decided not to reenlist. His Vietnam memories and his wife's religious testimony

15 This is the estimate of regular army Chaplain Les Thompson. Lester Thompson interviewed by Linder, 30 June 2004.

16 Eric Trezise interviewed by Linder, 10 July 2004, Australian battalions in Vietnam contained approximately 1,000 men.

17 Nicholas H. Cooper interviewed by Linder, 12 March 2001.

18 Bryan J. Nicholls interviewed by Linder, 16 March 2001.

launched him on a spiritual pilgrimage that led to his commitment to Jesus Christ and to the ministry. He enrolled at the Theological Hall of the Uniting Church of Victoria at Ormond College and was ordained to the ministry in 1994. His Vietnam experience became the focal point of his life and, following his ordination, a vital part of his Christian ministry. While pastor of the Uniting Church in Ballarat, Victoria, he reached a number of Vietnam veterans with the Gospel message of spiritual healing.

Bob May served in Vietnam in 1966 and 1967 as a signalman. He had been to the 1959 Billy Graham Crusade in Sydney and went forward in one of the meetings, but there was no follow-up and he drifted away from any pretence of a religious life. He acknowledges that in Vietnam he 'sank into the depths of depravity'. He was impressed by the Christian witness of five young men who lived exemplary lives and resisted the pressures to imbibe alcohol and visit the brothels. His war experiences gave him nightmares for years afterward. He recalls being caught in a minefield and watching some of his mates blown up a few feet away. He saw Vietnamese civilians lying along the roadside, like kangaroo road kill in the outback.[19] Discharged in 1969, May went back to his hard living lifestyle. However, he and his wife Sandy made a commitment to Christ in 1983. He trained at the Baptist Theological College of Queensland (now Malyon College) and came to serve as the padre for the Vietnam Vets Motorcycle Club in Brisbane. He believes that God used his Vietnam experiences to prepare him for this ministry, especially to Vietnam veterans.

Clarence Ormsby was a Kiwi. He served in Vietnam from 1966 to 1968 in a New Zealand artillery unit. He grew up in a Maori community in New Zealand, and after an early marriage, found himself responsible for a wife and child. Because the government offered strong economic incentives for those who joined the NZ Defence Forces, he volunteered for Vietnam, enlisting in 1966 at age nineteen. Shortly after arriving in Vietnam, he received a letter from his wife informing him that she was divorcing him and taking their daughter with her. Ormsby was heavily involved in combat field operations, and the carnage soon began to prey on his mind. The suicide of a close mate shook his rational and spiritual foundations. He came to believe that 'life had no purpose'. And, he reasoned, 'if no purpose, then there must be no God'. He felt 'a growing and pervasive sense of evil' in his life. He became reckless and suicidal. After the Tet Offensive of January 1968, he descended into the abyss of grog and drugs. He observed, 'I went into a killing mode. I went

19 Robert C. May interviewed by Linder, 9 June 2001.

out on a mission, killed, and came back to get staggering drunk.' One day he cracked and put his service revolver to his Commanding Officer's head. He later came to believe that he did not pull the trigger because God had work for him to do in the future.

Following his Vietnam experience, Ormsby continued his dependence on drugs and alcohol. His depression deepened, and he walked out on his second wife and children. The turning point began when, at his estranged wife's insistence as a precondition of reconciliation, he began to attend meetings of the Church of Christ in Gosford, north of Sydney, where he now lived. Then, on 13 November 1991, he suffered a massive heart attack. When he awoke, he found his wife and Eric Trezise, an old Christian friend from Vietnam, at his bedside. Trezise challenged him to embrace Christ. From that day the craving for cigarettes, liquor and drugs was gone. His depression lifted and the bitterness of the Vietnam years dissipated. Clarence Ormsby was a 'new man in Christ'.

This set the stage for a remarkable ministry. In preparation for the dedication of the Vietnam War Memorial in Canberra on 3 October 1992, Ormsby dreamed of creating a 'Vietnam Veterans' Memorial Bible' to give to each ex-Vietnam serviceman attending the dedication. He and his wife walked the streets of Sydney asking for donations to publish the 5,000 Bibles he hoped to hand out on the occasion in Canberra. One little girl gave five cents. The money was raised and the special Bibles printed. Ormsby and Bob Millard, a Vietnam veteran friend, arrived at 4:30 am to oversee the distribution. However, the Bibles had not yet been delivered when the time came for the march. According to Ormsby, providentially, the march was delayed for thirty minutes and the Bibles arrived ten minutes before the march began. The men and women began streaming out of the ceremonial area and some took a Bible and others said 'no thanks'. After about a hundred individuals had passed the Bible distributors, a crowd of children gathered and asked, 'can we help hand out Bibles?' As the children handed them out, not one veteran turned them down. Then a number of women appeared and offered to help distribute the special Bibles, and not one veteran refused them either. In three hours, the marching veterans had accepted some 4,500 Bibles. It had all gone so much better than he could have orchestrated that Ormsby was not really surprised to discover later that the Military Christian Fellowship Movement had been praying for his scheme to distribute the special Vietnam Veterans' Bible.[20]

---

20 Clarence Ormsby interviewed by Linder, 13 June 2001.

From 1992 Ormsby dedicated his life to helping his fellow Vietnam veterans. He operated a Vietnam Veterans' Christian Counselling Centre and visited jails seeking veterans he could help. His home in Gosford became a refuge for the abused wives of Vietnam veterans and as a place where veterans whose spouses had left them for various reasons could come for help and counselling. One such veteran found Christ and became a Pentecostal minister. Another cleaned up his life and eventually became an Army Reserve chaplain. Ormsby's various ministries aimed at battered Vietnam veterans and included a campaign to help victims of the chemicals used in the war.[21]

Fifty-five Australian army padres served in Vietnam. Sectarian rivalry between them was unknown. Francis Gorman (Roman Catholic), Howard Dillon (Church of England), and Clarry Badcock (Protestant Denominations) were so close that the soldiers, seeing them always together, whether on or off duty, called them the 'Holy Trinity'.[22] Among evangelical chaplains, Anglican Lester Thompson was invited to join the army by Alan Begbie, Chaplain General of the Australian Defence Forces and a Sydney Anglican minister. Thompson was one of nine Australian Army padres who were in Vietnam at any given time during the war. This meant that there was one chaplain for every 1,000 men and that they all saw plenty of combat. Thompson was involved in the Battle of Long Tan on 18 August 1966, in which 18 Australians died, and ministered to many wounded and dying men, and assisted in the burial of 245 enemy bodies.[23] He recalled hearing a corporal who was an evangelical believer ask a dying Digger if he was a Christian. The Digger replied, 'I wasn't this morning but I am now'. Others said the Lord's Prayer as they died.[24] When he held a service in the jungle under combat conditions, it was usually twenty minutes long, and included the Eucharist, a Bible reading and a ten-minute sermonette. He had a ready congregation: as Sergeant Bob Buick of Thompson's unit observed: 'Australian soldiers might not be perfect but they are imbued with basic Christian values, regardless of what they might say or how they might appear'.[25]

Not all evangelicals, however, were willing to condone or participate in the war. Far from it, they were well represented in the growing opposition to

---

21 Clarence Ormsby, 'Political Poison' http://www.crimehurts.org/politics-03.html (accessed 5 September 2016).

22 Michael Gladwin, *Captains of the Soul: A History of Australian Army Chaplains* (Newport: Big Sky Publishing, 2013), 226.

23 Gladwin, *Captains of the Soul*, 207f.

24 Lester Thompson interviewed by Linder, 30 June 2004.

25 Bob Buick with Gary McKay, *All Guts and No Glory: The Story of a Long Tan Warrior* (St. Leonards: Allen & Unwin, 2000), 218.

the conflict in the late 1960s. Anti-war feelings flourished in the evangelical radical discipleship communities established in Australian cities, including the House of the New World in Sydney and the House of Freedom in Brisbane.[26] Francis James, Sydney Anglican journalist, criticised the Vietnam conflict and worked against it through his much-read newspaper *The Anglican*.[27] James infuriated Prime Minister Robert Menzies in 1965 by breaking the news that Australian forces were to be sent to Vietnam. James had a mole in the cabinet – future Prime Minister William McMahon[28] who often provided James with the news before it was news.

In Victoria, Methodist evangelical clergy who opposed the war included long-time peace activists Frank Hartley, Rex Mathias, Darcy Wood and Elizabeth Wood-Ellem.[29] The NSW Methodist Conference in October 1967 called for an end to Australian military involvement. Bruce Lumsden, scion of a leading Melbourne evangelical family, World War II returned airman, was appointed headmaster of Caulfield Grammar School in Melbourne in 1965, and his school became a centre of debate and resistance to the war in Vietnam.[30] The use of napalm in Southeast Asia had become a moral issue to many. Kenneth Grigg and Geoff Forster, two Melbourne Baptist leaders, were particularly vociferous on this issue.[31] In 1967, both the Victorian Baptist yearly assembly and its Tasmanian counterpart pressed for an end to the war.

The Vietnam crisis divided the churches. In a famous incident, Broughton Knox, principal of Moore College, pulled the plug on one of Alan Walker's radio broadcasts. Walker's Central Methodist Mission had a regular live weekly broadcast of one of its Sunday services over Radio 2CH. The station was owned by the NSW Council of Churches, of which Broughton Knox was chairman. The topic for discussion on the afternoon of 12 November 1967 was 'Vietnam and the Senate Elections'. Walker urged his hearers in the Lyceum and his listening audience to vote only for Senate candidates who would pledge

26 Athol Gill, *The Fringes of Freedom: Following Jesus, Living Together, Working for Justice* (Homebush West: Lancer Books, 1990), chapter 9, 'Christian Peacemakers', 193–211.

27 The peak circulation of *The Anglican* from 1952 to 1969 was 93,000 copies. Francis James interviewed by Stuart Piggin, Margaret Lamb and Robert D. Linder, 19 June 1990.

28 McMahon was a Sydney Anglican who had once trained for the ministry at Moore Theological College. James and McMahon knew each other well. Francis James, interviewed 19 June 1990.

29 Wesley Hartley interviewed by Linder, 12 January 2004.

30 David Thomson, Obituary of Bruce Clyde Lumsden, *The Age*, 28 July 2004, 17.

31 Geoff Forster, 'War: A Challenge to Christians', *Australian Baptist*, 11 January 1967, 5.

to work to end the Vietnam conflict.[32] Knox still supported the war and was particularly riled on this occasion by Walker's one-sided presentation.[33] He phoned the radio station and ordered the attending technician to terminate the broadcast.[34] *The Sydney Morning Herald* made it front-page news. Its headline screamed 'ANTI-WAR PROGRAM CUT OFF AIR'.[35] Two days later the paper's editorial was highly critical of Knox's action. It insisted that Knox owed an explanation to both the Central Methodist Mission and the public for interfering with free speech, denouncing Knox as a censor.[36] Knox was impervious to such pressure as, consistent with Luke 12:32–34, he had long learned to be single-minded and free from fear.[37]

Victoria seems to have been the centre of evangelical opposition to the war. On 30 May 1971 evangelical students from Monash, La Trobe and Melbourne Universities participated in the third Melbourne Moratorium March, led by Labor Party leader Dr. Jim Cairns and Anglican Bishop C. Edward Crowther of South Africa. The Moratorium attracted more than 50,000 marchers. Bob Robinson of Ridley College, Alan Gijsbers the president of the Melbourne EU, and Bruce Wearne, who was to become the president of the Monash Christian Radicals Club, organised evangelical support for the event. They decided to provide coffee for the demonstrators at the end of the march, and EU workers distributed more than 500 cups of coffee accompanied by a leaflet which said: 'We believe peace is more than the absence of war. This cup of coffee is given to you in the name of Jesus, the Prince of Peace'. Alan Gijsbers later received a note from Jim Cairns: 'The bishop and I had just arrived at the end of the march route and he said to me, "That's over now. Wouldn't it be lovely to have a cup of coffee?" I have never known Episcopal power to be so immediate!'[38]

The evangelical movement was proving far from monolithic in its conservatism. A surprisingly large number of evangelical believers had come to question and/or oppose the war. Opposition to the war was particularly intense among

---

32 Alan Walker, 'Vietnam and the Senate Elections', *The Methodist*, 18 November 1967, 2.

33 Donald I. Wright, *Alan Walker: Conscience of the Nation* (Adelaide: Openbook, 1997), 186.

34 Alan Gill, 'God's Radical: Alan Walker on God, ASIO and Retirement', *SMH,* 25 March 1995, 4A.

35 *SMH*, 13 November 1967, 1.

36 *SMH*, 15 November 1967, 2.

37 D.B. Knox, *Justification by Faith* (London: The Church Book Room Press, 1959), 22.

38 Bruce Wearne interviewed by Linder, 7 July 2003. Also see *Crucible*, 4.1, April-May 1974, for examples of CRC thinking on the issues that evangelical Christian students faced in the 1970s.

Victorian evangelicals, especially among the Baptists. A returned Methodist chaplain found it hard to get a position in his own church because it had gone 'anti-war'.[39] Evangelical dissent was revived and the evangelical movement was divided by it. Many empathised with the soldiers who returned from Vietnam only to be berated by those who believed that Australia's involvement in Vietnam was a right wing disaster and those, ever increasing in number, who joined with the massive anti-war moratoriums.

By 11 January 1973, Australian involvement in the longest and most controversial war in the nation's history was over. The cost?

> Approximately 50,000 Australians served in Vietnam between 1962 and 1972. Of these, 501 were killed or listed as missing presumed dead, and 3,121 were wounded.[40]

Vietnam was a schism in the Australian soul. Bitter as it was, it did not last. By the late 1980s anti-war Australians who had vented their displeasure by reproaching Vietnam veterans repented of this injustice and were prepared to recognise the courage and self-sacrifice of those who had fought in Vietnam. The perspective of history will also be kind to chaplains of all denominations who served in Vietnam, who with very few exceptions, proved good and faithful servants of their master. Arguably, too, the 'spiritual instinct' did not desert the average Australian soldier. Vietnam was a severe test of authenticity akin to prisoner of war camps in World War II, and the leadership given by the faithful brought some hope to an apparently hopeless and deteriorating situation. This very Christian contribution was given in a very Australian way. Chaplains represented the Australian way of the interdependence, rather than the separation, of church and state. They were subservient to the state, but still engaged with it in the task of producing and preserving a military force, the morale of which was threatened by drug and alcohol abuse, sexual disease, and psychological despair. Again, the state looked to the church to strengthen the moral fibre of its soldiers, and the church welcomed the inclination of the state to supplement military might with financial and practical aid and, in a situation of total war, to have consciences sensitised to the need to minimise death and injury to the civilian population.

A lower percentage of the soldiers attended church parades than had been the case in World War II, reflecting the secularisation then evident in the wider Australian population. That was a challenge to the evangelistic instincts

39 Gladwin, *Captains of the Soul*, 230, 241, 245.

40 Jeffrey Grey, *A Military History of Australia* (Cambridge: CUP, 1990), 248–9.

of Christians, especially of evangelicals for whom evangelism was a primary goal. The pitiless reality of war reinforced concern for the eternal state of those who faced imminent death, but it also created such stress among survivors that pastoral care seemed a more pressing goal than evangelism. The extremity forced new solutions: surely evangelism was more effective when presented through pastoral care. Surely, too, it was more effective when it was an ecumenical work of all the denominations. The non-sectarianism of the work of chaplains in Vietnam was now the easier because of Vatican II's new hospitality towards Protestants. Whatever the feeling on the relationship between evangelism and pastoral care, there was unanimity in the view that the latter had to be done more effectively. Chaplains welcomed the increased professionalisation of care-giving through developments in psychology and social sciences and the deeper understanding they brought of the reality of post-traumatic stress. Professionalisation in caregiving was to become a mark of the new therapeutic evangelicalism of the end of the twentieth century.

The Vietnam experience was also an opportunity for Australian values to be reinforced by vital Christianity. Faith, hope and compassion were transformative in that context. They gave a distinctively Christian strain to the 'digger's ideal of mateship, unity and self-sacrifice'.[41] One who has reflected deeply on this relationship is Neville Clark OAM, English and History teacher at Geelong Grammar School and then Headmaster of Mentone Grammar School in Melbourne. On 6 August 1967, the 7th Battalion of the Royal Australian Army came under attack by Viet Cong in Phuoc Tuy Province. Clark, then a lieutenant with the 106th Field Battery, directed artillery fire against the enemy which was only 50 metres in front of him. Since the Australian howitzers were ten kilometres away, this was an extraordinary feat of precision, which Clark performed with such coolness in spite of the danger to himself, that he was awarded the Military Cross. A devout evangelical Christian, he was to become a much-acclaimed speaker at Dawn Services on Anzac Day at the Melbourne Shrine of Remembrance. At the 2015 service he spoke of 'the traditions of Anzac', a formulation of Australian values as a compound of Classical virtues and Christian values:

> The traditions of Anzac: courage and endurance ... traditions of duty before entitlement; self-reliance and initiative before complaint and victimhood; cheerfulness and wry humour rather than gloom and despair; unselfish team-playing; above all, standing by your mates,

41 Gladwin, *Captains of the Soul*, 245.

> who are beacons of hope, inspiring the rest of us every day Australians to do exceptional things in the spirit of Anzac.[42]

Secular Politics

The Australian Labor Party was probably more rapidly secularised than the wider community. In Federal politics, the Labor party, led by Gough Whitlam from 1967 to 1977, believed it could engage in mocking Christians with impunity. Gil Duthie (Labor, Tasmania) was a member of the New and Permanent Parliament House Committee, charged with the oversight of a new parliamentary building for the federal capital. On 2 March 1970, Duthie recorded in his diary the following observation on three other Labor members of the committee:

> Jim Cavanagh attacked the use of the word 'chapel' in the new Parliament & got it altered to 'meditation room'. Murphy and Cavanagh, both agnostics, said some frightening things & Gough Whitlam made the cynical comment, 'Anyway, there won't be any believers left by 2000 A.D.'[43]

Highly effective Labor premiers, Don Dunstan in South Australia and Neville Wran in NSW, repealed legislation designed in a less libertarian age to regulate behaviour in a way consistent with what were understood to be Christian values. Sunday observance was the first legally-sanctioned practice to go. The opportunities for gambling proliferated; hotels were opened on Sundays and hotel trading hours were extended; censorship collapsed, and pornography became a legal industry; abortion on demand became a legal reality; and homosexuality was decriminalised.

Don Dunstan (Premier 1967–68 and 1970–79) was an Anglican in his early days, participating actively in the Adelaide diocesan synod.[44] But his was an Anglicanism of the non-evangelical kind, allergic to the moralising of the wowsers or to any regulation of private behaviour. He became committed to extending personal liberty which, for him, meant repealing what he understood

42 Neville Clark's speech from the dawn service, Apr 26, 2015, accessed 31 July 2017, at https://www.reddit.com/r/melbourne/comments/33vm8l/neville_clarks_speech_from_the_dawn_service/.

43 Gil Duthie, *I had 50,000 Bosses: Memoirs of a Labor Backbencher, 1946–1975* (Sydney: Angus & Robertson, 1984), 241f.

44 David Hilliard, 'Anglicans in South Australian Public Life', *Journal of the Historical Society of South Australia*, 34, 2006, 5–16.

to be repressive laws. He liked to describe his Government as 'libertarian'. He extended liquor trading hours, decriminalised homosexual practice, and was quite happy to see the proliferation of sex shops, pornography, prostitution and nude bathing. He castigated the Christian 'wowser' as the 'drab-souled Philistine haunted by the memories of others' happiness.'[45]

In 1971 Dunstan appointed prominent nuclear physicist, Mark Oliphant, whom he had never met, as State Governor, believing him to be a radical nonconformist. Oliphant had an altogether more robust view of what was involved in liberty than freedom to sleep with whom you liked. In moral matters, he was conventional and quite unprepared for the bursting of the floodwaters of libertinism. A warning shot was fired across Dunstan's bows when Oliphant refused, on his appointment as Governor, to allow the Press to characterise him as an 'agnostic'. He was certainly unorthodox, with a distaste for 'most of the Old Testament' and 'St Paul's obsessions', but he still thought of himself as a 'christian',[46] and was esteemed by such radical clergy as Bishop Burgmann for his appreciation of the compatibility of the laws of nature with the thoughts of God.

In 1975, Paul Barnett, evangelical Anglican rector of Holy Trinity Church, Adelaide, wrote to the Governor to express his 'outraged helplessness' at Dunstan's new anti-censorship legislation. In taking this action, he was exploiting the special link he had with the Governor, who nominally appointed and confirmed rectors of Holy Trinity. Barnett pleaded with the Governor to intercede with the Premier to reconsider the legislation and suggested that he might view some of the material now removed from censorship if he doubted the seriousness of the matter. The Governor asked the Commissioner of Police for samples of the offensive material. He was so appalled that he requested Dunstan to call on him. Dunstan reiterated that his was a libertarian government and that, while he was Premier, there would be no censorship of what adults could read in private and, possibly unwilling to be lectured to, he beat a hasty retreat. In the opinion of Oliphant's biographers, this event was to prove 'the real parting of the ways' between Governor and Premier.[47] It contributed to the Governor's repeated threats of resignation before the end of his term in 1976 and to the damaging of the Government and its eventual fall in 1979. But the defenders of conservative morality were on the back foot, and their victories became fewer and harder won. The changes of a

45 Keith Dunstan, *Wowsers* (Melbourne: Cassell, 1968), 2.

46 Stewart Cockburn and David Ellyard, *Oliphant* (Adelaide: Axiom Books, 1981), 313.

47 Cockburn, *Oliphant*, 315.

type Dunstan championed normally operated on a 'one-way ratchet system'. They moved easily in the direction he sought; reversing them required more muscle than most of the churches then had. Barnett's 'muscular Christianity' was becoming exceptional.

Muscularity was more common among the secularists. Neville Wran, NSW Premier from 1976 to 1986, was possessed of a crusading zeal which could be illiberal and undemocratic. When in 1979 he legalised the opening of hotels on Sundays it was contrary to the overwhelming wish of the NSW public expressed in repeated referendums. In a political arena where special interest groups such as the liquor industry were able to focus pressure through lobbying, democracy was sacrificed.

What Christians – Catholic and Protestant – took to be excessive hedonism galvanised them into resistance. In South Australia where Methodism had once withstood the liquor industry, the Festival of Light was formed in 1973 to 'make a stand against moral decline'.[48] Based on the English Festival of Light which gathered 35,000 Christians in Trafalgar Square in 1971, it was supported not only by the 'wowsers', but also by Roman Catholics who had never in the past had a reputation for wowserism. The collaboration of evangelicals and Catholics was a dramatic demonstration of the death of sectarianism among even the most conservative of Christians after Vatican II and it vindicated such ecumenical endeavours by discharging increased moral energy into the community. Its analysis of the alignment of Australian values with the Judeo-Christian tradition coincided with the national debate on the nature of the Australian identity.

In 1974 Fred Nile was appointed full-time NSW Director of the Australian Festival of Light. His father was a King's Cross taxi driver and his mother a King's Cross waitress, thus accounting for his lifelong concern for the probity of Sydney's seediest district. Nile had graduated from the Melbourne Bible Institute in 1957. The following year, Elaine and Fred Nile were married at Revesby Evangelical Congregational Church of the Puritan Heritage, where Fred was converted. The call to full-time Christian service came through the preaching of John Ridley. From 1958 to 1963 Nile completed further theological and university courses and rejected 'the foolishness and barrenness of modernism'.[49] He was ordained in the Congregational Church in 1964 and in that same year succeeded the Rev Norman Pell as full-time National Director

48 Roger C. Thompson, *Religion in Australia* (Melbourne: OUP, 1994), 116; David Furse-Roberts, 'Keepers of the Flame: A History of the Australian Festival of Light 1973–1981', *Lucas,* 2.2, 2010, 46–66.

49 'A Call to Prayer and Action', Call to Australia, Leaflet no.1, 1991.

of the Australian Christian Endeavour Movement. In his connexion with the Festival of Light, Nile arranged for a number of prominent morals campaigners and Christian celebrities to visit Australia: Mary Whitehouse (1973, 1978 and 1984); Pat Boone (1974); the now converted Malcolm Muggeridge (1976); and Mother Teresa (1981). In response to Mary Whitehouse's September 1978 visit, Rupert Hamer, the Liberal Premier of Victoria, tightened anti-pornography legislation. Dunstan resisted, calling Whitehouse's campaign 'disgraceful'. But when SA Liberal MP Bruce Eastick remonstrated that *Just Boys*, a child pornography magazine, was as readily available in SA as the *Women's Weekly*, Dunstan was forced to introduce the Criminal Law (Prohibition of Child Pornography) Bill, which passed both houses of parliament without dissent.

The Call to Australia Party with Fred Nile as leader was formed in 1977 and Nile was elected to the NSW Legislative Council four years later. Defending a Christian nation required political power, and Nile developed appropriate words for the campaign. He insisted on calling Australia a 'Christian' or 'godly nation', opposed by a vocal minority. He was spokesman for the silent majority, Catholic as well as Protestant.[50] The culture wars required the end of sectarianism and the defence of what were now called 'Judeo-Christian values'. This tolerant, ecumenical descriptor signified that evangelicals had their own brand of political correctness. Thirty-eight years after his first election, Nile is the longest-serving member of the NSW parliament, and his party, now known as the Christian Democratic Party (CDP), at the time of writing holds the balance of power.

Aboriginal 'Self-Determination'

There was a decided increase in the momentum for 'Aboriginal uplift' in the 1960s. Two matters in the late 1950s had confronted all Australians with the problem. The December 1956 Grayden Report and a subsequent film made by William Grayden, a WA parliamentarian, and Pastor Doug Nicholls, shocked white Australians with damning evidence that malnutrition, blindness, disease and early death were common among the Aboriginal people of the Warburton Ranges in WA.[51] Then, in 1959, the legal struggle over the conviction of Aboriginal Rupert Max Stuart (see above, chapter 8) for the rape and murder of a young girl in Ceduna, SA, had sensitised many

50 Hugh Chilton, 'Evangelicals and the End of Christian Australia: Nation and Religion in the Public Square 1959–1979,' PhD, University of Sydney, 2014, 119, 122.

51 http://www.creativespirits.info/aboriginalculture/history/referendum-1967.html#ixzz1lrBXChTO, accessed 2 February 2012.

Australians to the dilemma of Australia's indigenous people 'caught between two worlds'.[52]

The Commonwealth Electoral Act was amended in 1962 to give the right to vote to Aboriginal people. In 1966 university students combined with Aboriginal people in the 'Freedom ride' headed by Charles Perkins. In the referendum of 1967 over 90 per cent of voters agreed that Aboriginal people should be counted in the census and that the Federal Parliament could make laws affecting Aboriginal people. The former enhanced their right to be considered citizens; the latter gave the Federal Government the power to make laws benefitting Aboriginal people. In 1973 Australia's new Labor Government under Gough Whitlam introduced the policy of Aboriginal self-determination. This meant that Aboriginal people were to decide for themselves the pace and the direction of their own development within the constraints of Australia's existing legal and social structures. In quick succession government policy for Aboriginal people had moved from 'protection' (1909) to 'assimilation' (1939) to 'self-determination' (1973) to 'self-management' (c1979).

In the 1970s the Department of Aboriginal Affairs implemented the 'homeland' movement, consistent with the policy of self-determination, encouraging the Aboriginal people to move 'back to country'. They would live in smaller communities than the old mission stations and set up small economies. They would thus be able to preserve a kin-based lifestyle. The trend towards support from the churches for this new policy was to be reinforced in the 1980s by liberation theology which stressed God's identification with the poor and marginalised, but by the 1990s this devolution had increased Aboriginal poverty by trapping them in uneconomical communities.[53]

Christian missionary agencies and churches were involved in all these activities, the more progressive pushing governments to go faster in the transition from one policy to another, and the more conservative bewailing the passing of a more paternalistic missionary era. The CMS Roper River Mission, now known as Ngukurr, was transferred in 1968 to the Welfare Branch of the Northern Territory. Its most revered leader was Michael Gumbuli Wurramara, the first Aboriginal to be ordained in the Territory (1973).[54] A gifted preacher and healer, he was involved with the translation of the Bible into Kriol. He had been encouraged in the days of assimilation not to submit uncritically

52 K.S. Inglis, *The Stuart Case*, (Melbourne: Black Inc., 2002), 328.

53 Diane Austin-Broos, 'Translating Christianity: some key words, events and sites in Western Arrernte Conversion', *Australian Journal of Anthropology*, 21.2010, 14–32.

54 Murray W. Seiffert, *Gumbuli of Ngukurr: Aboriginal Elder in Arnhem Land* (Brunswick East: Acorn Press, 2011), 226.

to government direction and he successfully fought to restrict alcohol at Ngukurr when it passed under government control.[55] With the formation of the Diocese of the Northern Territory also in 1968 the five CMS missions in Arnhem Land became parishes.[56] In 1974 funding provided under the Labor Government's policy of self-determination allowed the CMS Mission at Oenpelli to be transferred to the Aboriginal Community. The Presbyterian Mission at Ernabella was taken over by the Anangu people in the same year. Hermannsburg Lutheran Mission was transferred to the Aranda in 1975.

The devolution of power to Aboriginal people favoured by the Whitlam Government was resisted in Queensland by the conservative government of Joh Bjelke-Petersen.[57] In 1975 it took over the lands of the Aurukun Mission in Cape York. Founded by the Moravians in 1904, it had been a Presbyterian Mission. But the Presbyterians had come to regret their acquiescing in the takeover of their Mission at Mapoon (also at Cape York) by mining interests in 1963 when the village and James Ward Memorial Church had been burned to the ground by armed police. So, they fought furiously for the retention of the Aboriginal mission at Aurukun, and the Commonwealth Government supported them in the struggle. The wily Bjelke-Petersen outwitted them, but he was forced into a compromise with the Aboriginal community which became an Aboriginal-run shire council. Shaped by the rather stern paternalism of long-serving Presbyterian missionary superintendent, William McKenzie (1923–1965), Aurukun was still in the 1970s a 'liveable and vibrant society'.[58] But by 2000 it was a 'disaster zone', with alcohol, introduced in 1985, featuring in most of the suicides and murders which had become commonplace.[59]

Not all missionary work among Indigenous people was confined to fighting social problems. But, of necessity, even conservative missions could not ignore this dimension of their work. In 1969, Ralph Bell held crusades in Darwin and Elcho Island. Bell had been a gaol chaplain in the USA, and

---

55 Seiffert, *Gumbuli of Ngukurr*; Murray W. Seiffert, *Refuge on the Roper: The Origins of Roper River Mission Ngukurr* (Brunswick East: Acorn Press, 2008); Peter Berthon, *We Are Aboriginal: Our 100 Years: From Arnhem Land's First Mission to Ngukurr Today* (Ngukurr: St Matthew's Anglican Church, 2008); Keith Cole, *From Mission to Church: The CMS Mission to the Aborigines of Arnhem Land, 1908–1985* (Bendigo: Keith Cole Publications, 1985).

56 Ngukurr, Oenpelli, Numbulwar on the mainland and Umbakumba and Angurugu on Groote Eylandt.

57 Humphry McQueen, *Gone Tomorrow: Australia in the 80s* (Sydney: Angus & Robertson, 1982), 116–118.

58 Peter Sutton, *The Politics of Suffering: Indigenous Australia and the End of the Liberal Consensus* (Carlton: MUP, 2009), xv, 1.

59 Sutton, *The Politics of Suffering*, 1.

he became a close friend of Billy Graham who admired his rapport with the marginalised and made him an associate of the BGEA in 1965. He balanced the appeal to personal faith in Jesus with concern to address the problems of homelessness, crime and poverty. A decade after Bell's crusades in the NT the greatest revival in Aboriginal history began on Elcho Island.

In addition to growing awareness of Aboriginal needs, missions also increasingly realised that they should give greater responsibility to Aboriginal people themselves. Indeed, this was a factor in the generation of the Aboriginal Revival which began in 1979 and continued until 1984. The missions had been slow to baptise Aboriginal converts and then slow to ordain Aboriginal ministers. But those attitudes now passed with the recognition that Aboriginal people were among the most evangelised people on the planet, more likely to be professing Christians than white people. Much was made of their greater openness to the spiritual dimension to reality, and certainly they were far more effective in evangelising and nurturing their own than white missionaries.

Among the Aboriginal evangelists who did significant work in this period was Ron Williams. He was born in 1940 to Cissie, a Noongar woman from WA and was raised by his mother's parents. His grandfather loved him, but was unable to release him from the circle of poverty, alcohol and hopelessness. In 1958, he accompanied his niece to church and he was spoken to kindly by Frank Cole at the UAM at Gnowangerup near Perth. The other whitefellas Williams knew flirted with the Aboriginal women and/or sold sly grog, but Cole seemed to be different. He said to Williams 'God wants you to have the best, my son. He wants to put the best robe on you, like the prodigal son.' He gave Ron a Bible and a picture of Jesus carrying a lamb. Cole and Williams prayed together and Williams invited Jesus 'to change his life for the better and give him hope'.[60] Ron was never drunk again.

Williams then attended the first Aboriginal Bible college in WA. It was at Gnowangerup, and he then worked for a time for the UAM in the Warburton ranges, 1600 kilometres north-east of Perth. He was badly injured when he fell off a horse in 1963. The pain was so bad that he just wanted to die, but he heard a voice speaking through the pain, 'You shall not die, but live and proclaim what the Lord has done for you.'[61] The doctor who treated him told him he would never be able to learn how to drive as a result of his injuries. But in 1969 Dr Bruce Rowe, a one-time truck driver who trained as a doctor because he was sick of not being able to prevent many Aboriginal people

60 Diana Williams, *Horizon is where heaven and earth meet* (New York: Bantam Books, 2001), 55.

61 Williams, *Horizon*, 63.

around him from dying, helped Ron to learn how to drive. He also gave Ron his Land Rover, and by so doing set the direction of Ron's life. Ron drove all over Australia, especially up dead-end tracks, speaking with lonely people about the love of Jesus. It was an amazing ministry. He collected the stories of the people to whom he ministered, treasuring thousands of 'forgotten' dreams, and thus became the custodian of the longings of Indigenous people, a heritage for all Australians to be proud of.[62] In 1977 he was called back to Gnowangerup, there to become the first Aboriginal principal of a Bible college.

From 1974, Aboriginal Christian workers were able to receive training through the ecumenical Nungalinya College in Darwin or its extension in Queensland, Wontulp-Bi-Buya College. The foundation principal, Keith Cole, moved onto the college campus in Darwin just nine days before all the college facilities were destroyed by Cyclone Tracy, and the building process had to start all over again.[63] Torres Strait Islanders were trained at St Paul's Theological College on Moa Island until 1969 when the college closed. In 1989, it reopened on Thursday Island.

Training in Bible teaching and leadership was at the centre of another significant cross-cultural development by Australian evangelicals. On 16 September 1975, Papua New Guinea achieved independence from Australia. A decade earlier the Christian Leaders' Training College (CLTC) had commenced operations at Banz in the Western Highlands of New Guinea. This was in response to an appeal to evangelical organisations from the Unevangelised Field Mission (UFM), which had commenced work in PNG in 1932, to come together in support of a central Bible training school. On the initiative of Harry Orr and Alan Prior, who had worked as chaplains in PNG during the war, Australian Baptists had established a vital work in the highlands among the Enga peoples. Their earliest work was medical owing to the need to treat tropical diseases. Sister Betty Crouch who had worked with the BCA in Ceduna, South Australia, became the pioneer nurse in the highlands, serving there for 26 years.[64] But the rapidly growing Enga church, in need of Bible teachers and evangelists, sent students to the inter-denominational CLTC, contributing to its success.[65] Gilbert McArthur, a Baptist pastor, was appointed foundation

62 Williams, *Horizon*, 65.

63 Keith Cole, *'But I will be with You': An Autobiography* (Bendigo: Keith Cole Publications, 1988), 156–78.

64 Richard Ansoul, *Beautiful Feet: Australian Baptists enter Papua New Guinea* (Hawthorn: ABMS, 1981), 24–30.

65 Ken R. Manley, *From Woolloomooloo to Eternity: A History of Australian Baptists*, 2 vols. (Milton Keynes: Paternoster, 2006), 617–626.

principal. An 'orator of dreams' with 'a head for strategy', he had worked on missions in PNG between 1955 and 1959. CLTC commenced under the direction and control of MBI, receiving the indomitable support of second generation members of the 'Melbourne Clapham Sect' (see chapter five), including Len Buck, Vice President of MBI, clothing retailer and General Director and Chairman of UFM; Bill Clack, Men's Superintendent of MBI and President of the Missionary Aviation Fellowship (MAF); Alfred Coombe a wealthy grazier and Chairman of MBI and Wycliffe Bible Translators (WBT); and Ralph Davis Chairman of Mayne Nickless Transport. Appropriate younger personnel to staff the new college were to hand, riding the wave of spiritual blessing generated by the Billy Graham crusades of 1959.

CLTC was envisioned as a training centre for all the Melanesian peoples of the South Pacific. Students were required to accept the statement of faith of the Evangelical Alliance. The College was especially effective in training evangelists and in imparting knowledge of the Bible. From the start, its student intake included young Engas destined to play a leading role in the growth of the Baptist Church. Marked by community baptisms attended by thousands and by outbreaks of revival, Baptist leaders proved equal to the spiritual challenge of adapting Christian faith and practice to indigenous cultural norms.[66]

Control of the CLTC passed in 1973 from MBI to a locally-based council in good time before PNG achieved its independence. Expatriate representation on the new Council was still strong, however, and, while there were now eight Melanesian members of the Council, Len Buck was elected as foundation chairman.[67] Gilbert McArthur, foundation principal of CLTC, had moved on to become Field Director for the World Vision South Pacific Office based in Sydney. He established the Pacific Leaders' Fellowship. Aware that in the Pacific Islands almost every head of state and cabinet member and the most prominent business men had been educated in Christian schools and colleges, McArthur put together a team including Max Meyers, a former RAAF pilot and now with MAF,[68] to visit all these leaders and to encourage them to adopt Kingdom values. Most notably, they recruited the enthusiastic support of Sir Peter Kenilorea, several times Prime Minister of the Solomon Islands, and Ratu Sir Kamisese Mara, Prime Minister of Fiji.

66 Tony Cupit, Ros Gooden, and Ken Manley, (eds.), *From Five Barley Loaves: Australian Baptists in Global Mission, 1864–2010* (Preston: Mosaic Press, 2013), 219.

67 J. Oswald Sanders, *Planting Men in Melanesia* (Mt Hagen: Christian Leaders' Training College of PNG, 1978), 171; Ron and Gwen Roberts, *To Fight Better: A Biography of J Oswald Sanders* (Crowborough: Highland Books/OMF, 1989), 169.

68 Vic Ambrose, *Balus Bilong Mipela: The story of the Missionary Aviation Fellowship, Australia and New Zealand* (Melbourne: Missionary Aviation Fellowship, 1987).

In the early 1980s, McArthur, along with Len Buck, Bill Clack and Will Renshaw became involved with 'The Fellowship', a group of Christians who sought to foster Christian leadership in politics, operating in concert with the National Prayer Breakfast in Washington, DC.[69] The Americanisation of Australian evangelicalism thus took a step forward, but McArthur's desire to have the politics of the Pacific islands shaped by evangelical values predated his association with Americans with the same aspiration.

Women in Christian Ministry

Changes in social values and government policies were now as likely to divide evangelicals as theological and biblical questions. Gender and sexuality and state aid for church educational and welfare institutions became again the great issues they had been in the nineteenth century. But now they were resolved differently. The Bible was no longer accepted as foundational to societal views on sexuality by the wider public and yet governments no longer withheld state aid from church schools and welfare bodies.

The new feminism of the 1970s generated one of the most divisive movements within Australian evangelicalism. It was a feminism which was particularly potent in Australia as its most popular manifesto, *The Female Eunuch* (1970) was written by an Australian academic, Germaine Greer, who had been raised in a conservative Melbourne Catholic family. Her international best-seller was reinforced by a number of widely-read historical and cultural studies by other Australian women.[70] Greer had argued that the nuclear family, so defended by the church, was bad for women and for the raising of children. Women increasingly sought a role outside of the family. The traditional role of women in the church, attending to flowers, food and family, began to change as women entered the professions. Heroic examples of the old ways became rarer. The Baptist Ladies Luncheon Committee of the Baptist Union of Victoria had served 4,000 meals for the Union's Centenary Dinner in 1962. They provided a four-course luncheon in 1965 at the opening of Whitley College, the Baptist College in Melbourne, in the presence of Prime Minister and Dame Pattie Menzies. Not surprisingly, the Committee

69 David Price, *Live in Tents: Build only Altars: Gilbert McArthur – his Story* (Vermont South: MST Press, 2019), Chapter 11.

70 Beverley Kingston, *My wife, my daughter, and poor Mary Ann: women and work in Australia* (West Melbourne: Thomas Nelson, 1975); Anne Summers, *Damned Whores and God's Police: The Colonization of Women in Australia* (Ringwood: Penguin Books, 1975); Miriam Dixson, *The Real Matilda: Woman and Identity in Australia, 1788–1975* (Ringwood: Penguin Books Australia, 1976).

collapsed through exhaustion in the 1970s. Whitley was an environment where the ministry of women was especially encouraged, aided by visits from the international Baptist scholar, Thorwald Lorenzen.[71]

At the 1968 Lambeth Conference, Anglicans debated the ordination of women to the threefold ministry of deacons, priests, and bishops. Marcus Loane, Archbishop of Sydney, spoke strongly against the proposal. His principal argument was that such a move would further alienate men from the Church.[72] There were then no women in the Sydney synod. Bishop Jack Dain, later a firm supporter of women in ministry, was reported as having said of female membership of the Sydney synod, 'Perhaps it wouldn't be wise. I suppose men think there are some preserves they would like to keep to themselves.'[73] In 1972 the Sydney synod agreed to allow women to represent parishes, way behind Melbourne in 1924 and Adelaide in 1946. In 1973, the first woman was appointed to the Anglican General Synod – the Adelaide evangelical CMS worker, Irene Jeffreys. Another consistent supporter of female ministry was Mary Andrews who had served with CMS in China from 1938 to 1951. She was then Principal of Deaconess House and, though a member of 38 committees, had no seat in synod until 1990. But she was 'a tough lady and a politician',[74] and she let it be known that she was unimpressed by clergy, including bishops, who protested at every expression of feminist sentiment. Compared with the Japanese generals and Chinese Communists she had experienced, Anglican bishops were 'cream puffs'.[75] In China, she realised, there had been no more effective evangelists than 'Bible Women': discrimination against women, she insisted, weakened the Church in Australia.

In 1973, the General Synod's Commission on Doctrine unanimously reported that there were no theological objections to the ordination of women to the diaconate, and a majority reported that there were no theological objections to the ordination of women to the priesthood and the episcopate. Broughton Knox, however, penned a minority report in which he declared that there were indeed fundamental theological objections to the ordination of women as priests and bishops. To the astonishment of Sydney evangelicals,

---

71 Marita Rae Munro, '"A Struggle for Identity and Direction": A History of Victorian Baptists (1960–2000)', PhD, University of Melbourne, 2010,135, 139.

72 Ruth I. Sturmey, 'Women and the Anglican Church in Australia: Theology and Social Change', PhD, University of Sydney, 1989, 170.

73 *SMH*, 12 August 1968, 5.

74 Peter Jensen, address at the Remembering Mary Andrews conference, Moore College Library Day, 10 May 2014.

75 Margaret Rodgers, 'Mary Andrews: A Feminist before her time?' *Southern Cross Quarterly*, Summer 1996–97, 24–27.

however, Dr Leon Morris, principal of Ridley College in Melbourne, let it be known that as he was not convinced that the Bible was clearly opposed to the ordination of women, he would not oppose it either.[76] Within the Anglican part of the evangelical family, Sydney and Melbourne were in disagreement.[77] In 1976, while the Melbourne synod endorsed the principle of the ordination of women to the priesthood (sixteen years before it became a reality), Sydney synod defeated a motion to allow women to become church wardens. By this time:

> the content of the debate was beginning to show the differences that were to be so pronounced in later ordination debates. Sydney was primarily concerned with specific points of biblical interpretation and with the perceived practical and psychological problems of women working closely with men. Melbourne was concerned about the Church's witness to the community and with more general 'theological' issues such as the relationship between sexuality and the activity of God.[78]

The story of the Presbyterian response to the move for female ordination is both separate from and inextricably bound up with the Anglican story. Sydney Anglicans and Australian Presbyterians experienced a heightened clericalism from the 1970s, and the opposition to female ordination was a symptom of that. Both moved in a conservative evangelical, Reformed direction. Both since the mid-1970s had many of their new clergy trained at Moore Theological College.

Presbyterian women in Australia had served as missionaries and deaconesses since the 1890s, elders since 1916 in Western Australia and since 1967 in the rest of Australia, and as ordained ministers since 1974. The movement for the ordination of women in the Presbyterian Church owes much to the hard work of these female missionaries in areas where men were unavailable and to the good work in parishes of deaconesses who had given irrefutable evidence of giftedness for the work.

In 1969, the General Assembly of the Presbyterian Church referred the question of the ordination of women to a Victorian sub-committee then examining the nature of the ministry. The matter was transferred to another committee who appointed the Rev. Alan Smart of Blayney, NSW, to report

---

76 John Gaden (ed.), *A Woman's Place.* Papers prepared for the General Synod (Sydney: Doctrine Commission, AIO, 1976).

77 Robert Forsyth, 'Dispensing with Paul: Can we do without the texts where sex makes a difference?' *Interchange* 20, 1976; W.J. Dumbrell, 'The Role of Women – A Reconsideration of the Biblical Evidence', *Interchange*, 21, 1977.

78 Sturmey, 'Women and the Anglican Church in Australia', 173.

on the issue, which he did in 1970. By then, with the Methodist Church already ordaining women and the Presbyterians fast heading towards union with the Methodists, the Church moved quickly to affirm the theological principle that 'a Reformed Church … may admit women to the ministry of the Word and Sacraments', there being no possibility of excluding women from the ministry on the grounds of Scripture.[79] In fact, in 1967, 1970 and again in 1972 the Presbyterian Church declared that the doctrine of the Church was not at stake in discussions about women in the office of elder or minister. With the later hardening of opposition, it was suggested that there should have been a change to the Confession of Faith before the ordination of women was endorsed as it was in 1974. But the Confession does not deal with the subject, and therefore no such change was required.

The matter having been referred to the churches for a decision, the Presbyterian General Assembly in 1974 resolved to allow the ordination of women to the ministry of word and sacrament. It was approved by all six of the State assemblies and 50 out of 53 presbyteries. The dissenting presbyteries were Moree and Sydney South in NSW and Carpentaria in Queensland.[80] The first Presbyterian woman ordained to the ministry was Mrs Marlene Thalheimer in Melbourne in 1974. In 1976 Joy Bartholomew was ordained by the Presbytery of North Sydney. Dr Margaret Yee was ordained in 1977 by the Presbytery of Sydney. She served in the Parish of Roseville and Scots Church in Sydney, and was to serve as Chaplain of Nuffield College, Oxford, and as a Senior Research Fellow in Science and Religion at Oxford and a Templeton Scholar.[81] In a very short space of time, however, the overwhelmingly-supported decision to ordain women was reversed.

State Aid and Welfare

The prevailing popular belief in the rigid separation of church and state in Australia is one of the great myths of Australian history: there has rather been much reciprocity between church and state. This 'pragmatic pluralism' resulted in the dramatic expansion of church involvement in social welfare.

79 Muriel Porter, *Women in the Church: The Great Ordination Debate in Australia* (Ringwood: Penguin, 1989), 30–32.

80 Helen Clements, 'Brief Notes on Steps taken to train and ordain Women for Service in the Presbyterian Church. Time Period 1887–1988, Paper No.1,' Unpublished Typescript, 1988, 6f.

81 Margaret Yee interviewed by John Cleary, Sunday Nights, 23.4.2006, http://www.abc.net.au/sundaynights/stories/Dr_Margare_m1224828.Mp3, accessed 19 November 2016.

From about 1960 the Federal Government offered partnerships, including partnerships with churches, in the areas of welfare, education and immigration. They have been unstable partnerships: Federal governments have transferred the onus for welfare provision to state and local governments and to churches and then taken it back again.

Most evangelicals calculated that they had been as often helped as hurt by political power. They incorporated social concern as part of the Gospel, and skirmished with those who thought the Gospel required only evangelism, not action on social issues. In Melbourne, Ridley College, under the principalship of Leon Morris, 1964–79,[82] trained a large number of 'theologs', unexcited by the prospect of ordination, but very committed to the interaction of faith and society: Gordon Gray with interests in the media; Peter Stanton who was to work in Sydney Anglican Radio; Trevor Wilson who developed counselling for drug addicts; Thomas Stokes and his community counselling program; Stuart Taplin with his outdoor education and counselling; Alan Lewis who combined an interest in music and monasteries; and Dave Walker who established an inimitable counter-cultural ministry.[83]

Baptists veered from their traditional stance of separation from the state, accepting state aid in welfare and education. Blackburn Baptist Church accepted government funding to help it open in 1978 'Robinson House', the first local church-sponsored women's refuge in Victoria. By 1978 Baptist Social Services in Melbourne had a budget of $3.3m, mostly from government grants, and were running five aged care homes, a nursing service, a counselling centre, six opportunity shops, and ministries to needy children and immigrants.[84]

But social commitment from evangelical churches was always in jeopardy from those who thought that the Gospel gave primacy to evangelism. West Melbourne Baptist Church, for example, purchased a large house in Parkville to use as accommodation for children who were the victims of domestic violence. This soon collapsed through the opposition of those in the congregation who doubted its evangelistic effectiveness. At North Blackburn Baptist Church a large kindergarten was developed, but its future was jeopardised when a new minister asked for the contact details of all the children's parents so that they could be paid an evangelistic visit. Church welfare agencies were also jeopardised by government regulation. The Baptists in Melbourne opened in 1967 an acute medical/surgical facility, F.W. Boreham hospital, the first

82 Neil S. Bach, *Leon Morris: One Man's Fight for Love and Truth* (Milton Keynes, UK, Paternoster, 2015).

83 Richard Prideaux to Stuart Piggin, 19 October 1990.

84 Munro, 'Struggle for Identity and Direction', 260, 263, 265.

Baptist hospital in Australia, but were forced to close it twenty years later when it could not meet complex government regulations.[85]

Victoria was the only State where the Baptists had schools. Carey Baptist Boys Grammar School was formed in 1923 in Kew, Strathcona Girls Grammar School at Canterbury in 1941 and Kilvington at Ormond in 1947. These were all in Melbourne's affluent suburbs. In States where there were no Baptist schools, opposition to state aid remained strong among Baptists, but in Victoria there was a readiness to accept the proffered aid for science buildings and libraries on the grounds that it would be responding to a 'national need'.[86] In 1973 the Whitlam government categorised Carey as a Category A school and federal funding ceased. Strathcona was Category B and its funding was reduced. Both had to increase fees. The Fraser government, which came to office in 1975, increased government funding to private schools and thus reduced their independence. A study of six non-government schools in Victoria concluded that in those with a Protestant foundation the religious life of the school had been compromised.[87] Learning how to respond to the secular society was going to be a hard-won lesson.

Immigration brought another range of opportunities and challenges to the churches. They not only responded to new multicultural policies; they had also contributed to their development. Al Grassby, the flamboyant immigration minister in the Whitlam Labor government, is often credited with devising and selling the term 'multicultural'. He had launched the term on 11 August 1973 in a speech he gave at a symposium at the Cairnmillar Institute, a counsellor training centre then in the Collins Street Congregational Church, Melbourne. But the speech was written by James Houston, a public servant and Commissioner for Community Relations, before he became an Anglican clergyman. He grew up in Dulwich Hill, son of a victim of the Depression. He studied three languages at High School: French, Latin and German, and had a flair for languages. He was a member of the Sydney University Evangelical Union in his undergraduate days when he studied languages and became a French teacher before working for Grassby as a researcher. He read Canadian social research on bi-cultural Quebec and concluded that Australia, too, had developed a mix of language, culture and religion for which he coined the term 'multi-cultural'. Houston then commissioned the Immigration Department, where he was a bit of a subversive, to open a new file entitled

85 Munro, 'Struggle for Identity and Direction', 259f., 265.

86 Munro, 'Struggle for Identity and Direction', 240.

87 I.V. Hansen, *Nor Free nor Secular: Six Independent Schools in Victoria: A First Sample* (Melbourne: OUP, 1971), 141.

'Multiculturalism in Australia' of which he wrote: 'I am confident it was the first time the word had gained official entry in the Australian Public Service. Naming it is half the battle: well begun is half done.'[88] It facilitated one of Australia's most celebrated social revolutions, leaving the 'White Australia' policy behind and identifying areas of discrimination, exclusion and disadvantage to be addressed by both church and state.[89] Following the passage of the Racial Discrimination Act by the Whitlam Government in 1975, it was illegal to use race as a criterion for selection of immigrants. Multicultural immigration on a large scale developed with unsurprising speed and surprising harmony which lasted until the mid-1990s when a reaction set in. But ideology apart, the institutionalisation of cultural and ethnic diversity was an essential long-term response to demographic change.[90] For Australia's Indigenous people, however, nothing seemed to change. Houston went to Ceduna, South Australia, which he was told was 'the most racist town in Australia'. He talked with the locals, both black and white, to the clergy, especially to the Anglican minister, the Rev. Ken Rogers, who seemed alert to the situation and to the police who did not, although from them he was able to hear what racism was really like. He was told of the gin-jockeying on the sand-hills between drunken white workers and black women.[91] It was an almost hopeless task, with only eight in the Community Relations Office to address this rampant discrimination right across Australia. After seven years of under-resourced activity by the State, Houston was recruited by Archbishop Penman to foster the Church's multicultural ministry. Grassby went on to blot his copybook with the Christians.

The Cost of Activism: The Murder of Donald Mackay

The secular society was becoming less knowledgeable about religion and more prone to suspicion of the motives of those who professed religious faith. Within a decade two evangelical Christians – Donald Mackay and Lindy Chamberlain – were to become noteworthy for the wrong reasons, and on both occasions the secular society got it horribly wrong.

---

88 James Houston, 'Chapter 41, Prophet ahead of his tine?', unpublished autobiography, 2015, 1; James Houston, *A Multicultural Odyssey* (Bayswater: Coventry Press, 2018), 16, 178–188.

89 Mersina Papantoniou, 'Multiculturalism's challenge to Sydney Anglican identity: A study of a minority radical tradition', PhD, Macquarie University, 2016, 124–126.

90 Alison Bashford and Stuart Macintyre, (eds.), *The Cambridge History of Australia* 2 vols (Port Melbourne; New York: CUP, 2013), vol.2, 9.

91 Houston, *A Multicultural Odyssey*, 220–232.

'DRUG SLAYING FEARS' was the banner headline of the *Sun-Herald* on Sunday 17 July 1977, followed by the words: 'The key figure in a fight against marihuana growing in NSW is missing, feared gunned to death in a Mafia-style killing in the Riverina town of Griffith.'[92] Mackay was born in Griffith in 1933. The family moved to Sydney in 1943, where Don attended Barker College, Hornsby, an evangelical Anglican school. In 1957, he married Barbara Dearman in St. James's Church of England, Turramurra, where Don Mackay attended and was active in the youth fellowship. Barbara was an active member of another evangelical parish, St. Martin's Church of England, Killara.[93] They established their family home in Griffith and had four children. They joined the local Methodist Church and began to make an impact on their congregation and their community.[94] Both taught Sunday School classes, Barbara played the organ, and Don was a circuit steward. He was secretary of the Griffith Pioneer Lodge Committee, founded the local branches of the Sub-Normal Children's Welfare Association and the Australian Birthright Movement, and was an active member first of the Apex Club of Griffith and then of Rotary.

Mackay also took an interest in politics and, in the federal election of 1974, stood for Riverina. He did not win, but his preferences helped unseat incumbent Labor MP, Al Grassby, the afore-mentioned Labor minister for immigration. This earned Mackay Grassby's enmity and brought him to the attention of certain dishonest policemen and politicians who began to consider him a troublemaker. Mackay began to pass information to the Drug Squad in Sydney, precipitating a raid on 10 November 1975, where the police found the largest single marijuana crop yet discovered in Australia valued at $80 million. Unfortunately, during the subsequent trial, the judge ordered the production of an official police notebook in which Mackay was named as an informant. The disclosure may well have been his death sentence.

On the afternoon of Friday, 15 July Mackay phoned his wife and told her that he would be home by 7:00 pm in time to mind their three-year old son James while she went to a meeting. Those were the last words he spoke to

92 *Sun-Herald*, 17 July 1977, 1. On the Mackay case, see Lesley Hicks, *The Appalling Silence: The Mystery of Don Mackay* (Lane Cove: Hodder and Stoughton, 1979); Bob Bottom, *Shadow of Shame: How the Mafia Got Away with the Murder of Donald Mackay* (South Melbourne: Sun Books, 1988); Keith Moor, *Crims in Grass Castles: The True Story of Trimbole, Mr. Asia and the Disappearance of Donald Mackay* (Apollo Bay: Pascoe Publishing, 1989).

93 Hicks, *The Appalling Silence*, 12–18; Ron T. Jarvis interviewed by Linder, 20 June 2012. Jarvis knew Don Mackay personally.

94 Hicks, *The Appalling Silence*, 17–18.

her, and his body has never been found. The Woodward Royal Commission, appointed in 1977, was given the task of investigating links between the Mafia and the police and Mackay's disappearance. In his final report in 1979, Woodward found that the Riverina Mafia were responsible for his disappearance and murder.[95] In spite of the findings, it was not until 1983 that any progress was made in solving the case. Fred Bazley, a painter and docker and professional hit man, who was paid $10,000 to execute Mackay, was given a nine-year term for conspiracy to commit the murder.[96]

Theories concerning Mackay's disappearance abounded. Some said that he staged the murder himself in order to run off with drug money or perhaps with a woman. This attempt to blame the family for the murder reached its zenith in 1980, when Al Grassby orchestrated the accusation of Barbara Mackay, her son Paul, and Ian Salmon, the family's solicitor, of conspiring to murder Don Mackay. Grassby was forced to apologise unconditionally to the family and its solicitor.[97]

Barbara Mackay continued to live in Griffith until her death in 2001. She wrote a book entitled *Before I Forget* that covered events surrounding her husband's murder. It was scheduled for publication in 1997, but never saw the light of day based on legal advice. On the fact that she was never allowed to issue her book, she commented:

> For at no time in the last 20 years since my husband's murder have I had an opportunity in court to speak about some of the unanswered questions, cruel rumours and dreadful truths which have continued to have a profound effect on my life for so long …
>
> Now I have been told the defamation laws mean that the truth cannot be published and incidents can't be described, even when they have been on public record for years.
>
> My husband was effectively silenced, and now it is my turn.[98]

In a case eerily similar to that of the Chamberlains in the next decade, Barbara Mackay was pilloried for her apparent lack of emotion at the time of her husband's disappearance. However, as Lesley Hicks explained: 'Some

95 Bottom, *Shadow of Shame*, 80–99.

96 'Ghosts of Griffith', *The Australian Weekend Review*, July 12–13 1997, online at http://www.gwb.com.au/gwb/news/onenation/press/ghosts.html (accessed 20 June 2012).

97 Hicks, *The Appalling Silence*, 47–61.

98 Keith Moor, 'Mackay's Wife Dies Without Learning Truth', *Daily Telegraph*, 27 February, 2001, 15.

simply could not understand Barbara's composure before the cameras, perhaps knowing nothing themselves of the peace that God can give'.[99] In the year before Donald's disappearance, Barbara had become a Charismatic Christian which she believed helped her better to face the reality of her husband's death and the aftermath of innuendo.[100] Like the Chamberlains later on, the impact of the years of uncertainty, government intransigence, police incompetence, threats and bullying, judicial setbacks and dead ends, and growing public indifference, resulted in great family pain. In the case of the Mackays, at least one of the children abandoned his Christian faith.[101] In the final analysis, Don Mackay had to go where his conscience led him. In the end it led to his death.

* * *

Challenges to evangelical Christianity in the 1960s and 1970s were legion and lethal. They divided the movement by ideology and by region. They brought out its potential for reaction and withdrawal. But it is a tough, resilient movement, and did not then suffer numerical loss like liberal churches. Its moral stand against the most egregious descent into unbridled hedonism was not without community support and it promoted the end of sectarianism as Catholics joined hands with Protestants to protest against the decline in moral standards. The glacial secularism of the 1960s had already begun to thaw by the end of the 1970s as a new spirituality which owed most to Eastern religions was accompanied by a resurgence of spirituality focussed on the humanity of Jesus. Evangelical complacency and triumphalism were confronted, allowing for the recovery of the instinct and habit of dissent. The foundations were not shaken, but serious reorientation was initiated within the evangelical movement.

---

99 Hicks, *The Appalling Silence*, 78.

100 Hicks, *The Appalling Silence*, 64–6, 74, and 91.

101 Hicks, *The Appalling Silence*, 78, Jarvis interviewed by Linder, 20 June 2012.

Chapter Twelve

EVANGELICAL RESPONSES TO SECULAR AUSTRALIA, 1966–1979

'[Broughton Knox's] conviction about propositional revelation was the big thing to my mind. God has spoken and in a way that we creatures made in his image can read and hear.'
(Paul Barnett)

Donald Horne's judgment in 1964 was that Australian Protestantism had been 'drained of almost all serious intellectual and moral content'.[1] Demonstrably, however, evangelicals were very serious on both counts. Hugh Chilton has recently analysed the sheer variety and energy of evangelical responses to the challenges of the 1960s.[2] Some insisted on reaffirming evangelical foundations, adopting a more thoroughly Reformed theology. They were the last who needed to be told, but they were advised anyway by Dutch Protestant sociologist Hans Mol, that the best thing to do at a time of rapid social change was to be yourself:[3] the most faithful would prove to be the most relevant in the end, because in the end only the faithful would remain. A minority went for the ecumenical option, in the conviction that union among Christians was the best response to numerical decline. A surprisingly large number of evangelicals believed that the radicalism of the age meant that they, too, had to become radicals, creating the 'Jesus movement'. Those who longed most for an Aussie awakening – the Pentecostals and the Charismatics – organised for revival and began to grow dramatically, and their hoped-for divine solution to secularisation, namely revival, was experienced in places.

1 Donald Horne, *The Lucky Country*, 5th ed. (Ringwood, Vic.: Penguin, 1998), 57.

2 Hugh Chilton, 'Evangelicals and the End of Christian Australia: Nation and Religion in the Public Square 1959–1979', PhD, University of Sydney, 2014, 12.

3 Hans Mol, *Christianity in Chains; a Sociologist's Interpretation of the Churches' Dilemma in a Secular World* (Melbourne: Nelson, 1969), v.

Evangelism, the traditional evangelical response to unbelief and decline in churchgoing, was sustained in home missions, crusades, and cross-cultural missionary activity. Enthusiasm for the last faltered briefly in the early 1970s as the quest for a 'new nationalism', nurtured culturally by Manning Clark and Donald Horne and politically by Gough Whitlam, replaced the Western Christendom model associated with colonialism.[4] But evangelicals were more aware of Asia than most because of their generations of missionary endeavour. As the star of Asia rose, that of Europe had to sink: Christendom, the union of Christianity with political power and its identification with civilisation itself, seemed to be on the rocks at the same time as the British Empire. To many conservative Australians they were the same thing. It was a lot to lose and it hurt the more that the British themselves seemed little wedded either to their Christian heritage or to their former dominions, casting them aside in 1973 for the material advantages of joining the European Economic Community.[5] The pain felt by Australians at this severance arose from the reality that they had always put more than the British into maintaining the interdependence of dominion and metropole, and that this had been an effort which had generated creativity in the commitment rather than mere unthinking subservience which had never been the Australian way.[6] Now Australians felt alone perhaps for the first time. Now they would have to construct an Australia with no more than the memory of Britain. Australian Christians would have to imagine and construct a new Christendom, intentionally differentiated from Western Christendom. A variety of responses emerged.

There was overlap between some of these responses, but there was also a lot of disagreement. The evangelical identity was as much in dispute as the Australian identity. It became increasingly difficult to identify who was in the evangelical family or indeed if there was any longer one evangelical family. There seemed to be at least three major groups: Reformed, liberal and Charismatic. The diverse strands of the evangelical movement were beginning to unwind, as differences in theology and strategy surfaced. The story of evangelicalism in this period, then, is ironically the strengthening of its conservative, radical and Charismatic wings, and the weakening of ties between them. The movement was losing its centre.

---

4 Mark McKenna, 'The History Anxiety', in Alison Bashford and Stuart Macintyre, (eds.), *The Cambridge History of Australia* 2 vols (Port Melbourne; New York: CUP, 2013), vol.2, 574.

5 James Curran and Stuart Ward, *The Unknown Nation: Australia after Empire* (Carlton: MUP, 2010).

6 Deryck M Schreuder and Stuart Ward, (eds), *Australia's Empire, Oxford History of the British Empire* (Oxford: OUP, 2008), 11, 393f.

Noel Vose (1921–2016): 'the greatest statesman Australian Baptists have produced'[7]

In such a situation, outstanding leadership was required to respond to the reality of history in the making, to act across a range of options, and to have the mental stamina to reconcile the faith with the intellectual challenges integral to the construction of a secular world. One such was Baptist theologian Noel Vose, destined to become a national and then international leader of his denomination. His father was converted to Christ through the Exclusive Brethren, which he left after he married. He did not go to church, but loved the Bible and read it all the time. He would say, 'Don't put anything on top of the Bible'. As a boy Noel attended a Methodist Church in Northam, WA. He joined Christian Endeavour, and through it accepted Christ. He was baptised at age 14. He became very involved with Maylands Baptist Church, Perth, from 1941 to 1943. He was in the RAAF from 1943 to 1946, serving entirely in Australia.

Immediately after World War II, Vose spent four years studying for the Baptist ministry under Principal Morling at the NSW Baptist College, where he was senior student. Appointed pastor of East Fremantle Baptist Church, WA, he simultaneously studied at the University of Western Australia, graduating Bachelor of Arts and Master of Education. The EU group was the largest student group on the university campus with 300 members, thanks partly to the work done through Crusaders in schools, and it was through Crusaders that Noel met his wife, Heather.

Fred Carter, a New Zealand Baptist pastor, urged Vose to get further theological training so that he could run a theological college in WA. It was a sign of the times that the route to Vose's singular effectiveness as an evangelical leader lay, not through Europe or Britain, but through America. He completed another Master's degree in a single year at the Northern Baptist Theological Seminary in Illinois, USA. He enrolled there on the advice of Charles Troutman, whom Vose had got to know in his capacity as secretary of the University of Western Australia EU. Vose then transferred to the School of Religion at the University of Iowa. There Professor James Spalding specialised in Reformed and Puritan studies. The subject of Vose's PhD dissertation was 'Profile of a Puritan: John Owen, 1616–1683'. It placed Vose at

7 Rory Shiner, 'Vale Baptist Statesman Noel Vose (1921–2016)', The Gospel Coalition Australia, https://australia.thegospelcoalition.org/article/vale-noel-vose, accessed 7 September 2016.

the forefront of Reformed scholarship in Australia at a time when Reformed theology was galvanising evangelicalism with greater doctrinal rigour.[8]

In the meantime, plans for a theological college to serve the Baptists of WA had gone forward and Vose had been appointed its founding principal. By the end of May 1963, he was back in Perth ready to assume his duties. He arrived home just in time to greet what became the great student revolution and the era of protest over the Vietnam War. He would be the key figure in preserving Baptist unity during the theological controversies in the denomination in WA during the 1970s and 1980s.[9]

On returning to Perth, Vose found the college already in progress. It had opened its doors on 5 March 1963 with twelve students. Student numbers increased each year thereafter, but Vose remained the sole full-time faculty member until 1978. Even so, in 1970 he was allowed study leave, and accepted an invitation to attend the Baptist World Alliance education conference preceding the main BWA meeting in Tokyo. Vose was made a member of the Doctrinal Commission and was thus introduced to the larger world of Baptists. In 1975 he attended the BWA meeting in Stockholm. He was able to visit the USSR, and he attended a conference on the Anabaptists held in Zurich. He was President General of Australian Baptists, 1975–1978, and President of the BWA, 1980–1985. He retired from the college in 1991, his powerful mind and intellectual curiosity undiminished. None had made a greater contribution to helping WA evangelicals engage with the intellectual challenges of the age. The Baptist College of WA was renamed Vose Seminary in 2008.

International Evangelicalism: Tensions and Triumphs

At the Second National Assembly of Evangelicals held by the Evangelical Alliance in London on 18 October 1966, Martyn Lloyd-Jones dramatically called the evangelicals out of their denominations to join a United Evangelical Church.[10] He argued that 'separation from liberals was not schism, separation from fellow Evangelicals was'.[11] John Stott, who chaired the meeting at which

8 Richard K. Moore, *Noel Vose: Pastor, Principal, President* (Perth: Baptist Historical Society of Western Australia, 2010),117–22.

9 Noel Vose interviewed by Linder, 27 July 1995.

10 The address, 'Evangelical Unity: an Appeal', is published in D.M. Lloyd-Jones, *Knowing the Times* (Edinburgh: Banner of Truth Trust, 1989), 246–257.

11 Christopher Catherwood (ed.), *Martyn Lloyd-Jones: Chosen by God* (Crowborough: Highland Books, 1986), 23, 44, 45.

Lloyd-Jones made his electrifying call, was horrified. Historian and sociologist Rob Warner considers Lloyd-Jones's stand a disaster, a debacle, which marginalised him so that he never regained influence among the mainstream denominations.[12]

In Australia that was not true. Martyn Lloyd-Jones was appreciated by a growing number of evangelical clergy influenced by the Banner of Truth conferences, now being held annually in Australia. True, for most Sydney Anglicans, John Stott trumped Martyn Lloyd-Jones. Stott's word was law and lore in Sydney, probably because he was Anglican. But it would not always be so – Stott began to lose his hold on the Sydney Anglicans as he became increasingly speculative in his theology. He was to lose his hold on some British evangelicals, too – significantly those who were infected by an increasingly uncompromising strain of Reformed evangelicalism emanating from Sydney.

Stott, unlike Lloyd-Jones, was a warm supporter of Billy Graham. His partnership with Graham created a pan-evangelical movement institutionalised in international conferences: Berlin (1966), Keele (1967), Singapore (1968), Lausanne (1974) and Nottingham (1977). Berlin, Singapore and Lausanne were largely funded by the Billy Graham Evangelistic Association; Keele and Nottingham were national evangelical Anglican conferences (NEAC), which, though held in England, attracted evangelical Anglicans from around the world. These international conferences were opportunities to reorient the evangelical movement now that the old Christendom was in its death throes.

The 1966 World Conference on Evangelism, Berlin,[13] was directed by Billy Graham and Carl Henry. It provoked the liberal *Christian Century* to ask if evangelical ecumenism was being developed in opposition to the broader ecumenical movement.[14] It was a good question. John Stott convened the meeting of evangelical Anglicans at Keele in 1967. Its purpose was to redress a prevailing negativity about the future of the church combined with the need to consolidate the rising power of the evangelical party now that it had become the strongest party within the Church of England.[15] This was the ambiguous character of the evangelical movement in the 1960s and 1970s: awareness of its own strength within a Church declining over all.[16]

---

12 Rob Warner, *Reinventing English Evangelicalism, 1966–2001: A Theological and Sociological Study* (Milton Keynes: Paternoster, 2007), 40.

13 John Pollock, *Billy Graham* (London: Harper and Row, 1979), ch. 15.

14 *Christian Century*, 88, 2 March 1966, 264.

15 Timothy Dudley-Smith, *John Stott: A Global Ministry* (Leicester: InterVarsity, 2001), 77–79.

16 R.T. France and A.E. McGrath (eds.), *Evangelical Anglicans* (London: SPCK, 1993).

The Keele Congress was the work of Anglican evangelicals frustrated with a diet of purity without relevance, of platitudes without participation. They felt keenly the reputation they had for separatist party spirit within the Church of England and for intellectual and social obscurantism in the secular community. They shared the need for 'greater flexibility in this age of flux', as Congress convener, John Stott, put it, and to move beyond piety into policy and practice.[17] Near a thousand clergy and laity at the Congress reaffirmed the evangelicals' intention of staying in the Church of England.[18] The Congress *Statement* affirmed 'we do not believe secession to be a live issue'.[19] While not departing from any conservative evangelical doctrines, it also insisted that 'evangelism and social action belong together in the mission of God'.[20] In this, Keele anticipated Lausanne, which historian David Edwards acclaimed as the Vatican II of the evangelical movement.[21] The International Congress on World Evangelization, Lausanne, Switzerland, in July 1974 emphasised holistic mission, critiquing the Western missionary movement as a 'mono-cultural export system'.[22] It made evangelicals aware that they had been captive to their culture. Conservative evangelicals had hoped that, under the influence of Billy Graham, Lausanne would reaffirm proclamation evangelism. American delegates were especially anxious that the new radical evangelicalism was just an iteration of the old social gospel.[23] But the persuasive John Stott, aided by Jack Dain, Sydney Bishop and chairman of the conference planning committee, and another Australian delegate, David Claydon, called for the re-integration of evangelism and social action, and for an awareness of the distinction between gospel affirmations and their cultural expression. It did give a new face to the movement. It was now 'more self-critical, more holistic, and extricated from the ghetto of neo-fundamentalism'.[24] Evangelicals were now called to take political action against 'every form of alienation, oppression and discrimination'.[25]

17 Andrew Atherstone, 'The Keele Congress of 1967: A Paradigm Shift in Anglican Evangelical Attitudes', *Journal of Anglican Studies*, 9.2, 2011, 178.

18 Alister McGrath, *Evangelicalism and the Future of Christianity* (London: Hodder & Stoughton, 1993), 2, 39.

19 Catherwood, *Martyn Lloyd-Jones*, 24.

20 Quoted in Warner, *Reinventing English Evangelicalism*, 175.

21 Warner, *Reinventing English Evangelicalism*, 184

22 John R. W. Stott and Robert T. Coote, *Down to Earth: Studies in Christianity and Culture: The Papers of the Lausanne Consultation on Gospel and Culture* (London: Hodder and Stoughton, 1981).

23 Brian Stanley, *The Global Diffusion of Evangelicalism: The Age of Billy Graham and John Stott* (Downers Grove, Illinois: IVP Academic, 2013), 172f.

24 Warner, *Reinventing English Evangelicalism*, 184.

25 Quoted in Chilton, 'Evangelicals and the End of Christian Australia', 327.

Not all were happy.[26] Conservative evangelicals baulked at the revived social dimension to the faith, and two of the chief critics of this development were John Chapman and Paul Barnett.[27] They too were Sydney Anglicans, just like Dain who allowed the change and Claydon who encouraged it. Sydney Anglicanism, like the evangelical movement as a whole, was not monochrome: and its prophetic biblicism fostered a venerable, if minority, radical tradition within evangelicalism. Perhaps the majority of evangelicals the world over were uncertain and confused. In Australia, for example, Baptist minister, Alan Nunn, who had served in country Victoria in the 1970s, was disorientated when he returned to the city of Melbourne in 1980:

> I came back to a different climate ... all of a sudden social justice becomes the big issue ... which had never been part of our training ... and I felt somewhat of a leper ... you were either an evangelical or ... a social justice person.[28]

Lausanne might have confused some and entrenched others in reactionary postures bent on keeping the movement pure, but it allowed others to speak into the market place of ideas at just the time when Australia was seeking intentionally for its national identity. To the clamorous voices of the economic rationalists of the Right and the new nationalist culture-shapers on the Left, was added the still small voice of Christian idealism. Grounded in the person of Christ and given urgency by the international experience of poverty as witnessed by the movement's missionaries, it was a voice which called Australians to be more faithful to their Christian heritage.

The second NEAC conference, Nottingham in 1977, promoted a decidedly progressive evangelicalism. Tony Thiselton challenged his hearers, when reading the Bible, to remove their evangelical 'spectacles' and not to see the text 'only in a "Christian Union" kind of way'.[29] Tom Wright and Michael Sadgrove, from 2003 Bishop and Dean of Durham respectively, argued that the entire New Testament should not be viewed through the lens of the letter to the Romans, but that all the books of the New Testament should be allowed to speak with their own voice. They thus contended for 'a hermeneutic

---

26 Arthur Johnston, *The Battle for World Evangelism* (Wheaton: Tyndale, 1978), 302; Stanley, *The Global Diffusion of Evangelicalism*, 173–177.

27 Chilton, 'Evangelicals and the End of Christian Australia', 326.

28 Quoted in Marita Rae Munro, "'a Struggle for Identity and Direction': A History of Victorian Baptists (1960–2000)", PhD, University of Melbourne, 2010, 290.

29 John Thiselton, 'Understanding God's Word Today,' in John R.W. Stott and Bruce Kaye, *Obeying Christ in a Changing World* (London: Fountain Books, 1977), 104.

of diversity'.[30] Together Lausanne and Nottingham expressed the aspirations of more progressive evangelicals. It would prove too much for traditionalists: the serious cracks in the evangelical edifice were widening.

The Resurgence of Reformed Calvinism in the Denominations

The renaissance of Reformed Calvinism was nowhere more welcomed than at Moore College during the long principalship of Broughton Knox (1959–85). It was accompanied by a dramatic improvement in scholarly standards in the College. The College's increasingly staunch theology was therefore increasingly defended by academic firepower. The defence of the Moore College position was grounded in the intellect. This meant emotion-based pieties such as Keswick were discounted, and the Charismatic movement was ruled out for the same reason.

Gough's successor as Archbishop of Sydney, Marcus Loane, from 1966 led the diocese through the means which it prizes second only to theology, namely preaching. His sermons, delivered in the famous stentorian voice which lent dignity to all occasions, gave heart to those who wanted to believe that you do not have to cease being an Anglican in order to be an evangelical. But Loane maintained his opposition to Roman Catholicism. In 1970 he declined an invitation to attend an ecumenical service in the Sydney Town Hall with Pope Paul VI. The press waxed indignant, reporting that Loane was 'unwilling to pray with the Pope', which might be considered a fair interpretation of Loane's action. But he claimed it was a press invention. He pointed to five Catholic doctrines which are 'radically inconsistent with the New Testament as the sovereign rule of faith': the infallibility of the Pope; the intercession of Mary to procure God's favour; that justification depends partly on our own works; that tradition is equally authoritative with Scripture; and the Mass is a sacrifice for the living and the dead. 'There are questions of truth,' declared Loane, 'which must be resolved before we can share in common worship or in unfettered fellowship.' It was a stand which re-stoked the fires of sectarianism recently greatly dampened by the Second Vatican Council. Loane was as faithful to his Reformation heritage as any, but he regretted sectarian strife. No dissembling prelate, he was sincerely 'convinced that until there is an agreed doctrinal confession any get-togethers of this kind only increase the

30 Warner, *Reinventing English Evangelicalism*, 189.

elements of disunity'.[31] One of Loane's biographers claims that the 'matter did die down', but he concedes that 'many' remember only this action of Loane, 'as if he never did anything else of note'.[32] Response to the incident is evidence both of the strength of sectarianism and of Australian distaste for it.

Loane possessed a deep appreciation of the church's role in British history, and he cared that Australian society was becoming severed from its British roots without a clear understanding of what the 'new nationalism' of the 1970s would grow in its place. On 13 March 1977 Loane (Sir Marcus since 1975) preached at Morning Prayer in St Andrew's Cathedral, Sydney, in the presence of the Queen. The service was televised nationally and was part of the celebrations of the Queen's Silver Jubilee. There had been many social changes and moral challenges in the first 25 years of her reign. There would be many more in the next 25, and Loane did not like what he foresaw. He took as his text Hebrews 11.10: 'He [Abraham] looked for a city which hath foundations, whose builder and maker is God.'

> This is a city in which God Himself is the eternal Sovereign, and all its citizens acknowledge His rule.... There will be no room for a permissive society, or an alternate culture, or a wealthy élite, or a down-trodden minority; there will be no place for political intrigue, or public wrangling, or partisan interests, or power struggles ... Therefore let us pray that the Silver Jubilee of an earthly reign will enlarge our vision of all that lies beyond the frontiers of earth and time, and will strengthen our resolve to live our lives for the glory of Jesus Himself who reigns as King of kings and Lord of lords for ever and ever. Amen.[33]

Was Loane the last of the Archbishops able to make the throne of the United Kingdom a metaphor for the Kingdom of God? He personified a tension within Australian evangelicalism in the 1970s. His 'geographically-aware Christian humanitarianism' gave him a vision for mission to an Asia then substantially undeveloped and for hospitality to refugees from Asia, while his 'British-centred cultural paternalism'[34] led him to support an immigration policy that favoured the maintenance in the Australian population of an Anglo-Saxon majority.

---

31 Allan M. Blanch, *From Strength to Strength: A Life of Marcus Loane* (North Melbourne: Australian Scholarly Publishing, 2015), 244.

32 Blanch, *From Strength to Strength*, 246.

33 *Decision*, April 1977, 13.

34 Chilton, 'Evangelicals and the End of Christian Australia', 240.

Revived Reformed Calvinism also made its impact on post-war Presbyterianism, which had been weakened by liberalism.[35] When in 1966 New Zealand theology professor, Lloyd Geering, maintained that the resurrection of Christ was nothing more than 'a symbol of hope', NSW Presbyterians were reminded of their long, sorry struggle over Samuel Angus. It led to the separation from the Presbyterian Church of the Rev Grahame Kerr of Sutherland in Sydney and the creation in 1967 of the Presbyterian Reformed Church of Australia. A decade earlier his father, J.T.H. Kerr, Principal of the Croydon Bible College, had written off post-war Presbyterianism in NSW as the undisputed product of the 'godless liberalism' of Samuel Angus. Now his son interpreted his own stand against Geering as 'a necessary and overdue condemnation of Angus and his theology' and of the members of the Presbyterian Church of NSW who had tolerated Angus and were themselves apostates.[36]

Grahame Kerr's action was condemned by most as schismatic and few followed him. But his action did spur some in the Presbyterian Church to promote Reformed evangelical teaching. With the formation of the Uniting Church in 1977, attempts were made to ensure that ministers of the continuing Presbyterian Church of Australia were given a solid grounding in conservative, Reformed theology. The Sydney Theological Hall was moved out of St. Andrew's College and relocated first at Ashfield and then at Burwood under the Rev. J.A. Davies as Dean, while a number of Presbyterian candidates trained at Moore College. Dr Nigel Lee, a prolific writer and Professor of Theology at the Queensland Presbyterian Theological Hall, exuberantly led the resurgence of Reformed theology, while the venerable Calvinist, Robert Swanton, the long-serving minister of Hawthorn Presbyterian church in Melbourne, edited the *Reformed Theological Review*, and filled the Chair of Systematic Theology at the Presbyterian College of Victoria until the late 1980s.

The Ecumenical Response: The Uniting Church

The revival of Reformed theology was not conducive to ecumenism, but some leaders in the mainline denominations naturally looked to church union as the answer to declension. On 22 June 1977 elements of the Methodist, Presbyterian and Congregationalist traditions merged into the Uniting Church of Australia. It was a long time coming, and its arrival was just in time as

35 Rowland Ward, *The Bush Still Burns, the Presbyterian and Reformed Faith in Australia 1788–1988* (St. Kilda, Vic.: Presbyterian Church of Eastern Australia, 1989), 405.

36 Susan Emilsen, *A Whiff of Heresy: Samuel Angus and the Presbyterian Church in New South Wales* (Kensington, NSW: New South Wales University Press, 1991), 285.

the ecumenical spirit was dying fast: 'In fact union of the three Australian Churches would be the biggest and perhaps the final act of the ecumenical movement in the Western world.'[37]

Among the Presbyterians, the strongest mind in favour of union was Davis McCaughey, Master of Ormond College in the University of Melbourne, and later Governor of Victoria. He was the author of the 'Basis of Union' of the Uniting Church and was the first President of the Assembly of the new Church. For all his powers of persuasion, McCaughey was more effective in alienating conservative Presbyterians than winning their support.[38] The draft Basis of Union was voted on in 1972 with the Methodists and Congregationalists both polling over 80 per cent in favour of joining. It was not until May 1974 that the Presbyterian General Assembly decided to proceed to union, though with only 7 votes more than the three-fifths majority required. A considerable number of congregations stayed out of the new Uniting Church of Australia. Some of these were Congregational churches, but most were Presbyterian. Hence union in effect further fragmented the denominational scene, with those staying out predominantly evangelical.

Meanwhile the number of evangelical denominations in this period multiplied. It was no longer necessary for them to identify with either Calvinist or Arminian theologies. It was possible to occupy a 'broadly evangelical' position. A case in point is the Christian and Missionary Alliance. Formed by A.B. Simpson in 1887 in New York, the C&MA had made occasional forays into Australia, but it was not until 1969 that it established an ongoing work. American missionary Robert T. Henry formed a church in Chatswood, Sydney, and within eight years twenty C&MA churches were established within Australia. As the name implies, its chief emphasis is on missions. It grew out of a missionary movement and it seeks to remain one, and has evolved in Australia into a church with a key ministry to congregations of people of non-English speaking background (NESB).[39]

The Open Brethren, who in the interests of the unity they prized, had also avoided identifying with Calvinism or Arminianism, continued to nourish the wider evangelical movement with their commitment to missions and to the support of parachurch evangelical societies. In 1968 there were 260 Open

37 Sarah Martin, *Davis McCaughey: A Life* (Sydney: UNSW Press, 2012), 213.

38 Martin, *Davis McCaughey*, 209.

39 Russell Warnken, '"Missionary is our Middle Name": The Christian and Missionary Alliance in Australia,' in Mark Hutchinson and Geoffrey R. Treloar (eds.), *This Gospel Shall Be Preached: Essays on the Australian Contribution to World Mission* (Sydney: CSAC, 1998), 263–274; O'Brien, 'North American Wesleyan-Holiness Churches in Australia', PhD, 240–243.

Brethren assemblies in Australia, with 12,000 'in fellowship'. In fact, New Zealand was the source of much Brethren energy, just as it was to become for the Pentecostal and Charismatic branches of the evangelical movement.[40] In New Zealand in the same year there were about the same number of assemblies (250), but a much larger membership (25,000) and a missionary contingent (185) more than double the size of the Australian assemblies.[41]

Parachurch Responses

Alongside, rather than outside, the denominations, evangelical parachurch groups, such as IVF and the Convention movement, were significantly strengthened, while new parachurch developments proliferated in number. The parachurch development most distinctive of the age was the 'Jesus Movement' which took institutional shape within and outside the denominations.

Within the IVF, members imbibed the theology of the Reformation far more easily than they did the theology of the founders of evangelicalism. Only Methodists read Wesley's writings and then only if they were training for the ministry. Hardly anyone had heard of the greatest of evangelical theologians, Jonathan Edwards. The theology of the Reformation was learned not only through the popular writings of contemporary evangelicals, but also through the many Reformation and Renaissance history courses then taught in Australian universities. In them the writings of Luther and Calvin were required reading as they were in theological colleges. A third avenue for the acquisition of Reformation thought was the presence in Australia of Continental theologians, such as the Dutch Reformed scholar, Klaas Runia (1926–2006), and the German Lutheran, Hermann Sasse (1895–1976). Runia, Professor of Systematic Theology at the Reformed Theological College in Geelong from 1956 to 1971, was pleased to find that Australian evangelicals were just as capable of defending the inspiration of Scripture as the Westminster zealots in the USA.[42]

In the 1930s Sasse had joined Bonhoeffer and Pastor Niemoller in opposing Nazism from within the Confessing Church. In 1949 he migrated to South Australia to teach in the Immanuel (Luther) Seminary, Adelaide, where he remained until his death. He had been involved in the ecumenical

40 Stanley, *The Global Diffusion of Evangelicalism*, 195.

41 Ian McDowell, *A Brief History of the 'Brethren'* (Sydney: Victory Books, 1968), 55.

42 Troutman to Burnard, 9 May 1963, Charles Henry Troutman Papers, Collection 111, box 1, folder 38, BGA; Klaas Runia, *Karl Barth and the Word of God* (Leicester: RTSF Monographs, 1964).

movement from the 1920s and sought to unite Australia's divided Lutheran churches, and was involved in formulating their statements of faith. But he was so precise in theological matters, especially concerning the Lord's Supper, that some supporters of the union despaired of ever reaching agreement. Sasse maintained that the teaching on the Lord's Supper could not be compromised or watered down in order to achieve union, although he very much wanted that union. Whenever the significance of Holy Communion was rediscovered in its original strength, he argued, the Church experienced spiritual revival and growth.[43]

Sasse was elected IVF President in 1967 and he educated university students in the great principles of the Reformation. Confessionalism became a characteristic state of mind for educated young evangelicals who signed the EU doctrinal statement with relish, not tempted by the freedom offered by the SCM who required no such subscription. By then SCM was in chronic decline. Its members, finding it hard to marry theology with social action, opted for the latter, while their mentors at first sought to make SCM 'a university within the university', a noble aim, and then created Religious Studies departments.[44] Sasse taught that it is a terrible thing to lose doctrinal purity, and that it is always accompanied by the painful loss of the Church's spiritual power. When he said such things, it helped that he was known to have a sense of humour. Asked by a seminary student if it was a sin for a young man and his fiancé to hold hands during church, Sasse replied, 'I think it would be a sin'. He paused and then added, 'if that young man and his fiancé did NOT hold hands during church!'[45]

The old guard who founded and defended the EUs were glad to foster theological debate. But Reformed theology could not contain the student psychic and social unrest of the late 1960s and 1970s. EUs became places of ferment that was more than theological, and this did not please the old guard. At Monash University a breakaway group from the EU, 'The Christian Radical Club', was formed in 1972. Its supporters had been disappointed by Billy Graham's refusal to condemn the American presence in Vietnam and they also felt let down by the IVF leadership. They wanted to go back to the roots of Christianity and apply the Gospel to politics and culture. They were

---

43 Rosemarie Müller to Robin Ruys, 29 September 2011. Müller revered Sasse as one of her 'spiritual fathers and advisers'.

44 Renate Howe, *A Century of Influence: The Australian Student Christian Movement 1896–1996* (Sydney: UNSW Press, 2009), 275ff., 397.

45 Anecdote posted by 'Acroamaticus', 17 November 2011, accessed on 8 February 2012 on http://sassedotalist.blogspot.com.au/search/label/Anecdotes.

challenged by Sartre, Freud and Marx, and longed for guidance in developing a Christian worldview. They read Graham's bestselling *World Aflame* and, observed one, 'along comes Billy and pours on kerosene'.[46] Ian Burnard, IVF General Secretary, and staff worker Rod Marsh advised against the formation of the Christian Radicals. They argued that there was no such thing as a Christian political viewpoint and urged Monash EU students to stay the course and focus on evangelism and Bible Study as they had always done and not 'break fellowship'. Student leaders like Bruce Wearne believed that this 'pious bluster' was the Sydney EU line dictated by the very conservative Sydney Anglicans.[47]

The Christian Radicals remained evangelical, however, and agreed to disband as soon as the EU took up a more socially committed stance. But radicalism did not leave evangelical students unscathed. In 1979 104 members of the MUEU between 1967 and 1972 were surveyed about their faith commitment. Their ages then averaged 29. Of them 68 per cent had retained their evangelical faith, 24 per cent had liberalised, and 8 per cent no longer held any Christian belief.[48] The opinion was abroad that many Christian students sank under the pressure in these years, reaching the nadir in the mid-80s when it was considered that it was essential that they should be given more help by professional staff workers.

Conventions for the deepening of the spiritual life also had to adjust to the times. Numbers attending the Katoomba convention were in free fall. The last of the old-style Katoomba Christian conventions was held in 1973, with about 250 present. A new style of spirituality was needed. Keswick's rather pietistic, inward-looking spirituality was not as appealing as it had been. It seemed anaemic, stale, and unhealthily subjective. J.I. Packer, whose word was becoming law in Sydney, denounced Keswick teaching as 'Pelagian through and through'.[49] A more robust diet of straight biblical teaching seemed to be called for. John Reid, appointed chairman of the Katoomba Convention in 1971, initiated the necessary, but painful break with the Keswick tradition. It was Reid who in 1974 brought on to the council the most dynamic of strategists in late twentieth-century evangelical Anglicanism, Phillip Jensen. The year before, he had begun his extraordinary ministry as chaplain at the University of NSW. His declared purpose was to 'seriously teach the Word of God for

46 Wearne interviewed by Linder, 13 July 2003.
47 Wearne interviewed by Linder, 13 July 2003; 25 July 2004.
48 John Prince and Moyra Prince, *Out of the Tower* (Homebush West: Anzea, 1987), 50.
49 David Bebbington, *Evangelicalism in Modern Britain* (London: Unwin Hyman, 1989), 257.

this generation'. The Convention was to be sharply focussed on that in order to produce Christians who really were the salt of the earth.

The demise of the weeklong summer convention at Katoomba gave birth to the Katoomba Youth Convention (KYC) in 1974 on the Australia Day weekend in January. Dick Lucas, rector of St Stephen's Bishopsgate in London and a master of exegetical preaching, was the principal speaker. A new style of Convention preaching was born. Behind this transition was John Chapman, the best known of Sydney's Anglican evangelists. He was Director of the Anglican Department of Evangelism from 1969 to 1993, spoke at the Katoomba Convention on 12 occasions from 1970, and was a Council member in the critical years of transition from 1975 to 1978. He was Phillip Jensen's spiritual father and would have rejoiced at every sign of the prospering of Jensen's strategy and the exponential growth particularly in the KYC.

While some evangelical conventions were being reborn, others were born for the first time. Christian Women Communicating International (CWCI), an international, evangelical women's ministry, started in Australia in 1957 and became celebrated for its dynamic Bible teaching. It grew so exponentially that it had to move to a large convention site south of Sydney at Stanwell Tops where 12–15,000 attended. Among their number was Jean Raddon, a natural leader, who had learned to trust the Lord and his Word during the toughest of missionary labours as a nurse in Nepal – she once removed fifty-four leeches from her person! In 1972 she started a less intense program of Bible study run over a shorter period of time called *Know Your Bible* or KYB. This proved very popular in Australia. By 1977 seven thousand Australian women were studying the Bible using KYB. In 2007 there were about 2,000 KYB groups in Australia.

The parachurch development which most affected Australian society in the 1970s was the emergence of low-fee independent, mainly Christian, schools. They were the product of four developments: the availability of state funding; the perception that state schools were becoming increasingly inhospitable to Christian values; the suspicion that traditional church schools, already too élitist, were becoming secular; and the presence of Reformed and conservative evangelical models of Christian schools in other countries, especially the United States.[50] Among the associations who advocated this development were Christian Parent-Controlled Schools (Reformed), Christian Community

50 Ian Lambert and Suzanne Mitchell, (eds.), *Reclaiming the Future* (Sydney: CSAC, 1996).

Schools (an Australian development) and Accelerated Christian Schools (American).[51]

Some of the new parachurch groups, such as Zadok and Cornerstone, were genuinely indigenous Australian developments. Zadok was founded in 1976 as a national study centre to relate Biblical Christianity to contemporary Australian culture and values. Its aim was to develop a lay-orientated, biblical theology for the work place and the world rather than for the church and the home. The Cornerstone Community, formed late in 1970, is different from many evangelical groups in that it is rural-based and communitarian. It resembles a Catholic monastic missionary order such as the Franciscans, but the Cornerstone community was to be made up of families. It became a theological college with campuses in a number of rural towns including Broken Hill, Dubbo, Canowindra and Swan Hill in NSW, Emerald and Darling Downs in Queensland, Ballarat in Victoria, and Strathalbyn in South Australia. Students and members of the community were employed in local industries. Their search for an incarnation of the Kingdom of God in Australian country towns was also the theological motivation behind many of the contemporary social experiments, mainly in cities, associated with the Jesus Movement.

The Jesus Movement

Over the Australia Day long weekend in January, 1972, the Sunbury Pop Festival was held near Melbourne. About 40,000 long-haired youths attended. It was Australia's answer to Woodstock. Banners read 'Smash the Draft' signifying popular opposition to the war in Vietnam. Glena, the Plymouth Brethren wife of John Smith of God Squad fame was astonished by the spectacle. To her husband she quoted the words from Joel 3:13,14, 'Multitudes, multitudes in the valley of decision'. 'John here they are', she said through her tears, 'But where is the church?'[52] Thanks to John, the church was there. Jesus Freaks, Australians who identified with 'the Jesus movement' in America, were present and were baptised in a creek which ran through the property on which the festival was held. One, a hard-drinking member of a bikie gang, testified to the transformation which Jesus had brought to his life. The

51 On this, see further in chapter 17.

52 Kevin J. Smith, 'The Origins, Nature, and Significance of the Jesus Movement as a Revitalization Movement', Doctor of Missiology, Asbury Theological Seminary, 2002, 2. This thesis was published under the same title in 2011 by the Emeth Press, Lexington, KY.

naked swimmers heard him in silence, respectful of his sincere passion. Two evangelical groups, spawned by the Jesus Movement were also there, Theos and Truth and Liberation Concern (TLC).

Glena Smith was thus introduced to the culture which her husband, a one-time Methodist minister and son of a Methodist minister, had embraced the previous year. The Jesus Movement radicalised a new generation of evangelical leaders. It was not revivalistic and millenarian, like its American parent, though it was utopian. It was a dissenting counter-culture committed to changing the dominant culture and improving the lot of the marginalised in Australian society. It produced ministries characterised by enormous energy, optimism, and not a little creativity. They included The House of the New World (HNW) in Sydney, The House of the Gentle Bunyip in Melbourne, The House of Freedom in Brisbane, The Last Homely House in Perth, Truth and Liberation Concern (TLC), The Abode of the Gentle Toad, The Resurrection Community, Theos Coffee Shops, Jacob's Ladder, and God's Squad Motor Cycle Club.

Most of the leaders of these ministries, John Smith observed, were 'conservative evangelicals who experienced swift paradigm shifts and embraced the dissenting culture as visionaries and strategists as well as evangelists, communal organizers, and pastor teachers'.[53] The thought leader of the Australian Jesus Movement was probably the much-loved and much-suspected Athol Gill (1938–92),[54] a New Testament scholar of international repute.[55] A member of the staff of the Baptist Theological College of Queensland (1971–73), he was challenged by his students to create a community where the radical demands of Jesus could be practised or else to stop preparing them for frustration. So he established the 'House of Freedom', a coffee shop in the Brisbane nightclub district. He was opposed by conservative Baptists who effectively engineered his dismissal. At Lausanne in 1974 he was among the leaders of the radical evangelicals or subversives.[56] He insisted that salvation is 'personal, social, global and cosmic' and added that 'we must repudiate as demonic the attempt to drive a wedge between evangelism and social action'.[57] In 1975 he was

53 Smith, 'Jesus Movement', 403 n16.

54 Harold Pidwell, *A Gentle Bunyip: the Athol Gill Story* (Wests Lakes, SA: Seaview Press, 2007).

55 His scholarship was focussed on the gospels, especially Mark. His mature thought is found in *Life on the Road* (1989) and *The Fringes of Freedom* (1990).

56 Chilton, 'Evangelicals and the End of Christian Australia', 303, 320–338.

57 Athol Gill, 'Theological Implications of Radical Discipleship', in J.D. Douglas (ed.), *Let the Earth Hear His Voice: The International Congress on World Evangelization, Lausanne, 1974* (Lausanne and Minneapolis: World Wide Publications, 1974), 1294.

appointed Dean at Whitley, the Baptist College in Melbourne. Even then an attempt was made in 1984 not to reappoint him, and he had to defend himself before a large gathering at the Baptist Church in Kew, where he successfully won over the soft hearts of the Victorian evangelical Baptists![58]

In Melbourne Gill, responding to growing youth homelessness, created the 'House of the Gentle Bunyip'. Here an attempt was made to find dynamic equivalents to some traditional church practices. For example, the Australian meat pie with sauce was used instead of bread and wine. The House of the Gentle Bunyip had about 70 members living in community and it organised a wide range of ministries: a youth centre, short-term accommodation for street kids, a food co-operative, a crisis-care program for schizophrenics, an alternative primary school, a lunch program for the elderly, an arts and crafts school, and a peace and disarmament group.

Gill famously rejected the argument, attributed to conservative evangelicals that, while Paul's letters are prescriptive, the gospels are descriptive. Gill believed too many Protestants, by this rationalisation, made the teachings of Paul mandatory, while unconsciously domesticating the gospels, thus avoiding the ultimate demands of Christ on their lives. By contrast, for all their frenetic activity and anxiety, the leaders of the Jesus Movement spoke of Jesus as the 'still point in a turning world'. 'The passionate drive to make Jesus the topic of liberating conversation', concluded John Smith, 'was possibly the simplest, yet most profound of the principles of missiology successfully employed across cultural diversity by Jesus Freaks.'[59]

John Smith's TLC, because the mainstream churches were so alien to new converts, formed a new church movement, known as Care and Communication Concern (CCC) and St Martin's Community Churches. TLC/CCC organised over 4,000 visits to schools – government as well as Christian and Church schools, primary as well as secondary – to discuss the Christian message in seminars and forums during school hours. School administrators seemed to be only too pleased that someone was doing something for 'at risk' youth. The media too found it easy to make a story out of the work of these evangelistic social activists who rode Harleys, made outspoken condemnations of established authorities in church and state, and addressed pressing social issues of homelessness, poverty, youth suicide, and indigenous land rights.

These ministries had a high failure rate and it is not hard to see why. The optimism was too high. They sought to engage not only the counter-culture, but

58 Munro, 'Struggle for Identity and Direction', 108f.

59 Smith, 'Jesus Movement', 529.

also the sub-culture of the bikie world, which was far from the peace-loving, non-violent hippie world. The energy was all expended in a few years of extraordinary self-sacrifice from the late '60s to the early '80s. The leaders were much better at starting organisations than keeping them going. Many of their ministries collapsed through poor management and burn out. Because they condemned capitalism they did not receive the financial backing of those whose enterprise generated wealth. Because they departed from the traditional evangelical churches and parachurch organisations, they forfeited their support and attracted the criticisms which other evangelicals were so ready to offer. They 'rejected everything between Jesus' time and their own'[60] which seemed an ill-informed dismissal of the riches of the Christian tradition. They depicted Australian history as materialist and secular from its birth, thus dismissing as inconsequential the efforts of those who had attempted to bear witness to Christ over the previous two centuries. They found in Australian historian Manning Clark a congenial interpreter of the Australian story: sensitivity to spiritual and religious forces combined with a pronounced distaste for the churches' chronic betrayal of 'the image of Christ'.[61] In the end its counter-cultural nagging overwhelmed its capacity to revitalise. It came to wallow in condemnation, and disillusionment was added to the hopelessness it had sought to redress.

But its architects moved on – many back into the evangelical churches from which they had come – and their churches were never the same again. An example is Peter Corney, who directed The Master's Workshop, an alternative youth-training scheme for Theos. In 1976, he left that position to become vicar of St Hilary's, Kew, and developed it into the largest Anglican church in Melbourne with a strong youth ministry. Another is John Hirt, converted at the 1959 Billy Graham Crusade, a Baptist minister, who, in 1970 in Sydney, established HNW, with branches in Melbourne, Brisbane, Adelaide and Canberra. Among those who were affirmed in the Christian faith at HNW was 1972 Olympic swimming champion Shane Gould. She had laid her Olympic medals on the 'altar' of Gordon Methodist Church in Sydney in thankfulness for the talents she had been given. She committed her life to Jesus through the ministry of the Methodist Central Mission.[62] Hirt married the radical American Christian feminist, Carol Rowley, and when, after a little under a decade, the ministry collapsed (from within through 'power and ego battles'),

60 Ian Breward, *A History of the Australian Churches* (St Leonards: Allen & Unwin, 1993) 178.

61 Smith, 'Jesus Movement', 328.

62 'Free Slave talks with Shane Gould', *Free Slave*, 3.1, April 1975, 3.

he did not return to the Baptist pastorate, but instead entered the Uniting Church as an experienced and determined social activist.[63]

The Jesus Movement contributed to making this yet another time, like the 1890s, when the reservoirs of evangelical orthodoxy burst their banks and flowed into radical reforms and ideologies: the submerged movement surfaced in the public culture. It was a time, also like the 1890s, when Australia was seeking to find its national identity. Members of the Jesus Movement, like radicals of the 1890s, claimed that their view of Jesus was more authentic than that of the conservative evangelical churches. The latter cared too little for the Australian soul and cared too much for private religious experience. Gill castigated this as 'Decisionism instead of discipleship': 'The idea of accepting Jesus as saviour and later, perhaps, acknowledging him as Lord is totally foreign to the New Testament.'[64] Gill believed that Sydney Anglicans were guilty of this truncation of the Gospel. By ignoring the need for justice in the world, they drove a wedge between 'Saviourism' and 'Lordship'. The only form in which faith exists in the New Testament, Gill insisted, is discipleship. Thus Hirt records, Gill 'was a continual thorn in the side of "Jensonism" [sic] and enabled many of us to be wary of self-serving fundamentalist rationalism'.[65] For leaders of the Jesus movement, conversion was a call to action on behalf of others: 'Once freed by grace, we are released from recalcitrant "quietism" and non-commitment into the "must" of obedience – to heralding the reign of God.'[66] This required not only announcing but also enacting 'Jesus' liberation program in the world' which included 'the exorcism of demonisms like poverty, hunger, violence, exploitation, greed and environmental despoliation'.[67]

It is possible that the Jesus Movement contributed substantially to one of the major and most impressive developments in recent evangelical history, the recovery of a social conscience. A case in point is Steve Lawrence (1952–2012). His parents were Methodists with a strong social conscience. While they took a two-year course in theology at the Tahlee Bible College at Port Stephens, north of Sydney, they sent Steve to board at the new Anglican Illawarra Grammar School, but this only made him aware of the disparity in income between his own parents and those who lived in housing commission accommodation in

63 Smith, 'Jesus Movement', 358.

64 David J. Neville (ed.), *Prophecy and Passion: Essays in honour of Athol Gill* (Adelaide: Australian Theological Forum, c.2002), 273.

65 John Hirt, 'Catechetical Evangelism as Radical Discipleship in the Mission of the Church,' in Neville, *Prophecy and Passion*, 314n31.

66 Hirt in Neville, *Prophecy and Passion*, 310.

67 Hirt in Neville, *Prophecy and Passion*, 312f.

the Wollongong suburbs of Windang and Warilla. His parents gave away 60 per cent of their income and took into their own home those who suffered from drug and alcohol addictions. Steve was attracted to Alan Walker in the early 1970s and attended the Jesus Commune in East Sydney.

He studied Social Work at the University of NSW and then joined St Mark's Anglican Church in Malabar, which combined social radicalism with Charismatic spirituality, and which, influenced by the Fisherfolk, created a Parish community where incomes were shared. 'We used to be paid $5 a week pocket money – that was the money I could spend without asking anybody's approval. Anything beyond five bucks I had to work out with the folks in the house I was living in.'[68] He lived this way for 15 years while he worked for the Department of Community Services. He had grown up close to Aboriginal families in Windang, and at Malabar he was drawn to work among Aboriginal people at La Perouse. So he resigned from the Department of Community Services and was paid by the rector of Malabar to work with the Aboriginal people. He visited communes in India, Israel, Holland, England and America, before establishing a community in Queanbeyan in NSW. In 1979 he established an employment training scheme called WorkVentures. By 2008 it was employing 200 people with a turnover of $16m. It spawned JobFutures, an $80m operation. By this time he was something of a celebrity. In 2004 he was introduced to John Howard and Bill Gates, met Kofi Annan, Secretary-General of the United Nations, and Ernst and Young made him their 'Social Entrepreneur of the Year'. His was a vision of what the Kingdom of God should look like in Australia. It would leave no room for poverty or disadvantage.

Evangelism

National evangelistic missions continued: the Australian Council of Churches sponsored the Church and Life Mission in 1966, and Billy Graham returned in 1968–69 and again in 1979. It is commonly asserted that the 1968–69 Billy Graham Crusade was not as successful as the 1959 Crusade because supporters were complacent and did not pray as much. But the vigilantly recorded statistics testify to much effort: 11,000 gathered for a 'Meet the Billy Graham Team' pre-crusade rally on 2 November 1967; 8,500 enrolled in counselling classes; 25,000 visited 750,000 homes in Sydney to invite people to the Crusade. And the initial results were far from disappointing, especially among young people. The first Sunday meeting of the '68 Crusade in Sydney

68 *SMH*, 20 August 2008; 9 July 2012.

attracted 59,000, a record crowd for a first Sunday meeting. The next night 22,000 young people attended and 2,224 went forward, at over 10 per cent, the greatest ever known percentage response. In a little over a week 417,000 attended, and 22,420 went forward of whom 81 per cent were under 25. The 1969 Crusade in Victoria attracted 333,250 and 12,000 inquirers. Walter Smyth, director of Graham crusades, felt that proportionately the '69 crusade in Melbourne was greater than 1959.[69]

The 1968–9 Graham Crusade met with far more determined opposition than that of 1959, both from secularists and fundamentalists.[70] Australia was divided over the Vietnam War, and Graham was condemned for not stating a position on it. Opposition to Graham was also fomented by the Banner of Truth, which condemned 'revivalism' and 'decisionism', and by American fundamentalist Carl McIntyre who visited Australia and condemned Graham as a compromiser with liberals. One W. Bradbury of Petersham in Sydney shot off the following missile to the BGEA:

> I am only an Electrician but I'd love one or two hours with Billy Graham over the Word of God. NO spiritual man would drift like Sir Billy has … I judge him to be a man of MIXED PRINCIPLES AND NOT FIXED ONES … I WILL NOT WASTE TIME TO SEE OR HEAR HIM UNTIL HE BECOMES A FUNDAMENTALIST AND NOT A NEUTRALIST.[71]

The Methodists, who had been ambiguous about the 1959 crusades under Alan Walker, were far less obliging under the redoubtable radical, Bill Hobbin, President of the NSW Conference. Hobbin declared that he had serious reservations about Graham's emotionally-charged, manipulative presentation, and that he was more concerned to do something 'for human beings right here on this earth' than following Graham's preference for preparing them for the hereafter.[72] Graham, in truth, was concerned to do something for them in both worlds, but secularised Methodists, when asked why they did not give more time to saving souls, replied that this is exactly what they were doing, but they had a very different understanding of 'save' and 'soul'.[73]

69 John C. Pollock, *Crusades* (Minneapolis: World Wide Publications, 1969), 296.
70 Chilton, 'Evangelicals and the End of Christian Australia', 181–190.
71 26 April 1968, Collection 245, 7, 16, BGA.
72 Collection Box 10, folio 1, 26 May 1967, BGA; Bill Hobbin, Unpublished Autobiography, United Theological College, 270f.
73 Winifred Ward, *Men ahead of their Time* (Melbourne: The Joint Board of Christian Education, 1996), 5.

A third Billy Graham Crusade was held in Sydney from 29 April to 20 May 1979. Archbishop Loane in 1975 conceived of the idea of Graham's returning to Sydney on the 20th anniversary of the historic 1959 Crusade. His invitation to Graham came with conditions: it must not be a short visit; 1968 was too short (eight days); Billy must come for three weeks and four Sundays. The Crusade office was set up in the offices of St Andrew's Cathedral, so it was very much an Anglican show. There was a feeling that many of the organisers were going through their paces partly to please the Archbishop whose baby this crusade so obviously was. The meetings were held at the Randwick Racecourse in cold and wet conditions, and attendance was lower than anticipated. There were 21,331 inquirers in the three-week crusade, compared with 56,780 in the four weeks of 1959, and 22,000 in the eight days of 1968. Loane's 1981 assessment:

> The crusade did not make the breakthrough or the impact on the city at large in the way that one would have hoped, but I would say without reservation that it was a source of very great blessing to the churches, among church people and for those whom church people were personally responsible for praying.[74]

The importance attached to Billy Graham by Sydney diocesan leaders was still considerable, but by now not uncritical. There was declining enthusiasm for his crusades by evangelistic strategists[75] and waning confidence that Australia might yet see a revival which would make it, in Graham's words, 'the great religious super power of the world'.[76]

One keen to try new methods was the Rev Geoffrey Fletcher.[77] He was Director from 1966 to 1969 of the Department of Evangelism in the Diocese of Sydney. He understood that lay people felt the need for training in evangelism. In 1966 he attended the Conference on Evangelism in Berlin. There he met Bill Bright, founder of Campus Crusade for Christ, who had been involved in the development of transferable training tools in evangelism and discipleship-making. Equipped with these, Fletcher conducted the first Lay Institute for Evangelism (LIFE) on Anzac Day 1967 in Dundas, Sydney.

---

74 John Pollock, *To All the Nations: The Billy Graham Story* (San Francisco: Harper & Row, 1985), 142f.

75 John Gray, 'Evangelism in the Anglican Diocese of Sydney, 1959–1989', MA(hons), University of NSW, 1994, 84.

76 *The Canberra Times*, 21 May 1979.

77 Michael Orpwood, *Chappo: For the Sake of the Gospel: John Chapman and the Department of Evangelism* (Russell Lea, Australia: Eagleswift Press, 1995), 80, 87, 88.

The LIFE program was designed to teach lay people 'how to present Jesus Christ, how to avoid religious jargon, how to overcome anxiety in sharing, how to answer questions, how to avoid arguing'. Two booklets were commonly used to share the Gospel: *Have you heard of the Four Spiritual Laws?* and *Have you made the wonderful discovery of the Spirit Filled Life*? Fletcher made the Lay Institute non-denominational and it later became known as Campus Crusade for Christ Australia. But, because it was no longer an Anglican body and because it was perceived as competing with the IVF in universities, Campus Crusade did not suit those concerned with Gospel purity. By now back in America, an alarmed Charles Troutman advised Ian Burnard that the advent of the 'ultra-right-wing fundamentalist' Campus Crusade in Australia would divide the evangelical student movement.[78] Fletcher felt himself blackballed by the criticism of LIFE.[79] But he recruited the most successful of Sydney's evangelists, John Chapman. 'Chappo', then in the Diocese of Armidale, was experimenting with evangelism in meetings held in private homes, called 'Dialogue Evangelism'.

The chief beneficiary of the still-hearty appetite for evangelism in the 1960s was the local church. It now became far more intentional about evangelism.[80] In the nineteenth century churches had been centres of pastoral care and moral influence rather than of evangelism. But now many churches had experienced increasing their membership dramatically through referrals from the Billy Graham crusades and they were hungry for more. Two very effective parish builders were fellow students at Moore College in the 1950s, Dudley Foord and Harry Goodhew, both later bishops.

Foord's desire to understand more deeply the dynamics of parish health, the term he preferred to church growth, led him to resign from 17 committees to find the time to devote to his own parish, Christ Church, St Ives. He enrolled at Fuller Theological Seminary in the USA to help him probe these issues more systematically. Foord was not given to the uncritical endorsement of American church growth principles, but he thought Australians tend to be too slapdash and he applauded the American aptitude for organisation and the pursuit of excellence and bigness of heart and readiness to take risks. Between 1972 and 1984 his parish grew into one of the largest parish churches in Sydney.

---

78 Troutman to Burnard, 25 July 1962, Collection 111, box 1, f.38, and to Brian Dickey, 19 February 1963, Collection 111, box 2, f.4., BGA.

79 Geoff Fletcher interviewed by Margaret Lamb, 16 November 1989.

80 See the 1972 Sydney synod report, 'Looking into the Parish'. In 1973 the Sydney Anglican Clerical Society responded with 'Take another Look at the Parish'.

Harry Goodhew was rector of St Stephen's Coorparoo, in the Diocese of Brisbane, from 1971 to 1976. One parishioner recalled 'Harry took Coorparoo from a low church to a worshipping Christian family. It was absolutely wonderful. He brought Evangelism Explosion to the parish and we saw people converted every week. He had almost the whole diocese eating out of his hand and asking about evangelism.'[81] In 1974 Goodhew attended the Lausanne Congress on World Evangelisation and visited leading churchmen in America and England. It was then that he forged links with American church leaders which remained strong: Church growth guru, Bill Yaeger of Modesto; Jim Kennedy, founder of Evangelism Explosion (EE); Bill Hybels, who promoted seeker-sensitive services; and Dr Win Arn, one of the early exponents of church growth theory. His application of the knowledge he thus acquired to local churches gave parish leaders confidence that churches could grow and was the chief factor in his election as Archbishop of Sydney in 1993.

Revival

Although Geoffrey Bingham saw amazing scenes of revival in Pakistan in the late 1950s and returned to Sydney full of the joy of the Lord, he was not heard gladly by those nervous of anything which could be interpreted as Charismatic or sinless perfectionist. Bingham, hurt, left the rather cool and unwelcoming bosom of Sydney, went to South Australia, first as principal of the Adelaide Bible Institute (later Bible College of South Australia), and then as Director of the New Creation Teaching Ministry (NCTM), where he wrote, published and taught an ever-expanding army of devoted disciples, who attended conferences and schools. NCTM's doctrinal stance was: 'biblical and Reformed, without prejudice to the movements of God's Spirit which come at times of revival and renewal of the Church'.[82]

At some of the missions taken by Bingham, the fire of revival fell. In August 1969 a mission entitled 'Free Indeed' was held at Wudinna on the Eyre Peninsula in South Australia. The large crowd at the opening meeting startled the organisers and they moved to a hall, but even there many hearers had to stand outside and listen through the open windows. The atmosphere was one of heightened expectancy, the listening was intent, and many attended who were not thought to be at all interested in Christian things. There was a

81 Vic Smith to Stuart Piggin, 20 February 1993.

82 Undated notes on the Ministry of New Creation, prepared by Geoff Bingham and Team (digital copy of the archives of the New Creation Teaching Ministry in possession of the authors).

sense of the presence of God brooding over the whole geographical area. A farmer who had not been going to the meetings, although his wife was, was out on his tractor ploughing, when great conviction came upon him and he got down in the dust and gave his life to the Lord. The sense of wonderment came to characterise all the meetings. Crowds of people would just sit in awe for half an hour after the meetings were over without moving or saying a word. Many felt that it was like Pentecost, although without tongues. Over 400 people came to the last meeting. They came from as far away as Ceduna and Cummins. Of the final night, Bingham said 'like a great rain of beauty and silence and joy, it just descended on the whole congregation. It was quite remarkable. I'd have called it a very gentle but a very powerful outpouring of the Holy Spirit. And I can remember the joy in the worship and the praise that night.'[83]

In 1979 revival, of great power and unusual longevity, came at last to the neediest of the Church's flock, the Aboriginal people. This revival began in the Uniting Church in Elcho Island (Galiwin'ku). On 14 March 1979 about 30 people gathered with their pastor Djiniyini Gondarra. He thanked those few who had been praying for renewal and he said that he too had been praying for revival. He describes what happened next:

> I asked the group to hold each other's hands and I began to pray for the people and for the church, that God would pour out His Holy Spirit to bring healing and renewal to the hearts of men and women, and to the children. Suddenly we began to feel God's Spirit moving in our hearts and the whole form of prayer-life suddenly changed and everybody began to pray in spirit and in harmony. And there was a great noise going on in the room and we began to ask one another what was going on. Some of us said that God had now visited us and once again established His kingdom among His people.[84]

Nightly meetings were now held with upwards of 200 in attendance, some of which went on until 2 a.m. Backsliders and fence-sitters fell on their knees and implored those who had been liberated to pray for them. On one weekend 128 either accepted Christ or rededicated their lives to him. Not only was the worship reportedly sweeter, but there was also a change in the tone of the community: less drunkenness, petrol sniffing, and fighting; greater

83 Trevor Faggotter, 'Revival Fire at Wudinna,' *Renewal Journal*, 4, 1994, 50.

84 Cited in Jeanette Boyd, 'The Arnhem Land Revival of 1979: An Australian Aboriginal Religious Movement', unpublished paper, October 1986.

conscientiousness in work; an increased boldness in speaking out against social injustices. Males took over leadership of the Church from women and of the singing in worship, an event of great significance in Aboriginal society:

> It was not only in the camp but in the church and the community as a whole, in fact the relationships with the church, the council, with the departments, the foreman, the bosses, and the workmen, the family and the village life with wives, husbands and children, were affected. It just swept through as though God had turned on a tap and was cleansing out the power of darkness. All the time we could hear singing; people would go past talking about it and at night we could go to sleep hearing people still singing Christian choruses. It was just like Pentecost.[85]

Unlike most of the revivals in Australian history, this Aboriginal revival was neither localised nor short-lived. 'When we read the Scriptures', explained Djiniyini, 'of Peter and others when they received the power of the Spirit, they didn't stop, they went out. This was revealed to us and we started to minister to other communities.'[86] Using the facilities of the Missionary Aviation Fellowship the Elcho Islanders spread their good news all over Arnhem Land, and north and north-western Australia.

Charismatics and Pentecostals

In the latter part of the twentieth century the chief heirs of those evangelicals who expected and prayed for revival were Charismatics and Pentecostals. They are best identified as the offspring of the Methodist branch of the evangelical family, as that part of the family which privileges experience above doctrine. The Charismatic 'Renewal' in the mainstream churches is commonly said to have begun with the 1959 declaration of an Episcopalian priest, Dennis Bennett, to his Van Nuys, California, congregation that he spoke with 'other tongues'. His book *Nine O'Clock in the Morning* had an effect beyond his denomination, especially after *Newsweek* and *Time* magazines picked up on the story. The movement spread rapidly across denominations, through the United States, Canada and overseas, usually causing division and debate and occasionally resulting in expulsions. When Michael Harper, curate at All Souls, Langham Place, London, began promoting the Renewal from 1962, the intellectual and Charismatic ends of Church of England evangelicalism

85 Max Hart, *A Story of Fire: Aboriginal Christianity* (Blackwood: New Creation Publications, 1988), 50f.

86 Hart, *A Story of Fire*, 51.

came into direct conflict, in the form of a dispute between himself and his rector, John Stott. In June 1964 Harper resigned and established the Fountain Trust. This development required a position from Sydney evangelical Anglicans, particularly after the *Australian Church Record* carried banner headlines declaring 'Tongues Spoken' at the Picton Convention near Sydney which the Rev. J. Barry Schofield held during the month of March 1966.[87]

The impetus for the general mainline renewal within Australia seems to have been in Sydney in 1968, when two traditional churches aligned themselves with a Charismatic ministry. Alan Langstaff's Lugar Brae Methodist church and, down the road, Alan Alcock's St Luke's Anglican church, Clovelly, came into contact with a Youth with a Mission (YWAM) house in nearby Randwick, a nondenominational Pentecostal group under Dean Sherman. At one of Langstaff's Sunday afternoon prayer meetings, Alcock was swept away by the 'singing in the Spirit': 'I thought, now, that is not man … To me, it was just unexplainable other than that people were singing as the Holy Spirit led them.'[88]

Langstaff, who had been baptised in the Spirit at a Catholic meeting while being prayed over by a Pentecostal minister, suggested to Alcock that he needed to be 'filled with the Spirit'. Alcock objected on the theological grounds that such a filling occurs automatically on conversion. He went to his local bishop, John Reid, who directed him to his Bible. He also went to Paul Collins's Faith Centre, an independent Pentecostal ministry, to search for answers. Collins sensitively dealt with his questions and led him into 'the Baptism'. Shortly thereafter, several Anglicans came into Renewal, including Greg and Judy Blaxland of the South American Missionary Society, David Crawford at Malabar, and the rector of St John's Darlinghurst, Bernard Gook.

The mid-1970s were the halcyon days for the Charismatic renewal in Australia. Alan Alcock ran regular tours to American Charismatic centres, accompanied by those who would be key to the spreading of Charismatic renewal in various sections of the community. In January 1973, Alan Langstaff, with Howard Carter of the Logos foundation, organised one of the first major Charismatic conferences at the Australian National University, Canberra. Subsequently, Langstaff and Alcock organised the Temple Trust to act as a medium through which further overseas speakers could be invited. Speakers such as Michael Harper, David Du Plessis, Terry Fullam, and Francis McNutt came to Australia under Temple auspices. In January 1977 the Temple Trust organised in Sydney what was hailed as the

87 John Wyndham, interviewed by Mark Hutchinson, 26 January 1993.

88 Alan Alcock, interviewed by Mark Hutchinson, 2 February 1993.

most significant inter-denominational church conference in Australian history to that time, the International Conference on the Holy Spirit and the Church, with some 5,000 delegates. By 1979, when Du Plessis and Harper spoke at a Temple Trust conference, some 15,000 attended.[89]

But as the movement grew, so too did the opposition to it. As early as 1971 committees to study the Charismatic movement were appointed by the Sydney Anglican Diocesan Synod and at least three Methodist State conferences. Even though the chairman of the Anglican committee was the moderate, even-handed Bishop John Reid, the Anglican Charismatics (including the leader of the healing movement in Sydney, Canon A.J. Glennon) felt they were outnumbered, and that the report was a show trial.[90] What Charismatics called 'Baptism in the Spirit' the report suggested was simply 'part of the sanctifying work of the Holy Spirit ... [who] may do this dramatically in one person and slowly and steadily in another.'[91] The Bible was unclear, and on the grounds that 'if an experience cannot be positively identified biblically it must not be urged upon Christian people as helpful or desirable'.[92] It called for both Charismatics and non-Charismatics to fellowship together, and not cause undue division in local congregations.

The acceptance of the committee's report at the 1973 synod meant that the Diocese of Sydney now formally adopted an essentially anti-Charismatic stance. Sydney remained a hard place for Charismatics. Wherever the movement came into the open, there was a reaction against it. Within six months, for instance, Ian Jagelman, then an accountant, later pastor of Christian City Church in Lane Cove, Sydney, recalls, 'I lost every Christian friend I had', and he was pushed out of official positions in the Crusaders and Campaigners for Christ. Ian Holt, head of Crusaders, specifically warned him about the dangers of movements which, like the Tinker Tailor group, tended towards teachings of entire sanctification and even sinless perfection. Charismatic renewal was condemned to being a small minority movement within Sydney Anglicanism and did not do much better in other mainstream denominations.[93]

But while, for the most part, the mainstream churches refused to incorporate the Charismatic renewal into their life and worship, the Pentecostal churches

---

89 Alcock, interviewed by Hutchinson.

90 *Handbook of the Church of England in Australia*, Diocese of Sydney, 1973 and 1974.

91 *Diocese of Sydney: Committee to consider the Neo-Pentecostal Movement. Both Sides of the Question: Official Enquiry into Neo-Pentecostalism*, (Sydney: AIO, 1973), 8.

92 *Both Sides of the Question*, 9.

93 Three Charismatic megachurches have grown in Australia: Blackburn Baptist Crossway Church and the Careforce Church of Christ Church, both in Melbourne, and the Gateway Baptist Church in Brisbane.

did just that and were revived in the process. Those who could not accept the condemnation of the movement by their leaders forsook their churches. The Christian City Church, a mega-congregation at Dee Why, was built on 'North Shore Methodists and Anglicans' whose experience had been rejected in the mainline churches.[94]

The period 1937–77 is characterised by Pentecostal leader, David Cartledge, as the Assembly of God in Australia's forty years in the wilderness.[95] But they were about to enter the promised land, led by a new breed of heroes. In 1969 Reginald Klimionok was appointed Pastor of Mt Gravatt Assembly of God (later Garden City Christian Church) in Queensland, and the following year David Cartledge was appointed Pastor of Townsville Assembly of God, and Andrew Evans, Pastor of Klemzig Assembly of God in South Australia, which was to grow into Paradise Gardens, for a time the largest Protestant church in Australia. All three had enjoyed special experiences of God and been mentored by New Zealand Pentecostals. These three, pastors of the movement's three largest churches, brought unrelenting pressure to bear on their movement to change, by making the Charismatic renewal the new way for Pentecostals. In 1973, the same year as the Sydney Anglicans condemned the Charismatic movement in their synod, the Assembly of God appointed a Committee on Restructure, made up of Pentecostal leaders of the younger generation who endorsed the Charismatic renewal and were determined to have their entire movement embrace it. In the same year, Paul (later David) Yonggi Cho, Korean pastor of the world's largest megachurch, first addressed an Australian Assembly of God conference. He tipped the balance in favour of the 'new' Pentecostals and spoke at a number of such conferences in the next decade, including the 'World's Largest Church Growth Seminar' held in Adelaide in 1979.

In 1977 there was a revolution in the Assemblies of God resulting in the appointment of what is known as 'apostolic leadership': pastors who had a track record in growing churches replaced those who had not.[96] David and Marie Cartledge, whose church at Townsville experienced revival in 1971, organised what was to be acknowledged as a famous tour of Cho's Church in Seoul, Korea and Jerusalem, ingeniously the newest and the oldest sources of inspiration, to which Pentecostals were ever alert. Most of the leadership of the AOG in Australia went on this lightening tour from 12 to 18 July 1977.

94 Alcock interviewed by Hutchinson.

95 David Cartledge, *The Apostolic Revolution: The Restoration of Apostles and Prophets in the Assemblies of God in Australia* (Sydney: Paraclete Institute, 2000).

96 Sam Hey, 'God in the Suburbs and Beyond: The Emergence of an Australian Megachurch and Denomination', PhD, Griffith University, 2010, 26.

Consequent upon the apostolic leadership revolution, the movement enjoyed a resurgence which has been characterised as revival.[97]

As part of the 1977 revolution, Andrew Evans, an exponent of the Charismatic renewal, was elected Superintendent of the Assemblies of God in Australia and held the position for 20 years, during which time the movement expanded dramatically. In 1977 the AOG had 152 churches and fewer than 10,000 constituents. By 1997 it had 826 member churches and 115,000 constituents.[98] Shane Clifton has reviewed the reasons for this expansion: exclusion of the Charismatically-inclined from the older denominations and their switching to the new-style Pentecostal churches, the modernisation of worship, acceptance of broader social values, leadership which encouraged diversity, and the enthusiastic adoption of church growth principles (high view of Scripture, priority of evangelism and the spiritual over social or ethical transformation, belief in targeting those especially ripe for evangelism – 'seasons of harvest', and pragmatism).[99] These new Pentecostal churches prized cultural relevance and strong leadership. By the end of the 1970s, then, when Charismatics began to bail out of their denominations, classical Pentecostalism had renewed itself sufficiently to embrace them gladly. It was a remarkable development in such a short space of time and one calculated to snatch from the defeat of the Charismatic movement the victory of the Pentecostal churches.

In July 1977 the first service of Frank Houston's independent Pentecostal Church, the Sydney Christian Life Centre, was held. He had come across from New Zealand where he had pastored a megachurch in Lower Hutt near Wellington. Andrew Evans persuaded him to join up with the new-look AOG. By 1980 Houston was State Superintendent and by 1981 – that is within just four years – membership of his church had topped a thousand. He restructured his church to give authority for governance to the elders, but he appointed them himself. Australia's largest church – Hillsong – was in the making.

* * *

97 Cartledge, *The Apostolic Revolution.*

98 Shane Clifton, 'An analysis of the developing Ecclesiology of the Assemblies of God in Australia', PhD, Australian Catholic University 2005, 211.

99 Clifton, 'Ecclesiology', chapters four and five.

The Reformed did not welcome Charismatic renewal, but in reality, a powerful new ally joined those within the evangelical movement now seeking new ways of being Christian in 'a post-Christendom national public culture'.[100] Indeed, there was a lot of energy in the response of evangelicals to the challenges posed by an increasingly secularised culture. The Reformed sharpened their theology; parachurch groups multiplied and organised more efficiently; within the mainstream denominations, especially the Anglicans and Presbyterians, evangelicalism became a more powerful presence; attempts to follow Jesus' example generated self-sacrifice sufficient to challenge materialism; new methods of evangelism were tested; the opportunity to experience new dimensions of spiritual power was offered by Charismatic renewal. The chief feature of the response of evangelicals to the secularisation of the nation, then, was not its fragility or timidity, but its energy and diversity. Unity was not its strength, but the evangelical movement was still strong.

100 Chilton, 'Evangelicals and the End of Christian Australia', 31.

Chapter Thirteen

IDENTITY CRISIS, 1980–1989

'I enjoy Australia, and I love being there, but it is a community which brawls more than it should.'
(Sidney Nolan)

Australia's bicentenary in 1988 gave all Australians the opportunity to reflect on what it means to be an Australian. For evangelicals, the challenge of the 1980s was to work out how best to engage in a society increasingly secular, wary of fundamentalism, and feminist. It was an engagement negotiated in parliaments, law courts and universities as well as in churches. There was a new interest by evangelicals in politics: Pentecostals particularly engaged on the Right of politics, while progressive evangelicals engaged on the Left. Feminism's confrontation with patriarchal traditions was played out, not only in the long struggle within the mainstream churches for the ordination of women, but also in the trials of Australia's most vilified evangelical woman, Lindy Chamberlain, and in the triumphs of Australia's most esteemed evangelical woman, Eva Burrows.

Politics – State and Federal

The crisis in evangelical identity following the challenges to its hegemony in the 1960s and 1970s did nothing to remove the long standing evangelical unease with politics. The 1980s was a particularly difficult decade for conservative Protestants to thrive in politics. Secularist politicians such as Neville Wran, Premier of NSW (1976–86), loved to have a dig at Christians and remind them, whenever they made a stand for Christian principle, that the Established Church was a thing of the past. Evangelicals were unnerved by such mockery, fearing the charge of 'interference' in what they too readily accepted to be a secular society based on church/state separation. In 1987 artist Sidney Nolan said: 'I enjoy Australia, and I love being there, but it is a community which brawls more than it should'.[1] Not averse to fighting

1 *Times Literary Supplement*, 27 November-3 December, 1987.

each other, evangelicals were not then itching for a fight with their secular compatriots who were shaping up to fight with them.

Prevailing evangelical theologies did not help much either. The perfectionist demands of older conservative evangelicals with their keen sense of withdrawal holiness and their aversion to compromise made the role of the evangelical politician thankless. The newer so-called 'Knox-Robinson ecclesiology',[2] emanating from Moore College, with its insistence that the church was primarily for the fellowship of believers, did little to encourage Anglican evangelicals to develop an interest in civic responsibility, politics or social reform: 'the church as a meeting is entirely disassociated from the society where it is and, unless it is forced to meet in public, makes not the smallest impression on it'.[3] In a marked departure from the practice of Wilberforce two centuries earlier, evangelical leaders failed to get together with other Christians to express a common mind on social and political issues, fearing 'contamination' by non-evangelicals. The 1988 NSW elections were instructive. The leaders of both major parties were churchgoing Roman Catholics. It was a low point for evangelicals – not a Catholic plot, but an evangelical capitulation to secular opposition, which encouraged evangelical laity to settle for the pursuit of private affluence. The Protestant work ethic continued to come naturally to them at the expense of the ethic of civic engagement.

In state politics, evangelicals focussed on moral matters. Unable to persuade either of the major parties in Australian politics to take up their concerns with any enthusiasm, they had to devise and work through small, special interest parties. The Festival of Light, for example, formed the Call to Australia Party with Fred Nile as leader in 1977, and Nile was elected to the NSW Legislative Council in 1981, with 9 per cent of the primary vote. His wife, Elaine, was elected in 1988. But the Niles found it hard enough even to

2 D.W.B. Robinson, 'The Church Universal and its earthly form', *ACR*, 2 February 1956; 'The Church Universal and its earthly form – 2', *ACR*, 16 February 1956; 'The Church in the New Testament', *St Mark's Review*, 17, 1959, 4–14; 'The Doctrine of the Church and its Implications for Evangelism,' *Interchange*, 15, 1974, 156–162; 'The Church Revisited: An Autobiographical Fragment,' *Reformed Theological Review*, 48.1, 1989, 4–14; G. Cole, 'The Doctrine of the Church: Towards Conceptual Clarification', in Barry G. Webb (ed.) *Church, Worship, and the Local Congregation* (Homebush West: Lancer, 1987), 3–18.

3 Donald Robinson, 'The Church of God: Its Form and Unity', in *Donald Robinson Selected Works, Volume 1: Assembling God's People*, ed. Peter G. Bolt and Mark D. Thompson (Sydney: Moore College/Australian Church Record, 2008), 247. Robinson was easily misunderstood on this point. See Rory Shiner, 'Reading the New Testament in Australia: An Historical Account of the Origins, Development and Influence of D.W.B. Robinson's Biblical Scholarship', PhD, Macquarie University, 2017, 129.

win evangelical support. When Nile stood for parliament, Marcus Loane, Archbishop of Sydney, withdrew from the Festival of Light. Its high public profile and its resorting to political processes raised fears that Australia was turning to fundamentalism and many evangelicals, Loane included, did not want to be saddled with that. Better to have no engagement in politics than engage on the basis of a theology which could open the church to criticism.

Pentecostals were not so squeamish about being labelled as theologically unsophisticated, and, in Queensland, Howard Carter, founder of the Covenant Christian Church, became involved in Queensland state politics. His extreme right-wing agenda proved as unpopular as the National Party which was thrown out of office in 1989 after having governed Queensland for 32 years. Marcus Loane's judgment seemed vindicated: there was something unhealthily selective about the causes championed by groups with fundamentalist sympathies. Overtly evangelical forays into state politics in the 1980s were disappointing.

Evangelical initiatives in federal politics were more successful, but they too were characterised by the tentativeness of those unsure of the wisdom of mixing religion and politics. An early initiative came from that branch of evangelicalism more accustomed to political endeavours – the Methodists. Gil Duthie (ALP), for 29 years federal member for the Tasmanian seat of Wilmot, was a Methodist minister before entering Parliament in 1946. He finally succeeded in 1968 in forming, together with the Liberal member for Lalor, Merv Lee, the Parliamentary Christian Fellowship (PCF). Lee became its first President and Duthie its foundation Secretary. It organised an annual ecumenical church service and from 1986 national prayer breakfasts. It owed a lot to what evangelicals meant by 'fellowship' and was designed to be a non-partisan, cross-party opportunity to meet for prayer and to hear talks on 'the Word of God'.[4] It reflected the evangelical caution about being involved in social rights issues. It also predated the advent of Christian lobby groups designed to intervene in the political process such as emerged in the 1990s with the formation of the Lyons Forum, the Australian Christian Lobby, and other conservative pressure groups with an apparent (and occasionally a real) affinity with the Religious Right in America.

The PCF reflected the then insecurity of most Australian evangelicals with political involvement. Brian Howe, Labor member for Batman in Victoria from 1977 and Deputy Prime Minister from 1991 to 1995, and who had been, like Duthie, a Methodist minister, found the PCF too pietistic. He

4 Harry Edwards, Liberal member for Berowra, cited by Marion Maddox, *For God and Country: Religious Dynamics in Australian Federal Politics* (Canberra: Dept. of the Parliamentary Library, 2001), 121,2.

would have preferred it to focus on social amelioration. He commented that it felt more like the EU at University rather than the SCM.[5] The PCF also felt culturally alien to the Catholics who were well represented in the Labor Party. So the three Australian Christian cultures – evangelical, Catholic and liberal – worked against ecumenical Christian activity. Only over time, as the three branches of Christianity became more familiar with each other's cultures, did the PCF provide a viable forum, laying a foundation for the later more interventionist approach of Christians. The increasingly post-sectarian character of Australian society made that possible, while Australia's increasingly secular character made it necessary. Parliamentarians became more relaxed about belonging to the PCF, and at times over a quarter of all federal politicians belonged.[6]

On Monday 9 May 1988 representative religious leaders offered prayers at the opening of the new Parliament House in Canberra. The brief service was an afterthought. The prior thought was to have no religious involvement. At the subsequent opening ceremony neither the Prime Minister nor the Supreme Governor on Earth of the Church of England had anything to say about God's role in that righteousness which exalteth a nation. Admittedly, Prime Minister Bob Hawke spoke of spirits and ghosts, but he was waxing sentimental rather than mystical. He is no high priest of the civil religion as is the American President who at every inaugural since Washington has led his people into a covenantal compact with the Deity.

Twenty thousand people came to Parliament House for the opening, far short of the projected one hundred thousand. The previous Saturday on the same spot 35,000 Christians gathered, far in excess of the numbers projected by the Prime Minister. He said that they would not muster enough to surround a football field, let alone the grounds of the largest building in the southern hemisphere. The event, which was organised by such Charismatic groups as the 'Intercessors', 'Ministries of 10,000 Men', 'YWAM', and 'Fusion' (a group which grew out of the Jesus Movement), testified to the growing impact of the Charismatic movement in Australia and its integration with the mainline churches. The crowd, which may have been one of the largest ever to assemble in the capital, participated in a service of reconciliation with Aboriginal people and, linking arms, surrounded, six deep, the new sacred site with prayer. Among those who led the vast throng in prayer was Freda Whitlam,[7]

5 Maddox, *For God and Country*, 123.

6 Maddox, *For God and Country*, 122.

7 Anne Nanscawen, *With one Accord: The Beginning of an Aussie Awakening* (Sydney: Anzea, 1989), 124f.

sister of the Prime Minister who had prophesied Christianity's demise by the year 2000. The media was not as impressed with all of this as the Christians thought they should have been. But it was a gathering which presaged the far more extensive involvement of evangelicals in politics in the ensuing decades.

Joh Bjelke-Petersen: 'The Lord's Premier'

Meanwhile in Queensland, the 1970s and 1980s were dominated by a political colossus of undoubted evangelical persuasion and a much-debated reputation. Johannes 'Joh' Bjelke-Petersen was a devout evangelical Christian who often made other evangelicals, especially those outside of Queensland, uncomfortable. It is difficult to assess such a figure who had so many friends and enemies.[8]

Bjelke-Petersen was born in 1911, the son of Danish parents who migrated to Australia by way of New Zealand. He was two years of age when his family moved to the Kingaroy region of rural Queensland. Carl Bjelke-Petersen, Johannes's father, was a Lutheran pastor. However, he was primarily a failed dairy farmer. The family was devout, and young Johannes grew up in a pious Christian household in which Bible reading and prayer were regular features of family life. His early schooling was brief and rudimentary and truncated by a year's absence fighting polio. Nevertheless, through hard work and bulldozer-like determination, he conquered poverty and physical limitations to become a successful farmer-businessman.

Charles Adermann, another successful peanut farmer in the area, became Bjelke-Petersen's close friend, mentor and role model.[9] Adermann, an active Churches of Christ layman, served the Kingaroy area in the federal Parliament for thirty years and guided Bjelke-Petersen into the fold of the Country Party[10] and encouraged him to seek elective office. Electoral success came quickly. In 1946, he was chosen as Country Party member for Nanango in the Queensland Legislative Assembly. In 1950, he became the member for Barambah, and retained that seat until 1987. He spent eleven years in opposition because the Australian Labor Party controlled the state legislature from

---

8 Rae Wear, *Johannes Bjelke-Petersen: The Lord's Premier* (St. Lucia: University of Queensland Press, 2002); Hugh Lunn, *Johannes Bjelke-Petersen: A Political Biography* (St. Lucia: University of Queensland Press, 1984); Evan Whitton, *The Hillbilly Dictator: Australia's Police State* (Sydney: ABC Books, 1989); Raymond Evans, *A History of Queensland* (Melbourne: CUP, 2007), 219–48; Johannes Bjelke-Petersen, *Don't You Worry About That!: The Joh Bjelke-Petersen Memoirs* (North Ryde: Angus & Robertson, 1990).

9 Johannes Bjelke-Petersen interviewed by Linder, 17 November 1987. Also see, Bjelke-Petersen, *Memoirs*, 45.

10 The Country Party, founded in 1920, became the National Party in 1982.

1932 until, following a split in the Labor Part in 1957, the Country Party came to power, with the Liberal Party as a junior coalition partner. It was also in 1957 that Bjelke-Petersen, then forty-six years of age, married Florence 'Flo' Gilmour. She later became a significant figure in her own right as a federal Senator for Queensland.

Bjelke-Petersen served in the cabinet of two Country Party premiers before being elected to that office himself on 8 August 1968 – a position that he held for more than nineteen years, until ousted by his own party (by then the National Party) in a November 1987 coup. It was a record run for any premier in Queensland history. Bjelke-Petersen presided over an unprecedented economic boom in Queensland's history. When he abolished death duties, it led to a steady flow of retirees moving from the southern states to Queensland, bringing their capital with them. The rapid rise in population in the Gold Coast, Brisbane and the Sunshine Coast, aided and abetted by Queensland's inviting warmer weather, stimulated a building boom that lasted for three decades. The state's infrastructure was transformed, with improved highways and new farm-to-market roads, the construction of a string of dams that improved the quality of life and provided vital water for the growing population, and an electrified rail network that helped modernise transportation in the state. The coal industry experienced notable growth by securing enormous overseas orders and the tourist industry greatly expanded. The man from Kingaroy also was a major factor in bringing the 1982 Commonwealth Games and the World Expo 88 to Brisbane.

The economic expansion, however, came at the expense of Aboriginal rights, which Bjelke-Petersen chronically denied, removing the non-compliant Uniting Church from its missions at Aurukun and Mornington, and opening Aboriginal lands to mining. Economic growth also came at the expense of trade union power, which he loathed. In 1984 the Electrical Trade Union tried to extract a contract for a thirty-five hour week from the South East Queensland Electricity Board. A strike in February of 1985 resulted in nearly a thousand linesmen being sacked and losing their superannuation. The government's tough stand against strikers, along with a further round of electoral gerrymandering, resulted in fifteen new seats for the National Party in the November 1986 election and marked Bjelke-Petersen's zenith as a political leader.[11] But there were also charges of favouritism for estate developers who happened to be friends of the premier and/or patrons of his party as well as rumours concerning bribes and payoffs by special interests.

11 Evans, *A History of Queensland*, 238–41.

Worse was seemingly intractable corruption in the Queensland Police Force. Max Hodges, the Queensland Police Minister, hired Ray Whitrod, regarded by many to be Australia's best-trained and most honest policeman and administrator, to reform the Queensland Police. However, the job proved to be more daunting than Whitrod imagined. A Baptist layman, Whitrod tried systematically to introduce reforms, but was frustrated on nearly every front. As he pressed the Police Union for change, he feared for his safety and took to locking his bedroom door at night and sleeping with a firearm close to hand.[12]

Whitrod had heard of the Christian testimony of Bjelke-Petersen before he moved to Queensland and knew that the premier still taught a Sunday School class in his Lutheran church in Kingaroy almost every weekend. He had expected to get along well with this most Christian of premiers. But they never did form a meaningful relationship. Whitrod found the premier 'to be a complex character'. Finally, after experiencing seven years of frustration and failure to reform the system, Whitrod resigned and left Queensland.[13] In his final assessment of Bjelke-Petersen in his memoirs, Whitrod confessed that he left with 'very mixed feelings' about the Queensland leader:

> I'm sure Joh takes his problems to the Lord in prayer, but I wonder if he waits for any answer. Or, if there is an answer, perhaps the reception is very bad … I didn't see much of Joh during my seven years and on the few occasions I did meet him, we had pleasant conversations. But, from a distance, it seems to me that he treated me rudely, arrogantly and ignorantly … Joh dismissed many of my suggestions out of hand. It was treatment I had never experienced before.[14]

The paradox remains of the Christian premier who appeared to allow wide-ranging corruption in his government and who also publicly declared his Christian commitment and values. A 1992 interview with Richard Horne, editor of *On Being*, an evangelical Christian magazine, yielded interesting insights into the thinking of the former Queensland premier. It was evident that Bjelke-Petersen had embraced Jesus Christ as his Saviour, and that he prayed and read his Bible with regularity. But it appeared that Bjelke-Petersen had an Old Testament understanding of Christianity – an eye for an eye and a tooth

12 Ray Whitrod, *Before I Sleep: Memoirs of a Modern Police Commissioner* (St. Lucia: University of Queensland Press, 2001), 138–91.

13 Whitrod, *Before I Sleep*, 189–90.

14 Whitrod, *Before I Sleep*, 185–6.

for a tooth approach, and 'he who is not for me is against me'. When Horne asked: 'So it's right to fight against injustices and things said wrongly about you?' Bjelke-Petersen replied: 'You've got to resist them, you've got to try and counter them. That's exactly what I did'. Horne persisted: 'But at the same time, you would go out of your way to forgive people who've offended you?' Bjelke-Petersen responded: 'I would not go out of my way to say, "Oh, they're great guys, they're good guys, they're kind guys and they're truthful guys." I'd go and say they are liars and scamps and the system stinks. Because I've got the responsibility to tell people that what these people do is not right and true.' There is no turning of the other cheek apparent in this response.

To Horne's question: 'In what ways do you think you've made mistakes as a man of God over the years?' Bjelke-Petersen answered: 'Well, the press [have] said, "name one thing that you've done wrong." I said, "I can't think of one – you tell me one." And never once would they ever think of anything'. Then Bjelke-Petersen observed: 'But, of course, in politics, if you can't look after yourself nobody else will. They'll tramp on top of you. Your own mates will do that, as they did to me ultimately'. Horne probed further: 'I suppose, as you look back, there are places where you'd say, "If I'd have been more faithful to God, if I could hear God more clearly, I may well have done things differently'. Bjelke-Petersen's response was: 'No, I wouldn't say that. I don't know any instance of where I would say that I would have done something differently'. Then at the very end, Bjelke-Petersen confessed: 'We know that we fail God in a thousand ways all the time, and yet He forgives us as we seek his forgiveness and mercy'.[15]

Which was the real Johannes Bjelke-Petersen? Bjelke-Petersen and Flo had four children. All continued in the Christian faith, and one daughter (Margaret) married a Lutheran minister. All of the children regarded the premier as a 'wonderful father' and a 'dedicated Christian'. Neither Flo nor the children considered Bjelke-Petersen to be a 'hypocrite'.[16] Federal Treasurer, Peter Costello, reputedly hailed him 'as the outstanding premier of the 20th century'.[17] How can historians evaluate Joh Bjelke-Petersen and his premiership to convey a fair portrait of a powerful, combative politician who also claimed to be a devout Christian? Biographer Rae Wear observes:

---

15 Richard Horne, 'God & Sir Joh: Faith, Forgiveness and the Final Judgment', *On Being*, February 1992, 16–19.

16 Johannes Bjelke-Petersen and Florence Bjelke-Petersen interviewed by Linder, 29 July 2003.

17 *The Australian*, 27 April 2005.

'Antipodean Lutheranism taught piety, the value of hard work and an individualistic, rather than a social, morality'.[18] This view of Bjelke-Petersen's religious milieu mostly rests on John M. Harrison's 1991 doctoral dissertation 'Faith in the Sunshine State: Joh Bjelke-Petersen and the Religious Culture of Queensland'.[19] Harrison notes that name-calling and rage do little to help explain Bjelke-Petersen and his era. Therefore, designations like journalist Hugh Lunn's 'Lethal Lutheran' and Gough Whitlam's 'Bible-bashing bastard' do not peel back the curtain on Bjelke-Petersen's faith or the motives that flowed from his religious outlook.[20] Harrison's attempt to get to the heart of the matter, though tantalising, ultimately feels inconclusive:

> Joh Bjelke-Petersen was neither a fundamentalist, nor an exponent of the classical Lutheran doctrine of the Two Kingdoms – the idea that the spiritual and secular realms were each independent of the other. His faith formation predated fundamentalism; he was an evangelical pietist of a kind much more akin to 18th century Moravians and Methodists than the confessionalism of Lutheranism, or the propositionalism of fundamentalism.
>
> In this, he was at one with the religious culture of Queensland, where the 19th century patterns of immigration and settlement – Protestant and Catholic alike – fostered pietism in religious practice, and congregationalism in polity. Such a polity denied any role to church councils beyond the local congregation. Bjelke-Petersen's legendary antipathy towards bishops sprang from this.[21]

Harrison's analysis helps explain why Bjelke-Petersen publicly defended the status quo in Queensland religion, morals and mores. It helps us to understand why many Christians, evangelical and otherwise, supported him. It also helps us to grasp why Charismatic and Pentecostal Christians flocked to his colours during the 1980s when they came to believe that the future spiritual health of Queensland was at stake and that it was important as Christians to begin to participate in the public square.[22]

18 Wear, *Johannes Bjelke-Petersen*, 42.

19 PhD Thesis, University of Queensland, 1991.

20 John M. Harrison interviewed by Linder, 30 May 1987.

21 John M. Harrison, 'Sir Joh Bjelke-Petersen: A Political and Religious Paradox', ABC Religion Report, http://www.abc.net.au/religion/stories/s1354728.htm accessed 25 February 2006.

22 'The Faith of Sir Joh', *Logos Journal*, June 1987, 12–15; and 'Sir Joh's Followers Defend the Faith', *SMH*, 1 December 1987, 2.

Vicious attacks followed Bjelke-Petersen's fall from power in 1987 and again when he died in 2005. There were some who tried to defend him, but they were few compared to the critics. Some of the harshest remarks were tirades against Bjelke-Petersen the Christian rather than Bjelke-Petersen the politician, but there were plenty of both. The stark contrast between the way the press handled Bjelke-Petersen's passing and the demise of billionaire Kerry Packer in the same year was more than interesting. Both were given state funerals. Though Packer's fame was not based on public service, but on years of self-service and profligacy, the contrast between the modest circumstances of Bjelke-Petersen's funeral in Kingaroy and of Packer's extravaganza in Sydney was hard to miss.[23]

Bjelke-Petersen remains a puzzle to many friends and foes alike. A political leader's contribution invariably involves balancing the achievements against the failures. When the political and the religious elements are as mixed as they were in Bjelke-Petersen's life, the process of sorting it out is exceedingly complicated. Perhaps fifty years' distance from the events will yield more balanced judgments. In the meantime, when Bjelke-Petersen was asked in one of his last interviews how he would like to be remembered, he responded: 'As a fine Christian politician who did my best for Queensland'.[24]

Lindy Chamberlain: Witch-hunting in the Secular Society

The most spectacular legal odyssey in Australian history, the Chamberlain case, preoccupied Australians for much of the decade. On Sunday 17 August 1980 just after 8 pm ten-weeks old Azaria Chamberlain disappeared from her parents' tent at a camping ground near Uluru (Ayers Rock). An inquest found on 20 February 1981 that Azaria had been taken by a dingo. But late in 1981 the Northern Territory Supreme Court quashed the findings of the inquest and ordered a coronial inquiry which, on 2 February 1982, committed the Chamberlains to trial. On 29 October 1982 Lindy, Azaria's mother, was found guilty of murder and imprisoned. The father, Michael, was convicted of being an accessory to the murder, but was not imprisoned. Lindy

23 'Mourners Farewell Sir Joh', *The Age*, 3 May 2005, http://www.theage.com.au/news/National/Mourners-gather-to-see-off-Joh/2005/05/03 accessed 25 February 2006; 'Kerry Francis Bullmore Packer 1937–2005: The Man and the Myth', *SMH*, 18–19 February 2006, 27–8 and 41; and Richard Walsh, 'Only a Meaner Nation could turn Kerry Packer into a Secular Saint', *SMH*, 24 February 2006, 11.

24 Johannes Bjelke-Petersen and Florence Bjelke-Petersen interviewed by Linder.

was released on 7 February 1986, following the accidental discovery of baby Azaria's matinee jacket with dingo teeth marks, and a Royal Commission found on 22 May 1987 that the convictions were unsafe.[25] Justice Trevor Morling, son of G.H. Morling, principal of the NSW Baptist College, found not one fact consistent with their guilt, while a host of indications supported the correctness of their story. They were the victims of an appalling miscarriage of justice which deprived Lindy of freedom for over three years and destroyed her marriage. Even so, the Chamberlains had to wait years more for compensation and that was hardly generous, and it was not until 12 June 2012 that a coronial inquiry finally declared that Azaria had been taken by 'a dingo or dingoes', and the coroner expressed her sorrow to the Chamberlains for the death of their infant.

As evangelicals struggled in the 1980s to understand what it meant to be Christian in secular Australia, the Chamberlain case serves as a stark backdrop to that struggle. What does it reveal of the dark side of the Australian character that someone like Lindy Chamberlain was hated with such intensity? What irrational fears possess average Australians that they should make someone like Lindy Chamberlain a scapegoat? It would appear from the treatment of the Chamberlains that secularism is no safeguard against prejudice and is no guarantee of rational and enlightened assessment of religious belief. In this case secular distaste for religious faith opened the door to primitive paranoia akin to the persecution of witches.[26]

Lindy and Michael were Seventh-day Adventists. Michael was an SDA pastor. Many of the unpleasant rumours about the Chamberlains arose from popular prejudice against this then largely unknown expression of the Christian faith.[27] Lindy realised all that, later writing succinctly about the problem:

> … we had to contend with prejudice against our religion, too. Anybody who knows anything about religion is aware that Seventh-day Adventism is very much in the mainstream of the Protestant faiths: we believe in the Trinity – one God: Father, Son and Holy Spirit. We take the Ten Commandments literally, which is why we have Saturday Sabbath instead of Sunday services. We believe the dead are asleep until Jesus

---

25 *Royal Commission of Inquiry into Chamberlain Convictions: Report of the Commissioner The Hon. Mr Justice Morling* (Canberra: Government Printer, 1987), 340–43.

26 For a fuller treatment of this argument, see Stuart Piggin, 'Witchhunting in the Secular Society: Christianity's Australian Future,' in B. Hocking (ed.), *Australia towards 2000* (London: Macmillan, London, 1990), 162–79.

27 Alana Valentine, *Dear Lindy: A Nation Responds to the Loss of Azariah* (Canberra: NLA, 2017), 34–37, 39, 44.

> returns again, at which time they are resurrected, as II Thessalonians 4:16,17 teaches. We hold communion, and baptise by immersion, as Jesus was baptised, but not until people are of an age when they can choose. We dedicate our babies so we may set a good example as parents and give them a Christian upbringing.
>
> Australia isn't what you'd call a deeply religious country on the whole, and these small deviations from the so-called 'norm' cause people to think we were weird. I don't believe in ramming my religion down another's throat … but I know that I wouldn't have survived without knowing that God was looking after me. His guidance was always made plain to me when I needed it most.[28]

Education is no safeguard against rumour and anti-religious prejudice: it was a medical doctor who treated Azaria shortly after her birth who told Inspector Gilroy, who was in charge of the investigation into Azaria's disappearance, that he had found the name Azaria in a dictionary of names and meanings and said that it meant 'Sacrifice in the wilderness'.[29] In fact it means 'the blessing or help of the Lord'. Lindy had a discussion about it with a camper just before Azaria's death: To Judy West she said, 'Bubby's name is Azaria. Azaria means Blessed of God, you know'. 'I didn't know that', Judy confessed. 'Don't worry, neither did my mother', Lindy said. 'When I told her, on the phone, you know, from the hospital, she thought it meant another boy.' 'Two boys already, so you'd prayed for a girl?' 'Certainly did. Boys are such little monkeys. Fancy three of them. And bubby is just the girl we wanted.'[30] Inspector Gilroy, who found the same book mentioned by the doctor in his local library, could not find any mention in the book of 'sacrifice in the wilderness'. That same doctor said that Lindy did not act like a normal mother and that the nursing sisters were amazed that she had brought in her baby for a check-up dressed in black.

Soon the prejudice was a raging inferno, and a lawyer likened the second Inquest to the Inquisition. The black dress, in which Lindy had clothed Azaria, became, in the popular imagination, a sacrificial garment. The small black coffin which Michael had used as a prop for his lectures or sermons to help people chuck the smoking habit became a white coffin and was transported to Azaria's bedroom. Lindy, it was said, has 'killer eyes', and Aidan, her son, was

28 Lindy Chamberlain, *Through My Eyes* (Melbourne: William Heinemann, 1990), 235f.

29 John Bryson, *Evil Angels* (Harmondsworth: Penguin Books, 1986), 98; Ken Crispin, *The Crown versus Chamberlain, 1980–1987* (Sutherland: Albatross Books, 1987), 63.

30 Bryson, *Evil Angels*, 23.

said to have 'really weird eyes'. The family Bible, it was claimed, had a passage (Judges 4.21) underlined in red which spoke of one Jael, wife of Heber, driving a tent peg through an enemy's head. The Chamberlains, it was said, were linked to the cult which had led to the Jonestown mass suicide in 1978. They had a history of child abuse. They belonged to a strange sect which believed in child sacrifice.[31] The child had been sacrificed to atone for the sins of the SDA Church and a memorial erected as part of a religious ceremony. Then it was rumoured that a four-year old child had disappeared mysteriously while in the care of Lindy's sister some years earlier. Hence, it was established that the Chamberlain's despicable behaviour and their callous and cunning pathological lying, originating in a fanatical religion, was reinforced by genetic insanity. A rumour, gaining something with each dinner table it passed over, was that Azaria was the product of a stealthy and adulterous relationship, and that the jealous Michael had therefore despatched her. Another rumour was that she had been irreparably brain damaged by a fall from a shopping trolley, and that the Chamberlains would not allow her to have the blood transfusion required by her condition. This shows a confusion of Adventism with the Jehovah's witnesses.[32] Yet another rumour, also completely untrue, was that Lindy had written a thesis on dingoes at college and that she therefore knew a lot more about them than she was letting on.

The tidal wave of rumour generated hate. At the first inquest, which began on 16 December 1980, someone from the public gallery called the court office on the phone and said, 'I am going to blow that bitch away'.[33] It became a commonplace to describe her as a bitch. 'The bitch should be burnt', said a taxi driver to a group of journalists. Then someone threatened to blow up the Chamberlains' motel, and they had to be moved to a secret place.

The press and electronic media spread the rumours nation-wide and beyond. As Dennis Barritt, the coroner at the first inquest, later said: 'At a certain point, you simply lose the capacity to deal with the volume of superstition.'[34] In an attempt to stem the tide of innuendo, gossip, and suspicion, Barritt took the unusual step of allowing his findings to be televised live. He completely exonerated the Chamberlains and castigated the conservation authorities for not warning people of the danger of dingoes, the forensic scientists for their lack of objectivity, and the police for suppressing the opinion of an expert witness who supported the dingo theory. The coroner thus unwittingly forged a new

---

31 Chamberlain, *Through My Eyes*, 542.
32 Chamberlain, *Through My Eyes*, 542.
33 Crispen, *Crown versus Chamberlain*, 74.
34 Bryson, *Evil Angels*, 235.

weapon to be used against the Chamberlains: the hurt pride of the Northern Territory authorities who became obsessed with their quest for revenge.

At the second inquest the crown presented a case, or rather hatched a plot, against the Chamberlains of which they were given no warning. An apparently impressive array of forensic experts claimed that Lindy had murdered her baby in the car by slitting its throat and then stuffed the body in the camera bag. They declared that they had found blood all over the car, under the dash, on a pair of scissors, and in the camera bag. The crown did not suggest a motive, but played on the prejudice against religious fanaticism by suggesting that the Chamberlains would not let anyone into their car on the night of the murder, making it 'a sort of shrine'.

An element in the anatomy of prejudice is the idolatry of science, the religion of secular society. When the 'expert witness' forensic scientist, Joy Kuhl, declared that she had found blood all over the interior of their car, a Torana, it was all over for the Chamberlains. Science can never be that wrong.[35] Not only are scientists never wrong, but they have all the answers. Kuhl demonstrated that a mixture of paint and bitumen was not only really blood, but foetal blood at that. Never had the alchemists achieved so much. The jury accepted all this as gospel.

The complicity of medical doctors and forensic scientists and attorneys-general in the persecution of the Chamberlains is a good illustration of the fact observed throughout history that persecution has often started from the top and not from popular prejudice. The fate of the Chamberlains suggests that secularisation is no guarantee of increased toleration; secularists can be persecutors. This would not be news to the SDA prophetess, Ellen White, who labelled her secular opponents 'evil angels', from which John Bryson took the title for his book on the Chamberlains. During the relentless inquisition by the prosecuting attorney in their trial, Lindy and Michael may have recalled her words: 'The evil one is the accuser of the brethren, and it is his spirit which inspires men to watch for the errors of the Lord's people, and hold them up to notice.'[36]

Eva Burrows: General of the Salvation Army

At the other end of the spectrum of possibilities for Australian Christian women in the 1980s was Eva Burrows. In 1934 when she was a young child, Salvation Army Commissioner William 'Fighting Mac' McKenzie of World

35 Lindy knew that many Australians would think that way. Lindy Chamberlain, *Through My Eyes*, 221, 756f.

36 Bryson, *Evil Angels*, 501.

War I fame visited the home of Captain Robert Burrows, and his wife, Captain Ella Watson Burrows, in Maryborough, Queensland, where they were stationed at the time. As Robert was introducing each member of the family to his legendary guest, he said, 'This is Eva'. McKenzie placed his hand on Eva's head and prophesied, 'Captain and Mrs. Burrows, one day we will have another "Evangeline" in this little girl. Another Eva'. He was referring to Evangeline Booth, daughter of Salvation Army founders, William and Catherine Booth, and who was at the time the Army's commanding General. That impromptu prophecy followed Burrows into the future and from that time on she would often hear herself referred to as 'another Eva'.[37]

Eva Burrows was born on 15 September 1929 in Tighes Hill, NSW, a small mining community near Newcastle. Both of her parents were dedicated Salvationists. Feeling called to the full-time ministry following their marriage, they attended the Army's training school in Sydney in 1921, after which they were commissioned as Salvation Army officers and ordained. The Salvos were one of the first evangelical denominations routinely to ordain women to the ministry because they were convinced that the Bible did not exclude females who believed that God had called them to preach.[38]

Following their commissioning in 1921, the Burrows embarked upon a nomadic life of hardship. They lived simply at the same level of those to whom they ministered and thought little of it. Eva Burrows, the eighth of nine children, arrived on the eve of the Great Depression. As she herself noted, she was 'a child of the Depression': 'I would say we shared the life of poverty of the people around us'.[39]

The Great Depression was followed by the coming of World War II in 1939, another event that greatly impacted the Burrows family. The elder Burrows became a padre in the Australian Army and all four Burrows boys marched off to war. The absence of the senior Burrows in the military and the instability of wartime gave teenage Eva an opportunity to rethink her Salvation Army connection and for a time to reject it. The Salvation Army did not allow its adherents to attend dances or movies, and this impeded Eva's

---

37 Henry Gariepy, *General of God's Army: The Authorized Biography of General Eva Burrows* (Wheaton: Victor Books, 1993), 27–8.

38 Catherine Booth, the spouse of General William Booth and co-founder of the Salvation Army, had written a pamphlet, 'Female Ministry', defending the practice of women's ordination on biblical grounds. Eva Burrows interviewed by Robin Hughes, Full Interview Transcript, the Australian Biography Project, ABC Radio, 26 November 1996, 2. www.australianbiography.gov.au/subjects/burrows/interview1.html, accessed 1 July 2011. Hereafter cited as Eva Burrows, Interview.

39 Eva Burrows, Interview, 2.

road to popularity.[40] From age thirteen to eighteen, she did not attend church. When asked years later about this stage in her life, Burrows responded that she had become popular at the élite Brisbane State High School and enjoyed it.

Burrows returned to her Salvation Army roots while a student at Queensland University. During her first year at the university, a young man invited her to attend the Christian Union (CU), and she there discovered a lively group of young people having fun and worshipping Jesus. At a Bible Camp during the 1947 school holidays, a young Anglican clergyman named Marcus Loane spoke on Paul's letter to the Romans for the week. Eva Burrows observed: 'In those few days in that week he [Loane] had a tremendous impact on my life so that I really wanted my life to follow the Christian life'. A short time later she began attending Salvation Army church meetings again where one day she went forward and prayed at the 'mercy seat',[41] and dedicated her life to Christ. From that time on her mind was fixed on serving Jesus, as she put it, 'within the orbit of the Salvation Army'.[42]

Graduation from the University of Queensland in 1950 was followed by Salvation Army officer training and ordination, and by service in the Fortitude Valley area of Brisbane. At the end of 1951 she headed for London and more training. She earned a postgraduate Certificate of Education at the University of London in 1952. During this period she decided that God wanted her to remain unmarried in order to devote her entire energies to service in the Army. She would be from that time on, in effect, married to the Salvation Army. She soon left for Africa where she became a missionary-educator of African children and young people.[43]

Burrows joined the staff of the Howard Institute in what was then Rhodesia (now Zimbabwe), where she served from 1952 to 1970, first as an elementary teacher, then as Head of Teacher Training, and then as Vice Principal. In 1967 she was appointed Principal of the Usher Institute near Bulawayo, where at last she could run her own program. It was her first opportunity for unchallenged leadership, and she loved it.

Burrows was then summoned to London to be Assistant Principal and then Principal of the Salvation Army's International College for Officers from 1970 to 1975 when she was appointed Leader of Women's Social Services for Great Britain. In 1977, she became the Territorial Commander of the Sri

40 Gariepy, *General of God's Army*, 33; and Burrows, Interview, 38.

41 In Salvation Army practice, the 'mercy seat' was a special place at the front of the church sanctuary where one could go to 'pray through' some problem or decision.

42 Burrows, Interview, 8.

43 Gariepy, *General of God's Army*, 44–53.

Lanka Territory, followed in 1979 by appointment as Territorial Commander of Scotland Territory, and in 1982 as Territorial Commander of Australian Southern Territory. Each of these assignments was as commander of a larger and more complex area. By the time of her appointment to the Australian post, the fifty-three-year-old Colonel Eva Burrows had served the Salvation Army at every level with distinction and efficiency.

Burrows was elected the thirteenth General of the Salvation Army on 2 May 1986 and served in that capacity until her retirement in 1993. Her election meant that she became the first Australian woman to lead a world-wide Christian community. Because she was an ordained female minister, Burrows's election brought to the fore the issue of the place of women in the evangelical churches, especially the debate over women's ordination in the Australian Anglican Church. The Army could not operate without adequate funding of its many social programs, and Burrows's feats as a fundraiser were legendary. 'I was never averse to asking for money', she noted, and added, 'I even had opportunity to ask Rupert Murdoch once to help us out'. She remarked: 'So I was always ready to capitalise on opportunities to get money. And, I may say, a woman often has a greater advantage than a man in doing this. We won't say how'. When accused of flirting with Murdoch to obtain the cash, a flustered Burrows denied this, and said:

> I don't use feminine wiles, but I think a woman can have a style in approaching people which is again less confrontationist, and perhaps more with a sympathetic, compassionate sort of style. Not as a trick, no, no, no. But I think naturally. Our founder's wife, Catherine Booth, always said that women are not in competition with men. Women and men complement each other because women have their gifts, their psyche, and if you use those gifts which you have to the glory of God, then God has a wonderful way of turning them to great value.[44]

Burrows was a fierce proponent of female ordination and of women's rights in general. Although she denied that she was a 'feminist', she sounded like one on occasion, and she spoke with approval of much that the modern feminist movement had accomplished. She gloried in the fact that, since the beginnings of the Salvation Army, women have been ordained and preached and held any position equal with men in the ministry and the leadership echelons. She was proud of the fact that her Salvationist mother was an officer and an ordained preacher. She pointed out that Jesus 'treated women as equal' with men and

---

44 Gariepy, *General of God's Army*, 60–1.

discussed some of his deepest thoughts with them. She was widely read in feminist theology and took its arguments seriously. She agreed that women's place in society in general and in the church in particular had improved in recent decades in part because of the feminist movement and that it was only a matter of time before all Protestant churches ordained female ministers. She observed: 'And I think the fact that women are now receiving a greater freedom than ever before, I think Jesus Christ would approve of that very much.'[45]

Toward the end of her term as general, Burrows suddenly was confronted by the opportunity to reintroduce the Salvation Army into former Communist countries following the collapse of Marxism in Eastern Europe. It was decided to assign the Salvation Army in a Western European country to look after the re-establishment of the Army in a respective Eastern European country, a clever strategy to accomplish its goal. Therefore, Switzerland looked after Hungary, the Netherlands looked after Czechoslovakia, Sweden looked after Latvia, Finland looked after Estonia, and West Germany looked after East Germany. Soon the Salvation Army was once again present in most of the Eastern European countries.

Russia, however, was a special case. The Army had been expelled by the new Bolshevik regime in 1923.[46] Burrows decided to go directly to the hierarchy of the Russian Orthodox Church to ask for its help. The Orthodox Church along with the Baptist and Pentecostal churches had suffered sporadic but severe persecution at the hands of the Soviet regime, and all religious-based charities had been eliminated. Burrows travelled to Moscow in May 1992 to ask the hierarchy of the Orthodox Church if it had any objections to the return of the Salvation Army. She knew that the blessing of the Orthodox Church would be crucial if the Salvation Army were to be permitted to return. She argued that the Salvation Army wanted to help in the re-establishment of a Christian presence in Russian society and to provide humanitarian services for the Russian people. The strategy worked, and the Salvation Army was allowed to re-enter Russia in 1992.

Noting that the Salvation Army had extensive work in South Korea, Burrows attended two different congresses in that nation during her tenure as general. The first occurred in April 1988 when she attended what was billed as a 'Sunday morning holiness meeting' which 4,000 people attended. Burrows visited South Korea a second time in February 1992 and addressed a gathering of 6,000 delegates at what was described as a 'Pentecostal experience'. All of

45 Burrows, Interview, 100–2; Gariepy, *General of God's Army*, 203–6.

46 The Salvation Army originally had been established in Russia in 1913.

these meetings with Methodists, Holiness denominations and Salvationists with Pentecostal leanings were natural connections with fellow Wesleyans who grew from the theological seed of John Wesley. Burrows was determined to keep those connections strong.

Burrows worked hard to make certain that the Salvation Army understood its mission in the modern world. She called it back to its evangelistic mission while maintaining its humanitarian outreach and social concerns. In summing up what she believed to be the greatest challenge of the Salvation Army in the future, Burrows declared:

> Our social and evangelistic work are inextricably bound together. It is our business to be among the deepest hurts of our world … Every land is my fatherland for all lands are my Father's lands … I would like to feel that The Salvation Army is known more as a church and not just a social service agency. I would not mind so much if I'm forgotten as long as the Army has grown.[47]

Although so much of the Methodist Church in Australia disappeared with the formation of the Uniting Church in 1977, its evangelical spirit of reaching out in Christ's name, ministering to the disadvantaged and engaging in welfare services, lives on in the Salvation Army, along with the pursuit of Scriptural holiness. The Salvation Army continues to be a vital member of the evangelical family in the world. Eva Burrows, a citizen of the world yet a quintessential Australian, helped make this a reality. And the prophecy of 'Fighting Mac' was fulfilled!

The Feminist Challenge and the Ordination of Women

Within the Anglican, Baptist and Presbyterian denominations, some evangelical women in the 1980s took the road less travelled: to ordination. It was a struggle between two styles of evangelicalism: the conservative and the progressive. This was a tension now beginning to be felt in other parts of the evangelical world. But, in Sydney, when the cold waters of conservative exclusive evangelicalism collided with the warm currents of inclusive evangelicalism, it developed into a cyclone, ripping up trust and sweeping away friendships. A connection between Lindy Chamberlain's treatment and that of supporters of women's ordination was not evident at the time,

47 Gariepy, *General of God's Army*, 343–6.

but in retrospect both were condemned hysterically, unreasonably and with allusions to witches.

In the Anglican Church the women's movement developed in the early 1980s a focus on a single issue – the ordination of women to the priesthood. The movement was led by Dr Patricia Brennan who in 1983 established the Movement for the Ordination of Women (MOW), modelled on the English group of the same name. Brennan had worked as a missionary doctor in Nigeria with a conservative evangelical missionary society, the Sudan Interior Mission. She served in mission hospitals and for a number of aid agencies, such as the Ethiopian Famine Relief Fund. She was national president of MOW from 1985 until 1989 and was a foundation member of the General Synod Women's Commission. She increased her profile as presenter of the ABC TV social issues programs, 'Brennan's Way' (1986) and 'Brennan' (1987). She was awarded the 1988 Bicentennial medal of Australia, and in 1993 appointed a Member in the Order of Australia (AM) for her 'distinctive and pioneering role in the struggle by women for equality within the Christian Churches in Australia and beyond'. In her capacity for the great-hearted service of Christ, she was typical of the most devout of Sydney Anglicans. But in her prophetic giftedness and her remarkably forensic debating skills and in her powers of articulation, she was quite exceptional, and very attractive to tertiary-educated and professional women from all denominations, including Catholics. Not all professional women agreed with her, of course. The conservatives enjoyed the support of many articulate, committed women who thought the most important matters to stress in the debate were obedience to the plain teaching of the Bible and the sedimentary importance for human happiness of the differences between male and female. One such was Patricia Judge, who formed 'Equal but Different' to counter MOW. She insisted that she, too, was a feminist and an activist, and she, too, was both awarded the Bicentennial Medal and appointed a Member in the Order of Australia (AM). This emotional debate was a great example of the passionate trial of all options and a clear demonstration that social developments were undermining the 'common sentiment' of the evangelical movement.

The professionalisation of women and their increasing role in the work force called for new theological thinking on the role of women in the church. Susanne Glover, the theological student who was to be recognised as MOW's theologian, seized the opportunity at the Sydney diocesan October Synod of 1983, the 500th anniversary of Luther's birth, to nail (or rather attach by removable glue!) her Twelve Theses to the door of St Andrew's Cathedral in Sydney. They challenged the doctrine of male headship on purely theological grounds: 'As long as the doctrine of headship is used to limit or deny women the exercising of their spiritual gifts and calling, a wrong is being done to the Gospel of Christ.' In insisting on the doctrine of headship, Glover reasoned, other more important doctrines were being denied: the doctrine that women as well as men were made in the image of God; the doctrine of the new creation in which spiritual distinctions between male and female were abolished; the doctrine of the Spirit's role in the life of the church; the doctrine that nothing but the Gospel was to be believed for salvation. But the doctrinal strength of Glover's theses was overlooked by her opponents who believed that they were confronting emotion not theology and by her friends whose advocacy of female ordination was more passionate than theologically precise.[48] The Press reported that the theses voiced the conviction that 'A great wrong is being done in the name of God'.[49] For Glover the wrong was theological; for many of her collaborators it was emotional. Monica Furlong, the English author, visited Australia for MOW in May 1984, and wrote 'it was the adamant, wounding kind of opposition within the Sydney diocese that had got MOW started there, mainly by women from Evangelical backgrounds'.[50]

The 'adamant, wounding kind of opposition' was a description of the way the evangelical founders of MOW felt about the response to their challenge to be taken seriously. In her Twelve Theses, Glover had used Luther's words to invite a response, namely that 'all who are unable to debate with them verbally will do so in writing'. The few debates which resulted often descended into lectures on 'propositional revelation' from MOW's opponents. More commonly, those opponents sought to starve the issue of oxygen. Indeed, that is what gave birth to MOW. In 1982–83, Peter Jensen, then a Moore College lecturer, served on the Sydney diocesan committee on the question of women's ordination, along with 11 others, including Patricia Brennan. She handed Jensen the testimony of 19 women whom she had interviewed on the issue in the expectation of discussing it with him. He returned all of it to her without comment. Unimpressed, Brennan contacted Colleen O'Reilly of Anglican Women Concerned, and they called together the 18 women who formed MOW in July 1983.[51]

---

48 Mavis Rose, *Freedom from Sanctified Sexism: Women Transforming the Church* (MacGregor: Allira, 1996), 174.

49 Religion Report, ABC Radio National, 7 January 2009.

50 'Furlong catalyst for MOW in Australia', *Balaam's Ass: Movement for the Ordination of Women Newsletter*, August 1984, 4.

51 Patricia Brennan, 'Editorial', *Balaam's Ass*, October 1992, 3; Stuart Piggin, *Spirit, Word and World: Evangelical Christianity in Australia* (Brunswick East: Acorn Press, 2012), 208f.

MOW founding member, Eileen Baldry (then Eileen Diesendorf and, at the time of writing, Professor of Criminology at the University of New South Wales) made a study of why women were leaving the church in the 1980s. She took as her sample seven very committed women who had left after an average of 20 years' involvement in churches in the Diocese of Sydney. Ironically, each woman had begun her journey out of the church through attempting to become more deeply involved. They left the institution of the church, not faith. Each still thought of herself as a 'spiritual person' and four still thought of themselves as Christians.[52] Baldry found that the strength and depth of commitment and involvement were akin to marriage for them, and breaking it was like divorce.[53]

Susanne Glover had plenty to be disenchanted about in her experience of Sydney Anglicanism. Her rector made it plain that she asked too many questions – and so he placed her under 'Calvinistic discipline' for three years from age 16. She was expected to be in church every Sunday and every youth meeting and had to have an explanation for any absence. She was expected to sit quietly and receive the Word. She was 'under discipline' by two successive rectors of that parish. They should not have been in control of young people, she now believes. They wreaked havoc with her. But, though she lost any hero worship she may have held for the clergy in Sydney, she just loved Moore College, where she was able to do to her heart's content what she had always wanted to do, study theology. She had free range of the library and no-one troubled her. She went on 'a self-education course'. She did her BD, for which she was awarded first class honours, and then went to Sydney University where she completed a Master's degree, then a PhD.

Glover's thinking was not fashioned by feminism, as her opponents too readily assumed, but by the Bible. Her hero was not Germaine Greer, but Jesus, and her guide, she believed, was the Holy Spirit. Indeed Glover complained that her opponents in the debate, which was reported at length in the *Australian Church Record*,[54] were so busy advising her not to allow any place for social mores in her exegesis that they failed to notice that her case was

52 Eileen Diesendorf [Baldry] 'Women Leaving the Church', Master of Welfare Policy, University of New South Wales, 1987, 33f.

53 Diesendorf, 'Women Leaving the Church', 41.

54 Susanne Glover, Charles Sherlock and Gordon Preece for the ordination of women debated John Woodhouse and Robert Forsyth who were against. 'The Pain of Second Class Citizenship: MOW debates women's ordination', *ACR*, 11 June 1984, 6–7; Part 2, 'Men and Women, identical in Responsibility?', *ACR*, 25 June 1984, 6–7; Part 3, 'God Revealed – in the Bible or behind the Bible?', *ACR*, 9 July 1984, 6–7; Part 4, 'Headship, culture and last words,' *ACR*, 23 July 1984, 6–7.

built rather 'on the person and work of Christ, giving Him an interpretative role in Scripture which they fail to do'.[55] They thought she was basing her argument on 'the Gospel plus human tradition', whereas they claimed their argument was based on 'the Gospel alone'.[56] They concluded: 'Any decision to ordain women which does not in an obvious way honour "the Gospel alone" approach must be firmly rejected as thoroughly out of keeping with the revealed mind of God'.[57] But for Glover, this was a slogan, not an argument. Her authority was Christ as the key to the Scriptures – theirs was propositional revelation. She saw that when the key doctrine is propositional revelation 'any other article of faith will be compromised if necessary in order to safeguard it'. Here is the reason, she believes, why the opposition in Sydney to the ordination of women has drifted towards heresy. Her opponents in the *ACR* were quite willing to posit a hierarchy within the Trinity to safeguard their interpretation of 1 Corinthians 11.[58] Amazingly, she could see this as early as 1984, two decades before the Archbishop of Perth levelled the charge of Arianism at the Sydney Doctrine Commission's findings on the Trinity. She also charged *ACR* with spiritualising doctrines to the point where they were meaningless, specifically the line that we are all equal in the sight of God and that when we get to heaven we will all stand shoulder to shoulder. But, she reasoned, if we can't stand shoulder to shoulder now it is meaningless. 'There is nothing more meaningless than the supposed equality of women that is evidenced nowhere in the Church.'[59] Glover wanted to see spiritual renewal in the church, and for her that meant moving human relationships away from issues of power and authority to mutual service.

Glover recalls that the leaders of MOW Sydney used to have monthly meetings with Archbishop Donald Robinson. They were trying to build a pastoral bridge – to get the hierarchy to take responsibility. Their Sydney opponents had alienated a lot of women, reasoned Glover, causing distress and confusion, and they had done nothing about it except harden their hearts and shut the gates. She asked the Archbishop personally to be their pastor, and he said that he could not do it. But, he said, 'we moved on the diaconate'. She replied, 'If we hadn't pushed you, you would never have moved'. On 12 February 1989 Robinson ordained 14 Sydney women as deacons. Among them was Jackie

55 'Strictly "on the record"', *MOW Newsletter*, August 1984, 10–11.

56 'Editorial', *ACR*, 23 July 1984.

57 'Editorial', *ACR*, 23 July 1984.

58 *ACR*, 11 June 1984, 8; 23 July 1984, 6, and 'Editorial', 8.

59 'Strictly "on the record"', *MOW Newsletter*, August 1984, 10–11, cf. her words in *ACR*, 11 June 1984, 6.

Stoneman. She had been reluctant to join MOW because of its reputed 'aggression'. She had already made the calculation that so many women had to make in the Diocese of Sydney, namely that ongoing employment in the diocese depended on moderation in pushing the female barrow. But Stoneman recalls that the Archbishop said to them on that occasion that their ordination was taking place only because of the radicalism of MOW, and that radicalism is required before any change will come about.[60] Also among those ordained on that occasion was Narelle Jarrett, by then principal of Deaconess House, who expressed the hope that this would smooth the way for the ordination of women to the priesthood.[61] But this would not be a hope that she would feel at liberty to express for too much longer.

The MOW blend – feminist, ecumenical and international – was far too rich for the conservative Sydney palate which preferred a diet of patriarchy, sectarianism and parochialism. In the perspective of history, this was an ironical outcome, as evangelicalism had done so much to promote feminist causes in the nineteenth century; it had started the ecumenical movement with the foundation of the Evangelical Alliance in 1848, and its missionary movement, traceable ultimately to the Great Commission, was one of the earliest feminist movements in world history. There is a biblical feminism, biblical ecumenism, and biblical internationalism. Conservative evangelicals were denying some of the most important achievements and potential of their movement.

In the 1980s the theological debate focussed on biblical authority and hermeneutics. It was championed in Sydney by John Woodhouse and Robert Doyle ably supported by Peter Jensen and David Peterson of Moore College.[62] Woodhouse addressed himself to answering the question, how can evangelicals who believe the Bible is the inspired Word of God come to different opinions about the ordination of women? Among evangelicals known to be in favour of the right of women to publicly teach men were Leon Morris, principal of Ridley College in Melbourne, Paul Jewett, Fuller Theological Seminary, California, F.F. Bruce, Manchester University, and David Scholer, Northern Baptist Theological Seminary. The Sydney evangelicals contended that women could not have this public role of authority over men because that conflicted with the created order of man and woman (Genesis 2 and 3). This order was established before the Fall and was therefore not the result of

60 Jackie Stoneman telephone conversation with Stuart Piggin, 19 December 2011.

61 *Australian*, 13 February 1989.

62 Barry G. Webb, *Personhood, Sexuality, and Christian Ministry* (Sydney: Lancer, 1987).

sin or of patriarchal oppression. The real sin committed (Genesis 3) was not pride or disobedience but the inversion of this God-given order of creation. The sin of woman has now been located 'in precisely that behaviour of modern women which is most threatening to the traditional authority of men over women – women's increasing autonomy. Thus "feminism" has become the original sin.'[63] For the Sydney theologians the ordination issue became the platform from which to defend a high view of biblical inspiration 'to withstand the evil days of apostasy ahead'.[64]

Immediately before the 1985 General Synod of the Anglican Church of Australia, the Appellate Tribunal, the court of appeal on matters of faith, ritual, ceremonial or discipline, advised that the church's constitution did not have to be changed to allow the ordination of women. This was a great threat to the conservatives who had looked to legal processes to obstruct the ordination of women. At the Synod Archbishops Penman of Melbourne and Carnley of Perth put forward an enabling bill to initiate the practice of ordaining women to the three-fold order. Passed in the Houses of Bishops and Laity, it was narrowly defeated in the House of Clergy. Sydney introduced a bill to ordain women to a permanent diaconate from which they would not be permitted to proceed to priesthood. This was defeated, and Melbourne and Perth succeeded with an alternative bill to allow for the ordination of women to the established 'apprenticeship' form of the diaconate. In February 1986 Penman ordained the first women to the diaconate, and then a second group in May of the same year including Barbara Darling, later a Bishop in Melbourne.

Although Sydney synod adopted the deaconing canon, Archbishop Robinson refused to give assent to the legislation, creating a first – the first time that a Bishop had used his power of veto over the expressed will of the clergy and laity in synod. In 1986, the Anglo-Catholic Bishop of London, Dr Graham Leonard, the main opponent in England of the ordination of women, organised the Association for the Apostolic Ministry (AAM). Archbishop Donald Robinson accepted his invitation to be co-chairman. The ordination question was beginning to cause the realignment of the old church parties as conservative evangelicals found common cause with conservative Anglo-Catholics. Robinson then revealed the plan Sydney would use to protect itself against the movement to ordain women. He argued that there would be no need for

63 Ruth I. Sturmey, 'Women and the Anglican Church in Australia: Theology and Social Change', PhD, University of Sydney, 1989, 265.

64 Sturmey, 'Women and the Anglican Church in Australia', 212.

schism in the Australian Church 'as long as it is possible for individual dioceses to retain what they consider to be the proper apostolic order'.[65]

At Meroo, west of Sydney, in March 1988 a special conference of the Evangelical Fellowship of the Anglican Communion (EFAC) allowed Sydney and Melbourne evangelicals to compare their positions. It was not a happy occasion. On the Melbourne side clergymen Kevin Giles, John Wilson and David Penman and layman Allen Kerr were angry with Sydney's behaviour at the General Synod and argued that tickets such as Sydney evangelicals used to defend their power were ungodly. Sydney's Bishop John Reid chaired the conference and had not yet revealed the depth of his opposition to the Sydney conservatives. David Claydon, another Sydney clergyman, was a keen promoter of EFAC in Sydney, but it never really caught on. The ecclesiastical politicians, including Bruce Ballantine-Jones, feared that EFAC wanted to line up as an alternative to the Anglican Church League. They warned the supporters of EFAC not to develop a ticket or they would take EFAC over and 'gut it'. So they killed it politically at birth.[66]

At the Lambeth Conference in 1988 Archbishop Robinson's motion to prevent the ordination of women to the episcopate was resoundingly defeated. The Bishops instead voted that the Anglican Communion would not be split by any diocese which ordained a woman to the episcopate. What Robinson lost on the international stage, he would work hard and successfully not to lose on the home front. In the next two decades, while most Australian Anglican dioceses would support the appointment of women, first to the priesthood and then to the episcopate, Sydney would continue to oppose it.[67]

* * *

By the end of the 1980s issues within the evangelical movement were less resolved than ever. Indeed, it was beginning to unravel, as those who professed to belong to it no longer affirmed attitudes traditionally considered

---

65 *SMH*, 22 August 1987, quoted in Sturmey, 'Women and the Anglican Church in Australia', 180.

66 Bruce Ballantine-Jones interviewed by Stuart Piggin, 11 July 2012. For an account of his role in the Diocese of Sydney, see Bruce Ballantine-Jones, *Inside Sydney: An Insider's view of the changes and politics in the Anglican Diocese of Sydney, 1966–2013* (Sydney: Bruce Ballantine-Jones, 2016).

67 Stuart Piggin, 'The Diocese of Sydney: "This Terrible Conflict",' in Elaine Lindsay and Janet Scarfe (eds.), *Preachers, Prophets and Heretics: Anglican Women's Ministry* (Sydney: UNSW Press, 2012), 178–204.

foundational to it. Fred Nile, Howard Carter and Joh Bjelke-Petersen were among evangelicals who did not resile from seeking and using political power as the more timid majority had become accustomed to doing. The separation of church and state continued to be thought desirable by the majority of evangelicals and non-evangelicals, but the involvement of religion with politics was no longer as tentative as it had been. Lindy Chamberlain, devout and well trained in Scripture, refused to submit herself to the governing authorities as Scripture enjoined if that meant being 'nice' to the police and prosecuting authorities for whom she had no respect. Donald Robinson no longer refused to co-operate with Anglo-Catholics since he needed their support to defeat the clamour for female ordination which, by his calculation, threatened the authority of Scripture more than the sacerdotalism, Mariolatry and priestcraft of Catholics. Patricia Brennan and Susanne Glover argued that the authority and example of Christ was greater than the shibboleth of 'the Gospel alone' which was used to deny the importance of the demand for female ordination. A rift was opening wide between the prophetic faith in Christ as liberator and the Reformed belief in the Bible as conservator. Evangelical identity was in crisis, involving a loss of momentum, a failure of traction. For such reasons, movements die, but the seeds of a more prophetic, less sectarian movement were taking root.

Chapter Fourteen

EVANGELICAL RESPONSES

Defence, Evangelism, Welfare, Spirituality, 1980–1989

'Love talked about is easily turned aside;
love demonstrated is irresistible.'
(Stan Mooneyham, World Vision)

To the increasingly virulent secular challenge to vital Christian orthodoxy, the evangelical response was not uniform. Traditional responses included defending the faith, evangelising with more intentionality, increasing commitment to welfare and social service, and deepening spiritual commitment. While most evangelicals owned the need for action on all four fronts, and the decade witnessed significant enterprise in all of them, not all evangelicals were equally enthusiastic about all four. In retrospect it was a period of too little innovation and too much preoccupation with internal concerns, although in the heat of struggle new instruments to grow the movement were forged.

Defending the Faith

Defensiveness was part of the evangelical identity and remained so. In the realm of theology, there were more subtle challenges to biblical orthodoxy than overt liberalism. Whenever the Gospel was conveyed in non-biblical language in the interests of communicating to a post-Christian community, conservative evangelicals became nervous that the Gospel was being betrayed. Among those perceived as traitors within the evangelical camp were those styled 'therapeutic evangelicals' who departed from traditional biblical formulations of sin and redemption and replaced them with Jesus the friend whose chief mission is to give health, happiness and self-fulfilment. American evangelical James Davison Hunter characterised the theology of therapeutic evangelicals as 'psychological Christocentrism',[1] that is, driven by the desire to move faith out of the head and into the heart, thus replacing the objective truth with subjectivity.

The ongoing debate on fundamentalism now came to focus on biblical inerrancy. Popular liberal authors had given conservative evangelicals ample cause for concern in the 1980s. In Britain, Don Cupitt, philosopher theologian, had popularised theological liberalism through his TV documentaries, including 'The Sea of Faith', dedicated to 'exploring and promoting religious faith as a human creation'. The appointment of David Jenkins as Bishop of Durham (1984–1994) caused widespread distress in the household of faith. He ridiculed the veracity of the resurrection stories in the Bible with insouciance. Evangelicals were adamant that he should never have been appointed and were half inclined to believe that a concurrent fire, severely damaging York Minister, was a display of divine displeasure.[2] From the evangelical heartland of Sydney, Barbara Thiering, lecturer in Semitic Studies in the University of Sydney, shocked the conservatives with her increasingly radical reading of the New Testament documents in the light of her interpretation of the Dead Sea Scrolls.[3] She left evangelicals in no doubt that feminism was the opposite side of the liberal coin.[4]

The very radicalism of the liberals' claims precipitated a corresponding rapid descent into fundamentalism from the conservatives. Dr Carl McIntyre, who formed the International Council of Christian Churches in Amsterdam in 1948 as a fundamentalist alternative to the World Council of Churches, in 1980 visited Melbourne to protest against the WCC Congress which he condemned as a citadel of Satan. In November 1980 a National Congress of Fundamentalists was held in Sydney at which the principal speaker was the Rev. Ian Paisley.

Mainstream evangelicals also felt the need to reveal their sympathies with the fundamentalists. In 1982, the year in which he became Archbishop of

1 James D. Hunter, *American Evangelicalism: Conservative Religion and the Quandary of Modernity* (New Brunswick: Rutgers University Press, 1984), 95.

2 Stephen Bates, *A Church at War: Anglicans and Homosexuality* (London: I. B. Tauris, 2004), 91, 92.

3 *Redating the Teacher of Righteousness* (Sydney: Theological Explorations, 1979); *The Gospels and Qumran* (Sydney: Theological Explorations, 1981); *The Qumran Origins of the Christian Church* (Sydney: Theological Explorations, 1983); *Jesus the Man* (Sydney and New York: Doubleday, 1992).

4 *Created Second? Aspects of Women's Liberation in Australia* (Sydney: Family Life Movement of Australia, 1973); *Deliver Us from Eve* (Sydney: Australian Council of Churches, 1977).

Sydney, Donald Robinson, in his Presidential Address to the AFES, admitted that he had thought of calling his address 'Confessions of a Fundamentalist'. He said, 'I must confess that I've always liked the term as referring to that which is fundamental or the fundamentals to which the term clearly points.' Invited in the previous year to become President, Robinson had been reminded by AFES Secretary, Tony McCarthy, that he had to subscribe to the doctrinal statement before he could be appointed. Careful about everything and meticulous about doctrine, he worked through the issue of biblical inspiration once again. He was aware that his old professor at Cambridge, C.F.D. Moule, who was much revered within the Evangelical party of the Church of England, denied the infallibility of the Scriptures. Robinson had to think twice before parting company with his guide and friend. He was also motivated to address this issue by the unsympathetic treatment it had received at the hands of James Barr.[5] First published in 1977 and reprinted in 1981, Barr's *Fundamentalism* insisted on calling evangelicals fundamentalists on the grounds that even if they disowned the term, they still exhibited the frame of mind commonly associated with fundamentalism.

It must be observed that there is little that is 'closed' in Robinson's frame of mind. He wanted people to be sufficiently open to allowing the Bible to speak to them; he did not defend factual, detailed inerrancy, nor did he argue that it was necessary to insist on the canonicity of every book in the New Testament. Inspiration and infallibility are to be understood less literally. Inspiration means that God is in control of the whole process of declaring what his saving message is and of delivering this message to humankind. Infallibility means that it cannot fail in its purpose. Robinson's nuanced understanding of fundamentalism, however, could not save the term for continued use by evangelicals. Fundamentalism was a lion which conservative evangelicals could not tame. It broke out of the safe cage of theological precision into the more rabid arenas of inerrancy, creationism, and political fundamentalism.

In Australia the Baptists were the denomination most troubled by debates over Biblical inerrancy. In the 1960s and 1970s a number of independent Baptist churches were established throughout Australia which were premillennialist, dispensationalist and fundamentalist. By the mid-1980s there were about 100 such churches with a combined membership of about 4,000.[6] The unofficial magazine of the independent Baptists, the *Biblical Fundamentalist*, was first published in Queensland in 1977. The Baptist Revival Fellowship campaigned

5 (London: SCM).

6 Ken R. Manley, *From Woolloomooloo to Eternity: A History of Australian Baptists*, 2 vols. (Milton Keynes: Paternoster, 2006), 653.

strongly for biblical inerrancy, fomenting a storm of debate within Baptist colleges and denominational magazines. The storm was not calmed when in 1979 the NSW Baptist Union's statement on the Bible declared it to be 'infallible' rather than 'inerrant'.

Particularly violent squalls in the storm were experienced by Baptists in WA and NSW. The trouble in WA blew up in 1985 when Brian Stone, Professor of Mechanical Engineering at the University of Western Australia, resigned from Como Baptist Church when he could not get his way on the question. He was a Creationist, a critic of the theory of evolution, and he wanted to change the constitution of the church to reflect inerrancy. He was opposed by another member of the church, Richard Moore, Head of the New Testament Department at the Baptist College where Vose was principal. The North Perth Association declared that Moore's position was consistent with that of the Baptist Union. The squall became most violent in 1987 when Stone opposed Moore's reappointment as theology lecturer, and Vose had to defend Moore and himself against the charge of endangering belief in the inspiration of Scripture.[7]

In NSW Baptists were sensitive to all hints that they were being corroded by liberalism. In 1985 the Rev James Hogg, pastor of Stanmore Baptist Church in Sydney, a Reformed stronghold, protested against the participation of the Baptist Theological College (now Morling College) in the Sydney College of Divinity (SCD). He questioned participation in a consortium which had Roman Catholics as the largest collaborators. The Baptist Union of NSW therefore asked both the Baptist College and Hogg to state their cases. The College and the Executive Council of the Baptist Union obliged with a pamphlet entitled *Co-operation without Compromise*. To this Hogg responded with *Ecumenism: A Serious Cause for Dissent*. At its meeting on 22 February 1986, the Union passed (343–329) the motion that they should stay in the SCD with certain safeguards (such as 'no exchange of lecturers'). The Reformed magazine *Banner of Truth* observed on this outcome:

> The controversy is clearly by no means over and while some deplore it, others remember the words of Spurgeon, 'A dead calm may be our enemy, a storm may prove our helper'.[8]

The pressure of the Reformed forces was too great, and in 1988 the Baptist College withdrew from the SCD and joined the Australian College of

7 Richard K. Moore (ed.), *Baptists of Western Australia: The First Ninety* Years (Perth: The Baptist Historical Society of Western Australia, 1991), 205 n60, 232 n40.

8 272, May 1986, 1.

Theology. The intensity of the controversy among NSW Baptists over biblical inerrancy and ecumenism drove a number of enterprising ministers to Victoria so that they could get on with the job of growing churches, the new word for evangelism.[9]

If among the Baptists, the fundamentalists became angry with the evangelical mainstream for being too liberal, in Anglican circles it was those on the progressive wing of the evangelical movement who railed against the fundamentalists. In October 1986, in the middle of the annual Sydney synod, Don Meadows, Anglican rector of the Parish of Newtown, addressed an invited group, exhorting them to establish what he called 'Open Synod'. He identified the sources of power in the diocese as Moore College and the Anglican Church League (ACL). The principal of Moore College chooses his staff, who are all, he declared, biblical fundamentalists who are not the same as evangelicals. Sydney diocese was moving away from true evangelicalism to fundamentalism. Similarly, the ACL, which traditionally supported mainstream evangelicalism, had vacated the middle ground. It, too, had been taken over by fundamentalists.

If fundamentalism was one reaction to liberalism, the opposite reaction was to embrace it. The evangelical Anglicans and Baptists gravitated to the former, the Uniting Church to the latter. Queensland premier Bjelke-Petersen accused the UCA of embracing left-wing causes favoured by Communists, atheists and humanists, and the *Bulletin* magazine identified the UCA as one of Australia's three new radical left power bases along with *Choice* magazine and the Australian Broadcasting Commission.[10] In 1987, on the tenth anniversary of the founding of the Uniting Church, the National Fellowship for Revival warned:

> ... many members of the Uniting Church are disillusioned by the apparent drift from the basis of Union into a religion based upon human ideas and experiences instead of upon what we receive as revealed by God in the Scriptures.[11]

Fundamentalism was no longer only a part of the inner history of the evangelical movement or of denominations. All over the world (in Ireland, Iran, Fiji, USA) it became political in the 1980s. It was a far cry from the introverted fundamentalism of the 1920s. The journal *Biblical Fundamentalist* was published

9 M. Himbury interviewed by Linder 25 August 1987.

10 Susan E. Emilsen and William W. Emilsen, *The Uniting Church in Australia: The First 25 Years* (Armadale: Circa, 2003), 2.

11 National Fellowship for Revival News, 5.20, 1 September 1987, 2.

in Brisbane and was circularised widely. The Logos Foundation, headquartered first in the NSW Blue Mountains, and then in Toowoomba, Queensland, campaigned politically on behalf of the Religious Right. Queensland was also the home of the Creation Science Foundation Ltd which by the late 1980s boasted a mailing list of 12,000.[12] In 1981 Professor Tyndale John Rendle-Short, Professor of Medicine in the University of Queensland, published the CSA's first book, *Man: Ape or Image – the Christian's Dilemma*.[13] In Queensland, Mr. Lin Powell, Minister for Education, expected creationism to be taught alongside evolution in state school science courses.

Another manifestation of political fundamentalism occurred on 7 October 1987 when Colonel Sitiveni Rabuka declared Fiji a republic, invoked God's blessing on his decree, asserted that Christianity was Fiji's official religion, and insisted on Sabbath observance, even outlawing jogging and all other sports and recreations on that day.[14] Among the Australian evangelicals who sympathised with this move were right-wing politicians especially Neil Pickard, Liberal Member for Hornsby in the NSW Legislative Assembly, and Jim Cameron, Speaker of the NSW Legislative Assembly from 1973 to 1976. In 1984, Cameron was elected to the Legislative Council representing the Call to Australia Party, which later became the Christian Democrats. In 2007 Rabuka flew to Australia for Pickard's funeral. Jim Cameron and Neil Pickard were supporters of the Washington Fellowship which promoted, through Cameron's sons, Jock and Ross, the National Prayer Breakfast and the National Youth Leadership Forum in the Federal Parliament. Jim Cameron was a fellow law student with John Howard and, with a reputation for political nous, had a powerful impact on him.[15] Howard never identified with the Religious Right, but in the 1990s and into the next century as Prime Minister, he found them useful allies in the conservative social policies integral to his government's longevity.

That in the theological struggles of the 1980s Sydney Anglicanism was not for turning was demonstrated by its ongoing support for the evangelical Church of England in South Africa (CESA). It was a longstanding rival of

---

12 *SMH*, 14 November 1987, 13.

13 His father, Arthur Rendle Short (unhyphenated), was Professor of Surgery at Bristol University. He was the founder of the IVF and author of many works on Christian apologetics. He was a member of the Plymouth Brethren.

14 Eddie Dean and Stan Ritova, *Rabuka: No other way* (Sydney: Doubleday, 1988).

15 Wayne Errington and Peter van Onselen, *John Winston Howard* (Carlton: MUP, 2007), 34.

the Church of the Province of South Africa (CPSA) and never accepted by the rest of the Anglican Communion. In 1984 Archbishop Donald Robinson consecrated Australian Dudley Foord as Bishop of the CESA. It was a sign of Sydney's determination to identify with those who stood for evangelical convictions against those of a different tradition. It was an anticipation of the action taken by evangelicals at the turn of the twenty-first century to establish separate churches in non-evangelical dioceses in Australia and to foster a pan-evangelical movement within the world-wide Anglican Communion which would be prepared to break with Canterbury and other Anglicans if necessary.

Archbishop Loane, who preached at Foord's consecration, expressed the hope that a 'healing finger' would be placed on the wounds of the church in South Africa, and that the two churches might move to repair the causes of division. At the consecration, goodwill was expressed by both the Archbishops of Canterbury and Cape Town, but it did not last. It was all very well for those in high places to express the warmest desire to settle the dispute. It was another thing for the CPSA bishops and the CESA to live with it. Any hopes that the two churches might be reconciled foundered on the rocks of mutual suspicion, and the CESA (from 2013 The Reformed Evangelical Anglican Church of South Africa) has since galvanised its position as an outpost of the Sydney strategy. Foord's predecessor as bishop, the Australian Stephen Bradley (who as a student at Moore College, Paul White could never beat in examinations), and Broughton Knox represented a harder school within Sydney Anglicanism. They were not surprised, or disappointed that the opportunity for co-operation with non-evangelicals had failed. They never believed that such either could or should work. Three decades earlier, Bradley, following his many battles with Anglo-Catholics, had written to T.C. Hammond, with reference to the acceptance of a new constitution for the Church of England in Australia:

> Personally I had looked forward to the day when the rest of the church would break away from Sydney and possibly Melbourne to form the Church of the Province of Australia which would then have given Sydney the opportunity to send out missionaries into the terribly needy country dioceses and to plant there … her churches.[16]

---

16 Bradley to Hammond, 7 November 1957, CESA archives, letter copied by Peter Spartalis, cited in Bill Lawton, 'Australian Anglican Theology' in Bruce Kaye (ed.), *Anglicanism in Australia: A History* (Carlton: MUP, 2002), 183.

Foord withdrew from the post in 1987 although Robinson pleaded with him to stay.[17] In 1988, out of a sense of 'pastoral helpfulness', Robinson invited Foord's successor, Joe Bell, to visit Sydney. CESA was quite happy to go its own way and consolidate its own ministries. Its supporters were now convinced that the future was on their side, and that they should train their own ministers for a church which was then about the fastest growing denomination in South Africa. The following year, Bell, on Foord's advice, invited Broughton Knox who had retired from Moore College, to establish in Cape Town a new theological seminary, George Whitefield College.[18] Knox was succeeded in 1993 by another Australian, David Seccombe, himself a Moore College graduate.

Ultimately Sydney's support for CESA laid the foundation for a growing evangelical predilection for planting 'Gospel' churches in parishes and dioceses where it is considered they do not already exist. It is a characteristic of the Sydney strategy that local defensiveness is turned into global offensiveness. Its architects have been quite prepared to incur the scandal of destroying 'true fellowship within the denomination', undoubtedly on the grounds that one cannot have true fellowship anyway with one who is not in their definition evangelical. Champions of the Sydney strategy, however, would prefer not to split the Church, but to achieve evangelical control of it.

Evangelism

Preaching the Gospel remained core to evangelical identity in the 1980s. Huge international conferences addressed the need for urgency in the task; local churches incorporated evangelistic training in their church growth plans; local churches experimented with 'seeker-sensitive' services; house churches sought to meet the more intimate spiritual needs of those who found even local churches too big and impersonal for comfort; new ethnic churches worked at redressing the dislocation of immigration; new student Christian groups multiplied on university campuses; and cross-cultural missions rebounded from their post-colonial demise.

In the decade of the 1980s evangelism was the focus of a plethora of conferences, both Australian and international. John Stott was the star attraction at most of them. He was himself moving away from an understanding of evangelism as seeking to win the lost through the proclamation of the Gospel alone to a more holistic view. At the second Australian National Evangelical

17 Peter James Spartalis, 'From Silvertrees to Lambeth: the Australian connection and the Church of England in South Africa, 1933–1948', MTh., ACT, 1990, x, 179.

18 *Church Scene*, 2 September 1988, 1f.

Congress (Melbourne, May 1981), Stott 'tried to bridge the gulf between the two stereotypes of those who entirely politicize and those who entirely spiritualize the gospel'.[19] But the trend was decidedly towards the former end of that spectrum. The Gospel alone fortress was besieged even in Sydney.[20] It fell elsewhere. Whereas the International Congress on World Evangelization, Lausanne, Switzerland, in July 1974 had mandated 'the evangelization of the whole world in our generation', Lausanne II (Manila, Philippines, July 1989) called 'the whole church to take the whole gospel to the whole world'. This was far too ecumenical a view of the church and far too broad an understanding of the Gospel for conservative evangelicals. Lausanne II was attended by 4,300 from 173 countries. The Soviet Union and Eastern Europe were well represented as were women, the young and lay persons. They listened to the voice of the Spirit and the cry of the World's poor. The Congress Manifesto declared that evangelism and social action were inseparable.

Among those who addressed Lausanne II were inclusive evangelicals from Australia. Eva Burrows of the Salvation Army was one who believed that in Christ there are no divisions of culture, gender or race, and who therefore thought the evangelical movement could not afford to limit the ministries of women nor the cross-cultural ministries of the church. Other Australian evangelicals who shared Burrows's commitments and who spoke at the conference were Robyn Claydon and David Penman, Archbishop of Melbourne. Burrows, Claydon and Penman were inclusive evangelicals, and they received plenty of encouragement to believe that the two evangelical giants of their day – Billy Graham and John Stott – were in agreement with their inclusiveness.

Robyn Claydon, who was to become vice chair of the Lausanne Committee for World Evangelization (2000–2011) and Lausanne senior associate for women (1991–2010), spoke on 'Cooperation in Evangelism':

> … it is becoming an increasingly obvious fact that the whole gospel will not be taken to the whole world unless it is taken by the whole church. No one of us can do it alone. No denomination can do it alone. No mission body can do it alone. No country can do it alone. No gender, age or race can do it alone. It can, however, be done, if we work in cooperation with God and with each other.[21]

---

19 Timothy Dudley-Smith, *John Stott: A Global Ministry* (Leicester: InterVarsity, 2001), 307.

20 See John Reid's 'Preface' to Ian Mears (ed.), *The Christian and Social Concern: A Set of Ten Studies on a Biblical Basis for Social Involvement* (Sydney: The Board of Education, Diocese of Sydney, 1981).

21 http://www.lausanne.org/docs/lau2docs/212.pdf accessed 5 May 2012.

David Penman gave the Bible Studies on Romans 9–15. They were among the last addresses he gave. The coronary heart disease which was shortly to take his life affected his voice and he struggled to articulate his words, but his studies were warmly received as a conference highlight.[22] He recounted a tragedy which he and his daughter, Christine, experienced in the 1985 Ethiopian famine. 'On the day we arrived, 146 people had died from hunger, cold and disease. It was a terrible experience which defies meaningful description … The Lord Jesus died not only for us, but also for such people in every corner of our world.' The Christian's responsibility to such people, he insisted, is not exclusively spiritual:

> The decade my family spent working among Muslim peoples in West Africa and the Middle East continues to affect and influence my ministry profoundly. The whole area touches my heart and brings tears to my eyes every day. Not just because of a spiritual lostness, real though it is, but because of their overwhelming social and emotional needs as well.[23]

If conservatives were suspicious of the inclusive evangelicals' heart-felt compassion for the poor and persecuted, what they did share in common was the conviction that the Gospel was for the whole world and that its propagation was urgent. Penman observed that Romans 13:12 ('The night is nearly over; the day is almost here') is to be taken literally and as an imperative to action.[24] The urgency to be about the evangelistic task was unabated.

The evangelistic imperative also ensured that evangelicals constantly experimented with effective methods. The 1980s was the decade when the churches awoke to the Church growth movement. It is not concerned primarily with the growth of denominations, but with the growth of individual church communities. Within the Churches of Christ, Barry McMurtrie in Wollongong NSW grew the largest church within that denomination. He wrote a good book which explained in advance how he was going to do it.[25] He augmented the three Churches of Christ theological training colleges with a fourth, the Institute for Contemporary Church Leadership. It offered training in entrepreneurial models of church leadership, fostering an aspiration for 'senior

22 Alan Nichols, *David Penman: Bridge-Builder, Peacemaker, Fighter for Social Justice* (Sutherland, N.S.W.: Albatross Books, 1991), 216.

23 http://www.lausanne.org/docs/lau2docs/255.pdf accessed 5 May 2012.

24 http://www.lausanne.org/docs/lau2docs/265.pdf accessed 5 May 2012.

25 *Time Out* (Box Hill: Vital, 1980).

minister' status within large congregations.[26] Gordon Moyes, who, in the same denomination, had grown a large church in the suburb of Cheltenham in Melbourne in the 1960s and 70s, was appointed superintendent of the Wesley Central Mission in 1977, and grew it into the largest church in Australia in the 1980s.[27] He also preceded his time at Wesley with the publication of a good book on church growth, *How to Grow an Australian Church: A Practical Guide to Church Growth*.[28] At the Wesley Mission, worship, evangelism, Christian education and social service all received specialised attention, while the whole work was saturated in prayer, the evangelical heritage preserved, and secularisation consciously resisted.[29] Peter Kaldor, starting with a welfare perspective within the Uniting Church's Board of Mission, began publishing his studies of the churchgoing habits of Australians which was to evolve into the National Church Life Survey, the most comprehensive statistical surveys of churchgoing anywhere in the world.[30] In the 1970s, as we saw in chapter 12, Dudley Foord and Harry Goodhew pioneered among Sydney Anglicans American Church growth methods and applied them in their own parishes which grew dramatically. Goodhew wrote a Master's thesis on the leadership factor in Church Growth.[31] The technology of growing churches had become a favourite object for study.

But, especially for the conservative evangelical, theology always trumps technology. Church growth theory was critiqued by Australian evangelicals, not only because it was pragmatic, and American in its pragmatism, but also on the grounds that it was deficient theologically. Sydney's Archbishop from 1982, Donald Robinson, could not embrace church growth theory with

---

26 Dennis Nutt, *A Crucible of Faith and Learning: A History of the Australian College of Ministries* (Rhodes: Acom Press, 2017), 162–6.

27 Gordon Moyes, *Leaving a Legacy: The Autobiography of Gordon Moyes* (North Sydney: Art House Press, 2005).

28 (Box Hill: Vital, 1975).

29 Don Wright, *Mantle of Christ: A History of the Sydney Central Methodist Mission* (St Lucia: UQP, 1983), 225–229.

30 Kaldor's books published in the 1980s include *A gulf too deep? the Protestant churches and the urban working class in Australia* (Chatswood: Board of Mission, the Uniting Church in NSW, c1983); *Green shoots in the concrete: towards a more sensitive Christian presence in our cities* (Surry Hill: Scaffolding, c1985); *Stepping out: churches living out the gospel in a changing world* (Chatswood: The Board, c1985); *Who goes where? Who doesn't care?* (Homebush West: Lancer, c1987); *Where the river flows: sharing the gospel in a changing Australia* (Sydney: Lancer Books, 1988).

31 Richard H. Goodhew, 'The Role of the Leader: An Examination of the Influence of Ministerial Leadership on the Growth of Six Australian Churches from 1798 to 1989', MA (Hons), University of Wollongong, 1990.

enthusiasm. He was not, however, disinterested in evangelism. He implemented two evangelistic programs to grow the church in Sydney: 'Vision for Growth' and 'Vision 2001'. The former ensured that new churches were built in the developing western parts of Sydney and the latter was prosecuted in the next decade by his successor, Harry Goodhew, who was far happier than Robinson with both American church growth theory and pragmatism.

Two corollaries of his position on the Church characterised Robinson's episcopate: the need to 'make Sunday work' and the insistence that the local church was at the centre of the Church's work. Ironically, the Knox-Robinson ecclesiology had reinforced the low church, evangelical impatience with diocesan bishops and other traditions which are not based obviously on Scripture. The subtleties of Robinson's ecclesiology were not easily grasped.[32] But Knox's anti-ecclesiasticism was, and Moore College produced rectors who preferred a polity of congregational independency, who had trouble with infant baptism, robes, liturgical services and prayer books. They suspected that such traditions were not only unbiblical, but actually impeded the church's outreach to the unchurched. Constant pressure was exerted for relief from these encumbrances. A fiercer pragmatism for the sake of evangelistic success had entered the courts of the Church thanks to the popularisation of the Church growth movement.

Rapid demographic change in Australia in this period made evangelism and church growth increasingly problematical. In spite of their long commitment to cross-cultural missions, most of the evangelical denominations had been largely monocultural and were therefore challenged by the new multiculturalism which framed Australia's immigration policy from the mid-1970s. A theologcal issue was even more difficult for the evangelicals than cultural differences. Multiculturalism meant multi-faith. How to relate to those of other faiths was problematical for evangelicals who believed the Jesus' own claim that no-one came to God, the Father, except through him (John 14:6). Missionary statesman, Max Warren, had seen the problem coming a generation earlier: the challenge of other world religions, he argued, would shake Christian confidence more severely than the confrontation between the Bible and evolution.[33]

32 For in-depth evaluations of this distinctive ecclesiology, see Trevor Edwards, 'Developments in the Evangelical Anglican Doctrine of the Church in the Diocese of Sydney, 1935–1985, with Special Reference to the Writing and Teaching of T.C. Hammond, D.W. Robinson and D.B. Knox', Master of Theology Long Essay, University of Sydney, 1996; Rory Shiner, 'Reading the New Testament in Australia: An Historical Account of the Origins, Development and Influence of D.W.B. Robinson's Biblical Scholarship', PhD, Macquarie University, 2017.

33 Geoff Huard, 'The Phoenix of Petersham', DMin, Northern Baptist Theological Seminary, 1990, 71.

Always alert to social change, the Uniting Church, from its birth released from conservative evangelical control, in 1985 proclaimed itself as 'a Multicultural Church' and was quick to establish 'ethnic' churches, with 65 of them in NSW alone by 1989. Ironically, these churches were to be among the more conservative of that denomination's churches, resisting its liberalising momentum and strongly resisting moves towards the acceptance of homosexual ministers.

The Chinese, who had been most discriminated against by the White Australia policy, now stood to gain most from its abolition. Chinese churches in the evangelical tradition grew rapidly in this period reflecting the growth in the Australian Chinese population and the ability of their leaders to create Christian communities where a wide range of spiritual and social needs were met. By 1986 1.1 per cent of the Australian population claimed to have Chinese ancestry (that is 172,000 out of 15.6 million). By 1993 over 30 Chinese congregations had sprung up in Sydney alone.

At the Chinese Presbyterian Church in Crown Street, Sydney, average attendance at worship increased from 408 in 1982 to 767 in 1992. Because of the increasingly varied background of those attending, the Church's leaders had to make radical adjustments. Bilingual services were proving tiresome to attendees, so the Church introduced monolingual ministries, services entirely in English, Cantonese, Mandarin or Swatow. Among those appointed to lead the English-speaking services were Morris Key, born in South Africa and trained at Moore College, and Choong Seong Tang, born in Malaysia and also trained at Moore. In keeping with its commitment to evangelism, it adopted the most aggressive of American evangelistic systems, Evangelism Explosion. CPC's range of activities was typical of most growing churches in the age of Church growth, namely ministries for all ages and of many types: not one, but half a dozen different choirs, language classes, and links with a host of parachurch ministries including the Chinese Restaurant Workers' Christian Fellowship.[34]

The most monocultural of the Protestant churches, the Anglicans, produced the most ardent advocate of multiculturalism: Archbishop David Penman.[35] He created in Melbourne the Department of Multicultural Ministries in 1984, the first of the Anglican dioceses to do so. As his Advisor on Multicultural Affairs, he appointed Jim Houston who, as we have seen, had coined the term 'multicultural' a decade earlier. Penman served as Chairman

34 Wendy Lu Mar, *So Great a Cloud of Witnesses: A History of the Chinese Presbyterian Church, Sydney, 1893–1993* (Surry Hills: Chinese Presbyterian Church, 1993).

35 Brian H. Fletcher, *An English Church in Australian Soil* (Canberra: Barton Books, 2015), 226.

of the Australian Institute of Multicultural Affairs in 1985, the peak advisory body closed by the Hawke Labor government in 1986. On multicultural policy Penman was well ahead of governments and other churches, setting a new standard for evangelicals in public life in marked contrast to conservative Sydney evangelicals. Penman's biographer wrote:

> as time went on, David Penman, as an evangelical leader, provided an alternative definition across the Australian church of what an evangelical was, compared with the Sydney model. Sometimes it seemed as though some evangelicals would rather that there was *not* an alternative evangelical model, but that Sydney provided the 'only true-blue' example of what a trustworthy evangelical believed and said. But at other times there was a natural feeling of belonging among people who have the same mission and are committed to the same appreciation of the implications of the gospel.[36]

The Diocese of Sydney, however, was not without a radical minority when it came to social issues. Among those who professed to be evangelicals was a determined team of social activists, radicalised by their experience of Sydney's poor, including John Reid, Bishop of South Sydney; Allan Whitham, General Secretary of HMS; and Bill Lawton, Moore College lecturer. Lawton, who was to leave Moore College in 1989 to become rector of St John's Darlinghurst in Sydney's red light district, avoided the middle class inclination to gloss over the church's failure to address the harsh reality compounded by poverty and demographic changes. His diagnosis:

> In the migrant-dominated Protestant ghettos of inner-western and southern suburbs of Sydney can be heard the accents of hostility. Here are people left behind after the communal upheavals of the fifties and sixties, confined by sentiment, poverty and loneliness, they watch their neighbours move to retirement villages while a Lebanese or Greek or Italian ocean of newcomers engulfs the street. Their antagonism to the migrant and their fear of alienation echoes through Australian history.[37]

Reid and Whitham, with Penman's encouragement, established in Sydney in 1987 the Department of Cross Cultural Ministries (DCCM) and appointed Mersina Tonys-Soulos as its co-ordinator. The DCCM was attached to the HMS rather than the Archbishop. In 1989 the Archdeacon of Sydney and

---

36 Nichols, *David Penman*, 164f.

37 William Lawton, *Being Christian, Being Australian* (Sydney: Lancer, 1988), 36.

Cumberland, Geoff Huard, who had been rector of South Sydney, presided over a DCCM project to address the plight of the parishes in the Area Deanery of Petersham and to develop ministries appropriate to its immigrant populations of non-English speaking background (NESB).[38] Tonys-Soulos conceived and trialled what she termed 'the Christian community development' approach, including ESL ministries and other evangelism/welfare ministries to those of NESB background. They were not ministries contingent solely on government grants because it was important to the 'radical evangelicals' who shared her vision not to be circumscribed by bureaucratic ideologies which did not originate in the Gospel. The number of successful NESB ministries multiplied and the Social Issues Committee of the Sydney diocese gave its support to the initiative, publishing in 1989 a study on the detrimental impact of racism within the church.[39] But by then a conservative reaction to multiculturalism had already developed in the wider community.[40] It was a struggle, and the DCCM was closed in 1997. There were not then enough 'radical evangelicals' to support the initiative, and there was chronic opposition to the co-ordinator's vision on the grounds that it was not focussed on evangelism, then generally understood as preaching the Gospel in English. Two decades later the Anglican church has awoken to the reality that ministries in languages other than English are essential to the evangelism of immigrants of NESB.[41] Support by the Uniting Church for multicultural churches on the basis of justice was now duplicated by the conservative evangelical churches in the interests of effective evangelism. The embrace of multiculturalism in Australian history has been hesitant, with evangelicals contributing to both the embrace and the hesitancy.[42]

The House Church Movement

While the multiplying manifestations of evangelical Christianity and a crisis of identity opened the door to more experimentation, it was still difficult to break out of denominational and clerical strait-jackets. Thinking of greater

38 Geoff Huard, 'The Phoenix of Petersham', DMin, Northern Baptist Theological Seminary, 1990.

39 *Racism: A Barrier to Mission?* (Sydney: AIO, 1989).

40 A major element in the reaction was confusion by many Australians on what the term entailed. Hugh Mackay, 'A National Identity? Wait and See', in J. Beaumont (ed.), *Where to Now? Australia's Identity in the Nineties* (Annandale: The Federation Press, 1993), 22–25.

41 Mersina Papantoniou, 'Multiculturalism's challenge to Sydney Anglican identity: A study of a minority radical tradition', PhD, Macquarie University, 2016, 136–144.

42 Deryck M. Schreuder and Stuart Ward, (eds), *Australia's Empire, Oxford History of the British Empire* (Oxford: OUP, 2008), 16.

power and radicalism was required for that. Robert Banks was such a thinker. He was converted at the Billy Graham Crusade in 1959 and entered Moore College to train for the ministry the following year, and was to become revered as one of its brightest students. Its principal, Broughton Knox, persuaded him to go to Cambridge to study, not systematic theology, but biblical studies, so as to avoid the trap into which too many theologians fall of developing an understanding of theology more dependent on reason than revelation.[43]

Banks was ordained into the Anglican ministry, but he soon repented of that action. The Church of England had too many unscriptural practices and its churches were too distant from the New Testament pattern of church life. The challenge was to form churches closer to that pattern. Doctoral study at Cambridge in the late 1960s was followed by a research fellowship in the History of Ideas unit at the Australian National University in Canberra. Here he associated with Geoffrey Moon in the house church movement, then (1969) in its infancy in Canberra.[44] House churches met in private homes rather than church buildings, not only because this is what the early Christians did, but because the maintenance of church buildings was a dead weight on the resources and time of Christians. Typically, families would meet on a Sunday for about three hours. They would sing hymns, have a children's talk half way through the singing, pray, and, over morning tea, share in Communion. Then the children would be taken on a pre-arranged activity, and those who remained would read the Bible and share their understanding, or attend to teaching by a member, or discuss a book.[45] When numbers grew to 25 they would divide and start a new group. Each group was autonomous and there was no hierarchical leadership, but giftedness in pastoral care was valued.

Banks became, especially in the 1980s, the leading Australian exponent and theologian of house churches.[46] In his doctoral studies at Cambridge and as a lecturer at Macquarie University (1974–1979), he had shared in the exciting task of identifying the radicalism of the Apostle Paul[47] and applying that to the

---

43 Marcia H. Cameron, *An Enigmatic Life: David Broughton Knox: Father of Contemporary Sydney Anglicanism* (Brunswick East, Vic.: Acorn Press Ltd, 2006), 197.

44 Geoffrey Moon, *Household Church Groups in Canberra 1968–1971* (Melbourne: Keswick Book Depot, 1972).

45 Robert Banks and Julia Banks, *The Home Church* (Sutherland: Albatross Books, 1986); revised edition 1989 published as *The Church Comes Home: A New Base for Community and Mission,* ch. 1.

46 Robert Banks, *Going to Church in the First Century* (Parramatta: Hexagon Press, 1980).

47 Robert Banks, *Jesus and the Law in the Synoptic Tradition* (Cambridge: CUP, 1975).

remodelling of church and community.[48] House churches, or 'home churches' as he then preferred to call them, had numerous advantages over traditional mainstream denominational churches. In their autonomy, they would better foster the liberty which the Apostle Paul esteemed as integral to the Christian life and as a mark of a mature Christian community, maintaining diversity within the unity of the Spirit.[49] Indeed, what he understood to be the 'crisis' in denominationalism, was its failure to understand and obey the Spirit.[50] Because house churches were by definition indigenous, they would cause less friction with the community culture. They would thus be more effective in local evangelism. Because they had no ordained ministers, they allowed for the exercising of the gifts of those who belonged, thus allowing for the implementation of the biblical doctrine of the priesthood of all believers. It was a doctrine which worked in practice: clergy were insiders, too committed to the maintenance of the denominational line; but transformation in Christian movements usually comes from the grass-roots, from the margins, from without.[51] House churches were designed to be an alternative to the local church, and not just a small group within it. They were not meant to be a means to the denominational church's ends; they were an end in themselves.

Stemming from the success of house churches in Sydney as well as Canberra, Banks in 1989 was appointed the first Homer L. Goddard Professor for the Ministry of the Laity at Fuller Seminary in Pasadena, USA. In Robert Banks, Australian evangelicalism gave to the international church a leading theologian of the concerns of the laity (work, time, leadership, story-telling) and of the spirituality of everyday life. In the house church movement, evangelical Christianity forged yet another practical evangelistic instrument: its purpose was mission as well as community. And it was a welcome option to those more introverted, gentle souls who have difficulty with the church growth mantra that 'big is beautiful'.

A conference in Adelaide in 1983 to discuss the movement was attended by 180, but ominously, one of the presenters on that occasion confessed that he was aware that the Sunday congregation within his own parish church was growing more rapidly than the house churches for which he had become

48 Robert Banks, *Paul's Idea of Community: The Early House Churches in Their Historical Setting* (Sydney: Anzea, 1979; Grand Rapids: Eerdmans, 1980).

49 Robert Banks, 'Denominational Structures: Their Legitimacy, Vocation and Capacity for Reform', in David Peterson and John W. Pryor (eds.), *In the Fullness of Time: Biblical Studies in Honour of Archbishop Donald Robinson* (Homebush West: Anzea Publishers, 1992), 280.

50 Banks, 'Denominational Structures', 298.

51 Banks, 'Denominational Structures', 292.

an advocate.[52] For all the power of Banks's theology and the prevailing post-modern antipathy for institutions which signalled that its time had come, the house church movement did not appear to have attracted wide support. Maybe there was too much demand on modern families to sustain the commitment required to keep such churches going. But its foundational ideas would not evaporate. In the 21st century its evangelistic focus is found in the 'Missional church movement' and its cultural sensitivity is reflected in the 'Emergent church movement'.

Student Ministry

There were dramatic changes in the evangelism and nurture of university students in the 1980s. In October 1977 Tony McCarthy had become General Secretary of the Australian Fellowship of Evangelical Students (AFES) as the IVF was known from 1973. McCarthy, who began his professional career as an English/History teacher, had already served the evangelical student movement for almost a decade as secretary of the ATCF and a staff worker with the AFES. He remained as Secretary until 1984, by which time he had introduced a generation of students to a new Bible Study procedure known as *Manuscript Discovery*. On some university campuses there were up to sixteen different student Christian groups apart from the AFES, and McCarthy found himself presiding over an increasingly fragile movement. His power to address the issues was diminished by the decentralisation of the AFES which strengthened the regions at the expense of the national office.

By the mid-1980s conservative evangelicals argued that the AFES was in crisis. Andrew Reid, General Secretary from 1984, called for a radical rethink of AFES policy. He argued that modern students could not avoid being influenced by the materialistic and apathetic society in which they live, and are therefore less mature, independent, capable and persevering than previous generations of students. Neither were they on average as intelligent as the previous generation of students as far more of them were now in universities thanks to their rapid expansion in the Whitlam years. Reid therefore proposed a reversion to a more directive stance from better-trained staff workers and academics in order to procure for modern students the nurture, leadership, and instruction which they could not supply for themselves. The task of the AFES was clearly identified as giving

52 Dean Brooks (ed.), *House Churches: A Discussion Booklet,* (The Uniting Church in Australia: SA Synod Evangelism Committee, 1983), 18, 19.

students systematic Bible exposition, as increasingly they were coming from churches where the Bible was not systematically taught and where many basic biblical truths were ignored. Its old guard reacted against this model, arguing that it stultified student initiative.

Meanwhile, a vigorous new player had entered the game. Phillip Jensen was appointed chaplain of the University of NSW in 1975 and rector of nearby St Matthias, Centennial Park in 1978. His chief appeal was to tertiary students and young city workers. It was estimated that 90 per cent of his congregation was aged between 18 and 30. Even within that age bracket, he practised deliberate 'market segmentation', dividing tertiary students from city workers. At the University of NSW, his Campus Bible Study (CBS) with 300 members eclipsed and replaced the Christian Union which collapsed. CBS had no student leaders as did the EU in the University of Sydney: it was entirely run by staff workers or trainees of Jensen's Ministry Training Strategy (MTS). The CBS dispensed with faculty leaders and a president, thus creating a very different culture from that which operated at Sydney University, a culture more amenable to control by the strategic leader.

Jensen was acclaimed for being 'very biblical' and 'very Australian'. The latter meant that he was a great debunker: he was forever 'knocking', especially 'the bishops'. Within a decade he had established a Greek Church, a Vietnamese Church, an Asian Church, a City Workers Church and an Undergraduate Church. The members of his congregations spoke more than forty languages: they did not appear to be daunted by the fact that he was 'very Australian'. He had 28 team members by 1987, but he was unquestionably 'the mouth'. By that time more than 70 members of his congregations had become missionaries. Small groups were essential to the expansion of his church. In spite of the protests, he disbanded these groups every year to throw off the accumulated social interaction which was a distraction from their main purpose. When the AFES workers on the UNSW campus did not welcome his overtures, he simply started his own meetings. Jensen combined great personal skills in evangelism and Bible teaching with a grasp of the strategic importance of programmatic training in evangelism, modelled on American precedents, but adapted for the Australian setting. Critics grumbled about the new movement's biblicism and even bibliolatry by which they meant fundamentalism. He refused to swallow the criticism that he was anti-Anglican. Discerning that the Anglican church gave him the broadest base on which to erect a viable ministry, he became more, not less, interested in making Anglicanism work, and in the early 1990s, for the first time he became involved in denominational politics in pursuit of his goals.

Cross-Cultural Missions

Foreign missions, instead of declining as anticipated in a post-colonial age, actually grew in the 1980s, striking testimony to the ability of the evangelical movement to adapt to challenges. The Australian Baptist Missionary Society was one evangelical society which adapted successfully to the new situation. In the period from 1958 to 1983, it was led by John David Williams (or JD as he was universally known). On his appointment he confessed to being ignorant of missionary theory, practice and history. But he was well-trained theologically and he knew how to find out what he did not know, reading widely and deeply in missionary theory. He was unmarried which gave him a certain freedom and he wept a lot in public which gave him a certain reputation. He relished the challenges of his day which he did not see as problems, but only as opportunities to do things differently. The task of cross-cultural mission he saw clearly was to strengthen the national leaders through friendship and to vacate the scene as soon as possible. He said, 'We should not ask "How long can we stay?", but "How soon can we leave?" No work should be undertaken which cannot be continued within the foreseeable future by the church itself.'[53] The firm policy of the ABMS was to two commitments: the first, to leave a field as soon as the work was done; second, to partner with the national church.[54] JD crowned his decades in the role with a celebration of the centenary of Australian Baptist missions. 'The climax of the year was the service in the Flinders Street Church Adelaide on 26 October 1982, 100 years to the day since Ellen Arnold and Marie Gilbert had been farewelled in a service in the same building.'[55]

The Australian CMS also refused to accept that the days of the Western missionary were numbered. CMS General Secretary, Jack Dain (1960–1965), a very competent administrator, had restructured the society's committees at both the federal and state levels which stood it in good stead for two decades. Subsequent General Secretaries included the historian Maurice Betteridge (1973–78) and the brilliant Bible scholar, Canon Alan Cole (1979–1987). They maintained the good name of CMS in the affections of its supporters partly because they did not innovate. In 1988 David Claydon was appointed to bring CMS 'up-to-date'. Claydon was not only an efficient manager. He was

---

53 John D. Williams, 'Twenty-five years in the Australian Baptist Missionary Society', *Our Yesterdays* 5 (1997), 30f.

54 Tony Cupit, Ros Gooden, Ken Manley (eds.), *From Five Barley Loaves: Australian Baptists in Global Mission 1864–2010* (Preston: Mosaic Press, 2013), 423–432.

55 *From Five Barley Loaves*, 438.

also a strategic leader.[56] In the next decade he devised a vision for a threefold program of the Australian CMS: to reach out to students, Muslims, and to cities. The recruitment of missionaries started to grow again aided by a reinvigorated spirituality in the youth conventions. CMS became exemplary for its care of its missionaries: every missionary was visited by the General Secretary every year; candidates were profiled psychologically before acceptance and were debriefed when returning to Australia either on furlough or permanently; training at St Andrew's Hall in Melbourne, next door to Ridley College, was streamlined. CMS Summer Schools continued to be a major source of spiritual nourishment for evangelical Anglicans.

Rather than being a vestige of past colonialism, evangelical foreign missions were agents of future globalisation. Australian missionaries were among those who contributed to the international scene. One such was David Cummings who in 1981 was appointed International president of Wycliffe Bible Translators and Chairman of its Board of Directors. He served the mission for over half a century. Another was Sydney Anglican layman, Michael Olson, international chairman from 1981 to 1988 of African Enterprise (AE). It was founded by Michael Cassidy in 1961 for the evangelisation of Africa and was to prove instrumental in the downfall of apartheid. Cassidy believed that the organisation 'came of age' under Olson.[57] Whilst maintaining a primary focus on evangelism, in the best conservative, evangelical tradition, it successfully adopted a more holistic approach, adding three other ministries: Aid and Development, Peacebuilding and Leadership Development.

Social Welfare

The holistic evangelism of AE reflected the growing concern among evangelicals to manifest the love of Christ in action as well as in word. Its capacity to generate 'dynamic altruism' increased as its international perspective took it beyond attending only to the Australian soul. It graduated beyond cherishing responsibilities to advocating rights.

Among the Baptists, it was a layman who did most to develop that denomination's significant social services arm. Lawyer and man of business, Fred Church (1919–1995), rose to become President-General of the Baptist Union of Australia. With a sharp mind and an indomitable will, he was the chief architect of Baptist Community Services in NSW. As a young man, during

56 Cecily Paterson, *Never Alone: The Remarkable Story of David and Robyn Claydon* (Adelaide: SPCK Australia, 2006).

57 *New Life*, 17 March 1988, 4.

the Depression he was struck by the misery of the unemployed. He saw then that Christianity had to come to the aid of the poor. 'Things spiritual must be expressed in ways material. What we do and how we live it out is the thing that matters.'[58] From 1937 a member of the Baptist College Council, his business and legal acumen proved invaluable and he became a powerful presence in the Baptist Union of Australia and in the ABMS. He had to overcome popular resistance to social welfare activities among Baptists: such activities were considered outside the remit of the 1919 Baptist Union Incorporation Act. During the Second World War he established the NSW Baptist Homes Trust, with the aim of establishing homes for the elderly. He has been acclaimed as 'without doubt the most outstanding Baptist layman in twentieth century Australia'.[59] Fred Church, OBE, was a powerful presence. Deacon of Epping Baptist Church from 1944 to 1983, he remained wedded to the British Baptist tradition and was not swayed, as were many of his fellow Baptists, by influences coming from America which were, perhaps, less sensitive to social need.

For all that, the significant engagement of Baptists in social welfare since the Second World War cannot be attributed solely to Fred Church. Towards the end of World War II Baptist housing trusts were established in most Australian states. A Tasmanian Baptist layman, Athol Townley, served as Minister for Social Services in the Menzies Liberal Government, and in 1954 presented the Aged Persons Homes Act to the Federal Parliament. Dr Minnie Varley, granddaughter of evangelist Henry Varley, at the Assembly of the Victorian Baptist Union in 1944, said that Baptists had a responsibility to set Christian standards 'in education, marriage, the care of children, the infirm and indigent'. She declared it a reproach that the elderly should become wards of the State. She was supported by an army of women who invaded the Assembly for the purpose and her motion was carried with 'acclamation'.[60]

The 1980s presented aid organisations with unprecedented challenges. Mass famine in Africa, especially Ethiopia, called for a much bigger response quantitatively than evangelicals had managed hitherto, and the advent of AIDS called for a less judgmental, more pastoral response. In 1971 Leon Morris at a meeting of the Australian Evangelical Alliance persuaded the Board to establish an emergency relief fund. It evolved into Tear Australia, and from 1979 until 2004, Tony McCarthy, who had been General Secretary

58 G.B. Ball and J.W. Mallice, *Striving for Excellence* (Epping: Baptist Community Services, 2004), 10.

59 Ball and Mallice, *Striving for Excellence*, 50.

60 Manley, *From Woolloomooloo to Eternity*, 2, 551.

of the AFES, was its chairman. McCarthy said that Tear was an 'inclusive organisation', made up of disciples 'passionate about … seeking to express God's love and concern for the poor' and 'rigorous in exploring the scripture to learn and to inform both belief and practice'.[61] Leaders of the evangelical movement in Australia were increasingly insisting on the holistic Gospel of love in practice as well as in word.

The theology of a holistic Gospel of biblical truth and social compassion was consciously developed within World Vision, the most successful of evangelical overseas aid organisations. An Australian, Graeme Irvine, led the way in that development. World Vision was founded in the USA in 1950 by Dr Bob Pierce, especially to help needy children in Korea and China. In 1953 it began its child sponsorship program for which it is renowned. In the 1960s it added disaster relief and rehabilitation to its core mission. But this was still treating symptoms rather than causes. In the 1970s it expanded its concerns to include community development, and in the 1980s, reflecting the increasing sophistication of evangelical social engagement, it fostered a more collaborative approach to aid and development, focussing on empowerment of the urban poor. By the end of the 1980s WV accepted that fighting for justice, even if that had political overtones, was required of an organisation committed first to 'follow our Lord and Saviour Jesus Christ'. By the end of the 1980s WV was committed to the 'ideal of mutual accountability, common stewardship of ministry and equal dignity of all before God'.[62] Irvine preferred to see this, not as a novel development, but as the 'traditional evangelical theology' with 'a new heartbeat', and it came from seeing the world of suffering with new eyes, 'some might say with the eyes of Jesus'.[63]

World Vision Australia was established in 1966, and in 1968 Graeme Irvine became Australian director. He took a leading role in the formation in 1976 of World Vision International, a partnership of donor countries (USA, Canada, Australia, New Zealand). Irvine became acting President of World Vision International in 1989 and President from 1990. Converted in 1947 through the ministry of Bill Clack, Secretary of MBI, and, after serving for a decade as secretary of the YMCA in Tasmania, Irvine had all his Christian life believed in the combination of evangelism and social action. As President he led the organisation in its clarification of its mission achieved

---

61 'About TEAR', TEAR Australian website http://www.tear.org.au/about, accessed 30 March 2013.

62 Graeme Irvine, *Best Things in the Worst Times: An Insider's View of World Vision* (Wilsonville: BookPartners, Inc., 1996), 84.

63 Irvine, *Best Things*, 17.

through 'holistic commitment' to six core ministries: transformational development; emergency relief; promotion of justice; strategic initiatives; public awareness; witness to Jesus Christ. The last was understood as 'foundational to our understanding of holistic ministry and is the integrating principle for all aspects of our mission'.[64] So the evangelistic imperative was maintained within a holistic context.

WV's foundation commitment to caring for children and emergency relief was also maintained, but there was a shift from focussing on human need to adding a concern for human rights. Slowly, through experience and deeper study of the Scriptures, WV's partners came to the realisation that people needed more than food, shelter and clothing: they also needed, in the words of Irvine's daughter, Ros, 'freedom, safety, dignity, a future'.[65] This realisation grew out of a 1978 policy decision, suggested by Australian WV Board member, John Denton, that recipients as well as donors were partners in the work of WV. Hence, Irvine was able to insist that the organisation was 'accountable to the poor as well as to donors', and that staff had to 'think twice and spend once'.[66] Of necessity, WV had to learn how to work alongside governmental and other relief agencies and the increasing inclusivity troubled some of its supporters. 'Are we evangelical or ecumenical?' one Board member asked. 'It is my belief that we must be both,' responded Irvine, 'and it saddens me that the two are so often stated as if they are contrary positions.'[67] Similarly there were those in the organisation who were adamant that WV did not have a political agenda. Irvine agreed with them, but equally he insisted that WV's Christian and humanitarian agenda could have political consequences and that these must be faced.[68]

For 27 years Irvine walked among the victims of wars where most of the casualties are civilians and most of them are children. He and his mission cared most about the most vulnerable: children under five – their dire need was 'the very soul of World Vision'.[69] It was a need at three levels: first the need for survival (food and shelter, medical care and protection); second the need to be returned to family and community; third the need for specialised counselling to help them through the trauma. In the 1980s WV's capacity for overseas aid practically quadrupled: in 1979 the number of children sponsored

64 Irvine, *Best Things*, 202.
65 Irvine, *Best Things*, 234.
66 Irvine, *Best Things*, 216f.
67 Irvine, *Best Things*, 187, 203.
68 Irvine, *Best Things*, 147.
69 Irvine, *Best Things*, 170.

was 214,525 and its budget was US$38.1m; in 1989 the number of children sponsored was 833,583 and the budget was US$153.6m.[70]

Another evangelical overseas aid organisation which grew exponentially in the 1980s was Opportunity International, launched in 1979 by Australian David Bussau and an American Al Whittaker. Bussau had been raised in two Anglican orphanages in New Zealand, one of which (Sedgley) has since been identified as a site of child abuse. But, when asked, Bussau commented only on the abuse from bullying boys. He attended Sunday School and always believed that God was a father who loved him. At age 15, he rented a hot-dog stand, then rented hot-dog stands out to others. He always found it easy to make money and to organise others to work for him. He concluded that God had created him to be an entrepreneur. By the age of 35, now married and living in Australia, he was the millionaire owner of five businesses in the construction trade. When news reached him of the destruction of Darwin on Christmas Day 1974 by cyclone Tracy, he took a team of skilled workers to aid the reconstruction and settled in Darwin. Then he moved to Bali to aid with village reconstruction following an earthquake.

By then Bussau had made two discoveries and was about to discover a third. The first discovery was that, since God had created him an entrepreneur, he should use that gift to serve God and the needy. The second was what he called 'the economics of enough': he did not need all the money he was so good at making. The third discovery arose from his experience of the poverty of Indonesian villagers. He realised that for most, poverty was a matter of debt. The poor even mortgaged their own children to money lenders as collateral and then worked to pay off the mortgage. Bussau could see that giving the poor small loans at reasonable interest would allow them to work for themselves in modest enterprises instead of remaining in financial bondage to the money lender. He thus adopted a novel approach to third world poverty and set about persuading churches to accept the enterprise solution to poverty. Opportunity International became a highly successful microfinancing charity which by the year 2000 had raised five million people out of poverty. Microfinancing as Christian mission was developed on an extensive scale, and other evangelical entrepreneurs, such as Geoff Kells, Adrian McCombe, and Athol Murray, and politicians such as Harry Edwards (Liberal), became committed to it as a method of economic development.

Quietly spoken and practical, rather than talking a lot and theorising, Bussau nevertheless valued those who did theorise, and he sponsored the

---

70 Irvine, *Best Things*, 266, 268.

formation of the Oxford Centre for Mission Studies. He took a great interest in the conferences organised by the World Evangelical Alliance to promote an agreed approach of evangelicals to economic and political challenges. He later confessed that he was reluctant to dream because he came to believe that everything that could be dreamed was accomplishable. In 2003–04, with that strong, gentle confidence for which he is famous, he even spent time with North Korean officials about bringing prosperity to that impoverished nation through micro-economic reforms. In 2008 Bussau was made Senior Australian of the Year, having previously been awarded the title of Australian Entrepreneur of the Year and International Social Entrepreneur of the Year.[71]

Deepening Spiritual Experience

By the 1980s traditional evangelical disciplines associated with the pursuit of holiness felt tired and anaemic, while the spirituality of other movements tantalised. The New Age Movement sprouted in the 1970s and flowered in the 1980s promising spiritual experience unmediated by doctrine or discipline.[72] The instinctive evangelical response was to condemn it. John Heinenger, national director of the Australian Evangelical Apologetics Society, argued that 'People need to understand that the New Age Movement is nothing more than the "old occult" dressed up in a pin stripe suit … It represents a form of cosmic humanism that seeks to draw not only on human strength alone, but also on the "energies" of the cosmos.'[73]

Others recognised, however, that the New Age sought to meet genuine needs which the churches were then failing to do, and that evangelicalism could do better in that domain by plumbing the depths of Christianity's own rich spiritual traditions. 'Eremos' was founded in 1982 to do just that. Its twin aims were to deepen the spiritual experience of those who were left unsatisfied by the spirituality prevailing in mainstream evangelicalism and to give its members a deeper understanding of the nature of Australian culture and society. Eremos claimed to be both evangelical and Australian and a channel for Catholic and Orthodox models and practices of spirituality.

---

71 On David Bussau and Opportunity International, see Philippa Tyndale, *Don't Look Back: The David Bussau Story* (Crows Nest: Allen & Unwin, 2004) and related websites.

72 Hilary M. Carey, *Believing in Australia: a cultural history of religions* (Sydney: Allen & Unwin, 1996), 177–186.

73 *New Life*, 1 February 1990, 6.

Conservative evangelicals sought to address the spirituality deficit in their own way. In Australia the Katoomba Easter convention was turned into something of a Moore College convention. But it worked, both numerically and spiritually. Numbers in attendance rocketed. The first KYC in 1974 had attracted 600. By 1980 this had increased to 1,000; in 1982, 1,500; and in 1983, the year Phillip Jensen became Katoomba Convention chairman, they exploded to 2,400. In 1987 6,000 attended the weekend meetings. CMS and the SMBC, now experiencing an unexpected surge in applicants, reported that many of them attributed their missionary calling to the influence of KYC and specifically the ministry of Helen Roseveare, missionary survivor of much brutality in the Congo, who addressed the KYC in 1980, 1985 and 1988.[74] Following her first address, about 600 declared their desire to serve Christ wherever he called them.[75]

The great emphasis at the conventions became the careful handling of God's word. The goal was to teach the Scriptures accurately and carefully. Broughton Knox had complained at earlier conventions that the Bible was not being sufficiently carefully handled. But with such speakers as John Chapman and John Woodhouse there were no such doubts and Anglicans flocked to the convention. John Dykes, secretary of the convention, reports of the convention in the 1980s:

> The popular conception … of young people is that … they don't want to think seriously and they are not interested in the serious aspects of Christianity. That's not what we are experiencing. It's very heartening to sit there and see 5,000 kids who will sit for nine messages over a weekend and hear a pin drop! It does your heart good.[76]

Revival and Indigenous Liberation

One of the most vital of spiritual movements in Australia in the early 80s was the Aboriginal revival. It began in Elcho Island in March 1979 (see chapter 12) and it spread like wildfire among the communities of the more remote parts of Australia. At the Anglican Roper River Mission (Ngukurr) in eastern Arnhem Land, which had been reduced to a social disaster area by

74 John Dykes interviewed by Margaret Lamb, 13 November 1986.

75 Stuart Braga, *A Century Preaching Christ: Katoomba Christian Convention, 1903–2003* (Sydney: Katoomba Christian Convention, 2003), 136.

76 Dykes interviewed by Lamb, 13 November 1986.

the granting of a liquor licence, the revival came as a form of social salvation. Sister Edna Brooker exclaimed:

> New life has come to Ngukurr … half the population say they have turned to Christ and the transformation from alcohol, petrol sniffing and immorality is very wonderful.[77]

At Wiluna in WA crime dropped to zero, and the local publican had to put on free beer in an attempt to entice people back into his pub. In August 1981 revival came to Warburton in WA, and some white missionaries sought ministry from Aboriginal Christians and were greatly blessed. Arthur Malcolm, a Church Army evangelist and, from 1985, first Anglican Aboriginal Bishop, described the coming of revival to Warburton and Meekatharra, thus:

> God called all the Christians, and so-called Christians, together in a place called Cement Creek. There God called them to true repentance in heart and soul. The number of people there was 120. It's funny that that was the same number as in the Book of Acts. We wonder was God saying something with a sense of humour; anyway God began to work … doing wonders and miracles, and then the rain poured down to fill Cement Creek with water and the whole 120 were baptised. It didn't rain anywhere else – just where God began this work among the people … An arrow in the sky told them to go and preach in the town of Warburton. 3,000 people came to the Lord and then 5,000 as they went on towards Meekatharra. So this is a repeat of what happened in the Book of Acts. This is the work of the [underprivileged and powerless] people and the Holy Spirit. It was not a Convention or the Missionary way with people being ordered from here to there. You see, God used people with an open heart, people who were broken down but open to God, not people who were conformed to some other ways. This is a true story. AMEN.[78]

The Aboriginal revival offered a spiritual solution to a desperate cultural and social crisis. Indigenous Australians were suffering from what anthropologists call 'demoralisation': a disintegrating culture, accompanied by alcohol abuse, petrol sniffing, suicide, and violence. Factors in the revival bear on issues critical

---

77 Quoted in Jeanette Boyd, 'The Arnhem Land Revival of 1979: An Australian Aboriginal Religious Movement', unpublished paper, October 1986.

78 Harry Walker et. al., 'Minjung in Australia', *South Pacific Journal of Mission Studies*, 1.1, 1989, 8f.

to the dignity and liberation of Aboriginal people: the assumption of control of churches by native pastors; the use of the vernacular in worship and other expressions of indigenisation such as the composition of their own songs; the charismatic element expressed in healings, exorcism, tongues, and visions; the creation of fellowship groups for ministry to one another; the missionary enthusiasm to share the experience of liberation with others of their race; and the institutionalisation of the revival in such ceremonies as the Thanksgiving Weekend around 14 March when the revival began.

It is unlikely that the Aboriginal revival would have been as significant had not the Charismatic movement matured to the point that it was able to offer the Aboriginal people a range of ways of expressing their new-found faith consistent with their culture. John Blacket[79] reports miracles, sightings of angels, numerous visions of fire coming down from heaven igniting spot fires all over the continent, of a great river flowing from Elcho Island to towns in southern WA, of signs in the sky telling the Aboriginal evangelists and their teams where to go next, many dreams, visions, deliverances, even a resurrection or two! These 'Charismatic' features of this revival, which made many whites cautious at first, came to be seen as themselves time-honoured features of Aboriginal culture.

This was especially true of the visions which preceded the revival and which continued to feature as the years passed. In 1983 a small Aboriginal boy in kindergarten at Yarrabah, south of Cairns in Queensland, did a butterfly painting, putting paint on a piece of paper and folding it in half. When he opened it he gazed on a remarkable likeness of Christ with crown of thorns.[80] Djiniyini Gondarra, the Uniting Church pastor at Galiwin'ku on Elcho Island where the revival had begun in 1979, had a vision of crows and flying foxes (which are totems of himself and his wife, Gelung) and of a beautiful girl wearing lots of bangles, namely Queen Jezebel. Gondarra called out to his wife, 'Go to Jerusalem, get the blood and wash the cross'. She did so and, when she washed the cross with the blood, it turned into a flaming two-edged sword, and she thrust it through Jezebel who turned back into a flying fox and exploded. Then God said to Gondarra:

> You lay down every totem and ceremony. In each of them there is good and bad. All of them must come under my Lordship, be washed by the

79 John Blacket, 'I Will Renew the Land': Island on Fire, unpublished MS of history of the Aboriginal Revival, dated 18 May 1993; see also his '"Rainbow or the Serpent?" Observing the Arnhem Land Aboriginal Revival, 1979 and Now', in Mark Hutchinson and Stuart Piggin (eds.), *Reviving Australia* (Sydney: CSAC, 1994), 291–301.

80 John Harris, *One Blood* (Sydney: Albatross, 1990), facing page 783, cf. 850.

> blood of Jesus Christ, and then you will see a new Aboriginal culture. I don't want to destroy and leave you empty. I will restore and renew what is good.[81]

Djiniyini's vision gave him the clear cultural message that Christianity comes not to destroy but to fulfil the aspirations of traditional law. The revival is thus a dramatic step by the Aboriginal people towards self-identity. Once – during the two centuries of subjugation – they were no people; now they are a people, God's people. The revival is the power by which the Aboriginal people are moving away from subjugation towards autonomy and a genuinely independent Aboriginal Church. For a start, the revival itself was completely led by Aboriginal people. It was when white missionaries were away or had just left an Aboriginal community that revival came.

Pentecostal Successes and Disasters

The Charismatic element in the Aboriginal Revival was but one manifestation of a new spiritual power across the nation. In fact, the 1980s was a great decade for the Pentecostals. The movement was characterised by spectacular growth[82] and spectacular failures. Many of its leaders had grown up in more traditional evangelical churches, and their departure from them enabled them to throw off constraints to growth, but too many of them also threw off constraints to biblical doctrine and morality. The great threat to Pentecostalism's future was instability: would the movement collapse in the short-term or would the marriage of freedom to grow with biblical truth be one of fidelity, reaching maturity and longevity?

That was still an open question by the end of the 1980s, which was a decade in which churches, now led by a new cadre of dynamic leaders,[83] rode the church growth wave on top of the Charismatic renewal and reaped huge rewards. The Assemblies of God Australia appointed church growth departments in each state. The AOG's theme at its 1981 Conference was 'Every Town': its goal was to establish an AOG church in every town in Australia with a population over 1,000. Pentecostal churches, often occupying old cinema buildings, became conspicuous features of Australian country towns, especially in Queensland. In the cities, a number of Pentecostal churches, founded in the 1960s or 1970s,

---

81 Blacket, 'I Will Renew the Land'.

82 Census figures for Australians identifying as Pentecostals: 1976, 29,400; 1981, 71,148; 1986 107,007; 1991 150,619.

83 David Cartledge, *The Apostolic Revolution: The Restoration of Apostles and Prophets in the Assemblies of God in Australia* (Sydney: Paraclete Institute, 2000).

became megachurches in the 1980s: Christian Outreach Centre and Garden City (Brisbane), Christian Life Centre (Hillsong) and Christian City Church (Sydney), Riverview Christian Church (Perth), Paradise Community Church (Adelaide), and Waverley Christian Fellowship (Melbourne).

In Brisbane, Reginald Klimionok's Garden City church opened a new auditorium with seating for 900 in June 1983. Attendances exceeded 2,000 each Sunday.[84] Clark Taylor's Christian Outreach Centre opened in 1985 a new auditorium which seated 5,000. Taylor was as remarkable for his compassion as much as his passion, and the COC acquired a reputation for inclusion of marginalised, needy people: the homeless, drug addicts, and Aboriginal people who had difficulty finding a home in 'white' churches. Taylor was a legendary figure and it was not always clear if the legends were right. He was converted at a 1959 Billy Graham Crusade is one story which sounds conventional enough. But another account of his conversion is that he was being tossed around by the horns of a bull when he prayed for mercy and immediately an Aboriginal stockman quietened the bull and released Taylor from the horns of his dilemma. This would explain why Aboriginal people were so welcome in his church!

In Sydney Frank Houston's Christian Life Centre held a conference in 1983 with the modest theme 'Let's take the Nation'. In this same year Frank Houston sent his son, Brian, to pioneer a church in the Hills, a fast-growing district of Sydney. In 1988 its first worship album was recorded. These albums put Hillsong on the international map. Another Sydney Pentecostal church which owed much of its success to music was Christian City Church, whose pastor, Phil Pringle, was musically gifted. He arrived from New Zealand in 1980. Raised in the Assembly of God, Pringle represented all that was new in the movement: energetic, innovative leadership, and the combination of Pentecostal, 'Latter Rain' and Charismatic practices, including raising hands and dancing in times of worship. The culturally apposite worship was attractive to many in the surfing culture who had been largely untouched by the churches. But it also appealed to many in the churches who were wearied by the effort of making traditional methods work in an increasingly unchurched society and were in need of fun and refreshment. Within two decades, Sunday attendances at Christian City Church exceeded 2,000. It should not be concluded, however, that Pentecostal spirituality was limited to fun-seeking or to promoting the personal prosperity of believers. It was

84 The period of growth came to an end in November 1988 when Klimionok resigned after he was alleged to have misspent church funds (*Courier Mail*, 6 July 1988; 17 August 1988; 28 November 1988).

also capable of producing martyrs. Jackie Hamill, 36, from Christian City Pentecostal church at Girraween (a Sydney suburb) was serving as a missionary, teaching prisoners in the Philippines, when, on 15 August 1989, she was gang-raped and murdered.

Riverview Christian Church in Perth was established in 1979 by Brian and Valerie Baker, who, like many Pentecostal pastors, came from New Zealand.[85] They were trained in Oklahoma by Kenneth Hagin, the 'father' of the 'Word of Faith' movement. By the late 1980s the church was the largest in Western Australia with a membership of 3,200. In contrast to Sydney, Charismatic Christians were very active in WA in mainstream denominations and notably aware of themselves as constituting a movement. Barry Skellett, rector of the evangelical Anglican Church in the Perth suburb of Balcatta from 1985 to 1993, was chairman of ARMA (Anglican Renewal Ministries of Australia). A Charismatic body, ARMA was particularly strong in the WA Diocese of Bunbury because its Bishop, Hamish Jamieson, was a Charismatic. But Perth's Archbishop at the time, Peter Carnley, was not so open. He called them 'charismatic simplistics' and evangelicals he called 'fundamentalists'.[86] It was more comfortable for Charismatics to leave the mainstream churches and join the exciting new Pentecostal churches.

The AOG also approved the creation by member churches of their own Bible colleges. Andrew Evans, Superintendent of the AOG for two decades from 1977, argued that the proliferation of such colleges was one of the chief reasons for the growth of the Pentecostals: when a church was on a winner, it was a good way of duplicating the winnings. Ironically, it was David Cartledge, later President of the Southern Cross College which aspired to be the sole denominational training college, who initiated the practice of attaching Bible colleges to local churches. He had established the Rhema Bible College at Townsville in 1978. By the mid-80s Cartledge calculated that 4,000 had been saved through the Townsville Assembly. With the collapse of Soviet Communism at the end of 1989, Cartledge travelled widely in Eastern Europe, and established a Bible college in the Ukraine, and became an adviser to Pentecostal movements in the countries of Western Europe. He had developed a formula for growing churches which Pentecostal leaders

85 Perhaps New Zealand fostered a culture of innovation and entrepreneurial leadership from the 1960s, and such leaders, having started on this trajectory, looked for larger fields of operation in Australia. Brett Knowles, 'Is the Future of Western Christianity a Pentecostal One? A conversation with Harvey Cox', Paper presented to "The Future of Christianity in the West" Conference, Dunedin, 5–8 December 2002. Accessed 9 February 2017 at http://www.otago.ac.nz/chaplain/resources/otago017072.html.

86 Ken Frewer interviewed by Stuart Piggin, 21 January 1990.

in other lands needed and wanted. Australian Christianity was becoming increasingly confident of producing ministries of export quality.

The decade saw outstanding failure as well as outstanding growth. Too many of the megachurch developments were undone by failings in the leadership: unbiblical theology; immoral conduct; succumbing to the corruptions of power. The attribution of 'words of knowledge' and 'apostolic anointing' to leaders was based on questionable grounds biblically and was made to look ridiculous when too many of the leaders so designated were exposed for immorality: Reg Klimionok for misappropriation of church funds in 1988; Clark Taylor and Howard Carter for serial adultery in 1990; Frank Houston for paedophilia in 2000.

Howard Carter stands out as a pioneer of another strength and weakness of Pentecostal churches: political involvement on the extreme Right of politics. In the 1989 Queensland election, Carter spent $100,000 on a morals campaign akin to that of the Religious Right in America. He stood against pornography, homosexuality and abortion, and for capital punishment. He seemed to care little about the corruption in society and the Queensland police force unmasked by the Fitzgerald Inquiry. The people of Queensland, however, did care, tipping out the conservative forces in a landslide. Carter's abject political failure was followed swiftly by his fall from grace: while campaigning as a morals crusader, proclaiming Christ and the family as his two great commitments, he was having an adulterous affair. Exposed, he fled to Canada.[87] The Pentecostals built a big house in the 1980s, but whether its foundation was sand or the rock was still an open question.

* * *

The evangelical movement in Australia in 1990 was not as unified as it had been in 1980. Radical challenges to Christian orthodoxy did act centrifugally on evangelicalism. There were those, under the influence of new psychological theories, who sought in the Gospel the answer to the subjective needs of the individual. There were those, under the influence of Marxist thought, who located sin within social structures and preferred political solutions. There were those, especially within the Charismatic movement, who attired churchgoing

87 Much of this section on Pentecostalism is based on Sam Hey, 'God in the Suburbs and Beyond: The Emergence of an Australian Megachurch and Denomination', PhD, Griffith University, 2010, and relevant websites.

in the dress of popular culture. But the movement had to make all these experiments, and in the process of making them, most remained anchored to Jesus and the Bible. True, venerable evangelical spiritual disciplines, such as the Quiet Time, seemed to be imperilled. Specifically, the contribution which the Scripture Union had brought to evangelical unity promoted by large numbers of members reading the same passages of Scripture each day, was in jeopardy, as membership declined. And there had been a shift in the way many evangelicals worshipped Jesus: he was now more than ever lover and friend. But he was also still Lord and Saviour, and the Bible's integrity survived the worst ravages of the liberals. Jesus and the Bible were still easily evangelicalism's greatest centripetal forces. For all the changes, evangelicalism had not changed as much as society; maybe it had not changed enough. Australia's social mores no longer defaulted to Christianity. By 1990 it could no longer be assumed that the church's role in society would be an honoured one. Historian Manning Clark put it more dramatically: 'We have seen our society change from a group of cretinous puritans ... into a society which has become lively, interesting and creative.'[88] The question was whether or not the evangelicals, from whose ranks, no doubt, the cretinous puritans were drawn, could become themselves sufficiently lively, interesting and creative in response.

88 *SMH,* 22 August 1987.

Chapter Fifteen

THE STRUGGLE TO RECOVER EVANGELICALISM'S PROPHETIC VOICE, 1990–2000

'a religious belief ... you either take that ... view or you do not, in my opinion. I do take it. People who do not take it I do not think will ever be persuaded. But it is fundamental, I think, to the beliefs that have guided our society from the days of the Ten Commandments.'
(Peter Costello)

At the beginning of the 1990s evangelicalism, though it had a way to go, was on the road to recovery of its prophetic voice and its social concern. Consistent with this, evangelicals in the 1990s extended their already significant commitment to education, health, welfare and aged care. This signified their determination to remain engaged with their society and culture. The disengagement the secularists and the fundamentalists wanted to impose on them was not an option. But they could not agree on how to engage. The 1990s was a decade of evangelical disunity – not between denominations: evangelical Anglicans, Baptists, and Presbyterians had much in common – but between exclusive, conservative evangelicals, inclusive progressive evangelicals, and Charismatics and Pentecostals. The disunity was not manifest mainly in theological differences which were internal to the movement. The disunity was rather in the response to cultural and social developments. Evangelicals divided over what then preoccupied most people: postmodernism, and indigenous, political and, most divisive of all, gender issues.

Postmodernism, the new cultural paradigm of the age, emerged in the 1970s, but only became a heated matter for debate in evangelical circles in the 1990s.[1]

1 J. Richard Middleton and Brian J. Walsh, *Truth Is Stranger Than It Used to Be: Biblical Faith in a Postmodern Age* (Downers Grove: InterVarsity Press, 1995) popularized the debate among evangelicals.

It wedged evangelicals into three groups: Conservative, exclusive evangelicals engaged with postmodernism by condemning it; the progressive, inclusive evangelicals, attracted to Radical Orthodoxy, saw in it the opportunity to present the Gospel in a more favourable light; the Charismatics and Pentecostals embraced it as the main paradigm of their movement.

Postmodernists see 'truth' differently from modernists. Whereas for the latter, truth is expressed in objective, absolute propositions, for postmodernists everything is subjective, relative, and truth is found only in relational integrity. The postmodernist God is said to be 'true' because he is reliable in relating to humankind. There was a surge in theological interest in the Trinity precisely because the Trinity is God in relationship. Whereas modernism focusses on the mind and the will, postmodernism prefers emotions and feelings. Modernism categorises reality in terms of truth and falsity, employs controls to guide people into truth and away from error, and invites assent and commitment. Postmodernism allows people freedom to advance any opinions and has difficulty with commitment. It values variety and options. The postmodern world is irreducibly pluralist: there are not only many religious options, but there are many Christian options. There is a smorgasbord of ways of being Christian, even evangelical Christian. Modernism esteems science and logic; postmodernism critiques both, seeing them as constructs of people with power. Modernism prefers fact to fiction, whereas postmodernists blur the distinction. Postmodernists like stories which entertain, but not big stories (metanarratives) which explain everything.

Postmodernism struck at the heart of conservative evangelicalism. It declared invalid the philosophy of biblical interpretation employed by the conservatives known as 'foundationalism'. This is the view that language reflects objective reality and can be interpreted correctly by the reader using the power of reason. Philosopher Ludwig Wittgenstein argued that language had no objective meaning: a word only took on meaning by the way it was used. Building on this insight, the post-structuralist philosophers, Michel Foucault and Jacques Derrida, argued that commonly language is used by the powerful to oppress the weak and that it privileges discourse which is deemed to be 'scientific' and 'rational'. The Bible, it followed, was capable of endless interpretations, and its over-arching metanarrative – God's story of redemption – was essentially oppressive.

Christian Philosopher, Nicholas Wolterstorff, and Bible scholars from the progressive, inclusive school of evangelicals – such as Stanley Grenz in North America and Tom Wright in the United Kingdom – agreed with the condemnation of foundationalism. They used postmodernist thinking to argue for greater freedom in biblical interpretation and for stressing those parts of the biblical message which promoted liberation and dialogue and sensitivity to suffering. Conservative evangelical scholars were indignant, even horrified by the claims of the progressive evangelicals. Don Carson exclaimed: 'I cannot see how Grenz's approach to Scripture can be called "evangelical" in any useful sense.'[2] In his zeal to condemn the progressives, Carson put George Carey, the evangelical Archbishop of Canterbury, and even John Stott outside the camp.

Leading English progressive evangelical New Testament scholar, Tom Wright, used the Reformation's high esteem for biblical scholarship to remove evangelical theology from the legalistic framework which had come to imprison Reformation theology itself. He deconstructed interpretations of Scripture which had become trapped in a modernist, enlightenment worldview. He advanced the 'new perspective' on the apostle Paul, arguing that righteousness, previously understood as a forensic concept, whereby an individual could be accounted right by God the judge, should rather be understood in a relational and corporate way. He maintained that his new perspective was a more valid interpretation of Scripture than the old. Progressive evangelicals also rebuked the conservatives for denying them another principle, sacred since the Reformation, namely freedom of conscience and liberty of thought. The divide between conservative evangelicals and progressives widened. In Australia the conservatives sided with Carson in rejecting postmodernism; the progressives sided with Wright and embraced it; the Charismatics practised it. In the process they each developed new styles of worship, new methods of evangelism, and new welfare ministries.

The story is far more complex, of course, than this all-too-simplistic classification. Postmodernism might have destabilised the evangelical movement by wedging it into three groups, but those groups already existed, and not all were prepared to identify one philosophical system with theological truth: not all conservatives insisted that modernism was essential to the preservation of the Gospel. There were, for example, conservative evangelicals who welcomed the erudite covenant theology of Tom Wright, finding it a ready fit with their long-held conservative theological framework. Others warmed to postmodernism's liking for options – after all was that not a prominent feature of the Reformation in its break from the straitjacket of medieval Catholicism? Conservative preachers, too, found the postmodernist stress on relationships too valuable to forego and resisted the objections of those who believed that

2 D.A. Carson, *The Gagging of God: Christianity Confronts Pluralism* (Grand Rapids: Zondervan, 1996), 481.

it risked drowning the movement in subjectivity and relativity. Having a relationship with God through Christ and fellowship with other believers were too central to evangelicalism to be denied in order to resist the impact of postmodernism. One parishioner of a conservative evangelical church was so struck by the emphasis on relationships by a young Moore College graduate in the late 1980s that he made a count of the number of times the word 'relationship' was used in a sermon: 50 times in 25 minutes. This preacher's commitment to authentic relationships originated in the Gospel: it did not need postmodernism to initiate it and any encouragement it received from postmodernism would not be resisted. Postmodernism might have wedged the evangelical movement, but it also provided the essential fuel for the evangelical engine: animated debate on the engagement of the Gospel with culture.

Tim and Peter Costello: Case Study

Two of the three styles of evangelical Christianity – the progressive postmodernist and the conservative modernist – were personified in this period respectively by Tim and Peter Costello. Tim (b.1955) entered the Baptist ministry, prophetically identifying with the poor and calling for radical transformation of the social systems which oppress the poor and undermine community. From 2003 to 2016 he was CEO of World Vision Australia, and from 2016 its 'Chief Advocate'. Peter (b. 1957) entered politics as a conservative and championed the role of Christianity in inculcating personal responsibility and empowering individuals to achieve their own goals. Peter was a minister in the Howard government from 1995 to 2007, Australia's longest-serving Treasurer.[3] They are the sons of Methodist lay preacher, Russell Costello, a convert from Catholicism, and Anne, Presbyterian. After they married, Russell and Anne became members of the Blackburn Baptist Church in Melbourne's Bible belt because that was the nearest church to their home.[4] The church was described by Tim as neither liberal nor fundamentalist, and the pastors, David Griffiths and Rowland Croucher, impressed them with their positive, creative ministries.[5]

3 Tracey Aubin, *Peter Costello: A Biography, the Full and Unauthorised Story of the Man Who Wants to be PM* (Pymble: HarperCollins, 1999); Peter Costello and Peter Coleman, *The Costello Memoirs: The Age of Prosperity* (Carlton: MUP, 2008).

4 Tim Costello, *Streets of Hope: Finding God in St Kilda* (St Leonards: Allen & Unwin, 1998), 29–37; Marita Rae Munro, '"A Struggle for Identity and Direction": A History of Victorian Baptists (1960–2000)', PhD, University of Melbourne, 2010), 10.

5 Costello, *Streets of Hope*, 31.

Though both sons attended the prestigious Carey Baptist Grammar School, theirs was not a wealthy home. The brothers were taught history and politics at Carey Grammar by their own father, who also groomed them in debating political issues. Tim was given training in public speaking through his involvement in evangelism on Melbourne's beaches under the guidance of evangelist, Robert Coyle. He was mentored in the application of faith to the marginalised in society by John Smith, founder of God's Squad. Both sons were deeply influenced by their Baptist heritage.[6] It fostered not so much conservative or radical thinking, as independent thinking. Tim and Peter, though apparently at opposite ends of the political spectrum, were both strongly independent thinkers. As we have seen (ch12) student radicalism of the early 70s stirred up the EUs, especially in Melbourne universities. Monash, where Peter Costello led the EU, was a hotbed of student radicalism, and Peter demonstrated his independence in not being swept away by the radicalism. Tim, though loyal to the Baptist denomination in which he was raised, and which was perceived as socially conservative, took full advantage of its resources to develop his socially radical instincts. Together with the theologically progressive Athol Gill, Tim Costello studied at the Baptist Seminary in Rueschlikon, Switzerland.[7]

> It was a brilliant experience. There were over 25 nationalities. All the Italian Baptists voted Communist. The Scandinavian Baptists had different views on premarital sex to our Australian Baptists. The British Baptists drank and smoked. So suddenly you had to go, 'What's Gospel? What's culture? How have I just seen my faith as really a hand-me-down of an Australian, narrower church experience?' It pushed you to really think about your faith.[8]

While there, Tim was offered jobs in prestigious Baptist churches, but it was a humble letter from the 10-member, dying church of St Kilda, a socially-challenged Melbourne suburb, which he and his wife, Merridie, accepted as the call of God. There his ministry to the mentally ill, the drug addicted, and street workers made full use of his knowledge as a lawyer as well as of his compassion as a pastor. In 1993 and 1994, he was mayor of St Kilda. He believed that the family, the church, the law and local government should also serve each other to build community. He served on the

6 Tim Costello interviewed by Peter Thompson, *Talking Heads*, ABC 1, 15 June 2009.

7 Relocated to Prague in 1995.

8 Tim Costello interviewed by Thompson.

council to provide public housing for those threatened with the loss of their homes as the suburb was gentrified.

In 1995 Tim became the minister of Collins Street Baptist Church in the heart of the Melbourne CBD. There he developed a ministry called Urban Seed and, from its Credo Café, fed the homeless and the Indigenous who lived among the Corinthian columns atop its front steps. His appointment also allowed him to address the issues of the day affecting the city. He felt that his calling was not only to be a preacher, but a prophet, and he could not be a prophet if he became a politician. To be a prophet one has to speak against the culture, never a popular thing, and impossible for a politician.

As mayor of St Kilda, Tim Costello had campaigned against council amalgamations enforced by Victorian Liberal Premier, Jeff Kennett. Now as head of the Interchurch Gambling Taskforce, Costello singled out Kennett for particular criticism. Tim was stridently opposed to the use of gambling to fill the State's coffers, lamenting:

> It comes as a breathtaking denouement, and even more of a shock, to hear the Victorian Premier launch the Melbourne casino saying this 'represented the new spirit of Victoria', the future vision for the State. This debauched statesmanship laughed off empirical evidence about the hideous addictions and corruptive processes that might accompany a spanking new gambling house … That which was once illegal and belonged to the pigeon-hole of vice is elevated to the level of a political achievement of moral proportions.[9]

Kennett accused Costello and his supporters in the Victorian Interchurch Gambling Taskforce of being 'wowsers' and 'unVictorian'. But the wowser tag did not stick, as Victorians saw that the Taskforce was not moralising, but based its opposition to gambling on the demonstrable grounds that people who could not afford the habit were being exploited by a rapacious industry.[10] Kennett accused Costello of not being a 'real minister', but a politician in disguise, 'hiding behind the cloth'.[11] The premier did not know how much was being hidden behind Costello's cloth. Darrell Paproth, lecturer in church history at the Bible College of Victoria, recalls that Tim had told him that parliamentarians had come to him at night (like Nicodemus) seeking his counsel. They said they hated the gambling culture that was developing, but 'if they raised anything

---

9 Costello, *Streets of Hope*, 202.

10 Munro, 'A Struggle for Identity and Direction, 297.

11 Tim Costello, *Tips from a Travelling Soul-Searcher* (Sydney: Allen & Unwin, 1999), 58.

with Jeff' he would simply threaten them with not getting pre-selection at the next elections. So Paproth, together with Barb Allison, the dean of women at BCV, organised a prayer day to withstand the gambling onslaught. In the belief that Crown Casino and 'the whole gambling thing' was hurting many businesses and individuals, Paproth and Allison arranged for their students to travel to the city by train for a prayer walk. In ones or twos they walked unobtrusively around Parliament House to pray for the members. Then they walked to Collins Street Baptist Church to pray that its pastor, Tim Costello, would continue to be a thorn in Kennett's side. Costello addressed the students on the gambling problem. Then the students walked through the city, praying for businesses. Reminded by Paproth that in 1835, John Pascoe Fawkner, in his handwritten newspaper, had written about establishing a 'Christian civilisation' by the Yarra river, the students ended up at the Crown Casino over which they prayed before catching the train back to the college at Lilydale.[12]

Before the 1999 election which, with Costello's help, Kennett surprisingly lost, Liberal strategists detected that all was not well and agreed to cap the number of poker machines in Victoria from 90,000, which Kennett had wanted, to 25,000. It was too late for Kennett, but not for Tim Costello, who in 2004 became CEO of World Vision.

Peter Costello's journey has been significantly different. He married Tanya Coleman, daughter of journalist and Liberal politician, Peter Coleman, and thus became part of the Liberal establishment. Costello also changed his denominational allegiance from Baptist to Anglican. But, rather than watering down any of his Christian convictions in these transitions, he applied them fearlessly on the conservative side of politics, where they exercised considerable potency. He was candid and open about his religious convictions. Speaking in the House of Representatives in 1996 on the euthanasia debate, he said that opposition to euthanasia is:

> a religious belief … you either take that … view or you do not, in my opinion. I do take it. People who do not take it I do not think will ever be persuaded. But it is fundamental, I think, to the beliefs that have guided our society from the days of the Ten Commandments.[13]

In the past two decades, Christians in general and evangelicals in particular, have developed an interest in contributing to the wellbeing of society

12 Darrell Paproth, email to Stuart Piggin, 9 February 2017.

13 Quoted in Marion Maddox, *God under Howard: The Rise of the Religious Right in Australian Politics* (Sydney: Allen & Unwin, 2005), 55f.

through political processes and they have recovered their social conscience. In both – Peter in the former, and Tim in the latter – the Costello brothers have made substantial contributions. They have helped the evangelical movement to recover its prophetic role.

Indigenous Issues

Two matters dominated consideration of indigenous affairs in the 1990s: land rights and the 'stolen generations'. Both were intensely divisive issues which ensured that indigenous concerns received unprecedented attention and also shone the spotlight on Christian involvement with Aboriginal people. On land rights there were two major legal decisions. In 1992 the Mabo decision declared that when Australia was colonised it was not *terra nullius* (a land belonging to no one),[14] but was in fact occupied by Aboriginal and Torres Strait Islander peoples who had rights to their land which preceded white settlement and were not extinguished by it. The 1996 Wik decision found that leases on pastoral properties did not necessarily allow the leaseholder exclusive possession. The first decision meant that for the first time in Australian history the law recognised native title. The Wik decision opened the possibility that since settlement some areas of native title had not been extinguished.

Anthropologist and Uniting Church minister, Robert Bos, interprets the Aboriginal revival, beginning in 1979, as one of the means by which Aboriginal people were able to persevere in their campaign for land rights.[15] The States, along with mining and pastoral interests, howled with hysteria over the Mabo and Wik judgements, but the Aboriginal people, now strengthened by revival and strongly supported by the churches, were able to persuade non-indigenous Australians to seek truth and justice in this issue, rather than be ruled by self-interest. Together Aboriginal people and the churches have changed the national mood which has moved towards a desire for reconciliation between black and white and atonement for past wrongs.[16] The very terms, at the core of evangelical theology, reflect a growing conviction that ministry to the Australian soul mandated addressing Indigenous concerns.

---

14 John Harris, 'Mabo for Teachers: Distinguishing True History from False History,' *JCE,* 37.2, 1994, 11.

15 Robert Bos, 'The Dreaming and Social Change in Arnhem Land,' in Tony Swain and Deborah Bird Rose (eds), *Aboriginal Australians and Christian Missions* (Bedford Park: The Australian Association for the Study of Religions, 1988), 422–37.

16 See, for example, *Social Issues Update*, 3.2, October 1993, The occasional newsletter of the Social Issues Committee, Anglican Diocese of Sydney.

The state-sanctioned practice of removing Aboriginal children from their parents was an even more emotive issue.[17] The Keating Labor Government in 1995 authorised the Human Rights and Equal Opportunity Commission to inquire into the removal from their families of Aboriginal and Torres Strait Islander children. The Commission reported in 1997.[18] Missionaries were deeply implicated in the practice of removing Aboriginal children from their mothers. Nineteenth-century Protestant missionary ideology had given a partial justification for it. Aboriginal people, most missionaries believed, had to be 'civilised' before 'Christianised'. Since Aboriginal adults appeared to care little for 'civilisation', it was believed that the best chance for the Christianisation of the Aboriginal race was to separate the children from the adults when they were as young as possible so that they would be exposed only to European ways. Missionaries had other motives for raising Aboriginal children apart from their parents, including a humanitarian concern to care for children whose parents were incapacitated through the ravages of marginalisation.

The weight of evidence is that, while most Aboriginal children were apparently not abused at the Christian missions,[19] there was too much regimentation and some missionaries had a reputation for strictness. The commonest complaint made to the 'National Inquiry into the Separation of Aboriginal and Torres Strait Islander Children from their Families' was not about ill treatment, but that the missionaries did not take the Aboriginal people sufficiently into their confidence and explain what they were trying to achieve. A second criticism was that they were not ambitious enough for the Aboriginal people and did not help very able Indigenous people to aspire after higher education and professional status. Missionaries, however, had always believed in the potential of Aboriginal people as few others did, and they equipped those who emerged as leaders to deal with governments and mining companies.[20] Many had established lasting bonds of affection with their charges and were distressed and disorientated by the thought that they might have been part of a system which damaged their flocks. The CMS unreservedly

17 Peter Read, *The Stolen Generations: The Removal of Aboriginal Children in New South Wales 1883–1969,* NSW Ministry of Aboriginal Affairs: Occasional Paper (No 1), (Sydney: Government Printer, 1982; Peter Read, *A Rape of the Soul so Profound* (St Leonards, Allen & Unwin, 1999).

18 *Bringing them Home: National Inquiry into the Separation of Aboriginal and Torres Strait Islander Children from their Families* (Canberra: Australian Government Publishing Service), 1997.

19 John Harris, *We wish we'd done more: Ninety Years of CMS and Aboriginal issues in North Australia* (Adelaide: Openbook, 1998), ch. 5.

20 Harris, *We wish we'd done more*, 343.

expressed 'its sorrow and apology to the indigenous people with whom it has been associated for any inappropriate policies and action which have caused suffering to them'.[21] Through the National Inquiry, the Catholic, Anglican, Uniting and Baptist Churches all made similar apologies.[22]

From the early 1970s missionaries were no longer entitled to negotiate with mining companies on behalf of Aboriginal people – that had to be done directly between the companies and the Indigenous people. Critical issues, however, such as the relationship between faith and culture, the preservation of indigenous languages, and the translation of the Bible into those languages, continued to engage the concern of missionaries.

Steve and Narelle Etherington, CMS missionaries, worked among the Kunwinjku language people in Oenpelli, in Western Arnhem Land (East of Darwin) from 1977. They later moved to Tamworth in northern NSW and from 2012 were seconded to the Bible Society to bring to completion the translation of the New Testament into Kunwinjku. In the late 1990s, after two decades of mission work, they reflected deeply on the experience of the Kunwinjku.[23] Etherington understood that the 'old people' who taught the Law lost prestige with the coming of the white man. He was sensitive to the humiliation which Indigenous people felt at every contact with white people who adjudged them to be unemployable or confined them to work in the most marginal of jobs.[24] Dependency was their destiny, but that destroyed self-esteem, and when they felt so disempowered that they could not function either in their own or in white society, those on whom they depended sought to force them to conform. The commonest response to all the regulation and compulsion was resistance, so indirect that it did not result in positive change or political empowerment, and so subtle that whites – missionaries and politicians alike – were largely unaware of it. Solutions would not be found within the debates of whites, centred on the binary assertions of the need for greater intervention and control or greater liberty and independence for Aboriginal people. It would come only through the type of research Etherington had conducted which is based primarily on listening to Aboriginal people themselves.[25]

---

21 *Checkpoint,* Autumn 1998, 7.

22 *Bringing Them Home*, 1997, 289–291.

23 Steven Etherington, 'Learning to be Kunwinjku: Kunwinjku people discuss their pedagogy', PhD Thesis, Charles Darwin University, 2006.

24 Etherington, 'Learning to be Kunwinjku', 23.

25 John Harris, 'It's time to listen to Aboriginal Christians and time to respond,' in Peter Carroll and Steve Etherington, (eds), *One Land, One Saviour: Seeing Aboriginal Lives Transformed by Christ* (Sydney: CMS, 2008), 230–243.

As the missionaries were increasingly removed from positions of responsibility for Aboriginal welfare, the churches became more involved than ever with Indigenous issues. The International Year of Indigenous People (1993) saw Sydney's Archbishop Goodhew in his first synod call for strong support for the process of reconciliation following on from the Mabo decision of the previous year.[26] Sydney has the largest population of Indigenous people in Australia, so it was appropriate that in the 1996 Sydney synod a proposal to set up a trust to fund indigenous ministry was approved unanimously and $1 million was voted for the purpose.

Not everyone in the wider community sympathised with the Aboriginal push for land rights. A reaction, led by the Queensland politician Pauline Hanson, made it a particularly divisive issue around the time of the 1996 Federal election. Sealin Garlett, the Aboriginal minister of the Uniting Church at Coolbellup, a suburb of Perth, persuaded his congregation to pray for Pauline Hanson. Garlett was one of the stolen generation. In 1964, aged 7, he was placed in the Mogumber Methodist Mission. He was converted in 1979 through the ministry of Aboriginal evangelist Ron Williams at a rally of the Aboriginal Evangelical Fellowship. With the formation of the Uniting Aboriginal and Islander Christian Congress (UAICC) in 1985 he decided to train for the ministry 'as a Spirit-filled Christian to become educated in the Bible for his people'. He was 'confronted by God and His Holy Spirit' who urged him, 'Sealin, you've got to cross the line'. This he took to mean that he had to become a minister for all people, white as well as black, and that he had to embark on a lifetime of allowing healing to take place in his own heart. He found it felt good when he didn't 'see the colour'.[27] The Christian ministry he saw was a ministry of reconciliation and he became one of the leaders of the UAICC contingent in the 1997 Eighth General Assembly of the Uniting Church in Perth which supported recognition of the pain of members of the stolen generations.

Another Aboriginal pastor instrumental in the reconciliation movement following the land rights legislation was Sonny Graham, a pastor with the Churches of Christ. He trained for the ministry in the later 1950s at the College of the Bible in Glen Iris in Melbourne and became acquainted with Douglas Nicholls, the pastor who was to become South Australia's Governor. In the early 1990s Graham was pastor of the Church of Christ in Port Hedland, WA.

---

26 *Social Issues Update*, 3.2, 1993.

27 Catherine J. Kelly, 'Dreaming Dreams and Seeing Visions: An examination of the lives and work of some Christian Aboriginal leaders', History Honours thesis, UWA, 2000, 9–13.

He there met Don McLeod, a Communist, who had instigated the famous stockmen's strike in 1946 which had won better conditions for Aboriginal workers.[28] Graham understood his people's identification with the land and believed that they should be accorded Native Title consistent with the Act. But he believed that a way could be found to do this without alienating miners, pastoralists, or townspeople. Because there are many Aboriginal nations, he did not believe that a 'Treaty' was workable, but he argued for regional agreements as the best way of implementing Native Title. Graham felt for children of the stolen generation and understood their anger with missionaries who had colluded with government policy. But he was not himself 'stolen', and he was grateful to the missionaries for education and the Gospel which he said the tribal leaders always respected: 'Their own spirituality told them that here was something that was true'.[29]

Missions and missionaries were not critical to the flourishing of First Australians, but Christian faith and hope were. While there was a need for reconciliation and a belief in the role of the spiritual in human wellbeing, the ongoing participation of Christian churches in Indigenous communities would be critical.

The Religious Right

From 1983 to 1996 the Labor Party under prime ministers Bob Hawke and then Paul Keating was in power in the Commonwealth Parliament. It was a government which drew on the spiritual capital of the Christian heritage first in the reconciliation between labour and capital in Hawke's 'Accord' and then with Indigenous people in Keating's famous Redfern speech (10 December 1992). Impressively, too, the Methodist and Uniting church clergyman, Brian Howe, Minister for Social Security, effectively addressed poverty.

But a conservative reaction also gained momentum, and that too drew profoundly on Christian values. This is evident in the maiden speeches made by conservatives in the Federal Parliament in this period. John Anderson, an evangelical Anglican, served in the House of Representatives from 1989 as National Party member for Gwydir and as Deputy Prime Minister from 1999 until his resignation in June 2005. In his maiden speech Anderson spoke of the twin pillars of Australian society, the Christian heritage and the family. Jesus' teaching to 'render unto Caesar that which was Caesar's and to God

28 D.W. McLeod, *How the West Was Lost: The Native Question in the Development of Western Australia* (Port Hedland: The author, 1984).

29 Kelly, 'Dreaming Dreams', 14–19.

that which was God's', he argued, 'established in mankind's thinking the idea that limits should be set to the size and nature of government's claims on the lives of ordinary citizens'.[30]

Anderson was a frank admirer of Sydney Anglicans for the clarity of their teaching and their uncompromising stand for traditional Christian values. He owed a lot to them for his own spiritual development. A pupil at the King's School Parramatta he came under the sway of housemasters, Rod West, later headmaster of Trinity Grammar, and Michael Smee, later headmaster of Newington College. Anderson confessed that he lapsed after leaving school. He was restored to vital faith at the university church of St Barnabas Broadway in Sydney. He later thought that he should train for the ministry, but Peter Chiswell, Bishop of Armidale, advised him to enter politics instead.[31] He was not a typical politician. By temperament he was gentle, by conviction a conciliator. Because Prime Minister Howard and Treasurer Peter Costello valued his integrity, the government was steered by his moral compass, at least when the tempests of naked political opportunism were not blowing.

More robustly, the Presbyterian, Rod Kemp, elected a Liberal Senator for Victoria, 1990–2008, in his maiden speech in parliament attacked the view popularised by historian Manning Clark that the 200 years of white settlement in Australia was 'a brief, nasty interlude'. He called for an understanding of the progress and unity achieved in Australian history which would make the youth of the nation proud and motivate them to work for a better Australia. In all this, Kemp had been influenced by the treatment of historian Geoffrey Blainey at Melbourne University. Blainey had resigned in 1988 following the furore which broke out after his questioning of the current immigration policy and the lauding of multiculturalism. It was Blainey who coined the phrase, the 'black arm-band' view of history. The History Wars had begun, an Australian battle in the culture wars then raging in Western civilisation.[32] Conservative evangelicals were in some danger of enrolling as troops in the culture wars.

On the conservative side of politics, steps were taken to protect traditional values. The Lyons Forum, characterised by Marion Maddox as a

30 The Hon John Anderson MP, Member for Gwydir (NSW), First Speech in the House of Representatives, Parliament of Australia, 17 May 1989, *Hansard,* no. 168, (1989), 434.

31 Paul Gallagher, *Faith and Duty: The John Anderson Story* (Sydney: Random House, 2006), 41f.

32 D. Gare, G. Bolton, S. Macintyre, & T. Stannage (eds.), *The fuss that never ended: The life and work of Geoffrey Blainey* (Carlton: MUP, 2003); Richard Allsop, 'Blainey outlasts the History Wars,' *IPA Politics and Culture Review,* March 2010, 7–11.

'crypto-Christian pressure group,' successfully promoted a 'family values' social agenda in Australian politics.[33] The Forum, named after Dame Enid Lyons, a Catholic, was formed in 1992 by two Catholics, John Herron and Kevin Andrews.[34] The first chairman, however, was a Baptist Lay Preacher, Chris Miles, who was considered by some to be its real founder.[35] Other foundation members included Eric Abetz, a member of the Reformed Church, John Tierney, an Anglican, Alan Cadman (Hillsong), John Bradford (who later represented the Christian Democrats), and John Forrest. The membership was confined to the Liberal/National Party Coalition and its purpose was to strengthen the family as the basic unit of society and to review legislation in the light of traditional Christian values. Some evangelical parliamentarians, such as Baden Teague, joined the Forum, but left it because he considered it too right wing. Nearly all its members were also members of the Parliamentary Christian Fellowship, but the reverse was not true. Many members of the PCF, such as its chairman Senator John Woodley of the Uniting Church, supported an agenda of social reform and human rights rather than the personal moral and conscience issues raised by the Lyons Forum.

According to Maddox, the real significance of the Forum was that it promoted John Howard into the leadership of the Liberal Party and therefore into the Prime Ministership which he held for a period (1996–2007) second only in length to that of Menzies. Miles, Cadman and Bradford were particularly angered by the endorsement of the Sydney Gay and Lesbian Mardi Gras by the Liberal Leader, John Hewson. A Baptist in his youth, Hewson had developed left-of-centre social policy values, and he defended his support of the 1994 Gay and Lesbian Mardi Gras on the theological grounds that "God didn't say, 'God so loved the world excluding homosexuals.'"[36] Maddox argues[37] that the opposition to him on this point led not so much to his downfall – he was doomed anyway after losing the unlosable election. But it set the moral agenda for his replacement as leader on 23 May 1994 by Alexander Downer (who, though never a member of the Lyons Forum, was prepared to back their policies rather than enthuse over them) and then in January 1995 by Howard (who was never a member either, but was more enthusiastic about their policies and values).

33 Marion Maddox, *God under Howard,* 38ff.

34 Marion Maddox, *For God and Country: Religious Dynamics in Australian Federal Politics* (Canberra: Commonwealth of Australia, 2001), 204.

35 Maddox, *For God and Country*, 204.

36 *Canberra Times*, 4 March 1994.

37 Maddox, *For God and Country*, 218 -225, 230f.

Howard, raised in a Methodist household, in public remained fairly difficult to pin down on religious commitment, but within the party he was prepared to make the Lyons Forum's agenda the backbone of Liberal policy. Key to that agenda was a belief in state intervention in moral matters whereas Hewson was libertarian and opposed to state controls on private morality.[38] Evangelical Christians tend to favour an ameliorative role for the state and therefore support its role in civilising capitalism and in keeping a welfare safety net. So they had some difficulty with the 'Dry' economic policies of such Liberals as Howard, Downer and Peter Costello, but they agreed that the personal responsibility of the individual, basic to 'Dry' philosophy, has its roots in Protestant culture and theology. They are inclined to overlook or even approve market freedoms, particularly if their advocates are firm supporters of traditional, Christian moral values and are not afraid to espouse them publicly. Howard crafted his political philosophy perfectly to win the approval and therefore the votes of most conservative evangelicals. In particular, he grasped the sense in which Australia is and ought to be both secular and Christian at the same time. To this he married an unembarrassed understanding of an 'Australian value':

> I think an Australian value is that we are a secular society in the correct meaning of that term, which is that we don't have an established religion but not secular in the sense that our culture is not influenced by the Judaic-Christian ethic; it plainly is.[39]

Howard's 1996 electoral victory brought more evangelicals into federal Parliament including Ross Cameron, Liberal member for Parramatta, and Danna Vale, Liberal member for the nearby seat of Hughes in which is located her church, Hillsong. Cameron started a Monday night prayer meeting for federal politicians, which was attended by Labor member, Kevin Rudd, destined to be Prime Minister, 2007–2010. Cameron was also instrumental, with his brother Jock, in establishing in 1997 a National Student Leadership Forum on Faith and Values. It was concerned to demonstrate that effective leadership must be underpinned by the spiritual values of service. Jesus, Gandhi, Albert Schweitzer and Mother Teresa were studied as models of 'servant leadership'. It was designed to be evangelistic, but was not to be overtly political and Cameron sought the support of politicians of all parties. It was even supported

38 Maddox, *For God and Country*, 214.

39 Cited in Hugh Chilton, 'Evangelicals and the End of Christian Australia: Nation and Religion in the Public Square 1959–1979', PhD, University of Sydney, 2014, 363f.

by Mark Latham, a professed atheist, who was to become Labor Party leader, and who thought Jesus was 'incredibly charismatic and inspiring'.[40] Cameron was shaped in his view of the role of Christianity in politics by the American Religious Right. He served as an intern with US Senator, Mark Hatfield, a prominent leader of the conservative Christian political pressure group known as 'The Family'. It advocated the support of church bodies with government money, known as 'faith-based initiatives' and the 'privatisation of welfare'.[41] There was increasing support for church involvement in welfare delivery in Howard's time. Howard wrote in his autobiography:

> Another goal of mine was to involve the charitable organisations of Australia, mainly religious, not only in the provision of services but also the giving of advice to Government. Nobody understands better than a Salvation Army officer just how hard life can be for those in poverty. In addition, they know better than anyone in politics or the bureaucracy the value of the charitable dollar.[42]

Howard himself believed that the churches were often the best groups to administer charities, and Australia has the largest percentage of church-based charities in the Western world.[43] So this development cannot be attributed to American influence. Nevertheless, there was an increasing congruence with American Religious Right practice and malpractice, including the failure to match pro-family profession with practice.

Danna Vale's faith was quite capable of motivating her to oppose the policies of her own party when she disagreed with them on moral or humanitarian grounds. In 1997 for the first time in Australia, the Northern Territory Government introduced mandatory sentencing which resulted in a dramatic increase in the sentences of Indigenous people, who were already shamefully over-represented in the prison population. The previous year the federal Howard Government had intervened in the affairs of the Northern Territory, blocking the legalisation of euthanasia. But over mandatory sentencing, it refused to intervene. So Vale went to 'Plan B: the power of prayer'. She asked the churches in her electorate to pray that the Prime Minister and Cabinet would

---

40 Maddox, *God under Howard*, 287.

41 Jeff Sharlet, *The Family: Power, Politics and Fundamentalism's Shadow Elite* (Brisbane: University of Queensland Press, 2008), 381.

42 John Howard, *Lazarus Rising: A Personal and Political Autobiography* (Pymble: HarperCollins Publishers, 2010), 487.

43 Shurlee Swain, 'A Long History of Faith-based Welfare in Australia: Origins and Impact', *JRH,* 41.1, 2017, 81.

receive divine guidance on the matter. She even asked Sydney's Archbishop Harry Goodhew to pray to the same end. She sought to influence fellow members in the Party Room and she spoke against mandatory sentencing in the House: 'I didn't have a speech ready, so I just said, "Help me, Jesus." The speech went down so well, but I hadn't been prepared – I think God put the Spirit on the ears of the hearer.'[44]

God was coming back into politics in a way which astonished the secular commentariat. The Australian Constitutional Convention to consider a new constitution for the Commonwealth Parliament was held in Canberra on 2 and 13 February 1998. In contrast to the debates of a century earlier on the constitution, no voices were raised against the invocation of God's name in the proposed rewording of the constitution. The issue most at stake then was whether Australia would become a republic. No one feared that it might become a theocracy, and seemingly a wave of respect for all things spiritual swept across the nation. Prime Minister Howard observed: 'His Grace the Archbishop of Melbourne said God had had a pretty good convention.'[45] So ascendant were the forces of conservatism that the move to a republic was easily blocked and all talk of a new constitution was shelved. On 8 August 1999 Howard opened Phil Pringle's Oxford Falls Christian City Church. By the end of the twentieth century in Australia there was far more interest in the interaction of religion and politics than there was in the separation of church and state, a situation which continued for another decade. There was by now, in any case, less reason to keep the churches out of politics on sectarian grounds. As evangelicals recovered their social conscience, they found they had far more in common with Catholics and liberal Protestants who had never lost it! Evangelicals, like all Christians, were learning to speak the language of civic discourse, thus investing the body politic with a metaphysical dimension.

Sexual Politics in the Church

Second wave feminism, which burst on the scene in the 1960s, was now reaching its apogee of influence.[46] It sought to give women equal political power, employment and citizenship rights. It did not make sense to many women church-goers that they should be denied the equivalent of these rights in the church.

44 Maddox, *For God and Country*, 136.

45 Howard, *Lazarus Rising*, 326.

46 D Altman, 'The creation of sexual politics in Australia,' *Journal of Australian Studies*, 20 (1987), 76–82.

The Ordination of Women

But denied they would be. The Presbyterians were the first among the conservative evangelicals determined to undo the damage they believed had been done by the feminists to their church. They had accepted the validity of women's ordination in the 1970s: it took some time for the conservatives to marshal their opposition. But in September 1991 three women and about 200 men at the General Assembly, meeting in Sydney, resolved to reverse the Presbyterian Church's support for the ordination of women. The voting by states showed that in NSW alone, the majority (45 to 41) opposed the reversal. In Queensland 32 approved the reversal and only 3 opposed it. In Victoria 33 approved and 14 dissented. By a margin of 124 to 60, the Assembly determined to delete the clause that 'women shall be eligible for admission to the Ministry of Word and Sacraments'. Then by 116 votes to 61, it approved that 'men only shall be eligible for admission to the Ministry of Word and Sacraments'.[47]

The media were intrigued. This decision violated the Australian sense of fair play. What had these female ministers done that they deserved such treatment? And how, if the Bible is so clear that women cannot be ministers, can it be right to allow those already ordained to continue in the position? There was a feeling among church members that the Assembly, which revoked the ordination of women, was increasing in power at the expense of the presbyteries where the power to ordain had always resided.[48] The Presbyterian church was becoming increasingly centralised as the result of the takeover by an authoritarian party: the lower courts of the church were not even being invited to express their views let alone the membership as a whole. As far as the membership was concerned, a referendum on the ordination of women conducted in the NSW Illawarra Presbytery had 88 per cent voting for female elders and 77 per cent for female ministers. There was little reason to doubt that the result Australia-wide would be similar.[49]

The capacity of the ordination of women question to stir the deepest emotions in the church was demonstrated by the trial for heresy of the Rev Dr Peter Cameron, Principal of St Andrew's College in the University of Sydney. On 2 March 1992 Cameron preached a sermon, entitled 'The Place of Women in the Church', to a congregation of 300 at Ashfield Presbyterian Church. It was not so much for his views on female ordination, which he favoured, but for his view of the Bible, that Cameron was tried and on 18

47 *National Outlook,* October 1991, 21.

48 *The Presbyterian Review*, March, 1992.

49 *The Presbyterian Review*, March, 1992.

March 1993 convicted of heresy. In that sermon, in commenting on Paul's injunction to women to keep silent and not to teach or have authority over men, Cameron asked:

> Are we bound by his views? I think not. It's not simply that his views are time-bound, it is actually possible that he got things wrong. There is no reason why Paul should have been infallible – indeed I should admire him less if he were infallible. You don't learn very much from perfect beings: you learn most from people who are just a little better than yourself.

So much for the status of the argument against the ordination of women: however much people quote I Timothy 2.13, the answer should simply be: 'So what?'[50]

Such a cavalier view of the Bible embarrassed those evangelicals who favoured the ordination of women. Cameron went further, agreeing with a TV reporter's suggestion that parts of the Bible were 'rubbish'. It became difficult to imagine how, if a Church had any penalties for heresy, Cameron could escape those penalties. To ignore the Bible whenever it fails to accord with one's own preconceptions was to capitulate totally to the forces of secularism. The Presbyterians, however, were no longer capitulators as they had been in the days of Samuel Angus!

Meanwhile, the Rev Joy Bartholomew and the Rev Theodora Hobbs took the General Assembly's reversal on female ordination to the NSW Supreme Court. The case was heard from 13–15 August, 1992. The General Assembly had already decided that those women who had been ordained would remain that way since they had been ordained by God. So Judge J. Brownie accepted the argument of the Procurator, Garry Downes, that he should not even consider the matter as the pecuniary interests of the ordained females was not affected.[51] The decision was similar to that made at about the same time affecting Anglican ordinations, but with the opposite result, namely that the courts had no role in such a matter as no property was involved, and that therefore the court could not prohibit the ordination of women.

The effect of the decision on the few women who had been ordained in the Presbyterian Church invites analysis. They appear to have started as evangelicals. Did it become necessary to depart from their evangelicalism in order to

---

50 *SMH*, 25 November 1992.

51 *Bartholomew v Ramage*, Unreported, NSWSC Eq Div, Brownie J, 4 September 1992, No. 6148/91.

maintain their sense of calling to the ministry? It is possible that the answer to that question is 'no'. They were ordained for the most part in the 1970s before second wave feminism reached its zenith, at least in the church, and because they were not primarily motivated by feminism, they were not tempted to adopt its more radical antipathy to religion as a patriarchal construct.

Joy Bartholomew was the daughter of missionaries who had worked for the Sudan Interior Mission. Her parents were very conservative evangelicals, but both of them strongly supported her in her calling to the ministry. Joy believes that the move for the ordination of women in the Presbyterian Church owed much to the mission field and also to the influence of deaconesses and those women who had been allowed to become elders since 1967. She was not aware that she was influenced by the feminist movement in any way: second phase feminism seemed to blossom in the church after the move for female ordination had been approved. She suspects that opponents of female ordination were influenced by their own reaction to feminism more than proponents were influenced by the movement itself.

Bartholomew was ordained by the Presbytery of North Sydney in 1976, and served in West Wyalong, NSW, Newcastle, and for 15 years at the NSW rural town of Corowa as assistant minister to Arnold, her also ordained husband. At West Wyalong she was asked to do nothing 'ministerial', by which the elders meant that they did not want her to preach. So she didn't. She taught Scripture and was asked, indeed expected, to supply the pulpit (preach) in a large number of surrounding towns as far afield as Orange – just not in West Wyalong. At Corowa she always felt accepted. The members of her church were certainly interested in the experiment and they sympathised with her in 1991 when the Presbyterian Church reversed its decision to ordain female ministers. In 1999 she was appointed as head minister of St Andrew's Presbyterian Church, adjacent to Parliament House, Canberra, with Arnold as her assistant. There she did not feel at all constrained to move from her evangelical, biblical faith. The Mission Statement of her church read: 'To provide an effective witness to the Gospel of Jesus Christ in the Presbyterian and Reformed tradition within the ACT and beyond'.

Theodora Hobbs (1931–2011) also started her Christian life as an evangelical: she was converted at a Crusader Camp at the age of 12. She was ordained on 19 February 1988, the last woman to be ordained by the Presbyterian Church. She was by no means a typical conservative evangelical: her tastes were too broad. Serving on the Church and Nation Committee of the Presbyterian Church, she co-authored a minority report on the divisive issue of abortion, in which she parted company with the conservatives.[52] She was twice married and twice divorced, the second time to Ian Edwards, grandson of John Edwards, chief supporter of Samuel Angus, the most notorious of the Australian Presbyterian Church's 'heretics', even if he was never condemned as such. So Hobbs certainly had an appetite for flirting with heresy. Yet, even in her case, she may not have moved irrevocably from her evangelical foundations. Joy Bartholomew believes that Hobbs had not departed from evangelical faith, at least not in the last decades of her life when Joy knew her best.[53]

Dr Margaret Yee was ordained in 1977 by the Presbytery of Sydney. She served in the Parish of Roseville and Scots Church in Sydney. The growing opposition to her ordination distressed her. Her subsequent remarkable career may have owed something to her reaction to this opposition. But a bigger challenge was to come. She was highly intelligent and would probably have gone to Oxford anyway to study theology. But shortly after her arrival there she suffered a subarachnoid haemorrhage and almost died. In response to these twin challenges, she forged at Oxford a theology of hope. She studied for her doctorate the 'principles of knowing' in the theology of Austin Farrer. She concluded that both in science and theology the horizons were too circumscribed, by positivism in science and fundamentalism in religion. It is necessary to use intuition, imagination and life experience and to seek a holistic view of the convergence of research from many different fields. Near death, either of one's vocation or of health, is enriching if one remains open to the possibility of transcending it through the resources of faith. It is rather by crossing such a horizon, that is, through facing such difficulties, that transcendence is attained so that we can see new horizons and arrive at a stronger understanding of life and love. Jesus traversed those horizons by facing the horrors of pain and suffering.

It was an approach which she found in Schleiermacher and Tillich as well as in Farrer, and we do seem to have travelled a long way from her evangelical roots. Indeed, such a journey may have been initiated for her by Crawford Miller, the unorthodox theologian under whom she had studied in Sydney. Miller had opposed Billy Graham's 1959 crusades in Australia which was enough to put him forever outside of the evangelical camp. But Miller insisted

52 Theodora Hobbs, Sydney Thornton, and Vera Ryan, *Abortion: Factors to Consider: A Minority Report* (Sydney: Church and Nation Committee, NSW Assembly, 1991), http://www.churchandnation.pcnsw.org.au/Images/C%20&%20N%201991.pdf. Accessed 18 September 2016.

53 Joy Bartholomew interviewed by Stuart Piggin, 12 April 2013.

that Scripture should be used to straighten out wayward thinking, an approach which commended itself to evangelicals.[54] And Yee's mature position was also in a trajectory consistent with evangelicalism rather than away from it: she insisted, for example, that the heart of faith is not found only in our relationship with God's love, but is to be grounded in 'documentary factors', that is Scripture, and the 'images of revelation' which it alone contains.[55] Yee's 'theology of hope' was of practical import in a suffering world: The Japanese government, for example, employed her to bring positivity to the business world which in tough times economically had experienced an epidemic of suicide among entrepreneurs and employees. Yee was to serve as Chaplain of Nuffield College, Oxford, as a Senior Research Fellow in Science and Religion at Oxford and was awarded a Templeton Scholarship to study the relationship of science and religion.

The Anglicans were in a different situation from the Presbyterians. In the late 1970s the reaction to feminism was not nearly as fierce in the churches as it was to become in the 1980s and 1990s. The Presbyterians had ordained women before anti-feminism burned most fiercely. The Anglicans, by contrast, sought to ordain women at the height of the blaze, that is at the same time as the Presbyterians, now more conservative in the wake of the formation of the Uniting Church in 1977, sought to stop any more ordinations.

On 23 December 1991 Owen Dowling, the Bishop of the Anglican Diocese of Canberra & Goulburn, announced that he intended to ordain eleven women as priests on 2 February 1992. On 3 January Archbishop Robinson wrote under his episcopal seal, invoking the bishop's oath of obedience to him as Metropolitan, and directing him not to proceed. Dowling replied on 10 January that he was not obliged to obey the Archbishop's opinion. To this the Archbishop replied on 24 January, pointing out that he had not asked for his opinions to be accepted, but his direction.

The gloves were off. Behind the two combatants were the organisations which represented each side of the contest, including the Movement for the Ordination of Women (MOW) and the Association for the Apostolic Ministry (AAM). Behind them were the convictions and world views which made this perhaps the most divisive issue which the Church had confronted

---

54 Mark Hutchinson, *Iron in Our Blood: A History of the Presbyterian Church in NSW, 1788–2001* (Sydney: Ferguson Publications and the Centre for the Study of Australian Christianity, 2001), 319, 368.

55 Margaret May Yee, 'The validity of theology as an academic discipline: a study in the light of the history and philosophy of science and with special reference to relevant aspects of the thought of Austin Farrer', DPhil, Oxford, 1987.

in its Australian history. It was a dispute which caused new alignments in the Church: conservative Anglo-Catholics sided with conservative evangelicals to resist what they perceived to be a feminist onslaught, and evangelicals were divided among themselves.

It was a new and unnerving experience for Bible-believing Christians to be in such fundamental disagreement with each other. A growing number of evangelical scholars were identified with the pro-ordination movement.[56] Some argued that the proper understanding of the Scriptures and the Gospel of unity and liberation made it very important to ordain women. While recommending caution in cultures where women's rights are still largely unrecognised, they argued that, in societies where such rights are recognised, female ordination is essential for the prosperity of the Gospel: '… for the sake of the gospel we've got to move fast so we don't lose another generation of men and women who find church is something they can't stomach.'[57]

Archbishop Donald Robinson never wavered in his opposition to female ordination. He had not changed in his thinking since 1949 when he read in the *Reformed Theological Review* Donovan Mitchell's 'Women and the Ministry: Whither Exegesis?', an 'article I regard as the most important I have ever read on the topic'.[58] In an attempt to explain why New Testament scholars have failed to reach agreement on 'the mind of Christ' in this matter, Mitchell contended that scholars have dispensed with 'two instruments of thought' which Christ entrusted to the apostles, the apostolic tradition and the law or norm of nature. Robinson admitted that he found it difficult to take seriously any case for the ordination of women which neglected to take the apostolic tradition into account. He believed that the all-male priesthood is an essential part, not of the Gospel, but of the apostolic tradition (paradosis), of which the Gospel is but part. This apostolic tradition has three major strands: the Gospel (e.g. I Corinthians 15.1ff.); teaching on moral conduct (e.g. I Thessalonians 4.1–8); and teaching on church order or conduct in the congregation. The proposal to ordain women violates the last, but any violation of the apostolic

56 Michael Green and David Watson who were among the best-known of English evangelical clergy; J. Ward Gasque, Professor of New Testament at Regent College, Vancouver; Klaas Runia, Professor of Practical Theology at the Reformed Seminary, Kampen, Netherlands; John Buchanan, Principal of St John's College, Nottingham; Leon Morris, principal of Ridley College, Melbourne; Paul Jewett, Fuller Theological Seminary, California; F.F. Bruce, Manchester University; David Scholer, Northern Baptist Theological Seminary; and I.H. Marshall, Reader in New Testament Exegesis, Aberdeen University.

57 Elaine Storkey, sociologist and Director of Christian Impact, founded by John Stott, from the *Priscilla Papers,* published by Christians for Biblical Equality, 15.2, 1991, 14.

58 *Southern Cross,* March 1985, 7.

tradition is unacceptable because it is a violation of Scripture, to obey which is required by the Constitution of the Anglican Church.

On 16 January 1992 Dr Laurie Scandrett, a Sydney layman and two clergymen, Dalba Primmer from Canberra & Goulburn Diocese and David Robarts from Melbourne, commenced proceedings in the NSW Supreme Court to restrain Bishop Dowling from ordaining women without a General Synod Canon. They then asked Dowling to hold off the ordination until the matter had been heard. Dowling refused to give such an undertaking, so the plaintiffs applied for an injunction preventing Dowling from proceeding before the matter was determined. On 28 January Mr Justice Rogers dismissed the application. The plaintiffs then appealed to the Supreme Court of NSW Court of Appeal. On 31 January Justices Gleeson, Samuels, and Meagher upheld the appeal, and Dowling was restrained from the ordination pending the final determination of the proceedings.[59] Exasperated, he denounced 'the outlook and attitudes of the controlling faction in the Diocese of Sydney, the most conservative diocese in the whole of the world-wide Anglican communion … who turn questionable tradition into immutable law'.[60]

On 7 March 1992 Archbishop Carnley of Perth announced that he intended to ordain ten women to the priesthood anyway. An attempt by four plaintiffs to restrain the Archbishop failed, and Carnley, carried out the historic ordination. The symbolic significance of this step can hardly be over-estimated. It breached the dyke holding back the rising tide of support for female ordination, it was taken by the media as the event for which they had been clamouring, and, precisely because it snubbed its nose at the cumbersome procedures of the legalists, it gave heart to supporters who were longing for a bishop to take on the establishment. One small step for Carnley was a giant step for womankind.

On 27 June 1992 a Diocesan Conference, with speakers 'generally recognised as being within the evangelical tradition of the Anglican Church of Australia',[61] was held at St John's Parramatta. It was chaired by Bishop Harry Goodhew, soon to be elected Archbishop of Sydney, and the speakers included Chris Forbes, Macquarie University academic, and Kevin Giles, a Melbourne cleric, who gave the case for Biblical equality, and David Peterson and Glenn Davies, both Moore College lecturers, who presented the traditionalist case.

59 Scandrett v Dowling and Ors, Friday 31 January 1992.

60 *Church Scene*, 7 February 1992, 17.

61 10/91 Ordination of Women to the Priesthood: A Report to the Synod, paragraph 3. Online at https://portal.sds.asn.au/sites/default/files/reports/O/OrdinationOfWomenToPriesthood.1993.pdf?doc_id=MjY4MzE=. Accessed 27 September 2017.

The conference caused much excitement. It was attended by over 370 people, the majority favouring the ordination of women. The report of the synod committee who organised the conference claimed to be written 'firmly and unashamedly from an evangelical perspective'.[62] The issue was not whether the authority of Scripture should be accepted – it was accepted by all parties. Differences, then, between evangelicals are to be attributed to differences in exegesis (the understanding of Scripture in its original context) and in hermeneutics (the way the results of the exegesis are to be applied in today's world). The pro-ordination forces were heartened by the conference, and indeed the report is a worthy document which demonstrates, unlike any previous synod document, the strength of the pro-ordination case from a biblical viewpoint.

The impression that the tide was beginning to flow in favour of female ordination was reinforced by the secular court. The judges in the adjourned Scandrett v Dowling case ruled in July 1992 that the NSW Anglican Church of Australia Constitution Act of 1961 does not have binding force at general law except in regard to matters of Church property, and since no property issue was at stake, the judges dismissed the proceedings.[63]

From 6 to 10 July the General Synod met in Sydney. Brisbane Archbishop Peter Hollingworth proposed a canon to remove any English law which might prevent women from being ordained. Archbishop Donald Robinson declared that the bill was morally and theologically wrong and pleaded with delegates, 'Go back! You are going the wrong way!' The motion was passed and was sent to the Church's diocesan synods for comment. Because motions bearing on the ordination of women were not to become effective immediately, Susanne Glover, MOW's 'theologian', walked out of the Public Gallery and out of the Church, taking herself into exile. Patricia Hayward, Convenor of MOW (Sydney), could not recall the scene without tears.

On 21 November 1992 the General Synod of the Anglican Church of Australia met in Sydney. In his presidential address, the Primate, Archbishop Rayner of Melbourne, reminded members that the dioceses in favour of the ordination of women had acted with remarkable restraint and to deny them now the opportunity to proceed as they had wished for so long would stretch their goodwill to breaking point. He added that the overwhelming support of church members for the ordination of women was now evident, and that the Church of England and the Church of the Province of South Africa had both legislated to ordain women. It was not an impartial address and it distressed

62 10/91 Ordination of Women to the Priesthood: A Report to Synod, paragraph 6.

63 Scandrett & Ors v Dowling & Ors, 3 July 1992, Supreme Court of New South Wales Court of Appeal.

opponents of the ordination of women, but the Primate made it clear that he had had enough. He concluded:

> This question has been before us for almost twenty years. It has rightly claimed our attention, because it is an issue with profound human as well as ecclesiastical implications. But we have been distracted long enough from tackling other parts of our Christian mission. The time has come to resolve this matter and move ahead.[64]

Some Sydney delegates had one more card to play. They called for an open ballot rather than a secret ballot. They suspected that two of the Sydney delegates would not vote openly against their archbishop, but might do so in a secret ballot. Bedlam. The mover of the open ballot motion withdrew. The result was announced at 10 minutes to 5. The Synod resolved by just two votes to allow dioceses to ordain women as priests.[65] It was the crossing of the Rubicon, but Sydney diocese had no intention of doing what it was now allowed to do.

By the time of Harry Goodhew's election as Archbishop on 1 April 1993, most members of the Sydney Synod were exhausted by the debate on the ordination of women. They agreed to a moratorium on the debate for the first three years of his episcopate. The proposal for the moratorium was put by Tim Harris, a strong supporter of female ordination. It was a motion not supported by MOW, which argued that three years was too long for some women. Indeed, now that ordination to the priesthood in other dioceses was an option, Sydney women were leaving the diocese.[66] Janet Scarfe estimated in 1995 that by then one in five of the women ordained as priests in the Australian Church had links with the Diocese of Sydney.[67]

---

64 Keith Rayner, Supplementary Presidential Address, 21 November 1992, *Proceedings of the General Synod, Anglican Church of Australia*, 1992.

65 The voting was:
In the house of laity (99 members) 69 for and 30 against.
In the house of clergy (99 members) 67 for and 32 against.
In the house of bishops (22 members) 16 for and 4 against, 2 informal.

66 By October 1994 the following women from Sydney had been ordained to the priesthood in other dioceses: Sue Pain, Claire Percival, Sue Watkins, Sue Watson, Barbara Darling, Helen Granowski, Beatrice Pate, Robyn Payne, Peta Sherlock, Julia Perry, Judy Peterkin, Rosemary Perrott, Marie Kingston, Ruth Mills, Marcia Green, Lu Piper, Colleen O'Reilly. Two Sydney women ordained in other dioceses have been made bishops: Barbara Darling and Genieve Blackwell.

67 *SMH*, 2 December 1995.

In the three years of the 44th synod, 1996–98, the proposal was debated to allow ordination to the priesthood without headship of a congregation, where women could become priests, not rectors. The mover of the motion, Justice Keith Mason, was then Solicitor-General for NSW. Synod was a legal environment and judges were esteemed advisers in synod debates, but Mason's legal eminence was not appreciated by the conservatives who ensured that he did not get elected to Standing Committee during Goodhew's episcopate. Mason was seconded by the one on whose shoulders Patricia Brennan's mantle had alighted, Julia Baird, then a doctoral student and one of three co-convenors of MOW Sydney. It was not enough, however, to be legally astute or academically able to win the support of the conservatives: one had to be theologically strong as well. For the conservatives, the sole basis for opposition or support of female ordination was biblical. They were convinced that it was contrary to the Word of God and therefore they could not countenance it. They saw the Mason/Baird proposal as the thin end of the wedge and in the 1996 vote said 'no', by a considerable margin in the house of clergy, but 49 per cent of the laity supported the proposal. The diocese was clearly torn in two over the issue.

At the 1997 Synod Goodhew proposed that a special conference of Synod members be devoted solely to discuss the matter of female ordination. It was held at Trinity Grammar School on 16 May 1998. The pro-case was entitled 'Not Compromise; Not Uniformity; But Liberty: A Case for the Ordination of Women to the Priesthood'. The issue of the analogy of the subordination of the Son of God in the Trinity was raised for the first time in a Synod debate on female ordination. Just as Jesus is not subordinate to the Father in the Trinity, so women should not be subordinated to men in the Church. The opposition seemed to have been genuinely surprised and disconcerted by this argument. The Sydney diocesan Doctrine Commission undertook to investigate it. The next year, 1999, they produced their report 'The Doctrine of the Trinity and its Bearing on the Relationship of Men and Women'. Theologian Kevin Giles responded with a *magnum opus* on the subject, in which he suggested that the Sydney Doctrine Commission's report was in danger of falling into Arianism,[68] a charge anticipated by MOW theologian Susanne Glover in 1984 (chapter 13) and repeated in the

68 Kevin N Giles, *The Trinity and Subordinationism: The Doctrine of God and the Contemporary Gender Debate* (Downers Grove: InterVarsity Press, 1999).

next decade by the then Anglican Primate, Archbishop Carnley of Perth (chapter 17).

It was a robust affair. Goodhew thought the special Synod at Trinity was a failure. He made one more throw of the dice in his 1998 Synod presidential address. He said that he had been asked by some to make his own position plain. He concluded a long section on the employability of women with the words:

> So where do I stand? In fact I don't. I pray … However I am persuaded that convictions about the role of women in ministry are not to be placed in the category of beliefs 'necessary for salvation'. In our Australian Church it is possible for women to be made priests. Should the Synod of this diocese ever decide to act in that way, it could. If you ask me whether I would withhold my consent if such a decision were made, my reply … would be tentative but I would not withhold consent.[69]

The conservatives were shocked. Bruce Ballantine-Jones, an intrepid opponent of female ordination and President of the ACL, expressed his disappointment at the 'bombshell' of the Archbishop's announcement that he was prepared to sign a bill authorising the priesting of women. Now the conservatives would have to oppose not only the ordination of women, but the Archbishop as well. For fight on they must and 'never give up'. Upholding the Bible on this matter had to take precedence over concern for the feelings of those who 'lose'. Never before, contended Ballantine-Jones, had the diocese been put in a position where those who held the Archbishop dear at a personal level had to oppose him because 'loyalty to God demands it'. Furthermore, other Gospel causes would suffer as time and energy were expended 'on this terrible conflict'.[70] 'In my judgment,' Goodhew replied, 'people like Morris, Bruce, Runia, Fee, Stott, and Graham Cole, to mention but a few, cannot be brushed off as liberals with scant regard for Scripture or the ready victims of rampant feminism.'[71] He was concerned that the conservatives were becoming unreasonable and destructive in the practical outworkings of their position.

Thanks largely to Ballantine-Jones's efforts, the exclusives were now in a majority in the Synod and an overwhelming majority in the Standing Committee. Any efforts to raise the matter of female ordination in the last two years of Goodhew's episcopate were put quickly to the sword.

---

69 R.H. Goodhew, 'Presidential Address', 12 October 1998, *Yearbook of the Diocese of Sydney* (Sydney: Diocesan Registry, 1990), 350.

70 Bruce Ballantine-Jones to Harry Goodhew, 23 October 1998.

71 Harry Goodhew to Bruce Ballantine-Jones, undated, perhaps late October 1998.

Issues Arising from Homosexuality

Those opposed to the ordination of women were quick to claim that it would lead to the ordination of practising homosexuals.[72] Pressure for 'gay rights' had been gathering momentum since the 1970s. In NSW in 1984 Neville Wran's Labor Government decriminalised male homosexual behaviour.[73] In 1997 Tasmania decriminalised homosexual practice, the last of the Australian states to do so.[74] Sydney has one of the largest gay and lesbian communities in the English-speaking world. Their number exceeding that of church-going Anglicans in Sydney in the mid-1990s, they were a political force.[75]

Acceptance of homosexual practice and the ordination of homosexuals became the most divisive issues in church circles in the 1990s and beyond. The first instinct of most evangelical church congregations was to become increasingly conservative on both issues. NSW Baptists in 1990 objected to the 'indecent, blasphemous and obscene acts' exhibited in the annual Gay and Lesbian Mardi Gras in Sydney.[76] 'Freedom from homosexuality through the power of Jesus Christ' was the mission of Exodus, an evangelical organisation, the Australian branch of which was formed in 1987, and which offered to 'help liberate gays from their bondage'. Peter and Jenny Stokes, members of Crossway, Victoria's largest Baptist Church, established 'Salt Shakers' in 1994 to campaign politically against such destructive developments as poker machines and acceptance of 'the homosexual lifestyle'.

Most Christian denominations resisted the pressure to accommodate homosexual ministers. Sydney Anglicans were prominent in the decision made at the 1998 Lambeth Conference to declare homosexual practice incompatible with Scripture. Baptists in Victoria and WA resolved decisively in 1998 to refuse to ordain practising homosexuals.[77] NSW Baptists the following year also determined that a homosexual could not be a leader in its churches.[78] The Lutheran Church of Australia welcomed non-practising homosexuals as

72 David Hilliard, 'Sydney Anglicans and Homosexuality', *Journal of Homosexuality*, 33:2, 1997, 116.

73 Hilliard, 'Sydney Anglicans and Homosexuality', 101–123.

74 The first was SA, 1975.

75 Hilliard, 'Sydney Anglicans and Homosexuality', 101; David Hilliard, 'Australian Anglicans and homosexuality: a tale of two cities', *St Mark's Review*, 163, Spring 1995,12–20.

76 Ken R. Manley, *From Woolloomooloo to 'Eternity': A History of Australian* Baptists (Milton Keynes: Paternoster, 2006), 669.

77 Munro, 'A History of Victorian Baptists', 287.

78 Manley, *From Woolloomooloo to Eternity*, 2, 669–672.

members, but resolved not to ordain them. No Churches of Christ congregations approved leadership by homosexual ministers.

Only in the Uniting Church did the impulse to treat homosexuality as a social justice issue make headway against the resistance of the conservatives, and that was not finally achieved until the first decade of the next century. But the struggle was well and truly joined in the 1990s. The Sixth Assembly of the Uniting Church (1991) appointed a Sexuality Task Force to study the issue and bring a report to the 1997 Assembly. In 1996 it made an interim report to canvass reactions from members. It found members were totally divided on the issue:

> For some respondents the directions put forward for prayerful consideration in the Interim Report indicated 'a capitulation to the spirit of the age and a departure from received Biblical and Church teaching.' For others it indicated 'a new movement of the Spirit in the direction of a more gracious and inclusive Church.'[79]

The Task Force's final report, *Uniting Sexuality and Faith*, was based on thinking which unnerved conservatives. The 'Wesleyan Quadrilateral' which added tradition, reason and experience to Scripture as sources for understanding faith had always made conservative evangelicals uncomfortable. But the Task Force went further, suggesting that 'revelation' (reflecting the growing Charismatic presence in the Uniting Church) and 'culture' (reflecting the strong liberal faction) might be added to the other four. The report's authors referred to 'the writer to the Ephesians' rather than St Paul. They advanced a new understanding of 'ethics', departing from the traditional biblical ethics most members of the church would have accepted, and from the 'situation ethics' of which some may have become aware, to an 'ethics of character' with which few would have been familiar. It was evident that members of the Task Force had undergone a self-education programme on matters of sexuality which would have made them feel way ahead of church members, but with which, given time, most members would catch up. The formula beloved of the conservatives, 'Celibacy in Singleness and Faithfulness in Marriage', it criticised as underestimating the complexities of human sexuality (p.54). It affirmed (p.52) a person with a homosexual orientation is no less fit for ministry than a heterosexual person and (p.71) that it should not be a bar to ordination.

79 *Uniting Sexuality and Faith: Final Report of the Assembly Task Group on Sexuality For presentation to the Eighth Assembly of the Uniting Church in Australia, July 1997* (Melbourne: Uniting Church Press, 1997), 7.

The authors of the report confessed (p.7) that they had failed to engage the Uniting Aboriginal and Islander Christian Congress and ethnic congregations in dialogue. It was therefore not surprising that, when the report was debated at the Eighth General Assembly of the Uniting Church in Australia in Perth in July 1997, the Aboriginal contingent at the Assembly walked out in protest, arguing that homosexual practice was contrary to both their faith and their culture.[80] About 85 per cent of responses to the Report were against the proposals. This delayed, but did not halt, the push towards acceptance by the Uniting Church of the ordination of homosexual ministers. That action, taken eventually in 2003, was imposed on the majority of the church's membership by supporters of gay rights who achieved political ascendency in the General Assembly. It led to what the conservatives assessed as catastrophic haemorrhaging of the church's membership[81] (we will continue the story in chapter 18).

An interesting indicator of the pace of change in social and moral values is that *Uniting Sexuality and Faith* defined marriage as between a man and a woman. While it recommended (p.72) the development of resources to allow for the church affirmation of same-sex lifelong relationships, same-sex marriage as late as 1997 was not on the radar, even in the Uniting Church. But clearly changes were inundating traditional institutions far more rapidly than they were able to be processed. By the end of the second Christian millennium, the Christian church in general and evangelicals in particular were seriously divided on a range of moral issues. It remained to be determined whether or not the division would be permanent.

---

80 Kelly, 'Dreaming Dreams', 9.

81 Peter Bentley 'These Statistics Don't Lie – Church Members have Left in Droves', *Catalyst* (Sydney), December 2007, 12–14; Keith D. Suter, 'The Future of the Uniting Church in Australia', PhD, University of Sydney, 2013, 51f.

Chapter Sixteen

TENSIONS AND INITIATIVES WITHIN THE EVANGELICAL MOVEMENT IN THE 1990S

'the long-term capacity for sustainability and reconfiguration within the evangelical tradition resides not in any supposedly monolithic homogeneity and conformity, but rather in conflictual heterogeneity.'
(Rob Warner)

In secularisation evangelicals faced an enemy potentially lethal to faith. Failure threatened. By the 1990s traditional methods and strategies had ceased to deliver growth. Billy Graham was growing old and no heir had been found: mass evangelism had lost its drawing power. The Bible was still revered as the Word of God by all evangelicals, but the habit of reading it daily had died. At the beginning of the new century, John Stott insisted on the value of the Quiet Time, the daily prayerful reading of the Bible. But it was a discipline no longer prized or practised: sales of SU notes in Britain declined by more than 50 per cent in the fifteen years to 2000.[1] Biblical knowledge declined with it. A report prepared for the EA in Britain said, 'It is important to recognise that in our present culture there are no easy routes to fast and numerous conversions.'[2] In this post-Christian world, conversion 'has become a much longer journey than it used to be, and that requires a profound re-imagining of the tasks of evangelism and catechesis'.[3]

It was not that evangelicals had failed to experiment with new ways. The problem was that many experiments had been tried, but they chronically failed to deliver what they promised: 'church growth theory; the confluence

1 Rob Warner, *Reinventing English Evangelicalism, 1966–2001: A Theological and Sociological Study* (Milton Keynes: Paternoster, 2007), 87.

2 Warner, *Reinventing English Evangelicalism*, 105.

3 Warner, *Reinventing English Evangelicalism*, 106.

of healing and evangelism in a revival movement led by the 'neocharismatic' John Wimber; church planting; seeker services; intercessory prayer and "spiritual warfare"; cell church; restorationism; prosperity teaching; and even the traditionalist, unvarnished preaching of the Calvinistic gospel.'[4] All failed not because of inadequate effort, observed English sociologist Rob Warner, but because of inflated expectations which took insufficient notice of secularisation. Progressive evangelicals had invested in enthusiastic rhetoric in support of their new schemes, while the panacea of the conservative evangelicals was a combination of traditional ethical standards and the theology of the Reformers.

The Charismatic branch of the evangelical movement did best in this period with its culturally apposite music and worship services and its theology of encouragement addressed to human need. But by the 1990s the very rapid growth in Pentecostal churches was already in the past. In any case, the Charismatic solution was not open to traditional evangelicals: they believed that the special gifts of the Spirit (the pneumatica[5] of 1 Corinthians 12, including tongues, healings, prophecy) had ceased at the end of the Apostolic age and that the Bible should not be used as a self-help manual. But while many evangelicals were unenthusiastic about the Charismatic movement, they could not agree on what they ought to be enthusiastic about. In responding to the challenges of secularism, they were divided between those who wanted purity of faith (conservatives) and those who wanted a welcoming faith (progressives). Of the three clear camps now within the evangelical movement (conservatives, progressives, and Charismatics/Pentecostals), none seemed to have the answer. Indeed, the division into three camps created its own problem. Most evangelicals so strongly identified with one of the three that it looked as if the centre of the evangelical movement would no longer hold.

Evangelicalism has been rightly defined as 'culturally adaptive biblical experientialism'.[6] Now there were three distinct ways for biblical experientialist Christianity to adapt to the culture. The differing emphases of conservative, progressive and Charismatic evangelicals in their approaches to the Bible and doctrine are summarised in Table 3.[7]

---

4 Warner, *Reinventing English Evangelicalism,* 62,63.

5 The pneumatica (spiritual gifts) of I Corinthians 12 may be distinguished from the charismata (grace gifts) of Romans 12.

6 Mark A. Noll, *American Evangelical Christianity: An Introduction* (Oxford: Blackwell, 2001, 2. See also Mark A. Noll, *The Rise of Evangelicalism: The Age of Edwards, Whitefield, and the Wesleys, A History of Evangelicalism* (Downers Grove: InterVarsity Press, 2003), 47–50.

7 This table summarises the discussion in Warner, *Reinventing English Evangelicalism*, 221. Warner's own table, which deals only with the left and centre columns, is found on 222.

Table 3. Evangelical Groupings in the 1990s

Conservatives	Progressives	Charismatics and Pentecostals
focus on biblical propositions	focus on the Person of Christ	focus on the Spirit of Christ
doctrine: revelation codified	story: revelation narrated	imagination: revelation interpreted through experience
systematic homogenisation of Scripture	diversity within the unity of Scripture	search for Scripture's prophetic challenge to the present
absolutise the Reformation	relativise the Reformation	more comfortable with their own history
suspicious, oppositional	openly dialogical	confidently assertive; persistently positive
favour textual critical exegesis (lower criticism)	favour historico-critical exegesis (higher criticism)	favour eisegesis
exclusive	inclusive	open and shut
guard the boundaries	affirm the centre: Christocentric and Trinitarian	exploit the possibilities

The left side of the table tended to be favoured by systematic theologians who look for the unchanging and seek to be ever more precise in their definitions of key doctrines. Especially in Britain and America definitions of penal substitution and biblical infallibility and inerrancy were made ever more explicit by conservative evangelicals. In Sydney evangelical Anglicanism, both issues stirred the troubled waters, but not as vigorously as the issues of the ordination of women, lay presidency, and Prayer Book revision, all denominationally-specific, indeed diocesan-specific, issues. The real rift seemed to be between those who had an instinct for inclusion and those who were instinctively exclusivist. Nineteenth-century evangelical doctrine, under the influence of Nonconformity in its heyday, insisted on the right, even the duty, of private judgment. But in the twentieth century evangelicals tended to move away from that understanding as it fostered liberalism, just as for the same reason in the first decade of the twenty-first century conservative Catholics moved away from the sovereignty of conscience as a guide to moral action. Rather than the heterogeneity produced by private judgement, conservative evangelicals at the beginning of the 21st century prefer conformity, a serious departure from Reformation convictions.

Progressive evangelicalism was an attempt at saving evangelicalism from its fundamentalist instincts without succumbing to liberalism. The most controversial of the current crop of professional liberal Christians was John Shelby Spong, the Episcopal bishop of the Diocese of Newark in USA. In 1998 he published *Why Christianity must change or die*. He dismissed the dogmatic core of Christianity as superstition. But the change he called for caused the church to die more rapidly than the refusal to change of the conservatives. Membership of the Episcopal Church in the United States collapsed in the first decade of the 21st century, declining 23 per cent.

Sociologist Robert Bellah contends that at the end of the twentieth century the entrepreneur and the therapist were the two leading cultural features of American life and the churches bought into them, too.[8] Songs sung in most evangelical churches now had a short shelf life, longer than the typical pop song, but not nearly as long as the traditional hymn. Since much evangelical theology was gained from hymn-singing, this reduced the theological acumen of many younger evangelicals. This was the more so because, whereas in the past most hymns were written by clergy, now they were written by musicians who often had little theological training. The thinning of theological knowledge was accompanied by increased indifference towards denominational allegiances.

What was demanded by the lethal challenge of secularism, argued Warner, was the rigorous and reflexive analysis which would provide evangelicals with a coherent socio-political critique of secularised, pluralistic culture.[9] That was a tall order for evangelicals most accustomed to blaming internal weaknesses and infidelities in their movement for the by-now too-chronic failure, but numerous authorities were attempting to redress the problems.[10] In this chapter the ways in which the three evangelical camps in Australia understood and addressed the problems facing them will be explored.

Anglican and Presbyterian Trials and Advances

Among Sydney Anglicans the division into two camps – the one inclusive and entrepreneurial and the other exclusive and defensive – was personified in the two Archbishops elected by the Diocese in the next two decades. Harry Goodhew (1993–2001) was an inclusive evangelical; Peter Jensen (2001–2013), a conservative, exclusive evangelical.

8 Robert N. Bellah, *Habits of the Heart* (Berkeley: University of California Press, 1996).

9 Warner, *Reinventing English Evangelicalism*, 64.

10 David Hilborn, *Movement for Change: Evangelicals and Social Transformation* (Bletchley: Paternoster, 2004); Stanley Hauerwas, Michael G. Cartwright, and John Berkman, *The Hauerwas Reader* (Durham: Duke University Press, 2001); Duncan B. Forrester, William Storrar and Andrew Morton, *Public Theology for the 21st Century: Essays in Honour of Duncan B. Forrester* (London: T&T Clark, 2004).

If Goodhew was an inclusivist, and the most vocal, articulate members of synod were exclusivist, how did he get elected? The simple fact is that the majority of synod members were not exclusivist, and they were not exclusivist because the exclusivists, in their zeal to respond to the urgency of the times, over-played their hand just prior to the election. In 1992 they started a spot-fire which had threatened to burn down the whole edifice, and so the majority in the synod reached for the extinguisher. The threatening conflagration was REPA (the Reformed Evangelical Protestant Association),[11] and the incendiary was Phillip Jensen, exclusivist extraordinaire!

Phillip Jensen believed that the constitutional crisis in the Anglican Church of Australia, precipitated by the fight over the ordination of women, was a good opportunity to make a concerted stand for conservative evangelicalism within the Anglican Church. The 1992 Scandrett vs Dowling judgment allowed dioceses to go their own way without hindrance from the national church. Phillip Jensen saw this as a great opportunity for the Diocese of Sydney to separate itself from what he called 'the liberal Catholicism' of the rest of the Anglican Church of Australia.[12]

REPA was born following a visit which Phillip Jensen paid to the Anglican Primate, Keith Rayner, in Melbourne. Jensen offered the Primate his assistance in dealing with the crisis in the Anglican Church. But Rayner rejected the offer. He argued that, by his calculations, one-third of the clergy of the Sydney Diocese was conservative evangelical, one-third was 'Anglican', and there was a middle third which would be happy to go either way. Since the Diocese of Sydney was actually more Anglican than Sydney's conservative evangelicals would allow, argued the Primate, once women were ordained, the Diocese would settle down.

Bruce Ballantine-Jones, Anglican rector and ecclesiastical politician, maintains that Jensen was made the more determined to counter the national church as the result of this rejection, and REPA was formed in February 1992, by 18 clergymen, rectors of large Anglican churches. Jensen labelled these rectors 'the Colonels,' to distinguish them from the 'Generals', that is, the bishops. Phillip, consistent with the culture of Sydney Anglicanism, did not look to bishops, but to the clergy for change. He initiated the move by sharing with Ballantine-Jones that he wanted to start a revolution. Bruce's late wife, Raema, who was privy to this conversation, observed to Bruce afterwards that Phillip would make an excellent Archbishop. This may have

11 The REPA sources on which this discussion is based were collected by the Rev. Martin Robinson.

12 'The Way ahead for Christian Liberty', *Repaccusions*, 2, December 1992, 8.

been the beginning of the push to make Phillip Archbishop, a push with which REPA became inextricably bound in spite of the protestations of some of its members to the contrary. Its name was devised by Jim Ramsay, rector of Liverpool, on the spur of the moment as the founders needed a name under which to open a bank account. Ramsay came up with 'Reformed Evangelical Protestant Association'. The name was unashamedly theological, and the determination of the founders was to explore and implement changes flowing from that stance. Its opponents branded it as 'fundamentalist' and 'the Opus Dei of the Evangelical World'.

Phillip Jensen was not an ideologue. He was not motivated by the desire either to outflank Rayner or to defeat the more inclusive of the evangelicals. Others behaved as if politics internal to the Church was the main game, but Phillip did not. He believed that the role of the Anglican Church in secular Australia was diminishing to a vanishing point, and that the best way to reverse this trend was to have 'more and more people out and about preaching the gospel of Jesus Christ and gathering up those converted into evangelistically-minded congregations'.[13] He wanted churches to be more determined in their evangelism and more focussed in their methodical teaching of the Bible. This was also what Goodhew wanted. But Phillip Jensen would gladly have jettisoned Anglicanism to get it, whereas Goodhew believed there was more chance of getting it through maintaining evangelical Anglicanism. Jensen was also more disposed than Goodhew to emphasise the crisis facing the Church. 'We face a lack of confidence in the gospel', REPA members were advised, 'expressed by a futile clinging to institutionalism and authoritarianism matched with a great willingness to open ourselves up to every fad and fashion of human philosophy and heresy.'[14] It followed that the compromise had to be rooted out, and a good way of doing that was to conduct an audit of diocesan organisations to assess if they made a positive contribution to Gospel ministry. The main aim was radical reform, but some feared that, like Thomas Cromwell's audit of the monasteries under Henry VIII, its purpose was to close many organisations down altogether.

The storm of emotion unleashed by REPA was fatal to Phillip's prospects of election as archbishop. Politically, his supporters had overplayed their hand, alienating not only those in the Diocese who put Anglicanism ahead of evangelicalism, but also those who favoured inclusive evangelicalism. So, in the synod election for Archbishop in 1993, while Phillip was the choice

13 R.E.P. Association, Statement No.1, 6 March 1992, 3.

14 *Repacussions,* 1, September 1992, 3.

of the minority who wanted a strong leader, he was considered too radical for the majority, who elected Harry Goodhew.

Goodhew was also a radical. But he was radically inclusive, which was contrary to the prevailing Sydney Anglican culture. Goodhew's counter-intuitive appeal to be softer so that Sydney Anglicans could be stronger was rejected by the conservatives. They argued that he was 'not safe with the crown jewels'. The exclusives, accustomed to power, through the agency of the ACL, now regrouped and eventually outflanked the inclusives on all fronts, strengthening their representation on both synod and standing committee.

It is significant that the issues over which the inclusives and exclusives fought in Goodhew's episcopate were not the same as those fought by parallel groups in America or England. In Sydney the inclusives are conservative, too. There was no battle in Sydney over biblical authority or the penal substitutionary theory of the atonement. There was also no opposition to a range of initiatives in Goodhew's time which safeguarded and strengthened the mission of the Church. These included the development of a sexual abuse protocol, the opening of a dozen schools in the diocese which were low-fee Anglican schools, the devoting of much larger resources to indigenous ministry, and the strengthening of parishes. The last was one of the chief reasons for Goodhew's appointment. He did not disappoint there: he poured water on every initiative to grow churches, increased the opportunities for in-service training, and encouraged clergy and laity to attend evangelism and church growth conferences. The result was that at the end of his time in office, the number of people attending Anglican services of worship had increased by 11 per cent, contrary to the experience of every other Anglican diocese in Australia, all of which shrank, some alarmingly, in this decade of runaway secularisation. English sociologist, Rob Warner, argues that the times now favoured 'entrepreneurialism, pragmatism, experientialism and detraditionalisation'. By those criteria Goodhew was a man of his times.[15]

Goodhew's political opponents were distracted, not blocked, from their main agenda which was to grow biblical churches. Phillip Jensen, himself, was central to a momentum which would not be derailed by church politics. It was a momentum which increased the influence of conservative Sydney Anglican evangelicalism on the convention movement (as was seen in chapter 14), on other Anglican dioceses in Australia, on other denominations, mainly the Presbyterians and the Baptists, and in other countries, especially on Anglicanism's home base, England itself.

---

15 Warner, *Reinventing English Evangelicalism*, 236.

The influence of Sydney Anglican evangelicalism on other Australian dioceses took two major forms which now supplemented the contribution which BCA, the evangelical mission society, was making to those dioceses. The first was the strengthening of evangelical parishes in predominantly non-evangelical dioceses, for example Shenton Park in Perth, Holy Trinity Adelaide, St George's Battery Point in Hobart, or St Stephen's Coorparoo in Brisbane. These evangelical churches remained Anglican. But in the 1990s Sydney Anglicans, with Phillip Jensen's active encouragement, began to plant 'generic' evangelical congregations in other dioceses throughout Australia. These were not official diocesan church plants, but were commonly 'affiliated' with a Sydney parish which supported the exporting of 'Gospel ministry' to areas which allegedly were deprived of the same. The Central Coast Evangelical Church at Erina in the Diocese of Newcastle, for example, was openly supported by Christ Church, Gladesville, in Sydney.

Among other denominations, the Presbyterians of NSW had less trouble than most in identifying with the combative mentality of the Sydney Anglicans. Leading up to and following the formation of the Uniting Church in 1977, evangelical Presbyterians had developed links with Moore College to train their ministers. Many young potential ministers had trained with Phillip Jensen's Ministry Training Strategy (MTS). They thus put themselves at some risk of becoming a generic evangelical church rather than distinctively Presbyterian. There was a strong push to replace key leaders in the Presbyterian Church with 'Jensenites'. Difficult this experience may have been for those affected, but arguably it was necessary. The Presbyterian Church might not have survived in NSW were it not for the Anglicans.[16] Upon reflection, however, even those grateful to the Anglicans for helping them in the difficult transition after 1977 did not want to become Anglicans: they were very independently minded and there were things about Presbyterianism which they wanted to preserve, such as its theological understanding of worship.

In Victorian Presbyterianism, too, theological disputation was alive and well in the 1990s.[17] *An Appraisal of the so-called 'Five Points of Calvinism'*, published in 1994, asserted that 'most of "the five points" are simply not true' and '"The tulip theory" is also a doctrine of disunity.'[18] In the same year

16 Paul Cooper to Stuart Piggin, 26 October 2011.

17 Peter Barnes, 'Australian Calvinism: An Impressionistic Snapshot on the 500th Anniversary of Calvin's Birth', *Church Heritage*, 16.2, 2009, 118–126.

18 A.T. Stevens, *An Appraisal of the so-called 'Five Points of Calvinism'* (Brighton: The Burning Bush Society of Victoria, 1994), v.

H.A. Stamp's *The Word of God in the Bible* was published in which he argued that, though the Bible is inspired, it is not infallible.[19] To both these assaults on conservative orthodoxy, the Principal of the Presbyterian Theological College in Melbourne, Douglas Milne, replied ably.[20] No disciplinary action was taken, but the Presbyterians were putting their house in order. The Rev Stewart Gill wrote confidently that 'as the Presbyterian Church of Australia looks forward to the year 2000 there has been a real return to Confessional orthodoxy and the church that had once lost its way has found it again.'[21] 'Jensenite' Sydney Anglicanism had helped them to get there, even if they retained their Presbyterian polity and did not become a 'generic' evangelical church.

Internationally, Sydney Anglicanism was rampant. Phillip Jensen's MTS, 'A *vision*, a *strategy* and a *mindset* all in one', and 'passionate about recruiting and training workers for the vital task of Gospel ministry through ministry apprenticeships',[22] became an export product. By the beginning of Goodhew's reign in 1993 English evangelicalism had become both much stronger in the Church of England than the Liberal and Anglo-Catholic movements, but it was also more divided. Oak Hill College moved to the right, identifying with the conservative Reformed evangelicalism of the Diocese of Sydney, and Wycliffe Hall in Oxford, where Broughton Knox had been on the staff in the 1950s, was heading towards a Sydney takeover at the behest, not of strongly Reformed staff, but of students influenced by Phillip Jensen himself.[23] In 1993 conservative English evangelicals, influenced by Sydney, established the pressure group 'Reform' which has become in the present century the largest evangelical group in Britain.[24]

The solidifying of different styles or camps of evangelicalism may have constituted a crisis for the movement, but it was an opportunity for individual church leaders of entrepreneurial and pragmatic instincts, such as Goodhew

---

19 H.A. Stamp, *The Word of God in the Bible* (Brighton: The Burning Bush Society of Victoria, 1994).

20 Douglas Milne, *The Word of God is the Bible and an Affirmation of the Five Points of Calvinism* (Box Hill North: Presbyterian Theological College, 1994).

21 Stewart Gill, 'The Battle for the Westminster Confession in Australia' in J. Ligon Duncan (ed.), *The Westminster Confession into the 21st Century*, volume 1, Fearn: Mentor, 2003, p.301. Cited in Barnes, 'Australian Calvinism.'

22 Ministry Training Strategy website, http://www.mts.com.au/, accessed 27 March 2012.

23 Andrew Atherstone, 'Evangelicals Fragmented: Theological Tensions at Wycliffe Hall, Oxford, c.1980–95', *Christianity and History Bulletin*, 4, Spring 2008, 34–47.

24 Stephen Bates, *A Church at War: Anglicans and Homosexuality* (London: I.B. Tauris, 2004), 30,116–119.

and Jensen. Another such leader was Paul Harrington, from 1993 rector of Holy Trinity Adelaide, a bastion of evangelical conviction.[25] Converted through the Evangelical Union at the University of Adelaide where he studied law, Harrington had been curate to Reg Piper, the previous rector. Harrington was a strategic thinker who spent his early years as rector in careful planning before leading the parish in a number of successful church plants.

The first church in Adelaide, Holy Trinity had always been a conservative evangelical parish, and it had gone through long periods of going it alone in a High Church diocese, occasionally incurring the wrath of unsympathetic bishops. Harrington did not fear the wrath, and shortly after his appointment he invited Ian George, Archbishop of Adelaide from 1991 to 2004, to preach at a morning service. Afterwards the chairman of trustees was heard to mutter 'that man will never preach at Trinity again'. George presented three problems for the evangelicals of Holy Trinity: he was too liberal in his theology; he allowed practising homosexuals to continue as clergy; and he blocked the appointment of men from Trinity to other Adelaide parishes. But there was no way that Harrington would allow his parish to withdraw into comfortable isolationism. He came to the conclusion that Holy Trinity would have to engage in church planting and that it would have to do it without the Archbishop's blessing.

Contracting attendances and closing churches was a reality in Adelaide, but it was a reality which had to be reversed, not accepted. In the interests of evangelism, a church had to be engaged with the wider community. Successful engagement required deft leadership, and Harrington devoted a lot of time to the selection and training of those he appointed to implement his initiatives, especially extra services on the City site in North Terrace and church plants in other suburbs. As membership and finances grew, so too did the staff. Harrington groomed them for leadership at conferences which were labelled 'attacks' because the word 'retreat' was too defeatist and too high church. He was unsentimental about the trappings of Anglicanism if they interfered with growth. He dispensed with robes, and he even dispensed with the Parish Council whose members, because they were no longer influencing decisions, agreed that there was no point in meeting, and therefore voted the Council out

25 This section on Holy Trinity Adelaide is based on the research of Brian Dickey. See his '"We wanted to make the first one a winner": urban church planting and the origins of "Holy Trinity Hills"' in Geoffrey Treloar and Robert Linder (eds), *Making History for God: essays on evangelicalism, revival and mission* (Sydney: Robert Menzies College, 2004), 169–196; and *Holy Trinity Adelaide 1836–2012: The History of a City Church* (Adelaide: Trinity Church Trustees, 2013), 217–232.

of existence.[26] He retained the strengths of the parish which were critical to the success of all evangelical churches: the tradition of Scripture-based preaching; prioritising evangelism; well-planned Sunday gatherings; a whole-of-week and across-the-age range ministry that engaged everyone, including sustained support for youth work and cross-cultural missionaries. But he focussed on improving the quality of each of these elements. The preaching program, for example, was more carefully planned and sermons were submitted in advance to the critique of the preaching team.

Harrington did not rush in to planting new churches. He had to be fully aware of what was involved. In May 1998 he attended a conference on church planting in Sydney organised by Phillip Jensen. Then from October 1998 he went on a three-month study leave to Wheaton, Billy Graham's college, in Illinois, USA, and was there able to study comprehensively the technology of church planting. Reflecting on all the options, he identified the Hills district of Adelaide as the ideal site. Throughout 1999 and early 2000 he negotiated with the Archbishop who, no doubt eager to block the development, insisted that it should receive synodical approval. On 25 February 2001, in spite of the unresolved tension with the Archbishop, the new congregation, labelled HTA Hills as a marketing strategy, met in the community hall in Aldgate, the first gathering of the first church plant; 220 attended. By 2004 attendances exceeded 300. The minister was Chris Edwards, but he remained responsible to Harrington as his curate, and the church retained the distinctively Holy Trinity focus on evangelism, community service, equipping and ministry. Within the next decade a further four such churches were planted by HTA. By 2012 the number of attendees at HTA churches had doubled the 2000 figure from 800 to 1600. By 2018 there were nine churches in the Trinity Network.[27] It proved that success is achievable through strong leadership in a determinably evangelical church in spite of the hostile forces of secularisation and church politics.

Pentecostal and Charismatic Trials and Victories

Among the factors contributing to the rapid growth in Pentecostal numbers in the last three decades of the twentieth century (as explained in chapter 12)

26 Unlike most parishes, Trinity's Parish Council only existed at the permission of the trustees, since the parish was not governed by the diocesan parochial ordinance, but by its trust deed. It was therefore easier to abolish.

27 Trinity Church Adelaide; Trinity Church Aldgate; Trinity Church Brighton; Trinity Church Mount Barker; Trinity Church Modbury; Trinity Church Victor Harbor; Trinity Church Colonel Gardens; Trinity Church Unley; Trinity Grove.

was openness to the Charismatic renewal, when the mainline churches were hostile or ambiguous about it. The Charismatic renewal was followed by what was labelled by C. Peter Wagner, Professor of Church Growth in Fuller Seminary, Los Angeles, as the 'Third Wave'. The first wave, explained Wagner, was practising the spiritual gifts by Pentecostals, the second by Charismatics, and the third by evangelicals. The third wave was associated particularly with the name of John Wimber and the Vineyard Movement. Vineyard churches, it was claimed, were neither Charismatic nor Pentecostal, but rather 'empowered evangelical'.[28] While they did believe in such Charismatic gifts as healing, deliverance, and prophecy, they did not accept that there was a 'baptism of the Holy Spirit' separate from conversion, nor that 'speaking in tongues' was the only evidence of it. This exercise in differentiation was lost on conservative evangelicals who attacked Wimber with all the weapons they had amassed in their assault on the Charismatic renewal.

The Pentecostal churches did continue to grow strongly in the 1990s. But there were worrying signs. Pentecostal leaders and strategists were troubled by the declining rate of growth in membership of their churches. Whereas those identifying as Pentecostals in the census had increased by 50.4 per cent from 1981 to 1986 and then by 40.8 per cent between 1986 and 1991, it slowed dramatically to 16 per cent between 1991 and 1996 and 11 per cent between 1996 and 2001.[29] Although such a decline is understandable statistically given the low base of the initial figures (29,400 in 1976; 72,100 in 1981), Pentecostal leaders were not inclined to depart from growth as a priority. With 150,600 members in 1991 and 194,585 in 2001, they still had (in each case) only about 1 per cent of the population. They were eager for more, and they had the leader to deliver more.

On the retirement of Andrew Evans in 1997, Brian Houston became AOG's General Superintendent. He changed his title to 'President' and in 2000 he launched Australian Christian Churches (ACC) which showed by its title the nature of his aspirations: to become the biggest and most Australian church movement in the land.[30] But while Pentecostal leaders loved such visions, they were becoming increasingly aware that further growth in their movement would not come easily. They had to block the fallout which occurred when leaders failed morally, a too regular occurrence. They also began to see that to retain membership they would have to feed the flock with more nutritious

28 Rick Nathan and Ken Wilson, *Empowered Evangelicals: Bringing Together the Best of the Evangelical and Charismatic Worlds* (Ann Arbor: Servant Publications, 1995).

29 ABS data.

30 On ACC, see chapter 17 below.

food than was the average diet in the 1980s. Pentecostal theology was typically shallow and ill-defined. Grounded in experience rather than the Word, it was too open to popular psychology which reflected the culture, and too closed to biblical truth which transforms it.

Part of the problem was that pastors were not adequately trained. Whereas 49.9 per cent of Anglican clergy in Australia in 1991 had a degree or higher, only 14.6 per cent of Pentecostal ministers had such.[31] The cure for this was not the multiplication of church-based Bible colleges as was the first instinct of every pastor of a large church. Fewer but better colleges were needed. In Sydney in 1996 there were 60,000 members of Pentecostal churches and five colleges; the Anglicans had about 80,000 attending church each week with only one theological college – Moore – and another – the Sydney Missionary and Bible College – was accepted as providing healthy competition.[32]

That this situation must change was not evident to all Pentecostal leaders at the same time. Ahead of their time were Barry Chant and Dennis Slape, pastors within the Christian Revival Crusade. In 1979 they established Tabor College, a non-denominational liberal arts college in Adelaide. With Chant as founding principal, Tabor established campuses in Melbourne in 1988, Sydney and Perth in 1992, and in Hobart in 1999. But the campuses, consistent with their tradition, went their own way. Meanwhile another route to a national college in the Pentecostal tradition was navigated. In 1992 David Cartledge, whom we met in chapter 14, was appointed principal of the Commonwealth Bible College (CBC). Earlier he had destabilised CBC by encouraging local churches to establish their own bible colleges. He changed its name to Southern Cross College (SCC) – in 2009 it was renamed Alphacrucis after the brightest star in the Southern Cross.[33] Cartledge moved it from Katoomba to Chester Hill in Sydney 1996. He wanted it to be at the same time both a Holy Ghost college and the equal of the best universities. He led it for a decade with colossal energy which was almost, but not quite, equal to the heavy hand of accreditation requirements increasingly imposed on tertiary institutions. When the dean of an accrediting college proved difficult to satisfy, Cartledge accused him of élitism and prejudice against Pentecostals. SCC's future was not assured after a decade of his leadership. But a foundation had been laid

31 1991 Census, ABS data.

32 Ian Jagelman, 'Church Growth: Its Promise and Problems for Australian Pentecostalism', *Australian Pentecostal Studies,* 1, 1998, online at http://webjournals.ac.edu.au/journals/aps/issue-1/church-growth-its-promise-and-problems-for-austral/

33 Denise A. Austin, *Our College: A History of the National College of Australian Christian Churches* (Parramatta: Australian Pentecostal Studies, 2013).

which would allow the college to mature in tandem with the maturity of the movement it serviced, and that would require another decade of effort on behalf of those who supported the national college.

The 1990s probably represents the consolidation, even bureaucratisation, of an inherently unbureaucratic movement. It was a process, however, which left plenty of room for surprises. Among those surprises was a dazzling Charismatic efflorescence known as the Toronto Blessing. Another surprise was that 'Alpha' an instrument of evangelism in a Charismatic Anglican church in London enjoyed international acceptance in churches Catholic as well as Protestant. It met resistance, unsurprisingly, from the conservative evangelicals who also sought to extinguish the Toronto Blessing. A third surprise in this decade was that the world's most successful tennis player became the head pastor of a Pentecostal Church – nothing surprising that this pastor combined success, celebrity and sport – but this pastor was … a woman: Margaret Smith Court.

The Charismatic movement struggled in the mainline churches from the early 1970s, but it did experience in 1994–95 a volcano which gave Charismatics hope that they would yet see a great awakening. The Toronto Blessing[34] may have been the first religious mass movement in the English-speaking world transmitted through the new technology: it was known as 'the internet revival'. It is customary to date it from 20 January 1994 when an unprecedented and unexpected manifestation was experienced at the Toronto Airport Vineyard Church of which John Arnott was the pastor. By March 1995 it was computed that 100,000 seekers including 10,000 pastors had visited the Toronto Airport Vineyard. It spread into individual churches within the mainline denominations, although it was most eagerly embraced by Pentecostal churches. In Australia, however, Pentecostal leader and historian, Barry Chant, founder of Tabor College, subjected it to a sustained critique, an interesting sign that the Pentecostal movement was becoming more self-critical.[35] The main criticism he made was that it was embraced by those who sought the manifestations first and then sought for biblical justification of them. He argued that scriptural conviction must always precede experiences. This seemed like a restriction on the sovereignty of the Spirit, and it is unlikely that the majority of Pentecostals agreed with him.

34 Guy Chevrau, *Catch the Fire* (London: Marshall Pickering, 1994); Patrick Dixon, *Signs of Revival* (Eastbourne: Kingsway Publications, 1994); Tony Payne, 'No Laughing Matter', *The Briefing*, 152, 7 March 1995.

35 Barry Chant, *This is Revival: A fresh look at revival: Reliving the New Testament in the 21st Century* (Miranda: Tabor, 2013), 116–118. He here refers to criticisms of the Toronto Blessing which he made in 1995 in an unpublished typescript entitled 'The "Toronto Blessing": Priestly or Prophetic?'

It is claimed that the Toronto Blessing influenced 8,000 churches in America and 5,000 in Britain by 1995. The Australian churches influenced by it ranged from mainline denominational churches such as Randwick Baptist Church in Sydney, Northbridge and Bomaderry Anglican churches, both in the Diocese of Sydney; large Pentecostal churches including the Hills (later Hillsong) and Christian City Church then at Brookvale, on Sydney's North Shore; and small churches ministering to Aboriginal congregations, such as the Aboriginal Assemblies of God in Taree and a church in Ceduna, in outback South Australia, which was reported to have 'filled up' with Aboriginal people.

It is probable that the Toronto Blessing, because it spread so powerfully and extensively, did help churches generally to address the question: is a movement which purports to be spiritual a movement of God the Holy Spirit, or of Satan and demonic spirits, or of the human spirit/psyche? In what way does Scripture help us to understand and test such a movement? The 'Blessing' resulted not only in the closer study of Scriptural passages on the gifts of the Spirit (I Corinthians 12; Romans 12) and testing spirits (I Thessalonians 5.21; I John 4.1), but also the reviewing of revivals in the history of evangelicalism. Both those in favour of the Toronto Blessing and those opposed turned to Jonathan Edwards, the Church's greatest theologian of revival, for help in assessing the movement. The opponents failed to see the main point of Edwards's treatment of reported manifestations.[36] It is true that his secondary purpose was to get the enthusiasts to rein in their excesses. But his primary purpose was to get the rationalists not to dismiss a movement which was outside their experience just because it was characterised by strange phenomena. Edwards's main point was that all these phenomena added together do not disprove a genuine work of the Spirit of God.

The Toronto Blessing was commonly called the laughing revival. It was portrayed as a time of fun, of enjoying the Lord. It was characterised by phenomena labelled 'manifestations', represented by their supporters as the work of the Holy Spirit. These manifestations included falling down (sometimes called 'slaying in the Spirit', 'resting in Jesus', 'going over' and 'doing carpet time'); violent twitching and shaking; bouncing like a pogo-stick; walking like a chicken; barking like a dog; roaring like a bull; laughing apparently uncontrollably; crying; moaning; groaning and shouting.

The nature of these manifestations made the movement easy to criticise. True revivals accentuate the doctrines of grace. But the manifestations did

36 Payne, 'No Laughing Matter'.

not appear to do that: the gifts of the Spirit, however genuine, are not identical with the marks of revival.[37] Movements which create such interest in spiritual things are rarely wholly bad, however, and the Toronto Blessing was no exception. It strengthened the faith of many people in a wonder-working God. From among those who reported on their experiences at Randwick Baptist Church in Sydney, where the pastor was Greg Beech, it is evident that deep hunger and need was felt by those who, through the Toronto Blessing, sought the blessing of God on their lives. They testified that the 'Blessing' helped them cope with needs which humanly speaking were beyond them: anxiety in the work place, unhappiness at home, the limitations of human rationality, the impoverishment of spending years dead to the reality of God, the deprivation of love, exhaustion from working too hard, stressed, joyless lives, lack of self-esteem and the feeling that one is too unimportant for God to worry about. To deal with problems such as those are all good fruit. But, it was asked, was it the fruit of the Holy Spirit? Was it any more than a good psychologist could bring about? As well as psychological relief, many reported spiritual blessing in terms of an increased desire for holiness, experiences of meaningful prayer, power to resist temptation, greater freedom to witness, and waking to the power of God's word:

> Suddenly the Word of God was REAL to me – I knew that what God said He meant – unbelievable as it may seem, I realised that although I believed that the Bible was God's Word, and Truth, I hadn't somehow built my life on His Promises … How DUMB can one be for forty years!
>
> The Bible now seems to me to be an autobiography of my closest friend and passionate lover so I want to read more and more to know him more and more.[38]

Such testimonies suggest there was genuine fruit of the Toronto Blessing. It is not in the historian's gift to discern if interest in the fruit came to outweigh interest in the manifestations. But the Toronto Blessing did remind evangelicals that vital faith is to be found in the affections and that Christians are to be sensitive to the supernatural within their own experience as well as doctrinal truth in their own intellects.

---

37 Stuart Piggin, *Firestorm of the Lord: The History of and Prospects for Revival in the Church and the World* (Carlisle: Paternoster Press, 2000), 94.

38 Greg Beech, 'The Outpouring of the Holy Spirit at Randwick Baptist Church, 6 November 1994', Typescript, 10 January 1995.

It was in England in an Anglican Church that the Charismatic movement devised its most successful instrument of evangelism: the Alpha course. Postmodernism gave rise to a range of evangelistic methods to supplement older programs such as Evangelism Explosion, Christianity Explained and Two Ways to Live. Because the modern mind is postmodern, reasoned evangelistic strategists, it must be approached through relationships and openness to contradiction. Because it is secular, the communication process must be extended to allow people more time to learn and digest the Gospel. Charismatic evangelicals understood this first and developed in London the Alpha course which spread through the evangelical world and well beyond it like wildfire.

Born in the Anglican parish of Holy Trinity, Brompton (London), Alpha was devised by Charles Marnham, a curate at Holy Trinity, as an introductory course in Christianity for new church members. In 1990 teaching the course was taken over by Nicky Gumbel of Jewish background who had been converted from atheism in his first year at Cambridge. A barrister before ordination as an Anglican minister, he wrote a number of books related to the Alpha course. *Questions of Life*, which has sold over a million copies and published in 48 languages, was 'Christian Book of the Year' in 1994. By March 2001 over 7,000 churches in Britain had registered to use Alpha and *The Guardian* estimated that through it 250,000 had come to faith in Britain.[39] By then Alpha was being used in more than 17,000 churches in 121 countries and 34 languages. Alpha courses were often led by laypeople, and because of its conspicuous success, it gave heart to churches demoralised by the lack of response from increasingly secularised people to earlier evangelistic efforts.[40] It viewed conversion as a relational process, not a sudden event.

The chief problem with Alpha for non-Charismatic evangelicals was its 'pneumatology that overstates *glossolalia* and thaumaturgy'.[41] So Alpha was more successful in non-evangelical churches than in anti-Charismatic evangelical churches. The latter sought to devise programs of their own making, more consistent with their own theology. This meant typically moving away from the 'Holy Spirit weekend' at which Alpha promoters hoped that attendees would be especially blessed by the experience of the Baptism of the Spirit. In London at All Soul's Langham Place where John Stott had held high the

---

39 Warner, *Reinventing English Evangelicalism,* 115.

40 Warner, *Reinventing English Evangelicalism,* 120.

41 Warner, *Reinventing English Evangelicalism,* 135.

evangelical banner, Rico Tice developed 'Christianity Explored' in the late 1990s as an alternative to Alpha.

In Australia 'LifeWorks' was developed as an alternative to Alpha, as was 'Introducing God'. Like Alpha, these programmes are held over a number of weeks (up to 12), and they include a weekly meal in a congenial, non-ecclesiastical environment, followed by the presentation and discussion of a simple message. The emphasis is on answering the question, 'does it work?' rather than 'is it true?' LifeWorks was seen by many as a typically anti-Charismatic enterprise. But it was more than that. It was the product of a joint effort by evangelicals from a number of church backgrounds and it was based on a study of the condition of the unchurched in Australia in the 1990s. It did begin as a version of the Alpha Course. In 1995 Robert Forsyth, rector of St Barnabas Broadway, chaplain to the University of Sydney, and shortly to become the Bishop of South Sydney, visited Holy Trinity Bromptom where he met Nicky Gumbel and observed Alpha in operation. Forsyth then wrote and developed his own version which he called the Barney's Course. The need for such a program was conceived independently by Leigh Brown of the Billy Graham Association and John North of Ambassadors for Christ. They were joined by Frank Tully from the Navigators, and by a number of other Sydney Anglicans: Mamie Long, editor of the Aquila Press, Lindsay Stoddart from Anglican YouthWorks, and Ray Robinson, rector of St Paul's Chatswood. They wanted to develop an evangelistic program which was thoroughly evangelical, relevant and Australian: Alpha failed two-thirds of that test! LifeWorks was presented as 'an explanation of the Christian Faith' and was strong on teaching content about who Jesus is, on the purpose of his death and the fact of his resurrection, what God is like and how to have a relationship with him, and how to pray and read the Bible. It was based on the view that the unchurched are more unaware of Christian beliefs than previous generations, and that therefore pre-evangelism would have to be a process extended in time (years even) and not just one-off events like the old evangelistic rallies, and it sought to impart this teaching in the context of warm relationships. Questions were invited and the views and doubts of seekers were to be addressed with respect and courtesy. It was designed as an intermediate step between the world and the church. Its motto is 'walking with people towards Christ.'

At the same time, a further programme 'Introducing God' was developed out of the evangelistic experience of Phillip Jensen by Greg Clarke and Dominic Steele. It is promoted as 'Two Ways to Live … now available as a relational evangelistic course for postmoderns'. Jensen had devised 'Two Ways to Live' when he was chaplain at the University of NSW. It is a seven-session course on the nature of the Christian gospel. 'Introducing God' expanded the number of sessions to 12 and covered such subjects as 'our autonomy problem', 'the death that changes everything,' and 'the difference Jesus makes to our futures'. In the first decade of the twenty-first century it spread throughout the evangelical world, another successful Australian evangelical export.

On the other side of the continent, the Pentecostals witnessed one of their most vaunted achievements, the work of a leader who had experienced the heights of success and the depths of suffering. In 1995 Margaret Smith Court, commonly acclaimed the greatest woman tennis player of all time,[42] founded the Victory Life Centre in Perth and became its senior pastor. It was a departure from the norm. The way Pentecostals read the Bible, pastors should normally be men – and they normally are, although frequently their wives co-pastor the women in the flock. Some Pentecostals argued that she must have misunderstood the Spirit's leading as the Spirit would never lead a woman into such a role. But there were enough who did want to follow her lead to enable her to grow quickly one of the three Pentecostal megachurches in Perth.[43]

Born in Albury, NSW, in 1942, she won her first tennis tournament Grand Slam at the age of 17. She was the first Australian woman to win Wimbledon. No other tennis player, man or woman, has equalled her record: 64 major tournament victories, including 11 Australian Opens, 15 US Opens, and 3 Wimbledon Singles titles. She was ranked the top woman player in the world in 1962–1965, 1969–1970 and 1973.

In Perth in 1967 Margaret Smith met and married Barrymore (Barry) Court, the son of one Western Australian premier and the brother of another.[44] When Barry took Margaret home to meet his mother for the first time, Rita Court warmly welcomed her and asked whether or not she realised that she had the same name as 'that famous tennis player'.[45]

42 Harry C. J. Phillips, 'Margaret Court', in Wray Vamplew, et al. (eds.), *The Oxford Companion to Australian Sport*, rev. ed. (Melbourne: OUP, 1997), 113–4; *SMH*, Australian Open guide 2003, 20; Margaret Court with Barbara Oldfield, *Winning Faith: The Margaret Court Story* (Sydney: Strand Publishing, 2000), 30.

43 The other two are the Riverview Church and the Perth Christian Life Centre.

44 Court, *Winning Faith*, 25–7.

45 Court, *Winning Faith*, 26.

Raised a Catholic, her early religious training did not include a knowledge of the contents of the Bible. Sometime in 1973, when Court was in America, a friend gave her a book to read entitled *How to be Born Again*, which, to her own surprise, she read repeatedly. Then, on her return to Perth in late 1973, she found that her close friend Anne Edgar had become a 'born again Christian'. Anne took Margaret to 'a charismatic-style meeting'. Margaret responded to the altar call as a public confession that she had embraced Jesus Christ as her Lord and Saviour.[46]

But conversion did not solve all her problems, which on a psychological level, were very severe. In fact, they grew worse, and she experienced depression and was often paralysed with terror. A major turning point in her life occurred when she saw a video of Fred Price, an American Pentecostal minister and founder-pastor of the Crenshaw Christian Center in California. As she watched this video, she came to the understanding that the Word of God was the only way to grow in faith and to overcome the areas of defeat in life. She took pages of notes and studied the Bible passages that Price gave. She discovered a Bible verse she had not noticed before: 'For God has not given us a spirit of fear, but of power and of love and of a sound mind' (I Timothy 1:7). Court drilled this verse into her brain and declared that she began to take the Bible as her 'spiritual medicine'.[47]

In 1982, Court began her formal theological education at the Rhema Bible Training Centre in Perth.[48] She graduated the next year, assured that she had been healed in body, mind and spirit, and that ahead was a work to which God had called her, and that she now had an understanding of the Word which would empower her to help others. She spent the next seven years, 1983 to 1990, in what she called various 'ministries of helps': assisting in the church nursery, counselling, leading prayer and intercession groups, and hospital and home visitation of the sick and despondent.

During these years, she developed the basic spiritual philosophy of her future ministry. She affirmed the central teaching of the Reformation that righteousness is the gift by which God makes us right with himself, and that it comes through faith alone which is itself the gift of God. Her assurance that she was right with God came not from experience, but from Scripture

46 Court, *Winning Faith*, 36–8.

47 Court, *Winning Faith*, 52–8; Barbara Oldfield interviewed by Linder, 6 June 2001. Oldfield at the time was Margaret Court's personal assistant.

48 Court, *Winning Faith*, 60, 63.

which taught her that 'faith comes by hearing, and hearing by the Word of God'.[49] All very evangelical! Nevertheless, it was in the outworking of this right standing that she claimed more than the typical evangelical. Having received assurance that she could go fearlessly into the throne room of God in prayer and find grace and mercy in time of need, she now testified to the possibility of 'winning faith'. It was a faith which would not only win others, but would prosper believers themselves in 'all things': in their relationships, finance and business, in community and family life, and in favour with others,[50] and it was a faith by which to 'claim divine health'.

Margaret Smith Court was officially ordained to the Christian ministry early in 1991 by Pastor Ray McCauley of Rhema Bible Church, South Africa. She then established the Margaret Court Ministries, Inc. With Court as Senior Pastor, the Victory Life Centre (VLC) within a decade had six associate pastors and an average attendance of more than 1,300 people on Sunday. The VLC launched a wide range of activities in the Perth community, including the Victory Life Bible Training Centre, the Victory Life Community Services, the City Wide Youth Ministry, the City Wide Kids Ministry, the STAND Young Adults Fellowship, the Victory Life Bookshop and the Victory Life International Movement. These ministries helped provide services not supplied by the WA government. The Victory Life Community Services (VLCS) is the welfare arm of the VLC, established to serve and support the many needy people of Perth, and through it about 500 people were 'won to Christ' each year.[51]

Court has encouraged other women to become ministers. Three of the seven pastors of the church are women, including her own daughter, Marika, and women are especially prominent in the beehive of activity that characterises each day of the church's activities.[52] At the same time, Court emphasises the importance of the home and the family unit in the Christian faith. She was honoured by Fred Nile in 1999 in Sydney for her service to God and country when Nile proclaimed her 'Australian Citizen of the Decade'. In May 2001 Oral Roberts University in the USA awarded her an honorary Doctor of Laws for her contribution as a Pastor to the church and to the community.

49 Romans 10:17.

50 Margret Court with Owen Salter, *Our Winning Position: living in victory every day* (Ballarat: Strand Publishing, 2002), 62.

51 Oldfield interviewed by Linder; 'Community' page, Victory Life Centre website, http://www.victorylifecentre.com.au/community-services.html, Accessed 13 July 2011.

52 Oldfield interviewed by Linder.

But Court is not without her critics, both within and without the evangelical camp. Some have condemned her as a woman in an ecclesiastical leadership position over men. Some fellow evangelicals are not comfortable with the tongues and healing emphases of the Pentecostal churches. Others have pointed out her seeming identification with the so-called Word of Faith Ministries with its emphasis on words, as if they have some magical content: 'Say it; do it; receive it; tell it' as the mantra goes. But most of the criticism directed at Margaret Court and, indeed, at most Pentecostal and Charismatic Christians, is of what is generally called 'the Prosperity Gospel' or 'the Health and Wealth Gospel'. Those who embrace this doctrine stress that God provides material prosperity for those whom he favours. Court's secular critics have aggressively attacked her for her condemnation of homosexuality and abortion. In 1990 she spoke out against gay and lesbian players such as Martina Navratilova, whom she condemned for publicly promoting lesbianism. In 2012 gay rights groups threatened to target Court in a protest at the Australian Open, reportedly due to her religious views on same-sex marriage. She was advised that she might be banned from attending. But she responded defiantly:

> I don't run from anything … It is hard that they can voice their opinions but I am not allowed to voice my opinion. There is something wrong somewhere.[53]

Her experience was a dramatic demonstration that most Australians by the second decade of the twenty-first century saw little value in freedom of religion. As an overwhelming majority of Australians voted for same-sex marriage in a 2017 postal survey, Court would have concluded that something was wrong everywhere.

* * *

Commenting on British and American evangelicalism, Warner observed that the identity of the evangelical movement appeared more imperilled at the beginning of the twenty-first century than it was a century earlier. No group appeared strong enough to redefine the movement in a way acceptable to the majority.[54] But Sydney evangelicals, galvanised by the Jensen brothers,

53 Benge Nsenduluka, 'Margaret Court unintimidated by gay right protest at Australian Open', *Christian Today Australia*, 12 January 2012.

54 Warner, *Reinventing English Evangelicalism*, 241.

gave some evidence that they might be able to do what no group in Britain or America had been able to do. They would not be able to prune the Pentecostal branch which had grown out of the evangelical stem and which was powerfully led in Australia by some outstanding leaders. But there was a genuine possibility that they could bring the inclusive and exclusive branches back into realignment.

Chapter Seventeen

CRUSADING FOR THE SOUL OF THE CITY, THE NATION, AND THE WORLD, 2001–2014

'You do not live in a time of peace.'
(Peter Jensen)

The trifurcation of the evangelical movement into conservative, progressive and Charismatic/Pentecostal streams by the beginning of the twenty-first century was not purely the result of forces internal to the movement such as theological disagreements. It rather reflected different responses to external challenges. Some responses were in defence of the movement; others on how best to attend to the national soul. Evangelicals could not agree on how to address postmodernism, on the role of religion in politics, the acceptance of other faiths in an increasingly multicultural community, or gender issues, specifically the ordination of gay ministers or same-sex marriage. Such divisions normally weaken a movement, and robust divisions within evangelical ranks remained a feature of the whole movement. A house divided against itself cannot stand, but ironically the three houses which replaced the single house of the historic evangelical movement, may be stronger collectively than the one it replaced. Certainly the three streams in Australia were dynamically led. With the Jensens leading the conservatives, Tim Costello a standout among progressive evangelical troops, and Brian Houston commanding Pentecostal forces, the evangelical movement was not likely to subside quietly into oblivion. In spite of the strong convictions of these leaders, the dramatic story of their co-existence is more one of convergence than divergence.

The Jensen Brothers: Reformed Evangelicalism Rampant

When Peter Jensen became Archbishop of Sydney (5 June 2001), the diocese reverted to control by those who believed themselves to be its rightful rulers, the conservatives. The white-hot politics of the Goodhew era abated quickly. Jensen was able to focus the resources of the Diocese on a program known as 'The Mission' (which he personally led) and to train the weapons of the Diocese on the main enemy – secularism. The habit of politicking was too ingrained to be eradicated entirely, however, and, with the help of the media, who loved to report on skirmishes within the Sydney Anglican Church, there were several spectacular outings in Jensen's episcopate, beginning at the beginning. The election synod was more than ordinarily unpleasant; the Archbishop's preferred candidate for the position of Principal of Moore College was opposed by the College Trustees; a move to extend Jensen's term as archbishop was compounded with charges of nepotism by the media; the Primate accused the diocesan Doctrine Commission's understanding of the Trinity to be heretical; a disenchanted ex-Moore College lecturer used the internet to galvanise a well-supported demand for change in the diocesan culture; most seriously the Global Financial Crisis of 2008 deprived the diocesan administration of half its income. Lesser minds would have been absorbed entirely by these challenges, but the Jensens still strategised to advance the Gospel, ploughing through problems like Moses through the Red Sea. But the strait way they made for the Gospel, while clear to them, was not as easy for others to see as the waves which threatened along the way. Thus we will ride the waves first.

The Jensen brothers did not welcome opposition and responded vigorously to it. 'I think part of the Sydney psyche,' said Peter Jensen, 'has always been we're under threat.'[1] The Jensens learned how to defend the evangelical heritage against every threat. It was a skill they valued. They also learned how to be defensive, which is a lower order skill, since it perceives friendly analysis as assaults. They probably received more criticism than everybody else in the Diocese put together. Phillip received more than Peter, and a social psychologist has argued that Phillip deliberately cultivated victimhood in response to the criticism he provoked by his own aggression. In a case of role reversal, instead of repenting of his aggression, he claimed underdog status, and his followers united behind him. Phillip made them feel like fellow victims of a Satanic

---

1 Chris McGillion, *The Chosen Ones: The Politics of Salvation in the Anglican Church* (Crow's Nest: Allen & Unwin, 2005), 172.

system which always persecuted Bible-believers whether they be in university or church, government or the media.[2] A *Sydney Morning Herald* columnist diarised the antics of the Reverend Obadiah Jensen-Slope, the Dean of Sydney's St Jensen's Cathedral and the brother of Sydney's 'Archbishop-for-life'.[3] The *Herald* denied that it was conducting a vendetta – 'no other denomination or religion appears to hold this *Herald*-specific persecution complex'[4] – but their defence sounds as if they have caught the Sydney Anglican virus of defensiveness. In a particularly ugly fight between Phillip Jensen and the media the *Guardian* newspaper in Britain reported that Phillip accused Rowan Williams, the Archbishop of Canterbury, of being a prostitute.[5] The report claimed that Phillip accused the Archbishop of hypocrisy because he maintained the Anglican Church's stand against the ordination of gay clergy while privately supporting it, and that Phillip had branded this hypocrisy as a 'total prostitution of the Christian ministry' and that he should resign. Phillip claimed the report grossly misrepresented him and he demanded an apology. He subsequently gave an explanation to the Sydney synod, ending with the words:

> I am sorry that media reporting of my activities have caused embarrassment to Christians in Sydney over the last week. Our friends around the world are in great difficulty at this time and are looking to us for help. Their problems are much greater than embarrassment. We cannot ignore their pleas for assistance. We cannot be engaged in their battles without calling sin, heresy and corruption for what it is. We are engaged in a spiritual warfare and if the first casualty of war is truth you can be assured that a war with the father of lies must inevitably be encased in falsehood, rumours and lies.
>
> I am truly sorry if I have failed you in any way but I was only earnestly doing the shepherd and watchmen task to which I believe I have been ordained.[6]

---

2 Peter Herriot, *Phillip Jensen, Bible Believer: The Psychology of Fundamentalist Leadership*, Kindle edition (n.p., The author, 2013), chapter 6, 'Being Victim'.

3 Mike Carlton in *SMH*, 1 April 2006.

4 Kelly Burke, Religious Affairs writer for *SMH* to Chris McGillion, cited in McGillion, *The Chosen Ones*, 143.

5 Stephen Bates, 'Evangelicals call Williams a prostitute', *The Guardian*, 14 October 2004.

6 Phillip Jensen, 'Personal Statement given to the Synod of the Diocese of Sydney', Anglican Church League website, http://www.acl.asn.au/old/041019_phillip_jensen.html, accessed 26 September 2016.

Phillip's use of the word 'sorry' twice in his explanation did not amount to an apology. He was not in the wrong: his critics were. Fundamentally, this was because they did not believe in the Bible, and he did. This gave him authority derived from God; they were without authority. To the objection that the interpretation of the Bible is contested and that therefore Sydney's Bible teachers should not be so sure that they are always right and in the right, Phillip retorted 'it is a sinful belief that the Scriptures themselves are unclear rather than the readers confused.'[7] Sydney was now being led by Bible-believers who were never confused and rarely unclear.

Peter Jensen went into the 2001 election synod by far the strongest backed of the five nominated candidates. On the first night of the synod, three of the candidates were eliminated because they failed to receive the support of the majority in both the house of laity and the house of clergy. None of that was surprising. What was surprising on that first night was that Robert Forsyth, Bishop of South Sydney, received the support of majorities in both houses, whereas Jensen failed to receive majority support in the house of laity. The supporters of Forsyth saw victory in their grasp. But Jensen's supporters were galvanised into action by the prospect of defeat. Jensen was strongly backed by the conservatives, and they were determined this time round not to be defeated as they had been too often in Goodhew's time. They manned the phones, ringing the clergy, requesting them to work on the parish lay representatives to bring them into line in support of Jensen. McGillion observes: 'For an organisation that championed the role of lay people in such radical terms as their right to preside at Holy Communion, this attempt to use clerical authority to sway their vote was odd, to say the least.'[8] But it wasn't odd at all. Sydney evangelicalism is clerical,[9] and the clergy prefer the laity to share their ecclesiastical and theological passions to focussing on the implications of faith in the home or work place which are their more natural areas of interest. When Goodhew had become Archbishop with the strong support of the laity and a small majority of the clergy, he was not in nearly as strong a position as Jensen with the strong support of the clergy and a reluctant laity. In Sydney, recalcitrant clergy are rarely brought to heel and never were in Goodhew's time. Recalcitrant laity are easy pickings and were mainly ignored in Jensen's time.

Clerical zealots went one further step to get Jensen elected: on the second night of the synod election they impugned Forsyth's character, a new low in

---

7 Quoted in Herriot, *Phillip Jensen*.

8 McGillion, *The Chosen Ones*, 82.

9 Stuart Piggin, 'The Properties of Concrete: Sydney Anglicanism and its recent critics,' *Meanjin*, 65.4, 2006, 184–193.

archiepiscopal elections. But it was sufficient to knock Forsyth out of the race on the second night, wrong-footing his advocates who expected to be able to give their speeches in support the next evening, an opportunity which never came. The tactics of the ACL conservatives on this occasion were as lethal as any experienced in the history of the Diocese and could easily have left a bitter legacy. Forsyth's magnanimity in the face of the ill treatment handed out to him, however, defused the issue. But lest ACL tactics should be looked to as a precedent by any who want to repeat this history, it must be observed that the success of their tactics is dependent on the gracious magnanimity of their opponents which they received far more often than they gave.

Not all the internal struggles were detected by the media. Jensen was set on having John Woodhouse, rector of St Ives Parish, replace him as Principal of Moore College. The College Trustees were opposed, but gave way to avoid plunging Jensen's episcopate into the same animosity which had bedevilled Goodhew's episcopate. Jensen was thus able to enjoy the support of a like-minded college principal for most of his time as archbishop: Woodhouse stepped down only in the last year of Jensen's episcopate, leaving the conservatives with the opportunity to appoint another conservative ACL leader to the post, thus denying to Jensen's successor what had been granted to him.

Jensen's episcopate lasted longer than originally envisaged. Synod had resolved that its archbishops should retire at 65, which would have given Jensen seven years in office. But diocesan politician, Bruce Ballantine-Jones argued successfully in the Standing Committee on 20 April 2003, that Jensen's episcopate should be extended by a further five years, as the extra time would be needed to make a success of the Mission. The matter was not put to the synod as Standing Committee had the power to make the decision, and it was feared by the conservative majority in the Standing Committee that taking the matter to the synod would only result in unhelpful dissension in the Diocese. As it was, the matter was put to Standing Committee five months later than Ballantine-Jones originally intended. In late 2002 the press had accused Jensen of nepotism in finding diocesan positions for his wife, son, and his brother, Phillip, whom he appointed Dean of St Andrew's Cathedral and in charge of clergy post-college training, and Jensen asked Ballantine-Jones to postpone the proposal for his extension. Peter Jensen handled the media well, but he did not like it, and his brother liked it even less.

Peter Jensen had long believed that the best way to respond to the ordination of women question was to ignore it. The matter, he maintained, had been settled in the negative, and it should not be permitted to take up valuable synod time. But, in his 2004 book, *Reflections in Glass*, the Anglican Primate,

Peter Carnley, accused the Sydney Doctrine Commission in their 1999 report on the Trinity[10] of falling into 'the ancient heresy of Arianism'.[11] He argued that, in order to maintain the subordination of women to men, the opponents of female ordination had so subordinated the Son to the Father that they, like early fourth century heretic, Arius, had stripped him of his divinity, thus jeopardising our salvation. The media rejoiced that the Diocese of Sydney, so critical of the heterodoxy of others and who put salvation at the forefront of concerns, should be accused of heresy and of endangering the salvation of souls. Jensen reconvened the Doctrine Commission to consider the Primate's charge and to revise the report if error could be detected.

Jensen was doubly pained. Not only did Carnley accuse the members of the doctrine commission of Arianism, but he accused the revered T.C. Hammond, Principal of Moore College (1926–53) and one of the Diocese's most effective apologists, of the same error. Jensen reported the Commission's findings that Carnley's charges were rejected decisively.[12] But the suspicion remained that the Sydney conservatives were even prepared to flirt with doctrinal error and doubtful or at least, disputed, scriptural exegesis to maintain their hard line against women ministers.[13] The nadir of the whole sorry affair was probably reached at a public colloquium in Melbourne on 20 August 2004 when Peter Adam, Principal of Ridley College, observed that the Primate's accusations had spread 'ill-will and resentment'. With the Primate only metres away, Adam thundered:

> With respect, let me say that I do not think that this Colloquium is an example of 'ever-deepening communion'. It feels more like an attempt to drive even stronger divisions between the tectonic plates that form the Anglican Church of Australia. May I ask you: Is this appropriate behaviour for an Archbishop or Primate? Should not a person in the

10 Diocesan Doctrine Commission, Anglican Diocese of Sydney, 'The Doctrine of the Trinity and its bearing on the Relationship of men and women', (1999). https://www.sds.asn.au/sites/default/files/reports/T/TrinityDoctrineComm.pdf accessed 29 September 2017.

11 Peter Carnley, *Reflections in Glass: Trends and tensions in the Contemporary Anglican Church* (Pymble: Harper Collins, 2004), 234f.

12 Peter Jensen, 'Caleb in the Antipodes', The TC Hammond lecture presented by Archbishop Peter Jensen during his trip to Ireland in June 2005, www.sydneyanglicans.net/indepth/caleb_in_the_antipodes_peter_jensen, accessed 21 November 2016.

13 Stuart Piggin, 'The Diocese of Sydney: "This Terrible Conflict",' in Elaine Lindsay and Janet Scarfe, *Preachers, Prophets and Heretics: Anglican Women's Ministry* (Sydney: UNSW Press, 2012), 178–204.

> role of Primate try to hold the church together? Is attacking people and their ideas a very good way to do this? Are you not being divisive? For what purpose? With greatest respect, engaging in this public attack looks as if you are trying to pull the church apart.[14]

Kevin Giles, also present at the colloquium, and a much-published opponent of Sydney's position on women and the Trinity, expressed his frustration that Adam was not addressing 'the central issue in contention'. Adam responded by claiming that whether or not the Diocese of Sydney was Arian was 'a significant enough issue'.[15] Adam had made an erudite critique of Giles first book on the subject, to which Giles replied in 2006 with an amplified version.[16] Sydney evangelicals, Giles there contended, were following the line of evangelical systematic theologian Wayne Grudem, who argued for the combination of the Son's equality of **being** with the Father with his subordination to the Father in his **role**. Ontological equality and role subordination was an invention of the 1970s, Giles insisted, in response to the need to admit that women were equal in a new non-patriarchal world, but to keep them subordinate anyway. The squabble was like the pamphlet wars of the Puritan Revolution and about as successful in changing hearts and minds.

The demand for change in the diocesan culture had not ceased entirely with the retirement of Harry Goodhew as Archbishop. A campaign by Keith Mascord to change the culture unleashed a flood of responses overwhelmingly from those who agreed with him. Mascord had lectured at Moore College during the decade of the 90s and then became assistant minister at St Saviour's Redfern in 2002, which had an impressive ministry to Indigenous people. When in 2006 its senior minister, John McIntyre was appointed Bishop of Gippsland, the parish did not feel sufficiently consulted about his replacement or about the appointment of new members of the Indigenous Peoples Committee. Mascord, who himself desired the appointment, wrote an open

14 Peter Adam, 'Honouring Jesus Christ', Trinity College Melbourne, Colloquium on Subordinationism and the Doctrine of the Trinity, 20 August 2004, www.trinity.unimelb.edu.au/theology/colloquium04.shtml

15 Tom Frame and Geoffrey Treloar (eds.), *Agendas for Australian Anglicanism: Essays in Honour of Bruce Kaye* (Adelaide: ATS Press, 2006), 155.

16 Kevin N. Giles (2006) *The Father and the Son: Modern Evangelicals Reinvent the Doctrine of the Trinity* (Grand Rapids: Zondervan, 2006). See Stuart Piggin's review 'Evangelicals: Inventing a false image of God to suppress women?' *Market-Place*, 5 September 2006, 11. Giles, a graduate of Moore College, wrote two other books on the debate: *The Trinity and Subordinationism: The Doctrine of God and the Contemporary Gender Debate* (Downers Grove: IVP, 2002); *The Eternal Generation of the Son: Maintaining Trinitarian Orthodoxy* (Downers Grove: IVP, 2012).

letter to the Standing Committee about the need for a change of culture in the Diocese. He confessed:

> I am worried about the Diocese. I am worried about its future. I am worried about the all engrossing Mission which is producing its own pressures and disappointments. I suspect that one reason that the Mission is not yet thriving as we had hoped it would is because, as a Diocese, we are not sufficiently living in ways that are consistent with the gospel we preach. Not only will God not honour our efforts if we continue to be like this, the people of Sydney who we are seeking to reach are not attracted to this style of Christianity.[17]

So extensive was the data contained in the responses to his open letter that he invited an advisory group of five people to write independent reports on 276 of the letters he received from those who gave permission for this to happen. Among the five, Bill Salier, the newly appointed Vice-Principal of Moore College, came closest to writing a minority report. He conceded that the data under review did point to three major issues in the diocese: the refusal to ordain women was the cause of ongoing angst; the process for the appointment of rectors for parishes was open to centralised control which parishioners found irksome; and there was a perception of too much arrogance and too little humility. But, all things considered, Salier was not personally convinced that 'there is something rotten in the state of Denmark as opposed to the usual mix of good, bad and ugly that one might expect in any massed gathering of humanity, redeemed or otherwise'.

In October 2007 the Archbishop and members of Standing Committee received the second of Mascord's open letters.[18] It diagnosed with a keener eye the psychological dimensions of the diocesan culture. It bore interesting testimony to the fragmentation of the evangelical movement. Evangelicals were now divided into 'soft' and 'hard' evangelicals, another way of labelling progressives and neo-conservatives, or inclusives and exclusives, or liberal evangelicals and conservative evangelicals. Those who could not win acceptance as 'hard' evangelicals were no longer called brothers; they were 'cousins'. Mascord concluded that the majority of people in the diocese felt marginalised; and the majority wanted the culture to change. He summed up the Sydney culture under five heads: it was 'fear driven,' 'suspicious,' 'politicised,'

17 A copy of this 'Open Letter' is found on the website of the Rev. Dave Smith, http://fatherdave.com.au/tag/sydney-anglicanism/ accessed 26 September 2016.

18 http://fatherdave.com.au/sydney-anglicanism-its-time-for-change/ accessed 26 September 2016.

'monochrome(ising),' and 'un-self-critical.' To use fear to defend the diocese's prize asset, the Gospel, a high price was being paid:

> Fear of Pentecostal emotion creates emotionally constipated forms of faith. Fear of liberal slipperiness stifles theological creativity and inquisitiveness. Fear of the social gospel leads to socially disengaged, compassion-lacking and environmentally apathetic churches. Fear of feminism creates conditions where women are again repressed and their gifts devalued. Fear of postmodernism and the emerging church movement cements into place modernistic and intellectualist forms of Christianity. All such fear impedes the ability of a church to engage in healthy and on-going reformation of its life and doctrine – in line with the spirit of Luther's adage, '*ecclesia semper reformanda*'.

Archbishops are forever receiving advice, and Jensen received enough in the early years of his episcopate as to absorb him totally in responding to it had he been that way inclined. But his inclination was rather to set the agenda himself and not allow himself to be distracted by church politics. He believed it was important to understand how the politics worked and to use it when necessary. But he had a bigger target than his political opponents, namely the secular world.

'The Mission'

In the year before his election, Peter Jensen had been asked by ACL to give its annual lecture at the time of the synod. Jensen revealed that he was clear-eyed about the implications of the reality that Australia had become a post-Christian society:

> We are not living in an even nominal Christian society; but in an ignorant and rebellious culture. Genuine Christianity offends opinion-makers of this culture. We must expect the culture to demand that we change the gospel to suit its version of the truth [but we must] address the secular challenge by providing flourishing Bible-based, gospel-centred, people-nurturing churches in as many places as possible.[19]

To confront secularism with the Bible and its rebelliousness with the Gospel was the sum total of Jensen's mandate. The church as it existed was not the best instrument for doing that. Jensen was not at ease at his installation as

19 Peter Jensen, ACL dinner, 9 October 2000, cited in McGillion, *The Chosen Ones*, 76.

Archbishop on 29 June 2001. He considered the service 'hopelessly out of keeping' with what the church then needed.[20] He did not enjoy dressing up in episcopal regalia and was distinctively uncomfortable even in the much attenuated ceremonial garb he wore for the occasion. Further, he had doubts about the very purpose of such an event, and he shared his misgivings with the congregation, among whom he knew would be those who had misgivings about his appointment:

> You may be bored; you may be glad; you may be stirred – but some of you are afraid. This ancient pageant marks a transition to office, to power. All the pomp is intended to make the transition legitimate. Power is clothed in dignity to hide its menace. The outward show is intended to reassure us: human beings may validly possess authority. But the question of power remains.
>
> So you may be afraid. You may well wonder what I plan to do with this authority. You may well also ask, has this power come to the right hands?

The cathedral was clearly not for him the platform on which he wanted to rally his troops. Too many of those who heard him were jaded by past divisions and were anxious about a Jensen future. His words did not soothe them, though his candour must have disarmed them. He ended with words which are recognisable in retrospect as being more than conventionally spiritual and as indicative of the mission focus he intended to pursue regardless of opposition:

> What are my plans? Well, don't look to me; look to the Lord Jesus Christ. As for me and my house, we plan to follow his orders, and in particular his last order, to make disciples of all nations. That is my special business. That is what I hope that you will be expecting me and asking me to do. I hope that it will be your business as well, especially if you have been commissioned as a minister of God's word and sacraments. Follow his standing orders; above all, follow his last word, that you will make disciples of all nations; teach, trust and obey the word of God.[21]

The contrast with Harry Goodhew's joyful installation eight years earlier could hardly have been more marked. Goodhew was at ease with the traditions of worship enshrined in the service; Jensen was suspicious of them as the 'pomp' which masks 'menace'. An alternative installation was required – one which

20 McGillion, *The Chosen Ones*, 100.

21 Sermon found at http://sydneyanglicans.net/seniorclergy/articles/72a accessed 26 September 2016.

was a more appropriate cultural response to Australian culture. So, on 19 August 2001 a mass rally of four to five thousand people attended a welcome to the Archbishop at the State Sports Centre at Homebush Bay. It was styled as the 'Deep Impact' gathering: If Jensen's vision was to make a deep impact on Australian culture, he reasoned, it would have to be delivered in a stadium, not a cathedral.[22] His address on that occasion[23] was not addressed to those with a limited attention span. It was strong meat: powerfully argued; grounded in Australia's history; programmatic of what he planned to do; challenging in his appeal to his hearers to fall into step with his plan. He began by arguing that the Anglican Church in Australia as presently constituted was doomed: it could not survive in the modern world and it was no part of God's plan for passing on the Gospel. To be the nation God intended, a resurgence of 'serious Christianity' was required. Australia's problems were chiefly spiritual and yet the church has 'ceased to attend to the national soul'. The way to make a deep impact on the nation was to make disciples by proclaiming the Gospel. This is our mission; this is how we are to glorify God.

Jensen wanted God back on the agenda as he had been a century earlier at federation. The colonies then became one nation because, as historian John Hirst said, 'God wanted Australia to be a nation'[24]. But now, said Jensen, God is not mentioned in public life. It would be interesting to know if there were any relationship between these prophetic words and the flowering of God-language in the national parliament in the next six years. It is known that at least one federal politician, Deputy Prime Minister John Anderson, was a great admirer of Jensen and strongly supported his election. But in 2001 Jensen was at pains to explain why God was no longer a topic of public discussion. It was because, in the Enlightenment, human reason displaced divine revelation as the foundation for public policy and Christians lost the argument and then stopped making the case for Christianity's role in nation-building. Jensen reported the findings of historian of secularisation, Callum Brown, that by the 1960s, the British people stopped 'even thinking like Christians', and he thought Australians had gone the same way: the Christian story had faded from the mind. Churchgoing Anglicans in Sydney were now only about one per cent of the population. 'We are becoming invisible. It is almost as unusual to have a friend who is a church-going Anglican, as it is to have one who is an

22 McGillion, *The Chosen Ones*, 100.

23 Address found at http://sydneyanglicans.net/seniorclergy/articles/74a accessed 26 September 2016.

24 *The Sentimental Nation: The Making of the Australian Commonwealth* (Melbourne: OUP, 2000), 1.

animal-keeper at the zoo. We are poised to become exotic.' If we are to have any hope of having a deep impact on our society then we need to increase the number of well-informed Christians to 10 per cent of the population. So here was the rationale for announcing that the object of the projected 'Mission' was to increase the number of people in Bible-believing churches ten-fold.

This was a daunting challenge, but the diocese was not without the means to reach out to the population of Sydney. From the 1960s on the diocese had been training 'radically conservative' congregations in an understanding of the Gospel which was counter to the prevailing secular culture; Moore College was fuller than ever with committed, well-educated prospective ministers; the missionary spirit was alive and well in such initiatives as the Ministry Training Strategy. Jensen concluded his passionate manifesto by calling his hearers to commit to six actions: adopt the mission; pray for the nation; repent of materialism, that very Australian sin; train in communicating Christian truth; give generously of your sons and daughters as well as your money; put God on the agenda wherever you are. Jensen certainly put the Mission on the agenda wherever he was: in synod he spoke of little else throughout his entire episcopate.

'The Mission', officially launched at the 2002 diocesan synod, aimed to have 10 per cent of the population of the diocese in 'Bible-based churches' by 2010. The 'Fundamental Aim' of the Mission was 'To multiply Bible-based Christian fellowships, congregations and churches which equip and nurture their members and expand themselves, both in the Diocese and in all the world.' This was to be achieved by a four-fold policy which included praying for compassion for the lost, enabling parish churches to become mother churches of other congregations and fellowships to reach social structures untouched by parishes, multiplying the number of those well-trained to produce such congregations and fellowships, and reforming the diocesan culture and deploying resources to support such endeavours. To achieve this policy a total of 79 initiatives were recommended, including: 'each parish undertake an audit using an instrument such as the National Church Life Survey or the Natural Church Development program,' and 'each parish consider becoming involved with community organisations to input a Christian ethos'.[25]

An opportunity to put the Mission on the national agenda and to develop a public theology which resonated with the current age, was given by the Australian Broadcasting Commission. From 13 November

25 Peter Jensen, Presidential Address to Synod on October 14, 2002, http://sydneyanglicans.net/seniorclergy/archbishop_jensen/599a, accessed 21 November 2016.

to 18 December 2005, Peter Jensen delivered the ABC Boyer Lectures.[26] First broadcast in 1959 the annual Boyer lectures were given by prominent Australians on scientific, social or cultural issues. Jensen was invited to give the lectures by Donald McDonald, chairman of the ABC and a personal friend of Prime Minister, John Howard.

Jensen's six lectures were entitled 'The Future of Jesus'. He observed that the distinctive message of Jesus was becoming unknown at least at the conscious level among Australians, even Australian academics. He began by observing that four prominent Australian academics, in a book entitled *Imagining Australia*,[27] had attributed the saying 'a house divided against itself cannot stand' to Abraham Lincoln, apparently unaware that it originated with Jesus. Jensen said that his purpose was 'to provoke a national debate with the Jesus of the Gospels':

> I want you see what a surprising man Jesus is; I want to trace something of his impact on the world; I want to see whether there is a trajectory which suggests that more is yet to come; I want to see whether he can speak with something like his old power, to central cultural issues like personal freedom, human relationships and the future of our country.

He clearly wanted to get Australians to engage with the Jesus of the Gospels, the Jesus who was not primarily a moralist or philosopher, but the one who brought the Kingdom of God into engagement with this world. Because Australians had lost their familiarity with the Bible, 'the history book of Western culture', they had lost their sense of identity. A vacuum had developed in the national life in which people found it hard to find meaning, purpose and community. The four academics unacquainted with the influence of Jesus, had posited the story of Eureka as a national myth for Australians. But Jensen doubted this had the 'capacity to inspire and shape'. Challenged by an 'interested agnostic' to address the question 'how does Jesus enrich the life of an unbeliever?', Jensen argued that Jesus is the key to an understanding of human freedom which is of more value than that based on individual rights. Liberty of action and of speech is only really possible in a moral society, 'where good is honoured, and where love is the rule', and it is the rule of Jesus, the Kingdom of God, which is the demonstration in history of that truth.

---

26 Peter Jensen, *The Future of Jesus: Boyer Lectures 2005* (Sydney: ABC Books, 2005), also at http://www.abc.net.au/radionational/programs/boyerlectures/past-programs/subjects/index=religion-and-beliefs, accessed 26 September, 2016.

27 Macgregor Duncan, Andrew Leigh, David Madden, Peter Tynan, *Imagining Australia: Ideas for Our Future* (Crows Nest: Allen & Unwin, 2004).

He 'sharply' questioned the 'Australian humanism' proposed by the authors of *Imagining Australia* where mateship is to be understood in terms of the 'humanist ideals' of brotherhood, community and love. In so far as these had real value they seemed to come unwittingly from Jesus in any case. 'After all,' asks Jensen, 'why are brotherhood, fraternity, community and love suddenly humanist ideals? They sound rather familiar to me as a Christian.' In this last lecture, Jensen stated his own views more categorically:

> I would say, that we have far better chance of constructing a more moral society in the soil of Jesus and his kingdom, than in Eureka or even Gallipoli.

And:

> I will come absolutely clean. I am not really worried about the future of Jesus without this nation to support him; he will survive and prosper; but I am deeply concerned about the future of this nation without Jesus.... in losing touch with him I fear that we will not have the cultural resources to develop spiritual heath and a vision of the good life and the enjoyment of true freedom. I fear that we will not be able to give our children community, meaning, purpose and a sense of the transcendent.

In 2008 synod was presented with a 'Midpoint Report' on the Mission. There had been some striking developments since its beginning. The number of ordination candidates had increased dramatically at Moore College. Offerings in churches had increased from $34 million in 2001 to an impressive $54 million in 2007. Since 2002 136 new congregations had been started throughout the diocese. But the Report was candid about the problems. People aged between 18 and 25 were seriously under-represented in congregations. New ministers seemed to be well-trained theologically, but few had the entrepreneurial and management skills to initiate and manage growth. To reach the desired goal of 10 per cent of the population, the numbers attending Anglican churches would have to increase to 230,000, with a further 70,000 in other Bible-believing churches (defined as those with an historic connection with the 'Bible alone' teaching of the Reformation). The required figure for the Anglicans only was four times as high as the number then in church. In fact church attendance, instead of increasing by the desired 400 per cent, had plateaued and had only increased in the previous three years by 0.5 of a per cent. Such a small increase in spite of the dramatic increase in the number of church workers was concerning. There was little intentional outreach and those inside the church were ministering to each other instead of seeking to connect with those outside the church. 'There is no gospel value,' the Report declared soberly, 'in replacing voluntary ministry with large teams of paid workers in each parish caring ever more intensively for static or diminishing congregations.' The solution was 'Connect 09': parishioners would make a genuine connection with those outside the church in order to have the opportunity to share the Gospel with them. But Sydney conservative evangelicals were very out of practice at connecting.

Instead, 2008–09 brought the Global Financial Crisis. The diocese, which had departed from conservative investment policy in favour of risky leveraging, borrowing money to make money, lost a staggering sum, variously computed at somewhere between \$160 million and \$200 million. The loss diverted the attention of synod in particular from eternal to economic salvation. Bruce Kaye, retired Secretary of the General Synod, wrote: 'Gearing might not in itself be unethical. But doing so in the context of the kinds of long term trust responsibilities of the diocesan officers is fairly clearly a moral failure of significant proportions for which someone should presumably take responsibility.'[28] It was a responsibility which Jensen felt keenly and confessed at the 2009 diocesan synod:

> I felt both *let down* and yet *responsible* since this has occurred on my watch and in part within funds in which I have a special interest. I felt *doubt* about whether we had engaged in ethically dubious practices by gearing the Endowment. I felt deep *uncertainty* about what we should now do and how we could carry on. Above all, I felt *grief* – and this I have continued to feel – as the impact of these losses on many fine ministries and on the jobs and personal lives of friends and colleagues has become clear.[29]

By the time of Jensen's final synod in 2012, nowhere near 10 per cent of Sydney's population were in Bible-believing churches. Falling so far short of the stated aim makes it easy to come to negative conclusions about the Mission, but the statistics are not unimpressive. Jensen reported that the

---

28 Bruce Kaye, 'Acting on trust: the morality of Church investment practices,' *Online Opinion*, 14 December 2009, http://www.onlineopinion.com.au/view.asp?article=9801, accessed 21 November 2016.

29 'Presidential Address 2009', https://www.sds.asn.au/sites/default/files/synod/Synod2009/Presidential%20Address%202009%20FINAL.pdf, accessed 10 February 2017.

growth within a decade had been 'approximately 7.1%, from 75,000 to 80,000 regular attenders'. He added, 'The experts tell us that by comparison this is quite notable.' He reported 109 new church plants and congregations and the initiation of at least 105 other groups. While it was true that other churches were closing, the net gain was evidence of commendable experimentation and a thrilling reversal of the age of unrelenting church closures. The number of NESB congregations had increased from 18 in 2002 to 60 in 2012. The number of ordained clergy had increased from 480 to 604. Money given through the plate had increased 88 per cent from $47 million in 2002 to $89 million in 2011. Missionary giving to CMS had increased by 78 per cent in the same period.

Such solid growth is remarkable in a secular age, even if it did fall so far short of the 10 per cent goal. But interestingly it may be contrasted with the rapid growth of the Pentecostal churches in the 1970s and 1980s which also accompanied a concerted strategy by the leadership. This does raise questions about Jensen's hard-line insistence in his Presidential Address that the habit which he commended of picking a fight paid off in the long haul. Forty years earlier, he argued, a contest had been waged between 'charismatic arminianism' and the 'reformed faith', the outcome of which remained 'crucial to our identity and our ability to preach the gospel'. It might have been crucial to their identity, but it is less certain that it was crucial to preaching the Gospel as many Charismatic Arminians have at least recovered the Gospel and have grown exponentially at the same time. Sectarianism was still alive in Sydney evangelicalism, increasing its vulnerability and reducing its attractiveness.

Equally debatable was Jensen's insistence that Sydney's position on women's ministry was paying dividends. Known as complementarianism, it was, Jensen insisted, 'the clear teaching of Scripture'. Since many evangelical scholars dissented from this view, it was anything but clear. Jensen could not legitimately argue that the interpretation of Scripture was plain and that the plain man's view of Scripture should be preferred to that of the scholar because he played the academic card when it suited him. When Labor politician Kevin Rudd reversed his opposition to same-sex marriage in 2013 and argued his position was not incompatible with Scripture, Jensen responded: 'His discussion of the Bible is historically shallow and he may be too confident about the state of current research'.[30] In his synod report, Jensen maintained that 'a very significant number of women' were now to be found in teams of parish workers. 'God will bless such costly, counter-cultural obedience to his word and he

30 Quoted by Julia Baird, 'Rudd rethink keeps the Faith,' *SMH*, 25/26 May 2013, 'News Review', 12.

has done so already', he concluded. In fact, in 2010, only 45 of 925 licensed clergy in the diocese were women.[31] Rather than lament this tiny fraction, Phillip Jensen maintained that the number of men in the ministry would not have been nearly so great were women ordained.[32] When in April 2002 Peter Jensen had met with Elaine Peterson, Convenor of MOW Sydney, he said in response to her claim that probably the majority of the laity supported the ordination of women, 'I agree but I am going to work very hard to change that.'[33] His hard work appears to have paid off: the Sydney synod could not even get enough support to debate the issue, and, in Melbourne, where the movement to ordain women to the priesthood had received its earliest and strongest support, a group of evangelical clergy, some of whom trained in Sydney and identified with the New Cranmer Society, agitated for the Diocese to reverse its decision to ordain women and were reluctant to allow women to preach or to hold leadership positions within parish churches.[34]

If Jensen maintained the Sydney line against the Charismatic movement and biblical equality in the ministry of women, he did surrender another long-held position of the hard-line conservatives, namely that the Gospel could be separated from a concern for social welfare. The dramatic increase in the number of ministers was a change in the 'ministry structure'. In the first five years of the Mission the dramatic increase was in those committed to evangelistic ministry. In the second it was 'in the involvement of people in community service or welfare-related church activities'. This compelled Jensen to the conclusion that 'we are on the way to becoming more outwardly focused and hence more able to penetrate the community around us with the gospel. The Mission is working.' Jensen was not making any concessions, but it could equally be argued that for the Mission to work, Sydney Anglicans would have to make changes in their thinking, and a deeper appreciation of the relationship between the Gospel and social concern was one such desirable change.[35]

History is replete with ironies which establish the truth of the proposition that man proposes, but God disposes. Jensen looked to a dramatic expansion

---

31 Muriel Porter, *Sydney Anglicans and the Threat to World Anglicanism: The Sydney Experiment* (Farnham: Ashgate, 2011), 121.

32 www.phillipjensen.com/articles/the-ordination-of-women-as-presbyters/ accessed 21 November 2016.

33 Stuart Piggin, 'This Terrible Conflict', 194.

34 Barney Zwartz, 'Men lead, women obey?', *The Age*, 10 June 2010. Cf. Zwartz, 'Spreading the word too far south?', *The Age*, 24 December 2004.

35 'Presidential Address to Sydney Synod, October 2012', *Synod Proceedings*, October 2012.http://www.sds.asn.au/assets/Documents/synod/Synod2012 /SynodProceedings.2012.full.pdf accessed 21 November 2016.

of church membership within his own diocese via the Mission. This did not happen, but Sydney Anglicanism expanded dramatically overseas, which few foresaw. It was not a commitment to mission which initiated this, but the vexed issue of homosexuality which allowed evangelicals to leverage greater support. Indeed, only this issue was big enough to garner the support of many progressive evangelicals in the West as well as evangelicals in the developing world. It was this issue which, at least at the beginning of the twenty-first century, distinguished nearly all evangelicals from liberals and galvanised them again into one movement. It is a movement which could reset the parameters for the study of the role of evangelicalism in history.[36]

In the 1998 Lambeth Conference, the Anglican Church had held to a traditional line on homosexuality, opposing the ordination of openly gay clergy and the blessing of same-sex unions. Among the leaders who fought for that successful outcome were Archbishop Harry Goodhew and the other Sydney bishops. But since then, in Episcopal dioceses in both Canada and the United States, the blessing of same-sex unions and the ordination of clergy and the consecration of bishops who were practising homosexuals were approved. The watershed year was 2003, when the Diocese of New Hampshire in America elected Gene Robinson, a gay man in a committed relationship, as its bishop. The conference of bishops of the Episcopal Church of the USA (TEC) confirmed the appointment. For evangelical bishops this was a step too far. 'The Americans took a risk,' declared Peter Jensen, 'but it was a tremendous strategic blunder which has awoken the sleeping giant of evangelicalism and orthodoxy.'[37]

In Canada, at the forefront of the battle to resist these developments was David Short, rector of Vancouver's largest Anglican parish, and son of Ken Short, one of Sydney's bishops during the Robinson years. Short was ably supported by that lion of evangelical orthodoxy, J.I. Packer, then lecturing at Regent College, Vancouver. Sydney evangelicals rushed to the defence of David Short who was opposed by his equally adamantine Bishop, Michael Ingham, Bishop of New Westminster. Ingham, when in line for the position of bishop in 1993, had been asked if he would maintain the guidelines on sexuality approved by the Canadian church and which were consistent with

36 Brian Stanley, *The Global Diffusion of Evangelicalism: The Age of Billy Graham and John Stott* (Downers Grove, Illinois: IVP Academic, 2013), 229–234; Bob Tennant, 'The Sermons of the Eighteenth-Century Evangelicals,' in Keith A. Francis and William Gibson, (eds), *The Oxford Handbook of the British Sermon 1689–1901*, (Oxford: OUP, 2012), 115.

37 *SMH,* 5 July 2008.

those of the Church of England.[38] He replied that he would, while also working to change them.[39] Given that answer, it is surprising he was appointed, for his synod was warned. Sydney, quite prepared to go it alone when it came to defending the faith, found itself supported by an astonishing array of Primates throughout the Anglican world, particularly those from African provinces where the number of churchgoing Anglicans easily outnumbered Anglicans in the West. Chief among these episcopal potentates was Nigeria's Peter Akinola, one of the strongest men in the Church world-wide. Akinola joined with Peter Jensen in June 2003 in threatening to split the Anglican Communion if the appointment proceeded of gay priest, Jeffrey John, as Bishop of Reading. The appointment did not proceed.

From being the renegade ringleaders of a bunch of Australian ecclesiastical cowboys who were prepared, it was suspected, probably wrongly, to split the Church over lay presidency, the leaders of Sydney Anglicanism found themselves in the vanguard of one of the major developments in recent Anglican history. Even Cardinal Ratzinger, shortly to become Pope Benedict XVI, wrote in support of the conservative bishops.[40] Peter Jensen was hailed as 'the pin-up boy for church conservatives' and 'the talk of Anglicans worldwide'.[41] The *Bulletin* magazine had already adjudged him to be one of the 100 most influential Australians in our history, one of only three clergymen so acclaimed.[42] Jensen resolved to boycott the 2008 Lambeth Conference and to support the preceding Global Anglican Future Conference, which became known as GAFCON. It met in Jerusalem from 22 to 29 June 2008 'out of a sense of urgency that a false gospel' had 'paralysed' the Anglican Communion.[43] It was a truly global gathering, with 1,148 lay and clergy participants, including 291 bishops representing more than 35 million Anglicans. It was not a schism, its participants insisted. It was a network within the Anglican Communion. GAFCON was committed to the promotion and protection of 'the biblical gospel and mission to the world,' and affirmed that the authority of those who denied the orthodox faith was to be rejected – they were to be called on to

38 These were set out in *Issues in Human Sexuality: A Statement by the House of Bishops* (London: Church House Publishing, 1991).

39 Stephen Bates, *A Church at War: Anglicans and homosexuality* (London: Hodder & Stoughton, 2005), 157.

40 Bates, *A Church at War*, 198.

41 *SMH*, 5 July 2008.

42 *Bulletin*, 21 June 2006. The others are Archbishop Mannix and John Flynn (of the Inland).

43 'The Jerusalem Declaration', 29 June 2008, GAFCON website, https://www.gafcon.org/resources/the-complete-jerusalem-statement, accessed 28 September 2017.

repent.[44] To the initiating cause of GAFCON, the acceptance of homosexual unions both in marriage and in ordination in Canada and in the United States, it responded (item 8): 'We acknowledge God's creation of humankind as male and female and the unchangeable standard of Christian marriage between one man and one woman as the proper place for sexual intimacy and the basis of the family. We repent of our failures to maintain this standard and call for a renewed commitment to lifelong fidelity in marriage and abstinence for those who are not married.'

GAFCON was 'a fellowship … faithful to biblical teaching, more representative of the demographic distribution of global Anglicanism today and stronger as an instrument of effective mission, ministry and social involvement'.[45] The inclusion of 'social involvement'[46] showed that it was a movement broader than the most conservative of evangelicals, and indeed among its members were many who supported the ordination of women. Sydney's conservatism was its strength on the world stage, but it was a conservatism which did not insist on making primary secondary matters as it was able to do in Sydney. Indeed GAFCON celebrated 'God-given diversity among us which enriches our global fellowship', and it acknowledged 'freedom in secondary matters'.[47] Outside the cloister of Sydney, even the conservatives adjusted their rhetoric. Peter Jensen was heard to declare opposition to female ordination a second order issue, while homosexuality was a first order issue.[48]

Out of GAFCON grew the Fellowship of Confessing Anglicans (FCA), and Peter Jensen was appointed its first General Secretary, and the Diocese of Sydney funded its secretariat.[49] In December 2009, Mary Glasspool, who was in a long-term lesbian relationship, was elected as Assistant Bishop in Los Angeles. Jensen said that this confirmed that the Episcopal Church of America (TEC) was determined to walk a path contrary to Scripture and

---

44 The Jerusalem Declaration, article 13. See also Rupert Shortt, *Rowan's Rule: The Biography of the Archbishop* (London: Hodder & Stoughton, 2008), 408f.

45 GAFCON Press Release, 'Statement on the Global Anglican Future', 29 June 2008. This included 'The Jerusalem Declaration'.

46 'The Jerusalem Declaration' affirmed: 'We are mindful of our responsibility to be good stewards of God's creation, to uphold and advocate justice in society, and to seek relief and empowerment of the poor and needy.'

47 'The Jerusalem Declaration', article 12.

48 Peter Jensen's address at All Souls, Langham Place, in London on 1 July 2008, was reported on http://www.anglican-mainstream.net/2008/07/01/post-gafcon-at-all-souls-abp-peter-jensen/ accessed 26 September 2016.

49 Porter, *Sydney Anglicans and the Threat to World Anglicanism*, 2.

he called on the Archbishop of Canterbury to sever ties with the TEC and instead to recognise the Anglican Church in North America (ACNA). By 2013 ACNA had been joined by over 1,000 congregations in USA and Canada. TEC had tried to remain engaged with a society which was rapidly changing in its views on sexuality, but while engagement with the host culture was sought also by Sydney evangelicals, TEC, in Jensen's estimation, made two fatal mistakes: they went liberal and then they tried to force conformity to controversial decisions on women's ordination and recognition of gay rights, thus disallowing diocesan sovereignty and parish liberty, both of which were traditionally Anglican and certainly very Sydney. For that reason, Jensen and other GAFCON leaders rejected the so-called Windsor Process with its 'Covenant', an instrument devised to keep a fragmenting denomination from disintegrating by subjecting local autonomy to a measure of centralism, which would have only made it fragment more rapidly.[50] Jensen was in no doubt that the Anglican Communion had already fragmented: 'To use an analogy, partners have separated, although they have not divorced.'[51] Conservative evangelicals were happy with the separation, but not even they were happy with the prospect of such a divorce. It would not be clever to leave the Anglican Communion when they were closer than ever to achieving control of it.

Among those who disagreed that Anglicanism was doomed unless taken over by the conservatives were more liberal, progressive evangelicals who worked to reform and strengthen existing structures. Constructive leadership along those lines was given by the General Secretary of the General Synod of the Anglican Church of Australia from 1994 to 2004, Bruce Kaye. A graduate of Moore College, he also studied theology at Basel, and lectured at Durham University for fourteen years in the Faculty of Divinity. While Master of New College in the University of New South Wales (1983–2004), he continued his studies in the major theologians within the Anglican tradition and, through the Institute for Values Research at New College, fostered the application of Christian perspectives on contemporary and Australian issues. As General Secretary, he appointed three teams of scholars and practitioners to report on Anglican theology, Anglican history, and Anglican missiology. Meanwhile he wrote a stream of books on the Anglican identity, and administered the General Synod Office with meticulous care. Debates within the General Synod became less confrontational and more focused on equipping the church to

50 Bruce Kaye. 'Covenant and fundamental issues for Anglicans', email 28 February 2010.

51 Shortt, *Rowan's Rule*, 357

serve the nation.[52] Kaye's vision and strategy are as valid within the evangelical movement as the more iconoclastic perspective of the Jensens.

The Australian Christian Churches

The Australian Pentecostal movement was also well placed to expand on a global scale. Hillsong pastor Brian Houston became President of the Assemblies of God in Australia (AOG) and in 2000 he founded Australian Christian Churches (ACC). Its vision was to become 'the public face of a Growing Church: Australian Christian Churches is an alliance of contemporary churches committed to communicating Christianity within Australian society through vibrant church services, relevant preaching, and practical community care'.[53] At the February 2000 launch of ACC it had 170,000 members in 1000 churches – Assemblies of God, Apostolic Churches, Bethesda, Waverley Christian Fellowship of Victoria, Abundant Life Fellowship, the Riverview Community Church of WA and a number of other independent churches.[54] In the 12 months following the launch, approximately 10,000 new members joined churches affiliated with ACC. By the 2006 census, ACC had the second highest church attendance figures behind the Catholic Church. Approximately 200,000 people attended the approximately 1,200 churches affiliated with ACC every weekend. A number of Pentecostal churches chose not to join: COC, CCC, CRC, Foursquare Church. They were concerned about independence and doctrinal identity, as the ACC does not require baptism in the Spirit as an article of faith or an expectation of experience.

Hillsong was the flagship megachurch of the ACC. By the beginning of the new millennium the annual Hillsong Conference drew crowds of above 20,000. In 2000, the city and Hills churches merged into Hillsong Church, two worship centres in one church. By 2004 it had over 15,000 members and its income was $40 million; by July 2005, 18,000 members with an income of $50 million; by 2015, 34,000 members with an income of $100 million.[55] Hillsong's mission statement is 'To reach and influence the world by building a large Bible-based church, changing mindsets and empowering people to

---

52 Frame and Treloar, *Agendas for Australian Anglicanism,* xi-xviii, 123f., 205–211; Brian H. Fletcher, *An English Church in Australian Soil* (Canberra: Barton Books, 2015), 233, 251.

53 'About us', Australian Christian Churches, website, http://www.austChristianchurches.com.au/about.asp, accessed 25 April 2005.

54 *New Life,* 62.36, 2 March 2000, 1.

55 *Daily Telegraph,* 20 July 2015.

lead and impact every sphere of life.' Like Sydney Anglicanism, it is committed to 'impacting lives and influencing nations'.[56] By 2011 it had extended its ministry outside Australia with churches in Russia, England, the United States, South Africa, France and Sweden. Brian Houston's personal vision for Hillsong was explicit about its influence, size and growth: 'The Church that I see is a Church of influence, a Church so large in size that the city and nation cannot ignore it, a Church growing so quickly that buildings struggle to contain the increase.'[57] The 2005 Assemblies of God conference held at Hillsong had as its theme 'Take the Nation, Shake the World'. Australian Pentecostalism, like Pentecostalism everywhere was globally networked, but now it was able to export its brand of Pentecostalism. Phil Pringle's Christian City Church also became a robust export. Restyled the '3C Church Global', by 2018 it claimed to be 'a movement of 440 churches in 60 countries with a reach of 80,000 people worldwide'.[58]

Hillsong has been the butt of much criticism. Secularists and disenchanted ex-members have accused it of fundamentalism, opposition to freedom of thought, authoritarianism, and lack of financial accountability.[59] Conservative and liberal Christians have joined in the attack. Archbishop Peter Jensen said that Pentecostalism 'in its love affair with modern culture' had departed too far from historic Christianity to have much of a future.[60] What Hillsong has loved most about modern culture, as the name makes clear, is music. Hillsong's music ministry, directed first by Geoff Bullock and then Darlene Zschech, sold more than 12 million recordings across the globe between 1991 and 2011. Marion Maddox maintained that Protestant, mostly Pentecostal, megachurches are complicit in global capitalism.[61] She says that their members are instructed in the duty of becoming rich and that poverty is the devil's work. In the name of Christ these megachurches want to conquer the world, and, through them, 'consumerism is re-enchanting the world.'[62]

Hillsong is indeed increasingly engaged with the 'world' as well as the 'Spirit', but it has not all been negative. It has established a social welfare

---

56 'My Place in the Unfolding Vision': The Hillsong Foundation, 2011/12, brochure distributed at Hillsong, Vision Day, 2012.

57 'My Place in the Unfolding Vision'.

58 http://www.c3churchglobal.com/phil-pringle, accessed 10 March 2018.

59 Tanya Levin, *People in Glass Houses: An Insider's Story of a Life in and out of Hillsong* (Melbourne: Black Inc., 2007).

60 Porter, *Sydney Anglicans and the Threat to World Anglicanism*, 146.

61 Philip Hughes, *Christian Faith and the Economy in a Globalised World,* Christian Research Association, Research Paper No.10 (Nunawading: CRA, 2011).

62 Hughes, *Christian Faith and the Economy*, 8.

department, the Hillsong Foundation. It has a staggering array of programs: Drug and Alcohol Services, Foodshare, Street Team, Prison Ministry, Immigration Detention Centres ministry and Community Children's Clubs. It has a foundation for handicapped children in South Africa, another to feed and educate children in Mumbai, and yet another to rescue girls from the sex industry. Hillsong CityCare seeks to provide for the needy in Sydney and Brisbane. It provides emergency relief provision of food, electricity and water, counselling, playgroups, a drop-in centre offering mentoring and life skills program. Like the Salvation Army, Hillsong is now able to offer significant disaster relief.

In his interesting review of the 'prosperity gospel', Shane Clifton traces the development in Pentecostal thinking of 'affluence for the sake of influence', to the replacement of 'prosperity' with the less commercial, less materialistic concept of 'flourishing', and how this has helped Pentecostals to see the relevance of the Gospel not only for the spiritual realm, but also for social and political realms.[63] Clifton is less happy with the declining place occupied by tongues and the Baptism of the Spirit in Pentecostal teaching and practice, and he wonders, should it diminish much more, if the AOG will continue to be a Pentecostal fellowship in any meaningful sense. The preference for the ACC label suggests that might have already happened. Cultural changes in the ACC, Clifton concludes, have outpaced the capacity for critical theological reflection.[64]

The Emergent Church Movement and the Baptists

Australian Baptists were, like the Anglicans, part of a denomination with a global network of churches and it contributed to creative thinking on the nature of the church at an international level. NSW Baptists, in particular, were influenced by Sydney Anglicans in other respects. They were softer on the issue of the ministry of women and allowed individual churches to decide whether or not to have women pastors. The training seminary, Morling College, had a reputation for being less prescriptive than Moore College. But even here it could not be seen to depart too far from the strong stand for evangelical truth for which Moore was reputed. To attract students from an essentially conservative church culture, Morling had to emulate Moore in offering strong Bible teaching. Conservative American Bible teachers, such as

63 Shane Clifton, 'An analysis of the developing Ecclesiology of the Assemblies of God in Australia', PhD, Australian Catholic University 2005, 226f.

64 Clifton, 'Ecclesiology', 258, 267, 288.

Don Carson, who were revered in Sydney Anglican circles, were also invited to lecture at Morling.

The Baptists joined the Sydney Anglicans in their determination to give their churches a mission focus. Michael Frost, director of the Centre for Evangelism and Global Mission at Morling College, has been a leading exponent of the 'missional church' movement. He is explicit about one of the features of evangelicalism which distinguishes it from fundamentalism, namely the necessity of engagement with the wider culture: 'living out the gospel *within* its cultural context rather than perpetuating an institutional commitment *apart from* its cultural context'. He sees little hope for 'institutional' churches which have three flaws in their DNA: they are attractional, dualistic, and hierarchical.[65] Frost contends the church must be 'recalibrated' purely in terms of its mission.[66] Missional churches are centred on Jesus, the Gospel, and the Bible. They are incarnational in their ecclesiology. That is, they seek to become Christian communities in places where Christ is not known rather than creating 'sacred' spaces (attractional venues) to which people are expected to come. They have a Christ-centred life rather than a vaguely, and typically dualistic, spiritual one; and they have flat, rather than hierarchical, leadership aimed at unleashing the gifts of evangelism, leadership, prophecy, pastoral care and teaching.[67]

The report of a high-powered inquiry into the health of the Baptist denomination in NSW and the ACT was released in 2010.[68] With zero growth in membership between 1996 and 2006, it was behind Baptist growth in WA (19% increase), Queensland (18%), and Victoria (11%). Though the NSW and ACT situation was not healthy, it was better than all the other mainstream Protestant denominations. The Lutherans of NSW and the ACT had declined by 6%, the Anglicans by 7%, the Presbyterians and Salvation Army both by 13%, the Uniting Church by 17%, and the Churches of Christ by 30%. Only the non-affiliated, independent churches and the Pentecostals had increased, by 60% and 46% respectively.

In the NSW and ACT Baptist churches, members below 45 years of age were declining in number. The Baptists appeared to hold their own among

65 Michael Frost and Alan Hirsch, *The Shaping of Things to Come: Innovation and Mission for the 21st-Century Church* (Erina: Strand Publishing, 2003), 18.

66 Frost and Hirsch, *The Shaping of Things to Come*, ix-xi.

67 Frost and Hirsch, *The Shaping of Things to Come*, 12, 174,5.

68 Jonathan Pratt, 'Growing Healthy Churches: Voices from the Churches', Directions 2012 Research Project (Epping: NSW & ACT Baptist Churches, 2010). It was based on 15,846 respondents and interviews with 71 church leaders.

the Baby Boomers, but lost membership from Gen X (25–44 in 2006) and Gen Y (5–24 in 2006): the Baptists were losing their future leaders. There was less interest from members in Baptist distinctives: denominational consciousness was waning. The research found that church leadership was the most important factor in the health of a church and that 'Jesus- and Bible-centred' leadership was critical to conversion growth.

Recommendations in the report included changes to local church governance, presumably to address power struggles, and the creation of networks of churches committed to growth and serviced by 'Gospel-hearted' mentors. It was more important for the leader of the Baptist Union to be 'powerful and accountable' than to be passionate about distinctive Baptist doctrines and practices. In identifying Christ-centredness, the Gospel, the Bible and conversion as keys to growth, the report really underlined the proposition that the more evangelical a church is, the more likely it is to enjoy growth, but only if that church is well led and avoids power plays. There was no correlation between the growth of churches and leadership by male pastors of more than ten years' experience of pastoral ministry with a conservative evangelical theological framework who focussed on developing small Bible study groups. That is a formula which no longer guarantees success![69] It is not enough just to be evangelical.

New Immigrant Churches

The surest evidence that the denominations were moving away from their British Empire heritage towards an understanding of the Kingdom of God as embracing people from every nation was their adjustment to and endorsement of multiculturalism. Assimilation to English-speaking norms was no more likely to appeal to immigrants than it had to Australia's Indigenous people. The denominations had to facilitate the emergence of congregations for those of NESB in which the services were delivered in languages other than English. After a slow start, Sydney Anglican ethnic-based ministries proliferated in the first decade of the 21st century. By 2011 there were 61 language-specific congregations, including 36 Chinese, 6 Sudanese, 5 Korean, and 3 Vietnamese.[70] Meanwhile, Pentecostal churches for NESB people have multiplied so

69 There is some evidence, however, of a correlation between congregations which value Bible study and church growth. See Peter Kaldor, et al, *Taking Stock: A Profile of Australian Church Attenders* (Adelaide: Openbook, 1999), 10, 131, 135. This is not an easy statistical exercise, however.

70 *2011 Year Book*, Diocese of Sydney, 151–154.

rapidly and in such easy symbiosis with traditional churches, whose facilities they frequently utilise, that their presence has yet to be documented. Korean and Chinese churches deserve far more extensive treatment than is given here. Possibly 70% of Korean immigrants to Australia attend church. Many are not Christians, but they attend churches because they need information by which to survive and thrive in a strange land. In church they find, for example, the opportunity to learn English, to receive legal advice, a safe environment for their children, and there is always the right sort of food after the service. But these attractions only work because they are built on a spiritually vital foundation which is largely the product of religious revival in Korea. By the end of the first decade of the 21st century there may have been as many as 280 Korean churches in Sydney, 70 in Melbourne, 50 in Brisbane, and 20 in Perth.

In Sydney Woo Sung Chung pastors the Korean Full Gospel Church, which is a branch of the largest church in the world, that of Pastor Yonggi Cho in Korea. The Sydney Full Gospel Church has 4,500 registered members. About 2,000 attend each Sunday. Since the church building only holds about 500 people, seven services are held on a Sunday. Pastor Chung has planted 27 churches in Sydney, Melbourne and Fiji. Every morning at 5 o'clock a one-hour prayer meeting is held. Pastor Chung was a country boy in Korea, and his accent, it is said, is not pure! But he has been as successful as he is because he is very humble, he believes that 'salvation is of the Lord', and he preaches the Gospel so there are always those who are being converted. Pastor Cho, his mentor, teaches that a leader can be a 'Big Bamboo'. Apparently, it is not only the Korean soil which is conducive to the growth of big bamboos, but the beliefs of Korean Christians which have the same effect, if Pastor Chung is any guide.

The by-now well accepted recipe for church growth in modern secularised Australia is that churches should be Jesus-centred, Bible-based, and imaginatively-led, and for denominations as a whole, as distinct from individual churches, open to people of all ethnic and linguistic backgrounds. It needs to be observed that even such a simple recipe was only reached through historical experience:

> At the dawn of the twentieth century, many Christians anticipated that their religion would have to discard old dogmas to embrace new scientific truths. A hundred years later the most successful churches were those that modernised the medium but not the message.[71]

71 Graeme Davison, 'Religion' in Alison Bashford and Stuart Macintyre, (eds.), *The Cambridge History of Australia* 2 vols (Port Melbourne; New York: CUP, 2013), vol.2, 233.

To this recipe a further ingredient needs to be added. Ministry must be focussed above all on young people, as an analysis, directed by clear-headed evangelical businessman, Tim Sims, demonstrates.[72] The plain, if regrettable, truth is that in recent decades churches have not done well at recruiting adults. They grew almost exclusively through the addition to the congregation of children of Christian parents. From 1954 to 2006 there is a 92% correlation between the graph showing the rate of births to stable marriages and that of church attendance. If the divorce rate increases and the birth rate decreases the numbers attending church decrease. In defending the nuclear family and opposing divorce, churches may appear to be restricting their appeal, but in fact they are strengthening their own foundations.[73]

The single most obvious reason why the Anglican Diocese of Sydney, contrary to all other Australian Anglican dioceses, has held its own against the erosion of secularisation or even increasing in numerical support, is that it has far more extensive and effective youth work than other dioceses. According to the 2006 National Church Life Survey, in each of the age cohorts, under 12, 12–18, 18–25, the rate of satisfaction of young people with the youth programs they are offered in Sydney is twice as high as it is in the average of other dioceses. The Sydney Diocesan age profile, in that it follows fairly closely the national demographic age profile, is conspicuously different from that of other dioceses which are greatly weighted to the older generation, signalling imminent collapse. Sydney does remain worryingly underrepresented in the 20 to 50 year-old age group, but it is well represented among 15 to 19 year-olds. It, and those other evangelical churches and organisations, both independent and Pentecostal, which have significant ministries for the young, have a future.

An evangelical organisation which has worked successfully within the secular world is Scripture Union Queensland. Since 1990 it has been responsible for the administration of a chaplaincy program within state schools. It agreed to the stipulation that chaplains were to offer pastoral care only: they were not to engage in either religious education or proselytising. Secularists complained that chaplains could never abide such a restriction and some evangelical Christians, for whom evangelism is integral to faith, argued that

72 'Churchgoing in Australia: Current observations and possible implications', PowerPoint presentation based on the research of Tim Sims, John Bellamy, Robin Kinstead, and Guy O'Hanna, 2010. NCLS data supports these findings.

73 This reality appears to be overlooked by Muriel Porter in *Sydney Anglicans and the Threat to World Anglicanism*, 137f.

they should not. But the pragmatism of the evangelical movement came to the fore, and SU Queensland had little difficulty recruiting chaplains. The support of evangelical education professor Brian Hill gave credibility to the experiment, and incidentally reflected how far evangelicals had gone in taking the Word into the world:

> While there was an aberrant period in recent church history when personal evangelism was (and by some still is) represented as the church's sole business, the more general story has been one in which the church has followed its Lord in pioneering services in such areas as health, education, and economic critique as part of its concern for people in their total life situation.[74]

Since the 1970s the largest investment of the churches in ministry to youth has been in Christian schools. Before then the larger denominations, with the exception of the Catholics, were content to work largely within the state school systems which were secular, but not anti-Christian. Since then the Christian schooling movement has increased exponentially, particularly in the early 1980s and in the period from 1999 to 2006 when generous government funding for private schools became available. Among the associations promoting this development were Christian Parent-Controlled Schools (Reformed), Christian Community Schools (an Australian development with links to Pentecostal, Charismatic and other evangelical churches), and Anglican low-fee schools. In 2011, 30 per cent of all pupils in Australian schools were in private schools of which 94 per cent were religious foundations (the last figure is much higher than that for the USA). In NSW 34 per cent were in private schools, while in Sydney it was 44 per cent. Research has shown that these schools do not make students more intolerant. If anything the reverse is true as these schools inculcate an appreciation of cultural diversity. Aggressive secularism has been identified as more corrosive of the balance of social cohesion and pluralism required for stability in modern multi-cultural Australia, a significant finding if valid.[75] Christian schools do not seem to make pupils 'more religious' either; they do not appear to have an influence over and above the religious beliefs

---

74 SU Queensland website, http://www.suqld.org.au/about/index.php?page=76, accessed 4 April 2012.

75 Jennifer Buckingham, *The Rise of Religious Schools* (St Leonards: Centre for Independent Studies, 2010), 15.

and practices of parents.[76] The relationship between Christian schooling and the growth of the churches, therefore, remains an open one.[77]

* * *

By the middle of the second decade of the 21st century it appears that the three branches of the evangelical movement – conservative, progressive, Pentecostal – are no longer moving away from each other. Rather, in their common pursuit of church growth and international influence, they are adopting the same principles and strategies. All are moving away from insisting on matters distinctive of denominational identity. All accept that their churches must be Christ-centred, Bible-based, and strongly led. Both the Sydney Anglicans and the Hillsong Pentecostals aim to achieve numerical growth so substantial that they achieve the critical mass which they believe essential for influence in the wider community. Both are now committed to social welfare as integral to their ministries, after some conservatives fought against that understanding for decades and the Pentecostals largely ignored that responsibility until it became essential to their image as a caring community. All are accepting, too, of the reality that, in today's Australia, it is necessary to offer ministries which reflect the nation's increasingly multicultural population.

---

76 Buckingham, *The Rise of Religious Schools*, 15; Colin Symes and Kalervo N. Gulson, 'Faith in Education: The Politics of State Funding and the New Christian Schooling in Australia', *Educational Policy* 22.2, 2008, 231–249.

77 Marion Maddox, *Taking God to School: The End of Australia's Egalitarian Education?* (Crows Nest: Allen & Unwin, 2014).

Chapter Eighteen

EVANGELICAL INITIATIVES IN THE PUBLIC SPACE IN THE 21ST CENTURY

'For the pain, suffering and hurt of these Stolen Generations, their descendants and for their families left behind, we say sorry.'
(from Prime Minister Kevin Rudd's 'Apology' speech)

The story of Australian evangelical Christianity does not end with a whimper in the first decade of the 21st century. Not only did the movement achieve unprecedented successes on the world religious stage (as we saw in the previous chapter), but it attracted more attention in the media and politics than it had received for decades. Taking the intelligentsia (media plus academia) by surprise, the first decade of the new century saw astonishing desecularisation as religious issues became the stuff of federal politics and of the media as Australians searched for personal values and national identity.[1] At the same time, secularism in Australia became as aggressive as it had ever been, bolstered by the publications explosion associated with the new atheism.[2] Evangelicalism's instinct was always 'oppositive': typically, it was strengthened by opposition, based on the conviction that as it gets darker the light shines brighter. Now that the enemy came more clearly into focus, evangelicals rallied to the cause and were less interested in criticising each other.

1 *The Bulletin*, 8 August 2004, reported that God was the most talked about subject in the media.

2 Richard Dawkins, *The God Delusion* (London: Bantam, 2006); Christopher Hitchens, *God is not Great* (New York: Twelve, 2007); D.C. Dennett, *Breaking the Spell: Religion as a Natural Phenomenon* (London: Allen Lane, 2006); Sam Harris, *The End of Faith* (London: Free Press, 2006); *Letter to a Christian Nation* (New York: Knopf, 2006); Michel Onfray, *Atheist manifesto: the case against Christianity, Judaism, and Islam* (New York: Arcade Publishing, 2007).

But rallying to the cause, now that it was clearer what it was, proved difficult. That many Anglicans had forgotten or never learnt how to connect with the wider culture which they were now trying to engage through 'The Mission', reflected a problem in the evangelical movement much broader than Sydney. It is a reality more easily seen in the American experience. There evangelicals, in order to avoid modernism, had retreated from the social gospel into fundamentalism. When towards the end of the twentieth century it sought to re-engage with the wider society, it did so mainly through the political policies of the Religious Right, namely determined opposition to abortion, homosexual lifestyles and attempts to redress climate change. To re-engage, it did need to get political, but its overly-long absence from the political processes meant that it engaged with them in a reactionary way. In America it was surprisingly effective for a time in winning support. In Australia, while the Religious Right was also in the vanguard of getting the evangelical movement re-engaged in politics, it was weaker, and connected mainly to the more Pentecostal branch of the movement. Other evangelicals, including Sydney Anglicans, had expended most of their energy fighting against secularism and theological liberalism. They took longer to look to political opportunities, and when they did, they were too inexperienced to be effective. Christian politicians oscillated between chiding Christians for not lobbying more energetically in support of positions which they (the politicians) considered important and warning Christians to keep off the turf because they were too judgemental and did not understand political realities. As Peter Jensen explained:

> … we have been fully engaged in safeguarding the churches against virulent secularism and liberalism. We have had little time or energy left for social and political struggles. Indeed, modernity, globalisation and immigration have changed the nature of our society so dramatically that it seems impossible to know where to begin again. What we lack is … a broad sympathetic Protestant constituency able to … appeal to the common moral code which was one of the achievements of the Protestant ascendancy when that existed.[3]

It existed, as the first volume showed, until the beginning of the First World War. The Protestant ascendancy was replaced, claimed Manning Clark, by the

---

3 Peter Jensen, 'The Protestant Conscience: The Inaugural Bernard Judd Memorial Lecture', St Andrews House, Sydney, Tuesday, 5th April, 2005. Available via link at http://sydneyanglicans.net/news/royal_wedding_tolls_death_of_protestantism_dr_jensen, accessed 21 November 2016.

'brotherhood of man' (a label which would bring even less joy to the feminists than to the evangelicals) which 'works for the day when that wealth of love which used to be lavished on Him is turned upon the whole of nature, on the world, on men, and on every blade of grass'.[4] The evangelicals found over the next century 'that wealth of love' was no longer lavished on the God and Father of the Lord Jesus Christ. As the secular society moved away from its Christian heritage, Australians preferred to lavish that love on themselves. It was a society as much in need of the Gospel as it had ever been and more in need of Christian participation in nation-building and social involvement. The need to recover its social conscience was so strong at the beginning of the 21st century that even the most conservative evangelicals began to regret the decades of relative neglect. They began to honour those who, in the past, had not been seduced from action on behalf of the poor in the name of theological purity. Many Australians were not only uninterested in theological purity, but were increasingly of the view that the churches were no longer places where any kind of purity could be found:

> Secularization of the wider society was hastened by revelations about the historical abuse of women and children in the care of church organizations, and possibly also by press coverage of church resistance to the ordination of women and gay clergy.[5]

The secular society was progressing from the view that Christianity was irrelevant to the view that it was positively harmful.

Religion in the Federal Parliament

It was therefore the more surprising that the first decade of the 21st century witnessed an unprecedented preoccupation of Australian federal parliamentarians with religious issues.[6] By 2004 'the mention of God in Hansard had reached a crescendo'.[7] A study of the increased invocation of religion in Australia's federal Parliament, based on 2,422 parliamentary speeches, demonstrated that the 'proportion of speeches given by prominent MPs

---

4 C.M.H. Clark, *A History of Australia*, vol. 1 (Parkville: MUP, 1963), 380.

5 Hilary Carey, 'Religion and Society', in Deryck M Schreuder and Stuart Ward, (eds), *Australia's Empire, Oxford History of the British Empire* (Oxford: OUP, 2008), 209.

6 John Warhurst, 'Religion and Politics in the Howard Decade', *Australian Journal of Political Science*, 42.1, March 2007, 19.

7 Matthew Buchanan quoting Marion Maddox in 'Catholic politicians blessed with rise to top of parties', *SMH*, 5 December 2009.

containing Christian terms[8] increased from 9.1% in 2000 to 21.7% in 2006'.[9] Many more issues now debated in Parliament involved the interaction of religion and politics.[10]

John Howard, Liberal Prime Minister, from 1996 to 2007, and Kevin Rudd, leader of the Australian Labor Party from 2006 and Prime Minister from 2007 to 2010, were both churchgoers, overt in their Christianity and its relevance to the public square. Both courted what was understood as 'the Christian vote'.[11] We were introduced to Howard in chapter 15, along with his two evangelical 2 IC's, Treasurer Peter Costello and Deputy Prime Minister, Anderson. This troika of Christian politicians led the resurgence in advocacy of Christian values which featured so strongly in the first decade of the new century. They were helped by an apparent unwillingness by the Labor opposition to push aggressive secular policies.

Howard, raised as a Methodist, became an Anglican and, while Prime Minister, worshipped regularly in the parish church of Christ Church, Lavender Bay, North Sydney. He believed in the Protestant work ethic, capitalism and economic prosperity, and he thought the Protestant establishment had done a lot more to be proud of than ashamed in its contribution to Australian history. He was therefore happy to attend what some purported to be the wedding of capitalist materialism with 'the prosperity gospel'[12] when in 2002 he opened the new Hillsong convention centre in western Sydney.

Peter Costello, a committed evangelical who consciously modelled himself on William Wilberforce, shared Howard's conservatism. He supported the Lyons Forum, the Right-wing conservative think tank. He spoke strongly on the essential value to our society of the Christian heritage and the Ten Commandments at a National Day of Thanksgiving in Melbourne in 2004. In his overt support for reconciliation with the Aboriginal people, he departed from his leader, but he supported Howard's view that Muslims who could not support Australian values should not come here. He, too, courted the support for the Liberal Party of Australia's largest church, Hillsong, and opposed euthanasia on religious grounds.

8 'Christ, church, faith, pray, Jesus, Bible, spiritual, God and/or religion'

9 Anna Crabb, 'Invoking Religion in Australian Politics', *Australian Journal of Political Science*, 44.2, 2009, 263.

10 Speeches on 19 policy issues used religious language in 2000, 32 in 2006 (Crabb, 'Invoking Religion in Australian Politics', 264).

11 There was probably no such thing, just the vote of Christians.

12 Marion Maddox, *God under Howard: The Rise of the Religious Right in Australian Politics* (Crows Nest: Allen and Unwin, 2005).

John Anderson, leader of the National Party and Deputy Prime Minister from 1999 to 2005, was the most overt of evangelical Protestant Christians in the Howard Cabinet. He was a peacemaker between factions, and especially kept the relationship between John Howard and Peter Costello under control. On his departure, this became more fraught and the whole cabinet more fractious.[13] Anderson feels keenly that he and Costello should have worked harder at translating their personal friendship and their common debt to William Wilberforce into political potency.[14] Independently of each other, but dependent on their shared faith, Anderson and Howard both came up with the response to the 2004 Boxing Day tsunami which impressed the world and with which few Australians seemed to quibble, namely that Australia would make a billion dollar donation to disaster-afflicted Indonesia.[15]

Anderson was prone to see reality in terms of black and white, with most of the white on the conservative side of politics. When introduced in 1991 to Australian Democrat Senator Karin Sowada, on learning that she was an evangelical Sydney Anglican, he looked her in the eye and said 'I don't know how you can be a Christian and a member of the Australian Democrats'. Evangelical Christians, however, are found in all political parties, and 15 years later at the height of the Howard Government's hard line on asylum seekers, Sowada, on reading his biography, found herself wondering: What were Anderson's 'views when the Howard Government was lying over the children overboard and dissembling over the dreadful sinking of SIEV X with the loss of over 350 lives, including women and children?'[16] If Sowada's framing of her question is fair, the answer would be that Anderson would have found this very hard. He was not given to 'dissembling'; neither was he without courage. On the eve of the 11 September 2001 terrorist attacks on New York and Washington, Anderson had fallen out badly with Prime Minister, Howard. Anderson did not support the policy of off-shore processing of 'boat people'. The two were not on the best of terms when Howard went off to America leaving Anderson in charge as acting Prime Minister. In the middle of the night, Anderson received a phone call from a secret service agent, giving him a 7-digit phone number to ring. He was thus able to speak with the Prime Minister, who was then in a bunker under the Australian Embassy. The coolness between the two of

---

13 Paul Gallagher, *Faith and Duty: The John Anderson Story* (Milsons Point: Random House Australia, 2006), 234.

14 Gallagher, *John Anderson Story,* 245; John Anderson interviewed by Stuart Piggin, 21 April 2007.

15 Gallagher, *John Anderson Story*, 197.

16 Karin Sowada's review of *John Anderson Story*, *Southern Cross*, 30 January 2007.

them evaporated immediately as they together dealt with the emergency. The sinking of the SIEV X just five weeks later came in the middle of an election campaign. Most Australians then seemed to agree that the country faced 'an unprecedented situation' which made it easy for them to accept the horrible charge that asylum seekers had thrown their children overboard. It was a convenient charge for the government, but that does not prove that it was 'dissembling' to propagate it. The charge was later disproved, an outcome that did not enhance Howard's reputation. But the Bali attack a year later, which killed 88 Australians, validated Howard's belief that these were dangerous times, calling for vigilance in the area of national security. In that the Prime Minister received Anderson's unequivocal support. Howard later said of his relationship with Anderson, 'We trusted each other completely'.[17]

One keen to argue that the conservative Coalition parties did not have a 'monopoly on God' was Kevin Rudd.[18] Raised a Catholic, he became, like Howard, Costello, and Anderson, an Anglican, in his case without ceasing to be a Catholic! After the 2007 federal election, when he became Prime Minister, the press found him most accessible when he emerged from church each Sunday, usually St John's Anglican Church in Canberra. When in opposition, Kevin Rudd worked hard to counter the Coalition's capacity to win the vote of the large majority of those who are regular churchgoers.[19] He formed a discussion group within the Labor Party to educate its politicians on the relationship between religion and values. Keen to bring the Labor Party back to its roots, he demonstrated at a National Forum on Australia's Christian Heritage in 2006, that they owed a great deal to Jesus.[20] Rudd was an articulate spokesman for the prophetic tradition of Dietrich Bonhoeffer.[21] He wanted the prophetic voice of Christianity to speak into the political process. 'Throughout, this country's history,' he wrote, 'the church has been at its best when it has been both fearless and informed in its ethical critique of government and corporate behaviour.'[22]

---

17 John Howard, *Lazarus Rising* (Sydney: HarperCollins, 2010), plate 24.

18 Tom Frame, 'The Labor Party and Christianity: A Reflection on *The Latham Diaries*,' *Quadrant*, 50.1–2, 2006, 32.

19 55% of churchgoers voted for the Coalition in 2004; 33% for the Labor Party. Warhurst, 'Religion and Politics in the Howard Decade,' 21.

20 Kevin Rudd, 'Christianity, the Australian Labor Party and Current Challenges in Australian Politics,' in Stuart Piggin (ed.), *Shaping the Good Society in Australia* (Macquarie University: ACHNF, 2006), 159–170.

21 Kevin Rudd, 'Faith in Politics,' *The Monthly,* October 2006, 27.

22 Rudd, 'Christianity, the Australian Labor Party and Current Challenges in Australian Politics,' 162.

What was achieved by these Christians in politics? Howard's ministry achieved some striking social engineering along conservative Christian lines: generous support of Christian schools, chaplains in schools, more religion in the Australia-wide history syllabus, and resistance to same-sex marriage. In spite of Rudd's displacement by Julia Gillard as Prime Minister in 2010, the Labor government did not dismantle these policies. Ironically, Gillard, a professing atheist, while Prime Minister, maintained her opposition to same-sex marriage. Rudd announced in 2013 that he now identified with the 53 per cent of professing Christians who supported gay marriage,[23] and Julia Gillard also changed her mind, announcing in 2015 that she would now support same-sex marriage.[24]

On 29 June 2005, Bill Shorten, then federal secretary of the AWU, and from 2012 leader of the ALP, called on Peter Jensen, Archbishop of Sydney. 'So why have you come to see me?' Peter asked. Shorten answered, 'Because we can't pick your politics, we can't pigeonhole you.' 'That's right,' Jensen replied. 'I'm in no one's pocket.' Shorten was hoping to recruit the Archbishop in the campaign against the Howard Government's projected draconian 'Work Choices' legislation. He found Jensen was an easy convert even if he was in no one's pocket. Jensen had been preparing his Boyer lectures which were to be given in late 2005. For that he had read Judith Brett's *Australian Liberals and the Moral Middle Class*. This strengthened his understanding of the need for a new politics transcending the left/right divide, a biblical communitarianism based on freedom with responsibility, rather than the ideological individualism of Howard and Turnbull. Jensen's public theology was also being shaped by the thought of Christian philosopher and social entrepreneur, Michael Schluter. In Britain, Schluter had fought to keep Sundays special in face of the Thatcherite onslaught on any traditions which hampered round the clock commercial activity. Jensen was introduced to Schluter's thought by Lindsay Tanner, then Labor Shadow Minister for Transport, and from 1997 Minister for Finance and Deregulation. Jensen called him after reading his book on the impact of work on people's lives and a friendship grew.[25]

Jensen's preference for a prophetic rather than a partisan approach to politics was shared by his more outspoken brother, Phillip, from 2003 to 2014 Dean of St. Andrew's Cathedral. In 2007 the Howard government lost power to the Labor Party, led by Kevin Rudd. The new shadow treasurer, Joe Hockey,

23 Kevin Connects website, http://www.kevinruddmp.com/2013/05/church-and-state-are-able-to-have.html accessed 20 May 2013.

24 *SMH*, 26 August 2015.

25 Andrew West, *The Monthly*, December 2005 – January 2006, no.8.

a committed, Jesuit-trained, but liberal, Catholic, in 2009 gave an address to the Sydney Institute entitled 'In Defence of God'. By 'God' he meant the common faith and values of all people of goodwill and moderation. This was his formula for a civil religion which could be used to fuse an Australian democratic identity. It was his mechanism for managing religious differences in a multicultural society. The secular press was not impressed. Journalist Annabel Crabb has God demur: 'My quibble is that, like Kevin [Rudd], you adopt the bits about Me that you like, and don't mention the bits that you don't. I am to be used as 'an analogy of faith in all its forms'? For Goodness' sakes, Joe, man up! Is that the best you can do?'[26] Phillip Jensen was not fooled either. He was rarely fooled and never through any need to defer to the powerful. He attacked Hockey's argument unsparingly:

> [Hockey] noticed that the Opera House usually is playing music inspired by faith. But his kind of faith will not inspire such music. He noticed that members of religious organisations are nearly twice as likely to be community volunteers. But his faith will not lead to more community volunteers. He noticed the decline in religious observance in Australia. But he fails to notice that it is those who take their Scriptures seriously who are retaining adherents and growing.[27]

All good (demonstrably true) points, but the only good Jensen saw in Hockey's address was that it is 'great' that political leaders 'are raising the issue of faith in the public arena'. He concluded with the words 'Let's keep the conversation going'. But one would have had to relish martyrdom to attempt to converse with the then Dean of Sydney, and Hockey, though his nearest church was named after the first Catholic martyr in the South Pacific,[28] was not so inclined.

The Political Defence of Christian Values

Coming to the aid of Christians unused to engagement in the political process was the Australian Christian Lobby (ACL). Its chief critics were secularists who do not want Christians interfering in the political process and Christians who agree with the secularists in this respect. The greatest lie that Christians have ever believed, maintained ACL managing director, Jim Wallace, is that

---

26 Annabel Crabb, 'God's memo for Kevin and Joe,' *SMH,* 14–15 November 2009.

27 Phillip Jensen, 'Sugar and spice and all things nice: a safe god for politicians', *SMH,* 14–15 November 2009.

28 St Peter Chanel Catholic Church, Hunter's Hill.

they should not be involved in politics.[29] The ACL was formed in Brisbane by John Gagliardi, journalist and lay leader from the Christian Outreach Centre in Brisbane and founder of its Christian Heritage College. He had a vision for a parliamentary lobby group, representing all denominations, which he called the Australian Christian Coalition. It was launched in 1995 and changed its name to the ACL in 2001.

ACL appointed Jim Wallace as its managing director in 2000 and relocated to Canberra the next year to be at the hub of political life. After 32 years in the Australian Army, Wallace, then Commander of Special Forces, was in line for promotion to Major-General, and if he had stayed on he would have tripled his pension. Instead he retired to head the ACL, and drew no salary. It was hard going as many Christians, perhaps most, agreed with the secularists that it is unwise to mix church and state. But Wallace was himself an able media performer and clear strategist, and he had a succession of good people as chiefs of staff: Caroline Cormack, founder of the Brisbane Lord Mayor's Prayer Breakfast; David Yates who gave up a promising career in the Public Service; and Lyle Shelton, who had worked for a senator.

The ACL motto is 'voice for values'. Wallace believed that Christ wants Christians to influence nations and the world for Christ. He argued that people often say, 'Don't legislate your morality on me', but somebody's morality is always being legislated. Thomas Jefferson believed that democracy could only work with a religious people. Without a basic religious understanding, 'you get tyrants'. The Christian constituency has every right to exercise its influence, and therefore the challenge is to get politicians to take the Christian constituency seriously.[30]

The churches, Wallace believed, had been too narrow in their interests. They were increasingly committed to environmental and social justice matters, but they seemed to him to have lost their nerve when it came to moral issues. Wallace reasoned that Ephesians 5 says that Christians have to expose the ways of the world; the Church does not do that; so the ACL has to. It does it in three ways: by lobbying, by supporting politicians who espouse Christian values, and by training and educating Christian activists.

Its most outstanding lobbying achievement was the *Marriage Amendment Act 2004* which explicitly defined marriage as 'the union of a man and a woman to the exclusion of all others, voluntarily entered into for life'. In 2004 ACL jointly organised the National Marriage Forum, attended by over 1,000

29 Robert Law, 'Australian Christian Lobby,' *Trowel & Sword*, November 2004.
30 Jim Wallace interviewed by Stuart Piggin, 14 February 2012.

representatives of a wide cross-section of Christian denominations, to support this definition of marriage and procure its inclusion in an amendment to the Marriage Act and the Family Law Act. A Senate committee to review the marriage issue, received 16,000 submissions, a record for any parliamentary committee, 99 per cent of which were in favour of the ACL's position. Politics, observed Wallace, is largely about numbers, so the ACL played the numbers game and did it well.

Whilst opposing gay marriage and gay adoption and parenting, ACL supported the rights of same-sex couples to access Medicare, social security, superannuation benefits and inheritances. In defence of the family, ACL supported child protection and opposed the sexualisation of children. It campaigned against human trafficking and sex slavery, prostitution, pornography, euthanasia, poverty and homelessness. It organised a training program for people aged 18 to 26 involving mentoring and coaching in government and policy formation. To give Christians guidance on how to vote in federal and State elections, ACL issued voters' guides reporting responses of candidates to ten questions on a range of topics, and, during election campaigns, arranged Meet Your Candidate Forums. Before the 2007 election, both Howard and Rudd appealed for the Christian vote in a webcast streamed live by the ACL to a claimed 100,000 Christians in 700 churches across the country.

The third wing of the modern evangelical movement, the Pentecostals, had a simple approach to political involvement. Hillsong's Brian Houston insisted he was as open to Labor's message as to that of the conservatives. 'Hillsong does not have a political agenda,' he maintained. 'I do, however, support individual Christians who feel called to influence politics, just as I would a Christian having influence in business, the arts, entertainment or sport. I would encourage those on the Left of the political spectrum to try to gain a greater understanding of churches such as Hillsong. These are growing churches that represent a broad cross-section of people from various political persuasions. To polarise them as one kind of voter would be unwise.'[31] With Howard and Costello happy to attend Hillsong functions and court the Pentecostal vote for the Liberals, Houston also invited the leader of the Labor Party in 2004, Mark Latham, to attend. He refused, but there followed the defeat of Labor in the 9 October 2004 election and victory for Liberal candidate, Louise Markus, who was then a Hillsong employee. Labor, led by Kevin Rudd from 2007, could see that it would have to woo the Hillsong vote, and Labor Senator, Brian Faulkner, visited Hillsong.

31 Quoted by Andrew West in 'Labor's God Squad', *Australian,* 6 July 2005.

Most of the evangelical churches, however, were not involved in federal and State politics to any marked extent. The Howard Government fostered an increased interest from evangelicals, especially at first from non-mainstream conservative religious groups who favoured conservative social, and neo-liberal economic policies. Indeed, Howard at his most conservative, was to the left of the Christian Right which reached its apogee in 2004 when Steve Fielding was elected to the Senate in the Commonwealth Parliament.[32] A member of CityLife, a megachurch, then the largest in Melbourne,[33] Fielding was elected to represent the Family First Party, founded in 2002 by Andrew Evans, General Superintendent of the AOG. Fielding, his own person, at times distanced himself from Howard, the ACL and even churches, and Howard preferred conservative Christians who were more predictable. This did not include mainline churches, some of whom were critical of his right-wing policies on asylum seekers and First Australians. Howard was remarkably tolerant of groups outside of the mainstream, such as 'Catch the Fire Ministries', and more 'beneath the radar' groups such as the Exclusive Brethren.

Some of the Open Brethren, who never identified with the Exclusive Brethren, in 2007 renamed themselves the Christian Community Churches (Australia) so as to be no longer confused with the Exclusive Brethren. The involvement of the latter in politics was a reversal of a determination as old as the movement itself to stay out of politics on the basis of its fundamental principle of separation from the world. The Exclusive Brethren did not even vote, let alone support political parties financially. Dating back to 1832, the movement formally began at a meeting in Plymouth, England, led by John Nelson Darby. Pre-millennialist and dispensationalist, it encouraged its members to 'withdraw' from those contaminated by the world, which involved the separation of married couples when one spouse offended against the leaders of the movement.

By the end of the twentieth century, the Exclusive Brethren in Australia were led by John Hales (1923–2002) and his son, Bruce D. Hales (b.1952).[34] The latter, the 'Elect Vessel', in 2004, committed the Brethren to support for the Howard Government in its opposition to the Green agenda of same-sex marriage and withdrawal from Iraq. The 'Elect Vessel' also anonymously supported political parties in the United States, Canada, and New Zealand

32 Andrew Evans, the retired pastor of the 5,000 strong Paradise Community Church in Adelaide, was the founder of Family First, and he was elected to the South Australian Upper House in 2002.

33 Soon to be overtaken by Planetshakers City Church, founded in 2004.

34 Ian McDowell, *A Brief History of the 'Brethren'* (Sydney: Victory Books, 1968), 48–52.

known to oppose same-sex unions and to support American foreign policy, including the war in Iraq. He wanted voters in Western democracies to awaken to the reality that left-wing parties were committed to 'institutionalising immorality'.[35] In Australia, the Exclusive Brethren had a more pragmatic reason for supporting Howard. They conducted 33 of their own schools as they could not, for religious reasons, allow their children to be educated in public schools. The leader of the Labor Party from 2003 to 2005, Mark Latham, had an ideological opposition to the funding of private schools, and, though a 'rich, cashed-up sect', the Exclusive Brethren had good financial reasons for opposing a Labor government.[36]

Members of the Howard Government insisted on their right to deal with the Brethren on the grounds that they were a legal organisation and that the Australian Constitution enshrined freedom of religion. It is not a crime to meet with the Exclusive Brethren, insisted Treasurer, Peter Costello. 'In fact, the crime would be if a member of parliament refused to meet anybody on the basis of their religious convictions.'[37] Kevin Rudd, newly elected leader of the Labor Party, was happy to commit that crime. He condemned the Exclusive Brethren as an 'extremist cult' who break up families and he refused to meet with them.[38] Howard, always gracious to the Religious Right, met with their leaders readily, and they supported financially the successful Liberal campaign for re-election in 2004 and the unsuccessful campaign in 2007.[39] Rudd insisted that religious conviction could not be allowed to cloak illegal activity, but, after election as Prime Minister, he refused to concede to the request from the Greens and from disillusioned ex-members of the Exclusive Brethren for an inquiry into their activities: 'The Government believes that such an enquiry could unreasonably interfere with the capacity of members of the Exclusive Brethren to practise their faith freely and openly.'[40] Rudd even increased the funding of Brethren schools. Attempts by Greens leader, Bob Brown, to have a governmental inquiry into the Brethren were repeatedly defeated.

---

35 Nicky Hagar, *The Hollow Men: A Study in the politics of deception* (Nelson: Craig Potton Publishing, 2006), 18–39.

36 Bernard Doherty, "The 'Brethren Cult Controversy': Dissecting a Contemporary Australian 'Social Problem'," *Alternative Spirituality and Religion Review*, 4.1, 2013, 25–48.

37 Interviewed by Neil Mitchell, 3AW, 22 August 2007, quoted in Michael Bachelard, *Behind the Exclusive Brethren* (Melbourne: Scribe, 2008), 175.

38 Bachelard, *Behind the Exclusive Brethren*, 212.

39 Mike Clancy, *Howard's Seduction of Australia: Where to Now?* (Watsons Bay: Fast Books, 2007), 109f.

40 Press release, Kevin Rudd's office, 6 May 2008, quoted in Bachelard, *Behind the Exclusive Brethren*, 291.

Interdenominational prayer movements have ever been a feature of evangelical Christianity. But one started on 7 August 2000 was a traditional evangelical way of addressing new anxieties. 'Rise Up Australia' was established to promote prayer for the transformation of Australia. It was supported mainly by Pentecostal churches and stood for a conservative social program, opposition to the multifaith dimension to multiculturalism, and was to become vociferously anti-Islamic after September 11, 2001. It consistently emphasised that Australia is a Christian nation or a Christian democracy and encouraged Christians in other Western nations to remember their Christian heritage. Started in Melbourne, by 2009 it held monthly prayer meetings in more than 50 locations throughout Australia and it had also spread to North America, Britain and Africa, another manifestation of the international expansion of Australian evangelicalism.

Proposed changes in social policy divided the churches. When in 2008 the Race Discrimination Commissioner, Tom Calma,[41] through the Australian Human Rights Commission (AHRC), invited submissions to its discussion paper, *Freedom of Religion and Belief in the 21st Century,* he managed to offend most of the conservative Christian churches. 'There is evidence,' he reported on the ABC, 'of a growing fundamentalist religious lobby, in areas such as same-sex relationships, stem-cell research and abortion'.[42] Since Catholics, the Orthodox and Protestants were all concerned about such issues, Calma was branding all Christians as fundamentalists, complained David Palmer,[43] convener of the Presbyterian Church of Victoria's Church and Nation Committee. Jim Wallace of the ACL thought Calma's comments were 'outrageous' and should be 'roundly condemned'.[44] Morling College lecturer, Rod Benson, thought that Australian Baptists would support a strong condemnation of Calma's initiative as 'antithetical to the Australian way of life and detrimental to the fostering of a flourishing liberal democratic society'.[45] Moore College lecturer in ethics, Andrew Cameron, chair of the Social Issues Executive of the Anglican Diocese of Sydney, was released from his duties to work full-time on a response to the Freedom of Religion project. He could see the need for vigilance or the churches might be denied exemptions in anti-discrimination

41 http://www.humanrights.gov.au/news/media-releases/2008-media-release-supporting-declaration-next-step accessed 9 June 2013.

42 http://www.abc.net.au/news/stories/2008/09/17/2366511.htm?section=justin accessed 9 June 2013.

43 David Palmer to Jim Wallace, email 6 October 2008.

44 Jim Wallace to Robert Benn, Moderator General of the Presbyterian Church of Australia, email 17 September 2008.

45 Rod Benson to David Palmer, email 9 October 2008.

legislation, be subjected to anti-vilification laws, and might witness the erosion of religious freedoms through human rights legislation. But he counselled a 'polite and carefully argued' response. After all, the Human Rights Commission was only doing its job, the churches should assume that they would receive a fair hearing, and they should 'play a long game'.[46] Since legislation was not imminent the churches should educate the population just as the early Church overcame the Roman prejudice against Christianity.

Conservative Christians became the leading opponents of legislating human rights on the grounds that it would be used by anti-Christian groups to restrict freedom of religion. They argued that misguided governments put the Christian heritage at risk by seeking to legislate against perceived Christian intolerance towards people of other religions. Such 'intolerance' is far less than the intolerance of those who do not go to Church, they argue on the basis of values surveys.[47] It is not a problem, so why legislate on the matter? The legislation which has been passed so far in Australia (such as Victoria's religious vilification law) had done a lot more to increase religious intolerance than to reduce it.[48]

While the majority of Christians would have preferred a spiritual awakening, they were experiencing a political awakening. Precisely because in Australia it had not been illegal to discriminate against people on religious grounds, Christians just accepted it as part of what it meant to live in a secular state. But when the state contemplated outlawing discrimination against Muslims on religious grounds it was bound to alert Christians to what should long have been their rights. Lurking in the background was a propensity to support 'Muslim exceptionalism' by secular Australians in the habit of giving uncritical support to multiculturalism in all its forms. Privileging Islam in Australia when they represented less than 1 per cent of the population, while more than 60 per cent of Australians identified with Christianity, appeared absurd to conservative Christians. By awakening them to their heritage and their rights, it threatened the role which Christianity had traditionally played in Australian society as an agent of community harmony. Having to respond to Islam in the political sphere was certainly dividing Australian Christians. It even divided the Christian Democratic Party in NSW. Its two members in the NSW Legislative Council, Fred Nile and Gordon Moyes, personified conservative and progressive evangelicalism respectfully, and fell out spectacularly

46 Andrew Cameron to David Palmer, email 7 October 2008.

47 Gary D. Bouma and Beverly R. Dixon, *The Religious Factor in Australian Life* (Melbourne: MARC Australia, 1986), vi, vii, 51–58.

48 The same might also be true of Section 18C of the Racial Discrimination Act (1995).

over the former's hard line against Muslim immigration and Muslim schools. Nile complained that Moyes supported the Greens far too often, and Moyes responded that the Greens were 'far more Christian'.[49] Moyes withdrew from the CDP, became an Independent, then a member of the Family First Party, and lost his seat in 2011. Politics was an accurate barometer of differences in evangelical ranks over social issues.

Indigenous Developments

Evangelical Christianity in the public domain expresses itself in two major ways, to protect the weak and improve the lot of the needy, and to give justice and liberty to the oppressed. The former can be authoritarian and therefore makes progressive evangelicals anxious. The latter can be libertarian and makes the conservatives anxious. Both are evident in the two most prominent events in the Aboriginal history of the first decade of the 21st century: the 2007 'Intervention' and the 2008 'Apology'.

On 15 June 2007 the 'Little Children are Sacred' report, *Inquiry into the Protection of Aboriginal Children from Sexual Abuse*, was released by the Northern Territory Government. Children needed to be in school, the report insisted, for there they are safe from abuse, and alcohol consumption needed to be curtailed in the communities where they live. It also recommended education campaigns on 'the impact of alcohol, pornography and gambling on communities, families and children'. The federal government responded swiftly with the 'Northern Territory National Emergency Response Act 2007' or 'the Intervention' which received bipartisan support in the lead-up to the federal election (November 2007). The logistical force for implementing the government's response was made up of 600 soldiers from the Australian Defence Force. It seemed draconian and opportunistic given the impending election.

It was certainly urgent. Just two weeks after the 'Little Children are Sacred' report was released by the NT Government, there were troops in the Hermannsburg outstations. Pornography and alcohol were banned in communities of more than 100 people; welfare payments were quarantined and the people were taken off welfare; the permit system was dismantled and all property was acquired by the Government. The aim was to stop violence and abuse by reasserting government paternalism. Quarantining was necessary because children could not safely be allocated to others in the

49 *SMH*, 4 February 2009.

same community, and neither could they be taken away because of the stolen generations experience.

The evidence of sexual violence especially alarmed evangelical readers of the 'Little Children are Sacred' report. Roslyn Phillips, research officer for the Festival of Light, reminded the government that 17 years earlier (in 1990) four Aboriginal pastors had pleaded with federal MPs to 'Please ban X-rated videos. They are causing the genocide of our people, especially in remote areas.' She applauded the federal government's intention to ban X-rated videos and DVDs in the Northern Territory, 'better late than never'.[50]

Archbishop Peter Jensen was another who welcomed the Intervention, but only if done with sensitivity. He had read John Harris's epic study of the Aboriginal encounter with Christianity, *One Blood* (first published 1990), and was profoundly affected by it. The extremity of the problem suggested the need for extreme measures. But these had to be balanced by the need to respect 'the integrity of communities':

> A bureaucratic or urban mind-set around the issue of land tenure may do untold damage to indigenous communities, particularly when seen against the backdrop of decades of dispossession and relocation. Solutions that rely on racially discriminatory or heavy-handed arrangements will cast a shadow over any of the good that might otherwise come out of the Government's intervention.[51]

At the same time as governments and concerned white Christians debated the Intervention, Aboriginal Christians went about the business of discerning the Lord's will. Within a year, three major Aboriginal Bible translation projects were completed after more than thirty years' work: the Kriol whole Bible in northern NT and WA (May 2007); the Ngaanyatjarra Shorter Bible in Central Australia/WA (May 2008); and the Djambarrpuyngu New Testament in Arnhem Land, NT (June 2008). At the dedication of the last at Galinwin'ku where the Aboriginal Revival had begun three decades earlier, the following prophetic word came through Anne Aysom, who had lived on Elcho Island where her accountant husband worked for the Community Council:

> I feel the Lord is saying that what He has begun, He has now finished. His faithful workers have produced His Word for all the people to read. But now He is starting a new work that will affect all of Australia. It

50 'Porn Action 17 Years Late', *Festival of Light Australia*, 22 June 2007.

51 *SMH*, 24 September 2007.

> will start like ripples in a pond after a stone thrown into the water, and will become a tsunami, and it will come from the faithful expounding and teaching from this new Bible. People's hearts and lives will be changed and this nation will never be the same.[52]

If the Intervention provoked debate, the Apology was received with less ambivalence. Elected at the end of November 2007, Prime Minister, Kevin Rudd put his Christianity quickly to work. Asked how he wrote his apology to the 'stolen generations' of Australia's indigenous peoples (13 February 2008), Rudd replied that he went to Church and then he returned to the Lodge and there in his study he wrote the speech:

> For the pain, suffering and hurt of these Stolen Generations, their descendants and for their families left behind, we say sorry.
>
> To the mothers and the fathers, the brothers and the sisters, for the breaking up of families and communities, we say sorry.
>
> And for the indignity and degradation thus inflicted on a proud people and a proud culture, we say sorry.

The language of the speech is derived from the Bible, it has a liturgical cadence rarely found in public life, and it has brought some moral clarity to an issue which has bedevilled the nation. Don Watson, speech writer in the early 1990s for Prime Minister, Paul Keating, considered it one of the nation's great speeches:

> It was Kevin Rudd speaking and was therefore authentic, and it released authenticity. It was language with a biblical provenance, which the public language does not have. As a result of what happened on 13 February 2008 Australia is a different country, not greatly different, but still different. We now have a more certain moral compass to guide and assess relations with aboriginal people in the future. In this sense, his speech was Lincolnesque, in that its message will have to be considered in the future: it holds people to moral account.[53]

The apology was 'Lincolnesque' in its brevity, recalling his Gettysburg Address. But Rudd followed it with a twenty-minute speech to Parliament in which he catalogued what might be done at a practical level to improve the living

52 John Blacket, *Khesed News*, 74, September 2008.

53 'Saturday Extra' with Geraldine Doogue, ABC Radio National, 16 February 2008.

conditions of Indigenous people, otherwise all talk of reconciliation would be 'little more than a clanging gong'. Historian Geoffrey Treloar wrote:

> ... on this great day ... only an evangelical Christian could have spoken the way the Prime Minister did this morning. Apart from the reference to I Corinthians 13, it was clear to me that a deep understanding of pain at wrongdoing and also of the mechanism and transforming effect of repentance informed a truly great speech. The evangelical standpoint also enabled Kevin Rudd to do what none of his predecessors have been able to do. Nobody will say this publicly, I suppose, but I'm sure it is the case.[54]

To those given to discerning such things, the speech was 'evangelical', but why it should have been so is not so obvious. Rudd's Christianity is evidently Anglican (his wife's denomination) and Catholic (his mother's denomination), but not so evidently evangelical. The speech may have been more evangelical than Rudd himself because Rudd may not have written it by himself. It was written substantially by one more evangelical than he, namely Tim Dixon, his speechwriter between 2007 and 2010. Dixon, who had attended Trinity Grammar School in Sydney and was a lawyer and economist, sought divine aid to write the speech. He wrote to Glenda Weldon, a member of the Christian and Missionary Alliance Church, and one whom he respected as a woman of prayer, and asked 'for prayer because he had been given the job of writing that speech'. Weldon observes: 'No doubt Rudd did his thing with what he was given but Tim definitely wrote the speech.'[55] It is the congruence of the Christian convictions of drafter and speaker on a matter of crucial significance for the national soul that is significant here. Is it perhaps an example of the value which all the churches together can bring to the making of public policy?

It was in 2008, too, that the National Aboriginal and Torres Strait Islander Christian Alliance (NATSICA) was formed 'to restore order and direction to the church and the nation', and Andrew Forrest, the Christian CEO of the mining company Fortescue Metals, established a 'covenant' to employ and train 50,000 indigenous Australians.[56] For their part, some Aboriginal Christians, like their white brothers and sisters, were rediscovering and asserting the socially-radical dimensions of the Gospel. Pastor Ray Minniecon and other indigenous leaders, on 23 August 2008 on Possession Island, renounced the possession of Australia by Captain Cook. They affirmed in a

---

54 Geoff Treloar to Stuart Piggin, email 13 February 2008.

55 Stuart Piggin from Glenda Weldon, email 23 July 2013.

56 Andrew Burrell, *Twiggy: The High-Stakes Life of Andrew Forrest* (Collingwood: Black Inc., 2013), 249–254.

'Proclamation' that the authority of the Indigenous people over the land is God-given. But it is hard to generalise about Aboriginal Christians, just as it is hard to generalise about all Indigenous people, because they have many cultures. Alongside Minniecon's radicalism, there were other Aboriginal Christian leaders who were sceptical of government-backed support for the restoration of traditional Aboriginal culture and ceremonies. They believed these cultures had been twisted by Satan. They preferred to seek a God-given culture.[57] That remained an unresolved issue, but the apology, reconciliation, and employment initiatives were desired by all Indigenous people.

The Uniting Church and Homosexuality

Debate on Homosexuality, as seen in chapter 17, was the occasion for Sydney Anglicanism's spectacular advance on the world stage. It may also have been responsible for the spectacular collapse of the Uniting Church on the Australian stage. In spite of its reputation for liberalism, the majority of members of the Uniting Church were conservative on the question of the ordination of homosexuals, yet the Assembly of the Uniting Church was controlled by theological liberals who politically outmanoeuvred the conservatives and progressively opened their denomination to the possibility of accepting openly gay ministers. In 1997 the Report of the Sexuality Task Group advised that heterosexual and lesbian, gay and bisexual relationships should be accepted with 'love, caring and compassion' and, as we have seen, that practising homosexuality was not necessarily a bar to ordination. The response from the vast majority was categorically negative. The Task Group appointed social researcher Peter Bentley to process the responses. He reported that up to one-fifth of the entire membership had made submissions and of these over 91% were opposed. The strongest opposition came from South Australia and NSW; of the small numbers in favour most came from councils of elders in Victoria and Western Australia. Ministers were more liberal than lay persons, and women ministers more liberal than men. But still 66 per cent of ministers were opposed to the Report's recommendations.

Indigenous and 'ethnic' congregations were particularly vehement and uniform in their condemnation of the report.[58] This was an embarrassment

57 John Blacket, *Khesed News,* 74, September 2008.

58 Peter Bentley, Analysis of the Responses to the Interim Report on Sexuality, Uniting Church, February 1997, accessed 30 October 2017 at http://www.confessingcongregations.com/uploads/Liberalism_Sexuality_and_the_Future_of_the_Uniting_Church_by_Peter_Bentley.pdf.

to the liberals who were strident supporters of multiculturalism and were proud of the 150 migrant-ethnic groups from 26 different cultural traditions who worshipped in Uniting Church congregations in languages other than English. Liberals spoke of the importance of being engaged with culture, and indeed they argued that their support for homosexuals would make the church more culturally relevant. Mainly evangelicals, the ethnic ministers called the liberals to account: 'How can Assembly not express what we believe is the majority ethnic position, in a Uniting Church that desires to be a multicultural church?'[59] The liberals did appear to be more patient with the opposition which came from ethnic leaders rather than from other conservative ministers, apparently convinced that their opposition was cultural and would evaporate over time.

Attempts to ordain practising homosexuals in the Uniting Church dated back to 1981, and had been debated in various councils of the church since then. But it was not until 1997 that evangelicals realised that they should organise to resist this move. In advance of the 1997 Assembly, they formed EMU (Evangelical Members within the Uniting Church in Australia). A 'Response Form' to the Interim Report on Sexuality asked 'Is there anything you particularly want to say to the Task Group and the Standing Committee?' The response of Church historian Malcolm Prentis was typical: 'The Task Group should apologise to the church and resign.'[60]

Undeterred, the Assembly Standing Committee procured the passage of 'Resolution 84' at the 10th Assembly of the Uniting Church in 2003. 'Resolution 84', declared Prentis angrily, 'is the longest suicide note in Church history.'[61] The power to ordain practising homosexuals in a committed relationship the Assembly devolved to regional presbyteries. This was a shrewd political move by the liberals who controlled the Standing Committee. They calculated that they could not prevail to impose a radical policy on sexuality on the more conservative Assembly. So they referred the matter to presbyteries who, at first, refused to ordain known practising homosexuals, but who became more open to that possibility over time as liberals replaced increasingly disenchanted conservatives.

---

59 The Council of Korean Churches, Chairperson Rev H.K. Lee and All Korean ministers:

Statement from Ethnic Congregations within the Synod of Victoria and Tasmania in response to Assembly Resolution 84 (August 2003).

60 Malcolm D. Prentis, Interim Report on Sexuality: A Response (undated, but probably 18 December 1996).

61 A Response to Resolution 84 by Malcolm Prentis (2003), unpublished.

Liberals took genuine pride in belonging to such a progressive, mature and inclusive church. The politicians among the liberal 'oligarchs' who controlled the Assembly cleverly acknowledged that there were two opinions on this issue which should be accepted: namely 'CISAFIM' (celibacy in singleness and faithfulness in marriage) and 'right relationships' (which, according to the liberals, include long-term homosexual relationships). To the conservative evangelicals, these two opinions were irreconcilable and could not both operate in the same church. To the liberals, it was a sign of strength that the church could live with two polarised viewpoints. The problem was that so many of the church's members could not live with it and deserted the United Church in calamitous numbers. In September 2003, 34 EMU members and 39 others established Reforming Alliance. It was soon joined by over two thousand members and 160 congregations. In response, liberals declared that they were more concerned for justice than numbers. Whether rationalisation or genuine belief, it was costly. The problem was that most Uniting Church members were elderly and were conservative on matters of sexuality. The liberals hoped that their more tolerant policies would attract the young, but this did not happen. Most of the young in the Uniting Church were evangelicals and they were opposed to the new developments and left in droves for other, more conservative denominations. The young, who did embrace a more relaxed sexuality, tended not to embrace any church and so the Uniting Church did not benefit numerically from its stand.

By March 2005, the Reforming Alliance reported that nearly 6,500 members had left the church since 1997, 119 congregations had split, over 40 ministers had resigned or retired over the issue, and 40 new congregations had formed outside the Uniting Church. When the 2006 Assembly reconfirmed its liberal stance in 'Resolution 108', EMU and the Reforming Alliance formed 'The Assembly of Confessing Congregations within the Uniting Church'. It was established in only 140 congregations as the more conservative elected to abandon the sinking ship. The response was typical of evangelicals to liberal challenges: either embrace a biblical confession or leave. Evangelical members of the Uniting Church were doing both.[62] By 2006, it is true, most of the mainstream churches were suffering serious losses, but in the Uniting Church, where the liberal leaders believed in toleration or death, the losses were cataclysmic. It could achieve no unity in its diversity. The feud had lasted for a quarter of a century – a debilitating clash of world views which weakened the church. The liberals dumped the Bible in order to be relevant

62 'Sexuality and the Uniting Church', 'The Religion Report', ABC, 23 March 2005.

to the culture. That the culture with which they were seeking to connect was indeed the culture of the majority of Australians was demonstrated by the strong endorsement of same-sex marriage in the 2017 national postal survey. But it was a culture which did not reward the Uniting Church for its support, while the church's evangelical members concluded that the gospel of their church was that of the age, not of the ages. It was not a gospel which could sustain and grow a Christian denomination.

Welfare Initiatives

In reality Australia had long practised the complementarity, rather than the separation, of church and state. Governments frequently welcomed the participation of churches in the provision of health, education and welfare services. Australia, the so-called 'secular' country, has been far more dependent on churches for such services than the United States or Britain. In the United States in 2001 only 5 of the top 25 non-profit charitable organisations by income were Christian. In Britain in 2005 only 3 of the top 25 were Christian. In 2004–05 in Australia 23 of the top 25 were Christian.[63] In Australia governments have assumed responsibility for the payment of social security benefits, leaving to charities (of which the majority are Christian) the task of delivering most welfare services.

A well-researched case study of a modern Christian charity is afforded by HammondCare. From a local, if dynamic, charity[64] founded in the Great Depression by R.B.S. Hammond to provide housing for the families of poor and unemployed men (see chapter three), it was transformed under Stephen Judd, CEO from 1995, into one of the top Christian charities in Australia. In 2008 HammondCare took over two other health care providers, adding $46m to its annual revenue and doubling its staff to 2,100 and the number of people being helped by the charity to 2,600. Judd was a progressive, inclusive evangelical rather than a conservative. He had been instrumental in the election of Harry Goodhew as Archbishop in 1993 in the hope that he would change the diocesan culture to one more open to engagement with the society. HammondCare reflected Judd's convictions as he engineered its departure from more conservative evangelical institutions. Whereas they were

63 Stephen Judd and Anne Robinson, 'Christianity and the Social Services in Australia: A Conversation,' in Piggin, *Shaping the Good Society*, 111–115.

64 By 1933 Hammond's Social Services was 'the largest social services outfit in Sydney'. Stephen Judd, Anne Robinson, and Felicity Errington, *Driven by Purpose: Charities that Make the Difference* (Greenwich: HammondPress, 2012), 53.

committed to the moral reformation and religious conformity of residents and other clients, HammondCare came to focus rather on the culture of the organisation and the values and expertise of the staff.

Judd was comprehensively equipped to refashion Christian charity for a new day. First, he understood the legacy and the liability of the old days. He wrote his doctoral thesis on the history of the Anglican Church League and then he wrote a history of the Sydney Diocese. From the former he acquired a grasp of diocesan politics and a distaste for its restraint on independence of thought which he saw as a betrayal of the Reformation heritage. From the latter he came to the surprising conclusion that the Diocese owed its strength, not so much to its conservative evangelical churchmanship, as to the management of its resources.

The most striking feature of Judd's leadership of HammondCare was the clarity of purpose and strategic intentionality he brought to the role. One had to learn to work with one's environment which was fashioned by commercial realities and governmental regulations as well as the Gospel imperatives which came with being a Christian organisation.[65] Government policy had long supported a 'mixed economy of welfare', the partnership of governments and charities in welfare service delivery. Some charities accepted all government regulations and in that process lost their Christian identity. Others insisted on maintaining their foundation practices, thus becoming indifferent to developments in their industry and vulnerable to collapse. HammondCare sought a third way and flourished. It was determined to remain true to its foundation principles, but to be flexible about practices and programs, depending on changes to human needs and government policies.

Most critically, HammondCare resolved to specialise in dementia care, thus positioning itself to meet a growing need: by 2008 every day 160 new cases of dementia were being diagnosed in Australia.[66] HammondCare did so well from its focus on dementia that it was able to differentiate itself from the other 1,500 aged care providers in Australia[67] and set a new benchmark for the industry, not only in Australia but overseas, yet more evidence of the international expansion of Australian evangelicalism. It did not confine its ministry to dementia sufferers: it also offered palliative care, rehabilitation and sub-acute hospital care, it took up non-residential community care, and offered professional services (consultancy, education, and training) on a commercial basis.

65 Lake, *HammondCare*, 270.

66 Lake, *HammondCare*, 230.

67 Judd, Robinson and Errington, *Driven by Purpose*, 6.

The political context put compliance pressures on Christian charities which caused anxiety. But Judd preferred clarity and justice to a laissez-faire approach. Being interested in results, he did not attack the government in the media.[68] He preferred to negotiate with politicians and senior civil servants, but he was also at pains to make the Christian element in HammondCare's work more explicit than ever so that no-one, in the government or elsewhere, would be unaware of how public money was being spent. He also believed that it was fundamental to the 'respectful partnership' with government that the latter should realise that Christian organisations insisted on delivering services in Christian ways on the grounds that Christian beliefs added value to service delivery.[69] Being unashamedly Christian in a government-regulated industry was a model of how to be evangelical in a secular world and it made that world less secular in the process.

A major manifestation of Christian engagement in the world is the partnership which Christian Non-Government Organisations (NGO's) have with the Australian Government's AusAID to maximise the delivery of aid in the relief of poverty and other needs around the world. As of 2011 there were 43 accredited NGOs in Australia. Of these 26 were Christian organisations, and of these, some of the largest were predominantly evangelical organisations: Baptist World Aid, CBM Australia, Opportunity International, Tear Australia, The Leprosy Mission, Archbishop of Sydney's Overseas Relief and Aid Fund (ORAF), Habitat for Humanity Australia, Salvation Army International Development (SAID), and World Vision, the largest of Australia's overseas aid charities.

World Vision's CEO from 2004 to 2016 was Tim Costello, the older brother of the federal treasurer. Following the Boxing Day 2004 tsunami, while Peter had to find a billion dollars from the federal budget for relief of the disaster, Tim's World Vision Australia raised $100 million for the same purpose. Tim Costello is a strong exponent of inclusive evangelicalism with a holistic gospel which must express itself in social justice and welfare compassion as well as evangelism. He is critical of exclusive, conservative evangelicalism, and publicly opposed the election of Peter Jensen as Archbishop of Sydney in 2001 on the grounds that he would foment sectarianism within the wider church. Tim had been offended by an article in *The Briefing* which was the mouthpiece of Peter Jensen's brother, Phillip:

> A review in *The Briefing* of my book, *Tips from a Travelling Soul Searcher*, said: 'You can have either an evangelical Christianity with a message

68 Lake, *HammondCare*, 300.
69 Lake, *HammondCare*, 331.

> of salvation from sin, or you can have a social Christianity with its salvation from oppression and social justice. You cannot have both.'
>
> My considered response, which was not published, was that such 'either/or thinking' is completely foreign to the Bible. It is narrow and exclusive thinking that indeed leads to arrogance and aggressiveness.[70].

The gospel of the exclusive evangelicals, he argued, was too attenuated:

> The gaming industry, which has 10 per cent of the world's poker machines, preying on the most vulnerable in NSW has nothing to fear from this reduced Gospel. Neither have those who damage the environment. As long as the polluters are putting money in the plate to fund evangelism, they need not expect uncomfortable questioning or prophetic preaching.[71]

Tim Costello pushed back so hard against Jensen because he believed that Jensen offered 'a divisive, limited version of the rich evangelical tradition' and that, worryingly, too many Baptists agreed with Jensen's criticisms. NSW Baptists in particular had been influenced by 'Jensenism', and largely under its influence had formed in 1997 the 'Conservative Evangelical Baptist Fellowship'. It defended inerrancy and, like Jensen, was opposed to the ordination of women and maintained that social action was not integral to the Gospel. Michael Fisher, pastor of Australind Baptist Church, south of Perth, comprehensively attacked 'the Christianity of [Tim] Costello' in an article in Jensen's mouthpiece, *The Briefing*, charging him with universalism, preaching a social gospel, and holding a flawed doctrine of the atonement.[72]

At World Vision in his first year, Tim Costello was named Victorian of the Year, and in 2005 he was appointed an Officer of the Order of Australia (AO). He pursued World Vision's policy of seeking the support of all political parties to redress issues of poverty, child health, and climate change. World Vision, the purpose of which is to fight 'poverty by empowering people to transform their worlds', is committed to advocacy in the political arena: 'If you keep rescuing people from the river, eventually you have got to go upstream and see who is throwing them in.'[73] Progressive evangelicals have a taste for advocacy. In theological terms they can bring secular Australia and the Kingdom of God

70 *SMH*, 5 June 2001.

71 *SMH*, 5 June 2001.

72 Ken R. Manley, *From Woolloomooloo to 'Eternity': A History of Australian Baptists* (Milton Keynes: Paternoster, 2006), 707.

73 https://www.worldvision.com.au/about-us/faqs, (accessed 4 April 2012).

into productive interaction: since the 1980s World Vision has been esteemed as the 'the Australian people's' overseas aid agency.[74]

* * *

By the middle of the 20th century, the welfare state replaced charities in providing for the needy because the charities were not equal to the size of the task. But, by the beginning of the 21st century, Christian charities were operating on an astonishingly large scale. In 2012 Anglicare, the welfare agency of the Anglican Diocese of Sydney, had revenue of $98.5m of which $83.5m came from governments and clients, of which it had over 13,000, served by over 3,000 paid staff and volunteers. It had been in the business for 150 years. So too had Mission Australia which in 2012 was providing welfare services benefitting over 300,000 Australians. UnitingCare, the welfare agency of the National Assembly of the Uniting Church, in 2013 was providing services accessed by 2 million Australians. Its army of employees and volunteers numbered 59,000. Its mission was 'justice, hope and opportunity for all'. World Vision, Australia's largest charity, helps 20 million people with the support of 400,000 Australians largely through its child sponsorship program. The social capital contributed to Australia by Christian aid organisations with an evangelical heritage was quantitatively and qualitatively impressive, witnessing to the value of its partnership with governments as well as being the fruit of the Gospel. Australia in the first decade of the 21st century is a good illustration of the contention that secularisation is not an inevitable, irreversible process.

74 Judd, Robinson and Errington, *Driven by Purpose*, 11.

CONCLUSION

Attending to the Cure of the National Soul

'… many Indigenous Christians are more interested in Jesus as a tribal man and the stories he told than they are in King Henry VIII's split with Rome or Calvin's *Institutes*'
(Tom Mayne)

The conclusion of this study of evangelical Christianity in Australian history is that it has been a strong and pervasive influence on the shaping, not only of the heart and soul of the Australian nation, but also of its body. This claim seems preposterous because it has been so little recognised by historians,[1] but this has been a study of the role of the Gospel in nation-building. It is the story of how Jesus has stamped his image on the character and values of the Australian people.

At its birth in the eighteenth-century revivals, evangelical Christianity was characterised as 'true, vital religion'. That has come to be described in words more congenial to the modern mind as 'biblical experientialism', with the Bible as the path to truth and the experience of the Spirit as the means of vitality. The future of evangelicalism, Mark Noll has observed, depends on its capacity to 'maintain the vitality of fresh religious experience in balance with the stability of traditional biblical authority'.[2] Accordingly, its past history must be the story of how well it has done that, and the purpose of this book has been to analyse what effect doing that has had on Australian history and how well the movement has cared, not only for the souls of individuals, but for the national soul as well. This analysis is not an exercise in pure subjectivism. The experience which is essential to evangelical identity is not primarily a subjective one, but is anchored in the written Word which is itself

1 Among the few who have recognised the formative influence of the church on twentieth-century Australian history is Brian Fletcher. See his *The Place of Anglicanism in Australia* (Mulgrave: Broughton Publishing, 2008) and *An English Church in Australian Soil* (Canberra: Barton Books, 2015).

2 Mark A. Noll, *American Evangelical Christianity: An Introduction* (Oxford: Blackwell, 2001), 287.

appropriated inwardly in the fellowship of the church. This understanding which the evangelicals owed to the Reformation has an element of irreducible objectivity. Fellowship as the context for interpreting and applying the Bible, especially prized in the middle decades of the twentieth century, gave to its adherents a conviction that they were called to conspire together for time and eternity. They were addicted to action in the pursuit of truth and of souls.

This biblical and conversionist movement, it has been repeatedly noted, is reformist. It seeks to reform the church, the individual and society. It originates in a desire to replace nominal Christianity with vital Christianity and traditional Christendom, especially as institutionalised in the British Empire, with the Kingdom of God as a present and future reality. While its Australian representatives have ambitions for their locality and nation, it is a movement with international and multicultural aspirations. Its missionary movement, taking root in the 1790s, sought to make disciples of peoples of all nations. In recent decades it has produced two outstanding exports. Conservative Sydney Anglicanism and Hillsong are expanding globally apart from and in addition to the traditional missionary movement. In the case of the former, it has been able to build on a century of missionary endeavour by Australian evangelicals, especially in African nations where the majority of Anglicans are now to be found. It is integral to the emergence of a new post-colonial Christendom of the global South where the number of Christians is now greater than in the older Christian heartlands of the northern hemisphere.

Just as the concept of 'fellowship', which was not prominent in the nineteenth century, came to full flower in the middle of the twentieth century, so too did evangelicalism's commitment to evangelism. It helped that in Billy Graham it produced arguably the greatest evangelist in the history of the church and that Graham's influence on Australia was as marked as his influence on any country. Billy Graham was a great focus of unity in the evangelical movement and he moved it away from the more subjective spirituality of Keswick piety to a more outward-looking biblical activism.

The energy and confidence that the 1959 Billy Graham crusades generated in the evangelical movement came at a critical time in Australian history. The year before, the British Empire was renamed the British Commonwealth, and, two years after, Britain entered the European Economic Community. The certainties of both the Empire, the idea of which died overnight, and of Western Christendom, apparently in a state of inexorable declension, gave way to an undefined future. The challenge to find a new evangelical identity coincided in time with the search for a national Australian identity. Spiritual resources were needed for both searches, neither of which was to prove easy.

In the failure to find a replacement for Graham, the movement which enjoyed unprecedented unity in 1959, began to divide into three streams: conservative, progressive and Charismatic/Pentecostal. Their leaders were not always kind in their assessment of each other in the closing decades of the twentieth century. It felt like a resurgence of sectarianism. But it has been argued in this research that, within the evangelical movement, rivalry often took the form of holy emulation and sanctified competition. It may be that in these recent decades where the three streams circled each other warily, they did better overall than if they had remained as one. In any case, in the 21st century it is clear that the three streams are quietly borrowing what they find best in the other streams. The conservatives have accepted that the social compassion beloved of the progressive evangelicals is integral to the Gospel and helpful for evangelism which they have found increasingly difficult in a secular age. The Pentecostals have added the same commitment to their ministries to increase their legitimacy. Both the conservatives and the Pentecostals are moving towards the progressive centre. As denominationalism has become decreasingly significant, especially to the young and new converts, the members of all streams have largely given up on insisting on the beliefs distinctive of denominations. The largest churches in the ACC movement, for example, have stopped stressing the importance of the Pentecostal gifts. Yet the leaders of all three streams acknowledge the desirability of bringing a prophetic ministry to bear on social issues in order to achieve greater engagement with the wider society.

There emerged, not between the streams, but within them, some disagreement about the desirability of megachurches versus church planting, of size and power on the one hand, and intimacy and variety on the other. But basically, there was agreement across the streams on how to grow a church. This must be one of the most self-evident and powerful of evangelical contributions to the wider church. To survive and thrive in a secular context, local churches must be Jesus-centred, Bible-based, and imaginatively led. For denominations as a whole, two more ingredients must be added: social concern and ministries to people of non-English speaking backgrounds in this most multicultural of nations.

In the process of arriving at this reasonably-propitious state, the evangelical movement has passed through many vicissitudes. It has had to, in order to reflect the national experience. Evangelical religion has been prominent in the nation's decades of equipoise, such as the 1880s and the 1950s, and it valued and did much to promote the stability and orderliness of those times. But it was also prominent in the radical decades of national readjustment such as the 1890s and the 1970s. In both of those experiences, Jesus was understood as transcending orthodoxy and he was found to be engaged compassionately with those outside the middle-class churches. Evangelicals coped with those developments as well, for they, too, weary of ecclesiastical routine and, in their piety, especially the more progressive among them, much prefer Jesus to orthodoxy.

As a highly culturally-adaptive movement, then, evangelicals have participated, probably more energetically than creatively, in the oscillations of radicalism and conservatism which generate the national history. Yet another aspect of evangelicalism was to the fore in the years of extremity and struggle in Australia's twentieth-century history: 1914–18; 1930s; 1939–45. There it honoured sacrifice for the national good and was fertile in the creation of ministries to relieve the national pain. Admittedly, it was not as prophetic as it might have been in its assessment of the international calamity which afflicted the world, but the prophetic is always a minority occupation and there was a minority of evangelicals who bore witness to the pacifist alternative.

It remains to summarise evangelical perspectives on a range of issues of importance to the development of the Australian identity: church/state relations, secularisation, culture, welfare, women and First Australians.

The separation of church and state, assumed to be the norm in Australia history, has actually operated for less than half of its European history, from c. 1880 to c.1960. It was preceded first by an assumed Church of England establishment and then by a plural establishment under the Church Acts. As heirs of the Puritans who had maintained a political involvement with the state in order to reform it, evangelicals in the Church of England were not blind to the advantages of establishment, but their doctrinal sympathy with evangelical Dissenters, had made them ripe for experiments in evangelical pluralism in the nineteenth century. They did well, as did all the churches, from state aid under the Church Acts. When the state aid ended, however, evangelicals were not in the main unhappy with church/state separation. The established Church of England had foisted on them bishops who were not evangelicals who appointed clergy who were not evangelicals. Better to be in control of one's own house or diocese than be subject to state interference. But strict separation or the control of one over the other were not the only options. For the last half century, church/state separation, which never strictly operated anyway, gave way to pragmatic pluralism whereby governments funded churches to operate a range of educational, health and welfare services.

Because church/state complementarity in the interests of nation building, rather than church/state separation, has been the norm in Australia, secularisation has not had free rein. Ideological secularists insist on church/state separation, but the interdependence of churches and governments in Australia has been entrenched and extensive. Values surveys have demonstrated that governmental faith in churchgoers to serve in the public interest is not unjustified. These surveys have shown that churchgoers are exceptionally productive of social capital: they are less racist and more tolerant of cultural differences than non-churchgoers.[3] The sustained high proportion of Christian organisations in the charitable sector and the increasing role of Christian schools in the education sector demonstrates that secularisation is not inexorable in Australian history. On the other hand, pragmatic pluralism exacts a price. Evangelical providers, like all other providers, have to meet government standards, and, in pursuit of the government dollar, some evangelicals have put meeting government standards ahead of their own founding convictions. Secularisation can work through the connection as well as through separation. The recent shamefully-exposed incidence of sexual abuse in church institutions shows that churches benefit from government inspection, just as the nation benefits from Christian altruism. Rigid, ideological separation of church and state is not in the interests of either.

It would be wrong to conclude that, in its preference for pragmatism, evangelicalism has sold out to the prevailing culture of its day. It has rather consistently adapted to each shift in economy and culture because its transcendent dimension has enabled it to be surprisingly flexible about the mundane dimension. It has consistently made the adjustment to its environment which it believes maximises its opportunity to do what it most values, to evangelise, to spread gospel truth, to invite their fellow Australians to enjoy peace with God through the transforming personal experience of the Christ who died for their salvation. By identifying and enhancing the latent potential in all cultural expressions to be an earthen vessel for the communication of the Gospel, the evangelicals have formed Australian society more than they have known. As to its own strength, evangelical Christianity seems to thrive in an environment which allows it to express itself in unrestrained pluralistic, even sectarian, ways. The competition inherent in pluralism is good for it. The rich variety of evangelical options is good for the nation. They represent, not so much doctrinal differences, as compassionate responses to the threats to human fulfilment arising from modernity – alienation, anomie, loss of

3 Gary D. Bouma and Beverly R. Dixon, *The Religious Factor in Australian Life* (Melbourne: MARC Australia, 1986), vi,vii; Peter Kaldor, John Bellamy, Sandra Moore, *Mission under the Microscope: Keys to Effective and Sustainable Mission* (Adelaide: OpenBook Publishers, 1995), 18.

identity. Because it addresses those needs so radically, the evangelical movement will continue to thrive and continue to evolve, most obviously along the therapeutic lines which characterises its more recent history among progressive and Charismatic evangelicals. But it will also thrive in its more astringent, Reformed manifestation, emphasising the transcendence of God and the unchanging revelation of the Gospel of Jesus Christ, for unrelenting change in the mundane world can be soul-destroying. Conservative evangelicals (R.B.S. Hammond was a case in point) have often proved the most pragmatic, versatile and strategic of operators in the harsh world of human need.

There are signs, however, that there are limits to evangelicalism's cultural adaptability. Australian culture no longer defaults to Christian values and is increasingly open to secular values. Those evangelicals who feel called to maintain traditional Christian morality, such as supporters of the Australian Christian Lobby, have enrolled as combatants in what they identify as the 'culture wars', an import from American fundamentalism. Values surveys show that churchgoers are more tolerant than non-churchgoers on a range of issues, but homosexuality has been an exception.[4] Churches which openly supported the ordination of homosexuals and gay marriage suffered an attrition in membership. Multiculturalism is supported by the majority in churches, but one dimension of multiculturalism – multifaith initiatives – are rarely welcomed. It is hard to predict how the evangelical movement will emerge from these cultural challenges. In spite of the absence of clarity or consensus on such matters, evangelicals persist in their desire to be heard. They are often found to be vehemently supportive of both left and right wing perspectives on social policy, which is evidence of their belief that the national health is contingent on adhering to Gospel values. It also betrays a fear of irrelevance with which they are charged by secularists and which they themselves consolidate by speaking and listening to the 'narrative of marginality' about their own movement.[5]

Another unresolved issue in the evangelical movement is the role of women. The traditional role of woman as confined to that of wife, mother and guardian of the home is held in practice by a minority of evangelical women. Respect for family dynasties over the generations continues, however, and close family networks are as marked as ever within evangelical societies and churches. Most evangelical women feel called to more than domestic

4 Gary D. Bouma and Beverly R. Dixon, *The Religious Factor in Australian Life* (Melbourne: MARC Australia, 1986), 53, 66, 67.

5 Hugh Chilton, 'Evangelicals and the End of Christian Australia: Nation and Religion in the Public Square 1959–1979', PhD, University of Sydney, 2014, 356.

duties and their faith has given them opportunities to do more. Evangelicals have prized the ministry, not only of ordained male clergy, but also of lay men, women, and youth. By the end of the nineteenth century women were more numerous on the mission field than men, and they were more effective campaigners against liquor than men. Their competence in the missionary, lobbying and political spheres made evangelicals early supporters of feminism and lies behind the increasing demand for the ordination of women. It was a demand which at the end of the twentieth century split the evangelical movement like no other. Presbyterians agreed to the ordination of women and then reversed the decision. Sydney Anglicans held out against it. Progressive evangelicals favoured it, but conservatives and Pentecostals, among whose major founders had been women, preserved leadership roles in the church for men. A consortium of conservative evangelicals, the Gospel Coalition, formed in America in 2007 was duplicated in Australia in 2014, with 'an Australia-wide vision for promoting faithful, persevering, Christ-honouring, Bible-driven, Spirit-empowered, gospel-centred ministry'. Its confession affirms: 'The distinctive leadership role within the church given to qualified men is grounded in creation, fall, and redemption and must not be sidelined by appeals to cultural developments.'[6] This constitutes the most counter-cultural of current evangelicalism's beliefs and will continue to divide the movement. Gender was the biggest issue in Australian social life in the 1980s, but the majority of Australians have moved on, dismissive of current conservative evangelical and Catholic views, and ignorant of the major contribution which evangelicals made to the origins and early development of feminism. All concerned need a good dose of history!

The biggest gap between evangelical vision and its practical outworking has always been in ministry to Indigenous Australians. The vision of harmonious co-existence between the new arrivals and evangelised First Nations peoples has not yet been realised. The shortcomings of Christian missions contributed to this failure. But the vision could never die because it was based on the indestructible principle which the evangelicals brought with them to the colonies that the Creator 'had made of one blood all the nations of the earth'. Missionaries, who chronically complained that they felt isolated and unsupported by the churches, were often the only, and always the most vocal, critics of the murderous treatment meted out by settlers in their lust for land. But missionaries loved the Aboriginal people better than they

6 https://australia.thegospelcoalition.org/about/foundational-documents/confessional-statement accessed 29 September 2016.

understood them, and the dispossession itself did not receive the same condemnation by the missionaries. Their Eurocentricity left them insensitive to the nature of Aboriginal connection to the land and convinced most of them that First Australians had to be civilised before they were evangelised. Their Eurocentrism, however, was not racism, and in this, too, the missionaries were different from the majority of white settlers.[7]

Tragically, Indigenous people continued to be massacred on the frontier of white society until the 1920s and their children removed ('stolen') from them until 1970. Missionaries always condemned the former, but too rarely saw the injustice of the latter at a time when they accepted the government policy of assimilation, and for the same reason saw little point in studying Indigenous culture or languages. The need for change was recognised in the 1930s by graduates of MBI. They began to accept that, unless churches were led by Aboriginal people and the Scriptures translated into their languages, it would continue to be very difficult for them to acquire a strong Christian faith and yet retain their identity.[8] Paternalism remains a problem to Aboriginal people: they feel that white leaders, accepting the need for change, in their haste to make decisions on their behalf, are not willing to listen to them. The best ministry to Indigenous people will be done by their own, and, although it will require support from churches now that missions have been replaced by governments, it is a work with a future as love is increasingly matched by knowledge and understanding. Failure, then, must be understood as resulting from too little love, knowledge and understanding.

Evangelicals have no other way of understanding their failure to attend to the Australian soul which has been too common an experience for them. They believe they have no alternative solution. The love of God in the Gospel of Jesus Christ, they insist, has always been the most consistently compelling and only legitimate power in their ministry. Knowledge and understanding of the Bible and of the national culture and of the relationship between them and matching both with the divine love has been the evangelical prescription for the national health in Australian history. To attend to the Australian soul is to sensitise its conscience, strengthen its moral energy, inform its consciousness, and fire its imagination with a vision for the future. Those are central concerns of Christianity, and the evangelical conviction has always been that it is necessary to be 'more Christian' to do them better.

---

7 Tom Mayne, 'A Brief History of Indigenous Ministry in Colonial Sydney, in the Sydney Anglican Diocese and beyond and of the Sydney Anglican Indigenous Peoples' Ministry Committee', January 2016, typescript, 12.

8 Mayne, 'A Brief History of Indigenous Ministry', 14.

BIBLIOGRAPHY

Primary Sources

Unpublished Manuscripts

Angus, Samuel, 'Biographical Catalogue', January 1932, Samuel Angus File, Alumni Records Sequence Number 5272, Princeton Theological Seminary Archives, Princeton, New Jersey, USA.

Angus, Samuel, Folder 1922–29, Box 6/3, Ferguson Memorial Library, Sydney.

Anon., 'Report of the Billy Graham Crusades in Australia and New Zealand, 1959', typescript, Billy Graham Archives, Wheaton.

Babbage, Stuart Barton, 'Flotsam and Jetsam – a sequel to *Memoirs of a Loose Canon*', typescript, 2011 (in possession of the authors).

Barrett, John, 'Australian Army Questionnaire', Box 47, PR89/135, AWM, Canberra.

Beech, Greg, 'The Outpouring of the Holy Spirit at Randwick Baptist Church, 6 November 1994', typescript, 10 January 1995.

Bevington, R. S., Personal Record, RAN, Series A3978, NAA, Canberra.

BGEA Films and Video, Collection 113, BGA, Wheaton College, Illinois, USA.

BGEA Records of the Australia Affiliate, Collection 245, BGA, Wheaton College, Illinois, USA.

Bingham, Geoff, and team, Undated notes on the Ministry of New Creation, (digital copy of the archives of the New Creation Teaching Ministry in possession of the authors).

Burnard and Troutman Papers, Moore College Archives.

Campaigners for Christ, Minutes of the Executive Meeting, October 1939, Campaigners Archive, Dalby, Queensland.

Chaplain's Report, HMAS Perth, 15 January 1942, MP150/1, Item431/204/100–HMAS Ships, NAA, Canberra.

Clark, C. M H., Manning Clark Papers, MS 7550, Box 136, J. S. Garden/Percy Grainger file, NAA, Canberra.

Dadswell, Henry W., 'Diary of a Sapper', MS 828, 137, AWM, Canberra.

Ferm, Robert O., Papers, Collection 19, BGA, Wheaton College, Illinois, USA.

Harrison, Hector, Correspondence, Hector Harrison Papers, MS6277, Box 1, Folder 4, NLA, Canberra.

Hay Methodist Church, Quarterly Meeting Minute Book, 1906–1933, Q.M. Rolls, Box 1, F, F2/3/M4, Uniting Church Archives, North Parramatta, NSW.

Heaton, J. H., to T. J. Ryan, 23 August 1916, Home Office, COL/A1207, 6849 of 1916, Queensland State Archives, Brisbane.

Hobbin, Bill, Ms Autobiography, United Theological College Archives, North Parramatta.

Lockley, G. Lindsay, Biographical Card Index of Congregational Ministers in Australia, 1798–1977, Uniting Church Archives, North Parramatta, NSW.

Menzies, Robert G., 'Speech at the opening and dedication of Bible House, Canberra, 13 February 1960', Robert Menzies papers, MS 4936, Series 6 Box 258, folder 52, NLA, Canberra, available online at http://nla.gov.au/nla.obj-222158841, accessed 19 November 2016.

Morgan, Peter, recorded address given to the National Praise and Worship Conference, Lighthouse Christian Centre, Wollongong, NSW, 28 September 1993.

Nixon, Richard M., Pre-Presidential Papers, Federal Records Center, Laguna Niguel, California, USA.

Orr, Arthur Henry (Harry), Correspondence and papers 1944–1945, Baptist Archives, Morling College, Eastwood NSW.

Renshaw, William F., Curriculum Vitae; and War Service Diary, 16 Feb. 1944 to 31 Dec. 1945, 1–4. In the possession of Will Renshaw, Blackburn, Victoria.

Ridley, John G., 'The Romance of a Bible Class', n.d. typescript provided to the authors by Ruth Ridley, daughter of John Ridley.

Rockhampton Baptist Tabernacle, Church Minute Book, 1918, Rockhampton, Qld.

Ross, Lloyd, Correspondence, Lloyd Ross Papers, MS3939, Box 29, Folder 9, NLA, Canberra.

William and Barbara Ross (eds.), The War Diary of 2nd Corporal F.A. McLaughlin, M.M., 1918, MS in the possession of Barbara McLaughlin Ross, Blackburn, Victoria.

Skinner, Edward Kenneth, 'Roll of Honour', NX41647, AWM, online at www.awm.gov.au/people/rolls/R1700170, AWM website, accessed 10 October 2010.

Skinner, Edward Kenneth, War Record, B883, NX41647, NAA, Canberra, online at http://recordsearch.naa.gov.au/, accessed 12 October 2010.

Slinn, Geoff, 'War Diary', Typescript extracts in the possession of R.D. Linder.

Stanmore Baptist Church 40th Year Memorial Book, presented to Pastor C. J. Tinsley, 27 May 1941.

Sydney University Evangelical Union papers, acc.549 series 27, University of Sydney Archives, Fisher Library, Sydney.

Troutman, Charles Henry, Jr., Papers, Collection 111, BGA, Wheaton College, Illinois, USA.

Wray, F. W., 'Diary 1915 – 1916', Papers of Chaplain F. W. Wray, File 3, DRL 648, AWM, Canberra.

Published (Including Memoirs)

Andersen, Bill, 'This Is My Story', *The Baptist Recorder*, July, 1998, 4–8.

Anderson, John, First Speech in the House of Representatives, Parliament of Australia, 17 May 1989, Hansard no.168, 1989, 434, online at http://parlinfo.aph.gov.au/parlInfo/search/display/display.w3p;query=Id%3A%22chamber%2Fhansardr%2F1989-08-17%2F0154%22, accessed 19 November 2016.

Anglican Church of Australia. Diocese of Sydney, *Yearbook of the Diocese of Sydney* (Sydney: Diocesan Registry, 2011).

Angus, Samuel, *Alms for Oblivion: Chapters from a Heretic's Life* (Sydney: Angus & Robertson, 1943).

Angus, Samuel, *Essential Christianity* (Sydney: Angus & Robertson, 1939).

Angus, Samuel, *Man and the New Order* (Sydney: Angus & Robertson, 1942).

Angus, Samuel, *Religious Quests of the Graeco-Roman World: a study in the background of Early Christianity* (London: John Murray, 1929).

Angus, Samuel, *Truth and Tradition: a plea for practical and vital religion and for a reinterpretation of ancient theologies* (Sydney: Angus & Robertson, 1934).

Anon., 'Community' page, VLC website, http://www.victorylifecentre.com.au/community-services.html, accessed 13 July 2011.

Anon., 'God Has Broken the Curse', Healing and Revival Press website, 2006, www.healingandrevival.com, accessed 22 June 2009.

Anon., *Fight the Good Fight: In Memoriam, Revd. George Tulloch, E. D.* (Perth: St Andrew's Church, 1946).

Anon., *St. Luke's Church, Whitmore Square, Adelaide, 1855–1955, Centenary Booklet* (Adelaide: The Church, 1955).

Babbage, Stuart Barton, *Memoirs of a Loose Canon* (Brunswick East: Acorn Press, 2004).

Baptist Union of NSW, *Annual Report 1921–2*, Morling College Archives.

Bennett, Mary M., *The Aboriginal Mother in Western Australia in 1933* (Sydney: K.A. Wood, Printer, 1933).

Bennett, Mary M., *The Australian Aboriginal as a Human Being* (London: Alston Rivers, 1930).
Bennett, Mary M., *Christison of Lammermoor* (London: Alston Rivers, 1927).
Bingham, Geoffrey, *Love Is the Spur* (Parramatta: Eyrie Books, 2004).
Bingham, Geoffrey, *Twice-Conquering Love* (Blackwood: New Creation Publications, 1992).
Bjelke-Petersen, Johannes, *Don't You Worry About That!: The Joh Bjelke-Petersen Memoirs* (North Ryde: Angus & Robertson, 1990).
Boyce, Francis B., *Four Score Years and Seven: The Memoirs of Archdeacon Boyce* (Sydney: Angus and Robertson, 1934).
Brawner, Mina Ross, *Woman in the Word* (Melbourne: Victory Press, 1931).
Bryson, Bruce S., *My Father's House: The Bryson Story of Life on Four Continents* (Torrens Park: Gillingham Printers, 1993).
Carruthers, J. E., *Memories of an Australian Ministry, 1868–1921* (London: The Epworth Press, 1922).
Chamberlain, Lindy, *Through My Eyes* (Melbourne: William Heinemann, 1990).
Chennell, Percy H., *The Sport Without a Smile* (Adelaide: Gillingham & Company, 1934).
Church of England, House of Bishops, *Issues in Human Sexuality: A Statement by the House of Bishops* (London: Church House Publishing, 1991).
Clarence Ormsby, 'Political Poison: Agent Orange victims chronicle the effects on their lives', CrimeHurts.org website, maintained by Clarence Ormsby, Mannering Park, http://www.crimehurts.org/politics-03.html accessed 5 September 2016.
Clark, Manning, *The Puzzles of Childhood* (Ringwood: Viking Books, 1989).
Claydon, Robyn, 'Cooperation in Evangelism', (Lausanne Movement, 1989) http://www.lausanne.org/docs/lau2docs/212.pdf, accessed 5 May 2012.
Cole, Keith, *'But I will be with You': An Autobiography* (Bendigo: Keith Cole Publications, 1988).
Costello, Peter, and Coleman, Peter, *The Costello Memoirs: The Age of Prosperity* (Carlton: MUP, 2008).
Costello, Tim, *Streets of Hope: Finding God in St Kilda* (St Leonards: Allen & Unwin, 1998).
Costello, Tim, *Tips from a Travelling Soul-Searcher* (Sydney: Allen & Unwin, 1999).
Court, Margaret, with Barbara Oldfield, *Winning Faith: The Margaret Court Story* (Sydney: Strand Publishing, 2000).
Court, Margaret, with Owen Salter, *Our Winning Position: living in victory every day* (Ballarat: Strand Publishing, 2002).
Crowley, Frank K., *Modern Australia in Documents*, 2 vols. (Melbourne: Wren, 1973).
Daniels, Len, *Far West* (Sydney: Church of England Information Trust, 1959).
Diocese of Sydney, Committee to Study the Neo-Pentecostal Movement, *Both Sides of the Question: Official Enquiry into Neo-Pentecostalism* (Sydney: AIO, 1973).
Diocese of Sydney, Diocesan Doctrine Commission, 'The Doctrine of the Trinity and Its Bearing on the Relationship of Men and Women', (1999), http://www.sds.asn.au/assets/Documents/reports/T/TrinityDoctrineComm.pdf, accessed 21 November 2017.
Diocese of Sydney, *Handbook of the Church of England in Australia, Diocese of Sydney* (Sydney: The Diocese, 1973 and 1974).
Drummond, Henry, *Natural Law in the Spiritual World* (London: Hodder & Stoughton, 1883).
Dryburgh, Margaret, 'The Captives' Hymn' (1942), Singing to Survive website commemorating the 70th anniversary of the Women's Vocal Orchestra of the Civilian Internment Camp, Palembang, Sumatra, 1943, https://singingtosurvive.com/2013/05/03/the-captives-hymn/ accessed 23 August 2016.
Duguid, Charles, *Doctor and the Aborigines* (Adelaide: Rigby, 1972).
Duthie, Gil, *I had 50,000 Bosses: Memoirs of a Labor Backbencher, 1946–1975* (Sydney: Angus & Robertson, 1984).
Dyer, Arthur J., *Unarmed Combat: An Australian Missionary Adventure* (Sydney: Edgar Bragg, [c.1954?]).

Farrell, Monica, *Laughing with God* (Glebe: Protestant Publications, 1957).
Fitchett, William H., *A Tattered Bible and a Mutilated Christ: Ought a Christian Church to Accept This?* (Melbourne: Fitchett Brothers, 1922).
Fitchett, William H., *Deeds That Won the Empire* (London: Bell's Indian and Colonial Library, 1897).
Fitchett, William H., *Where the Higher Criticism Fails* (London: Epworth Press, 1922).
Freund, A. P. Harold, *Missionary Turns Spy* (Glynde: Lutheran Homes Incorporated, 1989).
Friend, Donald, *The Donald Friend Diaries: Chronicles & Confessions of an Australian Artist*, ed. Ian Britain (Melbourne: Text Publishing, 2010).
Fysh, Wilmot H., *Qantas Rising: The Autobiography of the Flying Fysh* (Sydney: Angus & Robertson, 1965).
Global Anglican Futures Conference, 'The Jerusalem Declaration', 29 June 2008, GAFCON website, https://www.gafcon.org/resources/the-complete-jerusalem-statement accessed 21 November 2016.
Glover, Susanne, 'God Revealed – in the Bible or behind the Bible?', *ACR*, 9 July 1984, 6–7.
Glover, Susanne, 'Headship, culture and last words', *ACR*, 23 July 1984, 6–7.
Glover, Susanne, et al., 'Men and Women, identical in Responsibility?', *ACR*, 25 June 1984, 6–7.
Glover, Susanne, et al., 'The Pain of Second Class Citizenship: MOW debates women's ordination', *ACR*, 11 June 1984, 6–7.
Gondarra, Djiniyini, *Let My People Go* (Darwin: Bethel Presbytery, 1986).
Goodhew, R. H., 'Presidential Address', 12 October 1998, *Yearbook of the Diocese of Sydney*, (Sydney: Diocesan Registry, 1999).
Gordon, Ernest, *Miracle on the River Kwai* (London: Fount, 1965).
Graham, Billy, *Just as I am: The Autobiography* (Sydney: HarperCollins), 1997.
Griffiths, Harry, *An Australian Adventure* (Adelaide: Rigby, 1975).
Hammond, Robert B. S., *With One Voice: A Study of Prohibition in the U.S.A.* (Sydney: NSW Alliance, McDonnel House, 1920).
Hammond, T. C., *Abolishing God: A Reply to Professor John Anderson* (Melbourne: S. John Bacon, 1943).
Hammond, T. C., *Fading Light: The Tragedy of Spiritual Decline in Germany* (London: Marshall, Morgan & Scott, [1942]).
Hammond, T. C., *In Understanding Be Men: A Synopsis of Christian Doctrine for Non-Theological Students* (London: IVF, 1936).
Hammond, T. C., *Reasoning Faith: An Introduction to Christian Apologetics* (London: IVF, 1943).
Hammond, T. C., *Reply to Dr Rumble: Marriage and Education* (Sydney: Criterion Press, n.d.).
Hammond, T. C., *The Case for Protestantism* (Sydney: The Author, 1960).
Hancox, Phil, *Cavalry or Calvary? The Christian Dilemma* (West End: Christians for Peace, 1984).
Hancox, Phil, *My Adventures in Evangelism* (Brisbane: Privately Printed, 1995).
Hasluck, Paul, *Light that Time has Made* (Canberra: National Library of Australia, 1995).
Hayden, Bill, *Hayden: An Autobiography* (Sydney: Angus & Robertson, 1996).
Henderson, Kenneth T., *Khaki and Cassock* (Melbourne: Melville & Mullen, 1919).
Henley, Thomas, *After the War: Christendom and the Coming Peace* (London: Hodder and Stoughton, 1917).
Horne, Donald, *An Interrupted Life* (Sydney: HarperCollins Publishers, 1998).
Howard, John, *Lazarus Rising: A Personal and Political Autobiography* (Pymble: HarperCollins Publishers, 2010).
Human Rights and Equal Opportunity Commission, *Bringing them Home: National Inquiry into the Separation of Aboriginal and Torres Strait Islander Children from their Families* (Canberra: Australian Government Publishing Service, 1997).

Jacob, John G., *Home Letters of a Soldier-Student,* 2 vols. (Adelaide: G. Hassell & Sons, 1919).

Jensen, Peter, 'Archbishop Jensen's address to the Deep Impact gathering', Homebush, 19 August 2001, Sydney Anglicans website, http://sydneyanglicans.net/seniorclergy/articles/74a accessed 26 September 2016.

Jensen, Peter, 'Presidential Address to Synod on October 14, 2002', Sydney Anglicans website, http://sydneyanglicans.net/seniorclergy/articles/599a, accessed 21 November 2016.

Jensen, Peter, 'Presidential Address to Synod, October 2012', in Standing Committee of the Synod Anglican Church, Diocese of Sydney, *Synod Proceedings,* October 2012, http://www.sds.asn.au/assets/Documents/synod/Synod2012/SynodProceedings.2012.full.pdf, accessed 21 November 2016.

Jensen, Peter, 'Sermon delivered by Archbishop Jensen at his Consecration and Installation Service', Sydney, 29 June 2001, Sydney Anglicans website, http://sydneyanglicans.net/seniorclergy/articles/72a, accessed 26 September 2016.

Jensen, Peter, 'The Protestant Conscience: The Inaugural Bernard Judd Memorial Lecture', St Andrews House, Sydney, 5 April 2005, available via link embedded in Madeline Collins, 'Royal wedding bells toll the death of Protestantism', News article, Sydney Anglicans website, http://sydneyanglicans.net/news/royal_wedding_tolls_death_of_protestantism_dr_jensen, accessed 21 November 2016.

Jensen, Phillip, 'Personal Statement to Synod of the Diocese of Sydney, 19 October 2004', Anglican Church League website, http://www.acl.asn.au/old/041019_phillip_jensen.html, accessed 26 September 2016.

Jensen, Phillip, 'The Ordination of Women as Presbyters', 9 October 2006, Phillip Jensen website, http://phillipjensen.com/articles/the-ordination-of-women-as-presbyters1/ accessed 21 November 2016.

Jones, Fletcher, *Not By Myself: The Fletcher Jones Story*, 2nd ed. (Cheltenham: Kingfisher, 1984).

Jordan, Arnold, *Tenko on the River Kwai* (Launceston: Regal Publications, 1987).

Keat Gin, Ooi (ed.), *Japanese Empire in the Tropics: Selected Documents and Reports of the Japanese Period in Sarawak, Northwest Borneo, 1941–1945*, 2 vols. (Miami: Ohio University Center for International Studies, 1998).

Kennedy, John J., *The Whale Oil Guards* (Dublin: James Duffy and Co. Ltd., 1919).

Kerr, Alan, *Guided Journey: Some Experiences of a Lifetime* (Gundaroo: Brolga Press, 1998).

Knowles, Brett, 'Is the Future of Western Christianity a Pentecostal One? A conversation with Harvey Cox', Paper presented to 'The Future of Christianity in the West' Conference, Dunedin, 5–8 December 2002. Accessed 9 February 2017 at http://www.otago.ac.nz/chaplain/resources/otago017072.html.

Knox, D.B., 'Propositional Revelation the only Revelation', *RTR,* 19.1, 1960, 1–9.

Lewis, Brian, *Sunday at Kooyong Road* (Richmond: Hutchinson of Victoria, 1976).

Lindsay, Norman, *The Scribblings of an Idle Mind* (Melbourne: Lansdowne Press, 1966).

Macintyre, R. G., *The Theology of Dr Angus: A Critical Review* (Sydney: Angus & Robertson, 1934).

Makin, Norman, *The Memoirs of Norman John Oswald Makin* (Adelaide: J. M. Main Bequest of Flinders University, 1982).

Mansfield, Bruce, *Summer is almost over – a Memoir* (Canberra: Barton Books, 2012).

Mascord, Keith, 'Follow-up letter', October 2007, reproduced in Father Dave's Article Directory, http://fatherdave.com.au/sydney-anglicanism-its-time-for-change/ accessed 26 September 2016.

Mascord, Keith, 'Open letter to the Standing Committee of the Anglican Church, Diocese of Sydney', 29 November 2006, reproduced in Father Dave's Article Directory, http://fatherdave.com.au/tag/sydney-anglicanism/ accessed 26 September 2016.

Mathew, John, *Napoleon's Tomb* (Melbourne: Melville & Mullen, 1911).

McCracken, John H., with Paul and Heather Shelley, *Summing Up: John Harold McCracken 1906–1999* (Aranda: Heather & Paul Shelley, 2003).
Menzies, Robert G., *Afternoon Light: Some Memories of Men and Events*, (Melbourne: Cassell, 1967).
Menzies, Robert G., 'The Forgotten People' (1942), Menzies Virtual Museum, http://menziesvirtualmuseum.org.au/transcripts/the-forgotten-people, accessed 19 November 2016.
Menzies, Robert G., *Letters to My Daughter: Letters 1955–1975,* ed. Heather Henderson (Millers Point: Pier 9, 2011).
Methodist Church of Australasia, Victoria and Tasmania Conference, *Minutes of the Twentieth Annual Conference* (Melbourne: Methodist Conference Offices, 1921).
Methodist Church of Australasia, *Minutes of Methodist General Conference*, 1935.
Morling, T. R., *Royal Commission of Inquiry into Chamberlain Convictions: Report of the Commissioner The Hon. Mr Justice Morling* (Canberra: Government Printer, 1987).
Moyes, Gordon, *Leaving a Legacy: The Autobiography of Gordon Moyes* (North Sydney: Art House Press, 2005).
Murdoch, Patrick J., *The Laughter and Tears of God and Other War Sermons* (Melbourne: Arbuckle, Waddell and Fawckner, 1915).
Murray, Andrew, *The Church Missionary Society and the deepening of the spiritual life* (Sydney: CMS Australia, n.d.).
Nalliah, Daniel, 'RUA Prayer' page, Catch The Fire Ministries website, http://catchthefire.com.au/rise-up-australia/ accessed 8 June 2013.
National Missionary Council, *Four Major Issues in Assimilation: a memorandum* (Sydney: NMCA, 1963).
Orr, J. Edwin, *All Your Need: 10,000 Miles of Miracle Through Australia and New Zealand* (London: Marshall, Morgan & Scott, 1937).
Peake, Arthur S., *A Commentary on the Bible* (Edinburgh: T. C. & E. C. Jack, 1919).
Penman, David, 'How Can They Hear?' (Lausanne Movement, 1989) http://www.lausanne.org/docs/lau2docs/255.pdf accessed 5 May 2012.
Penman, David, 'Love in the End Times', (Lausanne Movement, 1989) http://www.lausanne.org/docs/lau2docs/265.pdf accessed 5 May 2012.
Presbyterian Church of Australia, *Blue Book: Minutes of Proceedings of the Federal Assembly of the Presbyterian Churches of Australia and Tasmania* (Sydney: The Church).
Presbyterian Church of Australia, *The Procedure and Practice of the Presbyterian Church of Australia* (Sydney: Presbyterian Church of NSW, 1926).
Presbyterian Church of NSW, *Blue Book: Minutes of Proceedings of the General Assembly of the Presbyterian Church of NSW* (Sydney: The Assembly).
Rayner, Keith, 'Supplementary Presidential Address, 21 November 1992', *Proceedings of the General Synod, Anglican Church of Australia* (Sydney: The Synod, 1993).
Ridley, John G., *Milestones of Mercy* (Sydney: Christian Press, 1957).
Ridley, John, *The Passion for Christ* (Stanwell Tops: Ambassadors for Christ, 1963).
Robinson, Donald W. B., 'The Church in the New Testament', *St Mark's Review,* 17, 1959, 4–14.
Robinson, Donald W. B., 'The Church Revisited: An Autobiographical Fragment', *RTR* 48.1, 1989, 4–14.
Robinson, Donald W. B., 'The Church Universal and its earthly form- 2', *ACR,* 16 February 1956.
Robinson, Donald W. B., 'The Church Universal and its earthly form', *ACR,* 2 February 1956.
Robinson, Donald W. B., 'The Doctrine of the Church and its Implications for Evangelism', *Interchange,* 15, 1974, 156–172.
Report of the Royal Commissioner appointed to investigate, report, and advise upon matters in relation to the treatment of Aborigines, Perth, Government Printer, 1935.

Rudd, Kevin, 'Faith in Politics', *The Monthly,* October 2006, https://www.themonthly.com.au/monthly-essays-kevin-rudd-faith-politics--, accessed 21 November 2016.

Rudd, Kevin, 'Church and State are able to have different positions on same sex marriage', 20 May 2013, Kevin Connects website, http://www.kevinruddmp.com/2013/05/church-and-state-are-able-to-have.html accessed 20 May 2013.

Rumble, Leslie, *Dr Angus – Or Christ* (Sydney: E. J. Dwyer, 1934).

Rumble, Leslie, *Radio Replies in Defence of Religion* (Sydney: Pellegrini, 1934).

Schwarz, Fred, *Beating the Unbeatable Foe: One Man's Victory over Communism, Leviathan, and the Last Enemy* (Washington: Regnery, 1996).

Schwarz, Fred, *The Heart, Mind and Soul of Communism* (Long Beach: Evangelize America programme, [1952]).

Schwarz, Fred, *You can Trust the Communists (to be Communists)* (Englewood Cliffs: Prentice-Hall, [1960]).

Shayler, Kate, *Burnished: Burnside Life Stories* (Hazelbrook: MoshPit Publishing, 2011).

Shilton, Lance, *Speaking Out: A Life in Urban Ministry* (Sydney: CSAC, 1997).

South Australia: Parliament. *Official Reports of the Parliamentary Debates* (Adelaide: I.L. Bonython & Company, 1915).

Stewart, Alfred R. M., *Diaries of an Unsung Hero*, compiled by Margaret Willmington, (Blaxland: Mark Webb of B-in-Print, 1995).

Stott, John R. W., and Coote, Robert T., (eds.), *Down to Earth: Studies in Christianity and Culture: The Papers of the Lausanne Consultation on Gospel and Culture* (London: Hodder and Stoughton, 1981).

Strehlow, Theodor G. H., *Journey to Horseshoe Bend* (Adelaide: Rigby, 1969).

Thompson, John A. and Beasley, W. J., *These Extra-Ordinary Documents* (Melbourne: Australian Institute of Archaeology, 1948).

Thompson, John A., *Cities Walled up to Heaven* (Melbourne: Australian Institute of Archaeology, 1948).

Thompson, John A., *Luke the Historian* (Melbourne: Australian Institute of Archaeology, 1948).

Thompson, John A., *Records in Clay* (Melbourne: Australian Institute of Archaeology, 1948).

Thompson, John A., *Unearthing Solomon's Stables* (Melbourne: Australian Institute of Archaeology, 1948).

Treloar, John L., *An ANZAC Diary* (Armidale: Alan Treloar, 1993).

Urquhart, Carment, *Is the Bible True?* (Perth: Perth Bible Institute, 1929).

Walker, Alan, 'A Peace Manifesto', *The Coalfield's Chronicle,* November 1939.

Walker, Alan, *A Vision for the World: Alan Walker Tells His Story* (Wantirna: New Melbourne Press, 1999).

Walker, Alan, *Herald of Hope* (Sutherland: Albatross, 1994).

Walker, Alan, *Heritage without end: A Story to tell the Nation* (Melbourne: General Conference Literature and Publications Committee of the Methodist Church of Australasia, 1953).

Walker, Alan, *White Australia* (Glebe: Christian Distributors' Association, 1946).

Webb, B. Linden, *The Religious Significance of the War* (Sydney: Christian World, 1915).

Whitney, H.J., *The new heresy* [Katoomba, N.S.W.: H.J. Whitney, 198–?].

Whitrod, Ray, *Before I Sleep: Memoirs of a Modern Police Commissioner* (St. Lucia: University of Queensland Press, 2001).

Williams, R. M., *Beneath Whose Hand: The Autobiography* (South Melbourne: Macmillan, 1984).

Winton, Ronald, *Johnny Head-In-Air: Memoirs of a Doctor Journalist* (Glebe: Book House, 2002).

Wylde, Arnold L., *The Bathurst Ritual Case, with a Preface by the Ven. Archdeacon T. C. Hammond, MA, ThD* (Sydney: George M. Dash, [c.1948?]).

Newspapers and Periodicals

The Adelaide Advertiser
The Adelaide Register
The Age
Anglican Church Record
The Argus
The Australian
The Australian Baptist
The Australian Christian
Australian Christian Commonwealth
Australian Christian World
Australian Church Record
Australian Women's Weekly
Balaam's Ass: Movement for the Ordination of Women Newsletter
Banner of Truth
The Briefing (Matthias Media)
The Bulletin
Canberra Times
Catalyst
Checkpoint (CMS magazine)
Christian Century
Christian Today Australia
Church Missionary Gleaner
The Church Record
Church Scene
The Church Standard
Courier Mail
Current Affairs Bulletin
The Daily Telegraph
The Edifier: a Christian newspaper (Melbourne)
The Federal Independent
Free Slave (Rowland Croucher, ed., for the House of the New World)
Glad Tidings
The Guardian
Herald Sun
Hobart Mercury
Honi Soit
Illawarra Mercury
The Keswick Quarterly and Upwey Convention News
Khesed News (Khesed ministries, WA)
The Messenger
The Methodist
Nation
National Fellowship for Revival News
National Outlook
New Life
Presbyterian Review
The Presbyterian (WA)
The Queensland Baptist
Repaccusions (Journal of the REP Association)

The Riverine Grazier
Rockhampton Daily Record
Rockhampton Morning Bulletin
Social Issues Update (Social Issues Committee, Anglican Diocese of Sydney)
The Southern Cross
SU News
The Sun Herald
Sydney Diocesan Magazine
Sydney Morning Herald
Trowel and Sword (Reformed Churches of Australia)
The War Cry
The West Australian
The Zeehan and Dundas Herald

Oral History Interviews

Aberdeen, Dr John E. C., interviewed by Margaret Lamb, 8 December 1989.
Alcock, Alan, interviewed by Mark Hutchinson, 2 February 1993.
Andersen, Bill, interviewed by Robert D. Linder, 8 June 2001.
Anderson, John, interviewed by Stuart Piggin, 21 April 2007.
Babbage, Stuart Barton, interviewed by Stuart Piggin, 19 April 2012.
Ballantine-Jones, Bruce, interviewed by Stuart Piggin, 11 July 2012.
Bartholomew, Joy, interviewed by Stuart Piggin, 12 April 2013.
Bentley, Maurice Edwin, interviewed by Robert D. Linder, 24 July 2004.
Bjelke-Petersen, Johannes interviewed by Robert D. Linder, 17 November 1987.
Bjelke-Petersen, Johannes, and Bjelke-Petersen, Florence, interviewed by Robert D. Linder, 29 July 2003.
Bryson, Bruce, interviewed by Brian Dickey, 15 December 1988, Myrrh Digital Repository, Moore Theological College Library, https://myrrh.library.moore.edu.au:443/handle/10248/8768.
Buck, Leonard, interviewed by Margaret Lamb, 15 November 1986 and 18 May 1988.
Burrows, Eva, interviewed by Robin Hughes, 26 November 1996, Australian Biography Project, ABC Radio, Full Interview Transcript, Screen Australia Digital Learning archived website, www.australianbiography.gov.au/subjects/burrows/interview1.html, accessed 1 July 2011.
Chubb, Geoff, interviewed by Stuart Piggin, 9 July 2012.
Cooper, Nicholas H., interviewed by Robert D. Linder, 12 March 2001.
Costello, Tim, interviewed by Peter Thompson, *Talking Heads*, ABC 1, 15 June 2009, transcript at http://www.abc.net.au/tv/talkingheads/txt/s2593114.htm, accessed 19 November 2016.
Coulter, James, interviewed by Isla Macphail, 6 December 1995, 3–4, John Curtin Prime Ministerial Library, The John Curtin Centre, Curtin University, Perth, WA.
Ctercteko, Ray, interviewed by Robert D. Linder, 13 July 2006.
Dunn, John, interviewed by Stuart Piggin, 26 September 1986.
Dykes, John, interviewed by Margaret Lamb, 13 November 1986, Myrrh Digital Repository, Moore Theological College Library, https://myrrh.library.moore.edu.au/handle/10248/8758.
Fletcher, Geoffrey, interviewed by Margaret Lamb, 16 November 1989.
Frewer, Ken, interviewed by Stuart Piggin, 21 January 1990.
Gallagher, Frank, interviewed by Robert D. Linder, 16 July 2002.
Galloway, Laurie and Galloway, Ruth, interviewed by Robert D. Linder, 27 July 1995.
Gilchrist, Alex, interviewed by Margaret Lamb, 31 July 1986.
Hamer, Horace, and Thomas L. Wilkinson, interviewed by Robert D. Linder, 27 June 2000.
Hancox, Philip, interviewed by Robert D. Linder, 16 June 1998.

Harrison, Hector, interviewed by Mel Pratt, 2 October 1973, 1:1/43–1:1/44, John Curtin Prime Ministerial Library, The John Curtin Centre, Curtin University, Perth, WA.
Harrison, John M., interviewed by Robert D. Linder, 30 May 1987.
Hartley, Wesley, interviewed by Robert D. Linder, 12 January 2004.
Harvey, Robin, grandson of Francis Clemens, interviewed by Robert D. Linder, 25 October 1994.
Himbury, M., interviewed by Robert D. Linder, 25 August 1987.
James, Francis, interviewed by Stuart Piggin, Margaret Lamb and Robert D. Linder, 19 June 1990.
Jarvis, Ron T., interviewed by Robert D. Linder, 20 June 2012.
Jeffreys, Irene, interviewed by Robert D. Linder, 22 September 1987, Myrrh Digital Repository, Moore Theological College Library, https://myrrh.library.moore.edu.au/handle/10248/8588.
Knox, Peter, interviewed by Robert D. Linder, 13 July 2009.
Knox, Sheila Nicholson, interviewed by Robert D. Linder, 14 July 2009.
Langdon, Alan, interviewed by Robert D. Linder, 24 April 2001.
Makin, Harold, son of Norman Makin, interviewed by Robert D. Linder, 19 July 1995.
May, Robert C., interviewed by Robert D. Linder, 9 June 2001.
Morcombe, Brian, interviewed by Robert D. Linder, 17 July 1997.
Morgan, Keith, interviewed by Robert D. Linder, 24 July 2004.
Morris, Leon, interviewed by Margaret Lamb, 8 August 1986, Myrrh Digital Repository, Moore College Library, Sydney, https://myrrh.library.moore.edu.au/handle/10248/8662.
Morton, Stanley (Tex), interviewed by Robert D. Linder, 30 May 2001.
Nicholls, Bryan J., interviewed by Robert D. Linder, 16 March 2001.
Norris, Harold G., interviewed by R. W. Tippett, 25 July 1986.
Oldfield, Barbara, personal assistant to Margaret Court, interviewed by Robert D. Linder, 6 June 2001.
Ormsby, Clarence, interviewed by Robert D. Linder, 13 June 2001.
Playford, Rev. Tom, son of Tom Playford, interviewed by Robert D. Linder, 19 March 2001.
Prentis, Malcolm, interviewed by Robert D. Linder, 20 November 2008.
Renshaw, William F., interviewed by Robert D. Linder, 31 July 1998.
Robinson, Donald W. B., interviewed by Robert D. Linder, 28 May 2001.
Robinson, Donald W. B., interviewed by Robert D. Linder, 9 January 1995.
Ross, Barbara McLaughlin, daughter of Fred McLaughlin, interviewed by Robert D. Linder, Blackburn, Victoria, 30 July 1998.
Ross, Barbara, daughter of Frederick A. McLaughlin, interviewed by Robert D. Linder, 31 July 1997.
Syer, Florence Trotter, interviewed by Robert D. Linder, 16 August 1998.
Taylor, Raymond, interviewed by Robert D. Linder, 22 July 2004.
Thompson, John, interviewed by Robert D. Linder, 28 August 1987.
Thompson, Lester, interviewed by Robert D. Linder, 30 June 2004.
Trezise, Eric, interviewed by Robert D. Linder, 10 July 2004.
Vose, Noel, interviewed by Robert D. Linder, 27 July 1995.
Wallace, Jim, interviewed by Stuart Piggin, 14 February 2012.
Wearne, Bruce, interviewed by Robert D. Linder, 25 July 2004.
Wells, Rev. Max, interviewed by Robert D. Linder, 28 July 1995.
White, Paul, interviewed by Margaret Lamb, 3 March 1986.
Whitlam, Freda, interviewed by Robert D. Linder, 30 May 1997.
Wotton, Roy, interviewed by Robert D. Linder, 23 May 2001.
Wyndham, John, interviewed by Mark Hutchinson, 26 January 1993, Myrrh Digital Repository, Moore College Library, Sydney, https://myrrh.library.moore.edu.au/handle/10248/8687.
Yee, Margaret, interviewed by John Cleary, *Sunday Nights*, ABC radio, 23 April 2006, http://www.abc.net.au/sundaynights/stories/s1624937.htm, accessed 19 November 2016.

Personal Correspondence

Abbott, Len, to Margaret Lamb, 11 October 1990.
Adam, Peter, to the authors, 2 May 1990.
Andrews, Mary, to Stuart Piggin, 5 May 1989.
Ballantine-Jones, Bruce, to Harry Goodhew, 23 October 1998.
Benson, Rod, to David Palmer, 9 October 2008.
Bingham, Geoffrey, to the authors, undated letter c. September 1997.
Buck, Leonard, to Margaret Lamb, 14 December 1990.
Cameron, Andrew, to David Palmer, 7 October 2008.
Cooper, Paul, to Stuart Piggin, 26 October 2011.
Deane, Arthur, to Stuart Piggin, 16 April 1993.
Dickey, Brian, to Richard Donnelly, email 6 August 2008.
Dunkley, Win, to Margaret Lamb, 12 August 1990.
Etherington, Steve to Stuart Piggin, 11 November 1998.
Goodhew, Harry to Bruce Ballantine-Jones, undated, c. late October 1998.
Grant, Mary, to Stuart Piggin, 27 August 1993.
Hartley, Wesley, son of Frank Hartley, to Robert D. Linder, 1 October 2010.
Hopgood, Donald J., to Arnold Hunt, 9 September 1994.
Hunt, Arnold, to Robert D. Linder, 13 September 1994.
Lewis, Francis B., to Robert D. Linder, 19 October 1994.
Morgan, Keith, to Robert D. Linder, 10 October 2003.
Müller, Rosemarie, to Robin Ruys, 29 September 2011.
Palmer, David, to Jim Wallace, 6 October 2008.
Petras, Michael, to Robert D. Linder, 26 July 2010.
Prideaux, Richard, to Stuart Piggin, 19 October 1990.
Renshaw, William, to Darrell Paproth, 22 June 2012.
Smith, Vic, to Stuart Piggin, 20 February 1993.
Stoneman, Jackie, telephone conversations with Stuart Piggin, 19 December 2011.
Treloar, Geoff to Stuart Piggin, 13 February 2008.
Wallace, Jim, to Robert Benn, 17 September 2008.
Weldon, Glenda, to Stuart Piggin, 23 July 2013.
White, Rev. Hensley to Robert D. Linder, 15 December 1996.
Willmington, Margaret, to Robert D. Linder, 10 July 2000.

Secondary Sources

Books, Book Chapters and Articles

Adam, Peter, 'Honouring Jesus Christ', *Churchman*, 119.1, 2005, 35–50, http://churchsociety.org/docs/churchman/119/Cman_119_1_Adam.pdf, accessed 21 November 2016.
Adam-Smith, Patsy, *The Anzacs* (Ringwood: Penguin Books, 1991).
Adams, Damon S., 'Divine Healing in Australian Protestantism', *JRH,* 41.3, 2017, 346–363.
Ah Kow, Adelaide, *William McKenzie: ANZAC Padre* (London: Salvationist Publishing and Supplies, 1949).
Alleyne, F., and Fallding, H., 'Decisions at the Graham Crusade in Sydney: A Statistical Analysis', *Journal of Christian Education,* 3.1, 1960, 32–41.
Allsop, Richard, 'Blainey outlasts the History Wars', *IPA Politics and Culture Review,* March 2010, 7–11.

Altman, Dennis, 'The creation of sexual politics in Australia', *Journal of Australian Studies,* 11.20, 1987, 76–82.

Ambrose, Vic, *Balus Bilong Mipela: The story of the Missionary Aviation Fellowship, Australia and New Zealand* (Melbourne: Missionary Aviation Fellowship, 1987).

Angell, Barbara, *A Woman's War: The Exceptional Life of Wilma Oram Young, AM* (Frenchs Forest: New Holland Publishers, 2003).

Angus, David E., *Decisive Years: Experiences of Christian University Students* (Melbourne: David E. Angus, 2005).

Anon., 'Doug Nicholls', Collaborating for Indigenous Rights web exhibition profile, National Museum of Australia, http://indigenousrights.net.au/people/pagination/doug_nicholls, accessed 8 July 2009.

Anon., 'World War II: 1939–45', Conflicts: Boer War to Vietnam page, National Archives of Australia, www.naa.gov.au/collection/explore/defence/conflicts.aspx, accessed 25 July 2016.

Ansoul, Richard, *Beautiful Feet: Australian Baptists enter Papua New Guinea* (Hawthorn: ABMS, 1981).

Atherstone, Andrew, 'Evangelicals Fragmented: Theological Tensions at Wycliffe Hall, Oxford, c.1980–95', *Christianity and History Bulletin,* 4, 2008, 34–47.

Atherstone, Andrew, 'The Keele Congress of 1967: A Paradigm Shift in Anglican Evangelical Attitudes', *Journal of Anglican Studies,* 9.2, 2011, 175–197.

Atkinson, Alan, 'How do we live with ourselves? The Australian national conscience', *Australian Book Review*, 384, 2016.

Aubin, Tracey, *Peter Costello: A Biography, the Full and Unauthorised Story of the Man Who Wants to be PM* (Pymble: HarperCollins, 1999).

Austin, Denise A., *Our College: A History of the National College of Australian Christian Churches* (Parramatta: Australian Pentecostal Studies, 2013).

Austin-Broos, Diane, 'Translating Christianity: some keywords, events and sites in Western Arrernte Conversion', *Australian Journal of Anthropology* 21, 2010, 14–32.

Australian Dictionary of Biography, National Centre of Biography, Australian National University, online at http://adb.anu.edu.au/.

Babbage, Stuart Barton, 'Evangelicals in the Church in Australia', *Churchman,* 77.2, 1963, 114–119, online at http://churchsociety.org/docs/churchman/077/Cman_077_2_Babbage.pdf.

Bach, Neil S., *Leon Morris: One Man's Fight for Love and Truth* (Milton Keynes: Paternoster, 2015).

Bachelard, Michael, *Behind the Exclusive Brethren* (Melbourne: Scribe, 2008).

Baker, A. J., *Anderson's Social Philosophy* (Sydney: Angus & Robertson, 1979).

Bale, Colin, 'In God We Trust: The Impact of the Great War on Religious Belief', in Peter Bolt and Mark Thompson, *Donald Robinson selected works. Vol 3: Appreciation* (Sydney: Australian Church Record, 2008), 303–314.

Ball, G. B., and Mallice, J. W., *Striving for Excellence* (Epping: Baptist Community Services, 2004).

Ballantine-Jones, Bruce, *Inside Sydney: An Insider's view of the changes and politics in the Anglican Diocese of Sydney, 1966–2013* (Sydney: Bruce Ballantine-Jones, 2016).

Banks, Linda and Robert, *They shall see his Face: The Story of Amy Oxley Wilkinson and her Visionary Blind School in China* (Sydney: Acorn Press, 2017).

Banks, Robert, 'Denominational Structures: Their Legitimacy, Vocation and Capacity for Reform', in David Peterson and John W. Pryor (eds.), *In the Fullness of Time: Biblical Studies in Honour of Archbishop Donald Robinson* (Homebush West: Anzea Publishers, 1992), 277–300.

Banks, Robert, and Banks, Julia, *The Home Church* (Sutherland: Albatross Books, 1986).

Banks, Robert, 'Fifty Years of Theology in Australia, 1915–1965, Part One', *Colloquium*, 9.1, 1976, 36–42.

Banks, Robert, 'Fifty Years of Theology in Australia, 1915–1965', Part Two, *Colloquium*, 9.2, 1977, 7–16.

Banks, Robert, *Going to Church in the First Century* (Parramatta: Hexagon Press, 1980).

Banks, Robert, *Paul's Idea of Community: The Early House Churches in Their Historical Setting* (Sydney: Anzea, 1979; Grand Rapids: Eerdmans, 1980).

Banner, Horace, *The Three Freds* (London: UFM, 1938).

Banner, Horace, *The Three Freds and After* (London: UFM, 1961).

Bardon, Richard, *James Gibson, M. A. D. D.,* (Brisbane: W. R. Smith & Paterson, 1955).

Bardon, Richard, *The Centenary History of the Presbyterian Church of Queensland* (Brisbane: W. R. Smith and Paterson, 1949).

Barnes, Peter, 'Australian Calvinism: An Impressionistic Snapshot on the 500th Anniversary of Calvin's Birth', *Church Heritage*, 16.2, 2009, 118–126.

Barnes, Stanley, *All for Jesus: The Life of W. P. Nicholson* (Minneapolis: Ambassador Publications, 1996).

Barr, James, *Fundamentalism* (London: SCM, 1977).

Barrett, John, *Falling In: Australians and 'Boy Conscription', 1911–1915* (Sydney: Hale and Iremonger, 1979).

Barrett, John, *We Were There: Australian Soldiers of World War II tell their Stories* (St. Leonards: Allen & Unwin, 1995).

Bashford, Alison, and Macintyre, Stuart (eds.), *The Cambridge History of Australia* 2 vols (Port Melbourne; New York: CUP, 2013).

Bates, Stephen, *A Church at War: Anglicans and Homosexuality* (London: I. B. Tauris, 2004).

Bean, Charles E. W., *Official History of Australia in the War, 1914–1918*, 12 vols. (Sydney: Angus & Robertson, 1921–1934).

Beaumont, J. (ed.), *Where to Now? Australia's Identity in the Nineties* (Annandale: The Federation Press, 1993).

Beaumont, Joan, *Broken Nation: Australians in the Great War* (Sydney: Allen & Unwin, 2013).

Bebbington, David W., *Evangelicalism in Modern Britain* (London: Unwin Hyman, 1989).

Beer, D. R., '"The Holiest Campus", Its Decline and Transformation: The University of New England, 1946–79', *JRH*, 21.3, 1997, 318–336.

Bellah, Robert N., *Habits of the Heart* (Berkeley: University of California Press, 1996).

Bendle, Mervyn F., *Anzac and Its Enemies: The History War on Australia's National Identity* (Sydney: Quadrant Books, 2015).

Benson, C. Irving, *A Century of Victorian Methodism* (Melbourne: Spectator Publishing Company, 1935).

Benson, C. Irving, 'The Life and Times of Dr. William Henry Fitchett', *Heritage: A Journal of the Methodist Historical Society of Victoria*, 11, 1960, 9–10.

Bentley, Peter, 'These Statistics Don't Lie – Church Members have Left in Droves', *Catalyst* (Sydney), December 2007, 12–14.

Berthon, Peter, *We Are Aboriginal: Our 100 Years: From Arnhem Land's First Mission to Ngukurr Today* (Ngukurr: St Matthew's Anglican Church, 2008).

Blacket, John, '"Rainbow or the Serpent?" Observing the Arnhem Land Aboriginal Revival, 1979 and Now', in Mark Hutchinson and Stuart Piggin (eds.), *Reviving Australia* (Sydney: CSAC, 1994), 291–301.

Blacket, John, *Fire in the Outback* (Sutherland: Albatross Books, 1997).

Blainey, Geoffrey, *The Triumph of the Nomads: A History of Ancient Australia* (London, Macmillan, 1976).

Blanch, Allan M., *From Strength to Strength: A Life of Marcus Loane* (North Melbourne: Australian Scholarly Publishing, 2015).

Bleakley, Jack, *The Eavesdroppers* (Canberra: AGPS Press, 1992).

Bleby, Martin, *A Quiet Revival: Geoffrey Bingham in Life and Ministry* (Blackwood: New Creation Publications, 2012).

Bolton, Barbara, *Booth's Drum: The Salvation Army in Australia, 1880–1980* (Sydney: Hodder and Stoughton, 1980).

Bolton, Geoffrey C., *Dick Boyer: An Australian Humanist* (Canberra: Australian National University Press, 1967).

Bond, John, *The Army That Went with the Boys: A Record of Salvation Army Work with the Australian Imperial Force* (Melbourne: The Salvation Army, 1919).

Bos, Robert, 'The Dreaming and Social Change in Arnhem Land', in Tony Swain and Deborah Bird Rose (eds.), *Aboriginal Australians and Christian Missions* (Bedford Park: The Australian Association for the Study of Religions, 1988), 422–37.

Bottom, Bob, *Shadow of Shame: How the Mafia Got Away with the Murder of Donald Mackay* (South Melbourne: Sun Books, 1988).

Bouma, Gary D. and Dixon, Beverly R., *The Religious Factor in Australian Life* (Melbourne: MARC Australia, 1986).

Boyd, Robyn, *The Witness of the Student Christian Movement: Church ahead of the Church* (Hindmarsh: ATF Press, 2007).

Braga, Stuart, *A Century Preaching Christ: Katoomba Christian Convention, 1903–2003* (Sydney: Katoomba Christian Convention, 2003).

Brauer, Alfred, *Under the Southern Cross: History of the Evangelical Lutheran Church of Australia* (Adelaide: Lutheran Publishing House, 1985).

Brett, Judith, *Australian Liberals and the Moral Middle Class: from Alfred Deakin to John Howard* (Port Melbourne and Cambridge: CUP, 2003).

Breward, Ian, *Dr Harold Wood: A Notable Methodist* (Melbourne: Uniting Academic Press, 2013).

Breward, Ian, *A History of the Australian Churches* (St. Leonards: Allen & Unwin, 1993).

Brock, Peggy et al., *Indigenous Evangelists and Questions of Authority in the British Empire 1750–1940* (Leiden, Boston: Brill, 2005).

Brockis, Muriel, *A History of Trinity Congregational Church, Perth, Western Australia, 1914–84* (Leeds: W.S. Maney and Son, 1988).

Brooks, Dean, (ed.), *House Churches: A Discussion Booklet* (n.p.: The Uniting Church in Australia: SA Synod Evangelism Committee, 1983).

Brown, Callum, *The Death of Christian Britain: Understanding Secularisation, 1800–2000* (London: Routledge, 2001).

Brown, Callum G., 'What was the Religious Crisis of the 1960s?' *JRH*, 34.4, 2010, 468–479.

Bruce, F. F., *In Retrospect: remembrance of things past* rev. ed. (London: Marshall Pickering, 1993).

Brune, Peter, *A Bastard of a Place: The Australians in Papua* (Crows Nest: Allen & Unwin, 2004).

Bryson, John, *Evil Angels* (Harmondsworth: Penguin Books, 1986).

Buckingham, Jennifer, *The Rise of Religious Schools* (St Leonards: Centre for Independent Studies, 2010).

Buckley, Doug, *Fragments from a Forgettory* (Hartwell: Temple House, 2007).

Buick, Bob, with McKay, Gary, *All Guts and No Glory: The Story of a Long Tan Warrior* (St. Leonards: Allen & Unwin, 2000).

Burrell, Andrew, *Twiggy: The High-Stakes Life of Andrew Forrest* (Collingwood: Black Inc., 2013).

Cable, Ken J., 'The First and Second Book of Chronicles: A History of the Heretics Club', in William Emilsen and Geoffrey Treloar (eds.), *The Heretics Club 1916–2006* (University of Sydney: Origen Press, 2009), 1–28.

Cameron, Marcia, *An Enigmatic Life: David Broughton Knox, Father of Contemporary Sydney Anglicanism* (Brunswick East: Acorn Press, 2006).

Cameron, Marcia, *Living Stones: St. Swithun's Pymble, 1901–2001* (Wahroonga: The Helicon Press, 2001).

Cameron, Marcia, *Phenomenal Sydney: Anglicans in a time of change, 1945–2013* (Eugene: Wipf & Stock, 2016).

Cannon, Michael, *The Human Face of the Great Depression* (Mornington: M. Cannon, 1996).

Carey, Hilary M., '"The Land of Byamee": K. Langloh Parker, David Unaipon, and Popular Aboriginality in the Assimilation Era', *JRH*, 22.2, 1998, 200–218.

Carey, Hilary M., *Believing in Australia: a cultural history of religions* (Sydney: Allen & Unwin, 1996).

Carnley, Peter, *Reflections in Glass: Trends and tensions in the Contemporary Anglican Church* (Pymble: Harper Collins, 2004).

Carpenter, Edward, *Archbishop Fisher – His Life and Times* (Norwich: The Canterbury Press, 1991).

Carson, D. A., *The Gagging of God: Christianity Confronts Pluralism* (Grand Rapids: Zondervan, 1996).

Carter, Howard, and Sheldon, Ian, 'The Faith of Sir Joh', *Logos Journal*, June 1987, 12–15.

Cartledge, David, *The Apostolic Revolution: The Restoration of Apostles and Prophets in the Assemblies of God in Australia* (Sydney: Paraclete Institute, 2000).

Caterer, Helen, 'Australia's First Flying Padre', *Decision*, September 1982.

Caterer, Helen, *Australians Outback: 60 Years of Bush Church Aid* (Sydney: AIO, 1981).

Catherwood, Christopher, (ed.), *Martyn Lloyd-Jones: Chosen by God* (Crowborough: Highland Books, 1986).

Chambers, David, *Tempest-Tossed: The Life and Teaching of the Rev. C.H. Nash, M.A.* (Melbourne: Church Press Publications, 1959).

Chant, Barry, *Heart of Fire* (Adelaide: The House of Tabor, 1984).

Chant, Barry, *This is Revival: A fresh look at revival: Reliving the New Testament in the 21st Century* (Miranda: Tabor, 2013).

Chavura, Stephen and Tregenza, Ian, 'Introduction: Rethinking Secularism in Australia (and Beyond)', *JRH*, 38.3, 2014, 299–306.

Cheney, Sydney A., *From Horse to Horsepower* (Adelaide: Rigby, 1965).

Chevrau, Guy, *Catch the Fire* (London: Marshall Pickering, 1994).

Christians for Biblical Equality staff, 'Elaine Storkey Speaks to Colleges, Seminaries, and CBE Chapters', *Priscilla Papers*, 5.2, 1991, 14.

Clack, W. S., (ed.) *We Will Go: The History of 70 Years Training Men and Women for World Missionary Activity* (Melbourne: Bible College of Victoria, 1990).

Clancy, Mike, *Howard's Seduction of Australia: Where to Now?* (Watsons Bay: Fast Books, 2007).

Clark, C. M. H., *A History of Australia*, vol. 1 (Parkville: MUP, 1963).

Clark, Mavis T., *Pastor Doug: The Story of Sir Douglas Nicholls, Aboriginal Leader* (Melbourne: Lansdowne Press, 1972).

Clarnette, Dallas, 'An Historical Introduction' to W.H. Fitchett, *A Tattered Bible and a Mutilated Christ: Ought a Christian Church to Accept This?* reprint ed. (Ballarat: Harry Brown & Co., 1972).

Clarnette, Dallas, *50 Years on Fire for God: The Story of Walter Betts* (Kew: The People's Church, 1967).

Clifton, Shane, 'Pentecostal Hermeneutics and First-Wave Feminism: Mina Ross Brawner, MD', *The Pentecostal Charismatic Bible College Journal*, 2, 2006, http://pcbc.webjournals.org/, accessed 25 June 2009.

Cockburn, Stewart, and Ellyard, David, *Oliphant* (Adelaide: Axiom Books, 1981).

Cockburn, Stewart, *Playford: Benevolent Despot* (Kent Town: Axiom Publishing, 1991).

Cockburn, Stewart, *The Patriarchs* (Adelaide: Ferguson Publications, 1983).

Cole, Alan, 'Gabriel Hebert on *Fundamentalism and the Church of God*', *Reformed Theological Review*, 17.1, 1958, 11–20.

Cole, Alan, *The New Temple. A Study in the Origins of the Catechetical 'Form' of the Church in the New Testament* (London: Tyndale Press, 1950).

Cole, Graham, 'The Doctrine of the Church: Towards Conceptual Clarification', in Barry G. Webb (ed.) *Church, Worship, and the Local Congregation* (Homebush West: Lancer, 1987), 3–18.

Cole, Keith, *Commissioned to Care: The Golden Jubilee History of the Mission of St. James and St. John, 1919–1969* (Melbourne: Ruskin Press, 1969).

Cole, Keith, *From Mission to Church: The CMS Mission to the Aborigines of Arnhem Land, 1908–1985* (Bendigo: Keith Cole Publications, 1985).

Cole, Keith, *Oenpelli Pioneer: A Biography of the Founder of the Oenpelli Mission, the Rev. A. J. Dyer* (Melbourne: CMS Historical Publications, 1972).

Coleman, William, Cornish, Selwyn and Hagger, Alf, *Giblin's Platoon* (Canberra: ANU ePress, 2006).

Conrad, Edgar W., and Newing, Edward G., (eds.), *Perspectives on Language and Text: Essays and Poems in Honor of Francis I. Andersen's Sixtieth Birthday, July 28 1985* (Winona Lake: Eisenbrauns, 1987).

Crabb, Anna, 'Invoking Religion in Australian Politics', *Australian Journal of Political Science*, 44.2, 2009, 259–279.

Cribbin, John, *The Making of ANZACS* (Sydney: Collins/Fontana, 1985).

Crispin, Ken, *The Crown versus Chamberlain, 1980–1987* (Sutherland: Albatross Books, 1987).

Crocker, Walter, *Sir Thomas Playford: A Portrait* (Carlton: MUP, 1983).

Cryle, Mark, 'A "Fantastic Adventure": Reading *Christison of Lammermoor*' in F. McKenzie, Journeys through Queensland history: Landscape, place and society: Proceedings of the Professional Historians Association (Queensland) conference, Brisbane 3–4 September 2009 https://espace.library.uq.edu.au/view/UQ:202012/p9780646519197_3_223.pdf&bookreader=true#page/1/mode/1up accessed 27.4.17.

Cupit, Tony, Gooden, Ros and Manley, Ken (eds.), *From Five Barley Loaves: Australian Baptists in Global Mission, 1864–2010* (Preston: Mosaic Press, 2013).

Curran, James, and Ward, Stuart, *The Unknown Nation: Australia after Empire* (Carlton: MUP, 2010).

Cutler, Genevieve, *The Torch: story of the C.M.S. League of Youth* (Lilydale: Church Missionary Society, 1976).

Darling, Barbara, 'Shy Scholar a catalyst for Women's Ministry', *The Melbourne Anglican,* 481, 2010.

Darling, Pat Gunther, *Portrait of a Nurse* (Mona Vale: Don Wall, 2001).

Davies, Maynard, *Beyond My Grasp* (Sydney: Alpha Books, 1978).

Davis, R. V., *A History of the Church Missionary Society of Australia, SA Branch, including WA, 1910–1960* (Adelaide: CMS, 1960).

Davison, Graeme, *Narrating the Nation in Australia* (London: Menzies Centre for Australian Studies, 2010).

Dawkins, Richard, *The God Delusion* (London: Bantam, 2006).

Daws, Gavan, *Prisoners of the Japanese: POWs of World War II in the Pacific*, rev. ed. (Carlton North: Scribe, 2008).

Day, David, *John Curtin: A Life* (Sydney: Harper Perennial, 1999).

De Vries, Susanna, *Heroic Australian Women in War* (London: HarperCollins Publishers, 2004).

Dean, Eddie, and Ritova, Stan, *Rabuka: No other way* (Sydney: Doubleday, 1988).

Deenick, J. W., (ed.), *A Church En Route* (Geelong: Reformed Churches Publishing House, 1991).

Demography Bulletin (Canberra: Commonwealth Bureau of Census and Statistics), 83, 1966.

Dennett, D.C., *Breaking the Spell: Religion as a Natural Phenomenon* (London: Allen Lane, 2006).

Dickey, Brian and Martin, Elaine, *Building Community: A History of the Port Adelaide Central Mission* (Adelaide: Port Adelaide Wesley Centre, 1999).

Dickey, Brian, (ed.), *Australian Dictionary of Evangelical Biography* (Sydney: Evangelical History Association of Australia, 1994) online at https://sites.google.com/view/australian-dictionary-of-evang/home.

Dickey, Brian, '"We wanted to make the first one a winner": Urban Church Planting and the Origins of "Holy Trinity Hills"' in Geoffrey Treloar and Robert Linder (eds.), *Making History for God: essays on evangelicalism, revival and mission* (Sydney: Robert Menzies College, 2004), 169–196.

Dickey, Brian, *Holy Trinity Adelaide* (Adelaide: Trinity Church Trust, 1988).

Dickey, Brian, *Holy Trinity Adelaide 1836–2012: The History of a City Church* (Adelaide: Trinity Church Trustees, 2013).

Dickey, Brian, *No Charity There: A Short History of Social Welfare in Australia* (Sydney: Allen & Unwin, 1980, 1987).

Dixon, Patrick, *Signs of Revival* (Eastbourne: Kingsway Publications, 1994).

Dixson, Miriam, *The Real Matilda: Women and Identity in Australia, 1788–1975* (Ringwood: Penguin 1976).

Doherty, Bernard, 'The "Brethren Cult Controversy": Dissecting a Contemporary Australian "Social Problem"', *Alternative Spirituality and Religion Review*, 4.1, 2013, 25–48.

Douglas, J. D. et al., (eds.), *The New Bible Dictionary* (London, IVP, 1962).

Downes, Garry, 'Administrative Law and the Churches', Speech to the Church Law Forum, Wesley Mission, Sydney, 17 May 2007, online at Administrative Appeals Tribunal website, http://www.aat.gov.au/about-the-aat/engagement/speeches-and-papers/the-honourable-justice-garry-downes-am-former-pre/administrative-law-and-the-churches, accessed 19 November 2016.

Dudley-Smith, Timothy, *John Stott: A Global Ministry* (Leicester: IVP, 2001).

Dudley-Smith, Timothy, *John Stott: The Making of a Leader* (Leicester: IVP, 2001).

Dumbrell, W. J., 'The Role of Women – A Reconsideration of the Biblical Evidence', *Interchange*, 21, 1977.

Duncan, Macgregor, Leigh, Andrew, Madden, David, and Tynan, Peter, *Imagining Australia: Ideas for Our Future* (Crows Nest: Allen & Unwin, 2004).

Dunn, Peter, 'Allied Signal Intelligence Units and Other Secret Units in Australia During WW2', Australia at War website, maintained by Peter Dunn, http://home.st.net.au/~dunn/sigint/sigint.htm, accessed 7 June 2006.

Dunstan, Keith, *Wowsers* (Melbourne: Cassell, 1968).

Dunster, Nelson, *Padre to the 'Rats'* (London: Salvationist Publishing and Supplies, Ltd., 1971).

Edwards, Benjamin, *Wasps, Tykes and Ecumaniacs: Aspects of Australian Sectarianism 1945–1981* (Brunswick East: Acorn Press, 2008).

Edwards, David L., 'Evangelicals All', *Church Times*, 29 November 1985.

Ellis, Bob, 'King O'Malley', in Russel Ward (ed.), *The Greats: The 50 Men and Women Who Helped to Shape Modern Australia* (North Ryde: Angus & Robertson, 1986), 138–43.

Elphick, Peter, *Singapore, The Pregnable Fortress: A Study in Deception, Discord and Desertion* (London: Hodder & Stoughton, 1995).

Ely, Richard, 'Protestantism in Australian History: An Interpretative Sketch', *Lucas*, 5, 1989, 11–20.

Ely, Richard, 'The Forgotten Nationalism: Australian Civic Protestantism in the Second World War', *Journal of Australian Studies*, 20, 1987, 59–67.

Ely, Richard, *Unto God and Caesar: Religious Issues in the Emerging Commonwealth, 1890–1906* (Melbourne: MUP, 1976).

Emilsen, Susan and Emilsen, William W. eds., *Mapping the Landscape: Essays in Australian and New Zealand History in Honour of Professor Ian Breward* (New York: Peter Lang, 2000).

Emilsen, Susan, *A Whiff of Heresy: Samuel Angus and the Presbyterian Church in New South Wales* (Kensington: UNSW Press, 1991).

Emilsen, William W., and Emilsen, Susan E., (eds.), *The Uniting Church in Australia: The First 25 Years* (Armadale: Circa, 2003).

Errington, Wayne, and van Onselen, Peter, *John Winston Howard* (Carlton: MUP, 2007).

Evans, Harold E., *Soldier and Evangelist: The Story of Rev. John G. Ridley, M.C.* (Sydney: Baptist Historical Society of NSW, 1980).

Evans, Raymond, '"All the Passion of Our Womanhood": Margaret Thorp and the Battle of the Brisbane School of Arts', in Joy Damousi and Marilyn Lake (eds.), *Gender and War in the Twentieth Century* (Melbourne: CUP, 1995), 239–53.

Evans, Robert, *The Evangelisation Society of Australasia: The Second Period, 1919–1945* (Hazelbrook: the author, 2011).

Evans, Raymond, *A History of Queensland* (Melbourne: CUP, 2007).

Faggotter, Trevor, 'Revival Fire at Wudinna', *Renewal Journal*, 4, 1994, 43–52.

Faulkner, John and Macintyre, Stuart, *True Believers: The Story of the Federal Parliamentary Labor Party* (Crows Nest: Allen & Unwin, 2001).

Ferch, Arthur J., (ed.), *Journey of Hope: Seventh-Day Adventist History in the South Pacific, 1919–1950* (Wahroonga: South Pacific Division of Seventh-day Adventists, 1991).

Fischer, Gerhard, *Enemy Aliens: Internment and the Homefront Experience in Australia, 1914–1920* (St. Lucia: University of Queensland Press, 1989).

FitzSimons, Peter, *Tobruk* (Pymble: HarperCollins Publishers, 2006).

Fletcher, Brian H., *An English Church in Australian Soil* (Canberra: Barton Books, 2015).

Fletcher, Brian H., *The Place of Anglicanism in Australia* (Mulgrave: Broughton Publishing, 2008).

Forrester, Duncan B., Storrar, William and Morton, Andrew, *Public Theology for the 21st Century: Essays in Honour of Duncan B. Forrester* (London: T&T Clark, 2004).

Forsyth, Robert, 'Dispensing with Paul: Can we do without the texts where sex makes a difference?' *Interchange*, 20, 1976.

Frame, Tom, 'The Labor Party and Christianity: A Reflection on *The Latham Diaries*', *Quadrant*, 50.1–2, 2006, 26–32.

Frame, Tom, and Treloar, Geoffrey, (eds.), *Agendas for Australian Anglicanism: Essays in Honour of Bruce Kaye* (Adelaide: ATS Press, 2006).

France, R. T., and McGrath, Alister E., (eds.), *Evangelical Anglicans* (London: SPCK, 1993).

Franklin, James, *Corrupting the Youth: A History of Philosophy in Australia* (Sydney: Macleay Press, 2003).

Franklin, James, 'The Sydney intellectual/religious scene, 1916–2016', *St Mark's Review,* 242, 2017 (4), 20–54.

Frappell, Ruth, et al., *Anglicans in the Antipodes* (Westport: Greenwood Press, 1999).

Frappell, Samantha, 'Post-War Revivalism in Australia', in Mark Hutchinson and Stuart Piggin (eds.), *Reviving Australia: Essays on the History and Experience of Revival and Revivalism in Australian Christianity* (Sydney: CSAC, 1994) 249–261.

Frost, Michael, and Hirsch, Alan, *The Shaping of Things to Come: Innovation and Mission for the 21st-Century Church* (Erina: Strand Publishing, 2003).

Furlong, Monica, *C of E; The State It's In* (London: Hodder and Stoughton, 2000).

Furse-Roberts, David, 'Keepers of the Flame: A History of the Australian Festival of Light 1973–1981', *Lucas*, 2.2, 2010, 46–66. Gaden, John, (ed.), *A Woman's Place.* Papers prepared for the General Synod (Sydney: Doctrine Commission, AIO, 1976).

Gallagher, Paul, *Faith and Duty: The John Anderson Story* (Sydney: Random House, 2006).

Gammage, Bill, *The Broken Years: Australian Soldiers in the Great War* (Canberra: Australian National University Press, 1974).

Ganter, Regina, 'German Missionaries in Australia', http://missionaries.griffith.edu.au /introduction#whygermans, accessed 25 April 2017.

Gare, Deborah et al., (eds.), *The fuss that never ended: The life and work of Geoffrey Blainey* (Carlton: MUP, 2003).

Gariepy, Henry, *General of God's Army: The Authorized Biography of General Eva Burrows* (Wheaton: Victor Books, 1993).

Garnsey, David, *Arthur Garnsey: A Man for Truth and Freedom* (Sydney: Kingsdale Press, 1985).

Garrett, John, *Where Nets Were Cast: Christianity in Oceania Since World War II* (Geneva, Switzerland: WCC, 1997).

Garton, Stephen, *Out of Luck: Poor Australians and Social Welfare 1788–1988* (Sydney: Allen & Unwin, 1990).

Gelber, Katherine and Stone, Adrienne, (eds.), *Hate Speech and Freedom of Speech in Australia* (Annandale: The Federation Press, 2007).

Gibson, P. M., 'The Conscription Issue in South Australia, 1916–1917', in J. I. W. Brach (ed.), *University Studies in History,* 4.2, 1963–1964, (Nedlands: University of Western Australia Press, 1964).

Gilbert, Alan D., 'Protestants, Catholics and Loyalty: An Aspect of the Conscription Controversies, 1916–17', *Politics*, 6.1, 1971, 15–25.

Gilchrist, Michael, *Daniel Mannix: Priest & Patriot* (Blackburn: Dove Publications, 1982).

Giles, Kevin N., *The Eternal Generation of the Son: Maintaining Trinitarian Orthodoxy* (Downers Grove: IVP, 2012).

Giles, Kevin N., *The Father and the Son: Modern Evangelicals Reinvent the Doctrine of the Trinity* (Grand Rapids: Zondervan, 2006).

Giles, Kevin N., *The Trinity and Subordinationism: The Doctrine of God and the Contemporary Gender Debate* (Downers Grove: IVP, 2002).

Gill, Athol, *Life on the Road: the Gospel basis for a messianic lifestyle* (Homebush West: Lancer books, 1989).

Gill, Athol, *The Fringes of Freedom: Following Jesus, Living Together, Working for Justice* (Homebush West: Lancer Books, 1990).

Gill, Athol, 'Theological Implications of Radical Discipleship', in J. D. Douglas (ed.), *Let the Earth Hear His Voice: The International Congress on World Evangelization, Lausanne, 1974*, (Lausanne and Minneapolis: World Wide Publications, 1974), 1294–1296.

Gill, Stewart, 'The Battle for the Westminster Confession in Australia' in J. Ligon Duncan (ed.), *The Westminster Confession into the 21st Century*, volume 1, (Fearn: Mentor, 2003), 247–302.

Gladwin, Michael, *Captains of the Soul: A History of Australian Army Chaplains* (Newport: Big Sky Publishing, 2013).

Goldney, Donald V., *Methodism in Unley, 1949–1977* (Eagle Farm: William Brooks and Company, 1980).

Gow, Harold and Manley, Ken, *People with a Purpose: Epping Baptist Church, 1933–1983* (Epping: Epping Baptist Church, 1983).

Green, S.J.D., *The Passing of Protestant England: Secularisation and Social Change, c.1920–1960* (Cambridge: CUP, 2011).

Grey, Jeffrey, *A Military History of Australia*, 3rd ed. (Cambridge: CUP, 2008).

Grey, Jeffrey, and Doyle, Jeff, (eds.), *Vietnam: War, Myth and Memory* (Sydney: Allen & Unwin, 1992).

Griffen-Foley, Bridget, 'Radio Ministries: Religion on Australian Commercial Radio from the 1920s to the 1960s', *JRH*, 32.1, 2008, 31–54.

Griffiths, Alison, *Fire in the Islands: The acts of the Holy Spirit in the Solomons* (Wheaton: H. Shaw Publisher, 1977).

Hagar, Nicky, *The Hollow Men: A Study in the politics of deception* (Nelson: Craig Potton Publishing, 2006).

Haining, Peter, *The Witchcraft Papers* (London: Robert Hale, 1974).

Hall, Desmond, and Horner, David, *Breaking the Codes* (St Leonards: Allen & Unwin, 1998).

Hansen, I. V., *Nor Free nor Secular: Six Independent Schools in Victoria: A First Sample* (Melbourne: OUP, 1971).

Hardgrave, Don, *For Such a Time: A History of the Wesleyan Methodist Church in Australia* (MacGregor: A Pleasant Surprise Ltd, 1988).

Harding, Mark, and Nobbs, Alanna, (eds.), *The Content and Setting of the Gospel Tradition* (Grand Rapids/Cambridge: Eerdmans, 2010).

Hardy, Graham W., *Living Stones: The Story of St Stephen's Sydney* (Homebush West: ANZEA Publishers, 1985).

Harris, John, 'Anglicanism and Indigenous Peoples', in Bruce Kaye et al., *Anglicanism in Australia: A History* (Carlton: MUP, 2002), 223–246.

Harris, John, 'Counting the Bodies: Aboriginal Deaths in Colonial Australia', *Zadok Paper*, S115, 2001, 1–13.

Harris, John, 'It's time to listen to Aboriginal Christians and time to respond', in Peter Carroll and Steve Etherington (eds.), *One Land, One Saviour: Seeing Aboriginal Lives Transformed by Christ* (Sydney: CMS, 2008), 230–243.

Harris, John, 'Mabo for Teachers: Distinguishing True History from False History', *JCE,* 37.2, 1994, 5–23.

Harris, John, *One Blood: 200 Years of Aboriginal Encounter with Christianity* (Sutherland: Albatross, 1990).

Harris, John, *We wish we'd done more: Ninety Years of CMS and Aboriginal issues in North Australia* (Adelaide: Openbook, 1998).

Harris, Sam, *The End of Faith* (London: Free Press, 2006).

Harris, Sam, *Letter to a Christian Nation* (New York: Knopf, 2006).

Harrison, John M., 'Sir Joh Bjelke-Petersen: A Political and Religious Paradox', ABC Religion, http://www.abc.net.au/religion/stories/s1354728.htm, accessed 25 February 2006.

Hart, Max, *A Story of Fire: Aboriginal Christianity* (Blackwood: New Creation Publications, 1988).

Hartley, Benjamin L., 'Saving Students: European Student Relief in the Aftermath of World War I', *IBMR,* 42:4, October 2018, 295–315.

Hartley, F. J., *Sananánda Interlude* (Melbourne: The Book Depot, 1949).

Hastings, Adrian, *A History of English Christianity, 1920–1985* (London: Collins, 1986).

Hauerwas, Stanley, Cartwright, Michael G., and Berkman, John, *The Hauerwas Reader* (Durham: Duke University Press, 2001).

Hebart, Th., *The United Evangelical Lutheran Church in Australia* (North Adelaide: Lutheran Book Depot, 1938).

Hebert, Gabriel, *Fundamentalism and the Church of God* (London: SCM, 1957).

Henderson, Harold R., *Reach for the World: The Alan Walker Story* (Nashville: Discipleship Resources, 1981).

Henson, Barbara, *A Straight-out Man: F. W. Albrecht and Central Australian Aborigines* (Carlton: MUP, 1992).

Herriot, Peter, *Phillip Jensen, Bible Believer: The Psychology of Fundamentalist Leadership*, Kindle edition (n.p., The author, 2013).

Hicks, Lesley, *The Appalling Silence: The Mystery of Don Mackay* (Lane Cove: Hodder and Stoughton, 1979).

Hilborn, David, *Movement for Change: Evangelicals and Social Transformation* (Bletchley: Paternoster, 2004).

Hilliard, David, 'Anglicans in South Australian Public Life', *Journal of the Historical Society of South Australia*, 34, 2006, 5–16.

Hilliard, David, 'Australian Anglicans and Homosexuality: A Tale of Two Cities', *St Mark's Review,* 163, 1995, 12–20.

Hilliard, David, 'Church, Family and Sexuality in Australia in the 1950s', *Australian Historical Studies*, 27.109, 1997, 133–146.

Hilliard, David, 'God in the Suburbs: The Religious Culture of Australian Cities in the 1950s', *Australian Historical Studies*, 24.97, 1991, 399–419.

Hilliard, David, *Godliness and Good Order: A History of the Anglican Church in South Australia* (Adelaide: The Anglican Church of SA, 1986).

Hilliard, David, 'Religion in Playford's South Australia', in Bernard O'Neil, Judith Raftery and Kerrie Round (eds.), *Playford's South Australia: essays on the history of South Australia 1933–1968* (Adelaide: Association of Professional Historians, 1996), 253–74.

Hilliard, David, 'The Religious Crisis of the 1960s: The Experience of the Australian Churches', *JRH,* 21.2, 1997, 209–28.

Hilliard, David, 'The South Sea Evangelical Mission in The Solomon Islands: The Foundation Years', *Journal of Pacific History*, 4, 1969, 41–64.

Hilliard, David, 'Sydney Anglicans and Homosexuality', *Journal of Homosexuality*, 33.2, 1997, 101–123.

Hilton, Boyd, *The Age of Atonement: The Influence of Evangelicalism on Social and Economic Thought, 1795–1865* (Oxford: Clarendon Press, 1988).

Hinrichsen, E. C., *The Gospel under Canvas* (Melbourne: Austral Printing & Publishing Ltd, 1958).
Hirst, John, *The Sentimental Nation: The Making of the Australian Commonwealth* (Melbourne: OUP, 2000).
Hirt, John, 'Catechetical evangelism as Radical Discipleship in the Mission of the Church', in David J. Neville (ed.), *Prophecy and Passion: Essays in honour of Athol Gill* (Adelaide: Australian Theological Forum, 2002), 300–327.
Hitchens, Christopher, *God is not Great* (New York: Twelve, 2007).
Hobbs, Theodora, Thornton, Sydney, and Ryan, Vera, *Abortion: Factors to Consider: A Minority Report* (Sydney: Church and Nation Committee, NSW General Assembly, 1991) online at http://www.churchandnation.pcnsw.org.au/Images/C%20&%20N%201991.pdf, accessed 18 September 2016.
Hogan, Michael, *The Sectarian Strand: Religion in Australian History* (Ringwood: Penguin Books, 1987).
Hogg, Anna, 'Editorial', *The Journal of Christian Education,* 1.1, 1958.
Hogg, James O., *Ecumenism: A Serious Cause for Dissenting* (Stanmore: Stanmore Baptist Church, 1986).
Holland, Alison, *Just Relations. The Story of Mary Bennett's Crusade for Aboriginal Rights* (UWA Publishing, 2015).
Holland, Alison, 'To Eliminate Colour Prejudice: The WCTU and Decolonisation in Australia', *JRH*, 32.2, 2008, 256–276.
Holland, Alison, 'A Scottish Inheritance? Mary Bennett, the Aboriginal Cause and the Legacies of the Past', *Journal of the Sydney Society for Scottish History*,16, 2016, 85–110.
Horne, Donald, 'Celebrating Our Differences', *The Australian*, 9 February 2001.
Horne, Donald, *The Lucky Country*, 5th ed. (Ringwood: Penguin, 1998).
Horne, Richard, 'God & Sir Joh: Faith, Forgiveness and the Final Judgment', *On Being*, 1992, 16–19.
Houston, James, *A Multicultural Odyssey* (Bayswater: Coventry Press, 2018).
Howe, Renate and Swain, Shurlee, *The Challenge of the City: The Centenary History of Wesley Central Mission, 1893–1993* (South Melbourne: Hyland House, 1993).
Howe, Renate, A *Century of Influence: The Australian Student Christian Movement 1896–1996* (Sydney: UNSW Press, 2009).
Hoyle, Arthur, *King O'Malley: 'The American Bounder'* (South Melbourne: Macmillan of Australia, 1981).
Hoyle, Arthur, *Jock Garden: The Red Parson* (Canberra: Privately Printed, 1993).
Hughes, Philip, *Christian Faith and the Economy in a Globalised World,* Christian Research Association Research Paper No.10 (Nunawading: CRA, 2011).
Hunt, Arnold D., and Thomas, Robert P., (eds.), *For God, King and Country* (Salisbury: Salisbury College of Advanced Education, 1979).
Hunt, Arnold D., *This Side of Heaven: A History of Methodism in South Australia* (Adelaide: Lutheran Publishing House, 1985).
Hunter, James D., *American Evangelicalism: Conservative Religion and the Quandary of Modernity* (New Brunswick: Rutgers University Press, 1984).
Hutchinson, Mark, *Iron in Our Blood: A History of the Presbyterian Church in NSW, 1788–2001* (Sydney: Ferguson Publications and CSAC, 2001).
Hutchinson, Mark, *Pellegrini: An Italian Protestant Community in Sydney, 1958–1990* (Sydney: Australia Pentecostal Studies Journal, 1999).
Inglis, K. S., *C. E. W. Bean, Australian Historian* (St. Lucia: University of Queensland Press, 1970).
Inglis, K. S., 'Conscription in Peace and War, 1911–1945', in Roy Forward and Bob Reece (eds.), *Conscription in Australia* (St. Lucia: University of Queensland Press, 1968), 22–65.
Inglis, K. S., *Sacred Places: War Memorials in the Australian Landscape* (Carlton South: MUP, 1998).
Inglis, K. S., 'The Anzac Tradition', *Meanjin Quarterly*, 24.1, 1965, 25–44.
Inglis, K. S., *The Stuart Case*, New ed. (Melbourne: Black Inc., 2002).

Iremonger, John, Merritt, John and Osborne, Graeme (eds.), *Strikes: Studies in Twentieth Century Australian History* (Sydney: Angus & Robertson, 1973).

Irvine, Graeme, *Best Things in the Worst Times: An Insider's View of World Vision* (Wilsonville: BookPartners, Inc., 1996).

Jagelman, Ian, 'Church Growth: Its Promise and Problems for Australian Pentecostalism', *Australasian Pentecostal Studies*, 1, 1998, online at http://aps-journal.com/aps/index.php/APS/article/view/46.

James, Bob, '"Lots of Religion and Freemasonry": The Politics of Revivalism during the 1930s Depression on the Northern Coalfields', in Mark Hutchinson and Stuart Piggin (eds.), *Reviving Australia* (Sydney: CSAC, 1994), 233–248.

Janis, Irving, *Victims of Groupthink* (Boston: Houghton Mifflin, 1972).

Jauncey, Leslie C., *The Story of Conscription in Australia* (South Melbourne: Macmillan, 1968).

Jeffrey, Betty, *White Coolies* (Sydney: Angus & Robertson, 1954).

Jenkins, Philip, *The Next Christendom: The coming of Global Christianity* (New York: OUP, 2002).

Jensen, Peter, 'Caleb in the Antipodes', The T. C. Hammond lecture, Ireland, June 2005, Sydney Anglicans website, posted 14 September 2005, http://sydneyanglicans.net/blogs/indepth/caleb_in_the_antipodes_peter_jensen, accessed 21 November 2016.

Jensen, Peter, *The Future of Jesus: Boyer Lectures 2005* (Sydney: ABC Books, 2005), also at ABC Radio National website, http://www.abc.net.au/radionational/programs/boyerlectures/the-future-of-jesus/3339436, accessed 21 November 2016.

Johnson, Mark, *At the Front: Experiences of Australian Soldiers in World War II* (Melbourne: CUP, 1996).

Johnston, Arthur, *The Battle for World Evangelism* (Wheaton: Tyndale, 1978).

Johnston, George, *My Brother Jack: A Novel* (London: Collins, 1964).

Jones, T. E., *'These Twenty Years': A Record of the Work of the Bush Church Aid Society for Australia and Tasmania* (Sydney: BCA, 1939).

Judd, Bernard G., *He That Doeth: The Life Story of Archdeacon R.B.S. Hammond* (London: Marshall, Morgan & Scott, 1951).

Judd, Stephen and Cable, Kenneth, *Sydney Anglicans* (Sydney: Anglican Information Office, 1987).

Judd, Stephen and Robinson, Anne, 'Christianity and the Social Services in Australia: A Conversation', in Stuart Piggin (ed.) *Shaping the Good Society in Australia* (Macquarie University: ACHNF, 2006), 111–115.

Judd, Stephen, Robinson, Anne, and Errington, Felicity, *Driven by Purpose: Charities that Make the Difference* (Greenwich: HammondPress, 2012).

Judge, Edwin, '"On this Rock I will build my *ecclesia*": Counter-cultic Springs of Multiculturalism', in E. A. Judge, *The First Christians in the Roman World: Augustan and New Testament Essays*, ed. James R. Harrison (Tübingen: Mohr Siebeck, 2008), 619–668.

Judge, Edwin, *Engaging Rome and Jerusalem: historical essays for our time,* ed. Stuart Piggin (North Melbourne: Australian Scholarly Publishing, 2014).

Judge, Edwin, 'The Religion of the Secularists', *JRH*, 38.3, 2014, 307–319.

Kaldor, Peter, *A gulf too deep? the Protestant churches and the urban working class in Australia* (Chatswood: Board of Mission, the Uniting Church in NSW, c1983).

Kaldor, Peter, et al., *Taking Stock: A Profile of Australian Church Attenders* (Adelaide: Openbook, 1999).

Kaldor, Peter, *Green shoots in the concrete: towards a more sensitive Christian presence in our cities* (Surry Hills: Scaffolding, c1985).

Kaldor, Peter, John Bellamy, Sandra Moore, *Mission under the Microscope: Keys to Effective and Sustainable Mission* (Adelaide: OpenBook Publishers, 1995).

Kaldor, Peter, *Stepping out: churches living out the gospel in a changing world* (Chatswood: The Board, c1985).

Kaldor, Peter, *Where the river flows: sharing the gospel in a changing Australia* (Sydney: Lancer Books, 1988).

Kaldor, Peter. *Winds of Change: The Experience of Church in a Changing Australia* (Homebush West: Lancer, 1994).

Kaldor, Peter, *Who goes where? Who doesn't care?* (Homebush West: Lancer, c1987).

Kaye, Bruce, 'Acting on trust: the morality of Church investment practices', *Online Opinion: Australia's e-journal of social and political debate*, 14 December 2009, http://www.onlineopinion.com.au/view.asp?article=9801, accessed 21 November 2016.

Kaye, Bruce, with Tom Frame, Colin Holden and Geoff Treloar (eds.) *Anglicanism in Australia: A History* (Carlton: MUP, 2002).

Keith, Agnes Newton, *Three Came Home* (Boston: Little Brown and Company, 1947).

Kelley, Dean, *Why Conservative Churches are Growing: a study in the sociology of religion* (New York: Harper & Row, 1972).

Kent, Gary, and Reynaud, Daniel, *Faith of the Anzacs* (Warburton: Signs Publishing, 2010).

Kiek, Edward S., *Our First Hundred Years: The Centenary Record of the South Australian Congregational Union* (Adelaide: The S.A. Congregational Union and Home Mission, 1950).

Kimball, Roger, 'Who was David Stove?', *The New Criterion*, 15.7, 1997, online at http://www.newcriterion.com/articles.cfm/Who-was-David-Stove--3368, accessed 30 January 2012.

Kingston, Beverley, *My wife, my daughter, and poor Mary Ann: women and work in Australia* (West Melbourne: Thomas Nelson, 1975).

Kirkby, Sydney J., *These Ten Years: A Record of the Work of the Bush Church Aid Society for the Church of England in Australia, 1920–1930* (Sydney: Bush Church Aid Society, 1930).

Knox, D. B., *Justification by Faith* (London: The Church Book Room Press, 1959).

Knox, D. B., *The Doctrine of Faith in the Reign of Henry VIII* (London: James Clarke & Co, 1961).

Knox, D.B., *Thirty-Nine Articles* (Sydney: AIO, 1976).

Laffin, John, *Digger: The Legend of the Australian Soldier*, rev. ed. (South Melbourne: Sun Books, 1990).

Lake, Marilyn, *A Divided Society: Tasmania During World War I* (Clayton: MUP, 1975).

Lake, Marilyn, *Getting Equal: The History of Australian Feminism* (St Leonards: Allen & Unwin, 1999.

Lake, Meredith, *Faith in Action: HammondCare* (Sydney: UNSW Press, 2013).

Lamb, Margaret, '"Out of all Proportion": Christian Brethren Influence in Australian Evangelicalism', in Geoffrey R. Treloar and Robert D. Linder (eds.), *Making History for God: Essays on Evangelicalism, Revival and Mission* (Sydney: Robert Menzies College, 2004).

Lambert, Ian, and Mitchell, Suzanne, (eds.), *Reclaiming the Future* (Sydney: CSAC, 1996).

Langmore, Diane, *Prime Minister's Wives: The Public and Private Lives of Ten Australian Women* (Ringwood: McPhee Gribble, 1992).

Lawton, William, *Being Christian, Being Australian* (Sydney: Lancer, 1988).

Lawton, William J., 'The Winter of our Days: The Anglican Diocese of Sydney 1950–1960', *Lucas,* 9, 1990, 11–32.

Lawton, William J., 'Australian Anglican Theology' in Bruce Kaye et al., *Anglicanism in Australia: A History* (Carlton: MUP, 2002), 177–199.

Lees, Shirley, *Drunk before Dawn* (Sevenoaks: OMF, 1979).

Leske, Everard, *For Faith and Freedom: The Story of Lutherans and Lutheranism in Australia, 1838–1996* (Adelaide: Openbook Publishers, 1996).

Levin, Tanya, *People in Glass Houses: An Insider's Story of a Life in and out of Hillsong* (Melbourne: Black Inc., 2007).

Lewis, Brian, *Our War: Australia During World War I* (Carlton: MUP, 1980).

Lewis, Donald M., (ed.), *Christianity Reborn: The Global Expansion of Evangelicalism in the Twentieth Century* (Grand Rapids: Eerdmans, 2004.

Lightfoot, Daryl, 'A Cliff College Contingent and Rev. John Wilkinson of Narrabri: A WW1 Tragedy', *Archiv-Vista,* 1, 2015.

Linder, Robert D., 'Alan Walker among the Sharks: Why the Most Important Christian in Australia in the Latter Half of the Twentieth Century was not also a Beloved National Figure', *Church Heritage* 17, 2011, 2–23.

Linder, Robert D., 'Presidents, Prime Ministers and Evangelicals: Christianity and Leadership in Two Countries', *Lucas: An Evangelical History Review*, 32, 2002, 7–54.

Linder, Robert D., 'William Henry Fitchett (1841–1928): Forgotten Methodist "Tall Poppy"', in Geoffrey R. Treloar and Robert D. Linder (eds.), *Making History for God: Essays on Evangelicalism, Revival and Mission* (Sydney: Robert Menzies College, 2004), 197–238.

Linder, Robert D., 'Comrades in Arms: Australian Evangelical Cooperation in World War I, 1914–1918', *Lucas*, 18, 1994, 51–71.

Linder, Robert D., 'Galilee Shall at last vanquish Corsica: The Rev. B. Linden Webb Challenges the War-Makers, 1915–1917', *Church Heritage*, 11, 2000, 171–83.

Linder, Robert D., *The Long Tragedy: Australian Evangelical Christians and the Great War, 1914–1918* (Adelaide: Openbook Publishers, 2000).

Linder, Robert D., 'The Peaceful Evangelicals: Refusing to take up the Sword, 1914–1918', *CSAC Working Papers*, 1.18, 1994.

Lloyd-Jones, D. Martyn, *Knowing the Times* (Edinburgh: Banner of Truth Trust, 1989).

Loane, Marcus, *Archbishop Mowll: The Biography of Howard West Kilvinton Mowll* (London: Hodder and Stoughton, 1960).

Loane, Marcus, *Makers of Our Heritage: A Study of Four Evangelical Leaders* (London: Hodder and Stoughton, 1967).

Lockley, G. Lindsay, *Congregationalism in Australia*, (ed. Bruce Upham), (Melbourne: Uniting Church Press, 2001).

Long, Gavin, *The Six Years War: Australia in the 1939–45 War* (Canberra: AWM, 1973).

Lunn, Hugh, *Johannes Bjelke-Petersen: A Political Biography* (St. Lucia: University of Queensland Press, 1984).

Lutton, Wesley, *The Wesley Story: Centenary of Wesley Church, Perth, Western Australia, 1870–1970* (Perth: Western Australian Newspapers, 1970).

Macdonald, Aeneas, *One Hundred Years of Presbyterianism in Victoria* (Melbourne: Robertson & Mullens, 1937).

Macintyre, Stuart, *The Oxford History of Australia vol.4 The Succeeding Age, 1901–1942* (Melbourne: OUP, 1993).

Maddox, Marion, *For God and Country: Religious Dynamics in Australian Federal Politics* (Canberra: Dept. of the Parliamentary Library, 2001).

Maddox, Marion, *God under Howard: The Rise of the Religious Right in Australian Politics* (Sydney: Allen & Unwin, 2005).

Maddox, Marion, *Taking God to School: The End of Australia's Egalitarian Education?* (Crows Nest: Allen & Unwin, 2014).

Makin, Norman, *Federal Labor Leaders* (Sydney: Union Printing Party, 1961).

Manley, Ken R., *From Woolloomooloo to Eternity: A History of Australian Baptists*, 2 vols. (Milton Keynes: Paternoster, 2006).

Manners, Norman G., *Bullwinkel: The True Story of Vivian Bullwinkel, a Young Army Nursing Sister, Who was the Sole Survivor of a World War Two Massacre by the Japanese* (Carlisle: Hesperian Press, 1999).

Mansfield, Joan, *A Church on the Highway: Pymble Presbyterian Church, 1895–1977* (Pymble: Pymble Council of Elders, 1985).

Mar, Wendy Lu, *So Great a Cloud of Witnesses: A History of the Chinese Presbyterian Church, Sydney, 1893–1993* (Surry Hills: Chinese Presbyterian Church, 1993).

Martin, Allan W., *Robert Menzies: A Life* 2 vols. (Carlton South: MUP, 1993–1999).

Martin, Sarah, *Davis McCaughey: A Life* (Sydney: UNSW Press, 2012).

Martin, William, *The Billy Graham story: a prophet with honour* (London: Hutchinson, 1992).

Massam, Katharine and Smith, John H., 'There Was Another Weapon: The Churches on the Homefront', in Jenny Gregory (ed.), *On the Homefront: Western Australia and World War II* (Perth: University of Western Australia Press, 1996), 149–161.

McCalman, Janet, *Journeyings: The Biography of a Middle-Class Generation, 1920–1990,* (Carlton: MUP, 1993).

McCalman, Janet, *Struggletown: Public and Private Life in Richmond, 1900–1965* (Carlton: MUP, 1984).

McDowell, Ian, *A Brief History of the 'Brethren'* (Sydney: Victory Books, 1968).

McGillion, Chris, *The Chosen Ones: The Politics of Salvation in the Anglican Church* (Crows Nest: Allen & Unwin, 2005).

McGrath, Alister, *Evangelicalism and the Future of Christianity* (London: Hodder & Stoughton, 1993).

McKernan, Michael, *All In!: Fighting the War at Home* (St. Leonards: Allen & Unwin, 1995).

McKernan, Michael, *Australian Churches at War: Attitudes and Activities of the Major Churches, 1914–1918* (Sydney and Canberra: Catholic Theological Faculty and Australian War Memorial, 1980).

McKernan, Michael, *Here Is Their Spirit: A History of the Australian War Memorial, 1917–1990* (St. Lucia: University of Queensland Press, 1991).

McKernan, Michael, *Padre: Australian Chaplains in Gallipoli and France* (Sydney: Allen & Unwin, 1986).

McKernan, Michael, *The Australian People and the Great War* (Sydney: Collins, 1980).

McKernan, Michael, 'War', in Wray Vamplew (ed.), *Australians: Historical Statistics* (Broadway: Fairfax, Syme & Weldon Associates, 1987), 410–4.

McLeod, D. W., *How the West Was Lost: The Native Question in the Development of Western Australia* (Port Hedland: The author, 1984).

McMurtrie, Barry, *Time Out* (Box Hill: Vital, 1980).

McQueen, Humphrey, *Gallipoli to Petrov: Arguing with Australian History* (Sydney: Allen & Unwin, 1984).

McQueen, Humphrey, *Gone Tomorrow: Australia in the 80s* (Sydney: Angus & Robertson, 1982).

McQueen, Humphrey, 'The 'Spanish' Influenza Pandemic in Australia, 1918–1919', in Jill Roe (ed.), *Social Policy in Australia: Some Perspectives, 1901–75* (Stanmore: Cassell, 1976), 131–47.

Meaney, Neville, 'Britishness and Australian identity: The problem of nationalism in Australian history and historiography', *Australian Historical Studies*, 32.116, 2001, 76–90.

Mears, Ian, (ed.) *The Christian and Social Concern: A Set of Ten Studies on a Biblical Basis for Social Involvement* (Sydney: The Board of Education, Diocese of Sydney, 1981).

Middleton, J. Richard and Walsh, Brian J., *Truth Is Stranger Than It Used to Be: Biblical Faith in a Postmodern Age* (Downers Grove: InterVarsity Press, 1995).

Miller, R. S., *Fifty Years of Keswick in Tasmania* (Launceston: Tasmanian Keswick Convention, 1975).

Milne, Douglas, *The Word of God is the Bible and an Affirmation of the Five Points of Calvinism* (Box Hill North: Presbyterian Theological College, 1994).

Mitchell, Angus S., 'Those 'Y' Blokes', *The Rotarian*, 64.6, 1944, 32–3.

Mol, Hans, *Christianity in Chains; a Sociologist's Interpretation of the Churches' Dilemma in a Secular World* (Melbourne: Nelson, 1969).

Mol, Hans, *Religion in Australia: A Sociological Investigation* (Melbourne: Nelson, 1971).

Moloney, Frank, 'Review: *The Content and Setting of the Gospel Tradition*', *The Catholic Biblical Quarterly*, 74, 2012.

Moon, Geoffrey, *Household Church Groups in Canberra 1968–1971* (Melbourne: Keswick Book Depot, 1972).

Moor, Keith, *Crims in Grass Castles: The True Story of Trimbole, Mr. Asia and the Disappearance of Donald Mackay* (Apollo Bay: Pascoe Publishing, 1989).
Moore, Richard K., (ed.), *Baptists of Western Australia: The First Ninety* Years (Perth: The Baptist Historical Society of Western Australia, 1991).
Moore, Richard K., *A Centenary History of the Baptist Denomination in Western Australia, 1895–1995* (Perth: The Baptist Historical Society of Western Australia, 1996).
Moore, Richard K., *Noel Vose: Pastor, Principal, President* (Perth: Baptist Historical Society of Western Australia, 2010), 117–22.
Morice, Janet, *Six-Bob-A-Day Tourist* (Ringwood: Penguin Books, 1985).
Morris, Leon, *The Biblical Doctrine of Judgement* (London: Tyndale Press, 1960).
Morris, Leon, *The Wages of Sin: An Examination of the New Testament Teaching on Death* (London: Tyndale Press, 1955).
Moses, John A., and Davis, George F., *Anzac Day Origins: Canon D. J. Garland and Trans-Tasman Commemoration* (Barton: Barton Books, 2013).
Moses, John A., 'ANZAC Day as Religious Revivalism: The Politics of Faith in Brisbane, 1916–1939', in Mark Hutchinson and Stuart Piggin (eds.), *Reviving Australia: Essays on the History and Experience of Revival and Revivalism in Australian Christianity* (Sydney: CSAC, 1994), 170–84.
Moyes, Gordon, *How to grow an Australian church: a practical guide for church growth* (Box Hill: Vital, 1975).
Mukherjee, S. K., *Crime Trends in Twentieth-Century Australia* (Sydney: Australian Institute of Criminology & George Allen and Unwin, 1981).
Mukherjee, S. K., et al., *Source Book of Australian Criminal and Social Statistics, 1900–1980* (Canberra: Australian Institute of Criminology, 1981).
Murphy, D. J., 'Religion, Race and Conscription in World War I', *Australian Journal of Politics and History*, 20.2, 1974, 155–63.
Murphy, John, and Smart, Judith, (eds.), *The Forgotten Fifties: Aspects of Australian Society and Culture in the 1950s* (Carlton: MUP, 1997).
Murphy, John, *Imagining the Fifties: Private Sentiment and Political Culture in Menzies' Australia* (Sydney: UNSW Press, 2000).
Murray, Andrew, *The Church Missionary Society and the deepening of the spiritual life* (Sydney: CMS, [19 –]).
Nanscawen, Anne, *With One Accord: The Beginning of an Aussie Awakening* (Sydney: Anzea, 1989).
Nathan, Rick and Wilson, Ken, *Empowered Evangelicals: Bringing Together the Best of the Evangelical and Charismatic Worlds* (Ann Arbor: Servant Publications, 1995).
Nelson, Warren, *T. C. Hammond: His Life and Legacy in Ireland and Australia* (Edinburgh: Banner of Truth Trust, 1994).
Neville, David J., (ed.), *Prophecy and Passion: Essays in honour of Athol Gill* (Adelaide: Australian Theological Forum, 2002).
Newton, Kenneth J., *A History of the Brethren in Australia with Special Reference to the Open Brethren* (Indooroopilly, Qld.: Aberdeen Desktop, 1990).
Niall, Brenda, *Mannix* (Melbourne: Text Publishing, 2015).
Nichols, Alan, *David Penman: Bridge-Builder, Peacemaker, Fighter for Social Justice* (Sutherland: Albatross Books, 1991).
Nile, Richard (ed.), *Australian Civilisation* (Melbourne: OUP, 1994).
Nobbs, Raymond, *You Are God's Building* (Wahroonga: St Paul's Church, 1987).
Nongbri, Brent, *Before Religion: A History of a Modern Concept* (New Haven: Yale University Press, 213).
Noll, Mark A., *American Evangelical Christianity: An Introduction* (Oxford: Blackwell, 2001).
Noll, Mark A., D. W. Bebbington, and George A. Rawlyk. *Evangelicalism: Comparative Studies of Popular Protestantism in North America, the British Isles, and Beyond 1700–1990* (New York; Oxford: Oxford University Press, 1994).

Noll, Mark A., *The Rise of Evangelicalism: The Age of Edwards, Whitefield, and the Wesleys, A History of Evangelicalism* (Downers Grove: InterVarsity Press, 2003).

Noll, Mark A., *The Scandal of the Evangelical Mind* (Leicester: IVP, 1994).

North, Richard, 'Master Codebreakers', *The University of Sydney Gazette*, 30.2, 2002, 1.

Nutt, Dennis, *A Crucible of Faith and Learning: A History of the Australian College of Ministries* (Rhodes: Acom Press, 2017).

O'Brien, Anne, *God's Willing Workers: Women and Religion in Australia* (Sydney: UNSW Press, 2005).

O'Brien, Glen and Carey, Hilary M. (eds.), *Methodism in Australia: A History* (Farnham: Ashgate Publishing Company, 2015).

O'Brien, Glen, 'Anti-Americanism and the Wesleyan-Holiness Churches in Australia' *The Journal of Ecclesiastical History*, 61.2, 2010, 314–343.

Oats, William N., *A Question of Survival: Quakers in Australia in the Nineteenth Century* (St. Lucia: University of Queensland Press, 1985).

Oats, William N., 'The Campaign Against Conscription in Australia – 1911–1914', *Journal of the Friends' Historical Society*, 1989, 205–19.

Onfray, Michel, *Atheist manifesto: the case against Christianity, Judaism, and Islam* (New York: Arcade Publishing, 2007).

Orpwood, Michael, *Chappo: For the Sake of the Gospel: John Chapman and the Department of Evangelism* (Russell Lea: Eagleswift Press, 1995).

Orr, J. Edwin, *Evangelical Awakenings in the South Seas* (Minneapolis: Bethany Fellowship, 1976).

Otzen, Roslyn, *Whitley: The Baptist College of Victoria, 1891–1991* (South Yarra: Hyland House, 1991).

Packer, J. I., *Fundamentalism and the Word of God* (London: IVF, 1958).

Paproth, Darrell N., *Failure Is Not Final: A Life of C.H. Nash* (Sydney: CSAC, 1997).

Paproth, Darrell, 'Faith Missions, Personality, and Leadership: William Lockhart Morton and Angas College', *Lucas,* 27 & 28, 2000, 64–89.

Paproth, Darrell, 'The Melbourne Bible Institute: Its Genesis, Ethos and Purpose', in G.R. Treloar (ed.), *The Furtherance of Religious Beliefs: Essays on the History of Theological Education in Australia* (Sydney: Centre for the Study of Australian Christianity, 1997), 124–155.

Parker, David (ed.), *Pressing on with the Gospel: The Story of Baptists in Queensland, 1855–2005* (Brisbane: Baptist Historical Society of Queensland, 2005).

Parker, Joy, *A Vision of Eagles: Fifty Years of Crusaders in NSW* (Sydney: The Crusader Union of NSW, 1980).

Parnaby, Owen, *Queen's College, University of Melbourne: A Centenary History* (Carlton: MUP, 1990).

Paterson, Cecily, *Never Alone: The Remarkable Story of David and Robyn Claydon* (Adelaide: SPCK Australia, 2006).

Petras, Michael, 'The Life and Times of the Reverend William Lamb (1868 -1944)', *The Baptist Recorder,* 101, 2008, 1–11.

Pfennigwerth, H. Ian, *The Australian Cruiser Perth, 1939–1942* (Dural: Rosenberg, 2007).

Phillips, Harry C. J., 'Margaret Court', in Wray Vamplew, Katharine Moore, John O'Hara, Richard Cashman and Ian Jobling (eds.), *The Oxford Companion to Australian Sport*, rev. ed. (Melbourne: OUP, 1997), 113–4.

Phillips, W. W., 'Religion' in Wray Vamplew (ed.), *Australians: Historical Statistics* (Broadway: Fairfax, Syme & Weldon Associates, 1987).

Phillips, Walter, '"Six O'Clock Swill": The Introduction of Early Closing of Hotel Bars in Australia', *Historical Studies*, 19, 1980, 250–66.

Phillips, Walter, 'Gipsy Smith in Australia, 1926: The Commonwealth Evangelistic Campaign', in Mark Hutchinson and Stuart Piggin (eds.), *Reviving Australia* (Sydney: CSAC, 1994), 185–201.

Pidwell, Harold, *A Gentle Bunyip: the Athol Gill Story* (Wests Lakes: Seaview Press, 2007).

Pierard, Richard V. and Linder, Robert D., *Civil Religion and the Presidency* (Grand Rapids: Zondervan, 1988), 11–29.

Pierard, Richard, 'The Missionary Origins of the Bengal-Orissa-Bihar Baptist Churches Association', *American Baptist Quarterly*, 29, 2010, 31–45.

Piggin, Stuart, '"Not a Little Holy Club": Lay and Clerical Leadership in Australian Anglican Evangelicalism 1788–1988', in W. J. Sheils (ed.) *The Ministry, Clerical and Lay: Studies in Church History* (Oxford: Basil Blackwell, 1989), 367–83.

Piggin, Stuart, 'Australian Anglicanism in World-Wide Context', in Bruce Kaye et al., *Anglicanism in Australia: A History* (Carlton: MUP, 2002), 200–222.

Piggin, Stuart, 'Billy Graham in Australia, 1959 - Was it Revival?', *Lucas: An Evangelical History Review*, 6, 1989.

Piggin, Stuart, 'Billy Graham's '59 Southern Cross Crusade: Evangelistic Efficacy and Baptist Bonanza', *The Baptist Recorder*, 107, 2009, 1–13.

Piggin, Stuart, 'Evangelicals: Inventing a false image of God to suppress women?' *Market-Place*, 5 2006, 11.

Piggin, Stuart, 'The Diocese of Sydney: "This Terrible Conflict"', in Elaine Lindsay and Janet Scarfe (eds.), *Preachers, Prophets and Heretics: Anglican Women's Ministry* (Sydney: UNSW Press, 2012), 178–204.

Piggin, Stuart, 'The Properties of Concrete: Sydney Anglicanism and its recent critics', *Meanjin*, 65.4, 2006, 184–193.

Piggin, Stuart, *Faith of Steel: A History of the Christian Churches in Illawarra, Australia* (Wollongong: The University of Wollongong Press, 1984).

Piggin, Stuart, *Firestorm of the Lord: The History of and Prospects for Revival in the Church and the World* (Carlisle: Paternoster Press, 2000).

Piggin, Stuart, *Making Evangelical Missionaries* (Appleford: Sutton Courtenay Press, 1984).

Piggin, Stuart and Lee, Henry, *The Mt Kembla Disaster* (Melbourne: OUP, 1994).

Piggin, Stuart, *Spirit, Word and World: Evangelical Christianity in Australia* rev. ed., (Brunswick East: Acorn Press, 2012).

Piggin, Stuart, *The Fruitful Figtree: A History of All Saints Anglican Church, Figtree, 1888–1983* (Wollongong: All Saints Anglican Church, 1983).

Piggin, Stuart, 'Witch-hunting in the Secular Society: Christianity's Australian Future', in B. Hocking (ed.), *Australia towards 2000* (London: Macmillan, London, 1990), 162–79.

Piggin, Stuart, 'Power and Religion in a Modern State: Desecularisation in Australian History', *JRH*, 38.3, 2014, 320–340.

Playford, Irene Hart, *Man with a Violin and A Vision: The Story of Stan Drew* (Perth: Pilpel Print, 2004).

Pollock, John, *Billy Graham* (London: Harper and Row, 1979).

Pollock, John, *Crusades: 20 Years with Billy Graham*, (Minneapolis: World Wide Publications, 1969).

Pollock, John, *To all the nations: the Billy Graham story* (San Francisco: Harper & Row, 1985).

Porter, Brian, *Frank Woods: Archbishop of Melbourne* (Parkville: Trinity College, 2009).

Porter, Muriel, *Sydney Anglicans and the Threat to World Anglicanism: The Sydney Experiment* (Farnham: Ashgate, 2011).

Porter, Muriel, *Women in the Church: The Great Ordination Debate in Australia* (Ringwood: Penguin, 1989).

Powell, Alan, *War by Stealth: Australians and the Allied Intelligence Bureau, 1942–1945* (Carlton South: MUP, 1996).

Pratt, Ambrose, *Sidney Myer: A Biography* (Melbourne: Quartet, 1978).

Pratt, Jonathan, 'Growing Healthy Churches: Voices from the Churches', Directions 2012 Research Project (Epping: NSW & ACT Baptist Churches, 2010).

Prentis, Malcolm, *Science, Race and Faith: A Life of John Mathew* (Sydney: Centre for the Study of Australian Christianity, 1998).

Price, David, *Live in Tents: Build only Altars: Gilbert McArthur – his Story* (Vermont South: MST Press, 2019).

Price, David 'A Life of Service: Leonard E. Buck (1906–1996)', *Lucas*, 21 & 22, 1996, 129–35.

Prince, John and Prince, Moyra, *No Fading Vision: The First 50 Years of APCM* (n.p.: Asia Pacific Christian Mission, 1981).

Prince, John and Prince, Moyra, *Out of the Tower* (Homebush West: Anzea, 1987).

Prince, John and Prince, Moyra, *Tuned in to Change: A History of the Australian Scripture Union 1880–1980* (Sydney: SU Australia, 1979).

Putnam, Robert D., and Campbell, David E., *American Grace: How Religion Divides and Unites Us* (New York: Simon & Schuster, 2010).

Pybus, Cassandra, *Seduction and Consent: A Case of Gross Moral Turpitude* (Port Melbourne: Mandarin, 1994).

Rademaker, Laura, *Found in Translation: Many Meanings on a North Australian Mission* (Honolulu: University of Hawai'i Press, 2018).

Radi, Heather, Spearritt, Peter and Hinton, Elizabeth, *Biographical Register of the NSW Parliament, 1901–1970* (Canberra: Australian National University, 1979).

Rafferty, Judith, *Percy Chennell: The Man Who Killed the Lottery* (Malvern: Uniting Church Historical Society, 1990).

Read, Peter, *A Rape of the Soul so Profound* (St Leonards, Allen & Unwin, 1999).

Read, Peter, *The Stolen Generations: The Removal of Aboriginal Children in New South Wales 1883–1969*, NSW Ministry of Aboriginal Affairs: Occasional Paper (No 1), (Sydney: Government printer, 1982).

Reed, Colin, *Walking in the Light: Reflections on the East African Revival and its Link to Australia* (Brunswick East: Acorn Press, 2007).

Reeson, Margaret, *A Very Long War: The Families Who Waited* (Carlton South: MUP, 2000).

Reeson, Margaret, *Whereabouts Unknown* (Sutherland: Albatross Books, 1993).

Reid, Colin, *Walking in the light: reflections on the East Africa revival and its link to Australia* (Melbourne: Acorn Press, 2007).

Reid, John R., *Marcus L. Loane: a biography* (Brunswick East: Acorn Press, 2004).

Renshaw, Will, *Marvellous Melbourne and Spiritual Power: A Christian Revival and its Lasting Legacy* (Moreland: Acorn Press, 2014).

Reynolds, Henry, *The Other Side of the Frontier: Aboriginal Resistance to the European Invasion of Australia* (Ringwood: Penguin, 1982).

Ridley, John G., *C. J. Tinsley of Stanmore: A Love of the Evangel* (Sydney: Greenwood Press, n. d.).

Riseman, Noah, 'Diversifying the black diggers' histories', *Aboriginal History*, 39, 2015, 137–142.

Robb, Ron, *Bethel: A Tradition of Faith at Work* (Ashfield: Ashfield Baptist Homes, 2002).

Roberts, Ron and Gwen, *To Fight Better: A Biography of J Oswald Sanders* (Crowborough: Highland Books/OMF, 1989).

Robertson, J. R. 'The Conscription Issue and the National Movement in Western Australia', in Frank K. Crowley (ed.), *University Studies in Western Australian History* 3.3 (Fremantle: S. H. Lamb, 1959) 5–57.

Robinson, Donald W. B., 'The Church of God: Its Form and Unity', in *Donald Robinson Selected Works, Volume 1: Assembling God's People*, ed. Peter G. Bolt and Mark D. Thompson (Sydney: Moore College/Australian Church Record, 2008), 230–53.

Robinson, Donald W. B., 'The Reverend Bernard George Judd (1918–1999)', *Lucas: An Evangelical History Review*, 25 & 26, 1999, 178–183.

Robinson, Donald W. B., *Josiah's Reform and the Book of the Law* (London: Tyndale Press, 1951).

Rodgers, Margaret, 'Mary Andrews: A Feminist before her time?' *Southern Cross Quarterly,* Summer 1996–97, 24–27.

Rodgers, Margaret, 'Sydney Women should be Trail Blazers', *The Southern Cross*, August 2003.

Rogers, E. Ron, *George Henry Morling: 'Our Beloved Principal': Baptist Theological College of New South Wales Australia 1923–1960: a definitive biography* (Macquarie Park: Greenwood Press in association with the Baptist Historical Society of NSW, 2014).

Rogers, E. Ron, *George Henry Morling: The Man and His Message for Today* (Forest Lodge: Greenwood Press, 1995).

Rose, Mavis, *Freedom from Sanctified Sexism: Women Transforming the Church* (MacGregor: Allira, 1996).

Rowston, Laurence F., *One Hundred Years of Witness: A History of the Hobart Baptist Church, 1884–1984* (Hobart: The Hobart Baptist Church, 1984).

Rowston, Laurence F., 'The Influenza Epidemic and the Ware Street Mission', *The Tabernacle*, 40.3, 1998, 1–7.

Royden, Maude, *A Threefold Cord* (London: Macmillan, 1948).

Rudd, Kevin, 'Christianity, the Australian Labor Party and Current Challenges in Australian Politics', in Stuart Piggin (ed.), *Shaping the Good Society in Australia* (Macquarie University: ACHNF, 2006), 159–170.

Runia, Klaas, *Karl Barth and the Word of God* (Leicester: RTSF Monographs, 1964).

Runia, Klaas, *Reformed Dogmatics: Its Essence and Method* (Geelong: Reformed Theological College, 1957).

Salter, J. C., *A Padre with the Rats of Tobruk* (Hobart: J. Walch & Sons, 1946).

Sanders, J. Oswald, *Planting Men in Melanesia* (Mt Hagen: Christian Leaders' Training College of PNG, 1978).

Santamaria, B. A., *Daniel Mannix: The Quality of Leadership* (Melbourne: MUP, 1984).

Saunders, Malcolm, 'The Origins & Early Years of the Melbourne Peace Society, 1899–1914', *RAHSJ*, 79, 1993, 96–114.

Schedvin, C. B., *Australia and the Great Depression: A Study of Economic Development and Policy in the 1920s and 1930s* (Sydney: Sydney University Press, 1970).

Schild, Maurice, 'Carl Strehlow's Work on the Aranda and Loritja Tribes – A Plea to Publish', *Lutheran Theological Journal*, 34.3, 2000, 147–153.

Schreuder, Deryck M, and Ward, Stuart (eds), *Australia's Empire, Oxford History of the British Empire* (Oxford: OUP, 2008).

Scott, Ernest, *Australia During the War: The Official History of Australia in the War of 1914–1918* vol.9 (Sydney: Angus and Robertson, 1938).

Seiffert, Murray W., *Gumbuli of Ngukurr: Aboriginal Elder in Arnhem Land* (Brunswick East: Acorn Press, 2011).

Seiffert, Murray W., *Refuge on the Roper: The Origins of Roper River Mission Ngukurr* (Brunswick East: Acorn Press, 2008).

Sexton, E. R., *'Griff'* (Adelaide: SA Methodist Historical Society Publication, 1969).

Sharlet, Jeff, *The Family: Power, Politics and Fundamentalism's Shadow Elite* (Brisbane: University of Queensland Press, 2008).

Sheridan, Greg, *God is Good for You: A Defence of Christianity in Troubled Times* (Sydney: Allen & Unwin, 2018).

Sherlock, Peter, and Grimshaw, Patricia, 'One Woman's Concern for Social Justice: The Letters of Helen Baillie to Farnham Maynard, 1933–36', in Colin Holden, (Editor), *Anglo-Catholicism in Melbourne: Papers to Mark the 150th Anniversary of St Peter's Eastern Hill 1846–1996* (Parkville: University of Melbourne, Department of History, 1997), 85–98.

Sherrington, Geoff, 'Youth, State and Community: The Report of the Curlewis Youth Policy Advisory Committee in New South Wales', *Australian and New Zealand History of Education Society Twenty-First Annual Conference Proceedings* (Adelaide: St Mark's College, 1992) II:125–38.

Shaw, Mark. *Global Awakening: How 20th-Century Revivals Triggered a Christian Revolution* (Downers Grove, Ill.: IVP Academic, 2010).

Shiner, Rory, 'Vale Baptist Statesman Noel Vose (1921–2016)', The Gospel Coalition Australia website, https://australia.thegospelcoalition.org/article/vale-noel-vose, accessed 7 September 2016.
Shortt, Rupert, *Rowan's Rule: The Biography of the Archbishop* (London: Hodder & Stoughton, 2008).
Smart, Judith, 'The Great War and the "Scarlet Scourge": Debates About Venereal Diseases in Melbourne During World War I', in Judith Smart and Tony Wood (eds.), *An Anzac Muster: War and Society in Australia and New Zealand, 1914–1918 and 1939–1945,* (Clayton: Monash University, 1992), 58–85.
Smith, F. R., *The Church on the Square: A History of the Albert Street Church* (Brisbane: The Uniting Church Centre, 1990).
Smith, Kevin J., *The Origins, Nature, and Significance of the Jesus Movement as a Revitalization Movement* (Lexington, Emeth Press, 2011).
Souter, Gavin, *Lion and Kangaroo: The Initiation of Australia, 1901–1919* (Sydney: Collins, 1976).
Southwell, C. Hudson, *Unchartered Waters* (Hong Kong: Astana Publishing, 1999).
Spice, Irene M., *Carment Urquhart and His Vision, the Perth Bible Institute* (Perth: Privately Printed by Irene Spice, 1993).
Spong, John Shelby, *Why Christianity must change or die* (San Francisco: Harper, 1998).
Spurling, Kathryn, *Cruel Conflict: The Triumph and Tragedy of HMAS Perth* (Sydney: New Holland Publishers, 2008).
Stamp, H. A., *The Word of God in the Bible* (Brighton: The Burning Bush Society of Victoria, 1994).
Stanley, Brian, *The Global Diffusion of Evangelicalism: The Age of Billy Graham and John Stott* (Downers Grove, Illinois: IVP Academic, 2013).
Stevens, A. T., *An Appraisal of the so-called 'Five Points of Calvinism'* (Brighton: The Burning Bush Society of Victoria, 1994).
Stock, Jenny T., 'Farmers and the Rural Vote in South Australia in World War I: The 1916 Conscription Referendum', *Australian Historical Studies*, 87, 1985, 391–411.
Stone, Gerald, *1932* (Sydney: Pan Macmillan Australia, 2005).
Strachan, George, *Revival – Its Blessings and Battles: An Account of Experiences in the Solomon Islands* (Laurieton: SSEM, 1989).
Stringer, Col, *800 Horsemen: God's History Makers* (Robina: Col Stringer Ministries, 1998).
Strong, Rowan, *Chaplains in the Royal Australian Navy* (Sydney: UNSW Press, 2012).
Summers, Anne, *Damned Whores and God's Police: The Colonization of Women in Australia* (Ringwood and Harmondsworth: Penguin, 1976).
Sutton, Peter, *The Politics of Suffering: Indigenous Australia and the End of the Liberal Consensus* (Carlton: MUP, 2009).
Swain, Shurlee, 'A Long History of Faith-based Welfare in Australia: Origins and Impact', *JRH*, 41.1, 2017, 81–96.
Symes, Colin and Gulson, Kalervo N., 'Faith in Education: The Politics of State Funding and the New Christian Schooling in Australia', *Educational Policy* 22.2, 2008, 231–249.
Tacey, David, *Re-enchantment: The New Australian Spirituality* (Sydney: Harper Collins, 1999).
Taffe, Sue, *A White Hot Flame: Mary Montgomerie Bennett – Author, Educator, Activist for Indigenous Justice* (Clayton: Monash University Publishing, 2018).
Tampke, Jürgen and Doxford, Colin, *Australia, Willkommen: A History of the Germans in Australia* (Kensington: UNSW Press, 1990).
Taska, Lucy, 'The Masked Disease: Oral History, Memory, and the Influenza Pandemic', in Kate Darian-Smith and Paula Hamilton (eds.), *Memory and History in Twentieth Century Australia* (Melbourne: OUP, 1994), 77–91.
Tavan, Gwenda, *The Long, Slow Death of White Australia* (Melbourne: Scribe, 2005).
Tennant, Bob, 'The Sermons of the Eighteenth-Century Evangelicals', in Keith A. Francis and William Gibson (eds.), *The Oxford Handbook of the British Sermon 1689–1901* (Oxford: OUP, 2012), 114–135.

Thiering, Barbara, *Created Second? Aspects of Women's Liberation in Australia* (Sydney: Family Life Movement of Australia, 1973).

Thiering, Barbara, *Deliver Us from Eve: essays on Australian women and religion* (Sydney: Australian Council of Churches (NSW) Commission on the Status of Women, 1977).

Thiering, Barbara, *Jesus the Man: a new interpretation from the Dead Sea scrolls* (Sydney and New York: Doubleday, 1992).

Thiering, Barbara, *Redating the Teacher of Righteousness* (Sydney: Theological Explorations, 1979).

Thiering, Barbara, *The Gospels and Qumran: a new hypothesis* (Sydney: Theological Explorations, 1981).

Thiering, Barbara, *The Qumran Origins of the Christian Church* (Sydney: Theological Explorations, 1983).

Thiselton, John, 'Understanding God's Word Today', in John R.W. Stott and Bruce Kaye, *Obeying Christ in a Changing World* vol.1 *The Lord Christ* (London: Fountain Books, 1977), 90–122.

Thomas, Laurel, 'Ronald Richmond Winton: Obituary', *The Medical Journal of Australia*, 181.1, 2004, 26.

Thompson, Roger C., 'Pastor Extraordinaire: A Portrait of Hector Harrison', in Susan Emilsen and William W. Emilsen (eds.), *Mapping the Landscape: Essays in Australian and New Zealand History in Honour of Professor Ian Breward* (New York: Peter Lang, 2000), 168–84.

Thompson, Roger C., *Religion in Australia* (Melbourne: OUP, 1994).

Thomson, Alistair, 'The Anzac Legend: Exploring National Myth and Memory in Australia', in Raphael Samuel and Paul Thompson (eds.), *The Myths We Live By* (London: Routledge, 1990), 73–82.

Tidball, Derek, 'Post-war evangelical theology: a generational perspective', *Evangelical Quarterly*, 81.2, 2009, 145–160.

Treloar, Geoffrey, 'T. C. Hammond the Controversialist', *The Anglican Historical Society Diocese of Sydney Journal*, 51.1, 2006, 20–35.

Treloar, Geoffrey R., *The Disruption of Evangelicalism* (London: IVP, 2016).

Treloar, G.R. (ed.), *The Furtherance of Religious Beliefs: Essays on the History of Theological Education in Australia* (Sydney: Centre for the Study of Australian Christianity, 1997).

Treloar, Geoffrey R., 'The Heretics, 1916–2016', *St Mark's Review*, 242, December 2017, 6–19.

Trosky, Leon, *History of the New Apostolic Church in the Australian District* (Ipswich: Privately Printed, 1990).

Trumble, Robert, *Kenneth Thorne Henderson: Broadcaster of the Word* (Richmond: Spectrum Publications, 1988).

Tyndale, Philippa, *Don't Look Back: The David Bussau Story* (Crow's Nest: Allen & Unwin, 2004).

Udy, James S., and Clancy, Eric G., *Dig or Die* (Sydney: World Methodist Historical Society, 1981).

Valentine, Alana, *Dear Lindy: A Nation Responds to the Loss of Azariah* (Canberra: NLA, 2017).

Vamplew, Wray (ed.), *Australians: Historical Statistics* (Broadway: Fairfax, Syme & Weldon Associates, 1987).

Van Til, Cornelius *The New Modernism* (Philadelphia: Presbyterian and Reformed Publishing Company, 1947).

Walker, Alan, *Coal Town: a social survey of Cessnock* (Melbourne: OUP, 1944).

Walker, Harry, et al., 'Minjung in Australia', *South Pacific Journal of Mission Studies*, 1.1, 1989, 8–10.

Wall, Don, *Sandakan Under Nippon: The Last March* 5th ed. (Mona Vale: D. Wall Publications, 2003).

Walls, Andrew F., *The Missionary Movement in Christian History: Studies in the Transmission of Faith* (Edinburgh: T&T Clark, 1996).

Ward, Rowland, *The Bush Still Burns, the Presbyterian and Reformed Faith in Australia 1788–1988* (St. Kilda: Presbyterian Church of Eastern Australia, 1989).

Ward, Winifred, *Men ahead of their Time* (Melbourne: The Joint Board of Christian Education, 1996).

Warhurst, John, 'Religion and Politics in the Howard Decade', *Australian Journal of Political Science*, 42.1, 2007, 19–32.

Warner, Rob, *Reinventing English Evangelicalism, 1966–2001: A Theological and Sociological Study* (Milton Keynes: Paternoster, 2007).
Warnken, Russell, '"Missionary is our Middle Name": The Christian and Missionary Alliance in Australia', in Mark Hutchinson and Geoffrey R. Treloar (eds.), *This Gospel Shall Be Preached: Essays on the Australian Contribution to World Mission* (Sydney: CSAC, 1998), 263–274.
Watson, Don, 'Reflections on the Apology', 'Saturday Extra' with Geraldine Doogue, ABC Radio National, 16 February 2008, http://www.abc.net.au/radionational/programs/saturdayextra/reflections-on-the-apology/3284448 accessed 21 November 2016.
Watson, Don, *Recollections of a Bleeding Heart: A Portrait of Paul Keating PM* (Sydney: Knopf, 2002).
Wear, Rae, *Johannes Bjelke-Petersen: The Lord's Premier* (St. Lucia: University of Queensland Press, 2002).
Webb, Barry G., *Personhood, Sexuality, and Christian Ministry* (Sydney: Lancer, 1987).
West, Andrew, 'Enough Already!: Peter Jensen', *The Monthly*, December 2005 – January 2006, https://www.themonthly.com.au/monthly-essays-andrew-west-enough-already-archbishop-peter-jensen-surprise-scouge-john-howard-and-ma accessed 21 November 2016.
West, Janet, *Daughters of Freedom* (Sutherland: Albatross, 1997).
Whitton, Evan, *The Hillbilly Dictator: Australia's Police State* (Sydney: ABC Books, 1989).
Wilkins, F. J., *Baptists in Victoria: Our First Century, 1838–1938* (Melbourne: The Baptist Union of Victoria, 1939).
Wilkinson, John T., *Arthur Samuel Peake, 1865–1929: Essays in Commemoration* (London: Epworth Press, 1958).
Wilkinson, John T., *Arthur Samuel Peake: A Biography* (London: Epworth Press, 1971).
Williams, Diana, *Horizon is where heaven and earth meet* (New York: Bantam Books, 2001).
Williams, John D., 'Twenty-five years in the Australian Baptist Missionary Society', *Our Yesterdays*, 5, 1997.
Williams, Roy, *In God they Trust? The Religious Beliefs of Australia's Prime Ministers, 1901–2013* (Sydney: Bible Society, 2013).
Wilson, Libby, 'Ronald Rutherford Grant' in Stuart Braga, *All His Benefits: The Young and Deck Families in Australia* (Wahroonga: Stuart Braga, 2013), 243–246.
Wilson, Raymond A., *A Reminiscent History of Rockhampton Baptist Tabernacle* (Rockhampton: The Baptist Tabernacle, 1992).
Wood, A. Harold, *'Not Lost but Gone Before': Memories of 100 Christian Men and Women* (Mitcham: Meerut Publications, 1987).
Wood, A. Harold, *A. E. Albiston: Preacher and Teacher* (Mont Albert: Privately Printed, 1989).
Wright, Don I., *Alan Walker: Conscience of the Nation* (Adelaide: Openbook, 1997).
Wright, Don I., and Clancy, Eric G., *The Methodists: A History of Methodism in New South Wales* (St. Leonards: Allen & Unwin, 1993).
Wright, Don I., *Mantle of Christ: A History of the Sydney Central Methodist Mission* (St. Lucia: University of Queensland Press, 1984).
Young, I. E., 'A.C. Willis, Welsh Nonconformist, and the Labour Party in NSW, 1911–33', *JRH*, 2, 1963, 303–13.
Zwartz, Morag, *Fractured families: the story of a Melbourne church cult* (Boronia: Parenesis Publishing, 2004).

Theses and Typescripts

Anderson, Donald, 'Defending an Evangelical Society and an Evangelical Diocese, Sydney James Kirkby, 1879–1935', MA, University of Wollongong, 1985.
Bale, Colin, 'A Crowd of Witnesses: Australian War Graves Inscriptions on the Western Front of the Great War', PhD, University of Sydney, 2006.

Blacket, John, 'I Will Renew the Land': Island on Fire, unpublished MS of history of the Aboriginal Revival, dated 18 May 1993.

Boyd, Jeanette, 'The Arnhem Land Revival of 1979: An Australian Aboriginal Religious Movement', unpublished paper, October 1986.

Calvert, John D., 'A History of the Adelaide Bible Institute (ABI), 1924–1962, with Special Reference to the Development of Its Theological Education', MA Thesis, University of South Australia, 2000.

Chambers, Brian J., 'Need, Not Creed: A History of the Adelaide Central Methodist Mission, 1900–1952', MA Thesis, Flinders University, 1986.

Chilton, Hugh, 'Evangelicals and the End of Christian Australia: Nation and Religion in the Public Square 1959–1979', PhD, University of Sydney, 2014.

Clements, Helen, 'Brief Notes on Steps taken to train and ordain Women for Service in the Presbyterian Church. Time Period 1887–1988, Paper No.1', Unpublished Typescript, 1988.

Clifton, Shane, 'An analysis of the developing Ecclesiology of the Assemblies of God in Australia', PhD, Australian Catholic University, 2005.

Close-Barry, Kirstie, 'Transporting concepts of Indigenous land rights between Fiji and Australia's North', paper at Colonial Christian Missions and their Legacies conference, Copenhagen, 28 April 2015.

Darling, Barbara B., 'The Church of England in Melbourne and the Great Depression, 1929 to 1935', MA thesis, Department of History, University of Melbourne, 1982.

Diesendorf [Baldry], Eileen, 'Women Leaving the Church', Master of Welfare Policy, University of New South Wales, 1987.

Edwards, Trevor, 'Developments in the Evangelical Anglican Doctrine of the Church in the Diocese of Sydney, 1935–1985, with Special Reference to the Writing and Teaching of T. C. Hammond, D. W. Robinson and D. B. Knox', Master of Theology Long Essay, University of Sydney, 1996.

Etherington, Steven, 'Learning to be Kunwinjku: Kunwinjku people discuss their pedagogy', PhD Thesis, Charles Darwin University, 2006.

Gilbert, Alan D., 'The Churches and the Conscription Referenda, 1916–17', MA Thesis, Department of History, Australian National University, 1967.

Goodhew, Richard H., 'The Role of the Leader: An Examination of the Influence of Ministerial Leadership on the Growth of Six Australian Churches from 1798 to 1989', MA (Hons), University of Wollongong, 1990.

Gray, John, 'Evangelism in the Anglican Diocese of Sydney, 1959–1989', MA(hons), University of NSW, 1994.

Harrison, John M., 'Faith in the Sunshine State: Joh Bjelke-Petersen and the Religious Culture of Queensland', PhD Thesis, University of Queensland, 1991.

Hey, Sam, 'God in the Suburbs and Beyond: The Emergence of an Australian Megachurch and Denomination', PhD, Griffith University, 2010.

Huard, Geoff, 'The Phoenix of Petersham', DMin, Northern Baptist Theological Seminary, 1990.

Jensen, Peter, unpublished address at the Remembering Mary Andrews conference, Moore College Library Day, 10 May 2014.

Kelly, Catherine J., 'Dreaming Dreams and Seeing Visions: An examination of the lives and work of some Christian Aboriginal leaders', History Hons thesis, UWA, 2000.

Lawton, William J., '"That Woman Jezebel" – Moore College after 25 Years', Moore College Library Lecture, 1981.

Lukabyo, Ruth, 'From a ministry for youth to a ministry of youth: A history of Protestant youth ministry in Sydney, NSW 1930–1959', PhD, Macquarie University, 2018.

Mayne, Tom, 'A Brief History of Indigenous Ministry in Colonial Sydney, in the Sydney Anglican Diocese and beyond, and of the Sydney Anglican Indigenous Peoples' Ministry Committee', January 2016, typescript.

Munro, Marita Rae, '"A Struggle for Identity and Direction": A History of Victorian Baptists (1960–2000)', PhD, University of Melbourne, 2010.

O'Brien, Glen, 'North American Wesleyan-Holiness Churches In Australia', PhD, La Trobe University, 2005.

Papantoniou, Mersina, 'Multiculturalism's challenge to Sydney Anglican identity: A study of a minority radical tradition', PhD, Macquarie University, 2016.

Parker, David, 'Fundamentalism and Conservative Protestantism in Australia, 1920–1980', PhD, University of Queensland, 2 volumes, 1982.

Parker, David, 'The Bible College Movement in Australia', unpublished paper, 9th Conference South Pacific Association of Bible Colleges, August 1980.

Pear, David A., 'Two Anglican Responses to the Depression and Second World War in Melbourne: A Study in Churchmanship', MTh Thesis, Melbourne College of Divinity, 1985.

Prunster, U. E., 'The Pagan in Norman Lindsay', MA thesis, University of Sydney, 1983.

Rafferty, Judith, 'Till Every Foe Is Vanquished: Churches and Social Issues in South Australia, 1919–1939', PhD, School of Social Sciences, Flinders University, 1988.

Ruffels, Patricia Webb, 'B. Linden Webb', unpublished typescript, 6 July 1995, in possession of the authors.

Schaefer, Trevor, 'The Treatment of Germans in South Australia, 1914–1924', BA Honours, Department of History, University of Adelaide, 1982.

Shiner, Rory J.W., 'Reading the New Testament in Australia: An Historical Account of the Origins, Development and Influence of D.W.B. Robinson's Biblical Scholarship', PhD, Macquarie University, 2017.

Smith, Kevin J., 'The Origins, Nature, and Significance of the Jesus Movement as a Revitalization Movement', Doctor of Missiology, Asbury Theological Seminary, 2002.

Spartalis, Peter J., 'From Silvertrees to Lambeth: the Australian connection and the Church of England in South Africa, 1933–1948', MTh, ACT, 1990.

Sturmey, Ruth I., 'Women and the Anglican Church in Australia: Theology and Social Change', PhD, University of Sydney, 1989.

Suter, Keith D., 'The Future of the Uniting Church in Australia', PhD, University of Sydney, 2013.

Tippett, Rodney W., 'Greater Than We Thought: Australian Army Chaplains in the South West Pacific Area, 1942–1945', MA (Hons), UNSW, 1989.

Turnbull, David, 'Australia and Carey's Legacy', unpublished paper presented at the Conference of the New Zealand Association for the Study of Religion, Wellington College of Education, Wellington, 1992.

Underwood, Brian, 'The History of the Commonwealth and Continental Church Society', MA, Durham University, 1972.

Walker, Ian, 'Church, College and Campus: The Sacred and the Secular in the Foundation of Denominational Colleges in Australian Universities, with particular reference to certain colleges in universities established in the period 1945 to 1975', PhD, UNSW, 2001.

Westwood, Susan, 'A Study of the Attitudes and Activities of the Church of England in the Illawarra During the First World War', BA Honours, Department of History and Politics, University of Wollongong, 1980.

Wilson, Elisabeth K., 'Brethren Attitudes to Authority and Government With Particular Reference to Pacifism', MA Thesis, Department of History, University of Tasmania, 1994.

Yee, Margaret May, 'The validity of theology as an academic discipline: a study in the light of the history and philosophy of science and with special reference to relevant aspects of the thought of Austin Farrer', DPhil, Oxford University, 1987.

Young, Peter, 'Rev. Joshua Robertson', unpublished paper read to the Baptist Historical Society of NSW, 16 October 1980.

INDEX

A

C

E

F

G

H

I

J

K

L

M

N

O

P

Q

R

S

T

U

V

W

Y

Z